MÈS FRÈRES

24, Faubourg

TÉLÉPHO

Messrs. Cartier have
the pleasure of announcin
that in spite of the prese
abnormal circumstances they
have been able to receive
from their Paris house
a very large selection
of Xmas presents

FRANÇAISE DES CÂBLES TÉLÉGRAPHIQUES

NEW YORK
Executive Offices: 28 Broad Street
Telephone Broad 5526-7

la Paix. Paris
Bond St London W
nue New York

18/7/14

Relevant nos

in Mai

s avons l'honneur de vous
lus, notre facture détaillée s'é
somme de 426.55.

Toujours bien e
res, nous vous prion

PARIS
MAIN OFFICE: 53 Rue Vivienne

24 ROYAL EXCHANGE
8 NEW BRIDGE ST., E. C.
30 VICTORIA STREET, S.

LIVERPOOL:
HAVRE:
DRESDEN:
ANTWERP:
ST. PIERRE:

No. 4711
Bill 3277
Room 198-199

GRAND HOTEL LTD.,
CALCUTTA.

19.12.192

CH TELEGRAPH CABLE subject t
are ratified and agreed to.

DEC 271922

Received with the

Madame Jacques Cartier + Miss
Robertson

Rupees eighty-seven annas

R NY

SSANCE AMITIES TOUS DEUX

LOUIS

Please file any answer to this message at or
umpanied by Telephone for Cablegrams FRP

ssiste dans
te donne
eux, ne
que ta partie
dy, comme
tu es
n'oublie
m deve-
critiquable
ligne

712 FIFTH AVENUE
PHONE NO. 5670 Circle

20 Janvier 1916

Mon vieux Jack

CAMP ISÉNIA. SAINT JEAN DE LUZ

N°

er nombre de mots

EST GRATUIT. Le facteur doit délivrer
lorsqu'il est chargé de recouvrer

rangers, l'heure de dépôt est

Timbre
à date.

À DÉCHI

responsabilité à raison du service de la correspondance privée par la voie

THE
CARTIERS

THE CARTIERS

THE UNTOLD STORY
OF THE FAMILY BEHIND THE
JEWELRY EMPIRE

FRANCESCA
CARTIER BRICKELL

BALLANTINE BOOKS

NEW YORK

Black-and-white photo credits are located on pages 601–602.
Color-insert photo captions and credits are located on pages 603–608.

Hardback ISBN 978-0-525-62161-4
International edition ISBN 978-0-593-15809-8
Ebook ISBN 978-0-525-62162-1

Printed in the United States of America on acid-free paper

randomhousebooks.com

2 4 6 8 9 7 5 3 1

First Edition

Book design by Jo Anne Metsch

FOR MY GRANDFATHER

AND MY CHILDREN

CONTENTS

JEWELRY SPOTLIGHTS

Captions and credits for the first color insert can be found on pp. 603–605.
Captions and credits for the second color insert can be found on pp. 605–608.

THE
CARTIERS

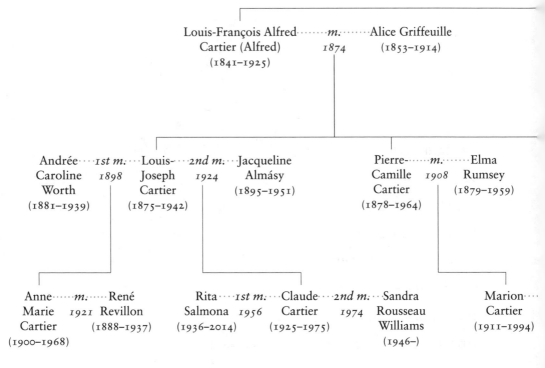

Pierre Cartier········
(1787–1865)

(+ 4 other siblings)

Louis-François Alfred······· *m.* ·······Alice Griffeuille
Cartier (Alfred)   *1874*   (1853–1914)
(1841–1925)

Andrée··· *1st m.* ···Louis- ··· *2nd m.* ··· Jacqueline   Pierre-······ *m.* ······Elma
Caroline   *1898*   Joseph   *1924*   Almásy   Camille   *1908*   Rumsey
Worth   Cartier   (1895–1951)   Cartier   (1879–1959)
(1881–1939)   (1875–1942)   (1878–1964)

Anne······ *m.* ······René   Rita··· *1st m.* ···Claude··· *2nd m.* ···Sandra   Marion····
Marie   *1921* Revillon   Salmona *1956* Cartier   *1974* Rousseau   Cartier
Cartier   (1888–1937)   (1936–2014)   (1925–1975)   Williams   (1911–1994)
(1900–1968)   (1946–)

Jacqueline······ *m.* ·····Sylvester
Cartier   *1939*   Prime
(1913–1991)   (1916–1987)

```
                    m. ························· Élisabeth Gerardin
                   1815                            (1794–1876)
      |
   ___|_____
                   |
              Louis- ·······m.······· Antoinette
              François     1840        (Adèle)
              Cartier                Guermonprez
             (1819–1904)             (1821–1902)
      _____|
                      |
                  Camille ········m.······ Louis Prosper
                  Cartier        1865       Lecomte
                 (1846–1922)               (1834–1881)
```

```
      _____
     |                                                |
  Jacques- ······m.····· Nelly              Suzanne ······m.······ Jacques
  Théodule      1912     Harjes             Cartier     1907       Worth
  Cartier               (1878–1972)        (1885–1960)            (1882–1941)
 (1884–1941)
```

```
···m.····· Pierre
 1933    Claudel
        (1908–1979)
```

```
      _____
     |                          |                                      |
  Alice ·····m.·····Carl    Jean-Jacques·······m.····· Lydia      Alfred ······m.······Elizabeth
  Cartier  1936   Nater     Cartier        1943      Baels       Harjes   1945       Conn
 (1915–2009) (1909–1997)   (1919–2010)            (1907–1990)   Cartier            (1911–1976)
                                                                (1922–1974)
```

The three Cartier brothers with their father.
From left to right: Pierre, Louis, Alfred, and Jacques.

FOREWORD

by Diana Scarisbrick

Many books have been written over the years on Cartier, but none have delved so deep into the true story of the family behind the firm. When the late Hans Nadelhoffer published his pioneering history *Cartier: Jewellers Extraordinary,* he told me how much he regretted having to "work in the dark," handicapped by the lack of personal information about the members of the family who created this international empire, synonymous with twentieth-century elegance and luxury. Thereafter, although the exhibitions on Cartier over recent decades have shown so many beautiful objects, almost all the people most responsible for designing, making, and selling them have remained in the shadows.

Now the veil has been lifted and the real story of the creation of Cartier has finally emerged. In this book, Francesca Cartier Brickell tells us of her dramatic discovery of old family letters and her ten-year quest to fill the gaps in the family history and provide new insights into both the business and the private lives of the personalities involved. *The Cartiers* follows four generations, from Louis-François, the scholarly founder, to Jean-Jacques, the author's late grandfather, but at its heart are the three brothers, Louis, Pierre, and Jacques, whose close bond and distinctive individual contributions coalesced to create one great name and style in the early twentieth century.

Through their own words, unearthed by Francesca's impeccable research, we can understand how Cartier survived revolutions at home and abroad, two world wars, financial crises, and the catastrophic recession of the 1930s, when so many rivals went under. Their history consists of a series of innovations closely linked to changes in fashion, social mores, and the prevailing economic situation. Yet whether in the traditional "garland" style of the Belle Époque, the modernist Art Deco style, or the sumptuous style of the post–World War II period, every item from the smallest tie pin to the grandest tiara was imbued with a look and finesse that were distinctly different from those of their rivals and could be identified immediately as Cartier.

As the great-granddaughter of Jacques and the granddaughter of Jean-Jacques, the indefatigable author has succeeded in bringing the Cartier story to life. No one could have done it better. Besides drawing upon the incomparable resource of her family's correspondence and journals, she has recorded many reminiscences from Jean-Jacques himself and tracked down veteran employees, who recalled nostalgically that working for Cartier was "like being part of a family." She has left nothing to chance, following in her forebears' footsteps from Paris, London, and New York to Sri Lankan sapphire mines and Middle Eastern bazaars. She has traveled to the palaces Jacques visited in India, met the descendants of his clients, and examined the jewels he sold them. Her achievement has been to synthesize ten years of intense biographical research into an engaging and accessible account of the greatest success story of twentieth-century jewelry. Jean-Jacques would be immensely proud.

INTRODUCTION

A few years ago, four generations of my family gathered at my grand-father's house in the South of France to celebrate his ninetieth birth-day. As we all sat on the terrace that warm July morning, enjoying our usual holiday breakfast of fresh croissants and jam, I barely stopped to think how this wonderful man at the head of the table had lived through more than we could imagine. Born in 1919, Jean-Jacques Cartier had—like so many of his remarkable generation—witnessed cataclysmic world events firsthand. He'd seen the devastating lows of the Depression and fought in the Second World War. He had expe-rienced more years of the Roaring Twenties than of the twenty-first century. And yet, that day, watching him open his birthday cards, he was simply Grandpa, with his neatly combed white hair and mustache and smiling blue eyes. But all that was about to change. I was just moments away from making a discovery that would bring me face-to-face with not only his past but the lives of many of my ancestors.

Finishing off the *cafetière* of coffee, we made relaxed plans for the day. We wanted to spoil my grandfather, but he hated being the cen-ter of attention. As usual, Grandpa just wanted the day to be about others. When we were younger, my siblings and I had been amazed at how he would rather give presents than receive them on his own birthday. One year it had been a large wooden sandbox that suddenly appeared on his terrace, another time a couple of bikes on which we could tear around his garden. This year, he announced he had been saving a bottle of vintage champagne.

Offering to fetch it for him, I headed down to his cellar. In the dim light, I scoured the shelves, and when I couldn't see the bottle, I began searching the rest of the room. My grandfather was known never to throw anything away, so there were plenty of things lying around, from boxes filled with manuals for long-defunct electrical appliances to cases of old clothes smelling of mothballs, along with umpteen copies of *Horse & Hound* magazine. Everything, it seemed, except the champagne. I was about to admit defeat and return empty-handed when, just as I was leaving, I noticed a large trunk in the corner nearest the door. Like most other things down there, it was covered with dust and a random mix of objects. It seemed unlikely to house the missing champagne, but I was intrigued.

I set to work removing a tall, thin metal wine rack holding a solitary bottle of out-of-date Orangina and made my way past some yellowing 1970s newspapers until the traveling trunk was revealed in its full battered glory. Black with brown leather straps, its surface was clear of any markings but its sides held clues to a different era: faded stickers from Parisian railway stations and exotic Eastern hotels. Kneeling, I carefully unbuckled the worn straps, willing them not to break off in my hands. And slowly, in that half-dark cellar, all alone, I lifted the lid.

Inside were hundreds and hundreds of letters. They were neatly arranged into bundles, each pile tied with a faded yellow, pink, or red ribbon and labeled in beautiful handwriting on a thick white card.

My grandfather had been part of the fourth generation of the Cartiers to join the renowned family business, and the last of that generation to run a branch before it was sold out of the family in the 1970s. His father, Jacques Cartier, must have been the original owner of the trunk. Here, I realized as I thumbed through the letters, was the story of a family firm that created some of the most revered jewelry of all time for the world's biggest names. That single case would, in time, open a window onto opulent Romanov balls, glamorous coronations, and extravagant maharajas' banquets. Royalty, designers, artists, writers, politicians, socialites, and movie stars would spring to life. I was soon to learn how King Edward VII of England, Grand

Duchess Vladimir of Russia, and Coco Chanel featured alongside the Duchess of Windsor, Elizabeth Taylor, Grace Kelly, and Queen Elizabeth II in Cartier's rich history. And how linking them all were the jewels. Emeralds as large as bird's eggs, ropes and ropes of perfectly pink pearls, cascades of rare colored diamonds, cursed gemstones, extraordinary sapphire tiaras, and the lightest, brightest diamond corsage ornaments.

But the letters also told a very human story. As I would discover, along with accounts of diamonds and glamour there were letters from homesick children and concerned parents. There were joyful telegrams on the birth of a baby and grief-stricken ones carrying news of deaths. There were love letters, angry missives, and correspondence colorful with news and excitement from foreign lands. There were pages written in hope and others scrawled in fear. There were words from a father offering guidance through new ventures, and there were airmail envelopes between brothers, squeezed full of shared problems, successes, and an unbreakable bond.

My grandfather had sometimes spoken of old correspondence passed down from his parents, but he had never been able to find it. He was resigned to the idea that it must have been lost or mistakenly thrown out in his move to France. As I returned to him on the terrace, without the promised champagne (later to be discovered in a cupboard under the stairs), I was able to surprise him with a bundle of the letters he had assumed were lost forever. He was thrilled.

I adored my grandfather. Generous to a fault, he was loving and kind and had an enormous belly-chuckle that would shake his entire body and dissolve us all into laughter. Very understated, he was perhaps not what one would expect from someone who had managed a famous jewelry firm. He was happiest at home, a quiet, introverted man who didn't speak about the business he had managed for decades unless we asked him. Even then it was usually only to sing the praises of his forebears or the talented craftsmen and designers who had worked for him, while playing down his own talents. Generally, he was more likely to want to listen rather than speak, to hear updates on the family, to know if everyone was well and happy, and if not, to find out what he could do to help.

Jean-Jacques had retired to France just before I was born. Each July, he would be waiting at Nice airport to collect us and whisk us back to the house he shared with my grandmother and, after she sadly passed away, in which he lived alone. Year after year, as we came through laden with bags, he'd be waiting there, standing unobtrusively at the back with his trademark pipe and cap. His face would light up when he caught sight of us, and he'd rush to help and lead the way out into that wall of heat and palm trees, toward the car. I loved that journey back to his house from the airport; it meant the summer had begun.

We would drive along the Promenade des Anglais with the glistening sea and happy beachgoers on our left before turning inland after several miles, toward the hills. Jean-Jacques' lungs, like his father's, were his Achilles' heel, so he had purposely chosen a place up in the mountains, where the air was fresher. As we left the coast and crowds, the scenery became more remote until we reached his small village. Past the boulangerie and the greengrocer's and the wood-fired-pizza van until, just moments away now, we would make the sharp turn onto the bumpy road leading up to his house and leave the real world behind. On both sides were goats munching on long, dry grass, and always Thérèse, the elderly goat farmer who lived in the beautiful tall stone cottage with tiny windows to keep it cool. Around a couple more sharp bends, and we were at the white gates that led to our holiday.

Inside, it was an oasis. The noise of the crickets would greet us as we leaped out of the hot car and ran across the pale gray gravel. The garden, into which Jean-Jacques had poured so much of his energy since retirement, was, in stark contrast to the parched dryness elsewhere, fresh and colorful and alive. The long green lawn stretched invitingly away from the terrace, the scene of childhood races and badminton games. To the left of the lawn, down one terrace, was the pool, surrounded by lavender and rosemary. And on the banks just below that were lemon, clementine, and grapefruit trees. Jasmine covered the old open-air pool house with its Provençal tiled roof, and beyond stretched a view all the way to the coast. On clear days, you could see boats in the Mediterranean Sea. At the bottom of the garden were the apricot trees and strawberry and raspberry plants. There were tomatoes, too, fragrant and juicy. Characteristically thoughtful,

Jean-Jacques had planted them and would dutifully water them each evening in advance of our arrival, even though he didn't like tomatoes himself.

The sky, the brightest blue in the midday sun, would turn a glorious gentle pink each evening. It was the sky of Matisse and Picasso and Cézanne. My grandparents had spent their honeymoon in the nearby hilltop town of Saint-Paul-de-Vence, famous for attracting artists before it became fashionable for tourists. It was no coincidence that my grandfather had chosen this area for his retirement. An artist himself, he was drawn to the light. In the last few years of his life, as he was losing his eyesight, I used to catch him staring out at the horizon over the sea. "I'm trying to take as strong a picture in my head as I can," he explained when I joined him on the terrace one evening. "I think if I go blind, I will miss that light terribly—not the sunset light but just before, when it's more subtle." Up in the garden, he had built an art studio. Modern for its time, it had sliding glass doors on one side and, above his artist's desk, a large rectangular picture window overlooking the sea. Filled with sketchbooks, design paper, perfectly sharpened pencils, and fine black pens, the studio was his creative retreat.

For Jean-Jacques, the excitement of his work at Cartier had never been about the biggest jewel. He was more interested in the quest for original design and exceptional craftsmanship. It was a philosophy that was also a way of life. Inside his house, each piece, whether it was a small bronze sculpture, an oil painting, or a Spanish dining table, was chosen for its intrinsic beauty and placed in just the right position. Everywhere were hints of foreign influence, from the Indian rugs to the Chinese coffee table to the Persian miniatures. The family firm had long used inspiration from all over the world in its jewels, and, just like his father and uncles, Jean-Jacques surrounded himself with eclectic works of art. But he wasn't trapped in the past. The innovative glass and metal bookcase, which he had designed for the back wall of the sitting room to hold his father's books, was a manifestation of his "less is more" philosophy.

Everything had its place, and yet when we all descended upon him, bringing chaos in our wake, there was never the slightest complaint. The opposite, in fact. If we broke something by accident, the only thing our grandfather would want to know was if we were okay.

"Don't worry, sweetheart," he would say as we apologized, filled with guilt. "Are *you* all right?"

Those holidays were heaven. And after we left our grandparents to head back to school in England, we would stay in touch via letters. When we were at boarding school, heavy with homesickness, those envelopes with his beautiful writing would bring with them a moment of relief. He understood so well that feeling of missing home, and, empathic to his core, he couldn't bear for others to be unhappy. He was dyslexic, and writing was time-consuming for him, so he'd use more images than words, filling the small pages with sketches of animals and amusing captions to make us laugh.

As we grew older and began to appreciate that this grandfather of ours might once have had his own life, we would ask him about his past. Though he didn't generally talk about himself, when questioned, he would sometimes share anecdotes with us. Like the time he fell asleep while waiting to see the British royal family in Buckingham Palace and was woken, absolutely mortified, by the Queen Mother. Or how, during World War II, his French cavalry regiment had been equipped with swords as if in Napoleonic times, even though they faced huge armored tanks. Sometimes he mentioned specific jewels, a vanity case he had enjoyed making for a princess, or a diamond necklace his father had made for a maharaja. And there were many stories about earlier generations of the family, especially his father and two uncles, the three brothers who had worked together to make Cartier the leading jewelry firm in the world.

By the time I discovered the trunk of letters, I had already started writing down some of my grandfather's memories, just for safekeeping, so they wouldn't be forgotten. In fact, it was someone else who first suggested I try to keep a record of those lunchtime chats when, as he munched on his baguette, my grandfather would open up about the past. My husband, new to our family gatherings and with no living grandparents himself, recognized what a privilege it was to be afforded such a window onto another world, and worried that, if no one started writing the stories down, they would just fade away.

My discovery in the cellar took a haphazard collection of anecdotes to a new level. After bringing up the trunk, I spent the remainder of that summer working through its contents with my grandfather. We tended to sit together in his sitting room, usually around teatime. Since moving back to France, he missed the English tradition of afternoon tea, and I would try (not always successfully) to make scones from my late grandmother's 1970s cookery book. As we read, we shared insights and I asked questions. I couldn't make my way through the letters fast enough, fascinated by this sprawling history I knew so little about. He tended to take them more slowly, absorbing each word gratefully. I'd often find him just holding a letter in his hand as he sat on his favorite chair looking into the distance.

Just the day before discovering the trunk, we had been looking through a jewelry auction catalog, as we often did together. When he spotted an interesting old Cartier piece, my grandfather would take the time to teach me something about it, how it had been made, where the inspiration had come from, or the problems the craftsmen had encountered making it. On that day, he'd pointed out several 1920s Egyptian-influenced jewels made under his father and told me how excited the world had been at the discovery of Tutankhamen's tomb, how it had made ancient history fashionable. After my discovery in the cellar, we joked about how the unearthing of the dusty trunk had been my own Tutankhamen moment. It would change the way I understood the past, transforming all those sepia photographs I'd grown up looking at into real, colorful and noisy characters. And though I didn't yet know it, it would also end up setting me on a new life course. The more I read, the more I realized that I couldn't bear that the letters might simply be packed back into their resting place for another few decades. I wanted to unravel the complicated Cartier history with my grandfather while he was still with us. The correspondence, after all, told only part of the story.

Turning to my grandfather one afternoon, I asked if he would allow me to record his memoirs. The odd story around the lunch table was wonderful but I would like, I explained, to have a more complete picture of his life and the lives of his ancestors in order that I might one day be able to write a history of the Cartiers. It was a big ask. Grandpa was incredibly discreet. He had consistently refused to speak to authors and journalists about the past. But he was elderly, and he recognized that if he, the last surviving Cartier of his generation, didn't share his memories, they would be lost forever.

He also felt that there were unsung heroes who shouldn't be forgotten. That though there were a huge number of gloriously illustrated books on Cartier, many of which he enjoyed, the full story had not yet been told. Sometimes, he would become frustrated when I suggested that his version of events didn't quite correspond to what I had read elsewhere. "It doesn't matter what the books say," he would harrumph. "I'm telling you what really happened and I was there!" And so, wanting the family history to survive beyond him, he agreed to help me.

Over the following months, I would visit my grandfather regularly. I would arrive late at night, having taken the last flight after work on a Friday evening, and he would be sitting in his small kitchen, at the white 1950s Formica table, just waiting to tell me all the stories that had come back to him since the last time I was there. It was as if my interest in him had inspired him to look back, to remember things and people half forgotten. He needed to tell me, to download his recollections, to bring them back to life.

And, wonderfully, I was also able to share with him what I had found. He didn't have a computer and had no idea how to search for old newspaper articles or track down people he'd known decades previously. I would arrive laden with material to show him: articles about his father, books that touched on his old clients, and recollections from those who had worked for the family firm. I was even able to locate some old Cartier London employees. Many of them, in their eighties or even nineties, and not good on the telephone, had assumed they would never again make contact with former colleagues. Sharing news and their best wishes through me was something that gave both them and my grandfather great delight.

So, as he assisted my own understanding of the past, I was able to help him remember and perhaps even enrich his memories. "I am so pleased there is a historian in the family," he used to say, even though I had never thought of myself like that before. After studying literature at Oxford, I had worked as a financial analyst covering the retail sector. Those long workdays in the City were terrible for my social life, but they did teach me how to analyze the factors that account for a company's success. It's one thing to produce top-quality products, but another challenge entirely to build an international brand over the course of decades. This journey started with a trunk of letters and a deep admiration for my grandfather. But the longer I spent researching my family's origin, the more I wanted to understand how my ancestors had built a small family business into one of the leading jewelry firms in the world. And I wanted to know why they had eventually sold it.

As I spoke to my grandfather delving deeper and deeper into the detail, I began to build a picture of how the firm had operated under over a century of family ownership. He showed me a timeline his father had drawn up decades ago so that he could learn the family history as a boy. He told me how his great-grandfather had struggled through revolution in Paris, how his grandfather had been brilliant with gemstones, and how his father and uncles had taken French luxury overseas well before the era of globalization. But for me, one of the most gratifying and unexpected rewards of this project was following him through his own life. In the place of the selfless Grandpa I'd always known, I came to see a little boy looking forward to his bedtime stories with his parents; a brave soldier; a young man mourning the loss of the father he had so admired; and a nervous boss taking over a business before he felt ready.

Finding that trunk of letters and recording my grandfather's memoirs were life-defining moments for me, but in many ways, they were just the beginning. For though I never doubted his version of events, I do recognize that no one's memory of the past is all-encompassing. Even the letters in the trunk tell just part of the story. So I have made every effort to seek out sources from all over the world in order to form, as best I can, a comprehensive view of the course of events. As I have turned over more stones, uncovering unexpected facts along the way, I have found myself constantly revising my view of the history and seeking out leads I had never considered.

I've tracked down fascinating family archives hidden in far-flung pockets of the world from St. Louis to Tokyo. I've visited addresses deciphered from spidery handwriting on faded envelopes in London, Paris, and New York, imagining what it must have been like to live in those grand old buildings in a different era. I've retraced my great-grandfather's footsteps through Eastern lands. I've visited the same sapphire mines, slept in the same buildings, walked barefoot through the same temples, and met descendants of those he knew, from Indian maharajas and Persian Gulf pearl sheikhs to Sri Lankan gem dealers and American heiresses. I've spent hours searching for hundred-year-old birth, death, and marriage certificates and studying them closely for clues into the lives of those long gone. And I have been lucky enough to meet some truly incredible people, from the ninety-year-old saleswoman who invited me to lunch and generously shared her remarkable stories, to the modest designer in London who treated me to Victoria sponge cake and regaled me with tales of eccentric client requests and the most fabulous royal jewels.

This book doesn't claim to be an official or the definitive history of Cartier as a family firm. I am mindful that there is always more to learn and much still to be discovered. It is simply a human story, based on personal memories, a huge amount of correspondence, and as much original source material as I have been able to track down. And, as an independent account of the family and the firm they founded, it ends when the last branch was sold by the Cartiers in 1974.

Sadly, my grandfather passed away a few years ago. Talking to him about the past had brought us very close over his final years, and I was devastated by his death. It took me a long time to be able to listen to the tapes I had recorded with him. I thought it would be strange hearing his voice again after he was gone, but it's been surprisingly comforting, as if he's still here on this journey with me. I think of him often: When one of the jewels he told me about pops up in an auction. When I read the letters he passed down to me or catch sight of that trunk in my house. And when the light in the South of France sky turns that gentle pink just before sunset. Before my grandfather passed away, more than a hundred years after the three Cartier brothers made a promise to one another to build the world's leading jewelry firm, I made him a promise to try to tell the story of the Cartier family as accurately as I could. This book is my attempt to honor that promise.

PART I

THE BEGINNING

(1819–1897)

I don't need to tell you that I long for your return. You and I are inseparable, so it hurts me to make you stay [away] for the length of time that you need to make the business achieve its greatest possible success. . . . I await good news from you. Believe me, my dear Alfred, your devoted father and friend.

—LETTER FROM LOUIS-FRANÇOIS CARTIER
TO ALFRED CARTIER, 1869

FATHER AND SON:
LOUIS-FRANÇOIS AND ALFRED
(1819–1897)

LIVING HISTORY

The auction room was buzzing. From five continents, jewelry lovers, collectors, and dealers had come to play their part in what *Town & Country* had billed "the jewellery sale of the century." Photographers lined the back wall, a large team manned the phones, and as the clock struck 10:00 A.M. on June 19, 2019, the first of five Christie's auctioneers took the stage at his podium in New York's Rockefeller Center for what would be an epic twelve-hour event. "It's not every day," *The Financial Times* enthused, "that a vast number of museum-quality jewels hailing from a single, world-famous collection finds its way under the hammer." Belonging to Sheikh Hamad Al Thani, the 388 lots up for sale in the Maharajas & Mughal Magnificence auction spanned five centuries and some of the most extravagant rulers in history. "An Aladdin's cave of treasures," *Forbes* had called them, if only one could "find a lamp with a genie to help finance a bid."

Many of the Cartier pieces came up in the afternoon session. Lot number 228, a 1922 bejeweled belt-buckle brooch made for the Marchioness of Cholmondeley, was always expected to garner significant interest. With its enormous 38.71 octagonal emerald centerpiece surrounded by diamonds, sapphires, and more emeralds, it was typical of Cartier's Eastern-inspired Art Deco creations of the period. Bidding started at $400,000. Rising initially in increments of $20,000 and then leaps of $50,000, it didn't take long for the digital ticker on the screen behind the auctioneer to surpass the jewel's $500,000–700,000 estimate. When the hammer finally came down, the price of over one and a half million dollars drew gasps and a round of spontaneous applause from the audience.

It wasn't the only Cartier piece to be fought over that day. From a Belle Époque diamond and platinum corsage ornament, to a 1930s Tutti Frutti brooch, a rare graduated natural pearl necklace, and a maharaja's ruby and pearl choker, there were twenty-one Cartier pieces in the sale. Eight of them reached over one million dollars. One exceeded ten million dollars. In total, the number of Cartier lots accounted for just 5 percent of the overall number but ended up contributing a quarter of the final $109 million value. A staggering result, and yet not altogether surprising.

Through the twenty-first century, antique Cartier pieces have been among the most coveted items of jewelry on the planet. "If you see an old jewel signed Cartier," one jewelry expert revealed, "you can triple the value. Those pieces are just in a different league." In 2010, the Duchess of Windsor's 1950s Cartier onyx and diamond panther became the most expensive bracelet ever sold at Sotheby's. When Barbara Hutton's 1933 Cartier jade necklace went under the hammer in Hong Kong four years later, it made history as the highest-valued jadeite jewel of all time. In 2017, Jackie Onassis's Cartier 1960s Tank watch sold for triple its estimate, while in the record-breaking 2016 sale of Elizabeth Taylor's jewels, it was a Cartier necklace that came out on top. With such illustrious worldwide recognition, it's perhaps hard to imagine that it was ever any other way. But the intense competition and willing parting of millions of dollars for jewels bearing that familiar italicized signature couldn't be further removed from how Cartier's founder started out. Exactly two hundred years before the headline-grabbing auction in New York, Louis-François Cartier made his entrance into a very different world.

THE APPRENTICE

As a child, Louis-François Cartier would have loved a formal education. He longed to study the classics, to delve into the sciences, to learn about great artists. But his immediate future was not up to him. There were seven mouths to feed in the Cartier family, and as the eldest son, he had a responsibility to play his part. After a rudimentary schooling, it was straight out to work. His father, Pierre, had managed to secure for him an apprenticeship in the jewelry trade. It would be hard work for little pay, but professional jewelers were part of the "six *marchands de Paris*," a prestigious group of skilled merchants and artisans who were considered middle-class. The prospects for the young Cartier would be far better than if he had followed his father into the metalworking industry.

Every day, Louis-François would walk the twenty minutes from his cramped family home in the Marais area of Paris, along the narrow streets with no sidewalks, toward Les Halles. Here, amid the bustle of the grain exchange and the smells of the oyster market, was where the city's jewelry craftsmen and specialists were based. His new boss, Monsieur Bernard Picard, a *fabricant* or maker of jewels, owned a well-established workshop on two upper floors of a large six-story building at 31 Rue Montorgueil, right by the church of Saint-Eustache.

Being a jeweler's apprentice was no easy undertaking. Workshop managers were renowned for treating their juniors "like the inmates of a kennel." The boys worked grueling fifteen-hour days for little reward. "We were not spared slaps, boxes on the ears, and kicks," recalled one of his contemporaries, Alphonse Fouquet, while elsewhere, craftsmen of the master jeweler Fabergé remembered how the most important instrument in an apprentice's set of tools was the whip: "no pupil has ever learnt without one." Not everyone lasted the distance, but Louis-François, who had witnessed his father rebuild his life from nothing, was fiercely driven.

A decade before the birth of his eldest son, Pierre, Cartier had been fighting for France in the Napoleonic Wars, when he'd been captured by Wellington's army. For years he'd been locked up in a disgusting, overcrowded, disease-filled prison hulk in Portsmouth harbor, wondering if he'd ever make it out alive. When finally freed after the defeat of Napoleon in 1815, he'd been twenty-eight years old with not a cent to his name, no prospects, and no living parents. Returning to Paris, he'd found work as a metalworker, married Élisabeth Gerardin (a washerwoman and the daughter of a merchant), and become a father. Now, with his son completing an apprenticeship, Pierre just hoped for a better life for the next generation.

Fortunately, for Louis-François, it was a reasonable time to be joining the jewelry trade. The French aristocrats who had fled the capital during the Revolution and the Napoleonic period had slowly returned under the new Bourbon monarchs, and their presence helped to jump-start renewed demand for luxury goods. Court life was still a pale imitation of the Marie Antoinette era, but there was a trend for smaller, more discreet items of jewelry, and Picard catered to this market. As Louis-François and his fellow workers completed items, they would stamp them with their master's *poinçon*, an official maker's mark certifying the provenance of a jewel. In Picard's case, it was his initials, BP, separated by the image of a river (a play on the French word *rivière*, which means both "river" and "diamond necklace"). But if any of the apprentices hoped to have his own stamp anytime soon, it was a distant wish. The chances of progression on that scale were limited. Even when Picard one day retired, he had his eldest son, Adolphe, to take his place.

A few months before his twenty-first birthday, Louis-François, unsure of his future prospects, married his eighteen-year-old sweetheart. Antoinette Guermonprez, known as Adèle, was not originally from Paris. Her father, a table maker, had moved to the capital from Roanne in search of work, and the extended Guermonprez family had joined him, several generations squeezed into one house together, not far from the Cartiers. It was in this Marais neighborhood, on a cold February morning in 1840, that the young couple said their vows in the large Gothic-style Catholic church of Saint-Nicolas-des-Champs. After the wedding, unable to afford their own home, they moved in with Adèle's parents. They would start their family here. An adored only son, Louis-François Alfred, always known simply as Alfred, was born a year later. And as he turned five years old, he was joined by a little sister, Camille.

Paris in the 1840s was a far from ideal place to be bringing up children, especially for the working class. Overcrowding had become endemic as the new inhabitants from the countryside settled in any space they could find, leaving no room for parks or recreation areas. Overflowing drains and open sewers were hotbeds of disease, and infant mortality rates were high. Louis-François worked hard for Picard, hoping desperately—as his father had done—to be able to offer his children a better future than his past. But for many years, it would be far from certain.

TWENTY THOUSAND FRANCS

In 1847, Monsieur Picard made an announcement that would change the life of not just Louis-François but also of future generations of Cartiers, and, in time, the entire jewelry industry. He wanted, he explained to his employees, to move his business to the more fashionable Palais-Royal part of town, but first he needed to sell his Rue Montorgueil workshop. Seeing the opportunity he had been waiting for suddenly appear so tantalizingly close, Louis-François seized his moment. With the support of extended family, he gathered together as much of the 20,000-franc sale price as he could (no small task at a time when the average wage was less than 2 francs a day). Lacking the full amount, not to mention the 1,600 francs required to cover the ongoing rent of the two-story workshop, he proposed to Picard that he pay the remainder in installments. And thankfully Picard, who had come to trust his hardworking employee over the years, agreed.

So it was that after years of struggling on the sidelines, the twenty-seven-year-old Louis-François Cartier became the proud owner of a business. He wasted little time registering his maker's mark, and by April he was able to officially manufacture jewels under his own name. Whereas Picard's *poinçon* had been a river through his initials, Louis-François designed a simple lozenge shape (a diamond on its side) with his initials, LC, separated by an ace of hearts. And by January 1848, when the annual Paris Trade Almanac was printed, *Cartier* appeared in the directory for the first time. His new firm, as Louis-François described it, was the "successor to M. Picard, manufacturer of *joaillerie* [gem-set jewelry] and *bijouterie* [gold jewelry], fancy decorations and novelties."

Cartier's first maker's mark, registered by the twenty-seven-year-old Louis-François on April 17, 1847.

As he had done under Picard, Louis-François kept making jewels in-house, but he also brought in pieces from elsewhere. In those early months of Cartier, his stock included crystal bracelets, flower brooches, baroque pearl accessories, and diamond earrings, which he sold to other workshops and jewelers (including the royal jeweler, Fossin, later Chaumet). Many were destined for the type of high-profile clients, from the Rothschild family to the Belgian Princesse de Ligne, that Louis-François would have loved to sell to directly, but for that he would have to wait. However attractive his jewels, his modest workshop was far from being distinguished enough to welcome the glamorous aristocratic set. Cartier's short-term focus at this point had to be on establishing its name in the trade. And though Louis-François' initial efforts were going well, the timing, as he was about to discover, couldn't have been worse.

"LONG LIVE REFORM!"

For some months, a background of bubbling discontent in France had been threatening to boil over. Bad harvests, potato blights, and a financial crisis in 1846 had led to a recession, with a third of Parisians out of work and struggling to feed their children. As the torrent of public anger against the king and government grew, the middle-class opposition held "political banquets" to discuss their ideas for reform. And when, in 1848, King Louis-Philippe decided to outlaw these banquets, it was for many the final straw.

Suddenly, cries of "Long live reform!" filled the capital as furious Parisians took their pent-up rage to the streets. Protesters erected barricades and fought with the king's guards. Soldiers fired into the crowd that had gathered outside the Ministry for Foreign Affairs, just ten minutes from Louis-François' precious workshop that he had yet to pay for in full. When the gunfire killed fifty-five citizens, the people erupted with uncontrollable fury, starting fires and marching toward the palace. The terrified prime minister, Guizot, immediately resigned. King Louis-Philippe rapidly followed suit, abdicating and fleeing to England.

The year 1848 would become known as the year of European revolutions, as uprisings against the monarchies spread through the continent. In Paris, the disturbances continued for many months. Louis-François, who had waited so long for the opportunity to have his own business, had no choice but to abandon his work. He feared, as his grandson later recalled, that it might be forever: "I can still remember my grandfather telling me during my youth that, when the revolution happened, he felt that he would probably not be able to continue the business he had just started."

Even afterward, once the flames of revolutionary anger had died down, the outlook was bleak. A new French provisional government turned out to be a disorganized disaster; wealth fled, credit became inordinately expensive, and the number of businesses in Paris halved. Desperate to start making a living again, Louis-François tentatively reopened the Cartier workshop, only to find most of his customers had either shut up shop completely or sought out opportunities elsewhere.

It was only really after the successful coup d'état by Prince Louis Napoleon three years later that things started looking up in Paris. Emperor Napoleon III, as he became known, brought with him a more modernizing leadership that boded well for business, and his authoritarian censoring of the press finally quieted the opposition. Louis-François, cautiously optimistic for the first time in years, considered a change in his business model. His jewelry workshop was reasonably located for selling items to retailers and other workshops, but he wanted to reach a more upmarket audience. Picard had moved because he had wanted to be in an area where he could sell directly to retail clients. Six years after founding Cartier, Louis-François followed suit.

"THROUGH THE CHAPEL, SIRE"

Within the world of luxury retail, location was everything. So it was that the ambitious Louis-François traded the hustle and bustle and

familiar oyster market smells of Les Halles for the distinguished
Palais-Royal area of town. It was here that the most beautiful Parisian ladies went in their carriages to shop, eat lunch, and be seen.
Cartier may not have been able to afford a showroom in the beautiful arcades, but from 1853 on, it would be a stone's throw away.
From his new second-floor showroom at 5 Rue Neuve-des-Petits-
Champs, above a fashionable restaurant and just across from the
exquisite gardens, the thirty-four-year-old Cartier founder started
welcoming those clients who would help spread his family name
within Paris. They didn't all come looking for jewels. Silver tea sets,
small bronze statues, ivory objects, and Sèvres porcelain were displayed enticingly alongside agate and obsidian cameos, decorative
buttons, pocket watches, and amethyst bracelets. The common thread
was simply that all pieces should meet Louis-François' high standards. After more than a decade working as a craftsman and overseeing a workshop, he knew exactly how to evaluate the creations of
others and was insistent that Cartier should be a shop where quality
was assured.

Finally the backdrop was positive. With France benefiting from
industrialization, the wealth of the upper and middle classes was on
the rise. Not only was luxury back in demand but, under the Second
Empire, the quality of jewels was on the rise too. As part of his reform program, Napoleon III had revolutionized the salary structure
of craftsmen, abolishing the previous strict fixed wages. As skilled
jewelers were rewarded with higher pay, the standard of jewelry settings took a turn for the better. To top it all off, there was also a
beautiful new empress on the scene, more than happy to play her role
in promoting French jewelry to a nation of admiring subjects.

Seduced by the beauty of the Spanish noblewoman Eugénie de
Montijo, Emperor Napoleon III had famously asked her, "How can I
reach you?" and her reply "Through the chapel, Sire" had resulted in
a very swift proposal of marriage. At their wedding in January 1853,
when the empress-to-be stepped out of the gilded glass coach that had
brought her from the Élysée Palace to Notre-Dame Cathedral, she
drew gasps from the crowds in her dress of white velvet with a "basque
bodice . . . ablaze with diamonds of the most costly description and
radiant with sapphires." Encircling her waist was a belt of diamonds,

"on her brow was the coronet of diamonds worn by Marie-Louise [Napoleon I's second wife] on her wedding day," and stretching down over her long train was a lace veil, fastened with a wreath of orange blossoms, which "mingled their pure loveliness with the gems."

The emperor would have many more of the French crown jewels reset for his bride, and a select few jewelers benefited enormously from the royal custom. The little-known Cartier was not among them, but the Empress's passion for richer, brighter gems, which used precious stones more profusely, gave a welcome boost to the entire French jewelry industry. And Paris, under the combination of Napoleon III's strong leadership and his sparkling bride, was becoming quite the place to be.

BE VERY KIND

To a client selecting her Limoges enamel brooch, ring, or cameo pendant, the jewelers dotted around the Palais-Royal would have seemed like rivals. In reality, apparent competitors (from Fossin to Falize to Boucheron to Cartier) knew each other well and often supplied one another with jewels. Sometimes a single necklace or brooch might have been produced by several workshops in tandem. This setup, with different jewelers buying from the same ateliers, invariably meant the range of items that Louis-François sold was not unique to Cartier. If he were to stand out from his peers, he was going to have to build his reputation in other ways.

"Be very kind," Louis-François would advise his son, Alfred, outlining a key tenet of his life's philosophy. "It is the easy way to keep friends whom we may need, however lowly or great their position." Everyone who entered Cartier, he believed, should be treated with respect. Louis-François may not have had the resources to fill his store with large diamond necklaces and ropes of pearls, and he couldn't afford a showroom in the prestigious arcades of the Palais-Royal. But he knew that the personal touch was one way in which his firm could distinguish itself. If clients left the showroom happy with their interaction with Monsieur Cartier, the chances were that they would be back, and might even tell their friends.

In Conversation with Jean-Jacques Cartier

Every client who walked through the doors of Cartier had to enjoy the experience. We used to have a wonderful doorman who looked a bit like Santa Claus and greeted every client with this enormous smile that took up his whole face. It was almost impossible not to smile back. It's a salesman's job to be discreet and helpful, that goes without saying, but people don't buy jewels if they're not feeling good. My father taught me that and it was a lesson passed down from his grandfather.

Two years into his new role as a retailer, whether by word of mouth or sheer good fortune, Louis-François would welcome his most important client to date. The forty-four-year-old Comtesse de Nieuwerkerke was the wife of Paris's superintendent of fine art. In 1855, the year of France's first Exposition Universelle, the Countess bought a cameo necklace and six buttons set with antique cameos, typical of the discreet fashions of the day. Over the next three years, she would visit Cartier's showroom regularly, buying more than fifty items. For Louis-François, the Countess's custom was most welcome, but even better was how she then spread the word. When she wore a recent Cartier purchase "inspired by an old jewel that the Louvre Museum has just acquired" at a "dazzling party," it was admired by her husband's lover, who also happened to be one of the most influential women in Paris: Princesse Mathilde.

THE MOST BEAUTIFUL NECKLINE IN EUROPE

"Had it not been for the great Napoleon," Princesse Mathilde Bonaparte once said of her uncle, "I should probably be selling oranges in the streets of Ajaccio." As it was, by the mid-nineteenth century, the Princesse couldn't have been more highly regarded in elite circles. After a short-lived and stormy marriage to the inordinately wealthy Russian Prince Demidov in 1846, at twenty-six years of age, she had fled to Paris where she tirelessly promoted the cause of her cousin Napoleon III. And once his place in power had been assured, so too had her position in society.

Nicknamed Notre Dame des Arts (Our Lady of the Arts), the cultivated Princesse Mathilde was celebrated for presiding over one of the most fashionable salons of the Second Empire from her mansion at 10 Rue des Courcelles. Her salon, "a court in itself," was described by her niece, Princesse Caroline Murat, as "the home and centre of Parisian intellect." Acclaimed writers from Guy de Maupassant to Gustave Flaubert to Alexandre Dumas fils would discuss politics and art alongside journalists such as Hippolyte de Villemessant, the publisher of *Le Figaro,* and scholars and scientists like Louis Pasteur. Friday night dinners were reserved for artists.

With her prominent standing in society, a reputation for having remarkable taste, and *"le plus beau décolleté d'Europe"* (the most beautiful neckline in Europe), Princesse Mathilde was every jeweler's dream model. When she asked Louis-François to repair a necklace for her in 1856, it boded well for the future. And when she started buying pieces from his showroom, he was well on his way to making a name for himself. Over the following years, she bought freely, with her purchases giving an idea of Cartier's diverse range of stock: a ruby and pearl necklace, Medusa-head cameos, amethyst-plaque brooches, a turquoise scarab brooch, an opal bracelet, a pair of earrings in the Egyptian style, and even a parasol handle. In all, there would be more than two hundred items in Cartier's ledgers ordered by the Princesse. There would also be those bought by the Count, more likely destined for his lover than for his wife.

But the Princesse and Louis-François had more in common than a passion for jewels. Both art lovers and appreciative of beautiful design, they also shared the same brilliant art teacher. Eugène Julienne had started out as a draftsman in the Sèvres porcelain factory before being spotted by the Parisian jeweler Jean-Paul Robin. Impressed by "his imagination [and] the brilliance with which he drew in a few minutes the compositions that were required of him," Robin suggested Julienne turn his hand to jewelry design. Before long, the draftsman was working for many of the leading jewelers and goldsmiths in the French capital, and in 1856, he started his own art school. High-profile private students included ladies of the court, but

Louis-François Cartier (left) and his most important early client, Princesse
Mathilde Bonaparte (right), who not only bought freely but also awarded the
firm its first *brevet* (royal warrant), which was proudly displayed alongside
Cartier's name on early invoices.

he also taught ornamental drawing to larger groups and Louis-
François, trained in jewelry making but not design, signed up for
evening classes. Once a week, he would walk the twenty minutes
from his Palais-Royal showroom to Julienne's studio on Boulevard
Saint-Martin to study with the great master. He was in good company. Fellow students included other jewelers, some of whom would
become suppliers to Cartier.

In just over a decade, Louis-François had progressed from a
poorly paid, overworked tradesman to a retailer who counted a princess among his clients. Life was never without its setbacks for long.
Three years after he'd opened his Palais-Royal showroom, a sudden
disaster threatened to end it all. In early 1856, when the chef in the
Cuvigny restaurant just below Cartier turned on the oven to start
cooking that evening, there was an explosion of such force that part
of the ceiling fell in. Shrieking diners, terrified as the rubble suddenly
covered their tables, were quickly evacuated. There had been an undetected gas leak in the pipes, and the flames spread quickly, invading
the third floor, where Cartier was located. Miraculously there were
no fatalities, and the firefighters, fast on the scene, managed to save
the building. After the necessary renovations, Cartier would reopen

as before. The experience, however, would change Louis-François. Not only would a fear of fire haunt him, but he would learn to prepare for the worst.

CARTIER GILLION

In the twelve years since it had been founded, Cartier had survived revolution, a disastrous economy, a coup d'état, and fire. But if anything, the adversities thrown in the way of Louis-François had simply made him even more determined. In 1859, six years after moving his business to the Palais-Royal, he took the biggest risk yet. On finding out that Monsieur Gillion, a sixty-five-year-old well-known Parisian jeweler, was considering retirement, the forty-year-old Louis-François approached the elder man with an offer for his business.

Far larger than Cartier's Palais-Royal premises, the Gillion building at number 9 on the busy Boulevard des Italiens included a shop on the ground floor with an entrance onto the street, a back shop, a mezzanine level, an attic with a maid's room, a cellar, and use of the water pump. Most significantly it was extremely well located for passing retail trade. One of the four main boulevards in Paris, Boulevard des Italiens was popular among the well-dressed elite. The Café Anglais, just two doors down at number 13, was considered the best restaurant in the capital and became such a landmark of the city that it would feature in novels by Zola, Proust, Balzac, Flaubert, and Maupassant.

The rental on the new Gillion shop was 8,500 francs a year ($45,000 today). Louis-François agreed to take on a ten-year lease, which, all going well, he could renew. The largest cost, though, was the stock, which, with the first rental payment, amounted to 40,000 francs ($220,000 today). It was double the price he had paid for Picard, but it was a far more established business. Gillion was known for its "brilliant rings, necklaces of pearls, jewels of all kinds set with perfect taste." And in keeping with Cartier's own broad offerings, the Gillion stock included more than jewelry. "There are also these sumptuous dishes and table services, which, by the brilliancy they spread in a feast, make good dinners better," one effusive journalist would enthuse, "for as man does not live by bread alone, the gourmet not

The busy Boulevard des Italiens, where Cartier moved in 1859,
with an example of what Louis-François sold there: a demi-parure
of enameled gold jewelry. The 1869 pendant locket, earrings,
and necklace were made by Fontenay but retailed by
"Cartier Gillion" in a fitted red silk box.

only eats with his mouth, he also enjoys with the eyes." In 1859, soon
after becoming the official owner of Gillion, Louis-François gave up
his old lease in the Palais-Royal and opened the doors to a much enlarged business. A huge part of the attraction had been in the name—
Gillion was acclaimed as "a talent of undeniable supremacy"—and
Louis-François marketed his new firm as Cartier Gillion, even print-
ing jewelry boxes with the new name.

As he settled into his new location, not everyone was doing so
well. For more than a decade Louis-François had modeled his business on what he'd learned from Picard. Like his former boss, he had
started out as a manufacturer, then changed locations to retail directly to the upper classes, and now he had plans to welcome his own
son, Alfred, into the business. Picard, meanwhile, was having problems. Highlighting the difficulties of running a family business, the
fifty-nine-year-old had recently been forced to dissolve his company
after infighting between his two sons from different marriages. The

year 1859 marked the moment when Louis-François stepped definitively ahead of his old master. It was also the year that he welcomed
his most significant client to date.

Since her spellbinding wedding with its jewels "on a scale worthy
of the most brilliant courts France has ever known," Empress Eugénie had changed jewelry fashions in France. Not only had she revived
the trend for wearing ropes of pearls in the evening, but, in contrast
to the more restrained look of the post-revolutionary period, she also
encouraged her circle to bedeck themselves in a multitude of gems.
"The Empress had a beautiful ballroom built out into the garden,
and it was there that she gave this really lovely fête," her friend the
Austrian socialite Princess Pauline Metternich would recall of one
glamorous ball. "I took part in the quadrille representing the Four
Elements, and was one of the group representing Air. There were four
women to every group. Those representing Earth wore nothing but
emeralds and diamonds; those representing Fire nothing but rubies
and diamonds; those representing Water nothing but pearls and diamonds, and those representing Air nothing but turquoises and diamonds."

Though far from being able to witness the regal balls himself,
Louis-François couldn't help but know of the Empress's passion for
gems. He'd been among the crowds awed by her wedding day and by
the grandeur of her gold, diamond, and emerald crown in the 1855
Exposition Universelle. So when, in 1859, Empress Eugénie stepped
foot inside his showroom, it was the ultimate accolade. Louis-
François Cartier, the son of a washerwoman and a metalworker, was
being called upon by the most important woman in France and possibly the best jewelry buyer in the world.

If, however, Louis-François had hoped the Empress was coming to
him for precious gemstones, he was to be disappointed. She bought
from Cartier a silver tea service. Nothing more. Still, that moment
was a pivotal validation, far more significant than the size of her invoice. Where she trod, other high-ranking clients would follow, and,
to the delight of Louis-François, there would soon be those from beyond France.

The following year, a visiting Russian royal, Prince Saltykov,
walked into 9 Boulevard des Italiens and bought an emerald bracelet
in a black-enameled gold setting. Again, the purchase was modest,

but a Russian client was an important development. After the First World War, America would emerge as the source of vast new industrial fortunes, but in the nineteenth century, Russia held much of the world's wealth and, with it, the world's best luxury clients. Saltykov's bracelet was an early vote of confidence from a country that, though Louis-François didn't know it yet, would play a hugely significant role in his firm's future.

PARISIAN GLORY

At 8 P.M. on the third Tuesday of every month, Louis-François would attend meetings at the Chambre Syndicale de la Bijouterie (Jewelry Union), alongside peers including Frédéric Boucheron, Alexis Falize, and Jean-François Mellerio. Also there was a young man by the name of Théodule Bourdier who would, in time, become closely linked to the Cartiers. Making connections had always been important to Louis-François, and the union (to which he was secretary for a time), was a tightly knit group. Its members were bonded by a passion for their profession and a sense that by working together to defend their industry, they could achieve more than they could alone.

In Conversation with Jean-Jacques Cartier

There's an assumption that jewelers were rivals, but it wasn't really like that. Certainly as a family, the Cartiers tended to get along with their peers. You see, we were in the same boat, shopkeepers to important clients. We didn't share everything, of course—we would keep our ideas for the next jewelry collection close to our chest—but you just need to look through my father's address book and correspondence to see how many jewelers he was friends with. The Fabergés are in there, the Van Cleefs, the Arpels, Charles Moore from Tiffany.

But throwing himself into the Parisian jewelry community was only part of Louis-François' working life. He wasn't blind to the need to also branch out on his own. In 1864, for instance, after hearing that the town of Bayonne was planning a large exhibition for the inauguration of Napoleon III's Paris-to-Madrid railway line, he packed up several suitcases of jewels and headed there himself. His aim was to display the gems in front of a new audience, and fortunately, his Parisian competitors hadn't made the same efforts. The exhibition welcomed tens of thousands of visitors, including the Emperor and the Spanish royals, but most important for Louis-François was the presence of the press. In Paris, Cartier had struggled to make it into the newspapers, but in the provinces, journalists were eager to share stories about the magnificent jewels from the capital.

One reviewer, erroneously referring to Louis-François as "Mr. Cartier Gillion," spoke of his "beautiful pieces, with a personal and unusual taste," remarking that "his diamonds are also very well set." An art journal, *L'Artiste,* delighted over the multipurpose features of one particular bodice ornament consisting of a bouquet of five diamond flowers mounted on silver: "It is a double fortune to own this luxurious jewel which is metamorphosed to infinity; from this rich bunch of flowers you can make five pretty brooches, a dazzling comb, a beautiful headband and an adorable bracelet; all these changes take place in a few minutes, without damaging the jewels."

As recognition of the Cartier name spread and Louis-François started to be hailed as "one of our Parisian glories," he was also moving up in social circles. Not only was he supplying silver and gold buttons to Charvet, the finest shirtmaker in France, but he could afford to wear their crisp made-to-measure shirts himself. Free from debt and ensconced in the middle class, he enjoyed fine wines and foreign travel (fulfilling his ambition to visit England, as well as Switzerland and Germany) and to invest in property. By 1865, when his nineteen-year-old daughter, Camille, was preparing to marry, he could proudly offer a handsome dowry of 40,000 francs ($215,000 today).

But the wedding would be tinged with sadness. When Camille Cartier walked down the aisle with the thirty-one-year-old Louis Prosper Lecomte in August 1865, there was one notable absence in the congregation. Pierre Cartier, Camille's seventy-eight-year-old grandfather, had died just three months earlier. For Louis-François, the passing of his father made him even more determined to turn Cartier into a successful family firm, and he offered his new son-in-law a role in the business. Louis Prosper, known to the family as Prosper, was successful in his own right as co-owner of a shop on Rue Lafayette and didn't accept immediately. But his time would come.

GOLD COINS

Since moving to Boulevard des Italiens, Louis-François had been joined by his son in the business. Alfred, now in his twenties, had learned to fill out the sales ledgers, sketching each item they sold as a visual reminder for the future. He'd been trained, too, to understand the finances, and, dressed smartly in a frock coat and Charvet shirt, to treat clients with deferential respect. It was in gemstones, though, that he found his niche, and before long, he would become known for his sharp eye and uncanny ability to spot fakes.

In Conversation with Jean-Jacques Cartier

Alfred was very good with gemstones. He had a technique when buying from dealers. After deciding which gemstones he wanted, he would play with gold coins as he talked about the price. He would repeatedly and obviously drop one, two, three coins slowly from one hand to the other and then back again. It reminded the dealer that a sale to Cartier meant instant payment. That was unusual for the time, and the dealers came to know about this Monsieur Cartier who paid up front. It meant they were eager to come to Cartier first with their best gemstones.

By the time Alfred started working alongside his father, Paris was a city buzzing with progress and improving by the day. Louis-

François, in his forties, had witnessed the capital's population double over his lifetime and, to cope with the changes, Napoleon III had ordered his prefect of the Seine, Georges-Eugène Haussmann, to re-design the city. Since 1853, overcrowded medieval neighborhoods had started to be replaced with wide avenues, perfectly manicured parks, and elegant squares. A new aqueduct dramatically increased the supply of clean water, and disease-filled areas had been tackled with the rebuilding of sewers. Railway stations and miles of railway tracks were added to link the capital with other cities. Bursting from its cocoon of construction, Paris once again became the adored Ville Lumière (City of Light), as it had been christened during the Age of Enlightenment. In the 1860s, the label was doubly apt as the boule-vards were lit for the first time with gas lamps, long before most other cities.

In 1866, when Napoleon III was at the height of his powers, Car-tier's profits for the year amounted to 48,244 francs ($250,000 today). The following year, when the 1867 Exposition Universelle became the greatest international fair ever held, a record 15 million visitors descended on the capital. It was a good time to be a jeweler in Paris, and the decade ended on a high note for the Cartiers. Louis-François, now grandfather of two little girls (the daughters of his daughter, Camille), was enjoying working alongside his son. And though his firm may not have been as highly regarded as jewelers such as Mellorio or Vever, it had earned the honor of being listed as a Notable Commerçant (notable merchant) with a royal patent from Princesse Mathilde.

Alfred, meanwhile, was proving a great addition to the small team in Paris and abroad. In 1869, he'd headed across the Channel with "beautiful merchandise" to sell in London. It hadn't been easy for the twenty-nine-year-old to break into a new market and Louis-François, vicariously living through his son's trials and tribulations via numer-ous letters, had been on hand to offer advice: "Go and buy cigars at Oberdoffers, 54 Regent Street. He welcomes the French in a skillful way. If you let him get a sniff of a discount, he will be able to advise you on selling your jewels." Inevitably some clients had been disap-pointed not to meet with their usual salesman ("Mme Burgess is a bit cross with me for not going to London," Louis-François admitted), but Alfred would win them over.

Among Cartier's most high-profile British clients were Lord and Lady Dudley. The fifty-year-old earl, a gem expert, had recently been president of the *Classe de la Joaillerie-Bijouterie* jury at the 1867 Exposition Universelle. He was also known to be an excellent buyer of jewels, especially since his second marriage in 1865 to the famously beautiful Georgiana Elizabeth Moncrieffe, whose "loveliness was something quite apart." Thirty years her husband's junior, Lady Dudley was something of a celebrity both at home and abroad (even Empress Eugénie and her court "confessed themselves completely outshone"), and the couple, who ordered a ring from Cartier in 1869, could not have been better ambassadors for the firm.

As his son helped spread the Cartier name further afield, Louis-François was feeling good about the future. Confident that he had built a business stable enough to pass down to the next generation, and reassured that Alfred was up to the role, he began to consider retirement. His optimism, unfortunately, would not last for long.

PARIS IS EMPTY

In July 1870, Napoleon III led his country into a badly planned and disastrous war against Prussia. The sixty-two-year-old emperor, suffering from ill health, commanded his troops into a succession of defeats. By August, Prussian forces had captured two French armies, including the one led by the Emperor himself at Sedan, and the fall of the Empire was proclaimed. Empress Eugénie fled to England with just one jewel, a locket that she gave to Lady Burgoyne, wife of the owner of the ship that took her to Ryde. It was her friend Princess Metternich, once a dancer in the bejeweled quadrant at the Empress's ball, who organized the safe transfer of the royal jewels to the Austrian embassy in London. Those same pearls and diamonds that had once symbolized ultimate power would become crucial insurance against an uncertain future.

Paris became an army camp: French soldiers within and Prussian soldiers without. For five months, the city was under siege. Luxuries disappeared first, followed by necessities. Food became scarce, and Parisians, who had initially been appalled by the idea of eating horse when the beef ran out, soon had to make do with eating far worse. Economic activity ground to a halt. "Business for France is everywhere broken up," wrote a journalist for *The Times* of London, "and one-third of the country is devastated and ruined."

By January 1871, with the prolonged war putting too much strain on the Prussian economy, the Prussian chancellor, Otto von Bismarck, ordered a bombardment of the French capital. The Parisians had gone to great lengths to protect their national treasures. External monuments had been moved underground, and sandbags covered the Louvre and other important buildings. But the shelling of the city was devastating, and the conflict would cause the most damage to the French capital in its history. Over twenty-three nights, the Prussians attempted to break French morale and force the city's surrender. As Communards were brutally massacred by French troops in Parc Monceau and Rue de la Paix, total casualties reached into the hundreds and many residents came perilously close to starvation. Within the month, Paris had surrendered. Bismarck honored the armistice by sending in trainloads of food, but insisted on retaining a Prussian garrison in Paris. Thousands of French citizens, from artists to aristocrats to revolutionaries, had either fled already or were planning to flee: "Paris is empty and will become even emptier," Théodore Duret wrote in May 1871 to the artist Camille Pissarro (who had escaped to London). "Anyone would think there never were any painters or artists in Paris."

Set against these scenes of chaos and desolation, business of any sort was almost impossible and Louis-François found his firm perilously close to the edge. Desperate, he hid away the firm's stock of jewels and fled to San Sebastián in the northern Basque region of Spain, writing to his son that he could not bear "to watch the Prussians parading up and down the boulevards in front of my window." Alfred, who was living in Paris, mostly surviving "on horsemeat, dogs, and rats," didn't leave for some time. Even after Cartier shuttered its doors, he sought out business opportunities in his city under siege, and he became known as a trustworthy buyer of gems for those needing to convert their valuable belongings into money. In the autumn of 1870, he was informed that the famous courtesan Giulia Barucci had died. Trapped in her house on Rue de Beaune during the

Paris Commune, she had succumbed to tuberculosis, leaving behind hundreds of thousands of francs' worth of jewels. Her heirs, of simple Italian peasant stock and keen to monetize their inheritance, agreed to Alfred's proposal to act as an agent on their behalf. For a commission of 5 percent, he promised to take the gems across the Channel and sell them to a British public mostly unaffected by the Franco-Prussian War.

In 1871, holding his jewelry cases close, Alfred left Paris and took a boat to England. Once in London, he found simple rooms in Argyll Street as the lodger of a Mr. Stammwitz, a wealthy tailor who had immigrated from Prussia and built a large, well-respected business in the British capital. Louis-François, who'd always hated being separated from his only son, realized that without overseas business, Cartier would not survive these disastrous times. "I don't need to tell you that I long for your return," he had written. "You and I are inseparable, so it hurts me to make you stay in London . . . for the length of time that you need to make the business achieve its greatest possible success."

VENUS DE MILO

La Barucci, or at least her jewels, would help keep Cartier afloat through the Siege. Not only were they magnificent but they also had that added allure of fame. The dark-eyed, golden-skinned Italian had been known far further afield than Paris. From an underprivileged background, she had become a celebrated courtesan at a time when courtesans, or cocottes as they were also known, often accumulated more power and wealth than their "respectable" counterparts. Stars of their day, they would appear in the best restaurants or at the opera *"en grande toilette,"* covered in jewels. Far from being ashamed or thinking themselves beneath the lofty aristocratic lovers they took, the cocottes received admirers, according to the contemporary chronicler the Comte de Maugny, "with the grave and imposing bearing of ambassadresses taking the air."

At the peak of her beauty, La Barucci had been considered the *"grande cocotte"* of her generation. *"Je souis* [sic] *le Vénus de Milo.*

Je souis [sic] *la première putain de Paris"* (I am the Venus de Milo, I am the number one whore in Paris), she would boast in her Italian-accented French. Only the wealthiest men could have afforded the exorbitant price of seeing her naked, and her lavish home at 124 Avenue des Champs-Élysées, complete with liveried footmen and a grand white-carpeted staircase, had been testament to the hold she exerted over fashionable Paris. She had collected jewelry and calling cards from her many male admirers. The jewelry, said to be worth a million francs in total, was proudly displayed in a cabinet for her visitors to admire. The calling cards, including gold-embossed ones from the court, crested ones from the imperial family, and others from almost every diplomatic corps in Europe, were kept in a Chinese bowl by her fireplace.

When she was asked to meet the Prince of Wales (the future King Edward VII) by the Duc de Grammont-Caderousse, she was instructed to turn up on time and behave politely. After swanning in forty-five minutes late, dripping in diamonds, she was presented to the infuriated prince as "the most unpunctual woman in France." Entirely unrepentant, she turned around and slowly let her dress drop to the floor without uttering a word. When she was later reprimanded by the Duc, she cried out in shock, "What, did you not tell me to behave properly to His Royal Highness? I showed him the best I have and it was free!"

By the time Alfred had arrived in London with La Barucci's jewels, the news of her death had reached the Prince of Wales via her brother, who had tried to blackmail the future king. He'd found among his sister's possessions intimate and compromising correspondence with *"votre Altesse"* and demanded £1,200 ($145,000 today) in order for it to be reclaimed. In the end, the matter was dealt with by the Prince's private secretary, who, after verifying the letters were real, managed to secure them for a quarter of the original asking price. Relieved, the future king was tactfully warned by his advisers to be more careful in future.

Among the courtesan's jewels that Alfred was tasked with selling were a ten-strand pearl necklace and, from inside her famous treasure chest with its separate compartments, a multitude of colored gemstones and diamonds. Having crossed the Channel from a city that was paralyzed economically, he happily found himself inundated with interested buyers. In contrast to those peers in the French capital who had dealt with the siege by simply shutting up shop, Alfred's journey overseas resulted in a sale of 800,000 francs ($4.2 million today) and a not insignificant 40,000-franc ($210,000) commission for himself.

For the following two years, Alfred spent more time in London than in his home city. He acted as a middleman between fellow French exiles forced to sell their gems to pay for their new lives and the English aristocracy whose daily rituals demanded a change of jewels for every meal. Though prominent French figures sometimes preferred to sell via an auction (Empress Eugénie chose Messrs Christie and Woods to sell "some splendid jewels, the property of a Lady of Rank"), others, less well known, came to rely on the affable Monsieur Cartier. He was no longer an unknown jeweler in a foreign city; the successful sale of La Barucci's jewels and the prior patronage of clients like Lord and Lady Dudley had raised his profile among both French sellers and English buyers. Before long, Alfred would even earn Cartier an accolade as an official supplier to the Court of St. James's.

Following his father's sage advice to always be kind, Alfred built up close friendships with his fellow exiles in London, regardless of class or circumstance. They were, in some cases, friendships that would later pay dividends. The French courtesan Léonide Leblanc, who appeared in several English theaters giving benefit performances for the French prisoners of war, was one of those grateful for the support that Alfred had offered her. When she returned to France and became the mistress of the Duc d'Aumale, she went on to become one of Cartier's most important patrons. The Duc was, after all, King Louis-Philippe's richest son and a key figure in Parisian high society. On one occasion Leblanc was said to have been traveling by train to her lover's château at Chantilly when she overheard three society ladies trying to outdo each other over how well they knew the Duc. "I'm lunching with the Duc tomorrow," boasted one. Another claimed that she was dining with the Duc next week, and the third said that she and her husband were staying at his château the following month. Leblanc didn't say a word until, as the train drew into the station, she alighted. Smiling sweetly as she closed the door behind her, she simply said, "And I, ladies, am sleeping with the Duc tonight."

HANDING OVER THE REINS

Once the Prussians had left his city, Louis-François Cartier returned to Paris and reopened his store. With Alfred still away, the fifty-four-year-old was helped by his son-in-law, Prosper Lecomte, whose own business had been among the many that had not survived the siege. Louis-François, happy with the idea of Cartier becoming even more of a family business, proposed that Prosper, Camille, and their children move into the apartment above the showroom on Boulevard des Italiens, and by 1873, they were comfortably installed there, with their maid in the attic.

"Prosper is drawing in the sales ledger . . . just as you would do," Louis-François wrote to Alfred in late August 1873 as he waited patiently for his son's return and considered the family's future. He had grandchildren from his daughter, but he wanted a Cartier heir and was not blind to the potential benefits of his son's marrying into money. Building a firm from nothing had been difficult. Though over the years Cartier had attracted several prominent clients, on the whole, they still came to 9 Boulevard des Italiens for smaller purchases (in 1873, the value of the rings and brooches in stock amounted to almost five times the value of the necklaces). Louis-François wanted more for his son.

In the autumn of 1873, soon after his thirty-two-year-old son had returned to Paris, Louis-François officially ceded control of the family firm. But he did not simply give the business to Alfred. Believing that his son would appreciate the firm more if he had paid for it, Louis-François sold him Cartier for 143,000 francs (around $640,000 today). Of this, it was the stock in the showroom—from rings, earrings, and necklaces to candlesticks and silver teapots—that made up the lion's share of the payment. The cost of the actual firm (defined as "the customers" and "the material that furnishes the store") was only one-third of the total.

Mirroring the favorable terms Picard had once offered him, Louis-

Having kept his business alive through revolution and war, Cartier's founder, Louis-François Cartier, spent his retirement studying everything from ancient Greek to stock market investing.

François proposed that Alfred spread the payment over ten equal parts, at 5 percent interest per year. Showing, though, that there was a limit even to the trust of a father for his son, the sale contract stipulated that Alfred could not "sell the business or assign the lease until he has paid the full price for this sale." And not forgetting his lucky escape, Louis-François also added a last proviso to the sale deed: The buyer had to "continue all necessary insurance against fires." Only then, with his son finally installed at the helm of the family firm, did Louis-François begin the retirement he had looked forward to for years: traveling widely, learning languages, and immersing himself in Paris's vibrant art scene.

In Conversation with Jean-Jacques Cartier

For the Cartiers, blood was thicker than water. There was a strong feeling that no one could be trusted as much as family. But they also felt that responsibility shouldn't be simply given. It had to be earned. My father taught that to me by making me work in the stables for an entire summer before I was allowed a horse of my own.

AN ARRANGED MARRIAGE

By the time Alfred became the owner of the Cartier store, Louis-François already had a prospective wife in mind for him. Alice Griffeuille was the youngest daughter of the late Joseph Griffeuille, a metal dealer from the Auvergne who had left a fortune of close to a million francs ($5.3 million today) to his family. In January 1872, Alice's only sibling, Marie, had married Théodule Bourdier, a forty-eight-year-old jeweler known to Louis-François for years through his connection with the Jewelry Union.

The Bourdier business was far better known in the Parisian jewelry world than Cartier, despite it having been founded almost fifteen years later. In 1872, it had been valued at 360,000 francs ($1.7 million today), more than twice the value of Cartier a year later. And Bourdier, as he told Louis-François, had plans to use his wife's substantial dowry for further expansion. Intrigued, Louis-François had made some enquiries about Marie's unmarried younger sister. And when he discovered that the widow Madame Griffeuille was keen to marry off her second daughter to a young man with similar prospects to Bourdier's, he set about ensuring that his son's finances would pass muster. It was part of the reason he had sold the business to Alfred in such a rush. They had an inside track on the Griffeuille family through Bourdier, but it wouldn't be long before other eligible young men heard of the dowry on offer. They couldn't afford to let this opportunity pass them by.

After several rounds of negotiations between Louis-François and Alice's uncle and brother-in-law, it was decided that Alfred and Alice would be married. Although an arranged union, the groom, eager to make the best of the firm he was taking over, was happy to go ahead with his father's proposal. The final dowry amount was confirmed at 100,000 francs ($430,000 today), and Alfred, who was bringing the Cartier business to the marriage, would see his net worth more than double. Just a week after the marriage contract had been inked, on Wednesday, July 1, 1874, the couple said their vows in the same church in which the twenty-one-year-old Alice had been baptized. The imposing Église Saint-Denys du Saint-Sacrement in Paris's 3rd arrondissement was just around the corner from the elegant Place des Vosges home where Alice lived with her mother. But Alfred, unlike his father, would not need to move in with his bride's family after the wedding.

The newlyweds set up housekeeping in the beautiful tall house that Louis-François had recently built at number 14 Rue de Prony.

The area, on the right bank of the Seine, had been part of the city's vast renovation project over the previous two decades. It fell in Paris's 17th arrondissement, one of the eight new boroughs created by Haussmann, and was considered his creation par excellence. By the time Alfred and Alice moved in, the road was filled with the upper classes, living in the "very well maintained" large houses that Émile Zola described in his notes of the time, "with footman, powdered concierge, imposing staircase, huge landing, couch, armchairs, flowers." At the end of their road, Parc Monceau was an oasis of calm that attracted aristocrats and artists alike with its paths wide enough for carriages, a bridge modeled on Venice's Rialto bridge, beautiful gardens, and ornamental gate.

Eleven months after walking down the aisle, Alice gave birth to Alfred's first heir. Named after both his grandfathers, Louis-Joseph Cartier was born at home, on Sunday, June 6, 1875, at eight o'clock in the evening. His entrance into the world was a ray of light for the extended family after a particularly devastating few weeks. Alfred's niece Jeanne, the three-year-old daughter of Camille, had died in April.

The Cartiers had come a long way in two generations. While Louis-François' mother was a washerwoman, his daughter-in-law came from a wealthy merchant family. Pictured here: Alfred, in his later years, and Alice Griffeuille around the time of their marriage.

It was a tragedy that had hit the fifty-six-year-old Louis-François hard. The very same day as his granddaughter's death, the patrician bought a plot in Père-Lachaise, the largest cemetery in Paris, to build a family crypt. The crypt (which still stands today) was not only a way of giving his loved ones the burial he felt they deserved but also a symbol of how far the Cartiers had come. His father, Pierre, would never have been able to afford such a monument. As soon as the building of the crypt was completed six months later, he transferred the bodies of both little Jeanne and his late father to rest there together.

THE FATHER OF HAUTE COUTURE

For Alfred the period after the birth of his son was a difficult one. The stability of commercial life under Napoleon III was a distant memory. After losing the Franco-Prussian War, France had been ordered to pay £200 million (over $24 billion today) in reparation costs to the Germans, putting huge pressure on the country. The advent of the Third Republic led to clashes between royalists and republicans, and, to make matters worse, the 1873 market crash in America resulted in a long depression on both sides of the Atlantic. Europe would struggle under a cloud of difficulty for the rest of the decade, with the gloom seeming to infiltrate even the creativity of the period. In contrast to the brilliant court of Empress Eugénie, suddenly "inspiration and taste seemed momentarily to have deserted the French jewellers." In 1875, just as Alfred was trying to repay his debt to his father, Cartier saw profits of just 39,200 francs, down from more than 48,000 francs nine years earlier.

Alfred was not one to simply look despondently on as the situation deteriorated. As he had done during the Siege, he bought from those desperate to sell, but he also sought out opportunities elsewhere. For some time the Cartiers had noted, with a degree of jealousy, that wealthy women favored couture over jewels. Increasingly aware of the money that was pouring into Parisian fashion, often from foreign visitors, Cartier decided to approach the city's most famous fashion house with a proposition.

Well before Chanel, Dior, and Yves Saint Laurent, Charles Frederick Worth was the first internationally renowned fashion designer.

Known as "the father of haute couture," Worth had turned the fashion industry on its head from his shop on the prestigious Rue de la Paix. He was the first to promote the crinoline and the *tournure* (a dress that was straight at the front and had a bustle at the back), the first stylist and artist to use live models, and the first designer in the world to hold fashion shows.

Born just six years apart, Louis-François and Charles Frederick Worth had both started out in the working class, but Worth's success had been stratospheric in comparison. He'd moved to Paris from England in 1845 aged twenty, speaking no French and with only £5 in his pocket. The textile apprenticeship he'd completed in London helped him secure work, and it wasn't long before his exceptional talent in dressmaking design was rewarded with prizes at the 1855 Exposition Universelle. Three years later, just before Louis-François bought Gillion, Charles Frederick opened his own fashion house. And when Princess Metternich wore a Worth creation to the Tuileries in front of Empress Eugénie, his future had been assured. "Worth was launched, and I was done for," the Princess later recalled. "No dress costing three hundred francs ever again saw the light of day."

In Worth's case, the Empress's patronage was far more visible than a silver tea service. As she modeled his dresses, his fame spread to women beyond the court, and to aristocratic clients beyond France. Over the following years and decades, Paris would become a regular shopping destination for princesses, empresses, and heiresses, principally so that they might purchase Worth creations. Then they spread the word by wearing them in front of admiring audiences back home.

When Alfred approached Charles Frederick in the 1870s, it was to ask if he could display some of his firm's jewelry in Worth's Rue de la Paix showroom windows for a small commission. Worth agreed, and the Cartiers' eyes were further opened to the vast fortunes of those who traveled to the French capital on a regular basis, especially those who came from America. Self-made industrialists and bankers from across the Atlantic were building fortunes to rival those of any European aristocrat. It planted another seed of an idea in Alfred. He would start advertising in English-language newspapers. Between May 1878 and January 1884, he placed more than a hundred advertisements for "Cartier Gillion" in the Saturday edition of the *American Register,* the first American newspaper published in Paris. And illustrating the

Alfred's marketing strategy included efforts to reach a wider audience by advertising in Paris's *American Register.* An early 1878 example (left) and one from 1884 (right) both highlight Cartier's offering at the time.

breadth of the firm's range at the time, the products advertised encompassed "curiosities" and "works of art" as well as jewelry.

TANTRUMS AFTER LUNCH

Louis Cartier's start in life was a far cry from the one his paternal grandfather had known. In contrast to the overcrowded Guermonprez house, the toddler Louis had space to run around and staff to attend to his needs. He could even play with other well-dressed little boys on the manicured grass of the neighboring Parc Monceau, at the same time that Claude Monet was inspired to capture its light in a series of early impressionist oil paintings.

But it wasn't all roses in the Cartier household. Alice was an opinionated wife who was, at times, unhappy with her role as a mother. When Alfred suggested she and two-year-old Louis spend the summer holidays out of Paris, she was not pleased. "It is I who has sacrificed herself in accepting this family life which ties me for the whole summer," she wrote to him, annoyed about being isolated in the seaside town of Le Tréport in northern France, far away from her friends in the capital. It had been a difficult couple of years for Alice. In November 1875, when Louis had been just a few months old, her adored mother had passed away suddenly, at the age of forty-eight, leaving her an orphan. "I often think of her, my mother, as she can't be replaced, and the void is as great as that lady was perfect." Five months later, mirroring the tragedy that had befallen Alfred's young niece, Jeanne, Alice heard that her sister's three-year-old daughter, Marthe Bourdier, had also died. Her sadness would have been understandable on its own, but on top of it, Alfred suspected she might be prone to excessive swings of emotion. "Today everything leads to sadness," she wrote, pregnant with their second child, "and . . . I have great difficulty in keeping myself from weeping."

Two-year-old Louis was showing all the signs of being as stubborn as his mother. "Your son had an enormous tantrum after lunch, over some beef in salad that I wouldn't give him, he had eaten a fried egg and some chicken, his appetite should have been satisfied, but he is becoming very greedy." Refusing to indulge him, Alice insisted on good manners, "and as he wouldn't ask my forgiveness he has gone to bed without dessert." A strong-minded woman, she insisted on being taken seriously: "When you are married and the mother of a family, you need authority and I will not give an inch." And yet for all her exasperation and moaning at her husband, she did love Alfred. Letters were affectionately signed "a big kiss from your little wife," and the couple would go on to have three more children together. The next one would arrive just as Louis prepared to turn three. Pierre Camille, a second boy, named after both Alfred's grandfather and his sister, was born in March 1878.

As the 1880s dawned, Alfred was not alone in hoping that the tough times of recent years were finally receding. Banks had started offering more credit and new businesses were founded. The Cartiers, financially prudent after the instability they had lived through, chose not to take out the cheap debt that was on offer, but they watched as others used the easily available cash to expand and confidence picked up. In 1883, Cartier recorded profits of more than 90,000 francs (more than double what they had been in 1875) thanks to an influx of clients who were optimistic enough to start spending on discretionary items. Alfred also increased his firm's range of products, buying far more stock than in the previous decade and becoming more experimental. Family records show Alfred taking a particular interest in platinum, for small, simple pieces such as studs and buttons.

But just as life looked to be picking up, there was another blow. Alfred's brother-in-law, Prosper Lecomte, unexpectedly passed away in the middle of the night at the age of just forty-seven. It was a huge loss, for the family and the firm, where Prosper had forged a role as Alfred's right-hand man. Camille was left a widow, with four fatherless children, all living above the Cartier showroom. Louis-François promised to look after them financially, but it was decided that it made more sense, given Alfred's position in the firm, for his family to live on Boulevard des Italiens. Camille and her children moved out into one of the properties owned by her father in the nearby town of Asnières-sur-Seine.

Alfred and Alice had two more children over the following four years. In 1884, a younger brother to nine-year-old Louis and six-year-old Pierre was born in the apartment above the Cartier showroom. Christened Jacques-Théodule, he was named partly after his uncle and godfather, Théodule Bourdier, and partly as a reference to the famous, albeit unrelated, French explorer who discovered Canada. A year later, in 1885, the final member of the Cartier family arrived. Suzanne became a much-adored little sister to the three boys.

"WITHOUT A CROWN, NO NEED FOR A KING"

The boom in Paris didn't last long. In 1882, the failure of the Union Générale, a French Catholic bank that had overextended itself, led to a crash in the stock market and widespread bankruptcies. Though the financially prudent Cartiers emerged largely unscathed, it became almost impossible to make decent money. Alfred kept the firm afloat by selling modest items, but profits suffered. Between the years 1883 and 1886, Cartier's income fell by 30 percent.

The following year, Paris was the center of an enormously controversial auction. The sale of the French crown jewels took place over twelve historic days in May 1887. Within the Louvre, visitors gathered to see the magnificent gems close up. Feelings were enormously divided. Those in charge claimed that a democracy had a duty to rid itself of frivolous objects of luxury "devoid of moral worth." But their real reason for instigating the sale was to stem royalist feeling and reduce the likelihood of a coup d'état: "without a crown, no need for a king." Others, meanwhile, looked on in horror to see the symbols of their country broken up (Princesse Mathilde would later ostracize women who wore the jewels from the auction in her presence).

Bidders included Tiffany, Bapst, Aucoc, Bourdier, and Boucheron. Cartier was not among them. Not only did Alfred have less liquid capital than his more successful peers, but he would not risk everything he and his father had achieved by taking on high levels of debt. The next generation of Cartiers would come to bid in the world's most historic auctions and would even acquire some of the jewels sold that day, but in 1887, forty years after the founding of the family firm, Cartier was still some way from playing in the big league.

HEAD IN THE CLOUDS

In the summer of 1889, Alfred and his family braved the unseasonable thunderstorms to visit the most impressive Exposition Universelle so far. After years of unwelcome instability, the French economy was again on an upward trajectory that would last, this time, for several decades, and the exhibition was fundamental in reinforcing Paris's position as capital of the cultural world. Welcoming a record 32 million visitors (compared to 5 million in 1855 and 15 million in 1867), it was held during the hundredth anniversary year of the storming of the Bastille. The tallest building in the world, the Eiffel Tower, was unveiled to awestruck tourists and locals alike as France presented itself as a progressive country in its prime.

The jewelry section of the exhibition had the draw of the Imperial Diamond, discovered five years earlier in India. At 400 carats before being cut, it was said to be the largest diamond in the world. Bourdier was awarded a gold medal by the fair's judging panel, but it was Boucheron, along with Vever, who came out on top this time, as his talents were recognized with the most prestigious prize of all: the Grand Prix for gem-set jewelry. As a retailer, yet to develop its own unique style, Cartier chose not to take a stand, but the showroom on Boulevard des Italiens included trinkets to commemorate the occasion, such as small Eiffel Tower charms.

In the couture category, Worth won the Grand Prix for his arresting Tulipes Hollandaises evening cape (now in the Metropolitan Museum of Art), which was revered for pushing the silk maker's art beyond what had gone before. By now, the sixty-four-year-old Charles Frederick had been joined in the business by his sons, Jean-Philippe and Gaston. Their creations at the Exhibition were, as was typical for Worth, not simply displayed on mannequins but worn by live models, including a particularly small one: Jean-Philippe's eight-year-old daughter. Andrée-Caroline was a love child, the result of an affair between her father and a house model at Worth. The young girl's standing in society would be tarnished as a result of her start in life, but her father, having no other children, had promised to bring her up as a Worth. Seeing her, just six years younger than his own eldest son, lit the spark of an idea for Alfred. Already, for the Cartiers, just knowing the Worths and having the opportunity to display jewels in their windows was positive for business. What if there was to be a real union between the families, a union of marriage?

For Louis Cartier, a self-confident fourteen-year-old, attending the fair alongside his father would leave him with a lifetime of vivid impressions. Inquisitive by nature, he marveled at the vast Galerie des Machines (Machinery Hall), the largest indoor space in the world, and the inspiring variety of new inventions and unusual sights, from locomotives to an Aztec temple. At his school, the Catholic École Stanislas on the Left Bank, he'd been reprimanded recently for not working hard enough, but his intelligence had never been in any doubt.

All three Cartier brothers benefited from the type of privileged education their grandfather had dreamed about as a child, even if Alfred feared his eldest son sometimes took it for granted. "He has a good heart but often seems cross," one school report read. "He does not pay enough attention to the remarks made about his character." Louis had received nine black marks that year, more than anyone else in his year group. The one subject in which he came top of the class was drawing. The teachers could see he was creative and admitted he had a good mind but despaired at his disruptive behavior. He was, they told his parents, too much of a daydreamer: "His head is in the clouds." Ironically, it was this very criticism, Louis' extraordinary powers of imagination and his refusal to follow the rules, that would enable Cartier to step definitively ahead of its peers in the era to come.

In Louis' defense, life at home was not easy. Alfred worried that his wife, Alice, was unwell. With four children, it was understandable that she sometimes felt overwhelmed, but as time went on, he feared it was more than that. Only much later was her deterioration linked to the onset of menopause. At the time, in the absence of effective med-

Curious and creative, the young Louis Cartier (right, as a law student in 1895) was interested in everything from new inventions and ancient civilizations to science and design. His father, meanwhile, was focused on securing him an appropriate future match and Andrée-Caroline Worth (left, as an eight-year-old modeling one of her famous grandfather's dresses in 1889) fit the bill.

ication, she was admitted to a sanatorium. Alfred was left looking after the children, and it was hard for them all. Fortunately, Louis-François, by now separated from his wife and living in a large apartment on Avenue de l'Opéra, was often around. His grandsons would later recall time spent with Bon Papa, listening to anecdotes of a very different kind of childhood.

In Conversation with Jean-Jacques Cartier

The three brothers were very close to their father. And their grandfather, too. There was a respect for the older generations, of course, but I think it was more than that. They would have done anything for one another. That's not to say they didn't come head to head on occasion! But they made up. Family came first.

A BELLE ÉPOQUE

Every time a new client walked through the doors of 9 Boulevard des Italiens, the Cartiers celebrated it as a small victory. By the late nineteenth century, with the firm's client base including notable aristocrats from the Prince and Princess of Wagram to Prince Pedro of Brazil and the Prince of Saxe-Coburg, the retired Louis-François was proud of how far his son had come.

Alfred, however, dreamed of bigger things. The reality was that most clients still tended to come to Cartier for small items and go elsewhere for their more important gems. While Bourdier had won worldwide acclaim for presenting an enamel egg containing a bouquet of diamond violets to the Empress of Russia, Cartier's biggest win of late had been a contract to make bronze medallions for the City of Bordeaux. Yes, it was good for business in terms of the ongoing revenue stream, but it was far from the type of prestigious work that would turn Cartier into a household name, and Alfred looked on his brother-in-law's success in Russia with some degree of envy.

The jewelry industry, meanwhile, had recently been upended by an unexpected discovery. Ever since a farmer's son had picked up a particularly shiny stone on the banks of the Orange River in the hot and desolate north of South Africa, the diamond business had exploded. That stone, found in March 1867, had turned out to be South Africa's first authenticated diamond. It weighed 21.25 carats, was brownish yellow in color, and would later be named the Eureka Diamond. Most important, though, it would lead to the discovery of vast diamond deposits over the next decade, and the founding of the De Beers mine by Cecil Rhodes in the 1880s. Previously, diamonds had been found only in small quantities in India and Brazil. Their scarcity had meant they were far more expensive than pearls. Now with diamonds far more freely available, the value of diamonds and pearls reversed, and high-quality natural pearls quickly became the most costly objects in the world.

The increased affordability of diamonds coincided with the international nouveaux riches seeking respectability through ostentatious jewels. Bankers, industrialists, and speculators from America, Germany, and England started to buy gems that would have put

Empress Eugénie and Princesse Mathilde in the shade (in some cases, they would even wear the Empress's old jewels). The aristocratic order was not so much collapsing as being enlarged to include those who could pay for its maintenance. Throughout the last decade of the nineteenth century, alliances between new, often foreign, money and blue blood became more and more common. When the impoverished nobleman Boniface (known as Boni) de Castellane married America's wealthiest heiress, Anna Gould, their wildly opulent parties would come to symbolize the very zenith of Belle Époque extravagance. And in England, when the railway heiress Consuelo Vanderbilt married the Duke of Marlborough, she became one of the first in a long line of "dollar princesses" shipped over from New York to transform the struggling finances of aristocratic landowners.

With the arrival of American heiresses to European shores came an influx of important gems and demand for new ones. The fabulous jewels Consuelo Vanderbilt brought with her included ropes of pearls that had belonged to Catherine the Great and Empress Eugénie. And though her diamond tiara may have "invariably produced a violent headache," it would raise the bar among jewelry buyers within Europe. Whereas size had previously been the overriding requirement for gemstones, increasingly there were well-informed purchasers from both North and South America who understood, and valued, quality more highly.

Against this backdrop, Alfred's expertise in gemstones would serve him well. Though Cartier might not be considered important enough for the dollar princesses quite yet, just being in an environment where there was such an interest in magnificent gems was good for business. Alfred had spent the last two decades building on the foundations laid by his father. Now, with the help of the next generation, he hoped to take it to the next level.

THE MAP

As he counted his takings for the day in the large showroom he had practically grown up in, Alfred could hear his children upstairs.

Louis, eighteen years old and enormously confident, had wanted to speak to his brothers about something important. Pierre, fifteen, sensible and eager to please, had been happy to oblige. And sweet Jacques, mature for his nine years, was, as usual, just thrilled to be included. The brothers' talk was of dividing and conquering, as though they were playing Risk, but there were no dice or toy soldiers. This wasn't a game.

Sitting in their bedroom, with its windows overlooking the busy Boulevard des Italiens below, the three brothers hunched over a map of the world. They knew that their time would come to take over the family business. When it did, they wanted more than anything to make their father and grandfather proud. "Never forget our dream," they would later write to one another in reminder of the pledge they had made that day, "to create the leading jewelry firm in the world!"

In Conversation with Jean-Jacques Cartier

The three brothers decided very early on that they wanted to take the business beyond Paris. My father told me how Louis had taken a pencil and divided a map of the world among them. Well, Louis was the eldest, and very much the boss of his siblings, so of course he had taken Paris, the headquarters, and he also wanted responsibility for the rest of Europe with all its important ruling families. Pierre had the Americas, both North and South. And my father was given England—that may not sound like so much, but it also included the British colonies. And India, you see, was particularly important when it came to gems.

The Exposition Universelle in 1889 and the huge influx of foreign visitors to Paris in the decade that followed had made the Cartiers more aware than ever of the possibilities outside France. Even the elderly Louis-François, not easily fazed after all he had gone through, had been astonished by the wealth from overseas. And the brothers started to realize they had something that their father and grandfather had never had. There were three of them. With three they could create scale. They dreamed of taking Cartier beyond Paris, to the world. Divide and conquer.

PART II

DIVIDE AND CONQUER

(1898–1919)

You know my two brothers are everything to me. Only together can we fulfill our dream and take our House to all four corners of the globe.

—LETTER FROM PIERRE CARTIER
TO JACQUES CARTIER, 1915

LOUIS (1898–1919)

A SPRING WEDDING

April 30, 1898. Springtime in Paris. Crowds were gathered outside the Church of the Madeleine, an imposing neoclassical building just to the northeast of the Élysée Palace, hoping to catch a glimpse of the sixteen-year-old bride as she arrived with her father. Inside, the Parisian fashion crowd were already at their pews. Eyeing one another's outfits and jostling for the best view of the aisle, they were eager to see what the granddaughter of the world's first celebrity designer would wear on the most important day of her life.

Up by the altar, the good-looking twenty-three-year-old groom was feeling uncomfortable. Under normal circumstances, Louis Cartier would have relished being the center of attention, especially surrounded by the crème de la crème of French society, but this was far from a normal day. Imploringly, he looked toward his father, who signaled encouragingly at the hundreds who had turned out to witness the union of two great families. Or rather, one great family, the Worths, and another family that still aspired to greatness. While the House of Worth was famous for revolutionizing Parisian fashion, the House of Cartier was still relatively unknown.

Just a few days earlier, Louis had gone to his father, Alfred, in desperation. He couldn't marry this girl, he had pleaded. She wasn't right. He understood that an alliance with her family would be good for their business, but what about his life? She would make him miserable. She wasn't like other girls: she was somber one minute, hysterical the next. His fourteen-year-old brother, Jacques, had spotted it too: "I spent several afternoons alone with her and I was struck by her strangeness, her melancholy, and her sense of not being completely there."

Later Jacques would recall how, soon after meeting Andrée-Caroline, she had insisted he read several morbid books, something that had surprised him given her young age. While he was reading, she "stayed silent for many hours and seemed completely absent of spirit. But occasionally she acted excessively gay for no apparent reason." He couldn't help but judge her to be "ill of mind." And he knew what he was talking about. "I have . . . witnessed the existence of nervous crises before." He was referring to his mother, Alice.

Louis had begged to call the wedding off. Alfred, who himself had

Louis Cartier as a twenty-three-year-old in 1898 (left);
Andrée-Caroline Worth, two weeks before turning thirteen,
in 1894 (right). Both photographed by Nadar.

entered into an arranged marriage over two decades earlier for the good of the family firm, would not hear of it. The two ended up having the almightiest row. Jacques, asked by Louis to be present, was shocked by the force of Alfred's reaction: "I attended a scene where my father pushed him into marriage, seizing him by the arms and forcefully expressing his concern over the future of the family and the business. . . . Without this obligation in which he was trapped, I am sure that my brother would have broken off the engagement."

But there was no way out. With Louis standing by the altar, the congregation looked back toward the large church doors where the silhouette of Andrée-Caroline appeared next to her father, and with every step that his bride-to-be took toward him, past the exquisitely arranged spring flowers on the end of each pew, Louis tried to master his discomfort. As he lifted her veil, he half-flinched to see a familiar absent look in her eyes. She would go through the motions of the wedding with "an unconscious air." Jacques, standing up by the altar alongside his brother, would later remember how Andrée-Caroline's "lack of reverence/recollection shocked me . . . I believe her to be ill, a young girl . . . to whom the idea of consent cannot have any value."

If that was so, the newspapers were blissfully unaware. The Paris broadsheets only gushed about the crowds gathered outside the magnificent Greek-temple-like church in order to watch a "deliciously pretty" bride in the "radiance of her sixteenth year." They were far more concerned with her family than anything else. She was, after all, descended from the great Monsieur Charles Frederick Worth himself, who "has rendered great services to France by developing— unbeknown to him—the luxury industry." Although the paper's comments on Worth and French luxury could have provided a neat segue into a brief description of Cartier as a family firm in the jewelry trade, neither the Cartier family nor firm was mentioned. In fact, so obscure was the young Louis Cartier that *Le Figaro* had to clarify, not once but twice—on consecutive days—that the groom of Andrée-Caroline was not the other, much better known Louis Cartier, the father of the Marquis de Villefranche.

This was why Alfred was so adamant that his eldest son had to follow his orders. Arranged marriages were not uncommon in French society, and this one would forge a lasting alliance between the relatively unknown (at least beyond Paris) Cartiers and the internationally celebrated Worths. After Charles Frederick Worth had passed away in 1895, his business had been taken over by his two sons, Gaston and Jean-Philippe. Under normal circumstances, the Cartiers would have struggled to marry into the Worth dynasty, but as Andrée-Caroline carried the stigma of having been born illegitimately, she could not marry into aristocratic circles. Jean-Philippe, keen to see his daughter taken care of by a respectable husband, had welcomed Alfred's interest on behalf of his eldest son. And just as Louis-François had negotiated his son's marriage contract with the Griffeuille family more than two decades before, so had Alfred negotiated Louis' future union.

The terms were favorable for the Cartiers. In return for Louis marrying his love child, Jean-Philippe offered not only a very handsome dowry of 720,000 francs (about $3.85 million today) but also introductions to the world's best luxury clients. When J. P. Morgan heard that the granddaughter of his late friend Charles Frederick Worth was to marry Louis, he called on the groom-to-be, promised him his future patronage, and bought $50,000 of jewels on the spot.

When Alfred first voiced the arranged marriage idea to his son, Louis had been happy to go along with it. Worth was one of the most famous names in Paris, and Louis, who didn't shy away from the limelight, wasn't averse to being linked to such celebrity. Though he hardly knew Andrée-Caroline, she was easy on the eyes (his nickname for her when they were courting was said to be So Pretty), and he was astute enough to see how the union would help his family business. The more time he had spent with his bride-to-be, however, the more his doubts had grown. By the time he had the confrontation with his father just before the wedding, he had made a decision. He would go ahead with the marriage only if his father would consent in advance to a divorce in the future, if as suspected the marriage turned out to be an unhappy one. Alfred, desperate that nothing should impede the arrangement he had made with Jean-Philippe, agreed to his son's sole condition but countered with an additional demand: If a divorce was sought by Louis, he would consent, but only after ten years. That would give the marriage a chance to succeed and also give Cartier enough time to benefit from an alliance with the House of Worth without upsetting Jean-Philippe too soon.

13 RUE DE LA PAIX

Ever since they were children, the Cartier brothers had dreamed about building the family business into the world's leading jewelry firm. By 1898, when Louis joined his father in the showroom at 9 Boulevard des Italiens, Cartier had a loyal domestic client base and a few faithful foreign visitors, but it was still some way off being known outside France. They longed for the kind of American grandes dames clients whose lives were summed up so succinctly by Alice Roosevelt Longworth. The Washington press recalled how they "bought clothes in Paris, came trotting back, perhaps went up the river for a brief moment, then to Newport, perhaps up the river again, New York for Christmas, worried through the winter, and then it was time to go to Paris again for more clothes and then to London. It was like living in a perpetual Christmas play."

Adjoining the majestic Place Vendôme, Rue de la Paix was the first port of call for luxury purchases in Paris. With Worth at number 7, the jeweler Mellerio at number 9, and the Hôtel Westminster at number 11–13, it was inundated with stylish ladies and wealthy admirers keen to impress them. Louis-François and Alfred had always known that location was key, and now Louis, having seen firsthand the caliber of clients who visited his father-in-law in the elegant Worth showroom, understood it too. He also, thanks to his wife's ample dowry, had the finances to make such a move possible. When part of the Hôtel Westminster was auctioned off in 1899, Cartier bought one of the two shops at number 13, with a lingerie firm taking the other half. The expansion into the wide-fronted store (encompassing the full 11–13 Rue de la Paix) would take place more than a decade later in 1912. For now, half of number 13 was quite sufficient. The new showroom was fitted out with all the latest modern technologies, including electricity (Cartier was one of the first firms to have electricity in Paris) and a telephone. They even had their own automobile for deliveries.

In Conversation with Jean-Jacques Cartier

The number thirteen has always been lucky for the Cartiers. I'm not sure if that superstition started before or after Alfred and Louis moved Cartier to 13 Rue de la Paix. Maybe that was why they had to have it! Anyway, by the time I came along, it was just the way it was.

On Boulevard des Italiens, Cartier had sold jewels and other decorative items bought in from external workshops or occasionally from individual clients. Now Louis would turn that old business model on its head. He didn't envisage Cartier as a retailer of others' creations. If his family firm was to stand out, he believed that its jewels must be unique and recognizably Cartier. They must be in the "Cartier style."

Louis started by building a team that would think differently. At school, he had been chastised for his "head in the clouds" mentality, but with a blank canvas to play with, his imagination became a huge asset. Bored with so much of the jewelry on the market, he didn't believe in hiring existing jewelry designers to join Cartier. He wanted "inventors," and before long his design team was made up of experts from a whole host of fields. Lace makers, bronze sculptors, and tapestry designers sat side by side up in the design studio with interior designers, architects, and ironworkers.

The fifty-seven-year-old Alfred, who had steadily steered the company since the 1870s, would continue to be involved in the business for the rest of his life. But with Louis' arrival in the firm, there was an injection of vibrant new blood, a defiance of the old ways, and an excitement for the future. Happy to let his son start making his mark, in August 1898 Alfred incorporated a new company, Cartier et Fils (Cartier and Son). And yet, as his own father had been with him, he was wary of giving Louis too much authority too early. His son had to prove himself first, and it wouldn't be until five years later, in 1903, that Louis would share a *procuration* (power of attorney) over the company's bank account. Louis didn't let it hold him back. Overflowing with ideas, he was impatient to set about modernizing all aspects of the firm, even if it sometimes meant clashing with his father.

Madame Ricaud was the first woman to work at Cartier. Alfred had hired her as a pearl stringer around the same time Louis joined the firm, with one proviso: She was not allowed to set foot inside 13 Rue de la Paix. She may have been a highly skilled employee, but as she was a member of the fairer sex, Alfred refused to sanction her presence alongside the male employee base in the main building and confined her to his own office at 4 Rue de la Paix just across the street. The result of the unusual setup was that near-priceless pearls were continually carted back and forth between buildings in the most inefficient manner. It wasn't long before Louis, not known for his patience at the best of times, had had enough. Marching across the street to see Madame Ricaud himself, he asked that she come and work, discreetly, at 13 Rue de la Paix. They wouldn't tell his father, he stressed, and she could string pearls in the small room (effectively a broom cupboard) under the stairs so she would be out of sight should Monsieur Alfred turn up unannounced. Madame Ricaud had little choice but to agree. She risked aggrieving either the young Monsieur Cartier or the elder one.

For a time the arrangement worked satisfactorily, until one day Madame grew thirsty and left her cubbyhole in search of a glass of water. Alfred, who had come to see his son, suddenly heard what sounded like the rustle of skirts. Confused, he followed the noise until he trapped the poor lady and furiously demanded an explanation. Terrified she would lose her job, the tearful pearl stringer tried to explain, diplomatically, that Monsieur Louis had asked her to work there. Alfred stormed up the stairs to his son's office and exploded with such fury that it could be heard throughout the building. Louis, still smarting from being forced into an unhappy marriage, was not prepared to keep conceding to his father. Especially not when he believed he was right. Sometime later Alfred came back down to the trembling Madame Ricaud and told her she could stay. Louis had won.

A JEWELRY REVOLUTION

Within a couple of years of Louis' joining his father in the family business, not only did Cartier have a foot in the door of perhaps the most renowned shopping street in the world, it was also becoming known for its unique jewels.

For some time, the artistic world had been buzzing with the rise of Art Nouveau, a style in the decorative arts that took its inspiration from free-floating forms in the natural world. Jewelers such as Lalique, Vever, and Fouquet used semiprecious stones, molded glass, and enamel to create pieces that were valued for their originality and design rather than the intrinsic value of the materials. But Louis had no particular interest in what his contemporaries were doing and no attraction to Art Nouveau. He wanted to create items that were timeless.

Known for marching his designers around the streets of Paris, Louis would urge them to look up and around rather than in the windows of other jewelers. He was particularly drawn to the idea of eighteenth-century France as a source of inspiration and encouraged his team to observe details of historical architecture: pediments above the doors, garlands of fruit on the Petit Trianon, and balconies on which wrought iron was shaped into wreaths and swags. It was the original eighteenth-century environment that was so exciting to Louis, not the more modern interpretation of it, and he and his team would fill notebooks with sketches of their surroundings. These, along with more detailed studies of eighteenth-century pattern books, would form the basis of what would become known as Cartier's "garland style." The Parisian wrought-iron balconies, as an example, with their decorative wreaths and delicate rise in the center, were tiaras on a larger scale. "In his eyes," Louis' grandson would later write, the French eighteenth century "portrayed France's past brilliance and influence." He wanted to evoke the spirit of the Ancien Régime and the brilliance of Versailles court life in his jewels, and in so doing appeal to a social elite looking to elevate itself from the crowd.

But the inspiration behind the jewels was only part of the creation. The challenge with the garland style was how to keep the designs light and airy when converted into metal and gemstones. Gold and silver, the traditional mounts for diamonds, were too heavy for the look Louis was trying to achieve. He wanted the mount to disappear, for the diamonds to be the star of the show. And so, ever the innovator, he started experimenting with different metals.

Still used predominantly for large-scale industrial purposes, platinum was not easily available for jewelers (who required only small amounts) in its pure form. And even when it was obtained, it was, as Louis would later point out, "no easy task to transform the thin, light metal into a support for precious stones." After all, it wouldn't work if the tiara looked stunning but

Queen Élisabeth of the Belgians in her 1910 garland-style diamond and platinum scroll tiara.

then you lost a diamond in your soup. In order to adapt the metal for use in jewelry, Cartier would have to think outside the box. Indeed, it was only when Louis looked in the unlikeliest of places—underneath a railway carriage—that he worked out what needed to be done. "It was not until we studied the mechanics of the springs and trusses that hold up the sleeping car that we were able to adapt the metal to our purpose."

In Conversation with Jean-Jacques Cartier

Louis was hugely creative and fiercely curious. He was an autodidact. He always wanted to know why and how. There are some people—most people—who are happy to watch the seasons come and go. Uncle Louis was one of those who wanted to know why they changed, how they changed. When I was a boy, he would always have some new scientific fact to tell me about.

Before long, Cartier had kick-started a revolution in jewelry through the use of this bright, strong metal. "The thick settings of gold, silver, and heavy woven strands that have been known since time immemorial were like the armor of jewelry," he explained. "The use of platinum, which became its embroidery, an innovation introduced by us, produced the Reformation." In reality, platinum had been used experimentally in jewelry since the eighteenth century, but not to anywhere near the same extent as Louis would go on to use it. He would source it directly from the platinum mines in Russia, and under his instruction it was transformed into a perfect light, flexible mount for diamonds, enabling Cartier to create delicate pieces that stood out from the heavy, often dowdy, gold and silver jewels of the time.

Later on, Cartier would produce its own type of hard platinum, by mixing the metal with nickel and iridium, and would gain a reputation for having the brightest platinum on the market. Visitors to 13 Rue de la Paix, from royalty to bankers, were impressed. Solomon Joel, a British financier who had made his money in South African diamond mines, specifically selected Cartier to make him jewelry that would show off his diamonds to their best advantage. The resulting 1912 *devant de corsage* (effectively a large brooch worn across one's bodice) with a 34-carat pear-shaped diamond at the center remains an example of exquisite craftsmanship and timeless design today. In 2019, it sold for over $10 million.

If ubiquity is the mark of a good innovation, Louis' use of platinum was a resounding triumph. For him, it was an accomplishment worth celebrating, primarily because it opened up whole new avenues of possibility. The strength, lightness, and flexibility of the metal enabled his teams to create far more delicate and lace-like jewels than would have been possible in silver or gold. Within the *colliers résille* (hairnet necklaces), for example, thin strands of platinum became the invisible wires that supported multiple diamonds, giving the impression of gemstones magically floating on the neck. Queen Alexandra bought one in 1904.

Most significantly, however, Louis' eighteenth-century-inspired diamond and platinum jewels marked the emergence of the "Cartier style." Just as he had envisioned, the family business was no longer a retailer selling pieces similar to those of other jewelers. It now sold unique creations that were recognizably Cartier. Among the devotees of the garland-style jewels were royals, aristocrats, and heiresses.

Tiaras, with jewels first to catch the eye of admirers (for the woman who wears a tiara towers above others), were an area of particular focus. An outward sign of privilege traditionally reserved for the elite, tiaras were not only de rigueur in British courtly circles but also in the French capital on Monday and Friday evenings, when ladies at the Paris Opéra would make their way in a bejeweled procession from the performance to dinner, known as *soirées de diadèmes*. Among the more influential clients who favored Louis' new garland-style tiaras were Anna Gould, Mrs. Keppel (mistress of Edward VII), Princess Marie Bonaparte, and Lady Astor.

And though, going forward, the Cartiers wouldn't always draw on eighteenth-century France as a source of inspiration, Louis' philosophy of going back to the original starting place, of truly understanding the period and culture he was representing in his jewels, would continue to play a fundamental part in the development of the Cartier style for years to come.

A DAUGHTER

Louis may have been making a name for himself professionally, but a couple of years into his marriage, life at home was not going so smoothly. He and Andrée-Caroline had moved into a townhouse belonging to her father in the upscale Avenue Montaigne. Though to the outside world they were a happily married couple who attended balls together and held dinner parties, Louis had confided in his brother that he was still concerned by her behavior.

In the winter of 1899, the seventeen-year-old Andrée-Caroline announced she was pregnant. If Louis had hoped for a male heir, he was to be disappointed. At 4:40 A.M. on August 9, 1900, little Anne-Marie, the first of the next generation of Cartiers, made her entrance into the world. After the birth, Andrée-Caroline became even more fragile. The twenty-five-year-old Louis, feeling trapped with a young baby and an unstable wife, spent more and more time away from home. His family didn't approve: "What a shame that Louis, with all his intelligence, is not blessed with willpower," his brother Pierre would write to Jacques. But they were wary of criticizing him. Louis was strong-minded and his siblings were well aware that he did "not like to change his ways or opinions." So instead of challenging Louis, the Cartiers tried to help by rallying around little Anne-Marie. The twenty-two-year-old Pierre, sixteen-year-old Jacques, and fifteen-year-old Suzanne were all smitten with their little niece, as was Alfred with his granddaughter, and they would remain fiercely protective of her throughout her childhood.

On the plus side of Louis' troubled marriage, his wife's family name continued to open doors to the cream of Parisian society. He attended events alongside prominent figures from the Comtesse Greffulhe, a renowned beauty and self-declared queen of the salons of Saint-Germain, to the Prince and Princesse de Polignac (the latter of the Singer sewing machine fortune). He joined prestigious clubs, such as the recently founded Paris Tennis Club into which he was invited by his cousin Jacques Worth (who would go on to win the doubles at Roland Garros twice). By 1907, he would be a proud member of the Cercle Hoche, the oldest fencing club in France, having been nominated by the Duke of Decazes (the father of the American socialite Daisy Fellowes) and Bernard Desouches, an industrialist who became a friend.

Along with the invaluable social connections, the ample and ongoing dowry from Jean-Philippe Worth was generous enough to help steady the marital ship in those early years. In addition to the initial lump sum of 200,000 francs paid to Louis on the day of the marriage, Jean-Philippe had promised his son-in-law a further 50,000 francs a year (plus interest) for ten years beginning April 1, 1901. Louis remained married in name but opted to spend as little time at home as possible and was soon known as a regular, without his wife, on the after-hours Paris nightlife scene.

A SECOND OFFICE

Louis Cartier was in his element at Maxim's. With its unmistakable red canopy on the outside and teeming with beautiful ladies inside, the fashionable Rue Royale restaurant was revered as the social and culinary heart of Paris. It was also, for Louis, a very convenient ten-minute walk from Rue de la Paix (somewhat ironically, past the Church of the Madeleine, where he had been married).

Growing up above the Cartier shop, Louis had crossed paths with the who's who of Paris, all the while aspiring to be among them rather than just on the other side of the counter. Resenting the way the blue-blooded circles generally dismissed his family as "trade," he enjoyed the mixed company of Maxim's, where artists, businessmen, and dukes could mingle over the delectable signature sole fillets and after-dinner liqueurs.

The real stars, though, were the courtesans. The owner, Eugène Cornuché, used to proclaim: "An empty room . . . Never! I always have a beauty sitting by the window, in view from the sidewalk." They turned up on the arm of their latest lover, dressed to the nines in an attempt to outdo their rivals. And jewels, of course, were a crucial part of their costume. For the gems they wore were an efficient way (in a time of no wealth tax) to proclaim to all potential admirers the high price of their charm and beauty. So overdressed were some female patrons that Cocteau is said to have recalled: "It was an accumulation of velvet, lace, ribbons, diamonds, and what all else I couldn't describe. To undress one of these women is like an outing that calls for three weeks' advance notice, it's like moving house."

In Conversation with Jean-Jacques Cartier

Uncle Louis definitely had an eye for the ladies. And he could get away with it, too, he was very good-looking and charming. I don't think my grandfather approved, he was a religious man, like his other two sons, but for the most part he let Louis get on with his life unless it affected the business.

It would have been hard for Louis to walk through Maxim's tables without spotting one of his own necklaces or corsage ornaments. Whereas, in the time of Alfred, the courtesan Léonide Leblanc had supported Cartier after the Franco-Prussian War by buying several small pieces, now Louis and his father were playing in the big leagues, and the courtesans came to 13 Rue de la Paix for more than small trinkets. The Spanish cocotte and actress Carolina Otéro, known simply as La Belle Otéro, was famously fond of gems. Fortunately, as the most sought-after woman in all of Europe, she also had a long line of impressive admirers—from Kaiser Wilhelm II to the King of Spain, the Shah of Persia, and various Russian grand dukes—to fund her habit. In 1903, she commissioned from Cartier a "technically astonishing" diamond and platinum *collier résille* that, even by today's standards, is quite remarkable. She supplied many of the gemstones herself, taking them from a bolero jacket that the jeweler Paul Hamelin had made for her.

Hugo, the notorious maître d'hôtel at Maxim's who knew everyone and everything, described a typical scene of extravagant catty rivalry between Otéro and Liane de Pougy, one of her prettiest fellow courtesans:

> The prize was given one night when the Spanish Otero arrived covered in gems, bracelets, necklaces, rings, a tiara and aigrette. What opulence. . . . She was vibrantly alive and the rubies, the sapphires, the emeralds, the diamonds by the kilogram sparkled! But the table of Madame de Pougy stayed empty. She finally arrived in a simple black dress, not a jewel to be seen. She had put all her jewels on her maid instead, who stood there with not a square centimeter not covered in sparkling gems. The whole of Maxim's was shocked! Madame de Pougy had won. Madame Otero stormed out, stopping at Madame de Pougy's table on the way, where she could not help but swear terribly in Spanish.

For Louis, struggling through an ill-fated marriage, evenings at Maxim's offered light relief. But to suggest his nights on the town were solely a way to spend time with the fairer sex would be to do him a disservice. He called the Club his "second office," and as spurious second offices go, it was at least a profitable one. Maxim's was the type of place where wealthy married men met their mistresses, so the possibilities of jewelry commissions abounded. And with almost every man came at least two opportunities for a sale: a diamond necklace for his lover, perhaps, and a guilt-driven tiara for the unsuspecting, or aggrieved, wife.

Sometimes this led to problems. On one early occasion, a Cartier salesman had made the gross error of asking a client's wife (who had popped in to 13 Rue de la Paix to have a tiara repaired) how she liked her new diamond necklace. When she replied that she had never received a necklace and her husband must have intended it for someone else, the mortified salesman tried desperately to backtrack, but it was too late. The husband had to put up with his wife's wrath that evening, and Louis lost a client the following day. Cartier changed the client record system after that. Discretion was crucial in this business.

In Conversation with Jean-Jacques Cartier

Instead of there just being a client card for the man who was buying the jewels, there would be separate cards for the recipients, too. The idea was that the salesmen would avoid slipups that way.

Cartier's client cards were said to be based on Hugo's secret little *cahier vert* (green notebook), detailing everything he needed to know about the courtesans, but it's hard to know which came first. It was a Cartier salesman's job to know multiple facts about his client, from his wife's birthday to his latest lover, and from the number of children he had to his skill on the tennis court. Even his favorite drink was logged on secret client cards alongside his latest Cartier purchase.

SANTOS

One of Louis' best-known early Parisian clients was in fact Brazilian. The pilot Alberto Santos-Dumont, son of a coffee magnate from outside São Paulo, had taken the French capital by storm since moving there in 1892. A regular competitor in flying races around the world, he delighted his admiring public with his vision that one day, everybody would be using airships to travel around town. He walked the walk too: In a display that would not be out of place in a futuristic movie, he would travel from Parisian restaurant to nightclub in his light airship, tying it to lampposts outside while he popped in for a glass or two of champagne. The *Baladeuse* (Wanderer), as Santos-Dumont named it, was his smallest flying machine, designed for urban travel, and it vaguely resembled a giant rugby ball on its side as it flew through the skies of Paris.

Fascinated by the novel idea of flying machines, Louis joined the blue-blooded Aéro Club of France, a society "to encourage aerial locomotion" that Santos-Dumont had founded along with Jules Verne and Henry Deutsch de la Meurthe. It held multiple competitions, from the Prix Deutsch de la Meurthe, which was a prize for lighter-than-air dirigible aircraft, to the later Gordon Bennett Cup for fixed-wing aircraft. Louis came to know Santos and became a regular at his little gatherings. The two men got on well, each admiring the other's innovative streak.

Santos-Dumont's dinner parties in his high-ceilinged Champs-Élysées apartment were legendary. Here one was as likely to be seated next to the daughter of the last emperor of Brazil as Edmund de Rothschild (whom Santos had first met when one of his planes had crashed into a chestnut tree in Rothschild's garden). But it wasn't so much the seating arrangement that attracted guests as the way they would be seated. Wanting to offer his diners an aerial experience, Santos experimented with suspending chairs and a table from the ceiling. While that worked for him and his almost unbelievably minute 100-pound weight, with a larger party the ceiling collapsed. Later, he commissioned a furniture maker to create extra-high chairs (accessible via little stepladders) and a very tall table to give the impression of eating in the sky. Nimble waiters would climb up and down the ladders to serve the meal.

On one occasion, when Louis and Santos were enjoying supper together at Maxim's, the pilot men-

Alberto Santos-Dumont in one of his flying machines. The Brazilian aviator was quite a celebrity in Paris. He had a vision that one day everyone would have their own flying machine.

tioned the difficulty he had faced during the Deutsch de la Meurthe race. The famous competition involved flying eleven miles from Paris's Parc de Saint-Cloud to the Eiffel Tower and back again in under thirty minutes. One of Santos's early attempts in the summer of 1901 had almost ended in disaster when his dirigible started to lose hydrogen. Much to the horror of his adoring fans looking up at him from the pavements below, Santos had crashed into the side of the Hôtel Trocadéro and had to be rescued by the fire brigade. Fortunately, he had survived unscathed, but his dirigible was declared irreparable. Santos immediately ordered the construction of a new machine so he could try again, and by autumn that same year, he had succeeded. The problem this time, though, as he explained to Louis, was that the Deutsch de la Meurthe was a race against time, and yet it was impossible to check his time while flying. Looking at his pocket watch required taking his hands off the controls. He simply couldn't risk that, not after the last crash.

Cartier's pocket watches were popular among fashionable men in the French capital. Flat and well proportioned, they fit smoothly into one's waistcoat and felt reassuringly solid in one's hand. But as Louis considered his friend's predicament, he started to imagine something just as stylish but even more practical. If he were to combine a smaller watch face with some kind of elegant built-in wrist strap, Santos wouldn't need to move his hands from the flying machine's controls.

Several weeks later, legend has it that Louis presented his friend with what he believed to be the first wristwatch for men. Bejeweled *montre-bracelets* had been favored by women wanting to draw attention to their pale wrists for centuries; Queen Elizabeth had worn one in the sixteenth century. But they had been a female decorative item: a tiny, often unreliable timepiece set within a round, oval, or square diamond frame and attached to the wrist with a black silk moiré band or sometimes a more extravagant diamond bracelet. Cartier had been creating these for its female clientele for some time, and they had even become something of a status symbol.

To suggest that the great Alberto Santos-Dumont should wear anything resembling one of these female decorations would have been absurd. Louis had to go back to the drawing board. In the

Franco-Prussian and Boer wars, soldiers had attached straps to pocket watches to create makeshift wristwatches, but Louis wouldn't have been happy putting the Cartier name to something so cumbersome. He wanted to create an object that was both functional and good-looking. He came up with a square, gold-rimmed watch face with lugs top and bottom so it could be attached securely to a sober, masculine leather braided strap. The only concession to his jeweler's background would be a plain sapphire winder on the right-hand side.

It was simple, and, as history would subsequently prove, timeless. But in the early twentieth century, it was a brave move to create something for men that had always been associated with female decoration. Louis had to effectively change the public's perception of a watch. Fortunately, he had the best brand ambassador in town. Santos wearing Louis' watch was the best brand endorsement Cartier could have wished for. The aviator was a global celebrity. Endlessly in newspapers, photographs of him reached countries on the other side of the world and his portrait image made it onto cigar boxes, matchbooks, and even dinner plates.

As interest in Santos-Dumont's elegant accessory spread through Paris, Louis set his preferred watchmakers the task of making more of these creations. But he kept them secret. It wouldn't be until 1911 that he would decide the time was right for a wider launch. In the meantime, he was forging a relationship that would enable him to create watches on a larger scale. He had a vision for the future of watchmaking, and his foresight here, as with his earlier adoption of platinum, would help Cartier stand out from its peers. Louis may have lacked the technical know-how and expertise to produce watches in-house, but he didn't let that stop him. One of his strengths was recognizing talent in others.

Since 1903, the forty-five-year-old watchmaker and inventor Edmond Jaeger had specialized in extra-flat watch cases by partnering with Lecoultre, the preeminent Swiss manufacturer of movements (the inner workings of a watch). Cartier became Jaeger's key client, solidifying this agreement four years later with a long-term exclusivity agreement. It was this collaboration that would, over many years, enable Cartier to "produce a series of exceptional watches which remain classics in the history of watchmaking."

When Louis released his new accessory for men onto the market in 1911, he rather brilliantly named it the Santos. Not only was his friend gratified by the recognition, but his fashion-conscious clients couldn't resist admiring a creation inspired by a style icon. It would be quite a few years before the wristwatch really took off among men (the war would play its part, as Louis would discover), but Santos would set Cartier apart as an innovative Maison for stylish gentlemen as well as their ladies.

THE PASSING OF A GREAT JEWELER

Though long since retired, the distinguished Louis-François had remained the wise patriarch of the Cartier family. As the firm he founded entered the twentieth century, Paris was booming and his grandsons, joining the luxury industry in an era of phenomenal wealth creation, found themselves in the right business at the right time. But they were also acutely aware that their dream of turning Cartier into the leading jewelry firm in the world was only within their grasp because of the foundations that their "Bon Papa" had painstakingly laid many years earlier.

Even in his eighties, Louis-François was a busy man. He may not have been involved in the day-to-day running of the business for many years, but he was not short of activities and social engagements to occupy his time. Sunday evenings, for instance, were spent over good food and fine wine with fellow members of the well-regarded Cercle Volney. Each week, Paul-Prosper Tillier, the club's eccentric president (and a renowned painter of beautiful women in varying states of undress), would lead lively debates about the Parisian art scene with members weighing in with proposals of up-and-coming artists to include in their next exhibition.

On the night of Sunday, May 15, 1904, the eighty-five-year-old Louis-François attended the lively meeting as usual. When it finished, shortly after 11:00 P.M., he bid his friends farewell and set off on the short ten-minute walk back to his spacious apartment on the Avenue de l'Opéra. Two hours later, a neighbor from the same building returned from an evening out as well. Finding it strange that the elevator was on an upper floor, she called it down. As it descended, she grew worried. She could see through the metal grille that something was wrong, and as soon as it reached the ground floor, she flung open the door. There, lying in a crumpled heap, was a distinguished white-haired gentleman, still in his overcoat and hat. A doctor was called but it was too late. Louis-François had suffered a stroke almost immediately after entering the lift and pressing the button for his fifth-floor apartment. The time of death was recorded as 11:30 P.M.

In contrast to his small wedding decades earlier, the church at Louis-François Cartier's funeral was packed. He would be buried in the Cartier crypt he had commissioned in Père-Lachaise Cemetery to mark the passing of his infant granddaughter twenty-nine years previously, the same year Louis had been born. In the week following his death, no fewer than seven newspapers would report the passing of Louis-François Cartier, the "founder of the great jewelery Maison of the Rue de la Paix." For the family, it was no less than the great entrepreneur deserved. They came together in their grief, reassured that their late patriarch had been happy with the success he had made of his life and driven forward by a desire to honor his memory.

A CLOCK MADE OF MYSTERY

Buoyed by the positive reaction to his wristwatch, Louis started spending more time on timepieces. In 1911, he engaged Maurice Couët, from a family of respected Parisian clockmakers, to work for Cartier. Together, the pair created a huge range of desk clocks with inventive features that still seem modern today, such as including the days of the week and the months, rotating dials, and diamond star motifs to mark the hours and minutes. But Louis wasn't content to stop there. He wanted to create a sensation. A clock so mysterious that no one would be able to fathom how it worked at all.

The "mystery" that he imagined with Couët was to create a transparent dial on which the hands of the clock appeared to hover in thin air, as if telling the time by magic. Inspired by the work of the illusionist Robert-Houdin, the first Cartier Mystery Clock took an entire year. No one except the clockmakers and the Cartier family were told how it worked. Even the salesmen were kept in the dark so that their sense of wonder was transmitted in the purest, most effective way possible to the confounded client.

In Conversation with Jean-Jacques Cartier

Uncle Louis had this idea to create a Mystery Clock. The clockmakers said it would be almost impossible to create one to his specifications, but that was like a red flag to a bull with Louis. If they said it couldn't be done, he would prove them wrong. That's the kind of person he was. That first clock took a year to make; a year is a long time when you're running a business! Louis kept sending it back to the workshop. The secret, you see, was that the workings were hidden in the base, but even when they had the mechanical part of it perfected, it had to be a thing of beauty. Oh, they were terrified of him in the workshops, he was so demanding! But he did it.

The banker J. P. Morgan was one of the few who could afford the finished product; he bought one of the earliest models, known as a Model A, in 1913. Recently, one of these models came up for auction. Made from rock crystal, black onyx, enamel, and diamond, it had previously belonged to the niece of Consuelo Vanderbilt. It ended up fetching over half a million dollars.

CLIENTS IN HIGH PLACES

Boosted by Louis' creative vision and insistence on the highest quality, Cartier's reputation spread further afield. In 1902 Louis' brother Pierre opened a showroom in London, and two years later, the firm received its first royal warrant from King Edward VII of England. As if one royal seal of approval was reassurance for other royals, it was swiftly followed by further warrants from Spain and Portugal. In 1907, Princesse Marie Bonaparte, the great-grandniece of Emperor Napoleon, chose Cartier jewels for her wedding to Prince George of Greece. The firm was so proud to have been selected for the bride's jewels that they even held an exhibition of them in the store, with the bride's Greek-goddess-like diamond and emerald olive wreath tiara the star of the show.

Most significant of all though, in terms of their spending power, were the Russian nobility. The Romanovs combined an insatiable desire for the biggest and the best, with the resources to make it possible. The Tsar was the richest man in the world, one of the few rulers who actually owned his country. He received an annual income of 20 million rubles a year (equivalent to around $260 million today), which was not always enough. It was quite common for him to delve into the royal coffers for top-ups. His offspring did well too. The grand dukes, who were his sons and grandsons, so more akin to European princes, had started receiving enormous annual sums from their twentieth birthday onward, while the grand duchesses' dowries were set at one million rubles ($13 million today).

In 1899, Grand Duke Alexei, the general admiral of the Russian navy and famous for his love of fast women and slow ships, had been among the first Romanovs to visit Cartier's Rue de la Paix store. In 1900, it was the turn of his sister-in-law, Grand Duchess Vladimir, who, with her love of jewelry and high standing within St. Petersberg, would go on to become the ideal client. In 1901, Louis welcomed Grand Duke Paul, Alexei's younger brother, just before his morganatic marriage and subsequent exile from Russia. The banished couple, who settled in Paris from 1902, would regularly grace the salons of 13 Rue de la Paix in the years to come. In her diaries, miraculously preserved in the Russian state archives, Grand Duke Paul's wife, Countess von Hohenfelsen, described typical shopping sprees in the chic Place Vendôme area, where it was not unusual to visit Cartier and Worth multiple times in the same day.

It wasn't long before Cartier was enjoying a stream of Russian visitors from the enormously wealthy Princess Vera Lobanov Rostovsky (who had exchanged her little hermitage in Moscow for Paris's Hôtel Ranelagh after the death of her husband) to the Dowager Empress's daughter, Grand Duchess Xenia (who visited in 1906). But it wasn't until 1907 that Louis welcomed the Dowager Empress Maria Feodorovna herself. Hugely influential, she was the widow of the late Emperor Alexander III and mother of the then-ruling Tsar Nicholas II. She was also the younger sister of Queen Alexandra of England, who was perhaps one of those who recommended

Cartier to her: Given that the two sisters sometimes even dressed in the same way (to emphasize how similar they looked), it's likely they would have also shared tips on fashionable jewelers of the time.

It is possible, too, that the Dowager Empress was, like so many other important clients, directed to 13 Rue de la Paix from the Maison Worth just a few doors down the road. She had been a loyal client of Worth for years and something of a muse for the late Charles Frederick himself. When he had been asked by a society figure why he couldn't design for others the same sublime dresses he made every week for the Empress, he had responded, "Bring me any woman in Europe—Queen, artiste or bourgeoise—who can inspire me as does Her Majesty, and I will make her confections while I live and charge her nothing."

The increasing number of glamorous visitors to Cartier's showroom justified a larger team. It was Alfred who, having long been impressed by the scale of Worth, suggested that they turn to Louis' father-in-law for advice. The Worth business was still vastly more prominent than that of Cartier, with a far greater pool of talent, and Jean-Philippe Worth, wanting his son-in-law to succeed in order that he might better support his daughter, had offered some of his recently trained employees. With the approval of their boss, the "very capable" administrator René Prieur (who became Louis' secretary in 1901) and salesmen including Paul Muffat (who joined Cartier in 1903 with a knowledge of gemstones from his father's lapidary work) left crinolines and corsets for diamonds and pearls. Importantly, they would bring some of their best clients along with them. Louis would be an exacting, authoritarian, and at times extremely difficult boss. He would also be hugely inspiring and motivating, capable of obtaining extraordinary results from his team.

Despite Louis' early successes, the early years of the twentieth century were not all plain sailing. The American financial crisis of 1907 had serious repercussions on the French luxury trade. As one rival later recalled, for over a year it depressed demand "for the most diverse objects: jewels, paintings, toilet articles, curios, antiques, etc., because we must never forget that America, a country of perpetual wealth creation, is Europe's best customer for all luxury goods." When Louis-François and Alfred had faced economic turbulence in the 1870s, they had looked to England for diversification. Now, with much of Europe and America struggling, they focused further on a country where the luxury-loving elite were wealthy enough to be un-affected by the storms of an economic depression: Russia.

OPERATION RUSSIA

It was around the time the Dowager Empress Maria Feodorovna first visited 13 Rue de la Paix in 1907 that the Cartiers decided to launch "Operation Russia" with full force. Alfred and Louis hired François Désiré Sarda, a bilingual Russian French businessman, to formulate a strategy for expansion within the land of the Romanovs. Based in St. Petersburg, Sarda's first job was to collate all the required paperwork for a royal warrant application. Having someone who spoke the language and understood the complicated requirements was a huge advantage, and before long, Cartier had made it onto the long list of recognized suppliers to the Imperial Court. Louis wasted no time in hanging the framed royal warrant alongside the others on the Rue de la Paix showroom wall in an outward affirmation of the family firm's growing prominence.

Next on Sarda's list of responsibilities was building up the Russian client base. He felt strongly that to best tap into the Russian market, Cartier should set up a permanent branch in St. Petersburg. The Cartiers disagreed, objecting that it would involve too much investment to start a new store and too much risk as they did not yet fully understand all the rules and regulations in Russia. Instead, they suggested that Sarda test the market for them by organizing a jewelry sale in St. Petersburg. In 1907, Sarda did as instructed, taking over a room in the Grand Hôtel de l'Europe to display Cartier's jewels, but as he had anticipated, the sale wasn't as much of a success as the family had hoped. He endeavored to explain the situation to Alfred and his sons: "Outside his own country, the Russian is indecisive and shy. Within three months he may easily spend seven-eighths of his wealth. In Russia, on the other hand, he is distrustful, and only on his third visit does he buy anything." The Romanovs might have been happy to spend their money while on holiday in Paris, but it appeared that buying foreign items in their hometown was a very different matter.

Disappointed, Pierre and Louis decided to take it one step further. As the 1907 recession in the West began to bite, tapping into Russia's wealth became more of a priority than ever. Sarda had been helpful as a contact on the ground, but they needed someone who was better networked. They recruited Paul Cheyrouze, a Parisian pearl expert who had been consulting with the French government on ways to better benefit from the pearl trade in Tahiti. He arrived at Cartier as a consultant, with a little black book of the very best addresses in Russia. "I'm in with the government, the police, the customs, immigration, the owner, with everyone," he boasted.

In early 1908, Cheyrouze wrote directly to the Dowager Empress, reminding her that she had acquired a tapestry portrait from him years earlier and lamenting the passing of her late husband, Alexander III, for whom he had had the pleasure of working. He went on to introduce his new employers: "Today I am attached," he explained, "to the impressive jewelry Maison Cartier, which Your Majesty already knows. I will soon be in Russia on business with the Head of the House, Monsieur Pierre Cartier, and Your Majesty would do me the greatest honor by agreeing to meet with us."

Without Cheyrouze's introduction, the Cartiers were little better than traveling salesmen in Russia. Yes, they had a royal warrant, but so did countless florists, bakers, and chocolate makers. It didn't make them worthy of a Romanov welcome. With Cheyrouze's help, doors started opening. On the Dowager Empress's recommendation, he was even granted an audience with the Tsar and Tsarina, the highest echelons of society. In the end they didn't buy much (the Tsarina, not as fond of opulent jewels as others in her extended family, felt obliged to favor local jewelers), but even the brooch they chose was an important endorsement.

For the 1908 Christmas season, the Cartiers decided to invest in a more significant sale in St. Petersburg. This time, rather than taking over a hotel salon, they rented premises from one of their best clients: Grand Duchess Vladimir. The building, in a splendid location on the banks of the River Neva with five windows looking directly onto the quayside, came at a reasonable price (900 rubles for a two-month period, equivalent to about $10,400 today), but inside it was very basic. Cartier employees from Paris, led by the former Worth salesman Paul Muffat, arrived a few weeks in advance of the opening with the brief of transforming it into a glittering salon worthy of the mighty Romanovs. Their days were filled with painting and decorating while their nights were spent on camp beds in the showroom, wrapped up in rugs against the bitter Russian cold. Finally, on December 9, the Cartier name was inscribed above the windows in smart black lettering, and the store opened for business.

To market the event, more than five hundred personal letters of invitation had been sent out, with precise instructions given to the delivery boy: He should be clean and intelligent and hand each letter to the doorman while concealing all the other letters "so as to give the impression that he has come for that purpose alone." Their tactics paid off, at least to some extent, and Cartier's early form of a Christmas pop-up store attracted several new clients. Jewelry was admired, sales were completed, and orders were sent back to Paris. Taken as a whole, however, the costs outstripped the takings and the season ended with a loss. Part of the problem was that the Grand Duchess Vladimir's not-to-be-missed Christmas bazaar was going on during the same period and many of the clients Cartier had hoped to attract were there instead. It was also hard to complete any commissions in the short matter of weeks the branch was open (the orders had to be made in Paris and then transported back to Russia). Sarda, frustrated by the timing and client issues, again stressed to Alfred and Louis that in order to succeed in Russia, the Cartiers must open a permanent branch there. Cartier's Parisian rival, Boucheron, had opened to acclaim in Moscow back in 1897, he reasoned, and there was still a space wide open for a luxury French jeweler in St. Petersburg.

Once again, Alfred and Louis refused. Apart from all of the other concerns about high fixed costs and unknown rules and regulations, Alfred particularly was adamant that every branch should be run by a member of the family. Three sons meant three branches. Louis' younger brother, Pierre, had recently opened a new showroom in London, so there was only one space left. The idea of a Russian branch, especially to the exclusion of, say, an American one, didn't hold water, at least not yet. Instead, Alfred felt they could achieve most of what they wanted with a couple of Russian sales each year, and Sarda (on the ground) maintaining the firm's interests for the rest of the time.

TROUBLES AT HOME

Ten years after the marriage between Louis and Andrée-Caroline, it was undeniable that, as Alfred had predicted, the alliance between the two families had been beneficial for Cartier. The reality, however, was that though Louis knew how to play the role of good husband if needed (the parties hosted by Mr. and Mrs. Louis Cartier, like the "elegant dancing evening" in Paris's Washington Palace in January 1907, often made it into the newspapers), the couple were increasingly estranged.

The Cartiers were not surprised. Letters suggest that though Andrée-Caroline's mood swings made her hard to live with, Louis was no piece of cake either. Confident, engaging, and charismatic in public, in private he suffered periods of great fury and impatience. And, while he was not averse to the strategic use of his wife's connections or spending her dowry, he lacked the enthusiasm to work on their marital relationship. He would, for instance, often leave his wife and daughter at Promenthoux, the Worths' fairy-tale castle residence on a lake in Switzerland, so that he might lead an almost bachelor-like existence in Paris. Pierre and Jacques may well have felt that their elder brother "does not always have a good sense of responsibility," but they would rarely say anything to his face. Louis had a temper and it was better for everybody that he stayed in a good mood. When Louis was "cheerful," Jacques would later write to Pierre, "it is good for business in 13 Rue de la Paix!" The inverse was also true.

Meanwhile, the outward bond between the Cartiers and the Worths was growing stronger. In 1907, Louis was a witness when his twenty-two-year-old sister, Suzanne, married Andrée-Caroline's cousin Jacques Worth. The other witness at the wedding was Jacques Lemoine, a jeweler just around the corner from Rue de la Paix on Rue de Castiglione who was married to the groom's sister, Renée Worth. Lemoine's family had been important Parisian jewelers since the Napoleonic era. The Cartiers were quick to spot the opportunity their extended family represented. In May of the following year, Lemoine wrote to all his clients informing them that he was merging his business into that of Cartier.

Several months later, on a wet day in late September 1908, Louis decided to take a short road trip out of town with a couple of friends.

He took his chauffeur along too, but being a keen driver with a passion for cars, he insisted on taking the wheel himself as they headed southeast out of Paris. Enjoying the feeling of speed, he accelerated along the narrow lanes around the historic forest town of Fontainebleau. And then in a split second the scene changed. He crashed into three cyclists, one of whom was thrown fifty feet into the air. Those in the car escaped with their lives, but not everyone was so lucky. According to one newspaper, one of the cyclists would later die from his injuries.

Louis was rushed to a hospital in agony, having broken his leg in three places. He wasn't able to walk properly for many months. It was a traumatic time, but he found himself, with the help of some good, fast-talking lawyers, excused from blame. Two months later, in November 1908, Louis was back in the papers, this time because his wife had demanded a divorce. Andrée-Caroline, driven to despair by her inattentive husband, finally wanted to close the chapter on their marriage. The divorce was made official the following March. Given the perceived wealth of the parties involved, the court made a very modest award to Andrée-Caroline of 300 francs ($1,300 today) per month for her daughter's maintenance.

Alfred, who had himself remained in an arranged marriage with Alice Griffeuille for decades, even after she started displaying signs of mental instability, was disappointed. But, nearing seventy now, he also wanted his children to be happy after he had gone. And fortunately, the links with Worth would continue through his daughter Suzanne's marriage with Jacques Worth. He was just insistent that Louis conduct himself properly when it came to looking after his eight-year-old daughter and his ex-wife. Since the death of Louis-François, Alfred had felt a duty to ensure that nothing, and no one, adversely impacted the reputation of Cartier.

The family firm was still his primary focus in life. He worked every day, was in charge of hiring new employees, and was often called on as an expert in the trade. In 1909, when the Turkish government wanted to value Abdul-Hamid's treasure chest of hidden jewels after the former sultan was deposed, Alfred was asked to consult on the matter. On his return, he was quizzed by the press for details of the gems (said to be worth 5 million francs, or $22 million today) and the likelihood of an auction. Knowing full well that a discreet press interview would help boost Cartier's standing at home and abroad, Alfred had dramatically put a finger to his lips and simply said, "I cannot speak. My report belongs to the Turkish government."

In Conversation with Jean-Jacques Cartier

Grandfather got on well with his sons, but Louis thought of himself as number one in the pecking order, and sometimes he had to be reminded who was boss. I'll give you an example. Louis would stop off at this one wonderful antiques shop on his way home from work. He became such a good client that the owner of the antiques shop joked that if Louis moved house, he would have to move his antiques shop too! Well, sometimes Louis would buy pieces and put them on the Cartier bill and then forget to pay—he was hopeless with finances. One time, after a few months when he still hadn't paid, the owner went around to my grandfather to let him know about the bill. Alfred hit the roof. He'd spent his life building up the Cartier name and would not have his son hurt the family reputation. Cartiers must always pay their bills on time. I don't think Uncle Louis made that mistake again!

A MEETING OF MINDS

After his divorce had been made official, Louis followed his father's advice and threw himself into work. Now living at 32 Avenue Marceau in the 8th arrondissement, between the Arc de Triomphe and the Eiffel Tower, he began an incredibly creative period, aided in no small part by a chance meeting with a gifted man who would become a major collaborator. Never one to follow convention, Louis Cartier found his greatest designer up a ladder.

Louis was taking a stroll along the wide tree-lined Boulevard Raspail, near his old school, when he spotted an exceptionally beautiful balcony being installed. Impressed by its avant-garde geometric style and sense of proportion, he called up to the workmen, asking who was responsible for its design. One of them shouted down that it was the work of their smart-looking companion on the ladder. He was onsite that day to ensure it was installed correctly. Louis again called up, this time asking if the young man could come down briefly. And eventually, the twenty-four-year-old Charles Jacqueau, frustrated at being interrupted, came down to talk to the man who was so incomprehensibly eager to speak to him.

Louis introduced himself as head of the Parisian jewelry firm Cartier. Not one to beat about the bush, he immediately asked the surprised Jacqueau to come for an interview. He had, he explained, already seen his ability to create beautiful objects in the iron balcony. He would be fascinated to see how the young man would tackle jewelry design. Jacqueau had trained at Paris's famous art school, the École des Arts Décoratifs, and knew of Cartier through one of his fellow students, Alexandre Genaille, who worked there as a senior designer. But he scoffed at Louis' suggestion. His professional expertise was in large metal structures, not in tiny gems. He wouldn't know where to start.

Louis, ten years older than Jacqueau and far more confident, was not used to taking no for an answer. He elaborated his pitch, explaining that jewelry was a form of metalwork and that clearly Jacqueau not only had real talent but also wasn't afraid to experiment with new ideas. He was exactly the kind of innovator that Cartier needed. Jacqueau, by now simply keen to return to the installation of his balcony, replied that he didn't have the time. He was under contract for another couple of months and couldn't just drop everything because some fancy jeweler spotted him up a ladder. Louis finally acquiesced, leaving his smart business card and suggesting that the young man drop by Rue de la Paix when he had finished his contract.

A couple of months later, when Jacqueau walked into Cartier, an excited Louis whisked him into his office and immediately began the interview. He laid out in front of Jacqueau a piece of paper, a pencil, and three piles of gems: one of rubies, one of sapphires, and one of diamonds. "Design me an item of jewelry," he instructed, explaining that he may use any or all of the gemstones in front of him. And with that, he stood up to leave Jacqueau alone with his imagination. Except

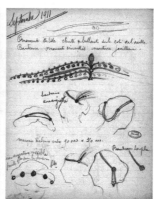

Charles Jacqueau, pictured here as an older man in Morocco,
alongside pages from his early design sketchbooks.

Jacqueau stood up too. He couldn't possibly do as Monsieur Louis
had asked, he objected; this whole idea had been a huge mistake.

Confused, Louis asked what was troubling him. "What if you're
setting me up?" Jacqueau replied. "You want to leave me in a room
with precious gemstones so that you can say I have stolen one. Then
you claim it on the insurance and I go to prison. I'm not as naïve as
you think." Louis laughed; he had trusted the young man from the
outset, but if it made Jacqueau feel more comfortable, he would
gladly sit with him, keeping watch while he worked. Jacqueau conceded and sat back down, quickly becoming absorbed in his task as
he put together a striking design. Louis, delighted his instinct had
proved correct, offered the younger man a job on the spot. And Jacqueau, intrigued by this new type of work and excited by the possibility of working for such a creatively brilliant boss, accepted.

A WORLD OF COLOR

It can't have been easy to get hold of tickets for the Ballets Russes'
1910 opening night performance of *Scheherazade,* but Louis managed it. The company's first season had been a sensation the previous
year, and Serge Diaghilev, the Ballets Russes' founder, had been the
talk of Paris ever since. The modern dancing, the lifelike sets, the
evocative costumes, the daring music—it was all so different from
the often staid and predictable traditional ballets.

As Louis took his seat alongside Charles Jacqueau, the energy in the Opéra Garnier was palpable. An audience made up of so many creative individuals, from Cocteau to Rodin to Chanel, was desperate to see what Diaghilev would do next. As the curtain rose and Léon Bakst's vibrant, sumptuous set was revealed, they were not disappointed. Billowing green curtains framed an opulent palace where hanging lanterns and tiled walls evoked the Eastern exoticism of *One Thousand and One Nights,* on which the performance was based.

As the ballet started, Michel Fokine's bold choreography and Rimsky-Korsakov's avant-garde music both enthralled and shocked the audience. It was Bakst's costumes, though, that had the most powerful effect on Louis and Jacqueau: brightly patterned pantaloons, midriff-baring tops, and strands upon strands of pearls. Diaghilev, being a perfectionist, had ensured that each outfit was made exactly as envisaged. Like Louis, he was known for being hugely demanding. And, as with Louis, the result was both spectacular and unique. The "extraordinary scenery, the even more extraordinary dresses, the most extraordinary color schemes," *Tatler* would remark, "upset all our preconceived ideas concerning ballet dancing and pantomime."

Always immaculately dressed under his fur-collared coat, when in Paris Diaghilev made sure to pop in to Cartier. Sometimes he was tempted by a new pearl tie pin for himself, other times it was a sapphire ring for his lover and premier danseur, Vaslav Nijinsky. Before long, he and Louis had become friends. With Paris a melting pot of art and new ideas, they were men of their time: both desperate to push the boundaries of fashion, both exacting aesthetes, both known for picking artists out of obscurity, and both with that "uncanny instinct for predicting the newest tendencies."

Like moths to a flame, Louis and Jacqueau were drawn back to the Ballets Russes performances, night after night, sketchbooks and pencils at the ready, hungry for new ideas. Bakst, famous for his use of dramatic color combinations, described how in *Scheherazade,* "against a lugubrious green I put a blue full of despair, paradoxical as it may seem," and Jacqueau was soon mirroring this in his designs. He would later recount in his diary how much he enjoyed the opportunity to create jewels compared with the earlier work he had been doing for Louis: "Recruited for the creation of precious objects, Monsieur Louis now thinks that in jewelry, I might also distinguish myself, [and] he has asked me to make some designs. The work itself is more interesting for me than having to work among eight other designers." It was a bold move for Jacqueau to break with the more subtle monochrome jewelry fashions of the day, but his decision to place blue and green side by side in his jewels (just as Bakst had done in his costumes) would attract trendsetters of the day. Among them, perhaps unsurprisingly, was Bakst himself, who picked out an emerald and sapphire ring.

Louis particularly loved the Persian style displayed in *Scheherazade*. A collector of Persian miniature paintings, he appreciated the oriental influence, and Cartier's jewels started to reflect his passion for the exotic. The more classic diamond and platinum garland creations remained popular with his traditional client base, but he added to them flashes of bright color. A brooch of little ruby and emerald fruits within an onyx and ruby bowl, for instance, was made in 1913 and sold to Grand Duke Paul of Russia. A bar brooch mixing emerald, jade, and turquoise with diamonds and a pearl, also made in 1913, was bought six years later by Baron Henri de Rothschild.

Cartier was not alone in coming under the spell of the Ballets Russes. Life (in Paris at least) soon began to imitate art. The Ballets Russes' costumes marked the start of a more modern era. The loose, flowing Arabian Nights–style outfits, so different from the tight corsets of the Belle Époque, provoked a new generation of couturiers to shake up traditional dress. In a promotional masterstroke, the French designer Paul Poiret hosted a lavish "Thousand and Second Night" party for three hundred guests, and it was such a roaring success that it was followed by a spate of oriental-themed balls. Countess Aynard de Chabrillan even took the idea to an entirely new level when she invited "nearly everyone prominent in Paris society" to her Paris residence, where Léon Bakst had painted the entrance court with frescoes of a Persian palace. The Aga Khan and the Maharaja of Kapurthala were among the twelve hundred guests in extravagant costumes and exotic jewels, while the Princess d'Arenberg made an entrance on a heavily bejeweled elephant.

But alluring though they were for many, the new trends at the turn of the twentieth century were too experimental for some. Worth, for instance, was unable to adapt to the wind of change that Diaghilev was blowing through Europe, and as designers like Poiret and Chanel began to make their mark, the star of Worth began to wane. Louis, in contrast, was determined not to rest on his laurels. Driven by a desire to keep innovating in Paris, he was also adamant that Cartier's good name should continue to be spread overseas. It was with this in mind that in December 1910, hot on the success of his Ballets Russes–inspired creations, he traveled to Russia. It was a trip that would not go exactly as planned.

ST. PETERSBURG, CHRISTMAS 1910

Oblivious to the winter wonderland view outside his window, Louis was beside himself with anxiety. With its large, sumptuous rooms, chic restaurant, and distinguished clientele, St. Petersburg's Grand Hôtel de l'Europe should have suited the thirty-five-year-old down to the ground. But the situation he found himself in was far from normal. "Everything," he wrote in desperation to his father, "has been leagued against my work and mental rest."

Just a few days previously, Louis had arrived by train from Paris with cases brimming with precious tiaras, clocks, and delicate objets d'art to sell over the Christmas season. The trip had started well with a personal invitation to call on his loyal client, Grand Duchess Vladimir. Head of the St. Petersburg social scene, the Grand Duchess was famed for making or breaking careers. Diaghilev, who had benefited from funding for his Ballets Russes performances when the Grand Duke Vladimir headed the arts committee, had found his sponsorship suddenly pulled from under his troupe's dancing feet when the Grand Duchess succeeded her late husband in 1909.

Fortunately for Louis, Grand Duchess Vladimir had something of an addiction to jewels. And not simply for their power to beautify. On her head and around her neck, diamonds and pearls became a political instrument, a powerful way of differentiating herself from the rest of society. At her wedding back in 1875, one American guest, Thomas W. Knox, couldn't help but remark: "Many a man would be willing to encumber himself with the princess just for the sake of the diamonds. . . . The loot of that woman, who probably never earned a sixpence in her life, would set up a first-class hotel."

That, however, had been just the beginning. As a young bride, the

Grand Duchess may have indulged, but as an increasingly well-known leader of society, she was unstoppable. The Grand Duke hadn't altogether approved of his wife's spending enormous sums on sapphire and emerald creations, but after he passed away in 1908, she was left with an annual allowance of a million francs (around $5 million today) and no one to stop her from spending it exactly as she pleased. When the American duchess Consuelo Vanderbilt was invited to the Grand Duchess's palace, she was given a special viewing of the jewels after dinner. Vanderbilt wasn't short on jewels or precious objects herself, but even she was blown away. Staring back up at her from the perfectly ordered cases in the Grand Duchess's dressing room were "endless parures of diamonds, emeralds, rubies and pearls, to say nothing of semi-precious stones such as turquoises, tourmalines, cat's eyes and aquamarines."

Louis had been particularly excited to be granted a private audience with the Grand Duchess, both for her personal love of jewels and for her standing in the Russian royal court. And the meeting had gone even better than he dared hope when she offered Car-tier a coveted spot at her annual charity Christmas bazaar. Louis would be permitted to select the exact location of his stall himself and he could, she proposed, borrow two Russian princesses as sales assistants for the four-day event. The 1908 Christmas sale Cartier had put on in the quay-side rented premises had failed to attract as many high-profile visitors as hoped because it had been in competition with this event. Now, with Cartier prom-ised a prime spot at the famous bazaar, Louis was hugely op-timistic. Everything the Grand Duchess was involved in seemed to be an overwhelming success: When she was hosting, as one

Grand Duchess Vladimir, pictured here at the February 1903 costume ball in the Winter Palace in St. Petersburg. Her headdress includes the famous suite of Romanov emeralds.

guest recalled, "one only met the prettiest and smartest women, the most distinguished men."

A loud knock at Louis' hotel room the following day had thrown everything into turmoil. Opening the door, Louis had been surprised to find himself face-to-face with several officious-looking men demanding to see his passport. Ignoring his request for an explanation, they had stormed past him to the bags of signature red jewelry boxes. Incensed, Louis had again demanded to know what was going on, but the men had simply seized his jewels and ordered him to follow them to the Customs Office. Once there, they informed him that they had reason to believe he had smuggled precious objects into Russia without declaring them properly. He was, they aggressively barked at him, a criminal, and he would be interrogated at length about his actions. It was very unlikely that either he or his jewels would be out in time for the Christmas bazaar.

The injustice of it all drove Louis into a rage. He knew that his Russian competitors resented his presence on their home turf. But for them to resort to false accusations to get rid of him was taking it too far. To be forced to miss the famous Christmas bazaar, after years of aspiring to have a stall there, was not even the worst of it. It would hurt this season's sales, of course, but that would be only a temporary setback. Far more damaging were the potential ramifications to Cartier's reputation. For decades the family had relied on client referrals to build their name into a luxury brand associated with the highest quality and utmost discretion. Cartier had become a name whispered among heiresses, countesses, and princesses, a name you could trust. Now, he fumed to his father, there were "rumors printed in the newspapers concerning this ridiculous affair of so-called smuggling" that threatened to reverse everything they had achieved.

Despite his protestations, Louis wasn't entirely without blame. He had failed to declare the gold in his stock on entering the country. The most valuable jewels he had brought with him to sell were platinum-mounted and therefore exempt from duties (platinum was yet to be designated a precious metal); however, there were several smaller gold items that should have been declared. Perhaps this was a genuine slipup, but the fact that gold was then taxed at 343 francs (more than $1,500 today) a kilo may have clouded his judgment.

With the help of his Russian contacts, Louis managed to have the smuggling charges cleared. Unfortunately, however, that wasn't the end of it. The authorities, acting in cahoots with his competitors, had him in their grasp and weren't going to let him go without a fight, especially with the Christmas bazaar just a few days away. If they could just keep his little red boxes impounded for another week, he would be forced to miss the entire season. "Dear Captain," he frantically wrote on December 22 to Captain Sawurski, the head of Grand Duchess Vladimir's staff, "I learned this evening that . . . in spite of the favorable view taken by the customs officer whom we saw together, the Petersburg jewelers are trying to obtain a decision prohibiting my firm from trading in Russia again. [I] suspect that another underhanded plot is being hatched against me."

He wasn't wrong. Next up was a charge of illegal hallmarking. Hallmarks, which varied from country to country, were official marks stamped on precious metals attesting to their purity. Cartier had been bringing jewels into Russia for years without any demands for Russian hallmarks, but suddenly he was told he was breaking the law. Unwilling to waste time arguing, he offered to immediately pay for any control required. That should have been an end to it, but the delays continued. Furious, Louis railed against the senselessness of the situation: "Part of my stock was returned to me, consisting of the cheapest pieces (mostly in gold), while on the other hand the expensive pieces consisting mainly of diamonds with very little gold were kept. To me this seems to be more incoherent. According to the law either all or nothing should have been hallmarked." Clearly feeling like a victim, he summed up the situation as he saw it: "I can only explain the senselessness of the present solution by a desire to harm a fine colleague unfamiliar with the national laws."

Louis didn't doubt the identity of the perpetrators behind the accusations. It was, he declared, a "conspiracy of my competitors which they created from the beginning." At the top of the list of his Russian competitors was his greatest rival, Carl Fabergé. Ironically enough (or maybe not), the year before, it had been the British Goldsmiths Association, perhaps pushed by jealous Mayfair jewelers, who had demanded that all Fabergé's London stock should be subject to stricter classification rules. It had ruled that Fabergé's stock should be stamped with a British assay mark to confirm their precious metal content. There had been no leniency for a "fine colleague unfamiliar with the national laws" that time. The whole experience had been highly disruptive to Fabergé's London business, and the idea that Fabergé might now want to cause the same chaos for a foreign competitor on its home turf was not altogether surprising. The tit-for-tat battle between the jewelers continued for several years until 1917, when Fabergé London, at that time a neighbor of Cartier London on New Bond Street, was forced to close its doors after the pressures of ongoing costly hallmarking restrictions combined with war and revolution became too much.

Louis' brush with the Russian authorities validated Alfred's often-expressed concerns about expansion into foreign markets. With a language they didn't understand, unfamiliar codes of conduct, and jealous local jewelers, Russia was still a large unknown. It may have been a country that was progressing rapidly—"wealth is edifying and the middle class are now growing rich," Louis had written to his father—but he also highlighted the downsides: "The lazy and pleasure-seeking character of many Russians, and the unending administrative formalities, prevent business from developing. To give you an idea, a bureaucrat from the imperial cabinet told me that the emerald mines are leased to a company that did not make a profit because of thievery—'every farmer, every worker, is a thief.'"

On the upside, Cartier's repeated run-ins with the authorities on this trip were proof of the firm's growing influence in Russia. It was surely no coincidence that the timing of the claims against Louis coincided with the preferential treatment he had started to receive from the Grand Duchess. A prime spot of his choosing at the sale of the season must have been like poison to the Russian jewelers used to being favored in their own country. "One hundred years after Napoleon," the papers declared bitterly, "there is another invasion of Russia by the French."

THE CHRISTMAS BAZAAR

Two days before Christmas, a hugely relieved and sleep-deprived Louis descended the palace staircase to see the crème de la crème of Russian society cooing over his jewels. At last, he wrote to his family, "the matter of a trial by the warranty seems averted." It had been a monumental waste of time. He should have been visiting clients and suppliers instead of explaining himself again and again to the customs authorities, but at least the Grand Duchess's bazaar, when it finally happened, was as fabulous as he had hoped with its "cathedral-like setting" and rousing music, which "filled the vast halls and seemed to rise up out of the depths of history."

The event took place over four days, from noon until midnight forty-eight hours of greeting people, smiling, selling. And there, presiding over the St. Petersburg aristocracy from the vast horseshoe-shaped sales counter, was Grand Duchess Vladimir herself. Known for obsessing over every tiny detail in the preparation of her own stall, she was a master saleswoman, "welcom[ing] everybody who approached with the same gracious smile, never pressing them to buy, but always managing to sell more than anyone else."

The bazaar thronged with deep-pocketed, glamorous shoppers, a few of whom Louis knew from their trips to Rue de la Paix but most of whom were new to him. "The crowd of onlookers surged everywhere," he later marveled, and yet "freedom and order prevailed." Laid out on the Cartier stand were some ninety brooches, nineteen necklaces, and thirteen tiaras for the Russian ladies to peruse. For the men, he had brought along clocks and pocket watches. The stall was popular, and in just four days it made 1.5 million rubles (about $18 million today). Louis had done it. After years of trying to break into the Russian market and countless attempts by others to prevent him from doing so, Cartier had finally made it into the inner circle and onto the royal Russian wish lists. He was also able to proudly show the Grand Duchess that her support of him was not in vain by presenting her with a sum of around 25,000 rubles (around $300,000 in today's money) to be distributed among the poor. Best of all, with the time-consuming customs problems finally behind him and the bazaar over, Louis was free to get on with what he had been looking forward to ever since he arrived in St. Petersburg: exploring Russia.

"REJUVENATION OF MY IDEAS"

"I am at a point of rejuvenation of my ideas and delighted to have come here," Louis wrote excitedly to his father after a trip to the magnificent Hermitage. The Paris branch would soon be enlarged and refurbished and his visit to Russia had provided valuable inspiration. "I think our new premises, to be justified in the eyes of our clients, needs to offer new pieces that I can hardly see possible in any other style than the Russian or the Persian." Just as the Ballets Russes had led him and Charles Jacqueau to experiment with an exotic mix of colors, so the St. Petersburg museums filled him with enthusiasm for all things Russian.

"The stay here is more favorable concerning ideas than in Paris," Louis explained. "There is in the Hermitage, in the private gallery, a wonderful collection of boxes, and diamond and emerald horse trappings, antique Easter eggs, fantastic watches in chatelaines, everything that interests our profession, except high jewelry, which is with the Empress." He even asked that Jacqueau be sent out to him because "it would be an excellent school for him regarding his department." Jacqueau set off from Paris immediately, and by January 1911, he and his boss were soaking up the wonders of Russian museums and galleries together. They traveled through the snow-covered country, accompanied by the senior salesman Léon Farines, stopping in Kiev and Moscow to visit workshops and suppliers. Jacqueau was never without his *cahier,* a brown drawing book, which he filled with sketches of the wonders he saw: brilliantly colored boxes, bejeweled belts and Easter eggs, crystal bowls and enameled frames, even a soldier's helmet and a golden chicken.

While Jacqueau's mind was opened to a whole new world of artistic possibilities, Louis rejoiced at the skill of Russian craftsmanship. Ten years previously, at the 1900 Exposition Universelle in Paris, he had seen the masterpieces of Carl Fabergé for the first time. Considered by some to be the greatest jeweler and goldsmith alive, Fabergé and the fourteen exquisite bejeweled Easter eggs he had brought with him to the Exposition had, quite deservedly, stolen the show. Ever since then Cartier had been exploring the possibilities presented by Russia. In 1904, Louis' brother Pierre had traveled to Russia to meet specialist suppliers and Cartier had started working with a few Russian workshops. Now, though, Louis saw he hadn't taken it far enough. Visiting the ateliers himself, he grew excited to see the intricacy of the craftsmanship, the brightness of the guilloche enamel, and the exquisite carving of hardstone ornaments. By the time he and Jacqueau returned to Paris in early 1911, they were full of new ideas for Russian-themed offerings. Small birds and animals sculpted from agate and smoky quartz would grace the windows of 13 Rue de la Paix alongside rose quartz parasol handles and enamel powder boxes. For those who had everything, there would be cigarette boxes, cane knobs, pencils, penknives, and scent vials, all beautifully enameled and with the option of personalization in diamond monograms.

Louis continued his experiments into timepieces too, creating geometrically-patterned enameled clock cases in shimmering pinks, blues, and violets. For a European audience in awe of the Romanovs, Cartier's Russian-inspired creations were enticing as much for their associations as for their intrinsic beauty. They sold well, attracting fashionable clients such as Consuelo Vanderbilt (who bought a Fabergé-inspired clock from Cartier in 1908) while helping to differentiate Cartier from many of its French peers.

Within Russia, Cartier's star was rising too. And this despite the danger lurking in the background in the years leading up to the 1917 revolution. During the 1911 Easter season, the Boucheron representative had been brutally murdered on a train by jewel thieves. Five months later, the prime minister (and Cartier's good client), Pyotr Stolypin, was assassinated at the Kiev Opera House by a leftist revolutionary. Clients, meanwhile, were still buying. Grand Duchess Vladimir spent 175,000 francs on a Cartier diamond and sapphire bodice ornament and diamond dog collar in 1910. Not unusually, she had requested a staggered payment schedule, and Cartier had agreed, allowing it to be split over four years despite the economic uncertainty. It was a well-known irony of the luxury trade that the richest clients generally took the longest to pay. Slow payments hurt Cartier's balance sheet in the short term, but Alfred, who had for years wanted to attract important Russians through the doors, insisted that his sons make every effort to win their custom.

It was a commitment that would serve them well as their reputation continued to spread throughout Russia. In 1912, Cartier's growing prominence hit a new high when the City of Paris, in an effort to strengthen ties between the two countries, selected a Cartier Easter egg as a gift for Tsar Nicholas II. This was a moment of particular satisfaction for Alfred, who for years had hoped to replicate the success of his late brother-in-law Théodule Bourdier's enameled Easter egg for the Russian empress in 1891.

The following year, just prior to the outbreak of war, the extensive celebrations to mark three hundred years of Romanov rule masked the rumblings of conflict. Luxury sales boomed. Cartier's platinum evening bags were a sellout item, Princess Yusupov indulged in several lucky (or not) charms, and her cousin Count Bilikin went all out on a showstopping emerald and diamond aigrette tiara, along with a pearl necklace. Grand Duchess Vladimir, tempted by several large diamond drops in the 15-to-21-carat range, held back until early the following year for the pièce de résistance: a 39.25-carat diamond at 45,600 rubles ($500,000 today). As usual with her large orders, she arranged to pay it in installments over three years.

Right up until the revolution, Cartier was on a winning trajectory in Russia. When Princess Irina, the daughter of Grand Duchess Xenia and niece of Tsar Nicholas II, married the insanely wealthy Prince Yusupov in February 1914, she chose a modern Cartier tiara of rock crystal. The wedding was such a major event that the publicity photograph of the bride in her diamonds had sold out before Cartier was able to acquire one for its Rue de la Paix showroom. A few months later, Cartier was selected above the usual Russian court jewelers of choice, Bolin and Fabergé, to design the ring for the high-profile wedding of Prince Sherbatov, the grandson of Count Stroganov, and the daughter of the late prime minister Stolypin. Indeed, by 1914, everything was going so well for the French firm in Russia that it even announced "as is fitting, we are now the leading firm in St. Petersburg."

PANPAN

The years leading up to World War I were, for Louis, particularly exciting ones. Professionally and creatively he was on a roll, but it was more than that. Single again, in his mid-thirties, he was considered quite a catch with his blue eyes, dark blond hair, and upturned mustache. He'd happily immersed himself in Paris's buzzing social scene with absolutely no intention of settling down again, when, quite unexpectedly, he met the woman who would become the love of his life.

Jeanne Toussaint, like Louis, was a regular at Maxim's in Paris. One evening she might be there with a gentleman companion, another time she'd be enjoying a girls' night with Coco Chanel at the expense of their obliging lovers. Always dressed immaculately, more often than not with a string of pearls around her neck and occasionally with her dark hair wrapped in a chic turban, Toussaint was known for her sense of style. Like Chanel, she was a strong, independent woman who'd come a long way from a childhood she liked to pretend never happened the way it did.

Jeanne had grown up in Charleroi, an industrial town on the banks of the river Sambre in the French-speaking region of southern Belgium. It had been a dreary place and her parents had been desperately poor. Her father, Victor Édouard, who had sold matches to make a living, had died when she was just seven years old, leaving her mother, a laundress, to look after five children. Jeanne was the youngest and had left home in the direction of Paris as soon as she could.

Since then, Jeanne had survived on a diet of wealthy admirers who had furnished her life in the French capital with apartments, dinners, and jewels. It was a world away from her impoverished beginnings and it suited her. She was born to be in this city at this time, and she was good at playing the game. Known as "PanPan" Toussaint, she mixed in the circles of the demimondaines (effectively ladies of the night, albeit in a socially acceptable way).

Presumably Jeanne had known exactly who Louis was when he first introduced himself. She was in her mid-twenties, twelve years younger than the suave jeweler, and had been supported financially for some time by a French aristocratic lover. Comte Pierre de Quinsonas had met Jeanne when he had fled to Belgium in 1909 to escape military service. They had fallen in love and he had promised to show her the world, even taking her to Africa (in 1912 and 1913), where he had given her the affectionate nickname PanPan as they watched the majestic panthers together in the wild.

Recently, though, Jeanne had become disillusioned with the Comte. She'd heard rumors that he was engaged to be married to an aristocrat and was hurt that he hadn't told her himself. Later, he would write a touching letter to ask for her forgiveness: "My dear

A young Jeanne Toussaint around the time she met Louis. She was
given the name "PanPan" because of her love of panthers.
Pictured here on safari in Africa in 1913.

PanPan, I'm sorry for all the pain I caused you. I didn't understand
early enough that you were the elite woman that you are. Thank you
for all the wonderful things you did for me." Jeanne may have ab-
horred Pierre's deceit, but part of her still loved him (she would keep
his love letters for the rest of her life). And his financial support was
not insignificant when it came to maintaining the lifestyle that she
had come to consider normal. Still, she was perhaps more open to the
advances of a good-looking jeweler than she might have been in earlier days. Louis would have no doubt put her at her ease; he was
practiced in the art of entertaining women. But he would soon find
that Jeanne was different from the others.

Perhaps it was because she was starved of beauty growing up that
Jeanne pursued it relentlessly as an adult. Not only did she exude
style, but she could see it everywhere. Louis was spellbound. Jeanne
didn't have a title, she wasn't as classically pretty as many of the
women he had courted, but she intrigued him. He wanted to understand the world through her eyes. And despite the warnings from
friends like Coco that Louis was a playboy who would end up hurting her, Jeanne couldn't keep herself from falling for him. As the political storm clouds of conflict gathered around Paris, they spent more
and more time together.

TWO ENEMIES: GERMANS AND MISERY

On a hot muggy day in late June 1914, news reached Paris of the assassination of the Archduke Franz Ferdinand and his wife by Serbian nationalists in Sarajevo. A month later, Austria-Hungary and then Germany declared war on Serbia, and in response, the Triple Entente (Russia, Great Britain, and France) returned the favor. In France, where the press and most political leaders advocated military action, a general mobilization was ordered on August 2 amid a wave of patriotic fervor.

It didn't take long for the German army to sweep through Belgium and march rapidly toward Paris. By the first week of September, the Germans were within a terrifyingly close thirty kilometers of Notre-Dame Cathedral, and the French president Raymond Poincaré was forced to declare that his government would temporarily relocate to safety in Bordeaux.

Louis turned up at the Paris war office, armed with his medical records. His right leg fracture from the car accident six years earlier, he explained, rendered him incapable of fighting, and he was initially given a desk job in Bordeaux. After sending his fourteen-year-old daughter, Anne-Marie, off to the Worths' Swiss château (a move that was criticized by his family), he traveled south to start his work alongside those in power. "I am staying in Bordeaux where I am assisting the minister of commerce, and all the government are here," he wrote to his youngest brother. "I am behaving as well as possible with all the bigwigs!" It suited him, a position of authority, or at least close to authority, away from the front. It also gave him the opportunity to see a specialist at the Bordeaux Faculty of Medicine about his leg troubles.

The biggest frustration was that he was far from both his business and Jeanne, to whom he was becoming ever closer. And the journey back to Paris was not straightforward. "If you want to travel by car, you need papers for the car and identity papers for everyone in the car," he explained to his family. "I am telling you all this as it's impossible to know it unless you have seen it for yourself as I have. I am going to Paris tomorrow by railway as I don't think I would be able to leave by car as the authorities would requisition the car." Even traveling by train was difficult: "To travel by railway you must get written approval from the commissaire de police as places are limited for civil travelers, buy food and drink as [there's] none on train, must order a car to pick you up in Paris as there are no cars and no lights in the night. It's really a city under siege."

As a result, the normally finger-on-the-pulse Louis was forced to take a back seat. He had to leave it to others and, as he advised his brothers, "don't worry about it too much!" Like most people, Louis couldn't imagine the war lasting anywhere near as long as it would. It was a devastating blow when his favorite uncle, General Roques, who had been a witness at his wedding, was killed in action while heading up the 10th Division in the northeast of France. "We have two enemies: Germans and misery," he wrote to his sister-in-law. "The death of Charles Roques is a huge loss for us, for both the family and the army."

While perhaps surprisingly relaxed about the state of affairs in the Paris Maison, Louis was concerned for his family. "Write to me of your news," he scribbled to his younger brother, Jacques, in 1914. "Tell me of your health, write to me at length of anything that interests you, do you have enough money?" It was, as he saw it, his role as an elder sibling to take charge of others. In this sense, he was a contradictory mix of traits: He could be caring and fiercely protective but equally irresponsible and self-centered. When he wrote to his elderly father, he advised him to travel to Bordeaux so they might see each other and then to go on to London to check on the Cartier branch over there.

This infuriated his brother Pierre, who wrote to Jacques in exasperation: "Why does Louis want to send Father . . . to London, passing through Bordeaux? It would be a long, painful journey. . . . If there is someone who should go to London, it is Louis. He is wasting time in Bordeaux getting to know government ministers, he should be with potential clients in London. Louis doesn't always have a good sense of responsibility." There was another thorn in Pierre's side too: his elder brother's ongoing relationship with Jeanne Toussaint. Like his father, he had never approved of Louis' dating a demimondaine, believing that his association with her demeaned the family name they were trying so hard to build. "And now he has sent for his little girlfriend to join him in Bordeaux!" he moaned in despair to Jacques.

For those left in Paris, life was challenging. Food was rationed and coal shortages made the freezing winter of 1916 particularly brutal. Though many shops stayed open, the cultural output of the city was significantly reduced. The fashion set tried to help out where they could. Worth offered its 7 Rue de la Paix building as a hospital, re-branding itself from *"Maison Worth"* to *"Hospital Worth."* The famed pianist and artist's muse Misia Sert set up her own ambulance unit by ingeniously requisitioning the delivery vans of Paris's couturi-ers. She was joined by Jean Cocteau, who, having been declared unfit for military service, had volunteered in the Red Cross ambulance di-vision but had no qualms about jumping ship to join his friend.

Cartier Paris kept going through the war years by adapting its product offerings. In the place of large gemstones, it sold smaller, more affordable pieces. There was a specific market for pendants, brooches, and charms in the shape of war-related objects like air-planes, with the red cross symbol or the year written in little pavé diamonds. Then there were the trophies of war, like the armlets cut from shells fired by cannons or *étuis* (cases) in the shape of military caps. But there was no getting away from the fact that this was a ter-rible market for a luxury business, and Alfred wrote in January 1915 to his sons complaining that "business in Paris, London and New York continues to be *nulles* [terrible]."

Number 13 Rue de la Paix was a ghost of its former self as many employees were called up to fight. Some stayed in touch with the Car-tier brothers by letter, eager for updates, nostalgic about the prewar days. Maurice Richard, Cartier's pearl expert, wrote from his regi-ment, "I hope I will again see Rue de la Paix like in the good old days—calm and long lasting. Actually this dream is a bit of an obses-sion of mine! Apologies for the long letter but it's a pleasure to think of Rue de la Paix." Of those that remained, M. Galopin was left in charge in Paris while René Prieur, Louis' personal secretary, was sent to New York to cover for the salesman Paul Muffat (who was later awarded the Croix de Guerre for his bravery at the Front).

In the midst of all this uncertainty, Louis received a telegram in the autumn of 1914 informing him that his mother, who had been in a psychiatric sanatorium on Rue Berton, not far from the Eiffel Tower, had passed away. While the war prevented both Louis and his younger brother Jacques from attending her funeral, Pierre managed to be there and wrote movingly to his siblings about it: "I descended on Father, who was remarkably brave. The service was beautiful and simple. Mother is looking down on us, looking after us all from heaven."

As the war continued, Louis changed roles multiple times. In 1915, he was mobilized as a driver in an airfield near Paris. "Louis is enjoying his service," Alfred wrote to Jacques; "he is without any great risk and is able to see different sides of this war—as interesting as if he was attached to a great major." The move to the capital had the added advantage of making it easier for him to secretly spend time with Jeanne Toussaint. There's a pencil sketch Louis drew for her at this time that still survives. It's small and simple, an image of a cat curled up asleep on a bed, perhaps not something one would expect this great woman of style to hold on to all her life. And yet it's also a strangely moving insight into their relationship. Louis was an acclaimed jeweler who promoted the use of precious stones by men looking to express their emotions—"for love expresses itself through these media," he observed in one interview—and yet with Jeanne he chose this personal, thoughtful gesture.

By early 1916, the military confirmed that Louis could stay in the auxiliary service due to ongoing complications with his knee and ankle. He wrote to family, friends, and clients to update them on his recent news. In an obsequious letter to Grand Duchess Vladimir of Russia in 1916, he enclosed several photographs "that I took at the front during my long stays in various locations," including one of seven soldiers leaning against the sides of a trench on the front line. Though he didn't actually fight himself, he commented on the solemn mustache-lined faces looking into the camera: "The soldiers seem more interested in having their photo taken than in the enemy!" He would later claim that it was on one such tour to the Front that he came up with the idea for what would become one of Cartier's most iconic creations: the Tank watch. And it was soon after this, in the spring of 1917, that the military agreed to release Louis from the war effort (on the basis that he was unable to drive a car), giving him the time to transform his idea into reality.

JEWELRY SPOTLIGHT: THE TANK WATCH

In December 1916, the French public had its first glimpse of the tanks used in the war when one appeared looming terrifyingly above a soldier on the front cover of *L'Illustration* magazine. Cartier's new watch was said to have been inspired by these mighty machines, with the watch brancards (the vertical side bars on each side of the dial) mirroring the tank's caterpillar treads on each side of the machine's cockpit. For Louis, the watch was not simply about telling the time, it had also to marry function and beauty in a harmonious whole, and the innovative design meant that the strap could be seamlessly integrated into the case. He was, first and foremost, a jeweler, and the watch, with its radiating roman numerals and cabochon sapphire winder, was a small work of art.

Whether the idea for Louis' new watch actually came from the tanks in the war or whether it was just an evolution of the earlier Santos, calling it the Tank was a stroke of genius from a sales perspective. It instantly tapped into the public's mood. Louis was said to have offered an early prototype of the Tank to the legendary American who helped win the war, General John "Black Jack" Pershing, commander of the American Expeditionary Force on the Western Front. Just as Alberto Santos-Dumont had helped popularize his namesake watch a decade earlier, so Pershing would have been the perfect international brand ambassador for the Tank.

As with the earlier Santos watch, part of Louis' problem when marketing the Tank was convincing men to exchange their very masculine pocket watch for an item that, at least in its smaller, more bejeweled form, had historically been the preserve of women. The Tank's simple geometric design already appealed to the male aesthetic, but Cartier pushed the macho angle even further by giving it a masculine pronoun. In French the word for "watch" is feminine, *la montre*; Cartier named their new creation *le Tank*.

In Paris, Boni de Castellane, the eccentric Belle Époque dandy, art dealer, now ex-husband of American heiress Anna

*Since its introduction
more than a century ago,
the Tank watch has
remained a perennial
classic, consistently
favored by some of the
most stylish people of
their time. Clockwise
from top, all wearing
the Tank, are Boni de
Castellane (who bought
one of the first Tanks in
1919), Rudolph Valentino
in* The Son of the Sheik, *and Jackie Kennedy
Onassis.*

Gould, and good friend of Louis Cartier, was one of the first to
adopt the new watch. He would wear it while schmoozing his
way through French high society. Later, Jean Cocteau, the artist and writer, would don his while dining out at Maxim's, and
across the Atlantic, Duke Ellington would wear his as he
played jazz onstage. Rudolph Valentino, actor and 1920s
heartthrob, famously insisted on wearing a Tank in the 1926
film *The Son of the Sheik* despite the glaring anachronism of
an Arabian prince wearing a French wristwatch in the desert.
Since its Hollywood debut, the Tank hasn't stopped appearing
on the silver screen, on everyone from Fred Astaire to George
Clooney. John F. Kennedy, who wore his Tank through most of
his term in office, once commented that the Cartier Tank was
"France's greatest gift to America since the Statue of Liberty."
    Of course, in time, the Cartier watch became fashionable
for women too. The Duke and Duchess of Windsor had matching his and hers versions; Elizabeth Taylor wore one herself as

well as giving it to all her husbands, and it was the watch favored by Princess Diana. When Jackie Onassis's Tank was sold in 2017, it smashed its $60,000–$120,000 estimate and sold for $379,500. (The buyer was Kim Kardashian West.)

Since Louis created the first Tank over a century ago, it has appeared in a myriad of different forms, from an elongated curved Tank *cintrée* to the Asian-inspired Tank chinoise to the JJC model (for Jean-Jacques Cartier). It is an iconic watch that has gone down in timekeeping history, and not just for timekeeping. When Andy Warhol was asked why he never wound his Cartier Tank watch, he exclaimed in shock. "I don't wear a Tank to tell the time . . . I wear a Tank because it is the watch to wear!"

THE RUSSIAN REVOLUTION

As the war dragged on in France, the Cartiers were receiving increasingly bad news from Russia, where one of their key salesmen, Léon Farines, was stationed as a French lieutenant between St. Petersburg and Arkhangelsk. The conflict in Europe had compounded many of the economic and social problems within Russia, and by February 1917, long-standing discontent with the regime, riots over the scarcity of food, and industrial strikes had erupted into revolution. The imperial government was overthrown, Tsar Nicholas II abdicated, and in October the Bolsheviks seized power. The following summer, the Tsar, his wife, and their five children were brutally executed while being asked to pose for a family portrait. Some claimed the girls took longer to die because all the jewels hidden in their clothes acted as a shield against the bullets.

Cartier's much-debated decision not to open a branch in St. Petersburg suddenly appeared enlightened. Grand Duke Paul, who had been a regular visitor to Louis Cartier's office while enjoying a comfortable existence in Paris several years earlier, was captured and imprisoned, along with four of his grand duke cousins. In place of a life filled with banquets, warm fur coats, and sycophantic admirers, the men were half-starved and treated like animals, locked in freezing individual cells for five brutal months. When they finally emerged on a January morning in 1919, they were ordered to take their places above a trench and ruthlessly shot dead.

Others, including Grand Duke Paul's children Maria and Dimitri, risked everything to flee the country, saving at least part of their fortunes by smuggling valuable jewelry collections over the border. The gem dealer Léonard Rosenthal remembered their desperate trips: "How many of them risked their lives to escape across the frontier with their jewels, the only thing they still possessed. Only under cover of darkness did they dare advance along the Finnish border, sliding in the snow and desperately clutching the small sacks which contained an entire fortune." Grand Duchess Vladimir would be among the last of the Romanovs to escape revolutionary Russia, as well as the first to die in exile, in 1920 in France.

Cartier's employees and consultants managed to escape in time. Carl Fabergé did not fare so well: His stock was seized and his company nationalized. He was forced to spend day after exhausting day appraising precious jewels for the same people who had murdered his royal clients. In late 1918, he escaped Bolshevik Russia, fleeing to safety in Germany. Later his sons, Alexander and Eugène, would move to Paris, where they would set up a new branch of Fabergé, making the same types of items their father had made, but to less acclaim. They would become friends with the Cartier brothers, with any earlier rivalry between the families dissolved by the force of their shared experience. They had been the lucky ones.

THE ARMISTICE: BACK TO WORK

On the eleventh of November 1918, the armistice that declared an end to fighting between Germany and the Allies was signed. After days of expectancy, it was announced to Paris soon after eleven o'clock in the morning by a salvo of five guns from the forts, and "in the twinkling of an eye, the entire aspect of the city changed. The incubus of four years' war fell from the shoulders of the capital like a discarded cloak." As the news spread, the capital erupted with years of pent-up excitement. Flags appeared everywhere. An Allied soldier would later recall the euphoria: "Paris without hesitation decided to do no more work for the day . . . It was a great and glorious crowd of humanity which surged along the grand boulevards. Everyone in khaki was enthusiastically cheered, and the whole-hearted manner in which the civilians grasped you by the hand, uttering a few words, showed the respect and honour they felt towards the man in uniform."

Crowds surged through the great streets around the Church of the Madeleine in which Louis had once been married and far down Rue Royale to Place de la Concorde. They carried the banners of all the Allies, singing "La Marseillaise" and "God Save the King." "It was the night, however, which for anyone to have witnessed will forever live in their memory. Arc lamps and signs which had not been used for four years shone forth and the crowd . . . gave vent to all the feelings which the emotions of the day suggested. Cheering echoed and reechoed through the streets and there was great rejoicing on all hands. Soldiers and civilians embraced to an extent that probably Paris had never before witnessed. The crowd took possession of taxicabs, lorries, or any other vehicles happening along. They climbed on to the roofs, clung to the footboards, and bestrided the bonnets."

Louis wasn't averse to riding the wave of patriotism to drum up business. His most prestigious war connection had come in July 1918, when Cartier was asked to design General Foch's commemorative field marshal's baton, a symbol of authority. The result, a "work of art destined to become a historical object," is today in Paris's Musée de l'Armée, alongside the baton Cartier designed for Pétain. Once the Armistice had been signed, 13 Rue de la Paix received more publicity when it displayed the original Allied flags personally autographed by the presidents of France and the United States and the prime minister of Great Britain. These historical souvenirs were then auctioned off to raise funds for the fight against infant mortality.

LOOKING TO THE FUTURE

Louis' romance with Jeanne Toussaint continued. After a difficult few years, she depended on him more than ever. Since the outbreak of war, Jeanne had lost three of the people she was closest to in the world. First, her mother, who had been living in London, died of pneumonia. Next, it was her former lover Comte Pierre de Quinsonas, who was killed in the most horrifically pointless wartime accident as a fellow pilot had swooped over him on the runway as a joke and, miscalculating, too low. And finally, in 1919, her adored older sister, Clémentine, contracted peritonitis and died in the French hospital in Soho, London. Perhaps it was these successive tragedies that forced Jeanne to build a protective shell around herself, or maybe the shell became stronger after each disappointment that life threw at her. Those who knew her later on, other than close family members, recalled that she could be cold. But never with Louis. The hard, independent exterior she showed to the world softened around him. She needed him.

Louis adored Jeanne, but the concerns Coco Chanel had expressed earlier were not unfounded. Deep down, Louis couldn't shake the feeling that Jeanne was not good enough for him. His family added fuel to the fire, Alfred and Pierre particularly. They had already suffered the turbulence of Louis' divorce from Andrée-Caroline, not easy for a Catholic family. And as time went on, the more concerned they became that Louis' affair with this, in their eyes, "inappropriate" woman would damage the family's reputation. Pierre repeatedly voiced his frustration in letters to Jacques: "You can see what will happen to Louis—he had a good role at the time of the divorce thanks to Father's good status, but now he's making lots of mistakes, living with this woman, not able to justify his actions." Jacques understood Pierre's concerns but didn't altogether agree with them. He saw how happy Jeanne made his elder brother and was of the view that they should marry. But he was the youngest. He didn't yet have the same influence as Alfred or Pierre.

In Conversation with Jean-Jacques Cartier

Jeanne Toussaint was Louis' soulmate. My parents thought he should have married her, that she made him truly happy. But there was a lot of snobbery back then. Class was a bigger thing than it is today. Grandfather and Uncle Pierre thought Louis could do better. And Uncle Louis was a bit of a snob too. He liked mingling in the right circles. With her past, perhaps he felt that she wouldn't have been right for his image. But he loved her. That was obvious.

Louis was not good at being told what to do. He was used to giving the orders. His sister-in-law described him as the type of authoritative sibling who would send his younger brother up the tree just to check that the branch didn't break and only then would he risk climbing it himself. But though he wanted to be with Jeanne, he wasn't blind to the perspective of his family. He saw that a close association with a woman widely known to be a demimondaine would not go down well in the royal and aristocratic circles that Cartier strove to impress.

Reluctantly, he assured his family that he would put the business first and end the relationship with her. The reality was not that straightforward. Not wanting to cut all his ties with the woman he still loved, he arranged for Jeanne to join the business as an employee in the handbag department. She had an eye for fashion, and he believed she would be an asset to the company. And secretly they would continue their romance in the shadows, away from the disapproving eyes of others.

In the workplace, the strains of war were subsiding. Expansion was the new goal. Cartier's reputation was growing stronger by the day, helped in no small part by the seals of approval from the ruling families of Europe (in 1919, Cartier received a royal warrant from King Albert I of Belgium, and the next year from King Victor Emmanuel of Italy and Prince Albert of Monaco). It was crucial that the firm could meet this increased demand. Cartier would not have its own in-house jewelry workshop in Paris until a decade later, but in 1919, with Maurice Couët, Louis established a dedicated Cartier clock workshop on Rue Lafayette. It would eventually employ some thirty specialists—stone setters, engravers, engine-turners—a team that would come to produce unique masterpieces like the Chinese-inspired mystery clocks.

As the 1920s dawned, Louis, in his early forties now, was nearing the peak of his creative powers. With his workforce returned from the war, he was freed up to focus on new innovations. In mid-November 1919, the first Tank watch models were entered in the stock register, with a total of six pieces built to mark the start of the esteemed new line. Next on the list was the geometrical style of jewelry that he and his protégé, Charles Jacqueau, had been pursuing before war broke out. Back then they had planned to exhibit a selection of their modern designs at the 1915 Arts Décoratifs exhibition. With the war, the exhibition had been postponed, but now back at their desks, they were eager to pick up where they left off. Women were demanding something more avant-garde, and Louis felt sure that this new Art Deco style was the way forward. Change was in the air.

PIERRE (1902–1919)

THE QUEEN OF AMERICA

Little did she know it, but Mary Scott Townsend's jaunts to Paris in the early years of the twentieth century would have a lasting influence on Cartier's future. Like many American heiresses, she was a frequent passenger on the luxury transatlantic steamliners and her regular pilgrimages to the French capital solidified her social standing back home. Not only could she talk eruditely about the impressionist works in the Louvre or Claude Debussy's operatic triumph, but she elicited envious glances from friends and guests thanks to her stylish pale pink crinoline number from Maison Worth and strings of natural pearls from Cartier.

As she arrived in Paris in the summer of 1905, Mrs. Townsend had more excuse than ever to stock up on the latest luxuries. Having re-entered society after years of mourning for her late husband, she was on the lookout for marriage proposals for her twenty-one-year-old daughter. Giving the beautiful debutante Mathilde the best chances of success required hosting a series of elegant parties. Mrs. Townsend knew all the right people to invite and had the perfect venue (their impressive Washington house was constructed in the style of the Petit Trianon in Versailles). No expense would be spared; tentative plans had even been made for a leading painter, John Singer Sargent, to paint Mathilde in time for the life-sized portrait to greet guests as they entered. She had visions of orchids and palms decorating the interior while hundreds of well-dressed ladies and gentlemen enjoyed the finest French wines, danced the cotillion in the ballroom, and went away with elaborate party favors like parasols made entirely from roses. It went without saying that mother, as well as daughter, had to look spectacular.

After a dress fitting at Worth, Mrs. Townsend wandered along Rue de la Paix to Cartier. Though debutantes themselves traditionally wore simple jewelry (Cartier advertised their pearl necklaces as ideal for "debutante daughters"), their mothers could be more adventurous in their choice of jewels. Seated comfortably opposite a suitably deferential senior salesman, Mrs. Townsend explained that she was looking for something truly magnificent. Nothing too old-fashioned— she was New World wealth, after all, not like those English aristocrats stuck in the past. The salesman nodded reassuringly; Monsieur Louis' delicate new creations would fit the bill perfectly. A delighted Mrs. Townsend ended up buying a striking diamond tiara in Louis' classic eighteenth-century style, which would look just fabulous against her neoclassical Washington mansion.

The following year, after no doubt many compliments back home, she returned to Cartier for more. This time she picked out a diamond choker inspired by garlands of flowers and foliage and a corsage ornament, in which entwined roses and lilies came to glittering life in diamonds and platinum. Wearing them together with the tiara, the overall effect of the sparkling gems at the head, neck, and breast would have been majestic. Forget aspiring to outshine her countess friends—in her new Cartier ensemble, Mrs. Townsend rivaled the Queen of England.

And that was exactly the aim. King Edward VII, unlike his late mother, Queen Victoria, had made a point of welcoming wealthy Americans to court, where he and his wife, Queen Alexandra, entertained in true regal style. For those aspirational heiresses born with no title, they had two choices: Either they could find an English lord to wed (by 1900, some fifty American women had married into the British peerage), or they could stay home and make up their own rules for social standing. Jewels were as good a marker as any, and many society ladies even had their tiaras remodeled to resemble specific European crown jewels.

Mrs. Townsend pursued both routes for her daughter. In 1906, she made sure to be vacationing in the same western Bohemian town, Marienbad, as Edward VII. Not leaving anything to chance, she ensured that the King found out about "a pretty American girl"—namely Mathilde—taking the curing waters at the bubbling springs each morning. The "highly amused" King, after receiving an anonymous letter about the debutante, took the bait. For three mornings, he assumed the best viewing spot of the guests at the springs. "The third morning," so the American press reported, "he was said to lift his hat with smiling grace and salute a group of ladies in which was a most charming American girl, Miss Townsend." And he was impressed enough to take the young beauty, along with her mother, to luncheon in nearby Carlsbad in his motorcar. But if Mrs. Townsend had hoped that it might lead to an opening into British high society for her only daughter, perhaps via a marriage proposal from one of the King's aristocratic friends, she was to be disappointed. There would be no title for Mathilde (who would end up marrying a U.S. senator and later an American diplomat), and it was back to relying on diamonds to demonstrate her superior position in society.

For the first six decades of Cartier's existence, the crowned heads of Europe had been the building blocks of the firm's brand. Mrs. Townsend was proof that this was changing. The wealth of the New World was compounding at a phenomenal rate. Self-made millionaires had riches to rival the royals, and generally a wife and daughter who were not shy about spending it. American society ladies might not have had a royal court, but the thirty-five boxes of New York's Metropolitan Opera House (where the music was far less important than the outfits) came a close second. This section was even nicknamed the Diamond Horseshoe as society queens like Mrs. Astor, always fashionably late, competed to outshine her fellow boxholders.

With every visiting American heiress or banker's wife who entered the doors of 13 Rue de la Paix (with an unspoken but all too evident brief to outrank her friends back home), the Cartiers were further tempted by the opportunity across the Atlantic. Their jewelry competitors might be content to welcome international visitors into their Parisian showrooms, but Alfred and his sons dreamed of expansion.

NEW BURLINGTON STREET

In 1900, a year after his elder brother and father had masterminded the move to 13 Rue de la Paix, Pierre Cartier joined the family firm. With his dark, neat hair and blue eyes, the eager twenty-two-year-old was good-looking in an earnest kind of way but lacked his brother's magnetism. Growing up, Louis, three years older, had always been one step ahead. At school, it was the elder Cartier who ended up with the better grades. Pierre was harder-working and more rule-abiding, but he became ill in his final years and couldn't finish his education. Then there was the creative aspect: Louis had been born with a heightened aesthetic sense and an ability to convert his visions into reality. Pierre appreciated beautiful objects but lacked that artistic streak. Even in their hobbies, Pierre was outmatched: He loved the idea of flying and was a keen follower of early motorcars, but it was Louis who had the fastest set of wheels and who had befriended the world's most famous aviator.

Pierre was close to Louis, but had never been in any doubt as to the family hierarchy: Louis, as the eldest son, was the heir apparent for the Paris store. So in 1902, a couple of years after he had fully joined the business, Pierre jumped at the chance to step out of his brother's shadow and set up a small Cartier branch in London. Though the family plan was that he would one day go to America and his younger brother would look after the English side of the business, Jacques was still too young to join the firm and Cartier couldn't afford to wait around. They had been asked by a particularly prestigious client to consider opening a London showroom in time for the most important event in recent decades.

King Edward VII was a style icon in turn-of-the-century Britain. Even before he was king, he would travel to Paris regularly, returning to London not only with the latest handmade suits, shirts, and high-end jewelry but also with new fashion rules for his country to follow. He invented the smoking jacket, popularized the tuxedo, and declared that the bottom button of a waistcoat should remain undone (handy for his ever-expanding waist). Put simply, Edward VII personified extravagance and style. So when he named Cartier "King of Jewelers and Jeweler of Kings," it was praise indeed. And when, after the death of his mother, Queen Victoria, in 1901, he suggested that perhaps the Cartiers might open a store in England in time for his coronation, they could hardly say no.

Ever since Alfred visited London to sell courtesans' jewels during the Siege, it had been a dream of his to have a permanent base in the English capital. Over the years, the Cartiers had traveled back and forth to put on exhibitions in Mayfair hotels and meet upper-class ladies in their Georgian townhouses, all the while learning about their tastes and the extensive English requirements for jewels. In her memoirs about a time when "the cinema star had not yet eclipsed the Duchess," the Duchess of Marlborough described hosting a royal gathering at Blenheim Palace in 1896 where the ladies were required to change their costume multiple times a day: a silk or velvet dress for breakfast, tweeds to go and meet the men in the hunting lodge for lunch, an elaborate tea gown in the afternoon, and a satin or brocade dress for dinner. Each change of dress, of course, had required a commensurate change of jewelry: natural pearls for breakfast perhaps, but a diamond corsage ornament and even a tiara for dinner. For a French jeweler looking to expand overseas, this level of demand for jewels was tantalizing. And to have the support of the future king was the icing on the cake.

When Pierre traveled to London to look for a store to rent, his father, Alfred, had been firm in his advice. To attract the best clientele, he felt strongly that the family should base their showroom in the high-end Mayfair district. Together with top salesman M. Buisson (who the following year would try, unsuccessfully, to expand Cartier's business into Germany), Pierre had initially used the smart Hotel Cecil by the Embankment as a base of operations. Here they met clients and discussed commissions for the upcoming coronation while simultaneously scouring the West End for a suitable location. They were even helped in their search by Alice Keppel, the influential British society hostess and a longtime mistress of King Edward VII.

New Burlington Street is one of the narrower streets in Mayfair, running east–west from Savile Row to Regent Street. Not as impressive as the wider and grander Bond Street, it nevertheless offered a very respectable start for the French jeweler trying to make an impression on a new audience. When the three floors of number 4 New Burlington Street came up for rent, Pierre initially dismissed the space as being too large and expensive for a London outpost. His father had been clear that they shouldn't pour too much money into the English venture just yet; the idea was to start small. But hearing of the potential opportunity, Alfred came up with a suggestion as to how it might work in a way that would be both affordable for Cartier and magnetic for new clients.

Since Louis' marriage to Andrée-Caroline four years earlier, Worth had been instrumental in building support for Cartier in Paris. Now Andrée-Caroline's father and uncle, Jean-Philippe and Gaston Worth, had ambitions for a British launch to conquer their late father's homeland. By combining forces, the Worths and the Cartiers would be able to afford the lease on the entire 4 New Burlington Street building. Worth could take the lion's share of the space (and the rent) and Cartier would benefit, again, from proximity to the world's most famous dressmaker. In March 1902, after several months of refurbishment, the building was open for business. WORTH OF PARIS, printed in enormous letters, stretched the width of the building outside the dressmaker's second-floor showroom. Cartier's discreet A. CARTIER & SONS on a small gold plate next to the entrance on the ground floor was almost invisible in comparison, but it didn't matter. The Cartiers knew that Worth was the main attraction. The entrance to the fashion house was via a side door on the ground floor, rendering it impossible to go upstairs for a dress fitting without a little glance into Cartier's ground-floor windows en route.

Pierre put together a small team to work in the new store. Some he brought over with him from Paris, such as Lucien Sensible and Victor Dautremont, but others, including the affable salesman Arthur Fraser, were hired in England. With his bushy upturned mustache and chic white cravat, Fraser appreciated the Cartier insistence on quality and discretion and would go on to dedicate the rest of his working life to the firm. Rather surprisingly, he had been a manure merchant before joining Cartier (Pierre had perhaps recognized that his talent for sales and making connections could be applied to jewels as readily as to fertilizer).

Pierre Cartier (left) opened the first Cartier London showroom in 1902 at 4 New Burlington Street (right), a building the firm shared with the better-known Parisian fashion house of Worth. Cartier was on the ground floor.

By the time Cartier moved into its new London base, the firm already had a large order book of jewels that were required in time for the coronation and related festivities. Dame Nellie Melba, the famous Australian opera singer, had been asked to sing at an Albert Hall concert in June as part of the celebrations. In preparation, she visited Cartier in April 1902 and went on something of a shopping spree, buying a diamond and platinum necklace (which, she proudly told her sister, had taken six years to make and "he [Cartier] says no Queen or Empress has anything finer") and commissioning two corsage ornaments. One of these, a diamond and pearl creation that could double as a necklace, would end up center stage as she sang the national anthem in front of thousands.

Pierre was thrilled with the publicity. Melba was one of the great celebrities of her day, who moved between luxurious rented villas and glamorous hotels in a puff of fur, jewels, and haute couture, surrounded by an entourage of assistants and admirers. She was the perfect ambassador for the new London branch, and Pierre, a fan of opera himself, would go on to lend her jewels for her sellout performances. Melba was only too happy to wear Cartier's gems before admiring audiences, but she was, after all, a diva and could be demanding. Victor Dautremont, the Cartier salesman tasked with personally delivering the jewels before each performance, was said to have been asked to carry them under his clothes in order that they be warm before they touched her delicate skin.

As Edward VII's big day grew closer, the number of jewels created in the Paris workshops to be shipped over the Channel multiplied to include twenty-seven tiaras. The Duke of Portland had supplied the firm with his family's magnificent rectangular Portland diamond, dating from the nineteenth century, and asked that it be made into the centerpiece of a tiara for his wife to wear at the coronation. On August 9, 1902, the Portland tiara, as it later became known, looked on from a particularly prestigious vantage point while Edward VII was crowned king in Westminster Abbey. At almost six feet tall, with a tiny waist and beautiful face, the Duchess of Portland would have stood out above the crowd anywhere, but at this event, chosen as one of the four canopy bearers, she (and her tiara) couldn't have been more in the limelight.

"After the monotony which had blanketed London in the latter years of the Victorian reign," Cecil Beaton would later remark, "there was to be a brief decade of dazzling seasons." King Edward VII's request for Cartier to open a British outpost in time for his coronation may well have been the impetus for the New Burlington Street branch, but even after the celebrations were over, the commissions continued to pour in. While France had lost its ceremonial court life a century earlier, for those in the elite circles of Edwardian Britain, a dizzyingly full social calendar offered multiple opportunities to wear extravagant jewels. Years later, Edward VII's grandson, the future Duke of Windsor, would look back on childhood Christmases at Sandringham as "Dickens in a Cartier setting." And like the royal family, many of their circle appreciated the light and modern style of platinum mounting that Louis had conceived of in Paris. The writer Vita Sackville-West, who would go on to become a friend of Jacques Cartier, wrote about a Duchess of Chevron character in her novel *The Edwardians* who "had the family jewels reset by Cartier, preferring the fashions of the day to the heavy gold settings of Victoria's time." And even the Countess of Warwick, who wrote disparagingly about "all these silly women . . . thinking life is bounded on one side by Worth and Cartier and on the other by Edward VII's court and bridge," was more than happy to wear a Cartier emerald tiara when the occasion called for it.

High-society trailblazers for the London branch included the Cuban-American Dowager Duchess of Manchester, whose 1903 flaming heart and C-scroll tiara (for which she supplied well over a thousand diamonds herself) sits proudly in the V&A Museum today, and her namesake goddaughter, Consuelo Vanderbilt. It was indeed a sign of how far Cartier's reputation had spread since the days of Boulevard des Italiens that Vanderbilt, the American dollar princess who had taken "society completely by storm by her beauty, wit and vivacity" since her 1867 marriage to the Duke of Marlborough, chose to patronize the store.

AN AMBASSADOR ABROAD

While Louis was at his happiest debating ideas with the designers, Pierre was a born networker. Tutored by his father in the business of buying and selling, he later recalled that it had been a tough training: "I was sometimes severely criticized by my father, who wasn't an easy boss to satisfy, and I recognized my errors willingly. I even thanked him for offering his valid observations as they would help me improve." He learned that the client's first impression of the firm started with him and so "dressed as carefully," one client remembered, "as any woman going to her first big ball!" He would wear a stiff white shirt, a black tie, a fresh cornflower in his buttonhole, and trousers so meticulously pressed that it was said that "you could have used the crease to cut butter."

Appearing as if he were going to a formal wedding every single day was Pierre's way of showing clients respect while conveying the notion that Cartier personified elegance. But beyond this, it was his approach to selling that was so exceptional. As one colleague recalled, his technique for negotiating, say, the sale of a pearl necklace was not at all what most people might imagine of the art of selling. "He never said 'This is a great buy, a necklace of X pearls of Y grains, perfectly matched and costs Z dollars.' He talked of painters of the seventeenth century who painted grandes dames with pearl necklaces, or he described the rich colors of the yellow and pink pearls that made up the matched necklaces. Or he discussed the difficulty of matching pearls or discoursed on India and her love of beauty and jewels." At the crux of it, he had an intuitive understanding of people's motivations.

Pierre may have been a great asset to the firm in England, but he'd never intended to base himself there full time. After renting an apartment in Marylebone's Seymour Street to use as a pied-à-terre when in town, he would travel back and forth to the Paris branch regularly. There was no doubt that 13 Rue de la Paix was still the Cartier hub (4 New Burlington Street was essentially just a showroom that sold items made in Paris), and Pierre didn't like being too far from the action. When the opportunity arose, however, he willingly volunteered for more trips to foreign lands. In 1903, he visited America for the first time, and in 1904 it was on to Russia, where he met possible suppliers and sought to drum up local business.

In 1906, Cartier et Fils (Cartier and Son) became Cartier Frères (Cartier Brothers) as the sixty-five-year-old Alfred deemed Pierre capable enough to take over his role as co-head of the firm. In reality, Alfred, not built for retirement, would continue as the patriarch of the family and firm right up until his death, but the change in company structure was a way of tax planning and safeguarding the future

Pierre Cartier on a sleigh during an early trip to Russia, 1904

of the firm as he grew older. Cartier Frères initially stood only for
Louis and Pierre (Jacques had just joined the firm and still lacked the
experience that Alfred deemed essential for a senior position within
the wider firm). Not wanting any arguments between his sons, Alfred
had a dispute resolution clause built into the firm's constitutional
documents. If there was a disagreement between Louis and Pierre, the
matter should be resolved by either Alfred or, interestingly, Louis'
father-in-law, Jean-Philippe Worth.

In the summer of 1906, just as Mrs. Townsend was stocking up on
jewels in Paris, the twenty-eight-year-old Pierre took the ship from
Southampton to visit America for a second time. Alfred was impatient to know if the time was ripe for expansion in New York, and he
didn't trust an employee to evaluate the situation. It had to be family.
Louis was far more interested in coming up with new design ideas in
Paris than in traveling overseas, but Pierre, who had dreamed of
doing business in America since childhood, had been excited to take
on his father's mission. He traveled with Victor Dautremont, the
salesman from the London branch who had lived in New York previously and, importantly, still had family based in Manhattan to help
with introductions.

The pair spent a busy three weeks in America scoping out the state
of the luxury market. If the Cartiers were going to open a branch
there, they needed to have an idea of the competition they'd be up
against, the retail rental market, and the American appetite for French
jewels. The days were filled with client meetings: discussing the latest
tiara creations with J. P. Morgan in his new library one day, meeting
Mrs. Cornelius Vanderbilt III (once scorned for eloping but by now
the elegant leader of New York society) in her West Fifty-seventh
Street townhouse the next.

Pierre enjoyed meeting people and was pleased to assume the role
of representative of the family firm without clients looking over his
shoulder to see if they might be able to speak to his elder brother instead. Cartier was not nearly as well known in New York as it was in
Paris, but among a select few, his name opened doors. American business, though, was slower than expected. The stock market—"the barometer of the jeweler," as his younger brother would later describe
it—had been on a downward trajectory for some time and it was
about to become worse. By the following year, widespread panic on

Wall Street would lead to a run on the banks as desperate workers feared losing their hard-earned wages. Eventually J. P. Morgan had intervened. In the same recently built library where he had met Pierre, he called a meeting of his fellow bankers and—the legend goes— locked the doors to prevent anyone from leaving until a solution had been found. He succeeded in urging them all to follow his lead by pledging a large amount of their own money to shore up the financial system. Disaster was averted, but the previously euphoric market had suffered a shock. It would take many months for the situation to return to normal.

For the Cartiers, previously so determined to spread their wings across the Atlantic, the Land of Promise would become a little less enticing. Financial prudence had been a recurring theme in the firm's history and one that had helped Cartier weather the bad times. As 1907 dawned and the American financial crisis intensified, Pierre couldn't ignore the fact that the risks of a New York venture might outweigh the rewards. That is, until a chance meeting changed everything.

A SERENDIPITOUS STORM

In the spring of 1907, Elma Rumsey, a thirty-three-year-old, well-to-do American from the Midwest, arrived in Paris with her mother for the season. A few days into her trip, she decided to head out for a solitary stroll through the romantic streets when she found herself caught in an unexpected downpour. For a while she kept walking, optimistic that the rain would stop. It didn't, and, absolutely sodden, she was forced to admit defeat and take shelter in the nearest shop. It was 13 Rue de la Paix. The Cartier sales assistants, assuming that this bedraggled lady dripping in their temple of luxury would not result in a commission for them, simply ignored her. Pierre, who had seen the incident out of the corner of his eye, was appalled. Having been taught by his father that everyone who entered Cartier deserved the utmost respect, he rushed over to greet her himself.

As he offered his assistance, Pierre couldn't help but notice that Miss Rumsey was a pretty woman, with chestnut hair that set off her dark eyes and fine, narrow mouth. And she was rather taken by the suave French gentleman with the thoughtful, attentive manner. As she would later admit to a probing reporter, it was love at first sight.

In Conversation with Jean-Jacques Cartier

Elma was lovely, very warm. She never cared as much for her appearance as Pierre did, so I can well imagine that she didn't look like anything special that day they met, but she came from a far more wealthy family than the Cartiers.

Elma Rumsey was the second of four children born to the St. Louis tycoon Moses Rumsey, Jr., who had made his fortune in plumbing, railroad, and foundry supplies. Although the four Rumsey children had never wanted for much, they had seen their father work hard and were not as spoiled as their vast wealth might suggest. Growing up, Elma and her two sisters had been described in the local press as "uncommonly likeable girls [who] pride themselves upon their originality and scornfully refuse to be exactly as the fashion plates demand." Living in St. Louis, away from the social hysteria of New York, had perhaps made Elma more down-to-earth than many of the American clients who graced Cartier's doors. She certainly couldn't understand the attention paid to aristocratic titles in Europe. "Personally I am too American not to admire one for what he can accomplish," she wrote, "but here [France] any old animal, [as long as] he drags a name out of the tomb of some titled old ancestor after him, has success with the ladies, and the American ladies are like the rest."

In 1894, thirteen years before she would meet Pierre, Elma and her elder sister, Marion, had been whisked off to Europe by their mother. Intent on creating well-traveled young ladies of the world, Mrs. Rumsey wanted to ensure that her daughters received a thorough education in art, music, and languages. Elma, then nineteen years old, had soaked it all in with abandon, especially the music, which would have a lasting impact on her.

By the time she met Pierre in 1907, both her sisters were married, she was a thirty-three-year-old spinster aunt, and her father had passed away. Her mother had been hoping that another trip to Europe might this time lead to a husband for her only unmarried child and had turned up in the French capital armed with calling cards and introductions to well-to-do families. Elma may have been a millionaire in her own right, but Mrs. Rumsey was keen to ensure that prospective suitors were not after her for her money.

During that summer, after their fortuitous meeting at 13 Rue de la Paix, Pierre spent a lot of time with Elma. He even invited her and her mother to the wedding of his younger sister, Suzanne. Mrs. Rumsey approved. Her daughter and the jeweler seemed to share the same values: the importance of family, the need to work hard for success, and the recognition that with wealth came responsibility. Before Elma boarded the ship back to America, Pierre gave her a special gift. One might have expected it to be a diamond bracelet, but instead, knowing her love of beautiful architecture, he commissioned a unique edition of a book on French châteaux with a personal dedication printed on the first page.

Pierre traveled over to America in the autumn on the pretext of business. He could meet potential clients and check out the economic situation firsthand for his father, who wanted to know if it was really as dire as the press were suggesting. While there, he would speak to the press, perhaps with Elma in mind, as he praised the style of American women: "Their taste in jewelry and method of wearing it are what I should term perfection. From a jeweler's point of view, of course, it might be wished that they would do more ornaments, but I must bow to their tastes. . . . They do not wear too many things at one time." But the principal purpose of Pierre's trip was unrelated to work. Along with the jewelry he brought over for Cartier's American clients, he packed a special ring.

By December of that year, the press on both sides of the Atlantic had announced the news of Pierre and Elma's engagement. "Well, I hardly know how to describe him," Elma gushed in a long St. Louis interview about the engagement. "He has blue eyes and dark hair, and is smooth-faced. How old is he? Well, really I do not know exactly, but he is under thirty. He is tall—taller than I am." *The New York Times,* meanwhile, boosted the Cartier family's standing somewhat in its article: "HEIRESS TO WED FOREIGNER . . . The prospective bridegroom, while untitled, belongs to an old and honored French family."

The couple tentatively planned a small wedding in Elma's home-town the following spring, assuming Pierre could get away from work. In the end, he couldn't. Louis was tied up with business in Russia and Jacques was in London, so Pierre was needed in Paris. Perhaps, he sug-gested, he would come over that summer so they could marry in The Owls, the Rumseys' vacation home on Nantucket Island. But that ended up being a short-lived plan. There was so much going on in Paris that he couldn't even spare the time to travel. In the end, they settled on a quiet family service at the Église Saint-Honoré-d'Eylau in Paris in the summer of 1908. Elma came over with her mother and sisters, and Pierre was joined by his delighted father and brothers.

The newlyweds decided to settle in Paris. They bought, from Comte René Chandon de Briailles, a large house on more than half a hectare of land in the chic Neuilly-sur-Seine area, just west of the capital. Facing the Bois de Boulogne, the property was perfectly lo-cated for an early morning ride, but still close enough to the center of town for Pierre to commute in to work every day. In "Our Home," as

Pierre (right) and Elma (center) would ride together in the Bois de Boulogne opposite their Paris residence. On occasion, Pierre's younger brother, Jacques (left), would join them.

they named their house, staff abounded, and everything—from the meals to the paintings on the walls—was evidence of Pierre's insistence on the very highest standards. Both the building and the decor were much admired by the many distinguished guests who passed through its doors, with the American journalist O. O. McIntyre praising it as "the only private residence I ever cared to own."

PATRIARCHAL SIGN-OFF

Alfred was overjoyed by the union of his son and the Rumsey heiress. He got on very well with Elma, who called him "Darling Père" from the start. But he was also not blind to the possible benefits she brought to the business. Louis' marriage to a Worth had helped the Paris branch, so now Alfred hoped his American daughter-in-law would bode well for expansion across the Atlantic. With this in mind, in November 1908, the sixty-seven-year-old patriarch decided to head to New York on a reconnaissance mission himself. With Louis still recovering from his car accident in Paris, Pierre busy preparing for the upcoming Christmas season, and Jacques in London, Alfred traveled with Louis' very capable secretary, the thirty-six-year-old René Prieur.

Stepping off the RMS *Oceanic* transatlantic passenger liner onto frosty American soil, Alfred was overwhelmed by the sheer scale of it all. "Everything seems so well laid out," he wrote later from his room on the seventeenth floor of the luxury Plaza hotel in awe, "but I'm seeing it from so far away, and in particular from so high up, I imagine myself to be living in the Eiffel Tower!" Alfred had done his research: The Plaza was *the* hotel to base oneself in, having been constructed just a year earlier at a then unprecedented cost of $12.5 million. Despite this, rooms were as little as $2.50 a night ($70 today).

Alfred and René wasted little time looking for a suitable headquarters. It didn't need to be large, just "one or two elegant rooms and a workshop for repairs." As with all Cartier branches, the most important feature was location. They settled on Fifth Avenue, which, having previously been largely residential, was increasingly dominated by high-end stores. "What wealthy Western family would be satisfied with any other than Fifth Avenue's stamp on its purchases?" observed *The New York Times* the following year. "The onlooker must be blind indeed if he fails to see the movement of our largest and best retail business houses to establish themselves [there]."

Of all the rental properties he viewed, Alfred singled out one less than five minutes' walk from the Plaza. Number 712 Fifth Avenue was not only perfectly positioned, a stone's throw from Central Park, but it was "the most French in appearance, Louis XVI in style and faced with dressed stone." Cartier would rent a single floor, sharing the building with an art gallery on the ground floor and the well-known Franco-American decorators Lucien Alavoine & Co. above. It was decided, too, that Alavoine would supply the wood paneling for the Cartier refurbishment (and later Pierre's desk) in order to maintain a French style within the store. Fifth Avenue might be a two-week journey away from Rue de la Paix, but a client of Cartier New York needed to feel they were walking into the same Cartier they knew and trusted from Europe.

By the following summer, Cartier New York was ready to open its doors. Pierre would not manage the New York store full-time initially, but he did plan to be there for a few months every year and traveled out for the launch. "We've had a shop in London for some time," he explained to *The New York Times,* stepping seamlessly into his new role, "and there seemed to be an excellent chance for one in New York, our work is so essentially different from that of the New York jewelers . . . I believe that we are the first French firm of jewelers to go to America." Not only was Paris universally accepted as the capital of the artistic world, but the expertise of French craftsmen was considered to be unparalleled. From the start, Pierre grasped that it was the firm's Frenchness that would set them apart, but he had his work cut out for him. Cartier was still unknown across the Atlantic. Along with the help of the press, he had to educate Americans about its status elsewhere. "Many of the most famous pieces of jewelry in the possession of the crowned heads of Europe, leaders of the American smart set, and celebrated actresses came from Cartier's," *The New York Times* excitedly informed its readers, telling them that "the Rue de la Paix is being moved to Fifth Avenue."

The Cartiers had initially planned that the new branch would import all stock from Paris, with just a small workshop for repairs. When they realized that margins would be hit by a devastating 60 percent import tax on high-end jewelry, they had to adapt their plans. Placing huge price tags on the jewels to compensate for the high taxes was not viable. If they were to expand in a new country, value must be the cornerstone of their organization: "Since the House of Cartier is destined to lead the world in jewelry, we must give our customers best value for money so as to obtain from them the confidence that is worthy of our company."

There was another negative with importing the stock, too: American firms like Dreicer & Co. just down the street could create lower-quality and less expensive copies of Cartier's latest Parisian designs and have them in their windows before the ship carrying the original Cartier jewelry had even left France. In order to avoid losing out to the American competition, Cartier needed a workshop on the ground. This was more difficult than it sounded. One couldn't simply find teams of skilled designers, setters, mounters, and engravers overnight. Especially not in America, where the jewelry trade was less developed than in France. It would take many years to train apprentices to the high standards that Cartier was famous for.

By 1910, the Cartiers had figured out a solution. They would still complete the bulk of the skilled creative work in Paris, and Pierre would import into America the jewelry broken down into its constituent parts (loose gemstones, sketches, molds, and settings). He would then hire a team of stone setters in New York who could reassemble them in-house, thus bypassing the import duties on completed jewelry. Together with Victor Dautremont, now to be his key lieutenant in New York, Pierre also brought over a small team of salesmen, designers, and craftsmen from Paris. This was crucial for maintaining that French allure in New York. When one saleswoman hired into a rival luxury firm proudly announced she was trying to lose her French accent, she was told to keep it: It was good for business.

Among the key employees who exchanged Rue de la Paix for Fifth Avenue in those early years were the salesmen Paul Muffat and Jules Glaenzer. Not only did they both speak English, but they had also already proved themselves in foreign environments. While the multilingual gemstone expert Muffat had overseen the St. Petersburg

Christmas sale the previous year, the fun-loving Glaenzer had toured Asia, where he had shown diamond necklaces to the King of Siam and his "little princesses" and sought out intriguing treasures (the bright blue kingfisher feathers he found in China would find their way into Cartier clocks). Also asked to make the move across the Atlantic was the craftsman Pierre Bouquet, who would head up the small workshop, and Jacqueau's designer friends, the brothers Alexandre and Georges Genaille. Though tasked with the job of creating pieces for an American audience, they brought with them an experience and appreciation of France that was crucial to maintaining the Cartier style. "One needs to breathe the air of France to create artistic models," Pierre explained. "Paris by its architecture develops a sense of proportion that one cannot get in New York. For instance, if we look at the buildings of Place Vendôme, there is a perfectly proportional symmetry, while in the United States you have very small buildings close to skyscrapers, and that contrast does not help the man who creates models to keep his sense of proportion."

SPREADING THE WORD

With the jewelry in place in the showroom and the eager French salesmen standing ready, the only element lacking in 712 Fifth Avenue was the steady stream of clients to which the Cartiers had grown accustomed in Paris. This was where Pierre came into his own. After inviting all those American clients who had visited Cartier in Europe to the launch of the New York branch, he turned his attention to those who had never heard of Cartier. John Pierpont Morgan was one of the wealthiest men he knew in New York; Pierre asked his lawyer for directories of other major New York bankers. He wrote to each one personally, suggesting that perhaps they and their wives might be interested in seeing the newest collection from a jeweler that was favored by European royalty.

As news of the Parisian jeweler spread through Manhattan, the bankers' wives were joined by the city's trendsetters. These included the well-known suffragist and wife of the financier Clarence Mackay, Katherine Duer Mackay (who would later cause a scandal when she ran off with the family doctor), and "the most picturesque woman in America," Mrs. Rita Lydig. Inordinately wealthy from her first marriage to the multimillionaire William Earl Dodge Stokes (who had been responsible for developing much of New York's Upper West Side), Rita was infamous for turning up at the Ritz in Paris each year with a hairdresser, masseuse, chauffeur, secretary, maid, and forty Louis Vuitton trunks.

Perhaps the most notorious of the Gilded Age clients, however, was Mrs. Stuyvesant Fish. Known as Mamie, Mrs. Fish was the wife of an American businessman whose large townhouse at the corner of Gramercy Park South and Irving Place was considered the center of the New York social scene. Not keen on following convention, Mamie was known for speaking her mind, especially to uninvited guests: "Make yourself perfectly at home, and believe me, there is no one who wishes you more heartily there than I do!" When she revolutionized the standard dinner party format by cutting it down from several hours to a brief fifty minutes, the rest of New York high society followed suit.

This small group of trailblazing ladies were the perfect advertisements for Cartier in America. When they wore their new Cartier necklace or brooch, their entourages clamored to do the same, and creations from the chic Parisian jeweler became something of a status symbol in Manhattan. When the contemporary novelist Elinor Glyn wrote *Elizabeth Visits America* the year Pierre opened his branch, she included twenty women at a ladies' luncheon in a New York mansion "all dressed in the most expensive, magnificent frocks from Paris and lovely jeweled Cartier watches." Pierre had grown up with the mantra that the best form of publicity was word of mouth, and here, just as in London, he saw it in action. Sometimes the one-upmanship took place even within the same family. The Vanderbilts were among the richest families in America, thanks to a fortune built from shipping and railroads by Cornelius Vanderbilt. His many heirs, hugely prominent in New York society, owned multiple houses on Fifth Avenue. In 1910, Mrs. William Vanderbilt, Sr., bought an *écharpe* from Cartier, effectively a large regal-looking sash made entirely of diamonds and pearls. Fixed to the shoulder and looped across the breast, it made an impressive statement. She followed it up with another one, this time all in diamonds, including five enormous pear drops, and kick-started something of a competition among the other Vanderbilt women. Consuelo Vanderbilt, Mrs. William Vanderbilt II, and Mrs. William Vanderbilt III had all been keen Cartier clients for some time, but following Mrs. William Vanderbilt, Sr.'s unveiling of her *écharpe,* Mrs. Cornelius Vanderbilt and Mrs. Frederick Vanderbilt jumped on the Cartier bandwagon, both ordering their own extravagant versions of the bejeweled shoulder sash.

With many of New York's wealthiest families accounted for, Pierre moved on to those American clients from farther afield who were visiting the city. Recognizing that they had probably never heard of a Parisian jeweler called Cartier, let alone knew it had come to New York, he contacted the company that made telephone directory cards for smart hotels and arranged for "Jeweler: Cartier, 712 Fifth Avenue" to be added to the list of local numbers. It was quite possible, Pierre believed, that a couple staying at the Plaza might be tempted to acquire a little memento of their time in Manhattan, or perhaps a lady staying at the Waldorf-Astoria had left her diamond tiara back home and urgently needed one for the opera the following evening. A quick glance at the directory card next to the phone in their suite overlooking Central Park and they would know whom to call. Pierre took the idea further: Bellboys of smart hotels and waiters in good restaurants were offered generous tips in exchange for information on particularly romantic couples. Flower delivery boys and fine chocolate shop assistants were rewarded when they updated Cartier on any significant orders. If a gentleman of means was even considering popping the question, Pierre wanted to make sure Cartier was his first port of call. Once Cartier had the inside information, a salesman would be dispatched to try to meet with the potential client.

Best of all, though, in Pierre's armory of marketing tools was Elma. Her standing helped elevate Pierre above that of a "foreigner shopkeeper" looking to cash in on his adopted country. "The man who 'kept a shop' was more rigorously shut out of polite society in the original Thirteen states than in post-revolutionary France," Edith Wharton would recall in her autobiography, quoting the example of a surprised Parisian bookseller whose Philadelphia shop was the meeting place "for the most blue-blooded of his fellow émigrés" and yet who never made the guest list for important events. Unlike the bookseller, Mr. and Mrs. Pierre Cartier weren't short of invitations. And when they invited others to their suite at the Plaza, they could be quietly confident that their table would be filled. Snooty politicians, diplomats, and businessmen who wouldn't have considered sharing a meal with a mere jewelry salesman graciously turned up for dinner with the millionaire heiress and her new husband.

As ever more prestigious clients rolled in, Pierre was insistent that the firm remain true to its original aim: "We must never lose our current reputation; in other words, we must sell only large jewels." It was with this in mind that, in 1910, he invested in a gemstone so large and important that it represented an enormous risk. If he couldn't sell it, Cartier would be left with a dent in its cash flow that could severely hamper the entire firm. And yet Pierre was in no doubt that it was a risk worth taking. As he had discovered in America, the fame and size of one's diamond was everything.

THE HOPE DIAMOND

Sometimes jewels carry a story with them that impacts all their owners. The notoriously cursed 45-carat blue Hope Diamond, once known as the Tavernier Blue, was one of these. Since its discovery in the Kollur mine in seventeenth-century India by Jean-Baptiste Tavernier, a French gem merchant, many of those who had owned or even been close to the stone were said to have suffered terrible fates. If you were to believe the stories, their horrific endings included being torn apart by wild dogs in Constantinople, being shot onstage and, in the case of Marie Antoinette and Louis XVI (who had enjoyed the diamond as part of the French crown jewels), famously being beheaded during the French Revolution.

Several months after Pierre opened the New York branch, Cartier bought the Hope Diamond in Paris. The gemstone had changed hands several times in the preceding few months. From Simon Frankel, a diamond dealer in New York, it had passed to a collector in Turkey (reportedly on behalf of Sultan Hamid of the Ottoman Empire before he was deposed), and then on to the French dealer Rosenau, from whom Cartier acquired it for 500,000 francs (around

$2.2 million today). Though the gem was magnificent, it was not easy to locate a client who was wealthy enough to afford it, fanatical enough about diamonds to need a large blue one, and brave enough to disregard the curse. Frankel, for example, hadn't been able to find a buyer for seven years, after which time his finances were in such a dire strait that he was forced to sell it at a distressed price.

This was where Cartier, with its multiple branches and increasingly impressive global client list, started to come into its own. The brothers could be hot on the buying scene in Paris, where so many of the best gemstones came to market, while simultaneously discreetly spreading the word of their new purchase overseas. They were well aware that an American heiress would relish the idea of parading a unique jewel from the chic French capital in front of her peers back home. In the case of the Hope Diamond, the Cartiers were confident enough of selling it that they were not to be deterred by the 1908 warnings in the press: "There are those who say [diamond dealers] will never regain their old position of supremacy in their trade as long as the Hope Diamond remains in their ownership." In fact, far from being put off by the curse, Pierre believed the gemstone's notoriety could act in his favor. He even had a client in mind who he suspected would be enticed by it.

The American heiress Evalyn Walsh McLean couldn't get enough of jewels. She was inordinately rich, thanks to her father, who had literally struck gold with one of the largest gold mines in America. In 1908, at the age of twenty-two, Evalyn married nineteen-year-old Ned McLean of the well-known *Washington Post* family. The young couple, it was widely reported, had far more money than sense. "It is no use to anyone to chide me for loving jewels. I cannot help it if I have a passion for them," Evalyn admitted. "They make me feel comfortable, and even happy. The truth is, when I neglect to wear jewels, astute members of my family call in doctors because it is a sign I'm becoming ill."

Evalyn had previously crossed paths with the Cartiers in 1908 when she was on her honeymoon in Paris. While at 13 Rue de la Paix, she had seen a necklace containing a large pearl, a 34-carat hexagonal emerald (a "thing I craved at sight"), and the pièce de résistance: the 94.8-carat pear-shaped brilliant Star of the East diamond. The price was 600,000 francs ($2.6 million today). She didn't hesitate. "We signed the bill," she would write in her memoirs, "and Cartier's sent us kids out into the world with the Star of the East."

In 1910, when Evalyn and Ned were back in the French capital, Pierre made an appointment to meet them in their hotel. Understanding from their previous purchases that the jewelry they sought out was large and significant, he was hopeful they would fall on the Hope Diamond like hungry wolves. "His manner was exquisitely mysterious," Evalyn remembered, as he placed an intriguing-looking package secured with wax seals before them. "I suppose a Parisian jewel merchant who seeks trade among the ultra-rich has to be more or less a stage manager or an actor." He was, as ever, perfectly dressed for the role: "His silk hat, which he swept outwards in a flourish, had such a sheen that almost made me believe it had been handed to him, new, as he crossed our threshold. His oyster-colored spats, his knife-edged trousers, his morning coat, the pinkness of his fingernails, all of these and other things about him were made by him to seem to be for me, Madame McLean, one French compliment."

Pierre retraced the gemstone's famous history for his captive audience, from its prominent place among the French crown jewels for more than a century, to a London lord and a Turkish sultan, and now all the way to their very hotel room in Paris. By the time he unveiled the gemstone, he had them on the edge of their seats. Unfortunately, though, it wasn't enough. Whether it was because the young couple weren't keen on the setting, or they had misgivings about the curse, or they had simply run out of that kind of spending money by the end of their trip that year, Evalyn and Ned left empty-handed.

Disappointed but determined his instincts were right about the McLeans being the perfect clients for the Hope, Pierre moved on to Plan B. He shipped the gemstone to America and changed the setting to an oval frame of smaller diamonds that enhanced the large blue Hope in the center. He again showed it to Evalyn, who, though more interested this time around, was still not convinced. Knowing his client's weakness for gems, Pierre proposed that she hold on to the necklace for a few days, suspecting that once she had it in her possession, it would be almost impossible for her to return it. She was used to getting things, not to giving them back. Evalyn took the bait and that evening, before she went to bed, she placed the diamond on her dresser. "For hours, that jewel stared at me, and at some time during the night I began to really want the thing. Then I put the chain around my neck and hooked my life to its destiny for good or evil."

The next day, Pierre received word that the McLeans would buy the Hope. The price was $180,000 (about $5 million today), of which the first installment was to be $40,000. The Cartier's were relieved: Having large gemstones in stock played havoc with the firm's cash flow until they were sold. But as with many privileged clients, the sale process wasn't as straightforward as it might have been. Several weeks after the agreed contract had been signed and the McLeans had taken possession of the gemstone, Pierre hadn't yet received a cent in payment. At his clients' request, he had even put a clause into the contract to assuage their worst curse-related fears (the "customer's privilege to exchange goods in case of fatality"), but still Evalyn procrastinated. At one stage, she tried sending the Hope back to Cartier. Pierre refused to stand for it and the necklace was returned to its owner along with a repeat demand for payment. By March 1911, two months after the sale had been agreed upon, Pierre was so frustrated by his clients' endless delaying tactics that a series of exchanges with Louis in Paris led the brothers to file a legal suit against the McLeans. Pierre, ever the bastion of discretion, refused to speak to the press, with *The New York Times* reporting that "extreme precautions appeared to have been taken to protect Mr. Cartier from possible visitors."

Finally realizing that there was no legal way out of the deal, Evalyn changed tack and decided that if she was going to buy the gemstone, she should at least take it to church for a blessing. She wasn't sure she believed in the curse, but May Yohe, the ex-wife of Thomas Hope and a previous wearer of the diamond, had publicly warned her against it in a March 1911 newspaper article, and she couldn't help but be spooked. The blessing took place in the church of Russel Monseigneur. The diamond was awaiting its blessing on a velvet cushion, when seemingly on cue, lightning flashed and thunder shook the building. Many might have taken this as a sign to back away, but not Evalyn. "Ever since that day," she would later declare, "I've worn my diamond as a charm." The sale was finally concluded in early

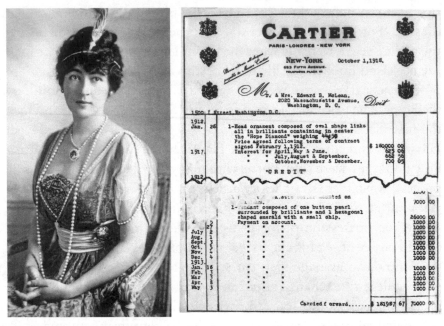

Evalyn Walsh McLean wearing the notoriously cursed Hope Diamond
that she bought from Cartier in 1912. The invoice shows the
agreed-upon price of $180,000.

1912, with the McLeans trading in the emerald from the Star of the
East pendant they had bought a couple of years earlier to help pay
for the Hope.

Financially speaking, the sale of the Hope wasn't a positive for Cartier. After all the legal fees, the firm ended up taking a loss. The board
meeting minutes noted, "Upon examining our legal expenses . . . we
have decided to be more strict. In future, we will have to think very
carefully before taking legal advice. We will avoid it as much as possible." And yet there was no question in Pierre's mind that it had been
worth it. Through this single transaction, Cartier became a household name in New York. After all, who wasn't secretly fascinated
by the exploits of the opulent and profligate McLeans? Add to that
the idea of a mysterious curse, and the gossip columns had struck
gold. The Cartier brothers may have shied away from taking out advertisements in the early years (Louis particularly felt they were beneath a great jewelry Maison favored by royalty), but they were more
than happy to have their name spread by the press alongside pictures

or social updates of their famous clients. And Evelyn McLean, who loved the stone's notoriety, never missed an opportunity to flaunt the spectacular Hope. She tied the diamond around the neck of her Great Dane dog, Mike, or held lavish garden parties where she hid it in the bushes and insisted the guests join in her favorite game: Find the Hope.

Evelyn held on to the Hope for the rest of her life, save for a brief moment during the Depression when she was forced to pawn it for $37,500 in a last-minute attempt to prevent a house foreclosure. On the day she had arranged to reclaim it, she took the train from Washington to New York and turned up at William Simpson's pawnshop entirely alone. No bodyguard for her, in fact not even a bag: She stuffed the diamond, along with a few other precious stones she was picking up, into her dress and set off uptown to meet some friends. After lingering too long over lunch, she rushed to catch her train, running "through the station so fast I thought I would be shaking the stones out of my bosom at every step." A far cry from the high security of the Smithsonian Institution, where the Hope sits safely on a turntable within a glass cabinet today, attracting more than seven million visitors a year and currently estimated to be worth around $350 million.

Over the decades that Evelyn owned the Hope, it was periodically sent back to Cartier to be cleaned. Once, in the 1930s, as the jewel was being carried down the back staircase on a green-felt-covered tray, the young employee ceremoniously carrying the tray tripped. Watching in horror, he saw the diamond leap from the tray and, with a heart-stopping clunk, land on the marble step before bouncing, seemingly in slow motion, toward the floor below. Remarkably, the diamond emerged unscathed, the Hope Diamond proving more charmed than cursed for him.

For the McLean family, though, the curse has always been more open to debate. While Evelyn never believed it, she suffered a fair amount of bad luck over her lifetime. Her husband, Ned, ran off with another woman and later died in a mental institution; their family paper, *The Washington Post*, went bankrupt; her son was killed in a car accident; and her daughter died of a drug overdose. Vagaries of life, maybe, but certainly enough to bolster the Hope's notoriety.

In Conversation with Jean-Jacques Cartier

"When I was at boarding school, I remember some of the other boys there teasing me about the Hope diamond. They'd read about the curse in a magazine and they knew the diamond had been in our family. I was worried after that and wrote to my father about it. He said the story of a curse made for a good story for a magazine but it was silly to believe that a stone can bring such bad luck."

"Do you think Pierre made up or exaggerated the curse?" I asked my grandfather, curious as to whether reports I had read about the origin of the curse were true.

"No, he wouldn't have made it up, that wasn't his nature. He was honest. But could I see him emphasizing it to a client? Well, yes, that's possible. Uncle Pierre was a fantastic salesman. He could have sold ice to the Eskimos. He had a knack of knowing what to say to each client to entice them without ever overdoing it."

Legal battles aside (and there would be others as well as the Hope case that temporarily cast a shadow over the firm), the years before World War I were good for Cartier's New York store, with sales boosted by significant interest in large gemstones. The verdant Colombian emerald Cartier had received from Evalyn McLean as partial payment for the Hope Diamond was quickly snapped up by Eva Stotesbury, the wife of J. P. Morgan's right-hand man in Philadelphia. She had the newly named Stotesbury Emerald combined with other precious gems to make a suite of jewels. (When the Stotesbury Emerald came up for auction at Sotheby's in April 2017, it sold for close to $1 million.)

On April 14, 1911, Elma gave birth to a daughter in the couple's New York home away from home, the Plaza. Both coming from large families, Pierre and Elma had wanted to have many children, but it had not been as easy as they had hoped and by the time little Marion (named after Elma's mother and sister) did arrive, the joy of a child was absolute. The press reported the news the following day, describing Elma as the daughter of the late Moses Rumsey and sister of Mrs. Bryson Delavan. Pierre, meanwhile, was referred to as a "wealthy Frenchman" and a "member of an old and honored French family." There was no reference to a jewelry firm at all, suggesting that, for all his efforts, Cartier was still relatively unknown within New York.

Soon after the birth, Pierre, Elma, and Marion returned to Paris. Frequent passengers on the vast ocean liners, they heard with horror about the sinking of the *Titanic* on Marion's first birthday, in April 1912, and yet they had no choice but to regularly make the transatlantic journey. They spent each winter in New York, but their main home remained in the French capital, where their *dîners dansants* regularly made it into the social pages. They even extended their "Our Home" property, giving their toddler more space to run around, by buying the adjacent house.

Pierre, who enjoyed being in Paris, was not immune to the growing burden of responsibility from the New York branch. He trusted his team on Fifth Avenue, but he also appreciated that when parting with large sums of money, important clients preferred to deal with "Monsieur Cartier" himself. Not wanting to relocate to America full-time, in early 1913 Pierre asked his younger brother, Jacques, to help manage the New York office for part of the year. Since officially taking charge of the London branch seven years earlier, the twenty-nine-year-old Jacques had been working between the English and French capitals. He'd cut his jeweler's teeth in the design and purchasing departments and learned more than either of his brothers about precious stones. A stint in the rapidly growing New York business would, Pierre suggested, not only be good for his training but also draw on his skills. He was right. Just as Pierre had envisaged, Jacques would end up being a great asset to the firm in America.

The Cartier brothers' ability to be in three places at one time was a critical factor for later success. Not for nothing did Pierre's business idols include the Rothschild family, about whom he had read a great deal. The Rothschilds had made money by having different members of the family in various financial centers around the world. In the days before instant communication, this gave them the advantage of being able to pass information among themselves faster than the governments. Pierre and his brothers weren't just focusing on financial information, but their presence in different financial capitals did give them certain insights that their Parisian peers would have lacked. It also meant they could share gemstones, designs, clients, and even employees. On one occasion, Pierre presented a friend with the book *The History of the Rothschilds,* explaining that he considered the Cartiers their counterparts. "We brothers are very close," he added; "that is our strength."

NO DANCING

In April 1914, as his daughter turned three years old, Pierre received the letter calling him up to his infantry regiment in France. He may have married an American and started a business in New York, but he was a healthy Frenchman and therefore obligated to serve his country. While he accepted his duty, he also felt a responsibility to the family firm. Fearing that if he was sent off to the Front he would endanger the dream he and his brothers shared, he dashed off a few letters to those in positions of authority requesting a safer war job. He offered his Neuilly house and grounds to the war effort, and donated his Mercedes-Benz, explaining that he no longer wanted to drive a German car. Pierre had a selection of the finest cars in Paris and was an excellent driver. Perhaps, he suggested, he could be a chauffeur to one of the generals?

His suggestions were accepted. Our Home became a recreation spot for the nurses and doctors working in the nearby American hospital. Pierre was appointed as a chauffeur, and effectively special aide, to Colonel (later General) Ponsard. Leaving his wife and daughter with his father in Paris, Pierre headed off to his position in Cherbourg-Octeville, about 350 kilometers away. Elma, who couldn't bear for them to be apart, followed him there, only to be sent back to the capital by her husband, who worried for her well-being. It was, Elma wrote to Jacques, "disappointing not to pass a few days with him, but I would travel no end of a journey for just a peep of his loved person." Still, he looked well, "even if he had his hair shaved close to his head and a bristly mustache."

By the end of August 1914, Paris no longer felt safe. Concerned for Elma and Marion's security, Pierre urged them to travel to America. Elma refused, not wanting to leave her husband or elderly father-in-law behind. But she recognized that wartime France was no place for a young child and made the heartbreaking decision to send Marion to her sister in New York. In an indication of how much Pierre trusted his head salesman, Jules Glaenzer, he asked him to accompany the three-year-old Marion, "the most precious jewel we own," across the Atlantic and ensure she made it safely to her aunt and uncle, the Delavans.

With little Marion in New York and Pierre in Cherbourg, Elma busied herself looking after Alfred in Paris. "Our treasured little daughter left August 2nd to sail on *La France*," she wrote to her sister-in-law. "Pierre and I thought it wisest so I may stay and watch Père's health and keep him company. . . . Of course, no one can live through the strong earthquake . . . that we have passed through and not show the marks. Why, I walk miles and miles just to be able to get some sleep at night, and Père walks quite a bit for the same reason."

Before long, it became clear that they, too, should leave the French capital while they still could. The front line was fast approaching Paris, and bombardments by German aircraft and artillery were not uncommon. Along with her sister-in-law, Suzanne, and various nephews and nieces, Elma agreed to Père's suggestion that they travel to his ancestral home, a remote village in the Auvergne, almost six hundred kilometers from Paris. "We left Paris on the evening of August 30th. Père, Suzanne, her 3 children, Renée and her maid, and I, eight of us in a 2nd class compartment . . . Crowds were swarming out of Paris, one had to guard the doors of the train, or we should have been crushed . . . the trip was a nightmare from which we did not awake until the following evening at about 6 o'clock." Once there, there wasn't much to occupy them. Elma, who couldn't stand sitting idle while others were suffering, volunteered at the nearby military hospital. Previously a summer hotel, it was now filled with injured servicemen. She had no training but came proudly armed with a Red Cross first aid book and a pair of bandage scissors from her brother-in-law, Doctor Delavan.

With his family away from immediate danger, Pierre's mind turned back to the business. He continually thought of the future, comparing the workings of the Paris, London, and New York houses from afar. Before the war, he had seen Paris as the central hub, but recent events had changed his perspective. That autumn, he wrote to Jacques of his new plans to focus on America: "I have been thinking about the effects of the war. After the war, I aim to continue in New York where I think we have the greatest chance of making big figures. That is my plan, the question is when will I be able to make it happen?"

He met with Louis and Alfred in Paris to brainstorm on wartime strategy. Jacques was harder to meet: first recovering in a Swiss sanatorium, then fighting at the front, he was almost impossible to track down, so Pierre wrote him endless letters. While some were about the business, others were more emotional amid the fear that they might not survive: "I want your life to be very rich. I have such a great affection for you. You have all the qualities I probably don't have in me. For now, the battle is getting closer. Take courage, dear old Jacques." Usually he was upbeat and positive, boosting his brother's morale, talking optimistically of the future, but occasionally he had what he called "a blue moment," and turned to his family to lift him out of his gloom: "I have not much courage anymore because recent events scared me—we need a plan against the Germans."

All three branches of Cartier had lost many men with the call to arms. Most survived, but there were, perhaps inevitably for a reasonably sized French firm, several losses during the four years of war. "The death of Bouquet hit me very hard," Pierre wrote to Jacques in 1915 about the gentle, talented Frenchman who had headed up the Cartier New York workshop. "Were you as affected by it?" The business became a juggling act for those employees who were left, as they were moved between branches. With Paris and London running at minimum capacity, it was New York that needed the most hands on deck: "[René] Prieur and Robinson go to New York on 21st, Prieur will take place of Muffat, Robinson will be salesman, I hope to make more important sales over there despite the war. Prieur is a very capable boy—[he] will be great for the firm." Even in war, Pierre worked around the clock, overseeing everything from lawsuits to staff changes.

Before news of war broke, American orders had been coming in faster than they could be fulfilled, and Pierre had been of the opinion that the New York branch should expand. He'd been thinking about larger premises for some time, somewhere with several elegant rooms for showcasing the collections and meeting clients and perhaps room for an in-house workshop as well. Glaenzer had been charged with keeping an eye out for suitable premises and asked to report back on any opportunities thrown up by the war. Pierre would be back soon himself, he reassured his right-hand man, predicting in one 1914 letter that the war would be over by next July.

But the conflict dragged on, and casualty numbers became far worse than feared. After the Allied troops checked the German advance at the First Battle of the Marne and mounted a successful counterattack, the invaders were driven back north of the Aisne River. Both sides dug into trenches, and the Western Front became the setting for a hellish war of attrition that would last more than three years. Friends and family like Jean-Charles Worth were injured ("thankfully superficially—shrapnel in his shoulder") while others, including Jacques Lemoine (Suzanne's brother-in-law) were taken prisoner.

While Pierre was in no immediate danger, his health was deteriorating. At the end of 1914, he had been diagnosed with severe appendicitis and taken out of active service for a couple of weeks to recover. Elma, dreadfully concerned about her "dear Pup," insisted on visiting him. "Traveling is so hard, I still have a crook in my neck," she wrote to her sister-in-law with news of her trip and advice on taking the train through war-torn France: "Take pillows and rugs with you and don't let your heads touch seats for fear of contagion—I know what I am talking about! I feel like we're living in a volcano, we have no idea where Pierre will be sent to next. I haven't relayed all sad news as I don't want to give you shakes and shivers." Once Pierre was back at his post, Elma managed to stay close to him by volunteering at the local Hôpital de la Gare Maritime. Pierre, though recovered from the appendicitis, was still weak and increasingly worried for the future. "We can't let the end of year go past without talking about events and how they might affect our firm," he wrote to Jacques. "The war is going on longer than expected—if it continues for much longer, we need to have a plan of action re. our firm. . . . Money situation is not good . . . we don't have anything to keep our operations going. Sorry to depress you with this dire financial situation but it's better you are under no illusions."

Elma, too, was scared, but more for her husband's worsening health. "I'm let down with worry," she confided to Jacques. "I don't want my beloved in a cage when with loving hands I might feed him for the rest of his life." From a photograph of Pierre taken around this time, it's instantly apparent why she was concerned. Sitting in his car, a chauffeur's hat perched on his head, his face is swollen to such a degree that he's almost unrecognizable. Sure enough, it was not long after this photo was taken that he was rushed to the hospital. His fever kept increasing, his headache was unbearable, but most frightening of all, he couldn't breathe properly. The doctors diagnosed diphtheria, a serious bacterial infection affecting the throat and nose. It wasn't usually life-threatening, but these were not ideal conditions. Medicine was in short supply and hospital beds were oversubscribed.

Fortunately, Pierre was one of the lucky ones. Able to receive the treatment he needed, he started to recover. By his side, Elma was herself ill, suffering from erysipelas, a skin disease causing fiery red swelling. Once Pierre had been discharged, the couple recuperated together at Alfred's house in Paris: "I've been a wreck but am slowly returning to my old self," Pierre wrote to Jacques. "It has made me very grateful for the love of Father, Louis, and you. I'm now recovering at Father's house in your old room. I can hear the one-step on the piano but there's no dancing. The view is very empty—like being at sea. Elma is very tired, she also needs a rest. And she misses our daughter terribly, she is thinking of traveling to America."

In the end they both went back to America. As a result of the diphtheria, Pierre was declared temporarily unfit for service and decided to take his sick leave in New York. "I think Pierre's illness is our heavenly father's blessing in disguise," Elma wrote in grateful relief to her brother-in-law. They traveled back in September 1915, a journey not without its risk. Just four months earlier, HMS *Lusitania* had been hit by a German torpedo off the coast of Ireland, killing 1,198 passengers traveling from New York. Among them had been some known to the Cartiers. Lady Marguerite Allan would survive, as would her Cartier diamond and pearl tiara (miraculously rescued by her maid), but devastatingly, her fifteen- and sixteen-year-old daughters would be among those who drowned.

As 1916 dawned, the war was becoming more brutal than ever. In the Battle of Verdun, which lasted the better part of the year, German and French troops suffered close to a million casualties. As the ever bleaker news reached America, Pierre and Elma wrote letters full of affection and optimism to buoy the spirits of their family left in France. "This war will surely be over soon and we can be together again." Under normal circumstances, Pierre should have reported back for duty once recovered, but by December, the French consulate confirmed him as being unfit for further service. The reason given was neurasthenic melancholy, a result of exhaustion of the central nervous system. Elma's brother-in-law in New York, the eminent surgeon Doctor Delavan, may have come in useful when writing the ultimate sick note. After arriving back in New York, Pierre and Elma had moved into the St. Regis Hotel on Fifth Avenue with their daughter. For Marion's fifth birthday that April, they threw a children's party in the library of the hotel that made it into the newspapers as thirty children were invited to view the French silent film *Cinderella,* followed by "tea and a frolic."

But for all the joy at being back in safety with his adored daughter, Pierre's mind never drifted far from the war. He threw himself into charitable work, first offering funds to the Union des Arts and then becoming its secretary. The organization, founded in Paris by the famous turn-of-the-century actress Rachel Boyer, had been initially set up to help needy actors and artists in France. When war broke out, it had turned its attention to funding soup kitchens in Paris, but raising money had become increasingly difficult.

At the request of Mrs. Boyer, Pierre joined the Union des Arts in the autumn of 1916 and helped launch a New York fundraising committee. Through subscriptions, events, and the sale of charms and bracelets, they raised considerable sums to send back to France. The fact that this put him in closer contact with the great and the good (like the Marquis de Polignac and Mrs. J. West Roosevelt, the cousin of Theodore Roosevelt) was a bonus. Mingling with the right sort of people was important to Pierre, both for the benefit of the business and for his own sense of self-worth. Having grown up in a society where aristocrats ruled the roost, he'd been frustrated, like Louis, at how his family had been looked down on by much of high society, and at one point had even hired a genealogist to prove (unsuccessfully) his family could be traced back to noble blood.

A STRING OF PEARLS

Pierre wrote to Jacques several months after arriving back in New York, "I thank heaven for circumstances allowing me to return because without my presence, our best interests would have been compromised." The men Pierre had left in charge in his absence, including Jules Glaenzer and Victor Dautremont, had quietly kept the wheels of the business turning without incident but equally without impressive sales. Louis' secretary, Prieur, whom the brothers had decided to send over from France during the war, had been adding value, but they missed Muffat, who had fought and been seriously injured when a bullet grazed his neck. He would survive, but it had been a close call: Had he not turned his head at the crucial moment, he would have been instantly killed.

For Pierre, back in the saddle, there were two items that took priority: finding larger premises and rescuing the faltering cash flow by selling some of the highest-value items in the showroom. Fortunately, there was a client just around the corner who would be the ticket for both, landing Pierre one of the biggest deals of his life.

In the early twentieth century, a perfect pearl was considered the most valuable object in the world. The discovery of one in the Persian Gulf was a major event. It would even throw the global financial market into a state of high alert by depressing the value of everything else. It didn't take long for Alfred and his sons to become wise to the power of the small iridescent gemstones. The wealthiest women in the world bought Cartier's pearls, but of all the well-known pearl transactions, one stood out as being particularly significant for the firm. It involved a spoiled young bride, Maisie Plant, and her doting elderly husband, Morton Plant, a railroad and steamship magnate who was also the commodore of the very prestigious New York Yacht Club.

In 1916, Pierre Cartier put what he believed to be the most expensive necklace in the world in his New York showroom. With two strings of fifty-five and seventy-three perfect pearls, it was worth more than a million dollars (around $24 million in today's money) and became an overnight sensation. Many admirers traveled to see it in the flesh, but the thirty-one-year-old Maisie Plant was more captivated than most.

One evening, Maisie Plant and Pierre Cartier were seated next to

Maisie Plant (left) wearing the Cartier pearl necklace for which her husband,
Morton Plant, exchanged his Fifth Avenue townhouse (right) in 1916.
After extensive renovations, the mansion would become
Cartier's New York headquarters.

each other at a dinner. She was extolling the beauty of Cartier's pearl
necklace but claimed not to be able to afford it. Pierre knew that
Morton Plant, in his sixties, was quite besotted by his much younger
second wife and would make it his mission to ensure that whatever
Maisie wanted she should have (much to the dismay of his grown-up
children, who had their suspicions that their new stepmother was a
gold-digger). Pierre also knew that Plant was considering selling his
Renaissance-style mansion at the corner of Fifth Avenue and Fifty-
second Street because he felt the area was losing its residential feel. As
both the five-story townhouse and the pearl necklace were valued in
the region of a million dollars, Pierre wondered if Mr. Plant might be
open to a deal: "Give me your townhouse, and I'll let you have the
necklace." Fortunately for Maisie, her husband accepted the proposal. A pearl necklace was exchanged for a set of keys. And Cartier
moved into the mansion.

A NEW HOME: 651-53 FIFTH AVENUE

"The new building is being transformed. The room dividers are being
demolished, the ceiling full of holes, there is plaster all up the stairs

but I am beginning to like our local future. We can start French luxury in New York!" So wrote Pierre to Jacques as he poured his energies and funds into renovating the new building. Only too aware that
war was still raging in Europe, he felt that focusing on the business
was the best thing he could be doing. Investing now (letters between
the brothers estimated the total renovation cost at $900,000, or $24
million today) meant reaping rewards later. And with sales in Paris
and London at rock-bottom levels, it was up to him to focus on underpinning future profits from the safety of America.

Pierre had shopped around for architects. He asked both Louis
and his sister-in-law for advice (her father had transformed a residential house on Place Vendôme in Paris into a bank). But eventually, he
had selected a well-known American. William Welles Bosworth, who
would go on to become a family friend, was instructed to create a store
worthy of Cartier's distinguished clientele while maintaining a touch
of the private house feel. The resulting store, Pierre insisted, must be
attractive to American clients while remaining in keeping with the
original Rue de la Paix showroom. It must still feel like Cartier.

Bosworth was not short of ideas, but ultimately this was Pierre's
kingdom. Every detail—from the choice of the carpet to the wooden
molding around the doors to the style of his desk—was run by him
for approval. Cartier might be known for large gemstones, but it was
above all a house of creativity and design: From the moment a client
entered, they must know they were in an establishment of superior
taste. Pierre may have lacked Louis' creative genius, but he was also
an aesthete with a highly attuned sense of style. Several months after
the refurbishment was completed, the Fifth Avenue Association
awarded the house a gold medal for the best-transformed building in
New York that year.

After months of renovations, on the morning of October 1, 1917,
Pierre sent several of his employees ahead to set up in advance of his
arrival. Edward Bell, his assistant, traveled the short distance between
the old location and the new in Cartier's van, squeezed in between two
police detectives on the front seat with boxes of jewels filling the back.
Jules Glaenzer meanwhile drove a little car into which he miraculously
crammed a heavy display case. The men arrived at the address at the
allotted time, where several office staff were waiting to help them

unload the items. Before long, all the precious cargo was piled up on the sidewalk just outside the new store.

The problem, they soon discovered, was that no one had the keys. Everyone in the group was under the impression that someone else had them, whereas in fact the builders had forgetfully walked off with them the previous day. They had to wait, the group of them, beside the little red boxes filled with rubies, emeralds, and diamonds, out on the sidewalk, while an office boy was dispatched to track the keys down. Glaenzer directed the situation with characteristic theatrical flair. The ladies of the office, in their large skirts, were instructed to make a circle around the precious cargo. Jules himself, trying to appear nonchalant, stood watch, fervently hoping that his society friends would not choose that moment to walk past. Cartier salesman Edward Bell later recalled "the feeling of relief when we were all safely inside. . . . We have now settled down to an effective organization, and Monsieur Pierre is delighted with the location—where it is certainly a pleasure to work—and I cannot but feel that Monsieur Pierre's satisfaction is the moral result of endless difficulties successfully overcome."

In Conversation with Jean-Jacques Cartier

Uncle Pierre made a great trade with that pearl necklace for the building, but you see, it wasn't as absurd as it sounds today. Buildings, after all, could be built or rebuilt, but finding a perfect natural pearl could take months, even years. And finding enough good-quality, perfectly matched pearls for a necklace, well, that could take decades.

In 1916, the same year of the Cartier building–necklace swap, the Japanese were awarded a patent for their revolutionary technique to artificially induce the creation of a perfect pearl, but it would take more than a decade to commercialize. In time, as cultured pearls saturated the market, the value of natural pearls would plummet.

On Maisie's death in 1957, her million-dollar necklace was sold for just $151,000. Conversely, the Cartier building would be declared a Landmark of the City of New York in the 1970s, and it remains the firm's American headquarters even today. That single savvy trade of Pierre's did more for the brand than any amount of advertising, securing Cartier's central position in the luxury capital of the New World.

AN AMERICAN MAISON

There may have been a war going on across the Atlantic, but as the new Cartier building opened its doors in 1917, it was to be business as usual for its American clientele. Customers approaching the store would have noticed the royal coats of arms on the exterior, carefully positioned to make them feel just a little bit royal by association. A uniformed doorman would greet them respectfully; touching his hat and bowing slightly, he would hold open the door to the impressive wood-paneled main gallery inside. One visitor to the store would later remember entering: "Men who I could only assume were salesmen, dressed and groomed like top diplomats, sat at small tables as though they were part of a stage setting." There wouldn't be any jewels on display, but after a discussion with the client to establish desires (and budget), the salesman would give the nod to the porters in dark blue suits who would, in turn, quickly bring over the required tray of bracelets, rings, or necklaces, always covered with a gray cloth. "In this establishment," Pierre explained, "discretion rules, for the jewelry business is based on discretion."

Pierre's personal office was not particularly large, for it was designed to foster an atmosphere of intimacy rather than aloof grandeur. He wanted his clients to feel comfortable as well as impressed. And here, like everywhere else in the building, the Maison's links with France were on display. His kidney-shaped Louis XV desk, for instance, had been built of rare French wood by Alavoine (the fashionable French decorator with whom Cartier had shared its previous Fifth Avenue establishment).

Upstairs, on the top two floors, were the designers and craftsmen. Cartier's in-house New York workshop was named American Art

Works. To begin with, it was relatively small, especially with many of the French craftsmen fighting in the war. Those who were there were mainly French rather than American, exempt from the war due to their age or health. Cigarette smoke filled the air, and any female employees, like the office secretaries or pearl stringers, were kept far away from the prying eyes of the oh-so-charming Frenchmen.

As the war drew to an end, Pierre, in his early forties, considered America to be home. He and Elma, who had just celebrated their tenth wedding anniversary, enjoyed a comfortable existence in Manhattan's Plaza hotel. They had also recently rented a cottage in New London, Connecticut. The air was fresher there, especially in the summer months when the city heat was unbearable, and seven-year-old Marion loved playing on the beach. A popular spot with the New York elite, it also had the added benefit of being good for networking. Pierre wrote to Jacques that the previous owners of the Cartier mansion, Morton and Maisie Plant, had an incredible vacation home just around the corner: "To give you an idea of the grandeur—before the war he employed 65 gardeners!"

The Cartier couple socialized endlessly, and with each dinner that they hosted or opera they attended, they became ever more integrated into the New York social scene. "I've been accepted as a member of the New York Yacht Club," Pierre wrote proudly to his brother; "the two people who put me forward were Morton F. Plant and W. K. Vanderbilt. It couldn't have been two better people and I received a very flattering welcome for our house and my humble self." With European economies depressed by four years of devastating war, he felt the responsibility more than ever for his part in the building of the family firm into a worldwide success story. "America will be the making of us," he wrote to his brothers, and that involved knowing the right people.

World War I had been brutal for employee numbers in Cartier New York as so many of the firm's staff were called back to their native France. With the declaration of peace came the opportunity to build up the team again. But employees like Muffat, the Genailles, and Rosier returned with a far stronger bond to Cartier than the one with which they had left. During the war, Pierre had often written to his employees at the Front or in military hospitals, sharing news from New York and offering support. When medical bills had needed to be paid for those who had been injured, he had offered to do so. Those same employees now returned weighed down by the past four years but with an intense loyalty to their firm. Cartier became like an extended family as staff were united by their shared experiences. It wasn't just the designers, craftsmen, and salesmen who became close, but their wives and children too. And over the years, it would become quite usual for multiple generations of the same family to work at Cartier.

With his team back around him, Pierre was keen to set about developing Cartier New York into a stand-alone organization rather than a foreign outpost of the main Paris branch. He talked to his brothers about his plans for the business: "Do not fear to criticize them, I trust your judgment." He explained that he wanted to incorporate the New York branch as a separate company from Paris. Not only would it offer more leeway to get around some of the more punitive tax laws recently introduced in America, it would also give him more independence.

Pierre, who had harbored a small but real concern that leaving the French capital and the Paris branch might diminish his position within the family firm, was increasingly sure he had made the right move coming to America full-time. During the wartime years, when the Rue de la Paix branch had been forced to almost shut down, Cartier New York had shown it could survive out of the shadow of its Paris headquarters. And each diamond necklace sold in the Fifth Avenue showroom was further evidence of the extraordinary wealth and appetite for luxury in this country. But if he was going to keep pouring every ounce of himself into the New York venture, he wanted to know that he had the power to instigate changes himself, and the right to reap the rewards directly.

The family agreed to his proposal for a separate company. In early December 1919, the New York branch was incorporated in Albany, New York, as Cartier Inc., with Pierre assuming the role of chairman. His very capable president was Joseph Hartnett, a family friend who had previously helped to run Elma's father's company in St. Louis. The two directors were Victor Dautremont, who had come with Pierre on that early reconnaissance visit to New York in 1906, and George van Tuyl, the founder of the Metropolitan Trust Company (of which Pierre also became a director). Paul Rosier, a New Yorker who had joined the firm in 1912, became the company secretary.

At the end of December 1919, a notice went out in *The New York Times,* among other newspapers, to announce that Cartier Inc. was raising funds for expansion of the American business. The circular noted that "Cartier are the well-known jewelers with stores in London, Paris and New York with agents in India and Russia." Alongside the forty thousand voting shares in Cartier Inc. held by the family, the placing (overseen by the Metropolitan Trust Company) offered up to forty thousand nonvoting preferred stock shares at $100 each (raising up to $4 million), with a 7 percent annual dividend. Rather grandly, Pierre announced that the placing and the incorporation of Cartier in New York were "for the purposes of becoming an American institution." For all the apparent lack of modesty, this is exactly what Cartier was now on its way to becoming.

JACQUES (1906–1919)

LONDON, 1906

In the autumn of 1906, Jacques Cartier arrived in England. He was twenty-two years old and, for the first time in his working life, away from the shadows of his family. Initially it had been his father, Alfred, and then his brother Pierre, who had forged the way across the Channel, but now he had been entrusted with management of Cartier's London showroom. Checking his pocket for the strong Turkish Abdullah cigarettes he smoked, he pulled out the small London map Pierre had left for him in the apartment and consulted it carefully. Motorized taxicabs had just been introduced to the capital, but unless he was running late, Jacques preferred to walk. He was a man who enjoyed immersing himself in his surroundings.

Tall, with dark hair swept off to the side, an elongated neat mustache, and the longest of all the Cartier long noses, Jacques was elegant rather than classically good-looking. And yet, if he lacked the obviously handsome features of his elder brother, Louis, he seldom gave it a moment's thought. Far more interested in the wonders of the world, his kind gray eyes looked at new sights with almost childlike awe. As he strolled alongside Hyde Park, he marveled at the beauty of John Nash's Marble Arch monument towering above him. His employees were expecting him for a morning meeting, but he still had time to reach into his top pocket for a pencil and the miniature notebook diary he always kept on him to briefly sketch the outline. He didn't want to forget the curve of the stone arch, so reminiscent of his hometown's Arc de Triomphe. He felt confident that London was going to suit him. Inspiring surroundings, an emerging business that needed his input, and the opportunity to make his own decisions.

In France, Jacques had never been able to act on his own when it came to the business. It hadn't particularly bothered him. In fact, if he'd had any say in the matter, he wouldn't even have joined the family firm. Since adolescence, he'd been more interested in religion than in diamonds and had fervently hoped to become a Catholic priest. But it wasn't up to him. "Never forget your duty," his brothers had reminded him in their letters time and time again. Instead of a life spent worshipping the Father, the Son, and the Holy Ghost, they insisted he form part of their fraternal triumvirate. "You are part of the trinity," Pierre would write to him. "We need you."

The second-youngest of the four Cartier children, Jacques had grown up in the background, quietly watching the inevitable family dramas. By the time he reached his teens, his mother had already started to display the signs of mental instability that would plague the rest of her life. His father was wonderful when he was around, but he was often preoccupied with work, and though his brothers could be tremendously loyal if needed, the perfect protectors at school, there was a large age difference. It was his sister, Suzanne, who was Jacques' closest childhood companion. With just one year between them, they'd bonded over childhood games as their father taught Louis the secrets of the trade. And though, as he grew older, Jacques became closer to his brothers, it would be many years before they would treat him as an equal.

Putting his dreams to go into the Church aside and bowing to his sense of familial duty, Jacques joined the business in February 1906. Like his brothers, he'd spent three years in military service (in his case, in the cavalry) before he started his apprenticeship in Paris. Those first few months on Rue de la Paix were busy ones. While Pierre had prepared for his visit to New York and Louis had been preoccupied with creations for important new clients like the Romanovs,

Jacques had moved from department to department, studying all apects of the trade. He had learned about pearls from the in-house expert, Maurice Richard; listened to the slick Jules Glaenzer for tips on salesmanship; and spent painstaking hours sorting rubies, sapphires, emeralds, and diamonds according to their color, quality, and size.

His favorite time had been in the design department, learning firsthand from Alexandre Genaille and Henri Chenaud, even the famously difficult Monsieur Rauline, who clashed frequently with Louis. Unlike his forthright elder brother, Jacques lacked the air of entitlement that could plague the next generation of a family business. He might not have been able to follow his Catholic calling in his day job, but he had vowed to live life according to the tenets of Christianity, and employees warmed to him. Alfred had been impressed with the progress made by his youngest son, especially when it came to his knowledge of precious gemstones. And nine months after joining the firm, Jacques had been deemed ready for London.

By 1906, the Cartier New Burlington Street showroom was already well on its way to becoming a staple in British high society. More than that, there was a feeling of optimism in the air that boded well for future business. With Britain ruling close to a quarter of the world, there was "an almost palpable sense of satisfaction that the state of the country was, if not perfect, then as near to that as God could make it." But there were problems too. Several clients had started to complain of delays for items shipped over from Paris. In a few cases, the plaster models (needed to confirm the setting and size) had broken en route, aggravating impatient ladies who then had to wait for new models to be made up and delivered. Other times, there had been issues with repairs and resizing. British clients, such as the financier and friend of King Edward VII, Sir Ernest Cassel, not unreasonably, expected the jewels they bought in Paris to be adjusted or repaired in London. At the end of 1903, Cassel had bought two platinum and diamond fern spray brooches from Cartier Paris as a gift for his sister in England. Typical of Louis' inventive focus, they could be ingeniously connected in numerous ways to form a stomacher, a necklace, a corsage ornament, or a tiara, and even came with a little spanner-head screwdriver to do so. But when Cassel brought back the red box across the Channel and presented it to Bobby, as he affectionately called his sister, it hadn't been quite right. She paid a visit to Cartier London to have the tiara section resized, and though a relatively simple job, it had—given the lack of a skilled team of Cartier craftsmen on the ground—taken far too long.

Then there was the location. Being below Worth had been great for business, but the Cartier showroom was on the small side and there was a risk that Louis' unhappy marriage could, at some point, lead to a souring of feelings between the two families. With all this in mind, Alfred proposed that his youngest son look around for a larger London premises independent of Worth, with space for craftsmen in-house. They would not start making their own jewels in England yet—Paris was still very much the hub of the creative side of the business—but they should have a few specialists for restringing and simple repair and resizing work. The new showroom should also, Alfred insisted, remain in Mayfair, close to the current branch. It took time to find the perfect spot, but in the end it was just five minutes away. Number 175–176 New Bond Street was leased as an art gallery when Jacques first inquired about it. By 1909, he had taken over the lease.

Jacques Cartier (left) moved Cartier London to new premises
at 175–176 New Bond Street (right) in 1909.

In Conversation with Jean-Jacques Cartier

My father had an intrinsic understanding of design. He appreciated beautiful objects on their own but could also see how they worked together. When he decorated our house or renovated the store, the result was really quite marvelous. He might have a Chinese tray next to an Indian table on top of a Persian rug. Things you might not think would work together, but they did. And his focus on the detail was phenomenal. Later on, my mother would learn to leave all the decorating to him, even down to the fabric for the curtains!

Alongside Alfred, who had wanted to be involved in the renovation work just as he had been with the Paris and New York stores, the twenty-five-year-old Jacques converted the ground floor of the new building into paneled showrooms: the main salon, the Louis XVI Room, and the White Room. The idea was that the new premises should enable Cartier to display many more items of jewelry as well as offering private spaces for individual clients to meet their salesmen. Outside, the building was smartened up with new polished red and black granite to give the right impression from the outset.

When the store opened on November 3, 1909, it failed to garner much attention. It was mentioned in the odd paper, such as the *Morning Post,* but mostly as an afterthought. Far more news-grabbing were occasions when the store welcomed royals, like the King of Portugal, who visited three weeks later along with the Marquis of Soveral, a Portuguese diplomat and a friend of Edward VII. But, for the upper-class English, its location alone was enough to attract their attention. Ladies from the grand Mayfair townhouses couldn't help but look in the Cartier windows on their morning stroll around the neighborhood with friends, while those who lived in country estates would stop in when they did their shopping in town.

The New Bond Street store may have lacked a full workshop, but it did promise clients a high standard of after-sales care. One could have a pearl necklace restrung (recommended at least twice a year), a diamond bracelet polished, or a clasp fixed without having to send off the item to Paris (or, heaven forbid, to a competitor in London). And though these services may have been relatively low-margin offerings, they were crucial in building client loyalty. Most ladies didn't plan to buy a new jewel every few months, but if they had the excuse to pop into Cartier to collect their restrung necklace or repaired watch, then they quickly built up a relationship with their salesman.

The design sketchbooks from 13 Rue de la Paix reveal how jewelry destined for London was generally simpler and more economical than pieces sold in Paris. Instead of the then fashionable diamond and pearl dog collar, for instance, it was thought that the British might prefer a version that could be tied around the neck with cost-effective moiré silk. Sometimes Jacques had a hand in the design process himself, meeting with the clients to discuss their requirements before sending his ideas over to Paris, where the jewels would be made up. The writer Vita Sackville-West, for instance, wrote to Jacques in thanks for a "beautiful hatpin" he had designed for her: "It's a marvel and I told my husband (who also thanks you for making me so happy) that I would have exchanged all my other presents for this pin. So you can see how happy I am, it will be the admiration of everyone!"

In Conversation with Jean-Jacques Cartier

You see, back then, jewelry was a part of a woman's makeup. It's not like today, when jewels are reserved for special occasions. It was a time when women wouldn't go out without necklaces, bracelets, brooches, corsage ornaments, or even hatpins. And in the evening, there would be more gems—tiaras, diamond necklaces, or ropes of pearls. They didn't always buy new pieces, but they did often have their old pieces remounted or restrung. There was a lot of work for jewelers back then.

In May 1910, just nine years after the death of his mother, Edward VII's bon vivant lifestyle finally got the better of him. After religiously smoking twenty cigarettes and twelve cigars a day for decades, he succumbed to a fatal mix of cancer, bronchitis, and several heart attacks. They may have been distressed by the news that their great royal patron had passed away, but the Cartiers had little time to dwell on it. The end of one reign meant a new coronation, and with it jewelry orders from all over the world. Princesses, maharajas, grand duchesses, and heiresses would all need elaborate accessories to pay their respects to the new monarchs, King George V and Queen Mary. Throughout the months leading up to the June 1911 coronation, the Paris workshops worked overtime to create, remodel, and repair in frantic preparation.

Jacques, who was in London at the time to be on hand to respond to the many coronation-related demands from his British clients, came up with an idea to capitalize on the big event. To his consternation, Cartier's rival Fabergé was taking over the lease at 173 New Bond Street, just next door. Keen that it should be his firm in the limelight, not the Russian jewelers also favored by royalty, Jacques approached several eminent British society ladies: Would they be willing to lend Cartier the tiaras they were planning to wear to the coronation? The previous year, Queen Mary's brother, Prince Francis of Teck, had died following an operation. All proceeds from Cartier's tiara exhibition would be going to the charitable foundation that had been set up in his memory for the endowment of the Middlesex hospital. Few could refuse the proposal in aid of such a good cause, and in April 1911, Jacques was able to display a collection of nineteen tiaras from high-society coronation guests including the Duchess of Marlborough, the Marchioness of Cholmondeley, and Lady Granard.

England, with its formal court life, had long been regarded as the home of the tiara, and news of the legendary exhibition spread far and wide. Thousands of visitors happily parted with a guinea—no small sum at the time—to see the very same tiaras that two months later would bear witness to the crowning of a new king in Westminster Abbey. In America, *The New York Times* reported that the tiaras on display at Cartier's in London represented "one of the most interesting collections of jewelry ever brought together" and estimated their combined value at a phenomenal $1.25 million ($34 million today).

The five-day event was a brilliant marketing move, playing to the sense of rivalry among the British elite and putting Cartier right in the heart of it all in the eyes of both its clientele and the public. This kind of discreet advertising, without Cartier directly courting publicity, aligned with Louis' and Pierre's early efforts. Louis had made sure his first wristwatch reached the public via its distinguished wearer, Alberto Santos-Dumont; Pierre had put Cartier New York in the press with the notorious Hope Diamond; and now their younger brother was ensuring that Cartier London made the headlines through a charity event. Going forward, Jacques would regularly align Cartier's name with that of various charities he considered worthwhile. Sometimes he would put on exhibitions, but other times he would lend or even give away jewels for a good cause. At the May 1912 Headdress Ball in aid of Westminster Cathedral, for instance, Cartier's magnificent diamond brooch was the much-publicized winner's prize (while Fabergé's diamond and enamel pendant was offered to the runner-up).

In the summer of 1911, with the tiara exhibition and the coronation commissions successfully behind him, Jacques returned to Paris. He moved back into his old room in his father's house on Rue de Pomereu, pleased to have all the family close by again. His sister, Suzanne, and her husband, Jacques Worth, were living on Rue La Boétie, in the 8th arrondissement, with their two children. Pierre and Elma, recently back from New York with their little baby, Marion, were happily installed in Neuilly and eager for Jacques to meet his niece. And Louis, recently divorced, was working hard and enjoying his single lifestyle (there were even rumors of an illegitimate child).

Jacques, meanwhile, was more focused on his work than on women. Louis had tried taking him out to Maxim's, but it wasn't his scene. In fact, he had quite resigned himself to a life of celibacy until the day he was requested to call on the Harjes family on Boulevard Malesherbes. One of the daughters, he was informed, was keen to discuss a new jewelry commission.

MERE TRADE

On paper, Nelly Harjes and Jacques shouldn't have been a successful couple. Whereas she was a loud, social thirty-three-year-old divorced

Protestant from a rich American banking family, he was a reserved, devout Catholic dedicated to his work. Had they not met in her family home and quickly discovered they shared a mutual friend, they might well never have given each other a second glance.

Nelly's sister, Louise, was married to Charles Messenger Moore, an American who had managed the Parisian branch of Tiffany since the 1880s. When she asked the charming Monsieur Jacques if he knew her brother-in-law, Jacques smiled. Although officially rivals, jewelers tended to stick together. Louis-François Cartier had strongly believed in working alongside one's peers, not against them, for the good of the wider industry, and it was a lesson that had been passed down the generations. Moore was an old friend of his father, Jacques explained—he'd known him for years.

Once they started talking, Jacques and Nelly clicked immediately. He appreciated her genuine interest in the arts and found her amusing and refreshingly honest. And she was fascinated by him, finding his modest manner much more attractive than the self-importance that characterized so many of the men she knew. As with Pierre and Elma four years earlier, the pair knew almost immediately that they had met the partner with whom they wanted to spend the rest of their lives. The problem, as Jacques would soon find out, was convincing Nelly's father.

John Henry Harjes had emigrated with his parents from Bremen, Germany, to Baltimore in 1849. Unqualified but determined to work in finance, the nineteen-year-old had taken the first related job he could find: filling inkwells in a local bank. By 1853 he had set up his own firm, Harjes Brothers, in Philadelphia and it wasn't long before he had attracted the attention of one of the country's most prominent bankers, Anthony J. Drexel (later the mentor of J. P. Morgan). Drexel was so impressed with the German immigrant's drive that he asked the young man to partner with him to start a banking firm in France.

John, together with his German wife, Amelia, and their two young children, moved back across the Atlantic. In May 1868, John proudly unveiled Drexel, Harjes & Co. on Paris's Rue Scribe. Unfortunately, the timing couldn't have been worse. As the 1870 Franco-Prussian War and siege of Paris crippled the city, the bank managed to stay open, but hardly any business took place. Instead, John Harjes turned his attention to charitable work and also helped arrange a significant

£10 million war loan (over $1.2 billion today) to the French government from a very wealthy American, Junius Morgan. When the millions arrived from America in the form of gold bars at the port of Le Havre, John and his wife were entrusted with collecting them in their horse-drawn carriage and delivering them to the French government in Paris. Terrified that they would be caught as they crossed Prussian-occupied Normandy, Amelia hid the gold bars under her huge skirts while trying to affect an insouciant expression. Miraculously, the Prussian soldiers didn't suspect a thing, and they made it through. It was this single trade that would end up linking the Morgans, Drexels, and Harjeses in a partnership that would last decades. The following summer, in 1871, Junius's son, the thirty-four-year-old John Pierpont Morgan, joined the Drexels in founding a modest merchant bank called Drexel, Morgan & Co. in New York. It would later become known the world over as J. P. Morgan.

In 1878, John and Amelia Harjes welcomed their sixth and final child into their very comfortable Avenue Henri Martin townhouse, at the corner of Rue de la Pompe. Anna Margaretha Nelly, or Nelly as she would always be known, was born during the cold February that year, the same winter that her future brother-in-law Pierre made his appearance into the world just a few blocks away. More like her father than her mother in many ways, Nelly was from childhood a strong character who knew her own mind. She grew up well educated, bilingual, and, despite her family's vast wealth, surprisingly down-to-earth.

In the summer of 1901, it was arranged that Nelly, then a twenty-three-year-old "very attractive young woman," should spend a season in America. The Drexels, by now longtime family friends, offered to host her at their Long Island home. It was here that she met her first husband at a dinner party. Lion Gardiner was a twenty-two-year-old Princeton graduate and part of the family that owned the not insubstantial three-thousand-acre Gardiner's Island off the east end of Long Island. Worth several million, the island had proved a sound investment for the Gardiners, who had first bought it from Wyandanch, a sachem (leader) of the Montaukett Native American tribe, for a large black dog, some gunpowder, and a few blankets in 1639.

Nelly and Lion were engaged by August and married that autumn, just a few months after meeting, and perhaps too soon for the young Nelly to appreciate her husband's true character. Two years later, their only child, Dorothy, was born, but already Lion was struggling with married life. Falling into debt, he became a gambler, a drunk, and occasionally violent. Ashamed, Nelly hid the truth from her family back in Paris, telling only her older sister, Millie. After one particularly bad episode, Millie let on to their father. Furious, John Harjes took the first ship to America to bring his daughter and young granddaughter back home to Paris.

It would be almost a decade after arriving back in Paris before Nelly would meet Jacques. After being rescued by her father, she moved back into her parents' family home and divorced Lion in 1908 (citing the fact that he had "misconducted" himself with another woman). Dipping her toes back into the Parisian social scene, she found that she was not short on suitors, but her father kept a close eye on her. Part of this was driven by his protective loving streak; after seeing his daughter hurt by a man who had married her for her money, he was wary of its happening again. The other part, though, had to do with the family name. Tongues were already wagging when Nelly came back from America as a single mother, and there was a stigma attached to divorce. John Harjes hated the idea that his family could be the subject of idle gossip. For a man who had built a business that relied on trust and discretion, reputation was everything.

So when, in 1911, Nelly mentioned to her father that she was interested in a young French jeweler, the eighty-one-year-old John Harjes was not impressed. And when Jacques went to ask John Harjes for his daughter's hand, the older man refused flat out. He feared the worst—another chancer out for his family's fortune. His son, Herman, didn't help matters. Viewing the Cartiers as shopkeepers, or "mere trade" as he referred to them, he considered Jacques far too inferior a match for the Harjes name with its lofty reputation in banking circles.

Nelly begged her father to reconsider. In the end, John Harjes came to a compromise. He insisted that Jacques prove his love by waiting an entire year before seeing Nelly again. If, at the end of twelve months, the two were still convinced they wanted to be together, then he would allow their union. Jacques, sensing Monsieur Harjes's genuine concern for his daughter, agreed to the condition. What was a year, he said to Nelly, in the scheme of the rest of their lives? Alfred, Louis, and Pierre were not so understanding. Outraged that a Cartier was not considered worthy marriage material, they were of two minds as to whether Jacques should go along with the older man's wishes. But they were not blind to the benefits of marrying a Harjes, and they did not object.

In Conversation with Jean-Jacques Cartier

My mother was furious with her brother, Herman, for dismissing my father as trade. As if he was trade, she used to say! The best jeweler in the world! She didn't speak to her brother again until he was on his deathbed. He was fatally injured in a polo accident, and it was only then that she went to his side. Even then it was more at the request of my father. He's the one who should have been cross, really, but he had a more forgiving character than my mother.

A JOURNEY EAST

Fortunately, Jacques had a particularly busy few months ahead to keep his mind off missing Nelly. The coronation of George V in Westminster Abbey earlier that summer was to be followed by another equally magnificent celebration. This time the festivities to mark the crowning of the new king would take place in India, the jewel in the British Crown. Planned for December 1911, the Delhi Durbar would welcome all the Indian ruling families in their full sumptuous glory. Jewels would be center stage, not only as adornments on the honored guests but also as gifts to the new king. It was, Alfred and Louis decided, not to be missed. Previously Cartier had sent salesmen to India, including Glaenzer in 1908, but this visit, with the new King and Queen of England also in attendance, was too important to entrust to someone outside the family. Jacques, who had already met several Indian rulers on their visits to London, would be the perfect representative of the family firm.

The Cartiers were not alone in recognizing the enormous opportunities emanating from the East. When Indian ruling families came to London or Paris, they didn't just stay in the best hotels, they took over entire floors of the best hotels. Traveling to or from London's Savoy, the Maharaja of Patiala insisted on a cavalcade of Rolls-Royces, while in Paris, the Nizam of Hyderabad was known for buying entire display cases of jewels at a time. And in Madrid, the Maharaja of Kapurthala had fallen in love with a beautiful Spanish dancer and wooed her with flowers, diamonds, and romantic dinners until she agreed to be one of his wives.

If the rumors were to be believed, back in their own country the maharajas were even more extravagant, filling their swimming pools with champagne and organizing enormous weddings for their pets. And of course there were the jewels: "They scattered pearls as confetti, they played marbles with emeralds as large as panther's eyes. . . . They put rubies in their navels and diamonds in their noses." The elephants in Baroda had anklets of solid gold, and Maharaja Ranjit Singh decorated his stallion's harness with emeralds. "Providence," as Rudyard Kipling wrote in 1886, "created the Maharajas to offer mankind a spectacle."

Society ladies hosting a glamorous party in Europe would fall over themselves to host an Indian ruler at their table. Forget wanting a beautiful duchess to add that touch of glamour—the maharajas were in a different league. Their lives were the stuff of fairy tales. For the Cartiers, the idea of building a professional relationship with the Indian rulers was about more than jewelry commissions, it was an opportunity to link Cartier's name with Eastern splendor for its clients back home, too.

So it was on a cold mid-October morning in 1911 that the twenty-seven-year-old Jacques, still counting the days until he could see Nelly again, boarded *Le Polynésien* for a two-week journey to the East. He traveled with Cartier's pearl expert, Maurice Richard, who had already visited India in search of gemstones a couple of years earlier. Between them they carried several heavily insured suitcases of jewels to tempt the Indian rulers, including one truly magnificent pearl that they hoped the gem-loving maharajas would fall over one another to own.

With no idea what to expect from the journey, Jacques was entranced by his changing surroundings. The boat stopped at "deserted and primitive" Yemen and "half European, half exotic" Port Said before sailing through the 190-kilometer Suez Canal and across the Gulf of Berbera. While Richard was happy to relax, Jacques took part in the different games organized each day after tea "to help break the ice" and ended up meeting a particularly interesting group of people. "If I wasn't so anxious to see India and to start my work," he would write in his diary, "I would be almost annoyed at leaving the *Polynesian*." Several passengers were connected in some way to the various Indian rulers. Mr. Triggs, an English architect, who had spent the last fifteen years living in Indore, revealed over dinner one evening that the Prince of Bhopul was a man who liked to bargain but that the Maharaja of Indore would probably be a keen customer. Another day, over a game of chess, Mr. Cornalba, who worked for the Gaekwad of Baroda, divulged that the ruler employed a staggering twenty-three people for the upkeep and restoration of his state's royal treasure.

Eighteen days after setting sail, on a hot, muggy morning in early November, Jacques at last spotted the southern Indian city of Bombay (now Mumbai). The coastal metropolis appeared on the horizon from afar as a "veiled lady," only vaguely visible through the haze caused by the cotton refining plants and lack of wind. "A large stripe of smoke remains permanently above the city, and from a distance seems to submerge it . . . it is almost a surprise to us all when the sun goes through it like an extra-light gauze. Indeed, once in the city, the sky is the purest blue."

Jacques and Richard checked in to the Taj Mahal Palace, the recently built luxury hotel overlooking the Arabian Sea in the south of the city. They were both eager to get to work, but selling jewels would have to wait. Their cases had been temporarily held by customs and it would take several long days of bureaucracy to free them. While Richard was dispatched to deal with the paperwork, Jacques set off to meet some clients and scour the local bazaars.

Before his younger brother had left, Louis, long fascinated by the East, had asked him to look out for beautiful Indian pieces with which to decorate the windows of Rue de la Paix. In Bombay, Jacques was disappointed by much of what was on offer, but later on, in other markets around the country, he found more to pique his interest.

Often these were pieces with little intrinsic value that he admired simply for their design or color combination or use of unusual materials. In Patiala, he discovered three cotton necklaces with acorn motifs that he envisaged "very pretty in pearls and diamonds." In Hyderabad he bought swords, antique books, silver boxes, and a horse bridle. Sometimes his purchases were destined to be gifts. When he sent a box of different objects back to Paris, he included a note saying that Louis' eleven-year-old daughter, Anne-Marie, could choose a trinket for herself, and that the Indian miniature was for Elma. He also wrote that if his brothers or father liked anything in particular, they were welcome to it. This sharing of ideas and findings across oceans would be crucial to the development of Cartier's style. Louis, who had been inspired by Persia since the Ballets Russes production of *Scheherazade* the previous year, was eager to hear Jacques' reports of "the real India," as he called it, and would, in time, transmute some of his brother's insights into his creations.

A CELEBRATION UNDER THE INDIAN SUN

Holding their cases of jewels close, Jacques and Richard disembarked from the train in Delhi, unprepared for the sheer scale of the Durbar arrangements that awaited them. "There is an officer who comes to meet us from the station. The bags go in military cars. At the hotel we are welcomed by the captain who is in charge of the hotel and the camp which depends on it. Two sentinels guard the door—the porter is a sergeant—and they're all so natural that you have a feeling they have done this job all their lives."

Each ruling prince had his own vast area consisting of multiple tents and exquisite gardens. There were "beautiful avenues lit by electricity in the evening" and even a specially built railway to get around, although that didn't eliminate the throng of automobiles, horses, and pedestrians everywhere.

The main event of the Durbar was to be the ceremony on December 12 at which the King and Queen were declared Emperor and Empress of India. All the Indian rulers were expected to approach their sovereigns one by one to pay respects and offer gifts. One maharaja's son would later recall the prominence of precious gems.

"First was the Nizam, who gave the king a ruby necklace, in which each ruby was as big as a pigeon's egg. Then the other princes followed—Baroda, Gwalior, Mysore, Kashmir—each presenting the king with other items of jewelry which must have been lying in their coffers for centuries, but which were unearthed and brought to life for this great occasion."

As just one of the twelve thousand attending the Durbar, Jacques didn't have an inside track at the ceremony. For him, the nine-day event was all about mingling with potential clients. The afternoon polo match turned out to be the perfect place to meet others in a relaxed setting. "On the first day," he remarked, "I was seated next to the Gaekwad of Baroda and we talked a long while." The Gaekwad mentioned that he had some jewels he would like to be reset and asked if Jacques could spare the time after the Durbar to come to Baroda. Jumping at the chance, Jacques accepted on the spot, relaying the news in an excited letter to his family later that evening.

Many important guests at the Durbar, however, proved more difficult to meet, and for these, Jacques enlisted the help of the widely respected jewelry and art dealer, Imre Schwaiger, whom he had met the previous summer in Europe. A tall Hungarian who had lived in India for years, Schwaiger knew all the country's best jewelry buyers. Brilliantly connected and famously discreet, he was also often the first point of contact for maharajas who wanted to sell their precious jewels without letting on to others that they needed the cash. He had a "marvelous shop" near Kashmiri Gate in Delhi but would spend much of his time traveling around the palaces, buying and selling.

Schwaiger, no doubt hoping for future work with Cartier, offered to introduce Jacques to his clients, and to give him a space in his gallery. "Today we had first the Vice-Reine, who, as soon as Schwaiger had told her about us, came to see us immediately," Jacques reported back to his brothers on December 1. "She was naturally excited by the big pearl and promised to bring the King to see it. After her, Captain Spencer Clay and his wife (the sister of Waldorf Astor) who bought a bracelet for the Viceroy, and five or six other visitors. . . . We are giving him [Schwaiger] a commission of 10% of all that we sell in his shop." Apart from a couple of other European jewelers near Schwaiger's shop, including Garrard, there was no real competition. The local jewelers seemed to Jacques to be more akin to pawnbrokers or junk dealers. Impressed with how Schwaiger managed to draw in impressive clients, Jacques thought of working again with him in the future: "I have in my head the idea to lend some London stock to Schwaiger next summer."

Schwaiger's shop may have been a magnet for wealthy Europeans in India, but the Indian rulers expected the trade, as Schwaiger and Cartier both were, to come to them. It was difficult, however, because Jacques could not turn up unannounced, and the ruler rarely granted an appointment without prior knowledge of the tradesman. Fortunately, Schwaiger was again able to help. With his letter of personal recommendation, sent along with a letter of introduction from Jacques and a sample of his wares (such as a Cartier pocket watch), a meeting would generally be granted. Once in the Rajah's camp at the allotted time, Jacques would then open his cases of jewels to reveal the valuable items he had brought from Paris.

The next problem, as Jacques soon found out, was that Indian audiences had different tastes from those of his aristocratic European clientele. Back in Paris and London, it had been the ladies who had worn the jewelry. In the East, the men were buying for themselves and they didn't want discreet little bracelets, feminine necklaces, or tiny diamond cocktail watches. They wanted either jewelry fit for a prince or the same simple accessories that chic Parisian men would be buying. In fact, as an incredulous Jacques wrote back to his brothers, the silver pocket watch he had sent along with his letter of introduction, in order to tempt the rulers to see him, turned out to be the most popular item of all.

THE VANISHING MAHARAJA

The Durbar opened up the world of Indian rulers to Cartier. Once it was over, Jacques traveled far and wide to meet them, from Calcutta to Baroda, and from Indore to Patiala. The distances between the palaces were long, far longer than distances he was used to traveling between clients in England. But the potential rewards were great, even if, as Jacques soon discovered, dealing with the maharajas was not always easy.

On a cold, sunny December morning, Jacques and Richard alighted from a train in the North Indian city of Patiala, two hundred kilometers from Delhi. They were there on the invitation of Maharaja Bhupinder Singh of Patiala, who had taken a liking to the large pearl they had shown at the Durbar and had wanted to see it again. A palace guide met them at the station and, after informing them the Maharaja would meet them the following day, showed them to the spartan bungalow where they were to be lodged. It was, Jacques admitted, not quite what they had been expecting. "The bedroom 6 m x 6 m and 10 m high would be considered a barn in France if it wasn't for the chimney and the strap bed. No bedding of course. Each traveler for himself. No towels, nothing." Food would not be included and in the place of the car they had requested, they were lent an uncomfortable cart pulled by an unwieldy horse. Next time, Jacques promised himself, he would bring his own car to India.

After a bad night's sleep and a wander around the local bazaars, Jacques arrived at the palace at the appointed time for his meeting with the Maharaja. It was, he wrote, truly magnificent. Delhi had been so busy, this was a calm oasis in comparison. Some two and a half hours went by as he waited patiently for his host when, suddenly, the squeal of car tires shocked him out of his daydreaming. Turning around, he saw a Rolls-Royce being driven worryingly fast toward him by a man in cricket whites, one hand nonchalantly on the steering wheel as he leaned out of the car precariously. It didn't take Jacques long to recognize the turbaned daredevil driver as Maharaja Bhupinder Singh himself. Screeching to a stop and leaping out of the Rolls—one of many that he owned—he greeted the Parisian jeweler brusquely and bade him follow him into the zenana, the female-only side of the palace. The guide was shocked. In more than twenty years of working for the Maharaja, he had never seen any adult males, other than his ruler or the guards, enter this area.

Jacques followed the Maharaja down seemingly endless corridors and through beautiful external courtyards before arriving at their secret destination. Six officials with six different keys had been there earlier to open all the treasure chests and prepare the room. Entering behind the ruler, Jacques found himself in a fairy-tale setting. All around him were jewels—glittering diamonds, strings of pearls, vivid emeralds, exotic turban ornaments. The Maharaja walked proudly to the end of the room where an altar-like table stood covered in the most fantastic gems of all. This, he explained, was his personal collection. He knew the price for the pearl was £40,000 (more than $5 million in today's money) and he wanted to add it to his treasures. But first, he proposed to sell Jacques some of the jewels in front of them.

Staggered by the ruler's collection, Jacques immediately offered to buy several items. He would have loved to show his brothers the magnificent turban ornament in the form of a large feather "at least ten inches long, made of diamonds. About the edge of this is a fringe of large, pear-shaped emeralds, each of which is almost priceless." But the Maharaja had no desire to sell that one. Instead, he offered an emerald jewel of lesser value. Jacques politely refused, but, understanding he was there to foster a good relationship and open the door for future relations, he did agree to buy a selection of gemstones at an inflated cost of £14,400 ($1.85 million today).

With the gems that Jacques agreed to buy deducted from the cost of the large pearl, the Maharaja was left with a bill for £25,600. Jacques had hoped the ruler might be able to pay it to him in cash before he handed over the pearl, but as he was fast discovering, business would not be that straightforward in India. The Maharaja of Patiala admitted that he didn't actually have the cash, because the Durbar had cost him £100,000 and he had to borrow money for the railways. So he asked to pay £14,000 then and there, the balance in March. "Naturally," Jacques wrote in his diary, "we politely refused. So he asked to think about it, he would see his bankers. But he asked to keep the pearl to show his women. I knew what he was trying to do, and even though it annoyed me, I let him take it. Tomorrow we meet at 2 pm. The first act is played out."

The following afternoon, Jacques returned to the palace for his appointment only to discover that the Maharaja was not there and wouldn't be able to see him until the next day. Instead, he had arranged for another European jeweler to meet Jacques to tell him that his pearl was overvalued. Slightly annoyed but not altogether surprised, Jacques went back to his spartan quarters for the night, where "with dinner in my room in front of a wood fire, one has a little bit the impression of being a prisoner of the state."

He trudged back to the palace the following day. Again, the Maharaja was not there. This time, Jacques was informed he had gone on a hunt and wouldn't be back until the end of the week. The charade continued. There was always another excuse. Finally, the Patiala State prime minister showed up in the place of the Maharaja to speak to an exasperated Jacques. "After four days of vain applications to see the Rajah, we received a meeting with the Prime Minister. He told us that he had been given control of negotiations for the purchase of the pearl. We told him that the terms had already been discussed and that they would not be changed. So he told us that he could pay all in cash but that the pearl must be first valued in Bombay by an expert of his choosing. There is no way to discuss this reasonably and so we refused. He said he would discuss with the Rajah and would let us know that evening. Naturally the evening passed without a word. The next day we went to him. He had left the previous evening for Calcutta."

At this point, the normally patient Jacques was becoming anxious and quietly incensed. He had given up hope that the Maharaja of Patiala would buy the pearl, but he had other appointments elsewhere in India and didn't want to create a poor first impression by being late. He needed to get back on the road but first he needed his precious pearl in his possession. Reflecting on his predicament, he came up with a plan. He sent a confidential telegram to his brothers asking them to wire him back, via the palace, requesting his presence with the pearl in Paris immediately. It worked. Once the palace received the urgent telegram from Cartier HQ, the Maharaja, now miraculously available, agreed to return the pearl to Jacques. Jacques paid for the items he had promised to buy at inflated prices and left Patiala bound for his next meetings, in Calcutta and Baroda.

BARODA AND ITS JEALOUS JEWELERS

When Jacques turned up at Laxmi Vilas, the magnificent Baroda palace built as a gift from Gaekwad Sarajirao III to his first wife, Chimnabai, in 1890, he was greeted by the Gaekwad's second wife, Chimnabai II. During the Durbar, the royal ladies had taken a back seat when Jacques had displayed his jewels, but in Baroda, he had the chance to speak to Chimnabai II directly. He liked her immediately, writing back home that she was a "superior woman," intelligent and thoughtful, who had from the first moment endeavored to put him at ease in this grand palace so far away from home.

Having started out as a farmer boy, Gaekwad Sarajirao III had been selected to become the future ruler of Baroda when the state was left without an heir. Whether it was this humble beginning that kept him grounded and wanting to do good throughout his life, or whether it was always in his stars to rule, he would go down in the history books as a remarkably progressive ruler and example to others. He built schools, colleges, libraries, and an exceptional museum in the palace grounds for the welfare and education of his subjects. Controversially, he offered women, starting with his wife, the opportunity to receive an education.

Part of one's instruction, the Gaekwad believed, should be to experience different countries and cultures, and he disregarded the long-held belief that devout Hindus would lose caste through contact with a multitude of non-Hindus outside India. In 1887, he and his wife traveled to Europe for the first time. They visited everywhere from palaces to sewage plants, with the Indian ruler taking notes along the way in order that his findings might improve his state back home.

Like Jacques, the Gaekwad also appreciated beautiful art and classic design. His home, four times the size of Buckingham Palace, boasted generous wide corridors, airy interior courtyards, intricate stone carvings, and open latticework where the light streamed through. Inside, everything was chosen with an innate understanding of how it would harmonize with the whole. Lush green plants surrounded cool pools of water, marble statues and grandfather clocks appeared in corners, and paintings of maharajas past lined the walls.

In his diary, Jacques drew beautiful, life-sized sketches of the Baroda jewels that the rulers showed him. The Gaekwad had been just twelve years old when he had assumed his regal role and worn them during the state visit to India of Edward, Prince of Wales (later Edward VII), in 1875. Back then, "the Little Gaekwad of Baroda," as the Prince referred to him, had dazzled his onlookers: "He was weighted—head, neck, chest and arms, fingers and ankles—with such a wonder of vast diamonds, emeralds, rubies and pearls, as would be the loot of many a rich town." Now Jacques was being asked to take a record of all those fabulous gemstones so he might propose how

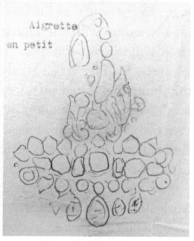

Jacques first visited Laxmi Vilas Palace, Baroda (top), in 1911.
Asked by the Gaekwad to come up with designs for the remounting
of Baroda's crown jewels, he drew them in order to have a record
to work from when he returned to Europe. Here his quick pencil
sketch of a diamond *aigrette* (turban ornament) is shown alongside
a photograph of the jewel.

they could be remodeled in more modern European platinum mounts.
Staggered by the quality laid out in front of him, he took notes alongside his sketches: "He owns the beautiful diamond, the 'Star of the
South.' This is used as a pendant on a diamond necklace made up of
three rows of diamonds, each stone weighing from thirty to forty
carats. The whole thing is easily worth £250,000. He has also a neck-

lace made up of five rows of pearls which, as to size and color, are absolutely matchless."

Alas, despite spending days and nights finalizing designs for the resetting of all the crown jewels, Jacques didn't end up securing the treasured commission on that first trip. As Louis had experienced in Russia a year earlier, suspicious local jewelers could make life unexpectedly difficult when trying to sell abroad. Even the Gaekwad hadn't anticipated the force of negative feeling from his court jewelers. So terrified were they that this European jeweler had come to steal their business that they created an enormous furor, effectively forcing Jacques out of their state. Jacques, who understood very well the politics of the situation, made a point of not complaining and remaining as neutral as possible. "As in all courts there are divisions. . . . Every time that I'm consulted, I agree with everyone while marginally siding with the maharani who is the head. . . . It is she who holds all the ropes in this court of tightrope walkers."

Jacques' approach was a good one. Before he left Baroda, the Maharani Chimnabai II had entrusted him with her largest necklace and a few other objects for remounting. It wasn't the huge commission he had been working toward, but at 30,000 francs, it was substantial. Leaving Baroda, Jacques was pleased he had been able to spend time with a royal couple he esteemed so highly. Their bond and respect for each other had reminded him of Nelly and how much he wanted to see her again. Before he could return to Paris, however, he had one more important mission to undertake.

PEARLS IN THE PERSIAN GULF

After four months in India, Jacques and Richard set off for the Persian Gulf. "My dear Louis," Jacques wrote home, "if I have understood correctly, the most important mission bestowed on me during this trip to the East is to investigate the pearl market and to report back on the most effective way for us to purchase pearls." As Cartier was well aware, natural pearls were like magnets for the wealthiest women in the world. Since the opening up of the South African diamond mines, the price of pearls had soared compared to diamonds based on their relative rarity. In the first decade of the twentieth century, one good-quality pearl (valued more for its round shape than its sheen) was priced four times more highly than a diamond of the same weight, and a pearl necklace could be more highly valued than a Rembrandt painting. Perfect pearls were almost impossible to find, but the best, the Cartiers believed, came from the Persian Gulf.

The value of pearl exports from the Persian Gulf had quadrupled in the twenty-five years preceding 1904. Even within ten years—from 1894 to 1904—pearl exports from Bahrain had risen from 3.7 million rupees to 10.3 million rupees. And yet it wasn't the Persian Gulf pearl sheikhs who were making all the money. It was the middlemen. They would buy the pearls from the Persian Gulf, ship them to Bombay (the world's gemstone trading center), sort and grade them, and then sell them on to international jewelers including Cartier for a huge markup. So far only one Parisian jeweler, Rosenthal Frères, had successfully managed to cut out the middlemen by buying directly from the Persian Gulf, and had become extraordinarily wealthy as a result (*The New York Times* estimated Léonard Rosenthal's fortune at $100 million in 1914, around $2.6 billion in today's money). Watching the Rosenthals enviously from the sidelines, Louis, Pierre, and Jacques had decided they wanted a share of the action too.

Like the Cartiers, the Rosenthals' strength was that they were brothers, able to be in multiple places at one time. In 1905, the younger brother, Victor Rosenthal, had traveled to the Persian Gulf and come back with 187,000 rupees' (around $1 million today) worth of pearls. The next year it was double that. It was impressive, but it wasn't enough for his elder brother. Léonard was the real brains behind the business, and he wanted to dominate the market. With the help of Victor's inside knowledge on the pearl sheikhs and their desire for security, he came up with a plan to ensure they always sold him their very best pearls.

In 1907, along with the financial slump that had postponed Cartier's expansion into America, there had been a simultaneous pearl crisis. At a time when most jewelers had been scared to make up-front payments, Léonard Rosenthal had spotted an opportunity. Persuading a banker to loan him several million francs, he had the entire amount converted into millions and millions of half-franc silver coins. He then sent them all, over the seas, to his brother, who was waiting in the Persian Gulf. On the day the ship arrived, the astounded Arabs watched as a seemingly endless procession of donkeys laden with sacks and sacks of shiny coins carried the money from the dock to Victor's house. The outlandish scheme convinced the pearl sheikhs that the Rosenthals were rich beyond comparison. From then on, all the best pearls were theirs for the asking. And, as Jacques would find out, it would not be an easy task to convince them to switch their allegiance to the Cartiers.

Jacques in the Persian Gulf, 1912, with his hosts, pearl traders and businessmen. Seated (top image) from left to right: Abdulrahman Al Ibrahim, Mugbil Bin Abdulrahman Al Thukair, Jacques Cartier, Salman Bin Hussain Mattar, and Yousif Bin Ahmed Kanoo. Later images from this trip (including Jacques' outing on a pearl fishing boat, pictured bottom right) would be used by the brothers to distinguish themselves from the competition as they marketed Cartier as "PEARL IMPORTERS" (bottom left).

Jacques spent several days with his hosts in the Persian Gulf, politely eating "edible without being appetizing" meals with them as they sat together on large Persian carpets and discussed the pearl trade. They communicated via Sethna, a Parsi pearl expert whom Jacques had hired as a translator in India: "The conversation wasn't very fast because I gave my message in English, Sethna translated it into Hindustani, while amplifying it slightly, and then Sheikh Youssef translated it into Arabic for the head sheikh, also adding his own comments. In this way, a discussion of fifty words took half an hour. And then the response came by the same chain, so the exchange went on for quite a while!"

While there, Jacques asked to see the pearl collecting process himself. It wasn't every European jeweler who had visited the Persian Gulf, and his brothers wanted to be able to tell their clients back home that Cartier had an inside track. Taking a trip on a pearl fishing boat, he watched in alarm as the divers dangerously weighed themselves down with buckets of stones in order that they might stay on the seabed for as long as possible collecting shells. Later, Cartier would use an image of the pearl diver on that boat as part of its marketing, with a caption claiming it was the "Cartier" boat. It all helped to boost the firm's reputation as "supplier of pearls" (as Cartier referred to itself on its letterhead and invoices). The reality, however, was that Jacques wouldn't be able to secure a special pearl trading agreement directly with the pearl sheikhs. The Rosenthals had gotten there first and it would prove just too difficult to knock them off the top spot.

In Conversation with Jean-Jacques Cartier

My father would tell us stories about the pearl divers. Terrible job—incredibly dangerous and they were hardly paid anything. One time, my father was on the boat an entire morning in the blistering hot sun and they collected about a hundred shells—but not one single pearl was found! Not even a bad one. Can you believe it? All that work and nothing to show for it. That's why natural pearls were so valuable.

RETURNING TO EUROPE

Sitting in Louis' Paris office in April 1912, a selection of Indian treasures laid out on the desk, Jacques recounted details of his voyage to his brother and father. He was optimistic for future relations with Indian clients, even if orders hadn't been as significant as they had hoped. India was a country, Jacques explained, where it would take time to build loyalty. The Gaekwad of Baroda, for example, wanted to stay in touch and had even asked Jacques to help him better understand the European jewelry market. He wanted facts and figures on everything from "jewelers' wages" to the "manufacture and refurbishment of jewelry" in order that he might learn from the best. Louis was pleased. He asked if the famous Baroda necklace was as wonderful as legend had made them believe. Yes, Jacques marveled, it was quite extraordinary. Seven strands, all perfectly matched. But he had seen so many miraculous jewels on his trip. When it came to pearls, which he had found to be the favorite gem in India, he felt that one of the finest collections was that of the Maharaja of Dholpur. He had a necklace reaching almost to the knees, consisting of five ropes of pearls caught together at intervals with single pearls of enormous size.

Alfred wanted to know about the new Nizam of Hyderabad. Would he be as good a client as his father, who had made the fortune of many men? Jacques told his father about the long trip he had taken to Hyderabad, only to be ignored for five days once he arrived. He had finally met the Nizam, he explained, at the Durbar. Unlike the other rulers, the Nizam had chosen to rent a house as well as an enormous camp for the duration of the Durbar to house his zenana of more than a hundred women. Jacques had been overwhelmed by the grandeur of it all, but it turned out the Nizam only wanted the two smallest items Jacques had brought along: a pocket watch and a cigarette case. Alfred was disappointed. He had considered the previous Nizam the best jewelry buyer in the world: "When he used to enter a shop, you didn't have to show anything or say anything. With his cane, he would point to an entire wall and say *'ceci est pour moi'* [I'll take this] without demanding the price—and he would pay in cash." Jacques was sure that the next trip over there would be better—the Indian clients just needed time to trust foreign jewelers, but the opportunities were enormous. "They pay in cash," he had noted with excitement. "It would be advantageous for us to visit them annually."

Speaking with his father and brother, Jacques explained why he felt strongly that a Cartier branch should be opened in India: not just for selling jewels but for buying them too. Though he had found a few high-quality gemstones on his trip, on the whole, the process had been difficult. He had been forced to buy large lots of gemstones, the bulk of which were poor quality. He'd tried to make his point by letter when still in India: "Since we must take these enormous lots in their entirety and the scrap (the largest part) is unsellable at Cartier . . . we must get rid of it in Bombay. The best would be to have an office here where Maurice Richard, or someone else, would spend four months of the year (September to December included) and the rest of the time we will leave there a local or two who will send us reports on the state of the market."

He had made good contacts, professionals like Schwaiger and Sethna, who could help out on the ground, and Cartier would just need to send out one representative from Paris, someone who really understood the inner workings and ethos of their House. It wasn't a dissimilar proposal to the one Sarda had earlier made for Russia. But just as Alfred had rejected the idea of a St. Petersburg branch, so Jacques' suggestion was dismissed. In Alfred's mind, it didn't make sense for his sons to be spread so thin. Jacques could travel east regularly and they could hold exhibitions in India as they did elsewhere. Perhaps they could even set up a temporary branch in Delhi with Schwaiger or sell from Schwaiger's shop. But they were not going to be investing large sums and taking business risks so far away without a family member there to oversee it.

Jacques was angry at first. He understood the family's tendency toward financial prudence and unwillingness to take on debt, but he felt strongly about the benefits of an Indian branch. He had written to Pierre in frustration, explaining how he had suffered a *"nuit blanche"* (sleepless night) at the rejection of his proposal, and yet he had little choice but to concede. He might have been twenty-eight years old but he still ranked below his two brothers in the Cartier

Frères structure. For now he would simply return to London and do what he could to spread the Indian word from there.

On the morning of Tuesday, May 28, 1912, 175 New Bond Street opened its doors for Cartier London's first Indian-inspired exhibition. Rather than being simply an attempt to sell jewels, the event was Jacques' way of conveying to his European clients the wonders of the East. Displaying a tiny sample of India's treasures in order to fire their enthusiasm, he excitedly told a journalist that his eyes had been opened to previously unimaginable wonders. "Among the collections which I saw I found some pieces which surpass anything similar to be found in the world."

The spring exhibition, titled "Oriental Jewels and Objets d'Art Recently Collected in India," was a resounding success. Long before traveling to the East had become fashionable among the elite, Monsieur Cartier had crossed the seas and brought back treasures worthy of magnificent princes. Carved emeralds, large pearls, and Mughal jades were admired by a crowd who had heard about the splendors of this opulent country and were desperate to see them for themselves. But it wasn't just the gemstones that were exotic; designs that incorporated lotus flowers, mythical monsters, and elephants were so different from Western motifs. It wouldn't be until a decade or so later that the full impact of India would appear in Cartier's jewelry— the First World War would ensure a lengthy interval between trips— but Jacques' exhibition was a significant early step in linking the firm's name with the enticing East.

THE WEDDING

The waiting was over. Buoyed by the success of his Indian exhibition, Jacques returned to Paris and his future wife—or so he hoped. First he had to face Nelly's father. As he made his way to the Harjes residence on Avenue Henri Martin, he was nervous. He didn't doubt that M. Harjes was a man of his word, but he wanted to be genuinely accepted by Nelly's family, not just out of obligation.

John Harjes duly listened to the jeweler's request for Nelly's hand. Jacques gave the older man his word that he would always provide for and protect Nelly and her little daughter, Dorothy. And, to prove that he was driven only by love, he vowed never to touch a cent of Nelly's money. Last, recognizing the difference in religion, he promised to marry her in a Protestant church and to bring up any children they might have together as Protestants rather than in his own Catholic faith. This, he felt, was the greatest sacrifice he ever made, a sign of the selfless love he felt for her. Years later, once the children were grown and he was nearing the end of his life, he would ask Nelly if she would consent to be remarried in the Catholic Church. She would agree willingly, and a great weight would be lifted from his soul, for up until then he believed he hadn't been properly married in the eyes of his Lord.

John Harjes accepted the young man's proposition this time. His son, Herman, was again furious, still believing that the Cartiers were not worthy of joining the Harjes family, but Nelly's father had given his word and would not go back on it. Jacques' entire family, in contrast, were overjoyed to hear of the engagement. For Alfred, it was more than he could have hoped for: another son married into the American elite. And they liked Nelly, she was fun, she had spark, and she brought out the best in Jacques. He was more ambitious since he had met her, more determined to do well by her. One week before the wedding, on December 20, 1912, Louis organized a dinner at home for the newly engaged couple so both families could get to know each other. After the unkindness she felt her family had shown Jacques, Nelly was especially grateful for this unconditional welcome into the Cartier fold. From this moment on, she would always refer to Louis and Pierre as her "brothers."

The big day dawned. On December 26, 1912, the day after Christmas, Nelly and Jacques said their vows in front of a small congregation. They hadn't wanted a big affair. Not only was this a second marriage for Nelly (in a world where it wasn't unusual for ladies of class to leave the room at the mere mention of divorce), but keeping personal affairs discreet would always be their way. They opted for the American Church of Paris on Rue Berri, where the proceedings were led by an American Congregational minister from Ohio. Nelly's daughter, Dorothy, now nine years old, was the bridesmaid.

In Conversation with Jean-Jacques Cartier

My mother's father was meant to walk her down the aisle, but he telegraphed a couple of days before the wedding to say he was feeling ill and wouldn't be able to make it. She was terribly upset—of course she suspected he wasn't really ill and that her snobby brother, Herman, had persuaded him to stay away. But her sister, Louise Moore, who was married to the head of Tiffany in Paris, came to the rescue. They hosted the wedding breakfast at their large house in Rue de la Pompe. I'm not sure if there were any photographs taken that day, but my mother kept that menu for the rest of her life!

After a wedding breakfast of foie gras, trout, breaded lamb cutlets à la Maréchale, and Alsatian-style ice cream, Jacques and Nelly bade farewell to their guests and set off for a short honeymoon just outside Paris. They spent a blissful few days in Chailly-en-Bière, a small village on the outskirts of Fontainebleau with a magical castle and imposing forests ("our woods," as Nelly would later refer to them). And just days after returning to work as a married man, Jacques approached his father and brothers about being more formally admitted into the main Parisian business. With a wife, a stepdaughter, and hopefully more children to come, he felt that he needed greater security. Alfred, Louis, and Pierre, who had come to rely on Jacques more and more, agreed. They might still look at him as the youngest and least experienced one in the family, but over the last year Jacques had proved himself in the East, and with his exhibition in London, and now he'd married well too. So in January 1913, Louis signed the papers finally admitting his youngest brother to the Cartier Frères partnership.

NEW YORK

Nelly and Elma had hit it off straightaway. Both more outspoken American than demure French in temperament, they enjoyed gossiping about mutual friends back across the Atlantic, and became nostalgic remembering lunches at the Colony Club and performances at the Metropolitan Opera. It had planted the seed of an idea in Pierre. Perhaps, he suggested, Jacques could help out with the Fifth Avenue branch as well as in London. New York was going to be crucial for Cartier's future success, and the London branch didn't need him there permanently, especially with all the items still being made in Paris. And if M. Jacques Cartier could spend at least a few months over in New York, it would free up M. Pierre Cartier to spend that time in Paris. Though Pierre and Elma were very happy to spend a season in New York each year, they still very much thought of Paris as home.

And so, nine months after their wedding, Jacques and a heavily pregnant Nelly arrived in America with ten-year-old Dorothy. It was September 1913, and the plan was for Jacques to build up an understanding of the New York business before they all returned to Europe in the spring. After a brief spell at the Plaza, they moved to a leased house at number 131 East Seventy-first Street. Nelly appreciated being close to many of her old friends, and for Jacques it was a pleasant twenty-minute stroll down the east side of Central Park to the Fifth Avenue store. He started off by organizing another Indian-themed exhibition that November.

It was a happy period. Jacques and Nelly's first daughter, Jacqueline, was born just a few weeks after their arrival in early October. Alfred couldn't hide his disappointment at another girl; it had been thirteen years since his first grandchild, he pointed out to Jacques, and still no grandsons to continue the Cartier name (he had been hoping that thirteen would be the lucky number). But Jacques didn't mind. From the moment she was born, he adored his little namesake girl. As she grew up, Jacqueline would prove difficult and headstrong, often driving her mother to despair. Jacques was almost miraculous in his patience with her. When she flew into a rage he would calmly listen to her point of view, never assuming that just because she was younger it was any less valid than his own. He was the only one who really understood her, and she adored him.

By March, the family had settled in so well to life in America that they were planning to accept Pierre's proposal that they should stay out there longer. Initially Nelly had wanted to return to France to be closer to her increasingly ill father, but after he passed away in February, she no longer felt so guilty about being abroad. She had even found a New York house for sale nearby, on the north side of Sixty-ninth Street, just west of Madison Avenue. Jacques had been about to sign the papers when a letter from France stopped him in his tracks. War was looking increasingly likely. His brothers advised that he return to France as soon as possible.

FROM TIARAS TO TRENCHES

Of the three Cartier brothers, Jacques was the only one who fought at the Front in the Great War. While Pierre was driving his commander around Cherbourg and Louis was mostly hobnobbing with the government in Bordeaux, Jacques was an officer in the cavalry. His brothers were furious with him for putting his life at risk: "Go and apply at Lausanne for a job not directly war-related!" Louis commanded, but Jacques refused, feeling it his duty to stand alongside his fellow countrymen in battle. It was one of the only times that he didn't put the wishes of his brothers before his own. Even when his longtime client and friend Prime Minister Asquith wrote to him from Downing Street offering him a way out over in England, Jacques prioritized his patriotism. Pierre was not impressed: "Louis told me of the offer you had received from Mr. Asquith to have any place you wanted in the English war effort. You seem to have turned him down without considering the many advantages—most important, your health. I understand and admire your patriotism—however, given your health, your responsibilities in life, and the profound affection we have for you, I think you should reconsider."

Pierre wasn't the only one concerned for Jacques' well-being. In the weeks leading up to war, Nelly had noticed that her husband had been losing weight, coughing too much, and generally looking exhausted. Jacques had played it down. He didn't want his wife worrying, especially in her condition. In August 1914, just days before he had joined his regiment in Luçon, Nelly had shared with him her suspicions that she might be pregnant again. It was bittersweet news, as the joys of another child on the way mingled with fears for the future. So Jacques put on a brave face despite his chest pain, dug out his army uniform, and kissed Nelly, Dorothy, and little Jacqueline goodbye, with promises to write and reassurances that he would see them all again soon.

He never did make it to the front line that month. As soon as he arrived in the western town of Luçon, he started coughing up blood. At the makeshift army hospital, the doctor suspected tuberculosis. The disease was highly contagious and often fatal; Jacques might have to be quarantined. He'd probably had it for some time in a latent form, perhaps even since his trip to India. He should never have been given a clean bill of health for fighting, but screening for soldiers in the First World War relied on a fallible chest examination for the detection of TB, rather than the much more definitive X-ray that was later used. The disease went undetected in thousands of men who would go on to spread it unknowingly among their regiments.

Jacques had been willing to give his life for the war effort, but he hadn't envisaged dying in an army hospital quarantine ward without the opportunity to play his part. He wrote to a private doctor in Geneva, Dr. Andrae, describing his symptoms and asking for advice on how to recover as fast as possible. The doctor's response was that Jacques should travel immediately to the mountains of Switzerland, where the hospital staff were trained in lung conditions and the elevated altitude would help his breathing.

By September 1914, just one month after leaving Paris at the call to arms, Jacques was in a hospital in Arosa, Switzerland. It was only at this point that he wrote to his wife to explain the news. From her daily letters, he knew she was struggling: "I must try to shake off the black," she'd written just three weeks after he'd left. "Oh Jacques my dear how I count the days. . . . Not a month ago I still had you. . . . Oh, don't you think of what could have been?"

Not wanting to add to her burden, he tried to stay upbeat in his responses, admitting he was in Arosa for his lungs but downplaying the severity of his condition. To his brothers, Jacques was more open, admitting he was feeling "blue." "*Pauvre vieux Jacques!*" Louis responded, "the pain you have endured for your patriotism!" But Jacques did not want sympathy. He wanted to discharge himself and go back to the Front. Pierre wrote to him with a mixture of tenderness and exasperation. He could not understand how his younger brother would risk his life when he had the family business waiting for him: "You are wrong when you say you are not indispensable in our house. You are the youngest and don't have the right to give up the work for which you are destined. Now you must focus on recovering. We have many wonderful days to live together. Even after our working lives are over, we have days in the Mediterranean to enjoy, as well as games of golf! Jacques, I count on you, and need you, with all the affection of a brother to another."

As 1915 dawned, Jacques started his fifth month of medical treatment in Switzerland. No one but close family knew he was there. There was a stigma associated with tuberculosis, and the brothers did not want to have to deal with reports in the press about how young Monsieur Cartier was fighting for his life. Meanwhile, Nelly, more than a thousand kilometers away in the relative safety of the vacation home her father had built in the seaside town of Houlgate, was entering her third trimester of pregnancy. Both had been told by their respective doctors to rest, and Nelly didn't see why they shouldn't do it together. She proposed that she join Jacques in Arosa and have the baby there. It was safer than France, she reasoned, and she couldn't bear to be apart from her "Monsieur sweetheart chéri" a moment longer. Jacques agreed. His brothers, who feared that a visit from Nelly would impede his recovery, did not.

Louis, in his characteristic controlling and intelligent manner, wrote to both Nelly and Jacques using different tactics to try to dissuade each of them from following through with their Arosa plan. To Jacques, he focused on the risks to Nelly's safety: "I am pleased that you are getting better," he scribbled from Bordeaux, "but don't ask Nelly to come to Switzerland. . . . It would be far better for her to stay in Houlgate where she can escape if necessary. . . . I'm the first to know that it is hard to be separated from your family but don't tempt fate, Nelly is safe where she is, it would be dangerous to take the train."

To Nelly, Louis appealed to her rational side, suggesting that if she truly loved her husband, she would leave him to recover: "I have been in constant contact with Jacques . . . he is better but still far from being healed. Don't forget that although he is honorable, his situation is unusual, and so we can criticize him—don't play with God. I know you, Nelly, you're intelligent and very balanced, and will understand the seriousness with which Jacques should treat the situation."

In the end, Nelly was summoned for a heated family council with Alfred and Louis in Paris to discuss the situation. She stood her ground and was eventually given their blessing to travel to Jacques, on one condition. The family feared that gossipmongers, hearing of Jacques' spending time in Switzerland with his wife, might assume he was shirking the war effort. He must therefore obtain an official consulate letter stating the obvious: "that you are not in a fit state to rejoin the army and that you were not in a state to travel at the time of the mobilization." The condition fulfilled, Louis helped Nelly arrange her travel through war-torn France into Switzerland. Jacques booked her a room in Arosa's Hotel Alexandra, and it was here, at the beginning of March 1915, just weeks after arriving, that she gave birth to their second child, Alice. "Still waiting for a grandson, for 15 years!" Alfred telegraphed in disappointment.

INTO BATTLE

Jacques didn't have long to enjoy his new daughter. Finally well enough to discharge himself from the clinic, he cabled his colonel to let him know he would soon be joining the regiment in Alsace.

It was decided that Nelly and the children should head to the seaside village of Saint-Jean-de-Luz in southwest France, where Jacques hoped the quality of life during wartime would be better than in the big cities. As the couple left each other again, Elma wrote to Nelly in sympathy. Pierre had told her that Jacques' sense of duty was too strong for his own good: "for that [sense of duty], I love him even more, but I feel for you, Nelly, all alone, and I wish I could be there to give you a hug of sympathy."

As it turned out, Jacques' time at the Front would be short-lived. Just days after taking his place in the trenches at Verdun in March 1915, his regiment was subjected to a terrible attack: mustard gas followed by a burst of enemy shells. Jacques was one of the survivors, but his already weak lungs struggled to cope with the gassing, and there was no way he could keep fighting. He was sent to the army hospital in Luçon, where the doctor feared a resurgence of the tuberculosis and ordered him to rest. It would be a full three months before he was deemed fit enough to rejoin his regiment.

Confined to a hospital bed for the second time this war, Jacques poured what little energy he had into work. He wrote to those left in charge on New Bond Street and Fifth Avenue, asking for updates. "Business is very bad," came the reply from a salesman across the Atlantic. "Everyone in New York is complaining. People are only coming in for repairs really." Many of the letters he received were from Pierre, who repeatedly stressed how much he needed his younger brother's help after the war: "I don't have any secrets from you—you know the workings of the Paris house, and the American house has to be an extension of that. The development of Cartier in America will be your work and you know the huge importance of conquering this country—it will be a matter of life or death for us."

From London, Arthur Fraser filled him in on business in Mayfair: "Things were upset after declaration of war but now all running smoothly." At the call to arms, Cartier New Bond Street had lost many men, to both the French and English armies, and jewelry sales would have been at a complete standstill "were it not for Americans stranded in London waiting shipment home." Since then many of the Americans had left and business was not good. Clients were hardly buying, and many of those who had bought before the war on installments had yet to pay in full. Nancy Astor, for instance, known for her "Ali Baba hoard" of jewels, had asked Cartier to reset the historic 55.23-carat Sancy diamond into a tiara just a year before the outbreak of war. It had been a large and prestigious commission (sixty-five years later, the Sancy diamond was sold to the Louvre for $1 million), but it was far from being the only one. "When she was dressed up to the nines for some function," her lady's maid would recall, "she turned to me and said: 'What do I look like, Rose?' Quick as a flash it came to me: 'Cartier's, my lady.' "And yet unfortunately, as Fraser explained to Jacques, the bank had been unwilling to cash Mrs. Astor's most recent large check in such economic uncertainty. Jacques wrote back proposing that the check be sent to America in the hope that it would be cleared over there.

Sometimes Jacques wrote to clients directly. Margot Asquith, the wife of the prime minister, was one of the many who wrote back: "Thank you for your kind wire. Unfortunately, one of my sons is unwell and I live in constant fear of the other one being killed in Flanders. You ought to think of some beautiful simple sort of order or medal in remembrance of this horrible war that men and women alike could wear on their watch chains." She ended that letter with a postscript: "I am grateful to you for fixing my account. I am very hard up and it has helped."

Before H. H. Asquith had become prime minister in 1908, his family had lived in an enormous house on Cavendish Square, complete with fourteen servants. Over the next couple of decades, no thanks to Margot and her spending, their financial situation had deteriorated so much that by the late 1920s she was forced to pawn her pearls. It would later improve, but she never forgot the kindness Jacques had shown to her when times were hard, and over the years they would become close friends.

By June 1915, Jacques had recovered enough to venture out of his hospital ward and explore the town: "You thrilled Elma with your long letter about your life in Luçon, we love hearing about it," Pierre wrote to him. The following month, he received the clean bill of health that he had been waiting for and returned to his regiment. The Dragons, still in Alsace on the Western Front, were responsible for the dangerous job of occupying the trenches of Burnhaupt and resisting the enemy advance on the nearby town of Belfort.

Through the hot summer, Jacques took his place on the front line, fighting alongside his fellow soldiers, and by the autumn, his regiment had moved to the Champagne region to play their part in the woodland battle of Trou Bricot. Though they showed commendable courage, and Jacques would go on to win the Croix de Guerre for conspicuous bravery in action, their hoped-for breakthrough never materialized and they were forced to abandon it.

Over the following year, Jacques completed machine gun training on the Atlantic coast and fought in Luçon, Lorraine, and Verdun. But his mind was also on the business. Passing through Rheims and seeing the large cathedral that now lay in ruins after explosives and fire had destroyed it in 1914, he wrote to his elder brother: "My dear Louis, I think you should send someone to Rheims to buy all the debris that he can find of the stained-glass windows from the cathedral. Other than small pieces which could contain a recognizable subject such as the head of an angel or a saint—the small pieces have lovely colors and would make attractive jewelry which the Americans would snap up after the war. The Archbishop or the priest might sell them directly. The pieces of glass could be set into jewelry—as it is such a special case, I don't think we will have to worry about it being gener-

Jacques and his two young daughters in Saumur, 1918. Nelly is looking on in the background.

alized. What do you think?" This idea of reusing beautiful, often symbolic, objects (often entirely unrelated to jewels) would remain a feature of Cartier's creations under the brothers. Stained-glass fragments meanwhile would find their way into jewelry made in the 1920s.

In the summer of 1916, Jacques was promoted to the rank of lieutenant, in charge of a troop of twenty men on horseback and several vehicles. After four months' leave in 1917, during which he celebrated his thirty-second birthday with his family in Saint-Jean-de-Luz, it was back to the Western Front for a further year. And then, in May 1918, much to the relief of his family, Jacques finally left the danger at the Front after being offered a prestigious army teaching position in Saumur. The town's famous riding school had been converted by the U.S. government into the Saumur Field Artillery School of Instruction, and Jacques, fluent in English, experienced in battle, and skilled on horseback, was chosen to be an army riding instructor for the American soldiers. It was a relatively safe and comfortable place to be stationed, and Nelly and the children would join him there.

Reunited in a house that Nelly rented on Saumur's Quai de Limoges, the family were grateful to be together again as the tremors of war still echoed around them. And for Jacques, teaching the American army was unexpectedly rewarding. "We were saying," Pierre and Elma wrote to him, "that even if you had followed your first vocation, the priesthood, it would not have presented so much to interest you or advantage you as you have found in the 'civilian' life." In his free time, Jacques would play tirelessly with his girls as they pretended they were his captains in the army. Sticks collected from the garden were their make-believe weapons. And sometimes he would simply sit with Nelly in the shade of a small army tent in quiet companionship. She would knit, he would study his army papers or read a book. The war was not over, but the worst of it was behind them, and after the traumas of the past few years, their time in Saumur was a period of quiet rejuvenation for them both.

A NEW CHAPTER

On a sweltering July day in 1919, the recently demobilized Jacques waited anxiously in the garden of the family's Saint-Jean-de-Luz home. Upstairs, his wife was in labor. Very soon, he would know whether they had delivered the only male heir to the Cartier business, or another daughter. Either way, he was happy. One month earlier, the Treaty of Versailles had been signed, marking the formal end of the war. To have come out the other side was a blessing, and he believed he owed it to his fellow countrymen who had not been so lucky to live each day to the fullest.

In Conversation with Jean-Jacques Cartier

My father was painting a picture in the Camposena garden when I was born. The nurse rushed down from my mother's room to tell him I had arrived, but he asked if he could have a few more minutes at his easel before coming up. The light, you see, it was about to change, and he wanted to capture it. After all, I was the third baby, he knew what to expect by then. . . . I'm not sure how impressed my mother was, mind you! But I totally understand that need to capture the light. I think I would have done quite the same thing.

Jacques and Nelly named their son Jean-Jacques. Telegrams came pouring in. Louis was thrilled: "At last a boy!" Pierre wrote from Paris. "Elma, Father, and I are delighted at your news—love to Nelly, must write news in social column." Even rival firms like the Van

Cleefs would write to congratulate Jacques and Nelly on the new heir to continue the Cartier dynasty.

Two weeks earlier, Jacques, with the approval of his brothers, had instructed Mr. Fraser, now the managing director in London, to file for the incorporation of a separate UK Cartier company. Up until then, the Cartier showroom in Mayfair had been, officially speaking, a part of the larger Paris-based firm, but in the summer of 1919, Cartier Ltd. was created "to take over the business of jewelers, gold and silversmiths, and watchmakers now carried on by Louis Joseph Cartier and Pierre Camille Cartier at 175/6 New Bond Street."

Jacques' experiences over the past few years had changed him, both personally and in the eyes of his family. Through India, the Persian Gulf, Paris, London, and New York, he had quietly shown he could stand on his own two feet, picking up loyal clients, sourcing the highest-quality gemstones, and managing a team of employees along the way. His journeys abroad had also given him the confidence to become more creative. Even Louis, famously demanding, had to concede that his little brother's colorful Indian-inspired ideas showed great promise. And then there was the war. Though Louis and Pierre had campaigned for Jacques to avoid the front line, they were more than happy to proudly inform clients that their younger brother had been awarded the prestigious Croix de Guerre for his bravery. Reputation was everything, and Jacques' was flawless.

And yet despite his successes, and even after lobbying for the formation of Cartier Ltd., it would be some time before Jacques would receive anywhere near the same economic share in the family firm as his brothers. In 1919, the London business, though it had become officially separate from the Paris business, was still controlled and owned, for the most part, by Louis and Pierre, with Jacques just one of the five directors. This situation would ultimately prove an unsustainable one against the background of Jacques' growing abilities and his wife's sense of injustice that her husband was underappreciated, but for now, Jacques was content. He was grateful to be home safe from the war, reunited with the love of his life and their growing brood. Besides, he had other things to occupy his thoughts: Pierre wanted him to come back to America. It was time for the next challenge.

PART III

NEVER COPY, ONLY CREATE

(1920–1939)

Had not our age witnessed an unprecedented succession of world-shaking events, such gems could not have been bought at any price.

—JACQUES CARTIER, REFERRING TO A 1931 DIAMOND NECKLACE COMMISSIONED BY THE MAHARAJA OF NAWANAGAR

5

STONES PARIS: EARLY 1920s

A FAMILY REUNION

In the summer of 1922, the Cartier family met for a reunion in the small French fishing village of Saint-Jean-de-Luz. Three generations, traveling from far and wide, came together in Jacques and Nelly's Camposena vacation home. Situated at the top of the village, it offered spectacular views out to sea and a much-needed breeze in the hotter months. It was also, handily for the young children, just a fifteen-minute walk down to the beach with Nanny. Past the boulangerie with the smells of fresh baguette, past the locals taking their morning café and croissant on little tables in the shade of the village square, and past the *pelote basque* courts with the continuous smack of the ball ricocheting off the burnt-orange wall. The walk back up the steep hill, sandy and salty in the blazing midday sun, was more painful, but it was worth it for the delicious lunches waiting on the large terrace. White tablecloths, freshly caught fish, home-grown runner beans, fat red tomatoes, and bowls of sweet strawberries for dessert. And Grandfather Alfred always had a sugared almond in his pocket if you were well behaved.

For the adults, vacations in the southwest were just as heavenly.

Over the course of their lives, three of the four Cartier siblings, Louis, Jacques, and Suzanne, would have houses in the Basque region. But this trip wasn't just about relaxing. In the days before air travel, the problem with running an international business was that it was almost impossible for Louis, Pierre, Jacques, and Alfred to be in one place at one time. They needed to discuss their business strategy and to plan for the future.

After their siestas, as the wives took tea under parasols in the garden, the men stood for a photograph. They were happy to be together, easy in one another's company, and grateful to have emerged from the dark years behind them. Since joining their father in the family firm, the brothers had witnessed vast changes in the world. Four years of fighting had disrupted the balance of society, and Cartier's key clients along with it. France, so recently considered almost the center of the world, may have emerged victorious against Germany but it was now weighed down by national debt, inflation, and high unemployment. Russia, previously home to Cartier's top clients, was now Communist. Other reigning families, along with the Romanovs, to lose their thrones included the Habsburgs in Austria-Hungary and the Hohenzollerns in Germany. The Ottoman Empire had been broken up, ending the historic power of the sultans. And of those European kings and queens who still remained, many had become, as King Alfonso XIII of Spain so aptly put it, "the *nouveaux pauvres*." In their place, the American nouveaux riches across the Atlantic were turning out to be more influential by the day.

Alfred and his sons had long known how important it was for Cartier to be a geographically diverse firm, and their decision to open an American branch well before their Parisian competitors had proved prescient. After the war, when it became obvious that a European luxury firm should follow the money across the Atlantic, there were others who tried to set up shop in New York, but by then Cartier already had an impressive head start. And, of course, Cartier's connections with America, and the American elite, had by this time been further strengthened by two very beneficial—and happy—marriages.

As Elma and Nelly chatted together over tea and madeleines, they looked at their men in the limelight. A photograph of Louis, Pierre, Jacques, and Alfred taken that day would make it into countless books about Cartier for decades to come. Yet the women who had been quietly supporting the Cartier men for years would remain in the shadows. Alice, Alfred's late wife, had provided the funds for the firm's nineteenth-century expansion. Andrée-Caroline had enabled Louis to leapfrog on Worth's gigantic success to join the big leagues in Paris and London. And now Nelly and Elma were quietly playing their part. If they truly wanted to succeed, Alfred had always believed, the Cartiers must be pragmatic. Marrying well had almost been part of the business plan.

When the photographs of the men were finished, Alfred asked the photographer to stay for one last picture with his only grandson. A maid was dispatched into the kitchen garden to retrieve the three-year-old Jean-Jacques from the game of *cache-cache* he was playing with his sisters. He was brought to his grandfather, who smiled at this young heir with his head full of blond curls. Jacques came into the shot to turn his son gently in the direction of the camera. But there was too much going on, and Jean-Jacques was distracted by his mother and aunt. Alfred pointed at the camera, indicating where his grandson should look. Under a large black piece of cloth, the overheated photographer captured the moment. Three generations immortalized.

There was a sense, on that hot day in 1922, of the family coming together to look forward. A sense that the time had come for the elder generation to make space for the younger ones in the picture. The men had recently updated the company structure to be more long-lasting, to survive beyond them. When the London and New York branches had initially been set up, they had been conceived as small outposts and so had fallen under the original Cartier Frères business based in France. Since then, they had been formally registered as separate British and American companies (Cartier Ltd. and Cartier Inc. respectively), and in 1921 the remaining Cartier Frères company had been replaced with Cartier S.A. (effectively Cartier Paris). Previously Cartier Frères had been set up as a legal partnership, not intended to survive its founding partners and with a short fifteen-year expiry. Its replacement, a limited company with a ninety-nine-year term, reflected the family's confidence and their optimism for the future.

In Conversation with Jean-Jacques Cartier

The agreement the family made after the First World War to officially split the branches into separate companies but for each brother to retain a financial share in the others' branches was critical to their success. It meant, you see, that each brother could be kingpin in his own kingdom but that they were also united. Not simply because they loved one another but also because there was a financial reward for them if the other brothers' companies did well.

The fact that each brother had a financial share in the others' branches was a powerful motivator. It was worth each one helping the others sell an important jewel or clock because they all benefited from the commission. They also shared the name and reputation equally, so a glowing press report of, say, a Cartier exhibition in New York, or a Cartier charity event in London, would reflect positively on the Paris firm as well. As Alfred had always told them, their strength was in their bond. In order to fulfill their dream and become the leading jewelry firm in the world, they had to work together.

When the brothers were apart, as they often were, they stayed in touch by letters and telegrams. The telegrams were dotted with codes, from the names of the brothers (Louis was LOUTIER, Pierre was CAPICAR, and Jacques was JACTIER) to the names of the branches: Paris was STONES, New York was MOICARTIER, and London was PRECIOUS. Throughout the 1920s and '30s, telegrams were far cheaper than placing long-distance phone calls and much faster than the postal service, but they lacked the privacy of a sealed letter. The brothers needed to share information about clients, jewels, and prices among themselves (and a few senior employees who were deemed trustworthy enough to know the codes) without the risk of anyone else's knowing what they were talking about. If, for example, a competitor caught on to the fact that Cartier was planning a new season of jewels in sapphires, then they might also start to buy sapphires, pushing up the price for the precious blue stone at a time when Cartier still needed to buy more to finish its collection. Codes were also a way of protecting clients' privacy. Cartier might well be privy to very personal information, such as when an important gentleman was considering a proposal of marriage, or had taken a new lover, or was forced to sell heirlooms because of financial difficulties. For a business that prided itself on discretion, it was crucial that this remained absolutely hidden from the outside world.

Cartier was growing faster than Alfred had imagined possible, but he continued to insist that there should be no additional branches unless they were run by a family member. They simply couldn't trust an outsider to the same extent, he explained. Though he and his sons had revised the legal structure so the firm might survive beyond the third generation, there was no doubt in any of their minds that it should remain in the family after their deaths. So far, only Jacques had given Alfred a grandson, but there were other ways to keep the business in the family. Anne-Marie had recently married, and Louis had high hopes for his new son-in-law.

RENÉ REVILLON

Anne-Marie first met René Revillon at a dinner hosted by her uncle Pierre and aunt Elma in their Neuilly-sur-Seine house, on the outskirts of Paris. It was the summer of 1920 and she was nineteen years old, excited by the promise of a long future stretched out in front of her. Seated next to the good-looking and self-assured René, she talked animatedly, radiating an almost childlike enthusiasm for life. René, twelve years her senior, was smitten. "Her exquisite vivaciousness of spirit, her simplicity, and delicious sentiments are just as you had described to me," he wrote elatedly to Pierre after the dinner.

In fact, the dinner party had been something of a setup. For several years, René had been working in New York for the American branch of his family firm, Revillon Frères. Just as Worth was known worldwide for its dresses, so Revillon was revered for its furs, at a time when the fur trade meant big, global business. Founded in 1723, it was one of the few family firms that the Cartiers truly admired. The young René, a Revillon Frères vice president, was someone for whom Pierre felt it was definitely worth making time. Inviting him around for meals, the Cartiers welcomed René into their family, and it wasn't long before Pierre had become something of a mentor to the younger man. Both in the luxury business and with shared clients, they would update each other on relevant developments in their sector. Elma meanwhile assumed the role of a welcoming aunt, and Marion became like a little sister whose "sweet nature and delightful pretty ways have won me for ever." The New York Cartiers were, in effect, surrogate guardians for him away from home. "Thank you for indulging me," he wrote in one letter to Elma in July 1920; "you have been more than a confidante."

The Cartiers and Revillons may have operated in the same circles, but there was no doubt who had the upper hand: Revillon far outstripped Cartier. The firm had been around longer, was better known, and had a larger international scope. This was partly the result of genetics. While the Cartiers had to wait until the third generation to have three brothers, Revillon's founder, Louis Victor Revillon, had a brother and four sons who were able to set about spreading their family name far and wide from the mid-nineteenth century.

By 1871, Revillon had expanded beyond Paris to have a boutique on Regent Street, London, and by 1880 they had one in New York. In 1889, when Louis-François and Alfred considered Cartier too small to exhibit at the Exposition Universelle in Paris, Revillon was awarded the Exposition's illustrious grand prize. By 1900, Revillon Frères was the largest fur trading company in the world, with capital of 30 million francs ($150 million today), offices as far afield as Montreal and Moscow, and three thousand employees in its Parisian factories.

But that wasn't all. The Revillons also had an envy-inducing aristocratic edge: René Revillon was descended from Comte Revillon d'Apreval, who had been a minister for Louis XV before the Revolution. It was no wonder that the Cartiers looked to the Revillons as they had to the Worths, as promising marriage material. And with his own daughter still far too young for marriage, Pierre thought instead of making a match for Anne-Marie. This wasn't a big leap. He and Jacques had been very close to their niece since she was a child, when they had felt that Louis hadn't always taken his role as father as seriously as he might have. During the war, for example, it was Elma who had proposed looking after Anne-Marie and taking her to safety in the Auvergne when Louis was too busy "living with another woman" in Bordeaux. Likewise, Jacques and Nelly, seeing how much Anne-Marie enjoyed being part of a large family and worrying that she might be lonely, would regularly invite her to stay.

Pierre's matchmaking dinner worked out, with Anne-Marie falling for René just as much as he did for her. René had to return to his job in New York at the end of the summer, but by early 1921, he was back in Paris to ask Louis for his daughter's hand in marriage. Louis accepted happily. His daughter seemed besotted, and the pragmatist in him couldn't help but be gratified to suddenly have a son-in-law with the best possible credentials in international luxury. The wedding date was set and invitations proudly dispatched. At midday on the thirteenth of April, Anne-Marie Cartier and René Revillon said their vows in the Roman Catholic church of Saint-Pierre-de-Chaillot in the 16th arrondissement. It was, the papers declared, the event of the Parisian social season. With a congregation that encompassed key figures from the world of luxury, it was not unlike Louis' wedding to Anne-Marie's mother twenty-three years earlier. But it was a far happier affair. The union might have been orchestrated by an offstage uncle, but the couple who walked down the aisle together this time loved each other.

After the wedding, Louis suggested that his new son-in-law might like to join him in the Cartier family business. René was tempted. Though he felt a loyalty to his own family firm, he feared his career progression was limited there: He was relatively senior, but his cousins, being more directly related to the firm's founder, were more likely to take the top spots going forward. There was also the issue of squeezed margins hurting salaries; Revillon had invested heavily in Russia before the war and was now feeling the effects. As he set off on his hon-

Anne-Marie Cartier and René Revillon setting off on their honeymoon, April 1921.

eymoon, bound for America on the SS *France,* René promised Louis he would think about his proposal.

WHAT PARIS DOESN'T TAKE AWAY

For Louis, with his creative spirit, Paris in the 1920s couldn't have been a more invigorating environment. In contrast to before the war,

Royal visitors to 13 Rue de la Paix often drew crowds. Around 1922, King Alfonso XIII of Spain was captured leaving the store (above), while a visit by the Prince of Wales (the future Duke of Windsor) made its way into a Georges Goursat "Sem" illustration (right) in 1927 entitled *Le Prince Charmant.*

when the French capital had attracted grand duchesses, heiresses, and European royals, now it became an even stronger magnet for fun-seeking expats and artists. American soldiers lingered on and wrote back to their friends that this city was the place to be, especially as the low value of the franc against the dollar made housing and food affordable for foreigners. Artists and intellectuals migrated to the City of Light, finding a freedom of existence and an exhilaration of thought unlike anywhere else in the world. "It's not so much what France gives you," said American novelist Gertrude Stein, then living on Rue de Fleurus. "It's what it doesn't take away."

The Montparnasse area of Paris especially drew in writers, artists, and musicians during what became known as *les années folles* (the crazy years). Communes like La Ruche made up for no running water, rat infestations, and damp, freezing studios with the promise of low rent and the chance to mingle with fellow imaginative minds. There was an energy in the air, a sense among those collaboratively working to push the boundaries of creativity that they were in the right place at the right time. Hemingway would meet Fitzgerald late at night in Le Dingo bar on Rue Delambre. Around the corner in Le Dôme café, where a pretty good Toulouse sausage and mashed potatoes could be found for a dollar, regulars included W. B. Yeats and Ezra Pound. The fact that so many of the city's most freethinking minds had no money was almost a badge of honor; poverty was, as Cocteau remarked, "a luxury in Montparnasse." In the Café de la Rotonde, frequented by Picasso and Modigliani, the owner, Victor Libion, would look the other way when starving artists broke the ends off a baguette in the bread basket. He'd also accept paintings as collateral for hot meals (returning them once the artist had come up with the money), so the café became something of an ever-changing art gallery.

For Parisians like Louis, the presence of all these great minds on their home turf constituted proof of their city's destiny to resume the world's cultural leadership, the *mission civilisatrice* that Victor Hugo had hailed some fifty years earlier. They were in this together, rebelling against convention and feeding off one another's brave new ideas. As modern paintings veered away from impressionism and toward cubism, so Cartier's creations migrated away from the romantic flowing garland style toward more geometric Art Deco shapes. They were helped by changes in gemstones: The new rectangular "baguette" cut of diamonds popularized in the 1920s opened up a whole new spectrum of possibilities when it came to the design of more linear jewels.

Fashion, too, was changing at a phenomenal rate. And, as the "slave of the dressmakers," jewelers had to keep up. After all, Louis would ask rhetorically, "Do we not design for the dressed rather than the undressed woman?" Prior to 1914, many of Cartier's clients had lived to entertain, be entertained, and look attractive. During the war, when women had tended to injured soldiers in makeshift hospitals, been secretaries for generals, or worked in factories, they had found a purpose outside their own little circle. Elma and Nelly were just two of thousands who had shed their expensive dresses and professionally styled hair for a more basic look and more practical clothes as they helped out. For many, it had been a revelation, as a new world of possibilities opened up beyond their previous existence.

As attitudes and expectations shifted, designers from Coco Chanel to Jeanne Lanvin created new fashions to better reflect the modern woman. Dresses got shorter, waistlines disappeared, and hair was bobbed. Taking inspiration from masculine outfits like sailor suits, Chanel created boyish clothes for women, and the flapper dress was born. Gone were many of the Edwardian restrictions of the court and, accordingly, jewelers could be more daring in their creations. In the place of heavy, tall tiaras that sat on top of large hair up-dos (adding height and importance to the wearer) came more discreet bandeaux that were worn on the forehead and worked well with shorter hair. The *devants de corsage* that had been pinned onto thick corsets no longer worked on the new lighter-fabric dresses, while the large statement necklaces and chokers that fell above the décolleté made way for sautoirs (long necklaces) that emphasized the more elongated silhouette.

Alongside Louis, Charles Jacqueau rose to the challenge at Cartier, churning out design after fabulous design. Louis would sketch his ideas for jewels in little notebooks he carried around with him. He might come up with several vague ideas for hair clips, cigarette boxes, or necklaces, based perhaps on an ancient Chinese plate, a stone carving, or a painting at the Louvre. He would pass on his half-finished ideas to Jacqueau, who would draw them life-sized in beautiful intricate detail. Every Wednesday, at the 13 Rue de la Paix design meeting, Louis would choose which designs should be made into a finished piece and which should be set aside. Those that made it beyond the drawing room floor were marked with *"A Ex"* for *"À Exécuter"* (to action) and the initials of the senior employee who was approving the design. There were multiple designers, but Jacqueau was Louis' favorite. And with good reason.

In Conversation with Jean-Jacques Cartier

Every piece was unique. So the designer, you see, was very busy. It wasn't as if he did a design and then we made a hundred items based on that design. No, generally for each design there was just one item made, whether it be a brooch or a ring or a cigarette case.

Jacqueau shared his boss's aesthetic sense. His creations were works of art in their own right, demonstrating his intrinsic understanding of symmetry, proportion, and color. Like Louis, he wasn't afraid to break with convention and move away from what was in vogue at the time. He knew how to maintain a sense of timelessness, and his creations—from an emerald necklace to a diamond hair clip—would withstand the test of passing fashion. He and Louis were a powerful team, sparking ideas off each other, both of them unwilling to settle for anything less than the best. They understood each other implicitly, and though their relationship was clearly defined as boss and employee, the respect went both ways. Louis could be a tyrannical Head of House, prone to angry outbursts for little reason, but there was rarely an angry word between him and Jacqueau. He simply admired him too much.

THE BEGINNING OF A RENAISSANCE

Louis put on several exhibitions to unveil Cartier's avant-garde take on accessories. For one, just after the war, he consulted the illustrator Georges Barbier over the invitation design. He wanted it to reflect the modern woman, young and fresh and carefree, a world apart from the unrelatable old-fashioned regal figures dripping in diamonds at court. The art dealer René Gimpel later recalled how enchanted he had been to receive it: "I'll certainly be going to Cartier's. . . . It has been left to Barbier to attract me in by sending me one of his charming reproductions, a chic Parisian girl in a short blue skirt patterned with large pink flowers. . . . Coming from Cartier's, she demurely shows off their delightful wares: on her arms, over long suede gloves, she has slipped two red and black bracelets. . . . A long necklace of green beads loops down from her neck, rounded off by a green cameo of hard rectangular stone. Long earrings, also green, frame her face. So this Parisienne will be getting me to Cartier's . . . it's the beginning of a renaissance in the art of jewelry. Cartier has fixed a day."

But it wasn't just jewelry that Louis was updating for the postwar world. Under his management, Jeanne Toussaint was creating small handbags for day and night. Louis hadn't lost his feelings for Jeanne, but he continued to try to keep their on-and-off relationship under wraps. Alfred still believed that a romantic liaison between his eldest son and a woman previously known as a demimondaine could seriously damage the good Cartier name. And Louis, knowing how much his father had sacrificed and how hard he had worked to build that reputation, didn't want to upset him. He resigned himself to the idea that the relationship with Jeanne would never lead anywhere. And that it must be kept secret.

In Conversation with Jean-Jacques Cartier

When Toussaint started out at Cartier, Louis put her in the handbag department because she was good with fabric. Within Rue de la Paix, she was known for being able to almost miraculously transform one piece of antique brocade or silk into two bags. She could cut it in the most effective way so as not to lose an inch. Louis admired her for that.

Jeanne, like Louis, mixed with an arty crowd. They may not have had the funds to buy the biggest pieces, but when Jeanne Lanvin bought a Cartier necklace and some lotus-themed spectacles, or Coco Chanel selected a sapphire and emerald ring, it was an important validation to Louis that his fellow innovators approved of his work. When René Gimpel was looking for a present for Marcel Proust to congratulate him on being awarded the Légion d'Honneur in 1920, he, too, went to Cartier, where he purchased a little diamond and ruby cross.

Proust, who had mentioned Cartier's stylish watches in his mammoth work *À la recherche du temps perdu* (started eleven years earlier in 1909), was enchanted. He wrote to his art-dealer friend with an enjoyably long-winded explanation as to why his thanks were late: "The day before yesterday . . . the firm of Cartier asked for my new address, having a delivery to make to me . . . I sent my chambermaid's sister for the object . . . Cartier declared after an hour and a half's search that there must have been a mistake, that there was nothing for me. So I sent again this morning (Friday) and at 9 this evening, when I had just got up, the delivery comes of the ravishing jewel which moves me more than I would know how to tell you. . . . Where will I hide your ravishing cross? I cannot display it. I don't go to official receptions. I shall look at it sometimes in secret, in recollection of the sentiments whose most affectionate expression I implore you to find in these lines, Marcel Proust."

If his home crowd lacked the funds for Cartier's more significant creations, Louis was unconcerned. Cartier was about both style and substance. Sleek minimalist designs were required to step ahead from the competition in Paris. Elsewhere in the world, there was a client base who could afford the large, flawless diamonds and ropes of perfectly matched historic pearls. During wartime, given the uncertainty, Louis had been forced to hold off buying precious gemstones, but he was only too happy to dive back in now. Fortunately, there was no shortage of supply; the cataclysmic financial disruption of the past few years had shaken the established order like an earthquake, bringing precious family heirlooms glittering to the surface.

COVERT TUNNELS AND DIAMONDS HIDDEN IN ROCKS

Before the war, Cartier had depended on Russian clients for its largest commissions. By the 1920s, Louis was relying on those same buyers to supply him with gems. "The art of the jeweler," he would later announce, "is a necessity as well as a luxury and the jewel is a symbol of convertible wealth as much as a platinum ring is the symbol of marriage." Since the Revolution, millions of francs' worth of jewelry had made their way to Europe from Russia. Those gems that had once been symbols of power, prestige, and love would become "convertible wealth" as their owners rebuilt their lives far from home. "Today the token of love the Russian nobleman gave his bride 20 years ago," Louis would explain, "has, perhaps, saved their lives when they fled to alien shores." Fleeing Russians hid their jewels inside opulent hairdos and sewed them into clothes. Others even swallowed them in desperation (the stomach being "the only hiding place that could not be opened"), leaving nature to take its course once they had made it to safety.

It was not, however, always possible to take one's jewels while fleeing to safety. Especially if there was a rather large amount of them. Grand Duchess Vladimir, Louis' former patron and queen of the St. Petersburg social scene, was among those forced to leave their many treasures behind. Eager that they should not fall into the Bolsheviks' hands, she later called on an old friend, Bertie Stopford, to retrieve them, giving him precise instructions on how to find them without arousing the suspicion of the palace guards. In a James Bond–style heist, Stopford would make his way through covert tunnels to her boudoir, unlock the safe, and escape with two Gladstone bags bursting with jewels.

The Dowager Empress Maria Feodorovna also succeeded in keeping her gems out of the hands of the Bolsheviks. Imprisoned in the Dulber palace with her extended family, she discovered that the guards, in a curious adhesion to Russia's dynastic law, believed that those not part of the royal bloodline were not worthy of capture. This freed up her daughter, Grand Duchess Olga (who had divorced her first husband to marry his nonroyal aide-de-camp, Colonel Kulikovski), to come and go as she pleased. Olga proposed to smuggle her mother's jewels out of the palace prison in small cocoa tins. Not having anywhere safe to deposit them, she took them down to the beach and stuffed the tins holding the same diamonds and sapphires that had once glittered their way around candlelit balls into the beach's rocky crevices. In 1919, when the Dowager Empress finally

THE
CARTIER
STYLE

"NEVER COPY, ONLY CREATE. . . .
INSPIRATION COULD AND SHOULD COME FROM
EVERYWHERE—EXCEPT FROM EXISTING JEWELRY."

—JEAN-JACQUES CARTIER

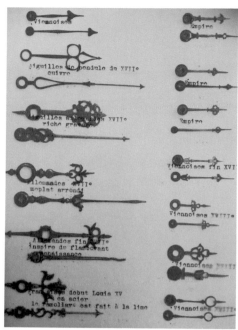

LA BELLE ÉPOQUE

1898–1919

THE JAZZ AGE

1920s

"YES, THE STYLE IN JEWELS DOES CHANGE OFTEN,
AS THE JEWELRY HAS TO ADORN THE GOWNS
THAT ARE CREATED EVERY SEASON."

—PIERRE CARTIER

caved in to the demands of her sister, the Dowager Queen Alexandra, to flee Russia, she retrieved the buried treasure and escaped initially to England. Just like Empress Eugénie fleeing the Siege of Paris half a century earlier, far away from home and a life of extravagance, those same jewels became her pension.

Through the 1920s, the Cartiers were privy to levels of trust from the Romanovs that would have been impossible to reach had they not visited their family homes prior to the Revolution. As a result, they were often the first to learn when exiled Russians were keen to sell their imperial jewelry, a fantastic advantage over their peers. But not all the Russian jewels coming onto the market were being sold by their previous owners. For all the gems smuggled out of Russia, there were many more left behind that had been seized by the Bolsheviks. A vast number of these would appear on the market in London and Paris. In one instance, the gem dealer Rosenthal was examining a string of emeralds for sale when he noticed a tuft of blond hair in the clasp. "I had no doubt," he later exclaimed, "that a brutal hand had snatched this necklace from the neck of a victim."

With such a large boost to the number of important gemstones floating around European jewelry markets, one would perhaps have expected prices to decline. In fact, the reverse was true. As the auction of Princess Lobanov de Rostovsky's hugely important jewelry collection in 1920 would illustrate, there was enormous pent-up demand for significant jewels after the war. And that single auction was an event that would set the tone for the next decade.

THE BEJEWELED PRINCESS

In 1920, Louis was named as one of three jewelry experts in the will of Princess Vera Lobanov de Rostovsky. Born into one princely family, the Dolgoroukys, and married into another, the Princess was the proud owner of a spectacular fortune by her early forties following the death of her husband. Her palace in Moscow, which she called her "little Hermitage," was surrounded by a great park and filled with historically significant furniture, artwork, and artifacts from all over the world. Soon after the assassination of her good friend Grand Duke Serge in 1905, she had left Russia to settle in Europe, splitting her time between a magnificent *hôtel particulier* in Paris and villas in Menton and Vevey, Switzerland. A lover of jewelry, she had become a frequent and welcome visitor to 13 Rue de la Paix and bought with what some might have considered abandon. To her critics, she retorted: "They are wise investments; I am not squandering anything; on the contrary, I am building a second fortune from the first one."

In April 1919, aged eighty-three, the Princess died in Switzerland, brokenhearted at the destruction in her motherland. Multiple auctions were organized for her vast collections, with the enormous jewelry sale planned for January 1920 in Lausanne, on the shores of Lake Geneva. Taking place over six days, the sale would offer one of the greatest private collections ever to come to the market in the twentieth century. Dealers, experts, and important members of society, from the Prince of Hesse to the former Queen of Greece, made their way from all over the globe to see for themselves the fabulous pieces that had graced the Russian princess and in some cases might even have been touched by a tsar. The highlights were a 118-carat diamond brooch and a three-rope necklace comprising one hundred seventy-one pink pearls (weighing about 2,000 grains, or 130 grams) that Emperor Nicholas I had bought for his favorite daughter, the Grand Duchess Marie.

Having valued the items, Louis helped decide the order in which they would be auctioned and was quick to propose that the pearl necklace (which he planned to bid on himself) should be the first lot. He hoped that if he, as an expert, was seen to bid high at the start, others would follow suit, and the 1920s jewelry market would be off to a flying start. It was, as it turned out, a good tactic. He bought the necklace for 533,100 Swiss francs ($900,000 today), and the auction, as he explained in a letter to his father, was a "great success. . . . The sale itself reached nearly double the figure that we had hoped for, the prices hit the imagination of all and sundry, and the news spread not only all over Europe but across the world."

In total, the auction made 3.47 million Swiss francs (more than $6 million today), kick-starting the huge demand for historic pieces that would continue over the following decade. "I foresee a large rise in the prices of precious stones in a short time," Louis would tell a U.S. reporter later. "Pearls, emeralds, very large rubies, sapphires and diamonds . . . will, as they have for so long a time, dominate the fashion in jewelry, [and] it is a question as to where the stones of the future will come from, as our best examples of precious stones come from old mines."

The Cartiers would play an important role in this booming market. Letters between Pierre and Jacques reveal their desperate attempts to acquire as many historic Russian jewels as possible before their competitors did. Understanding that selling one's family heirlooms was a sensitive topic, they would not be so brazen as to pitch for any pieces but would tentatively stay in touch, hoping they would be the first to be called upon when the surviving Russian exiles needed to sell. And they often were. So even as the Bolsheviks closed Russia away from the world, the country's influence on Cartier's history continued. The Romanovs, who had once, through their prolific custom, bathed Cartier in their reflected glory, now imbued the jewelry they were forced to sell with a prestigious provenance. And as the Cartiers knew well, there would be many an international client, Americans especially, who would be more than happy to pay over the odds to wear the same tiara that had once graced the head of a blue-blooded grand duchess.

653 FIFTH AVENUE

The new structure of Cartier, with each brother having a financial share in each Maison, was good for business. It meant that Louis had an incentive to keep doing what he was good at—creating—and his brothers were motivated to look for buyers in their more prosperous markets. But it didn't mean there were never any arguments. No matter how close the brothers were, there was nothing like money and power to confuse matters.

The Fifth Avenue building was jointly owned by Louis and Pierre. Six years after it had been acquired (in exchange for the pearl necklace), they were in discussions about what to do with it going forward. Pierre felt it made sense for him to own it outright, given his role as president of the New York branch. For his half share, he offered Louis half a million dollars, pointing out that it would be an excellent deal for his elder brother: "The exchange rate [into francs] will triple the capital you have put down." Wary of missing out on a future uptick in value, Louis was unconvinced. He also felt that when calculating the current value of the property, they should take into account the $900,000 in renovation costs that had been incurred to convert the residential home into a business. He was, he declared, only prepared to sell Pierre, "my old brother and associate," his half share of the building (for half a million dollars), if his brother would commit to sharing any future profits (one-third to Louis, two-thirds to Pierre) when the building was eventually sold.

Pierre's response was to backtrack, claiming that he wasn't really interested in buying the business after all, despite its being his idea in the first place. Perhaps he hadn't expected his normally less business-savvy brother to be so sharp: "I was suggesting I would buy your shares in order to do you a favor, but nothing would be more agreeable to me than to keep the status quo." He acknowledged that while the value of 653 Fifth Avenue might have increased in the short term, property values over time were very changeable, going so far as to claim outrageously that "the lifetime of a New York building is only about thirty years. It has about fifteen years left to live."

The two couldn't find a solution. Pierre didn't agree with Louis' figures, or his assertion that the renovation costs had increased the property value, believing that "this expenditure was absolutely necessary to adapt a private home to our type of business." He claimed to be driven primarily by his concern for the reputation of the American business, Cartier Inc., in which they each had a 50 percent share: "I am thinking more of Cartier Inc., in which I have only a half [share], than of my own personal interests." Louis didn't entirely believe him, nor did he agree with Pierre's claims about the renovations not affecting the building's value or with his assertion that the property would soon start to decline in value.

Both strong-minded men, both used to getting their own way, Louis and Pierre hit an impasse. They could reason all they liked, but they shared the same stubborn self-belief and fear of being taken advantage of. United, these were powerful characteristics, but set against each other, they impeded progress. Pierre suggested that they might ask their father to intervene. Alfred, seventy-two years old, was still heavily involved in the business and seen as the voice of unbiased reason and experience. For now, though, they agreed to put the matter on hold. Pierre had to travel to Canada for work and Louis was off to Budapest. He had recently met a rather enticing Hungarian countess.

THE COUNTESS

In the winter of 1921, Louis had taken a short break from work in the Normandy seaside town of Deauville. Known as the Parisian Riviera, two hundred kilometers west of the capital, Deauville was a fashionable resort for French high society. Throughout the year, well-to-do ladies and gentlemen would escape the city and flock to vacation villas or hotels to take in the Atlantic views and enjoy the scene. There would be polo matches at the Duc de Gramont's polo club, cocktails at Le Bar du Soleil, blackjack at the Grand Casino (founded by the owner of Maxim's), and dinner parties at fabulous private residences.

It was at one of these dinners that the forty-six-year-old Louis found himself sitting next to Jacqueline Almásy-Bissingen. Twenty years his junior, she was, so the press reported, quite a beauty: "Young, slender, with skin as milky white as that of a rare Oriental Pearl, eyes glittering like twin sapphires and hair like a golden halo." She was also, crucially, aristocratic. Born in the southeast of Hungary, Jacqueline was the daughter of Count George Almásy and Countess Zinaida Zichy.

Though titled, the Almásys, like many aristocratic families, had seen their wealth dwindle over the years. While Jacqueline's grandparents' generation had considered it entirely normal to send one's laundry from Budapest to Paris once a week, or to order fresh croissants from France for breakfast, by the 1920s, what were once warm, well-stocked palaces filled with staff had become drafty half-empty buildings.

Growing up, Jacqueline and her cousins had spent depressing summer holidays in the gloomy castle of their blind grandmother. Countess Jacqueline Zichy was a formidable woman who saw no reason for affection or home comforts. Her grandchildren may have been blue-blooded, but in her house there would be no tea served with a silver spoon and on her estate they would be forced to do for themselves. One of the few rules was that they were forbidden to learn the local Slovak language for fear they might associate with the village children. It didn't work; they found other ways to interact, with Jacqueline proving she was no cosseted wallflower: "We kept up a relentless feud with them, with sticks and stones as weapons, yelling at the top of our lungs whenever we detected one of them gathering dry branches or walnuts on the property."

It was an unconventional childhood, but it made for interesting adults. One cousin married the man who would become president of the first Hungarian Republic (much to Jacqueline's disgust, as a staunch monarchist), while another became a motorist, aviator, and desert explorer, and was the inspiration for the lead character in the book and film, *The English Patient.* Jacqueline grew into an incredibly self-possessed woman who held strong political views. In 1917, she had married a fellow Hungarian aristocrat, Count Charles Bissingen-Nippenburg, but just one year later, at the age of twenty-three, she had become a war widow.

Sitting next to her at that Deauville dinner, Louis was captivated. Jacqueline was young, beautiful, and titled, but the attraction was based on more than that. She couldn't have been more different from his first wife. Where Andrée-Caroline had been disinterested and absent, Jacqueline was articulate and sure of her own mind. Louis decided to extend his stay in Deauville. Every morning, the press reported, the jeweler would send the Countess flowers. Every evening, he would take her to a smart dinner in an exclusive nightclub. He courted her unreservedly. Although a part of him would remain in love with Jeanne Toussaint, he had decided long ago that he could never marry her. For all the outside world knew, the Countess included, he had divorced his first wife thirteen years ago and not yet fallen in love again. And as a good-looking, charming millionaire who was famous for creating some of the most spectacular jewels in the world, he was a particularly eligible bachelor for a noble-born lady likely living beyond her means.

In Deauville together, Louis and Jacqueline would drink champagne, eat oysters, and dance. She would smile sweetly, no doubt laugh at his jokes, but that's as far as it went. The Countess wouldn't be his lover. Mature for her twenty-seven years, she knew her worth. "I believe in marriage," the papers dramatically reported she had cried to him as her train pulled out of Deauville station, Hungary-bound, "and only in marriage." It didn't take long for Louis to follow her. Staying with a mutual friend, Prince Ludwig von Windischgraetz, in Budapest, he continued to court her there. By the spring of 1922, the Hungarian papers were announcing news of their betrothal.

Louis' family was delighted to hear of the impending nuptials, especially his father, who for years had feared his eldest son might disgrace the family name by marrying Jeanne, with her checkered past. Now that Cartier's standing was assured, there was no longer a need to marry into money, but the addition of an aristocratic title in the family was something that filled Alfred with pride. Others, however, were less complimentary about the engagement, and the cutting remark *"c'est lui qui a les bijoux et elle les quartiers"* (he has the jewels, she has the coat of arms) rippled through the upper classes. Despite the widespread changes in society after the First World War, an innate snobbery persisted in blue-blooded aristocratic circles. Louis, though he had no intention of going back on his proposal, was riled by the negativity and determined to prove his accusers wrong. He employed a genealogist to verify his own noble origins (research that, to his embarrassment, was later proved to be erroneous). He even, remarkably, changed his name by deed poll to reflect his apparent newfound bloodline. In August 1923, Louis Cartier officially became "Louis Cartier de la Boutière, Baron de Saint-René."

The wedding took place in Hungary in January 1924. Jacqueline's mother was gravely ill, so the Almásys had decided that it should be a small and discreet affair and Louis, who had already endured the spectacle of being the groom at one large public wedding, was more than happy to oblige. It wouldn't be until several months later that the French papers caught on to the news, belatedly announcing in the summer that Countess Almásy had married "M. L-J Cartier, a knight of the Légion d'Honneur" earlier that year. Interestingly, the article did not use his new "Baron de Saint-René" title. It boosted his standing more authentically by highlighting the prestigious Légion d'Honneur award he'd received in 1923 for his contributions to the jewelry industry. The marriage, the article reported, had been kept in the strictest privacy due to a recent family bereavement (Jacqueline's mother had died that May).

By all accounts, those early years of married life were happy ones. In a hard-to-beat romantic gesture, Louis bought a palace in Buda-

Louis Cartier in the 1920s (right), and his second wife,
the Hungarian countess Jacqueline Almásy (left)

pest, located at Tarnok Utca 5, for his bride, which he would restore
and fill with valuable furniture and wonderful artworks. He even
commissioned a well-known artist, Halim, to paint Jacqui (as he now
called her), proudly telling Pierre how pleased he was with the resulting portrait. The couple would live, Louis promised, at least a few
months of every year in her native Budapest. But for now, Paris remained the center of his working life, and Jacqui was quite happy to
enjoy the French capital's magic. "The Cartiers' life in Paris was a
most glamorous one," the press recalled. "Dinners, balls, receptions—
and in the constant merriment, the beautiful Countess was bearing
herself with all the majesty of the East European aristocrat." But it
wasn't all champagne and dancing. The year 1924 was one of the
busiest of Louis' working life. He had an exhibition to prepare for
and a million ideas to turn into reality.

BLUSHER AND CIGARETTES

In February 1924, a month after his wedding, Louis opted to stand
down from the board of directors of Cartier S.A. He would continue

to be the innovative force behind the firm, and he remained the majority shareholder alongside Pierre, but he didn't enjoy being tied down with administrative functions. He proposed that his place on the board be filled by his son-in-law, René Revillon, who had taken him up on his offer to join the firm. At just thirty-six years old, René was appointed as an *administrateur délégué* (managing director) for an initial term of one year (later extended) to execute the will of the board, specifically "the hiring and laying off of workers, fixing the wages and governing all current operations of the company." Up until this point, it had been Alfred who had looked after the employee side of the business but as he entered his eighty-second year, he admitted he lacked the energy he once had and Louis needed someone to take his place.

Louis' brothers were concerned that giving René so much authority at such a young age might upset some of the more senior employees in the firm, but Louis had been insistent: René was family now. His marriage to Anne-Marie had already resulted in a grandson for Louis. It was only right, he felt, that René should be promoted into the heart of the Cartier family empire.

The board reshuffle allowed Louis to focus on more creative projects. Recently he had been inspired by some of the Asian antiques he'd seen in various stores around Paris, such as those belonging to the Chinese dealer C. T. Loo. Loo, who would later build a bold five-story red antique pagoda shop in the upscale neighborhood of Parc Monceau, sold to museums and important collectors across Europe and America. But he was not popular back in China, where he was seen by his fellow countrymen as looting his home country of precious artifacts (he would later claim that had he not removed those precious historic objects, they would have been destroyed in the Communist Revolution). Louis, once inspired by the Ballets Russes to create objects in the Persian style, now turned to Asia for inspiration. For instance, 1922 saw the creation of the Tank Chinoise, a variation on the classic Tank watch inspired by Chinese temple porticoes.

For those in the West who had suffered through a terrible war, the idea of the exotic East was a form of escapism. Just as Persian-themed balls had been quite the fashion in the prewar period, a decade or so later the West went wild for all things Chinese. CHINESE

FASHIONS CAPTURE EUROPE, *The Brooklyn Daily Eagle* reported in the fall of 1923. "Following the Russian and Egyptian crazes, the smart woman now favors the Oriental in her wardrobe." From Loo and other Asian dealers, Louis bought trays of lacquer panels, the glossy black lacquer inlaid with iridescent mother-of-pearl engravings of classic Chinese scenes. Finding them intensely beautiful, Louis had the perfect idea of how to use them in his creations.

Before the war, it had been frowned upon for women to wear makeup in public, let alone apply it in public. It was the same with smoking: Tobacco packets may well have featured alluring women seductively appealing to the male audience, but prior to 1914, a woman caught smoking in a hotel or restaurant might well be asked to leave. By the 1920s, perception throughout civilized circles had changed. Smoking and applying makeup had become a way for women to show their independence. Now they just needed somewhere to store their rouge, lipstick, and cigarettes. Cartier was quick on the uptake, and those lacquer panels that Louis had discovered deep within the antiques shops of Paris would find their way onto some of the most sought-after vanity cases of the century.

JEWELRY SPOTLIGHT: VANITY CASES

A 1920s Art Deco gold, onyx, enamel, and diamond vanity case.

Cartier hadn't been the first to come up with little vanity cases. The early 1920s *nécessaires*, as they were known, dated back to the 1720s, when they had held everyday necessities and been attached to clothing via a chatelaine. Louis had long enjoyed playing around with them to make them even more practical and stylish, on one occasion telling a magazine about "a mirror that may be carried in a woman's pocketbook and is so cunningly devised that it will enable her to see the back of her head and even the shape of her neck as well as her face. Naturally, in these days of bobbed hair, the back of her neck is as important to her as the rouge on her lips."

The only problem with these *nécessaires*—elegant though they were dangling from a ring or one's arm, or perhaps just placed envy-inducingly on the table—was that they were rather small (often no larger than 4 cm by 10 cm). When Florence Gould, the American railway magnate's wife, couldn't squeeze all her essentials inside, she ended up carrying them around with her in a box. So later the jewelers went bigger, creating *minaudières*, with space for everything from powder, lipstick, and comb to a retractable watch, dance card, pencil, pillbox, and handkerchief.

Charles Jacqueau worked on many of the designs for the cases, enjoying the space they offered for him to be creative. The craftsmen, though, weren't always so keen. It took multiple experts to create one finished piece, and each stage had to be perfect before it was passed to the next specialist. The decorative outside often required different techniques (from engraving, enameling, and stone setting to lacquer work, chasing, and polishing), but that was just part of it. The inside was a true feat of engineering, not only fitting a specific combination of compartments and objects inside in the most efficient way possible, but also ensuring that the retracting elements worked perfectly so the lipstick would, for example, pop up helpfully as soon as the box was opened but disappear smoothly when it was closed.

Cartier's vanity cases, essentially predecessors to the handbag, encompassed a whole host of themes, from traditional Chinese and Japanese scenes to Egyptian faïences embedded into Art Deco designs to bejeweled animals. In 1920, Pierre bought a sleek black onyx vanity case for Elma decorated with three diamond greyhounds standing in front of two stylized emerald North American cedar trees. It symbolized their family of three (which they referred to as "the Three Pups") in America. Many cases were personalized. When the Duke of Westminster commissioned one for his lover, Coco Chanel, he chose a simple C monogram in black and white. And in 1927, when Jacques sent his niece Marion a gold and cream enamel vanity case to celebrate her debutante season, he included her initials MC in small diamonds.

Of all Cartier's small cases, the ones featuring traditional Asian scenes on antique lacquer panels remain among the most sought-after today. At a 2015 Bonhams auction in London, one of these (measuring just 8 cm by 5 cm) came up for sale with an estimate of £30,000–£40,000. Featuring different scenes on each side (a Chinese nobleman on horseback on the front and two Chinese figures in a landscape on the back), it also had an engraved gold border, and a carved emerald and diamond sliding clasp. Though compact (especially compared to a handbag), when opened, it incorporated a lipstick holder, two covered compartments, and a mirror. The idea of a vanity case may be old-fashioned in today's world, but that didn't stop the bidders. This small one—a work of art within a work of art—sold for double its estimate, reaching over £65,000.

The interior of a 1920s Chinese-themed laque burgauté *and gem-set compact.*

Along with its often intricately decorated vanity cases, Cartier's more simple cigarette cases for men also became increasingly popular through the 1920s. While smoking for men had been de rigueur for decades, it had been pipes and cigars, rather than cigarettes, that were traditionally associated with the idea of masculinity. The war, however, had changed this. Not only had prepackaged cigarettes been more convenient in trench conditions, they had also represented a small luxury in a time of need. Sent in care packages to soldiers at the Front, they had become a currency: two cigarettes was the price of a haircut in the British trenches. And when, around the same time, cigarette advertising started in earnest, it didn't take long for cigarette smoking to become ubiquitous. Louis was a smoker himself. Cigarettes during the day, cigars after dinner. After all, every time he offered some high society chap a cigarette from his chic Cartier case, or a light from his gold Cartier lighter, he was advertising his own products.

FRAGMENTS OF THE MOON

Sometimes it would be Louis who came up with the ideas for Cartier's creations. Other times it would be his designers. Occasionally it would even be the clients themselves. Jean Cocteau, a man "to whom every great line of poetry was a sunrise, every sunset the foundation of the Heavenly City," was one of these clients. One day, Cocteau described to Louis a dream he had experienced. Perhaps under the influence of opium, to which he was becoming increasingly addicted, the acclaimed writer and poet explained that he had envisaged the rings around Saturn and was inspired by their magic. He wondered if Louis could somehow transmute their likeness into a ring for his little finger. The idea of something so large and universal being represented by something so small and personal entranced him.

By 1924, Louis was able to present his friend with a prototype of what would become a cult accessory. Made initially in platinum, yellow gold, and rose gold (later the platinum would be replaced with white gold), the ring's pared-back simplicity—not a gemstone in sight—was a brave departure from the more extravagant jewelry in fashion at the time. Cocteau was entranced, proclaiming that Cartier was "a subtle magician who captures fragments of the moon on a thread of sun." The artist, who by now was already famous in literary circles but would soon become known throughout France and farther afield, wore the ring stylishly on his little finger, helping it earn iconic status in the world of accessories for both men and women. At that time, it wasn't known as the Trinity ring, but rather the *bague trois ors* (triple-gold ring) or the *bague trois anneaux* (triple-ringed ring).

Cocteau, born into a prominent French family, was, unlike many of his fellow artists, able to afford Cartier's creations himself. He had planned to order one of Louis' new rings as a gift for his lover, the poet Raymond Radiguet, before his untimely death in December 1923. Instead he would later give one to the beautiful Russian princess Natalia Pavlovna Paley, sixteen years his junior, with whom he enjoyed a short, passionate affair in the early 1930s.

Soon after creating the ring, Cartier experimented with other triple accessories. The first triple bracelet was bought by Elsie de Wolfe, the well-known American interior designer, in 1925. American *Vogue*

wasn't far behind on the uptake. In 1925, it released an Edward Stei-
chen photograph of a stunning dark-haired model wearing "the new
Jewelry from Cartier." The matching Trinity bracelets and ring she
wore were not only "amazingly chic," so *Vogue* reported, but happily
also "very moderate in price." Of course, Cartier hoped that its clients might then progress up to the costlier items in the store: the
Vogue model also sported earrings "cut from one piece of onyx with
diamonds coming out like drops of water and pear-shaped diamond
pendants," while in her Trinity-ring-wearing hand she held up a fantastic crystal brooch to the light. But the idea of pieces that were
more "moderate in price" was one that Louis and his brothers had
increasingly been pursuing in the postwar market. It had even led to
the creation of a whole new department.

DEPARTMENT S

Art Deco diamond jewels, mystery clocks, and one-of-a-kind vanity
cases produced under the controlling eye of Louis were among Cartier's most exceptional pieces in the interwar years, but as the brothers well knew, they had a limited audience. In an attempt to reach a
wider client base in New York, Pierre started an in-house stationery
department in his Fifth Avenue store. His idea had been that even
those who couldn't afford jewelry could come into the store and receive the same high level of service as they ordered calling cards, invitations, or Cartier's signature sea-green high-quality writing paper.
Several years later, when they had either made some serious money or
perhaps married someone who had, Pierre hoped that they would
feel a certain loyalty to the store where they had ordered their first
headed paper and come back for the gems.

Louis was skeptical of his brother's idea at first, fearing that offering a lower-cost product would demean the Maison's reputation.
But later, he adopted it in Paris, said to have justified his actions with
the remark "If the King of Spain buys his stationery here, and the
Maharaja of Kapurthala his calling cards, I hardly feel as though I am
lowering myself." Certainly the idea of offering his clientele something
practical at a lower price point made good sense in the postwar envi-

ronment. In 1923, leapfrogging off the stationery idea, Louis created a whole new division, Department S, to provide a larger range of beautiful but relatively affordable and functional objects. The S stood for "silver," and though objects were not limited to silver, the idea was that they should be made from less valuable materials than, say, platinum, diamonds, and precious gemstones in order to keep the prices down.

Louis gave Jacqueau a largely free rein in the new department. Enjoying the opportunity it afforded him to be creative, he came up with designs for unusual objects from letter openers that incorporated a watch and cigarette cases with incorporated lighters to fountain pens with calendars on the cap and mechanical pencils with built-in flashlights to write in the dark. Other writing instruments included Chinese-style pencils in coral and Japanese-style Namiki pens, made of costly lacquer, that would end up furnishing the desk of the writer Rudyard Kipling as well as that of Louis himself. Sometimes these innovations would end up being too expensive to remain in the lower-priced Department S, but they were born of that same aim: to link functionality with beauty.

Not everyone was happy with the idea of a separate creative department. Jeanne Toussaint didn't appreciate the fact that her work in the handbag department now fell under a division that was effectively championed by Louis' protégé. It was no secret in 13 Rue de la Paix that there was a bitter undercurrent of rivalry between Toussaint and Jacqueau. Now it burst into the foreground. Louis, for the most part, went about his business, choosing to ignore the rumblings of conflict in his team, regarding them as a tiresome and unwelcome distraction. He was busy and anxious enough already without having to deal with managerial grumbles. The Exposition des Arts Décoratifs was just around the corner and Cartier's offerings needed to be perfect.

In 1925, the year of the exhibition, he came up with a solution that, at least temporarily, stopped the arguments. Louis promoted Jeanne Toussaint to head of Department S, thereby satisfying her creative aspirations, and simultaneously asked Jacqueau to focus on designs for the more important (non—Department S) high-end work. With the two rivals separated, and one administrative weight off his mind, Louis was freed up to work on ideas for the exhibition. But his anxiety remained a constant companion. As he made increasingly brilliant pieces, more and more was expected of him. There were times when he felt he just needed to get away from it all.

In Conversation with Jean-Jacques Cartier

Mademoiselle Toussaint was jealous of Jacqueau. She was used to being number one in Louis' eyes, but in Rue de la Paix, she had competition. She wasn't a designer, you see, and Jacqueau, well, Jacqueau was quite exceptional. There was no one like him. It was more than that, though. He really understood Louis. The two of them sparked ideas off each other, they were a team. Well, Toussaint couldn't stand that, of course. But she was very political, and she liked working at Cartier. She knew that Louis wouldn't like it if she said anything bad about his favorite designer, so she held her tongue in front of him. And later she was promoted. Before, everyone had been scared of her because she was Louis' lover—later they were scared because she had real power!

THE BEST VIEW IN THE WORLD

Though not short of houses, soon after his marriage Louis bought another one. Villa San Martin, looking out to sea from the mountainous Basque region of Spain, was a haven from both the pressures of work and the long arms of the tax man. Located in the stylish resort town of San Sebastián, it was just across the border from France and a short drive from Jacques and Nelly's Saint-Jean-de-Luz house where the family had met for their 1922 reunion. It was an iconic spot, home to "the Best View in the World," encompassing the vast panorama of the immense Cantabrian Sea with its surrounding Gipuzkoan coastline and the hills beyond. It was so magnificent, and so far removed from the frenetic pace of working life in Paris, that no other place, a Spanish interviewer would later write, could "satisfy the anxiety of the restless spirit of Louis Cartier, who needs to see the sun of Spain, from his villa in Monte Igueldo, to be completely happy." Even here, however, he was known to lose his temper, one time so enraging his cook that she stormed out (he then sent the governess to Paris to hire another one for the rest of the summer).

San Sebastián suited Louis well. Not only was it warm and beautiful, it was also a thriving cosmopolitan town filled with a fashionable crowd. In the late nineteenth century, the Regent Queen María Cristina, King Alfonso XIII's mother, had chosen the sleepy fishing village as her summer residence, commissioning the royal palace of Miramar on La Concha Bay in 1893. Following the Queen's lead, others flocked to enjoy the area, and hotels, palaces, and villas soon sprang up along the coastline. By the start of the First World War, visitors to San Sebastián were as diverse as the imperial Romanov family, the revolutionary Marxist Leon Trotsky, and the notorious exotic dancer, courtesan, and German spy Mata Hari. It was also a town with a Cartier family link, as Louis' grandfather had spent time there in self-imposed exile during the 1870 Franco-Prussian War.

Five years before Louis moved to Villa San Martin, Cartier had been in San Sebastián to present an exhibition at the newly built Hotel Maria Cristina (named after the Regent Queen). It had been quite a show, with the views stretching out to the deep blue sea competing for attention with the world's largest cut sapphire. Originally from Ceylon (now Sri Lanka), the 478.68-carat cornflower-blue gemstone had formed the centerpiece of a diamond and sapphire necklace. The Queen of Spain, Victoria Eugenia (known as Queen Ena), had tried it on, but it was on this occasion that her husband famously remarked of the 1.25-million-franc price tag: "Only the nouveaux riches can afford such luxuries . . . we kings are the *nouveaux pauvres* of today!"

"*Pauvres*" or not, Louis still enjoyed mingling with the aristocrats. Especially now that he had married one of them and considered himself officially part of their tribe. Prior to his second marriage, his continued efforts to reach the most elite social circles had generally been met with humiliation and exclusion. Coco Chanel herself recalled being on the same receiving end of the upper-class snobbery as the Cartiers, observing that "there was a social custom that one did not entertain one's tradespeople." In her memoirs, she remembered meeting Louis, tall and dressed in a frock coat, at the house of Baron Henri de Rothschild, the French playwright. The Baron's wife, who had helped build the reputation of the House of Chanel, had invited Chanel to see "heaps of old-fashioned jewelry." While she was looking at the spectacular necklaces laid out on a velvet pad in the Baroness's boudoir, Louis Cartier was shown in. He was, Chanel recalled, treated no better than the domestic help, like "an obviously superior servant."

So it was with much happiness, and no small amount of smug self-satisfaction, that after his marriage, Louis found himself accepted into many of those same circles that had previously ignored him. From Budapest to Paris to San Sebastián, important clients started to see Monsieur Louis Cartier in a new light. Unfortunately, though, not everyone felt the same way.

PISTOLS AT DAWN?

A few years after his marriage, Louis was delighted to receive an invitation to a party held by the Baron Maurice de Rothschild. The fact that the Baron had never shown the jeweler any previous courtesy just made Louis' joy all the greater. Here, at last, was evidence he had crossed the boundary from shopkeeper to peer.

Maurice, "one of the gaudiest ornaments of the spectacularly rich tribe," had inherited a fortune from a doting aunt. He married into another fortune (his estranged wife's family owned the Crédit Mobilier bank). His residences included an enormous estate outside Geneva where even the fish were treated as VIPs (the aquarium blue trout were served a meal of fresh bull heart daily) and a vast Parisian townhouse. Along with his multimillionaire status, Maurice also belonged to a family that the Cartier brothers had always admired. He may have been several generations removed from the legendary Rothschild brothers who had made their fortune in finance by being in different cities at a time when no one else was thinking globally, but he was still a part of that all-important dynasty. Louis had been looking forward to meeting him properly, if not as a complete equal, then at least not as a servant.

The Cartiers had been at the Parisian party for some time before Maurice spotted Louis. Jacqui by this time was already on the dance floor. The following description of the meeting between the host and his guest comes from a newspaper article that made it all the way over to America:

> "What are you doing here?" the Baron demanded gruffly, as soon as he saw the jeweler.
>
> "I am here because you invited me," replied Monsieur sharply.
>
> "You are mistaken," said the Baron coldly, while a circle of guests listened in amusement to the conversation.
>
> "Your invitation was addressed to Monsieur and Madame Cartier," declared M. Cartier rather hotly.
>
> "Well, anyway, I don't want you here," responded the Baron, and walked away.
>
> M. Cartier, flushed with anger, called his wife, who was dancing at the time, and they walked out of the house.

It was unclear why Louis had received the invitation, which the Baron claimed never to have sent. Some newspapers suggested that Rothschild might have meant to ask Louis' wife, the Countess, while leaving her husband off the guest list. Chanel herself claimed that the invitation was in fact intended for the Belgian diplomat Baron Cartier de Marchienne. Either way, it had not been Louis' mistake. Enraged at such a public dressing-down, he returned home in a fury.

Sifting through the many invitations on his fireplace mantel, Louis found the one in question. He had been right. It had been addressed to "Monsieur et Madame Louis Cartier." The injustice of the situation drove him mad: Not only had he been humiliated in front of a crowd he desperately wanted to impress, but the Baron, acting like a king, was just a descendant of humble merchants himself. Louis had at least earned a title, Chevalier de la Légion d'Honneur, for his service to France. What, he fumed, had the Baron ever done that was worthy? Livid, he called two friends to his house and spoke with them long into the night. He needed to avenge his honor, he explained, and the only way to do so properly was the old-fashioned method: a duel. He would even allow the Baron to choose the weapon: traditional swords, or more lethal pistols.

In a scene reminiscent of the one in Fitzgerald's *Tender Is the Night* in which McKisco keeps a desperate all-night vigil before the duel, Louis prepared for morning. But whereas Fitzgerald's contrite McKisco regretted his violent temper, Louis was unwavering. He was literally willing to risk death, to leave behind a widow and a leaderless company, just to redeem his honor. The high levels of recognition and success he had achieved were all for nothing if he didn't have the respect he craved. He had married Andrée-Caroline because his father had said the union would be good for the Cartier name; he hadn't wed Jeanne Toussaint for fear of how the match would reflect on him. Now, in the embodiment of his worst fear, he was being humiliated even after marrying an aristocrat. By dawn, he had worn down his more reasonable friends and they had agreed to be his seconds in the duel.

Immediately after sunrise, he sent them over to the Rothschild house. Eventually waking the bemused Baron and handing him the invitation as evidence, they explained the jeweler's wish that old-fashioned justice be done. In a rather patronizing anticlimax, the Baron just laughed uproariously in their faces, leaving the tabloids desperate to know what would happen next: "The affair still hangs in suspense with all the upper crust of Parisian society anxiously waiting to see what will happen. He [the Baron] has just left Paris to take a month's cure at Marienbad, however, and the jeweler can do nothing except gnash his teeth until his opponent returns."

Nothing would come of the teeth gnashing. The duel would not take place, and the Baron would not acknowledge the jeweler as anything other than a lowly shopkeeper. But that obsession Louis felt with impressing high society, that need for social acceptance, continued to plague him. It was the same fire that drove him, through the 1920s, to create some of the most innovative and beautifully made jewels of all time for the best clients in the world. If he was to be judged alongside other luxury shopkeepers, then he could at least ensure that his Maison came out on top.

JEWELRY SPOTLIGHT: THE MYSTERY CLOCKS

*Art Deco rock crystal, onyx, and diamond
"Model-A" mystery clock.*

The mystery clocks Louis had started experimenting with in the 1910s, whose hands appeared to hover in thin air, had been among his biggest challenges. A decade later, he sought to take them one step further. Throughout the 1920s, working with the skilled Couët clockmakers, he experimented with different forms, building on the original Model A. There were those in which hexagonal rock crystal clock faces rose above their onyx bases on black and gold pillars. Others boasted rectangular dials of carved Chinese jade and delicate rose-cut diamond hands. There were large ones designed as freestanding oriental gateways, and those so remarkable and rare that they have been compared to Fabergé's eggs: the figurine mystery clocks.

For these, inspired in part by the eighteenth-century *pendules à sujet* in which a clock was set on the back of an animal figurine, Louis would incorporate an ancient artifact, such as a jade goddess, a coral turtle, or an agate chimera. The brief to his team was that the final creation should not only be a reliable, working clock, made in complete collaboration with the Couët workshop (so that the Cartier designer fully understood where the workings would be hidden and could design the clock accordingly), but should also reflect the individual artifact being used. For a jade carp clock made in 1925, for instance, the two jade carp fish swim through frosted rock crystal "water." The mother-of-pearl "waves" are edged with blue enamel and studded with small emerald cabochons while the diamond hour hand is shaped like a seahorse-dragon. This idea of remaining true to the spirit of the original piece, of the jade fish immortalized in a bejeweled sea, was fundamental to the Cartier style. The brothers had been brought up with a great respect for past civilizations, and they would use ancient objects in their work only if the resulting creation enhanced their overall meaning and beauty.

The highly complex mystery clocks, Louis believed, couldn't have been made anywhere but Paris, the indisputable center of craftsmanship. But through the 1920s, the clients with the deepest pockets were more likely to be found overseas and Louis called on his brothers to help sell the clocks in their markets. Pierre and Jacques rose to the challenge. Among the American clients to purchase one of the rarest horological creations of the twentieth century, "seemingly woven from moonbeams," were Ganna Walska, Anna Dodge, and George Blumenthal. English aristocratic fans included the Duchess of Westminster, although hers, "an exquisite little thing which seemed to work by magic," met a rather sad end during a marital argument (her husband's lovers included Coco Chanel): "One night, during a nightmarish argument, it was hurled against the wall and shattered into a thousand pieces." And in 1928, Jacques would sell one of the most fabulous models of all, a gem-studded jade elephant supporting a coral, onyx, pearl, and rock crystal pagoda-shaped clock, to his best client and good friend, the Maharaja of Nawanagar.

Prior to this 1928 "Le Ciel" mystery clock appearing at a Bonhams auction in 2006, featuring jade carp under a translucent night sky dial, dotted with diamond stars, it had been thought that there were only twelve Cartier figurine mystery clocks. This clock marked lucky number 13.

JEWELS AS A "LIVING REALITY"

As the spring sun dissolved the last of the frost, travelers started descending on the French capital by the thousands. The 1925 Exposition des Arts Décoratifs, originally planned for 1915 but repeatedly postponed because of the war, was about to open. From April to October, it would take place over an enormous area surrounding the large glass and iron Grand Palais pavilion. Encompassing everything from architecture, furniture, and interior design to glassmaking, fashion, and jewelry, it promised to highlight the new modern style. Fifteen thousand exhibitors from twenty countries would have the opportunity to showcase their latest creations in front of a global audience.

Thirteen architects had been chosen to design the thirteen entrances. Inside, French and foreign pavilions of all shapes and sizes, each conceived by a different architect, would compete for visitors' attention with sculptural friezes and daring metal murals. The Japanese pavilion, constructed of traditional materials, was made in Japan, dismantled, transported to France, and rebuilt by Japanese workers at the event. But the architecture was only part of it, as within each pavilion would be even more feasts for the eyes: refined lacquer decoration, Austrian modernist sculptures, illuminated Lalique crystal fountains, and Le Corbusier furniture. With many thousands of avant-garde designs across a huge range of applied arts presented for the first time, it was to be a groundbreaking event. For Cartier, with its focus on innovation, it was an ideal venue to impress an international audience.

Louis, who had been working on the Exposition for many months, was proud to be vice president for the jewelry category and a member of the jury for the awards. Alfred was delighted. Throughout the nineteenth century, he and his father had chosen not to present Cartier's wares at the many international exhibitions held in Paris, as they had been more retailers than makers of jewels. Now to see his sons not only present in exhibitions but also be on the judging panel was a source of enormous pride.

The plan was for the fashion houses to present their collections in the Pavillon d'Élégance (the fashion pavilion designed by Rateau and Lanvin), with the jewelry houses occupying a dedicated section within the main Grand Palais. Louis, ever the trailblazer, had other ideas. As early as 1923, he had submitted a provisional application to "exhibit gem jewelry, fine timepieces, etc." as "part of an overall presentation concerned with ladies' attire, including dresses, hats, evening hairstyles, etc." He asked for Cartier to be separated from all the other jewelers and moved to the Pavillon d'Élégance alongside the *grands couturiers*. His firm's creations were designed to be worn with haute couture, so, he reasoned, they should be viewed alongside it too.

Fortunately, Jeanne Lanvin, the acclaimed designer and president of the Fashion Category, agreed with him. An admirer of Louis' work and owner of a Cartier pearl, diamond, and crystal necklace herself, she recognized that his creations were a form of "living reality" as much as her couture. It felt right that they should be seen on mannequins, in bobbed hair and alongside dresses, rather than in cold display cases. "Modern decorative art in all its forms is to be understood as a living reality," the exhibition documentation claimed. "A ceramic tile or a wallpaper can only properly be judged in situ—a desk lamp only when actually alight on the table."

The rules for all entrants to the exposition were strict: "Admitted to the exhibition are works of new inspiration and genuine originality, by artists, craftsmen, industrial and fashion designers and publishers, as long as they are in tune with the decorative and industrial arts of today." Cartier wasn't short of pieces in the modern aesthetic. From as far back as the 1910s, well before Art Deco had a name, Jacqueau had been experimenting with geometric shapes and bold color combinations. Recently the style had taken off, and by 1925, the time of the exhibition, the vast majority of Cartier's clients were fans of the cutting-edge and yet highly wearable fashion.

If anything, it was hard to know what to choose. Some objects, like the mystery clocks and the Egyptian and Chinese vanity cases, were out of the question, given the fashion-based context of the exhibition. Beyond that, Louis came up with a hundred fifty items that expressed the exhibition's theme. A few had been made several years previously and had to be borrowed back from clients who had bought them. Most pieces, though, were made specifically for the event.

In Conversation with Jean-Jacques Cartier

Uncle Louis really was an incredible innovator. His motto, one that the brothers shared, was "Never copy, only create." The idea behind it was that inspiration could and should be taken from everywhere, except from existing jewelry.

Pushing the boundaries of design and technical virtuosity, Cartier's contribution to the event impressed even its competitors: "Among the outstanding pieces," Georges Fouquet announced of his rival's collection, "were . . . a large brooch with a carved emerald, necklaces of engraved emeralds or carved coral, a ravishing coral comb, and a bracelet made of little barrels of diamonds and black enamel." There were three-dimensional "panther skin" orchid blossoms to be worn in one's hair, in which pavé diamonds and onyx had been astonishingly combined by Cartier's highly skilled setter over complicated curved surfaces. There was a novel *fermeture de corsage,* designed to replace the conventional fastening at the front of a dress but made of jewels. Two stems with stylized flowers in diamonds, onyx, and pearls were joined at the base, where two emeralds formed a point. It was perhaps not the most practical item, needing to be "fastened at intervals to the corsage with needle and thread," but the fashion world, unconcerned by the practical, loved it. *Vogue* featured the piece in its September 1925 issue with the caption "Cartier sponsors this new jeweled ornament to outline the front opening of the bodice." It would spur a run of less expensive imitation versions from other jewelers.

For a firm focused on design in an exhibition based on design, the display of Cartier's stand was almost as important as the creations themselves. Louis used mannequins, skillfully arranged in front of mirrors, to expose the back of the jewels as well as the front. This was especially important for the showstopper central piece of the exhibition. The Berenice "necklace shoulder ornament," as it was known, was a whole new take on the idea of a necklace. A band of black enamel, pearls, and diamonds, interspersed with three large carved emeralds, was designed to stretch from shoulder to shoulder (one emerald on each shoulder, with the largest emerald resting just between, and slightly below, the collarbones). The bejeweled band didn't join behind the neck as a traditional necklace would; it continued over the shoulders and down each side of the back, ending in two long tassels of pearls, emeralds, and diamonds. It was a hugely original and much-admired creation, and an illustration of a short-haired blond model wearing it even made it into the special Pavillon d'Élégance edition of the *Gazette du Bon Ton.* But, like many of Cartier's most fantastic pieces in the Exhibition, including the diamond and pearl *fermeture de corsage,* it didn't sell and was later broken up.

For Louis the inventor, it was worth creating, and then dismantling, extraordinary jewels just to make a mark for his firm in the world of jewelry and art. He had fought to have a center-stage position in the exhibition of the decade, and he wasn't going to waste it by playing it safe with pieces already in the Rue de la Paix shop windows. Working alongside some of the most skilled designers and craftsmen in the world to create pieces that would never sell may have hurt Cartier's balance sheet in the short term, but Louis was driven by something far stronger than a desire to make money. Ever since he had attended the 1891 Exposition Universelle as a boy of sixteen, back when the Eiffel Tower had been unveiled for the first time, he had wanted to play his part among the world's leading innovators. This was his time.

A CELEBRATION OF SUCCESS

In mid-September 1925, fresh from a break in San Sebastián, Louis and Jacqui threw a large dinner in Paris. The guests of honor were Pierre and Elma, who had been visiting for the summer and were due to head back to New York later that week. It was a happy affair, not least because Jacqui was seven months pregnant, and Louis hoped a Cartier heir was on his way.

The exposition, now drawing to a close, had been visited by 16 million people. That was publicity on an enormous scale. Countless artists had shown what could be done without relying on the Greco-Roman tradition, and though the term "Art Deco" was not yet used, a new style had been born. In the years that followed, variations of the art and design showcased at the fair would find their way around the world, from the skyscrapers of New York to the ocean liners that crossed the Atlantic.

Creatively, the Cartier stand represented perhaps the pinnacle of Louis' career and was among the most impressive selections of jewels on display in the exhibition. Because Louis was a member of the judging panel, Cartier was prohibited from competing for awards. Critics, however, hailed Cartier's novelty of design and technical supremacy. Baron de Meyer, *Harper's Bazaar*'s chief photographer in Paris, spoke of the stunning originality and "dangerous" color combinations, while Fouquet praised the "subtle taste of Monsieur Louis." The Cartier brothers, he announced, were "without doubt among the *bijoutiers-joailliers* [high-end jewelers] who have done the most to revive the techniques of jewelry." Louis had achieved everything he set out to accomplish.

And yet his elation at the recognition was mixed with concern. It had been wonderful for the brothers to come together in Paris for the exhibition, but they'd all noticed how frail their father had become. Alfred's eyesight had dimmed so much that he could barely see his eldest son's new creations. His usual determination had been replaced with exhaustion and resignation. The eighty-three-year-old thanked his family for their concern and dutiful sending over of various newfangled medicines but reasoned that it was pointless: "My chief illness is the accumulation of years . . . I ask to carry on only as long as it pleases the good Lord." It wouldn't be long. On October 15, 1925, just two weeks before the end of the seven-month exhibition, Alfred, the adored patriarch of the Cartier family, passed away.

MOICARTIER NEW YORK: MID-1920s

THE PASSING OF A PATRIARCH

Pierre heard about his father's death by telegram. The news hit him hard. Like his siblings, had he adored and admired Alfred, and the feeling had been mutual. "Kiss [your family] for me and keep an affectionate embrace for yourself from your father" was the standard sign-off on his many letters. His passing would leave an enormous void.

As far back as Pierre could remember, Alfred had been the axis around which the Cartier family firm rotated. Though he had "retired" to give his three sons space in the business, he could always be relied upon as the unbiased mediator and the firm hand of experience in the face of difficult decisions. When he was tough, as with Louis' first marriage, or in teaching his sons his work ethic, he had the firm's and the family's best interests at heart. Alfred had taught his sons far more than the trade; he'd fired their ambition, fostered their love of family, and instilled in them his drive. "Up to a few months ago," the papers reported on the day of his funeral, "M. Cartier . . . had never missed a day from his labors in his offices in Rue de la Paix."

Pierre wasn't able to make it back to Paris from New York in time for the funeral but read in the papers how the Église Saint-Honoré-d'Eylau, the church he knew so well from attending Sunday mass, had been squeezed full of "personalities from the world of high fashion and industry." Louis and Jacques had been among the mourners, along with their wives. After the service, the coffin procession had made its way along nine kilometers to Père-Lachaise Cemetery, a maze of headstones and vegetation extending over 106 acres. It was here that Alfred's father had begun building the Cartier crypt for his three-year-old granddaughter fifty years earlier, and here that both Louis-François and his father, Pierre Cartier, had been buried. Now Alfred joined them. Pierre arranged for a simple stone memorial plaque from the Cartier New York branch his father had helped to found. Louis and Jacques provided similar plaques from Paris and London and each one was inscribed with a dedication from *le personnel* (the staff). Above the words, stretching across the top left-hand corner, was a three-dimensional fern leaf carved from stone, recalling the diamond and platinum fern-leaf jewels that had helped mark the emergence of the Cartier style twenty-five years earlier.

The passing of their father would inspire the three brothers to create a new Cartier crypt, far bigger than the last, with room for them all and their families when the time came. This one was not to be in Père-Lachaise, where it was difficult to secure a large enough plot, but in the less densely populated Cimetière des Gonards in Versailles. Jacques, who had visited the Versailles cemetery with his wife (as her family's large and imposing Harjes family crypt was located there), suggested the location to his brothers, and they had agreed. Once they had secured the right to build a mausoleum in the verdant northeastern corner, Louis worked on the plans with an architect. Design was in his blood, and his talents stretched beyond jewelry: The final plans of the two-story Monument Funéraire, as he called it, were works of art in themselves. It would not be until two years after Alfred's death that the new family resting place was ready. Three coffins would be moved from the Cartier crypt in Père-Lachaise: those of the brothers' grandfather Louis-François, their mother, Alice, and their father, Alfred.

Within a month of hearing of his father's passing, Pierre received another family telegram. This time it bore happy news. Louis and Jacqui announced the birth of a longed-for son, Claude Cartier. Alfred would have been so pleased, and the family rejoiced—finally, an

The Cartier chapel and crypt in the Cimetière des Gonards, Versailles. Louis designed the building in 1927 with the help of the acclaimed architect Walter-André Destailleur.

heir for the Paris branch. At fifty years of age, Louis wasn't the young father he had been to Anne-Marie, but in place of youth, he had time. Two decades earlier he'd been ceaselessly striving for greatness; now he'd achieved it and was on the cusp of retirement. Pierre, on the other hand, at forty-seven, was still getting into his stride. With no son to follow in his footsteps, he was throwing everything he had into the business. The idea of slowing down was inconceivable to him. America was ramping up by the day, and he couldn't afford to lose focus for a moment.

BOOM TIME IN AMERICA

The 1920s were an age of dramatic social and political change in America. For the first time in the country's history, more Americans lived in cities than on farms. The Gilded Age of the late nineteenth century had been dominated by those very few who had made fortunes from railroads, ships, and banks, families like the Astors, Vanderbilts, Morgans, and Rumseys. Now their place in society would be challenged by a new breed of upstart tycoons in emerging mass-market industries like film, radio, chemicals, and cars.

In part, this massive wealth creation was driven by a slashing of American taxes. At the end of World War I, the highest marginal tax rate was 77 percent. By 1928, under Presidents Harding and Coolidge, it had fallen back to 24 percent. Unemployment had halved and the nation's total wealth had doubled. This unprecedented economic growth swept many Americans into an affluent but unfamiliar "consumer society." "This nation has definitely become a land of multimillionaires," reported one United Press dispatch. The new moneyed population didn't hold back when it came to spending, and if they could outshine their neighbors in the process, all the better.

Horace Elgin Dodge was a classic example. Coming from nothing, he'd started out as a mechanic and married a piano teacher from Scotland. In 1901, aged thirty-three, he and his brother founded the Dodge Automobile Company, which supplied engines and parts to car manufacturers. When one of his clients, just starting out at the time, had been unable to settle his $10,000 bill for the car parts in cash, the Dodge brothers had accepted his offer of a minority shareholding in his fledgling company instead. That man was Henry Ford. Fifteen years and a lengthy legal battle later, the savvy redheaded Dodge brothers sold their $10,000 stake back to Ford for $25 million ($590 million today).

Though he became a multimillionaire with a fabulous red sandstone mansion on the banks of Lake St. Clair in the fashionable Grosse Pointe area outside Detroit, Dodge continued to be looked down on by high society. With his uncouth and aggressive outbursts, many felt that he hadn't learned the behavior befitting a man of wealth. But in 1920, much to his delight, doors previously closed to him started opening when his daughter announced her engagement. Through marriage to Jim Cromwell, Delphine Dodge would link her family name with that of her new mother-in-law, the society queen Eva Stotesbury.

Since meeting Edward Stotesbury, known as Ned or "the richest man at J. P. Morgan," on a cruise to France, Eva Stotesbury had enjoyed the best of everything. She had been reasonably well off with her first husband, Oliver Eaton Cromwell (a descendant of Oliver Cromwell), but Ned opened her eyes to a whole new level of spending possibilities. Her outfits and jewelry were discussed at length in the society columns—long silk dresses, a showstopping purple opera cloak with white fox fur at the collar and cuffs, $500,000 in diamonds gifted by J. P. Morgan, coils and coils of pearls, and "the most beautiful [tiara] ever seen at the Metropolitan Opera House."

And then there were the houses. El Mirasol, a Spanish Colonial

Revival palace in the sand, was the largest property in Palm Beach when it was built in 1919, and even included a zoo. Whitemarsh Hall in Philadelphia, completed in 1921, took five years to build. It was the largest, most extravagant residence the city had ever seen, with 147 rooms and 45 bathrooms. Its three basements housed bakeries, laundries, a tailor shop, a barbershop, a gymnasium, and a movie theater. The gardens alone required a staff of seventy. Parties there were legendary. For their grand opening, in bold defiance of Prohibition, they constructed four bars in the corners of the rotunda: one for cocktails, one for whiskey, one for champagne, and one for any other drinks that took one's fancy. There were four orchestras, two seated and two strolling. Ned Stotesbury even had a go on the drums.

For all her party-throwing skills, though, Mrs. Stotesbury was not popular. Philadelphia high society found her spoiled and ostentatious, no doubt partly jealous that their local millionaire hadn't married a hometown girl. And yet, as her son Jim Cromwell later revealed, the vast spending was more Ned's idea: "Father was the show-off—not my mother. He was of a generation of men who want to show the whole world how important they are. . . . His theory was: If you've got it, flaunt it." Ned's wedding present to Eva had been a $100,000 sapphire necklace and "a rope of pearls so long that, if worn as a single strand, it would have extended to the floor." Horace Dodge was impressed. When he and his wife had visited the Stotesburys prior to the wedding of their children, they had both been suitably "goggle-eyed" at the house and its magnificent interiors, but it had been Eva's jewelry collection that really made an impact on Horace. While Anna Dodge would later hire the Stotesburys' architect to transform their house, Horace was focused on outshining the Stotesburys in the short term. His son-in-law would later recount the story of his quest for the perfect wedding jewels:

> Not long before the wedding, Mr. Dodge took his future son-in-law aside. "Jim," he said, "I'm worried about Mother." "What about her?" Cromwell wanted to know. "Well, Mother doesn't have the kind of pearls your mother has. In the church, people are going to notice that kind of thing. Where does your mother buy 'em?" Cromwell mentioned Cartier. "Never heard of him," Dodge said. "But get me an appointment with this fella."

And so Cromwell arranged a meeting between Pierre Cartier, Horace Dodge, and himself. At the meeting, Cartier—whom Mr. Dodge persistently called Mr. Car-teer—produced several trays of pearl necklaces[.] "No, no, Mr. Car-teer," said Mr. Dodge. "I want something bigger than that for Mother. Something to match Mrs. Stotesbury's pearls." Finally Cartier said, "Monsieur Dodge, I do have one very fine set. They belonged to the Empress Catherine." "Never heard of her," said Mr. Dodge. "But let's see 'em." Cartier then brought out a magnificent strand of pearls the size of robin's eggs. "That's more like it," said Mr. Dodge. "How much?" "Ah, Monsieur Dodge," said M. Cartier, "that necklace is one million dollars." "I'll take it," said Dodge, pulling out a checkbook and writing a check for $1,000,000.

CATHERINE THE GREAT'S PEARLS

The necklace, five strands of 389 perfectly matched natural pearls with one enamel clasp portraying a Russian empress and two diamond alternate clasps, also had a magnificent heritage. It was said to have been owned at one time by Catherine the Great, the Russian empress renowned for her sumptuous collections of artworks, artifacts, and jewels.

Needless to say, Dodge's wife, Anna, dazzled in the Empress pearls at her daughter's wedding the following month in front of three thousand guests and the entire Detroit Symphony Orchestra. As Dodge had hoped, his daughter's big day helped propel his family name into the spotlight, and pictures of the happy bride were splashed across the papers. Gaumont even produced a silent film, set to jaunty music, showing large crowds lining the streets around the Jefferson Avenue Presbyterian Church in Detroit, with the bride and her bridesmaids laughing happily together at the family home. Well-heeled wedding guests quick-stepped their way around a large dance floor set up in the Dodge garden before bidding farewell to the bride and groom leaving for their honeymoon trip on their not insubstantial yacht, *Delphine I.*

Apart from the profits on the sale, the Dodge necklace brought unexpected publicity for Pierre. A high-profile lawsuit against Cartier hit the papers in January 1922, courtesy of two reputed Egyptian art dealer brothers who had sourced the jewelry. The Benguiat brothers had been among the many dealers to descend on Russia after the revolution in order to buy from the Soviets. Their main business, however, was importing rare Eastern rugs, not pearls, so after buying the necklace, they passed it on to Cartier in exchange for a $500,000 down payment and a promised half-profit share. Once Cartier had sold the necklace to Mr. Dodge, they filed a suit alleging that they had been shortchanged.

Claiming that the necklace had in fact been sold for $1.5 million, they demanded several hundred thousand dollars' worth of additional sale profits for themselves (while also alleging underpaid luxury taxes). In the end, the matter was resolved only when the executor of the Dodge estate declared that the price his client had paid was in fact $825,000 ($8 million today)—not the $1.5 million mentioned in the lawsuit and not the $1 million that Dodge's son-in-law had claimed. This played well to public perception of Cartier (who had refused to comment on the sale all along) as both an honorable business and one devoted to client confidentiality.

Alas, Horace didn't make it much past the wedding, dying along with his brother during the influenza epidemic of 1920, aged fifty-two. Anna lived on until she was 103. At her death in 1970, her jewelry collection was estimated at $6 million, excluding the Catherine the Great necklace, which was broken up and divided among her descendants. In December 2008, a portion of the notorious necklace, consisting of 224 pearls and only three strands out of the original five, resurfaced when it was sold at a Bonhams auction in New York for $600,000. Ten years later, in 2018, it reappeared in a Christie's auction and sold for $1.1 million.

A PUBLIC RELATIONS PIONEER

Despite the success of the Dodge sale, the fact that his client had never heard of Cartier was something that Pierre badly wanted to change. His ambition was for Cartier to become a household name in America, not just known to a select few. He still hoped, of course, to be selling the historic million-dollar necklaces to glamorous heiresses, but he also sought to appeal to the increasingly affluent middle-class buyer looking for a simpler engagement ring or chic pair of cuff links.

After an introduction via one of his lead salesmen, Pierre hired the marketing consultant Edward Bernays in 1922 to learn more about the mysterious arts of marketing and public relations. A nephew of Sigmund Freud, the Austrian American immigrant Bernays would later become known over a forty-four-year career as "the father of public relations," with corporate clients including General Electric, Procter & Gamble, and the American Tobacco Company. He was a pioneer in the marketing industry's use of psychology and social sciences to design its campaigns to shape public opinion. As Bernays asked, somewhat eerily, in his 1928 book: "If we understand the mechanism and motives of the group mind, is it not possible to control and regiment the masses according to our will without their knowing about it? The recent practice of propaganda has proved that it is possible, at least up to a certain point and within certain limits."

When Pierre first met Bernays, the thirty-one-year-old was relatively inexperienced but keen and full of ideas. Over the next few years, the partnership between the pair would prove an incredibly fruitful one. Together they created an in-house marketing committee for Cartier New York, even if its cynics suggested it was designed to foster "the illusion that Monsieur Cartier's decisions were democratically arrived at." Every Wednesday morning, Pierre would sit at the head of a large table flanked by his secretary and chief of staff and surrounded by his department heads. Every subject would be discussed with the utmost precision and formality.

Initially, Pierre had rejected the idea of magazine advertising, just as Louis had always done. He was, however, happy to respond to magazines such as *Vogue* and *Harper's Bazaar* when they asked for images of jewels. The fact that they considered Cartier the arbiter of good taste was recognition that Pierre was keen to encourage. He would respond deferentially to all their letters (whether regretfully rejecting their invitation for advertising or agreeing to send them pictures and data for their articles) and would always sign off with the same nineteenth-century closing, "I am your obedient servant."

With Bernays's guidance, Pierre refined his view on marketing. He came to recognize that in a competitive business facing an era of mass communication, there was a need for advertising, provided that it was "discreet" enough for the firm to maintain its sense of prestige and exclusiveness. Creating brand awareness within a large modern market called for a new approach. Theater tickets were considered an appropriate medium: Cartier was one of the first to place a formal advertisement reading simply "Cartier, Jewelers at 52nd Street and 5th Avenue" on the ticket envelopes. Simultaneously, they would quietly suggest to the theater producers that referring to the leading lady's necklace as a "Cartier pearl necklace" might enhance the play's overall prestige.

One area where Pierre was already light-years ahead of his peers was in the use of what Bernays called "strategic intelligence" in selling. All through the 1920s, while Louis was creating jewels over in Paris, Pierre was creating a jewel of his own, a vast and detailed index of current and prospective clients. He was rigorous in ensuring that his salesmen gathered and stored information that they could then use in sales approaches. Index cards were used to note engagement dates, marriages, births, and deaths, all culled from newspapers, society publications, and the Social Register (which detailed family relationships). And wills filed in the surrogate court were rather lugubriously scanned, with salesmen on the lookout for bequests of important jewels, which might be purchased by Cartier for resale.

In Conversation with Jean-Jacques Cartier

Pierre understood that his clients appreciated French luxury; that was what he was selling. But he also understood the American culture. He was interested in it, in the different areas and accents. In fact, he was incredibly talented at recognizing accents from all over the country. He could tell from a short "Hello" or "Good morning" exactly where his client was from.

So successful were Pierre and Bernays's techniques that demand started to outstrip supply. Pierre needed to increase production. Part of the reason behind his earlier decision to start an in-house workshop had been to fight back against his main competitor. Dreicer had been a fellow Fifth Avenue jeweler who, to Pierre's intense frustration, had copied the designs of jewels sold on Rue de la Paix and sold reproductions faster than Pierre could obtain the originals from Paris. Even more infuriatingly, Dreicer's storefront had been designed to resemble 13 Rue de la Paix.

For over a decade and a half, Dreicer had been poaching Cartier's potential clients. In 1921, the heads of Dreicer, a father-and-son team, both passed away. Without clear leadership, Dreicer started to deteriorate and by 1925, it was being liquidated. Pierre, ever the dealmaker, was able to buy the bulk of his competitor's stock for $2.5 million. He didn't plan to sell Dreicer's stock as his own, but he could dismantle the jewels and recycle the constituent parts. Importantly, the purchase would also prevent another opportunistic jeweler from acquiring the stock and picking up where Dreicer had left off.

With one aggressive competitor out of the way, and orders pouring in from clients, Pierre invested heavily in the New York workshop American Art Works. It was led by the highly experienced Paul Duru, who, in the winter of 1920, had been handpicked by the Cartiers to come over to New York from Paris. He worked alongside Maîtrejean, an expert diamond setter who had helped Bouquet set up the original small workshop before the war. Under the fifty-one-year-old Duru, the team was quickly expanded to include around thirty skilled jewelers and craftsmen by 1922, a number that would later grow to as high as seventy. The workshops were strictly single-sex; most of the craftsmen were men, but there was a separate room for the women, who tended to be pearl stringers and polishers. Alongside them worked talented designers like Alexandre Genaille, who by now was senior enough to be tasked with not only coming up with designs but also overseeing a team and producing the price estimates to be presented to the client. He wrote extensive instructions for each new designer to join the firm, including small details on how to bring their painted designs to life, such as "To bring out the light in the colored gemstones, add a layer of varnish." Genaille, who had attended the very best French design schools before coming to America, couldn't help but be impacted by the scale and boldness of New York, but that elegant Parisian sense of style, the very reason Pierre had brought him over, remained with him.

"Yes, there is a difference jewelry-wise in the tastes of American and European women," Pierre would proclaim in a speech later in life. But this didn't mean Cartier should lose sight of its French heritage. Rather, there were ways to maintain the same Cartier style and keep clients on both sides of the Atlantic happy by making small adjustments: "Generally French women attach more importance to the mounting of the stones, and they insist on extremely light mountings, the metal must practically disappear to please the French women." In contrast, he noted that in the United States, "the mountings must be stronger in structure and the stones should be extremely securely set as American women travel a great deal and cannot extend the same care to their jewels."

In 1925, with American demand on the increase, Pierre expanded his in-house supply capabilities even further by starting a second workshop. Marel Works (a combination of the first names of his daughter, Marion, and his wife, Elma) specialized in goldwork. As non-bejeweled gold objects, such as cigarette cases and picture frames, required different skill sets from the more jewelry-based work, it made sense to create a separate workshop. From early on, it was run by Albert Klauss, who would work for Cartier for more than thirty years. Originally a silversmith from southwest Germany (he'd fled the Weimar Republic in the late 1920s), Klauss was a good-humored, kindly boss but a fastidious disciplinarian in the workshop. "He taught me how to very carefully put the screws in my gold frame handbags," one of his junior employees remembered of her time working under him. "I did two under the pressure of his watchful eye. My respect for what appeared to be a simple job changed. If I missed and scratched the gold it would have to be completely repolished . . . not good." When Klauss was unhappy with the quality of work produced in his workshop and became upset, the employee would recite "Die Lorelei," the famous German poem by Heinrich Heine, to calm him down. He would laugh. He appreciated, after all, that his nationality made him something of a novelty within a building that often felt more like "the last French outpost of the New World" than a Manhattan jewelry store.

THINGS OF EXQUISITE BEAUTY

Sometimes for Cartier, being French in New York had its drawbacks, not least because the client struggled to pronounce Cartier's name. In 1923, Cartier's had to write to the manager of a local taxi firm, noting that several out-of-town clients had found it difficult to explain to their drivers where they wanted to go and asking whether, in their common interest, "you would not care to put on the bulletin board which your drivers see, a card stating that the location of Cartier is at 52nd Street and Fifth Avenue, and that the pronunciation of the name is Car-tee-ay. By so doing, you will help your passengers, your drivers and all concerned."

But there were bigger problems with being a French firm in postwar America. Traditionally, France had been associated by Americans with all things wonderfully stylish. Unfortunately, that positive sentiment had soured somewhat after the First World War. There was a sense among some Americans that the war had not been worth the loss of lives, and France had become something of a scapegoat. Pierre was not alone in wanting to reverse this ill feeling, and in 1923 he and other French retailers in New York formed a plan.

The French Exposition in New York would take place in April 1924. Designed to revive the sense of glamour and romance once associated with France, it would feature the A to Z of all things luxe: from automobiles to china, from furs to gowns, and from jewels to perfumes to shoes. Whereas the 1925 Exposition des Arts Décoratifs in Paris was focused on innovation and included major progressive exhibits from some twenty countries, the French Exposition in New York was designed to showcase stylish French items from all periods. There was some overlap: French designers such as Worth and Lanvin sent over their latest creations to entice stylish Americans in two fashion shows daily. But a large part of the New York exhibition was backward-looking. The French government shipped across porcelain from Sèvres, Gobelins tapestries, and historic jewels that had been housed in the Louvre.

In Paris, Louis had been asked to be on the admissions committee for the 1925 exposition. For the New York exhibition, Pierre took an even more senior role as part of the main board, and offered an office in Cartier for their meetings. After months of preparation, the ten-day event was opened to much fanfare on April 22 by the French ambassador and friend of Pierre's, Jules J. Jusserand. Excited guests packed the Grand Central Palace auditorium by the thousands as the band played the American and French national anthems, and Jusserand was dramatically escorted to the stage by a police guard. He spoke of the recent war but observed that France was "working now with might . . . not to win a war, but at her looms, at her plow and her wheels and mills, and here it is your privilege to see displayed many of her most useful and her most beautiful products."

Pierre went all out in his display, spending a small fortune on the wood-paneled replica of the Fifth Avenue store. He wasn't alone. Looking at the event pictures, one would be forgiven for assuming an entire luxury shopping center had been built, not a temporary display that would be dismantled in less than two weeks. But as Pierre and his peers knew very well, the event wasn't about making money. It was far more important to impress the audience, and to link the ideas of France and beauty in the minds of the many thousands who visited. The exhibitors, Pierre included, were investing in their brands, and in that respect, it was a home run. "It was a gala opening night," *The New York Times* reported the following day; ". . . whatever the war did to France, it did not rob her of her power to create and fabricate things of exquisite beauty."

There were, *The New York Times* continued with glee, over $1 million (around $15 million today) worth of jewels to be seen, "so much of value that a special police guard keeps a vigilant eye upon [it] day and night": oriental pearls, diamonds, pearl tiaras, and a necklace of emerald pendants valued at $85,000. Recognizing that Americans appreciated French luxury because of its heritage, Pierre even included the silver service that Napoleon I had once owned, valued at $100,000.

It was typical of Pierre to work on something that not only boosted Cartier's standing but helped build relations between his adopted and native countries too. In this respect, as Bernays later observed, he was a trailblazer, well ahead of his time: Pierre "anticipated by years corporate image building by asserting his leadership in improving United States and French relations. Today most corporate executives . . . are aware that leadership in one area carries over into another. This truth was not generally recognized in the early twenties."

In Conversation with Jean-Jacques Cartier

Pierre was a brilliant businessman. He didn't have Louis' creative vision, but then again, Louis didn't have Pierre's ability for selling or his understanding of finance. Louis used to say, "It suffices for me to buy a share in a company for it to plummet in value. I buy, it goes down!" But Pierre understood the markets and he understood people's motivations. Cartier needed the mix of different talents, you see, that was one of the reasons that it did so well.

In another life, the family joked, Pierre would have been a diplomat. Certainly, he relished the opportunity to connect important individuals and improve international relations in any way he could. Recalling his list of achievements, it becomes entirely understandable why an exasperated Elma felt he generally took on too much. He was awarded the Légion d'Honneur for his fundraising efforts during the war, he was president of the French Hospital in New York (an organization for which he also tirelessly fundraised), and he founded and headed the Franco-American Council for Trade and Industry. He was president of the French Chamber of Commerce in New York (giving them their headquarters rent-free in a Cartier-owned building next to the Fifth Avenue store) and president of the Alliance Française. And all this in addition to his day job.

15 EAST NINETY-SIXTH STREET

Entertaining at home offered Pierre the opportunity to introduce high-profile figures to one another. For one evening event, at which both the French ambassador and a French cardinal were to be present, Pierre sent out invitations to several friends, many of whom also happened to be rather good clients. In a society based on whom one knew, the drawing card of an influential senior figure was a powerful one: "It is with a feeling of much honor that I look forward to meeting the French Ambassador and Monseigneur Baudrillart," Harold McCormick replied to Pierre's invitation on April 21, 1927. Though not designed as work events, these evenings had the beneficial effect of building client loyalty. After all, if Mr. McCormick had helped himself to a cigarette from the silver Cartier box on the table, or Mrs. McCormick had admired Elma's new necklace over the fish course, they would be likely to have Cartier on their mind the next time they were in the mood for a shopping spree.

Pierre and Elma's house was the perfect venue for their endless stream of stylish dinners. A handsome five-story Beaux Arts–style mansion on Ninety-sixth Street, it was a stone's throw from Central Park, in between Fifth Avenue and Madison Avenue. Designed by the fashionable architect to the elite Ogden Codman, Jr., it had been commissioned by Lucy Wharton Drexel Dahlgren in 1915 after she divorced her philandering husband, Eric. Lucy Dahlgren was a banking heiress (her father, Joseph W. Drexel, co-founded Drexel Morgan and was an old business partner of Nelly's father). She had lived in her Ninety-sixth Street mansion for several years with her eight children before renting it to Pierre and Elma.

It's not hard to see why the Cartiers first leased the property and then, when the opportunity arose six years later, bought it. The limestone façade, the intricate wrought-iron balcony, and the slate mansard roof turned it into a slice of Paris in Manhattan. The house offered thirty rooms, including eleven bedrooms and bathrooms. There were carved fireplaces, a sweeping marble staircase, an octagonal dining room with two elaborate wall fountains to rinse wineglasses between courses, and the all-important Estey organ in the drawing room. In the interior courtyard, Marion could play with the puppy Nelly had given to her as a birthday gift ("You have made me the happiest little girl in the world!" she had written joyfully to her aunt). To accommodate Pierre's motorcars, there was a ground-floor carriageway leading through the courtyard to an automobile turntable at the back of the property. There was even an elevator to allow cars to be stored in the cellar.

Dinner parties in the comfortable home were a regular occurrence. Marion could look down from her bedroom window as distinguished guests pulled up in their motorcars. Ladies would be modeling

Left: Pierre and Elma with their fifteen-year-old daughter, Marion, in 1926.
Right: their New York home, 15 East Ninety-sixth Street, in the 1920s.

the latest silk dresses from Paris on a warm summer evening or wrapped in the best Revillon furs during the harsh winters. Except, as Pierre was finding out, there were fewer and fewer clients around in the depth of winter. Those with the money and the connections shared a secret, and Pierre and Elma had just been let in on it.

WHERE SUMMER SPENDS WINTER

Once just a sparsely populated part of Lake Worth, Palm Beach had started out as a resort at the turn of the twentieth century, thanks principally to the Herculean efforts of Henry Flagler, a co-founder of Standard Oil. In pursuing his dream of a new "American Riviera," he had built the first hotels and made what was an Atlantic Coast barrier island accessible via the Florida East Coast Railway. With holiday accommodation and transportation needs met, it did not take long for Palm Beach to grow in popularity.

As money poured into the land where "summer spends winter," a building boom swept through the region and architects were commissioned to build ever more fabulous residences. Chief among them was Addison Mizner, a Renaissance man and worldwide traveler who contributed perhaps the most to the architectural opulence of Palm Beach's Gilded Age. Mizner "brought his love of Mediterranean architecture from Europe to Palm Beach: arches, clay tile roofing, intricate stonework flooring, pecky cypress ceilings, and imported massive fireplaces."

Pierre and Elma's earliest jaunts to Florida didn't actually include Palm Beach. Elma's brother, Lee Rumsey, had retired to the region before the war and regularly invited family down to his fabulous house on Belle Isle, just off the coast of Miami. It was the perfect retreat for a relaxing family vacation, except that, as Elma well knew, her husband wasn't very good at relaxing. Before long, news that friends and clients were just up the coast in Palm Beach lured the workaholic Pierre away from the generous hospitality of his brother-in-law.

Pierre liked what he found, particularly the newly constructed Everglades Club on Worth Avenue. Originally designed by Mizner as a hospital for injured soldiers, Everglades had been turned into a highly exclusive members club once the war was over and there was no longer any need for a soldiers' retreat. Paris Singer, the club's founder, chose the initial members, and it wasn't long before the well-connected Pierre counted himself among them.

Back in 1918, when Singer first conceived of Everglades, Worth Avenue was a dirt road. As Everglades transformed into the preeminent social club in Florida ("If you have to ask where it is, you don't belong here"), it didn't take long for retailers to catch up. After all, behind those secret club walls where men played golf looking out to sea and ladies took tea on the Marble Patio were some of the best clients in the world. They may have been on vacation, but, as the couture houses were well aware, there would be no pause in the social schedule just because they were away from home. And a constant stream of cocktail parties, costume balls, garden luncheons, and afternoon teas required a serious wardrobe.

As a luxury retailer himself, Pierre couldn't help but be taken with the potential of the area. In 1923, he took a long-term lease on one of the fashionable Beaux-Arts shops on Lake Trail, which he tried for a season before subletting to Charvet et Fils (the luxury Place Vendôme shirtmaker his grandfather had been so fond of). He had already decided he wanted to be closer to Everglades. He wasn't alone. Fashion designers were lured to Worth Avenue by the hope that they might be able to present their new season's collection at the club's weekly fashion shows (which would later serve as a launch pad for new designers including Valentino and Givenchy). Costume stores, meanwhile, opened principally to provide outfits to guests who had been invited to the legendary annual Everglades Fancy Dress Ball.

By 1928, Cartier's had established a seasonal store at 249 Worth Avenue on the corner of Hibiscus Avenue. Headed up by long-term Cartier New York employee Paul Rosier, it would open in the warm winters and close in the stifling summers. All the stock for the Palm Beach showroom was sent from the New York headquarters. There was no in-house workshop, just a couple of salesmen and a craftsman for repairs. On occasion, when an important client requested it, Pierre would send down one of his designers from New York to discuss a commission. And they weren't short on important clients down there. It was Marjorie Merriweather Post, one of the best jewelry buyers of all, who recalled the fabulous gems that sparkled under the Palm Beach sun: "You can't conceive of the amount of jewels in those days that were worn there, huge diamond rings, pins, and such necklaces as you wouldn't believe."

MARJORIE MERRIWEATHER POST

Marjorie Merriweather Post was one of those discerning Cartier clients who bought jewelry with the eye of a true collector. Not only was she knowledgeable, she also knew exactly what she wanted, often leaning toward important or historic gems. She was also one of the few ladies able to afford them.

Born to a pioneer in the hugely profitable cereal industry, Marjorie became the owner of the Postum Cereal Company and one of the wealthiest women in America after her father's death in 1914. She was twenty-seven years old at the time, had two young daughters, and was nine years into her first marriage (of four). Five years later, she had divorced her investment banker husband, Edward Close, and found a new one. Edward Hutton was an alluring financier who had founded his own stockbroking company. He met Marjorie at a Palm Beach houseboat party and they were married amid much pomp and ceremony in 1920. Together they built up her company through a series of mergers into the General Foods Corporation while simultaneously dazzling high society. Always elegant, Marjorie enjoyed entertaining, whether out at the Westbury races, over in Paris for a luncheon, or at her fully staffed 207-acre "rustic retreat" on Upper St. Regis Lake in northern New York State, where each guest cabin was staffed with its own butler. Everything was top of the range, the biggest and the best: from *Sea Cloud,* the most enormous yacht in the world, to Mar-a-Lago, her lavish seven-acre Palm Beach estate.

Even by privileged Palm Beach standards, Mar-a-Lago was opulent. Fifty-eight bedrooms, thirty-three bathrooms with gold-plated fixtures (easier to clean, Marjorie believed), an eighteen-hundred-square-foot living room with forty-two-foot ceilings, and three bomb shelters. "Its 110,000 square feet glinted with gold leaf, Spanish tiles, Italian marble, and Venetian silks." Over the three years of its construction starting in 1924, she spent $7 million, all told (north of $100 million today). Her husband at the time, Edward Hutton, joked: "You know, Marjorie said she was going to build a little cottage by the sea. Look what we got!"

In the same year construction started on Mar-a-Lago, Marjorie took a trip to England and saw a carved Mughal emerald brooch in Cartier London. The piece had been made a year previously and sold to a Mr. Godfrey Williams, who had subsequently returned it. This was not unusual. The brothers prided themselves on satisfied clients; if a client was not happy with his or her purchase, the jewelry could generally be returned or exchanged, no questions asked. There was little risk; another buyer would almost always come along before too long. In the case of the emerald brooch, Mrs. Hutton, as she was then known (a Cartier salesman had to be au courant with the latest divorces, remarriages, and changing surnames of his clients), was that other buyer. She appreciated the mix of the old gemstones within Cartier's more modern setting as seven carved Indian emeralds were complemented with diamonds and mounted in platinum. The central hexagonal emerald was particularly distinguished, dating from the Mughal period and bearing an inscription linking it to the Persian ruler Shah Abbas II.

Palm Beach was a holiday destination for many of Cartier's best clients, including Marjorie Merriweather Post (left), dressed for the exclusive Everglades costume ball in 1929. Her Juliet costume, complete with Cartier emerald necklace and the emerald brooch as a pendant, won first prize.
Top right: Marjorie's Palm Beach "cottage by the sea," Mar-a-Lago.
Bottom right: Cartier's early Palm Beach branch on Worth Avenue.

In Conversation with Jean-Jacques Cartier

For me, the Persian or Indian style, where, say, an antique Indian carved emerald or even several old gemstones were mounted within a more modern Art Deco setting, well, that was typically Cartier in the twenties and thirties.

Marjorie brought the brooch back to America, where she later took it in to Cartier New York for modification. Instead of the circular diamond top, she had it changed to more of a doorknob shape.

Either way, it was awe-inspiring, and, according to *Vogue,* on trend: "Perhaps the most outstanding new note in jewellery is the size and importance of brooches." Generally, jewelry that was pinned to one's dress in the twenties was lighter than in the prewar corset years, but not this piece. It is likely Marjorie's dresses would have had to be reinforced to support it. In a portrait painted in her Washington home, Hillwood, she sits with her young daughter, the enormous emerald brooch stealing the show. Over her lifetime, Marjorie would patronize a whole host of different jewelers as her tastes and collecting styles developed, but she always remained loyal to Cartier. Not driven by a need to make a status statement, she considered her jewels to be works of art. On her death she left an immensely valuable jewelry collection to the Smithsonian and her own Hillwood museum, hoping others might gain the same enjoyment and appreciation of them that she had.

JEWELS FROM JULES

Marjorie Merriweather Post wasn't alone in having residences around the country. A salesman at Cartier had to be prepared to be on the move at a moment's notice should a client request it. Pierre tried to make it down to Palm Beach for a couple of weeks in the winter, and over to Paris for a month in the summer with his family, but he couldn't afford to leave the office and his responsibilities in New York for much more than that. He needed someone he could trust to do the bulk of the traveling for him. Jules Glaenzer was that man.

Glaenzer, three years younger than Pierre, had joined Cartier around the same time as he. A truly brilliant *vendeur,* he was also, as one society columnist remarked, "one of the last of a rapidly disappearing human species of boulevardier and bon vivant." Descended from a prominent New York family (his father was a well-known art dealer), Glaenzer was brilliantly connected among the clientele to whom Cartier aspired. He regularly entertained Broadway composers, Hollywood artists, and industry tycoons in parties that became the talk of the town: "His studio in New York was the scene of many a brilliant party to which came the most prominent members of the theatrical and literary as well as the social worlds."

Glaenzer's parties (more than two hundred a year) were "considered so important socially by some people that an individual unlucky enough not to have received an invitation is compelled to leave town for a week so that he will have a good excuse to explain his absence." Like Everglades, he hosted costume balls that became legendary, not least because of his spectacular outfits, such as the embroidered coat given to him by a maharaja. No wallflower, Glaenzer craved attention. Regular sessions in the gym ensured that he looked fit, pinstripe suits and a colorful tie gave him a certain standout style in the office, and perfectly practiced dance moves set him apart in the nightclubs. He was a gourmet, a wine connoisseur, and a proud collector of brandy (he had seventy varieties, one of which dated back to 1807). He was a student of the cocktail, and his invention, the Glaenzer Special, was a potent concoction of rum, peaches, and limes.

His little soirées at home, where his well-known musician friends George Gershwin and Richard Rodgers were prone to break into impromptu performances in front of everyone from the Vanderbilts to Charlie Chaplin, were also good for business—so much so that Pierre even paid the rent on Glaenzer's five-room duplex apartment on East Sixty-fifth Street. Much like Maxim's for Louis in Paris, Glaenzer's home (and party venue) in New York acted as a kind of unofficial second Cartier office. It went without saying, of course, that the clients must never feel they were being sold something. They were at the cocktail evening because they had been lucky enough to be invited and because it was not to be missed. If they happened to pop in to Cartier the following week to see Jules and ask if their old diamond necklace could perhaps be remounted into a brooch similar to the one Marjorie Merriweather Post had been wearing at his party, that was entirely their own idea.

It was Marjorie who had introduced Jules to his first wife, Edith Adams. The couple had married in the winter of 1916 in a hotly anticipated New York society wedding. A son soon followed, but within five years, the marriage had broken down. Despite rumors that Glaenzer was homosexual, the divorce petition stated that he had been found with an unnamed woman at an apartment at 741 Fifth Avenue, just down the street from Cartier's. Perhaps unsurprisingly, his ex-wife, Edith, had gained custody of their only son. More unusually, the punitive terms of Justice Morchauser's divorce decree had stipulated that, in light of the clear blame that fell on his side, Glaenzer was forbidden to remarry during Edith's lifetime, even though Edith herself was allowed to do so.

For some time, this wasn't an issue. Glaenzer, turning forty, continued merrily on the party circuit, enjoying bachelor freedom. Three years after his divorce, however, in the fall of 1924, Glaenzer fell in love again, this time with a twenty-one-year-old professional dancer. Miss Luella Kendall Lee had come to Jules's attention when she had modeled several Cartier creations for *Vogue* (including the new Cartier Trinity jewels). She was, as he later found out, a direct descendant of General Robert E. Lee, making her a daughter of both the American Revolution and the Confederacy. Blue blood, lively feet, and fantastic beauty. Needless to say, Glaenzer was smitten.

When Miss Kendall announced in January that she was heading to Palm Beach for the season, Jules pulled out all the stops and arranged a "very swank" farewell party with "heavenly dance music and such food!" Unable to await her return to New York, he followed her down to the sunshine and pursued her relentlessly. By the end of March, the deed was done, and their engagement was announced by Miss Lee's mother. The problem, naturally kept under wraps by Jules, was that it was illegal for him to remarry.

Glaenzer called on his boss to quietly help him overturn the in-

Left: Jules Glaenzer with his bride, Luella Kendall Lee, on their honeymoon in 1925. Right: Kendall models "the New Jewellery from Cartier" for *Vogue*, including the cutting-edge Trinity bracelets and a Trinity ring.

convenient court order. Emergency affidavits of his good character had to be given not just by Pierre, but also by other prominent figures including the president of Revillon Frères and United States Attorney William Hayward. Fortunately for Glaenzer, his ex-wife, Edith (who had since remarried), did not oppose the petition, and the earlier court order was overturned. A month later, in the spring of 1925, Jules was in St. James Lutheran Church on Madison Avenue, watching as his beautiful bride in ivory satin and a lace-trimmed veil of tulle was escorted by her brother down the aisle toward him. Within a decade, however, Glaenzer would be divorced again, with the former Miss Lee alleging cruelty.

Despite his eccentricities, Jules Glaenzer was highly valued by Pierre. Among his fellow employees, he could be considered something of a self-absorbed prima donna at times, but to his clients he was never anything short of charming and infinitely obliging. A gifted salesman, he was brilliantly creative when it came to convincing clients that they simply must have this Art Deco necklace or those fabulous emerald earrings. At the opening of Marilyn Miller's hotly anticipated theater performance in the Ziegfeld Follies, he not only arranged for the stars of the play to wear Cartier jewels onstage (with a classy little credit in the program), but he went one step further: He invited several carefully selected clients to attend the performance in a special box with him. They all accepted gratefully, but what they didn't know was that Glaenzer had selected the jewels for the actors with these clients' tastes in mind.

After the show, he went backstage with his guests to meet the actors and collect the necklaces, bandeaux, and bracelets. He then announced that it would be too risky to carry home such a huge amount of valuable jewelry. Instead, he proposed that each of his female guests select an item to wear for the remainder of the evening, and that he would collect it from each of them the following morning. He then took his guests out to a nightclub, where, as intended, their jewels were much admired. The next day, a Cartier delivery boy called at the homes of the guests for the jewelry only to find that each of the women had decided to buy what she had been wearing the previous evening.

This technique was typically Glaenzer, for whom his life was his work and his work was his life. Every night out on the town was enjoyed with great gusto, but always with an eye to boosting his future commissions. Each time the luxury ocean liners crossed the Atlantic in May, "telegrams from Jules prepared Louis Cartier for the imminent arrival of Mrs. George Gould on the *Lusitania*, Mrs. Clarence Mackay on the *Kronprinzessin Cecilie*, and Mrs. Rita Lydig and Mrs. Vincent Astor on the *Mauretania*." Sometimes he would be on the ocean liners himself. On one occasion, Pierre's PR consultant, Edward Bernays, had a lunch booked with Glaenzer for a Wednesday. "On Tuesday, he [Glaenzer] telephoned me. 'I'm terribly sorry. I'm leaving for a trip to Europe on the same ship with Edsel and Henry Ford.' " A tip had come in that the Fords would be on the boat, and he decided he simply had to be there (he would become a good friend of Edsel Ford). There was, he had discovered, nothing like a long journey in a confined space to inspire the desire to buy a new accessory or two. And the great dining halls on board the *Queen Mary* or the *Aquitania* were the perfect backdrop to show off one's pre-dinner purchase. That boat trip alone made Cartier hundreds of thousands of dollars in fabulous sales to the Fords, to the despair of its rivals waiting patiently in their chic Parisian showrooms.

It was no surprise to anyone when, in 1927, Pierre promoted Glaenzer to the leadership team as vice president in recognition of his talent. Over the eighteen years he'd been with Cartier New York, Jules had been Pierre's secret weapon, mingling in all the right circles and selling everything from historic necklaces to Art Deco vanity cases. Above all, though, Jules was good with pearls, which he loved. "Nothing can be added to fine pearls to make them more beautiful," he would say, "except a lovely woman." And shortly after his marriage to Miss Lee, he scored an enormous coup, securing the purchase of perhaps the greatest pearl necklace of all time.

THE THIERS NECKLACE: DYING FOR A PEARL MOTHER

The Thiers pearl necklace had been bequeathed to the Louvre in 1880 by its late owner, Élise Thiers. In 1833, the fifteen-year-old Élise, a daughter of a Parisian banker, had married the thirty-six-year-old French minister of the interior, Louis-Adolphe Thiers. With the help of her family's funding, Thiers had gone on to become the interim president of France during the Third Republic following the defeat of Napoleon III. Élise was an ardent supporter of her husband, collecting and compiling his speeches in a book after his death.

He, in turn, was very fond of his younger wife. As a wedding present, he had given her a gift of three rose-tinted oriental pearls. They were to be the beginning of a collection. With the help of Bapst of Paris, longtime jewelers to French royalty, she started looking for pearls with the same pink hue. She and her husband had a deal: Whenever he received 50,000 francs from his broker, she was to be given 1,000 francs to spend on pearls. In the end she was able to construct an exquisite triple-stranded necklace of 145 perfectly matched natural pearls.

The necklace was dutifully displayed in the Louvre's high-vaulted Galérie d'Apollon for more than forty years. In 1922, the Louvre decided that the necklace was no longer of sufficient "artistic character" or "educational value" to remain in its prominent spot. But that wasn't the only reason it needed to be removed from its case. The necklace was said to be losing its color and luster behind glass, or, as the journalists sensationally put it, the pearls "were withering and dying" and their value was shrinking. "Nothing could save them . . . but a 'pearl mother.' They wanted to be loved." It was essential, the pearl experts agreed, that the pearls be worn, be shown daylight, and be held close in order to revive them.

The problem was that Madame Thiers had insisted that they should remain in a display case in the Louvre. In order to remove them, the French government was forced to pass a law allowing the pearls to be extracted from their glass case. Then the museum started looking for a "pearl mother." After much discussion, the Louvre decided upon Lilian Greuze, a beauty of the Opéra-Comique, due to "her velvety skin and even temperament."

Each day at three o'clock, Mlle Greuze would appear at the Louvre, where the pearls would be placed around her neck. Accompanied by policemen, she would ride down the Rue de Rivoli and on to the Champs-Élysées. There, she and the pearls would sit at a little table in a famous café taking refreshment. Later, she would return to her apartment in her hotel opposite the Tuileries Garden and spend an hour "caressing and fondling the pearls, holding them against her velvety cheek, whispering sweet nothings to them, loving them as a mother would her child." After wearing them out to dinner or the opera, Greuze would return them each night to their case in the Louvre. And so it was that the Thiers pearls were saved.

Not long after, the French government decided that the pearls should be sold. The proceeds would be divided equally among the Louvre, the Thiers Foundation, and another charity. Having ears close to the ground, the Cartiers heard early on about the jewelry auction planned for the summer of 1924. Discussing it with his brothers, Pierre decided the necklace would fare best over in America. So he, rather than Louis or Jacques, proposed to bid for it. Jules Glaenzer was sent over to France to mastermind the operation. Of course, if Cartier Inc. won, they would lend the necklace for display in the Rue de la Paix branch. If it attracted interest from a Parisian client, Pierre and Louis would share the commission, but Pierre's principal thought was to display it in New York. The import duty would hurt margins, but it would be worth it to build his firm's association with historic jewels in a nation where high society was still drawn to heritage like bees to nectar.

The sale took place in June 1924, in the majestic Salle Denon, one of the great halls of the Louvre Museum, in the presence of more than a thousand spectators. At the 1887 auction of the French crown jewels, also in the Louvre, Louis-François and Alfred had looked on from the sidelines as their more successful peers bid on the famous lots. It was a sign of how far the next generation had come that they could now compete for a prestigious slice of their nation's history. But Cartier faced tough competition in the Thiers pearls auction, and the crowd looked on in disbelief as the bidding rose by hundreds of thousands and eventually millions of francs.

Initially, each of the three strands of pearls and the diamond-studded clasp were called out separately in order for the auctioneer to establish whether bids for the individual sections would be greater than bids for the necklace as a whole. The longest strand, containing fifty-five pearls, reached 5 million francs, the middle strand 3.2 million francs, and the shortest, forty-one-pearl strand 2.7 million francs. All were bid on by separate jewelers and pearl dealers, but not by Cartier. The clasp was also singled out, with the winning bid falling to one of Cartier's preferred gem dealers, a Mr. Esmerian. Finally, the whole necklace was then auctioned again, this time as a single piece.

The sum of the parts had been just shy of 11 million francs, so bidding for the entire necklace had to exceed that amount in order to void the previous bids. It did. The bidding war, won by an agent for a mystery absentee bidder, reached 11.3 million francs (equivalent to more than $7 million today).

Rumors abounded that the auction had been won by an American. Two days later, the press was able to report that the buyer was Cartier New York. Glaenzer had been in Paris for the auction but had preferred to bid from afar so as not to ignite too much interest. If fellow bidders had known the renowned international jewelry firm Cartier was interested, they might well have bid higher themselves.

The following month, the celebrated necklace started earning its keep, attracting "a constant stream of visitors" to 13 Rue de la Paix, where it was placed on view. "An inner salon has been set up apart as a shrine for the precious pearls and the public pass by in almost death-like silence." In an interview, Glaenzer boasted that the Prince of Wales, the Queen of Spain, and the Queen of Romania had all examined the three strands of perfectly matched pearls. When the press asked if they were potential buyers, Glaenzer rather sniffily echoed King Alfonso's comments in San Sebastián a few years earlier. "No, they are too poor," he explained. "Their governments may buy them as crown jewels, but the monarchs are not as rich as they once were."

The following January, the necklace arrived on Fifth Avenue. As in Paris, the idea was to display it in the Cartier showroom. Clients of the store received an elegant square invitation with a smart raised border announcing a "Pearl Exhibition including the Famed Thiers Necklace from the Musée du Louvre." The press spread the word further afield, announcing with excitement in January 1925 that the famed necklace had finally arrived on New York soil, that it had "passed the customs and is now in the custody of the Cartier galleries," where it "will be exhibited next week." The exhibition would last five days, from 10:00 A.M. until 5:00 P.M. each day, and entrance would cost one dollar. But all for a good cause, or rather two good causes: the Big Sisters organizations, headed up by Mrs. William K. Vanderbilt II, and the French Hospital, chaired by Pierre Cartier. Open to all, the event was a way of building excitement among the American public. In most cases, Cartier would discreetly buy and sell historic jewels, but here, ordinary folk were being given a once-in-a-generation opportunity to see a truly spectacular piece with a remarkable heritage up close. They took the bait, descending on Cartier by the thousands: "New York society, the wealth of America, the gem seekers of the world and thousands of others are visiting this little room at Cartier's and are viewing not only the Madame Thiers necklace, but full seven or eight million dollars' worth of other pearl necklaces."

Sadly, for lovers of near-perfect pearl necklaces, the Thiers necklace was never to be seen publicly again. The pearls were said to have been sold to the anonymous wife of an American millionaire, and the necklace was later dismantled with the pearls incorporated into other pieces of jewelry (Cartier's centenary exhibition in 1947 would feature "pearl necklaces holding many of the famous Thiers pearls"). For Pierre, though, the enormous success of the exhibition, which helped spread the Cartier name far and wide in America, validated his belief that heritage was a powerful marketing tool. Just a couple of years later, he took it one step further, using not only historic jewels to attract attention to his House, but to the royalty who wore them, too.

INTERNATIONAL STARDUST

"Dazzlingly fair, with lovely features, the bluest of eyes and a luscious figure," Queen Marie of Romania combined good looks with perfect pedigree. The granddaughter of both Queen Victoria and Tsar Alexander II of Russia, she had not grown up short of suitors, and had ended up rejecting a proposal from the future George V of England to marry the future King Ferdinand of Romania in 1893. She would go on to become hugely popular in her adopted country after successfully speaking up on its behalf at the Paris Peace Conference. Romania had been left severely weakened by the First World War, not only looted by Germany and its allies but also having received a declaration of war from Russia (which confiscated its gold reserves). Queen Marie negotiated emotionally for her country and emerged triumphant, with an enlarged territory for Romania.

To compensate his wife for her many jewels seized by the Bolsheviks, King Ferdinand proposed to help her replenish her collection. The couple became an excellent client of Cartier, purchasing several important pieces including an exquisite diamond tiara with pear-shaped pearls suspended from arches. Most spectacular of all, though, was the enormous 478-carat sapphire that Louis Cartier had first displayed within a sautoir necklace in the 1919 San Sebastián exhibition. Despite attracting significant interest, it had remained unsold until 1921, when King Ferdinand bought it, remounted as a pendant on a diamond and platinum necklace, for 1.38 million francs ($1.2 million today), payable in four installments. Receiving it as a gift for her coronation, Marie wore it often, especially as it went so well with the Cartier sapphire *kokoshnik* tiara she had bought from her sister's mother-in-law, Grand Duchess Vladimir.

As queen, the glamorous and dynamic Marie was one of the first royals to truly become a modern celebrity, thanks to her willingness to engage with people of all backgrounds and readiness to publish books and articles. In 1926, she decided to undertake a diplomatic tour of the United States to "see the country, meet the people and put Romania on the map." (It would also provide her with the perfect excuse to spend time away from what she described as "this quiet godforsaken little country of mine.")

Traveling to New York in the fall with her two youngest children, she was welcomed enthusiastically, with "whistle of steamers, roar of guns in white smoke puffs against gray fog, voices cheering in a stinging rain." There followed a zigzag tour across America and Canada, lasting more than seven weeks and covering 8,750 miles in her special train, the *Royal Rou-*

Queen Marie of Romania wearing the 1909 Cartier sapphire tiara previously owned by Grand Duchess Vladimir and the 478-carat sapphire set in a Cartier sautoir. After her 1926 visit to America, she wrote in her diary, "I know, as long as I live, breathe and think, the love for America will beautify my life and thoughts."

manian. Visiting "horse shows and balls and luncheons and chambers of commerce and libraries and museums and schools," she was seen by an estimated six million people and took America by storm.

The trip was due to be cut short on account of continuing reports of the ill health of her husband (who would die the following summer), but when her visit to New York prompted a media frenzy, Pierre was determined to capitalize on the royal allure before she departed. He was, as she wrote in her diary, "very eager that I should visit his shop." Much to his delight, she agreed. She was perhaps the biggest celebrity ever to walk through Cartier's New York showroom. Escorting her to his comfortable office, Pierre displayed for her a few items from his latest collection and listened "attentively" while she told him how she had invented the fashion for wearing head jewels with the new bobbed hairstyles. He may have secretly doubted her story, especially as his brother had been creating bejeweled hair clips for years, but this was no time for pedantry.

Not content to simply sit back and enjoy the headlines linking his store with a fashionable queen, Pierre went one step further to ensure that the royal magic remained long after the press had died away. As he had done after Queen Élisabeth of the Belgians' visit in 1919, Pierre had a plaque made that he attached to the Louis XIV chair that Queen Marie had sat upon, reading: "On this chair sat her Majesty, Queen Marie of Rumania, when she paid a visit to the House of Cartier." Pierre instinctively understood that by impressing a potential client, he was halfway to a sale. Displaying the royal coat of arms on the Fifth Avenue building had appealed to affluent Americans for the past decade. The now royal-infused chair took that idea to a whole new level.

AMBASSADOR OF LUXURY

Pierre may have been on his most formal behavior with Queen Marie, but he treated all clients with extreme deference. He greeted those who walked into his office with a handshake and slight bow, not dissimilar to how one would expect an ambassador to behave. His formal "How do you do, Mr. . . ." would reveal a slight French accent, but he spoke English perfectly. And once a client was sitting on *the* chair (Pierre knew that it would be a rare client who forgot the experience of sitting where a queen had sat), he could begin his pitch.

If, for example, a client asked for an emerald, Pierre would press a button and convey his request to a uniformed attendant. Before long, a selection of emeralds on a tray covered in soft dark cloth and bound in silk would be ceremoniously carried in and placed on his desk. Pierre would casually pick out one of the gemstones and mention its price. "This is one of our less important emeralds," he might say of a $35,000 specimen; "we have of course much better ones." The client's expression gave him the clue for the next step. If he could afford it, the client asked for the best emerald in the house, and Pierre would gratify his wish. If not, the customer would have to make do with what his money could buy. Regardless of the level of the purchase, at every stage of the process the client was made to feel special. Cartier prided itself on having some of the highest-quality jewels and objets d'art in the world, but, recalling his grandfather's words, Pierre recognized that client satisfaction went beyond the objects they were buying.

Sometimes he had in his office a special item he knew a particular client would be especially interested in. In the case of Prince Christopher of Greece, the husband of Nancy Leeds and son of Grand Duchess Olga of Russia, Queen of Greece, it was the Romanov marriage crown. A hugely significant and emotional jewel for the Romanovs, the crown had been auctioned at Christie's on the instruction of a Soviet syndicate in 1927. Soon after, Pierre had found it in a Paris antiques shop, and, recognizing that there would be far more demand for it in America than Europe, he had brought it to Fifth Avenue, where he planned to quietly show it to a few select clients.

Prince Christopher of Greece later recalled the moment Pierre revealed it:

At the time, I was in New York, visiting Pierre Cartier in his office. Suddenly he said: "I would like to show you something." He took a velvet case from his private safe, laid it on the table, and opened it. Within lay a diamond crown with six arches rising from the circlet and surmounted by a cross. "Do you recognize it?" he asked me. I nodded wordlessly, seized by a sense of melancholy that rose from the depths of my memory. It was the crown of the Romanovs.

My mother had worn it and her mother before her, it had adorned all the princesses of the imperial house on their wedding days. All at once, it seemed to me the room was full of long-dead brides.

Pierre's position as a buyer and seller of famous jewels was a difficult one, especially if at one point in their illustrious past they had been seized from their rightful owners. On the one hand, Cartier was keen to bolster its reputation as a purveyor of important gems; on the other, the firm risked being criticized for benefiting from the misfortune of others. The crown was a particularly sensitive piece because of its turbulent recent history (rightfully a Romanov piece, stolen by the Bolsheviks). As with so many of the post-revolutionary Russian pieces that came his way, Pierre knew he must personify discretion if he was to gain and retain the loyalty of those needing to sell their family heirlooms. They must trust him. Fortunately, in most cases they did. In his memoirs, Prince Felix Yusupov described sailing to America with his jewels in November 1923, and once there calling on Pierre: "a helpful and loyal man . . . I could count on him to act in our best interests." Prince Felix was known among European high society for a great many reasons, including his penchant for cross-dressing, his being at one time the richest man in Russia, his beautiful Russian princess bride, and his role in the murder of Rasputin. But to Pierre, he was simply an excellent client, who, like many of his fellow Russian exiles, was forced to sell his family's magnificent jewels to fund his new life in Europe.

Pierre hadn't been Prince Yusupov's first port of call. His friend Elsie de Wolfe, the celebrity interior designer, had offered her shop, and Yusupov himself had arranged his jewels and trinkets in her window "as I had always seen them placed in the window of my father's study at St. Petersburg; reminiscences that did not go without melancholy." When they didn't sell, however, he had turned to Pierre; "I ended up entrusting everything to the Cartier House." There was a huge amount: watches and snuffboxes, miniatures in diamond frames, and oriental daggers with handles enriched with precious stones. There was the Polar Star diamond that had belonged to Joseph Bonaparte, the diamond earrings of Marie Antoinette, and the "Sultan of Morocco," a 35.67-carat steel-colored diamond. There

Senior Cartier New York salesman
Paul Rosier with the fabled Romanov
wedding crown (right), Prince Felix
Yusupov with his wife, Princess Irina
(left), two of the many exiled Russian
royals who sold jewels to Cartier after
the revolution.

were jewels too that had belonged to Catherine the Great, including the "Ram's Head" light rose diamond on a striking black pearl
necklace.

They were exactly the type of important historic pieces Pierre
sought out for his American clients. The issue with promising discretion, however, was that it made spreading the word impossible. Not
able to openly advertise the fact that he had Yusupov's jewels, he
could ask a few select clients who he thought might be interested, but
other than that, he had to be patient and wait for the appropriate
buyers to come to him. In the case of the black pearl necklace, it was
bought by the daughter of the lady who had helped inspire Cartier to
start a New York branch in the first place: Mathilde Townsend (by
then Mrs. Peter Goelet Gerry, wife of a former United States senator). The price was $400,000 ($6 million today), over five times the
$75,000 advance Cartier had paid Yusupov in the intervening period.

Fortunately, not all historic pieces demanded such secrecy. If they
were bought via an auction or a dealer (such as the Hope Diamond
or Thiers pearls), Pierre had always been open to linking Cartier's
name with them in the press, and in time, Bernays took this basic idea

to a whole new level with a technique he called triangulation. When Cartier bought a newsworthy historic jewel in Paris, it would be mentioned in the Wednesday marketing meeting and studied from the perspective of an American audience. If it was interesting enough, Bernays would write an article about it, which he would send to Paris for release over there. The Cartier Paris branch would then turn the story over to the Paris correspondents of U.S. newspapers, whereupon the article would be cabled back to New York and published in the United States under a Paris dateline. If, as hoped, the piece ignited interest among Americans, the New York press would generally approach Cartier New York for comment, and Cartier's noteworthy Parisian purchase would hit the headlines on both sides of the Atlantic far more forcefully than if Cartier had simply written its own press release.

Often Cartier clients found their own way into the news, at least in their local papers. There might be a sighting of Marjorie Merriweather Post wearing her Cartier diamond and sapphire Art Deco necklace in the *Palm Beach Daily News,* or the Stotesburys at the opera in Philadelphia. In Chicago, though, it would, more often than not, be the McCormicks hitting the local headlines.

JEWELRY SPOTLIGHT: THE ROMANOV EMERALDS

In 1874, on the occasion of her marriage, Grand Duchess Vladimir received a set of jewels from her father-in-law, Tsar Alexander II. It included a necklace that featured ten extraordinary emeralds, each one set in a double border of diamonds in the traditional Russian style. And its center was the most impressive gem of all: a hexagonal emerald of 100 carats. Composed of detachable sections, the necklace's emeralds could be worn in different ways, and in 1903 they were immortalized within a staggering headdress in a photograph taken at the Bal de Costumes Russes. But with the 1917 Russian Revolution came an end to that extravagant life and the emeralds were among the many jewels smuggled out of the country under the cover of darkness.

On Grand Duchess Vladimir's death in 1920, her gems would be divided among her children. It was Grand Duke Boris, her second-eldest surviving son, who inherited the emeralds and, needing to fund his exiled existence in France, promptly sold them to Cartier. It was here that the geographic reach of the brothers came into its own. While the Paris branch, weakened by war, lacked the rich jewelry buyers it had once known, over in America Pierre had plenty of stylish and wealthy Jazz Age clients crying out for a genuine slice of European history. Cartier combined what the press described as "the finest collection of emeralds available" with 1,657 diamonds, and the resulting sautoir necklace was snapped up by Chicago heiress Edith McCormick, for $550,000 ($8 million today).

A decade later, it was all to change again. On Edith's death in 1932, the executors of her will entrusted the emeralds back to Cartier to find a buyer. By now, the Roaring Twenties had given way to the Great Depression, and selling them would not be so easy. It wasn't until 1936 that the press announced the executors of the will had finally agreed to a price of $480,000. The buyer was Barbara Hutton, the Woolworth heiress. (The press later erroneously reported that she had bought them for $1 million.) Ignoring criticism for extravagant spending during a depression, Hutton had the emeralds shipped over to her neo-Palladian London mansion. And this time it was the turn of Cartier's London branch to remodel them into a massive necklace, plus earrings and a ring.

Barbara Hutton wearing the Romanov emeralds set in an oriental-style headdress at Sidi Hosni, her Tangier palace, in 1961.

The Second World War turned fashion on its head, and those big necklaces of the 1930s were no longer all the rage. After the war, when Hutton was living in Paris, she called on her favorite salesman at 13 Rue de la Paix, André Denet, and requested

another remodeling of the emeralds. This time, the French
Cartier designer Lucien Lachassagne came up with an
oriental-style necklace that could double as a headdress. Barbara Hutton, dressed in a sari, would wear it as a tiara as she
greeted guests at her legendary parties in her Tangier palace.

In the mid-1960s, as Barbara Hutton split from her seventh
husband, she sold the notorious gems. This time the buyer
was Van Cleef & Arpels, which decided, perhaps because of
the difficult environment for luxury goods at the time, to break
up the headdress and sell the emeralds individually. And
those magnificent gems that together enjoyed such a prime
position within some of the most glamorous locations and moments of the twentieth century started the next chapter of
their remarkable existence apart.

CHICAGO ROYALTY

Harold Fowler McCormick was the privileged son of Cyrus Hall
McCormick, Chicago's "Reaper King," who had revolutionized farm-
ing by inventing the first commercially successful mechanical reaper.
Edith was the youngest daughter of John Davison Rockefeller, the
co-founder of Standard Oil and probably the richest person in modern history. Together, they were Chicago royalty. Perhaps this was
part of the reason their marriage was doomed to fail: "The legendary
joining of two great American fortunes has not happened all that
often in American history, but it happened in the McCormicks' case,
and the result was that there was no way one partner in the union
could bring the other into line."

The McCormicks' house at 1000 Lake Shore Drive was filled with
all manner of museum-worthy objects, from a rug that had belonged
to the Shah of Persia to a fifteen-thousand-volume library of rare
books. The furnishings had been collected to recall the days of the
French royal court, and the dinner parties were like state occasions.
Behind each of the two hundred guests stood a footman, and on the
tables were French menus engraved in gold. One could even eat from
the thousand-piece golden dinner service that Napoleon had given

his sister. Every detail was designed to impress, and yet, as Edith observed to her husband, her events seemed "forced and formal." Harold gently explained why they lacked that element of fun and spontaneity: "My dear, don't you realize these red-blooded young Chicagoans are used to having their liquor? They simply must have their wine, their highballs and cordials." But Edith had promised her late teetotal father that she would never either touch alcohol or serve it in her home. She would not go back on her word, and she would not let anything disrupt her idea of appropriate behavior. In fact, she was so strict that when her young son died of scarlet fever during a dinner, the servants were unsure whether to tell her. In the end they decided to quietly let her know. She, "appearing more annoyed by the interruption than by the news, merely nodded, and the dinner party continued."

Even without the merriment, however, the McCormicks' gatherings were not invitations to be turned down. The couple were Chicago's hottest celebrities. When the opera-loving Edith decided to attend the Chicago Opera on a given evening, it would guarantee a sellout performance. Not unlike the reaction to chart-topping divas today, crowds would be waiting outside to catch a glimpse of her as she arrived in her plum-colored Rolls-Royce (driven by a chauffeur in a plum-colored uniform). Stepping out of the car in her famous ermine cape (composed of a phenomenal 275 skins), she made sure always to display a glimpse of her favorite feature, her ankle, often encircled by a gold anklet. It was, however, generally what was hanging around her neck that attracted the most attention. One Cartier necklace she owned contained ten large emeralds spaced along a rope of 1,657 diamonds, while her pearls had cost $2 million.

And yet, though the couple dazzled society at their parties, at the opera, or out on the town, behind the scenes it was not such a happy picture. Harold, dapper in his colorful shirts with contrasting collars, embroidered waistcoats, and Cartier cuff links and tie pins, was notoriously unfaithful. By 1913, after eighteen years of marriage, Edith was close to the breaking point and decided to check herself in for treatment of depression under a psychiatrist she had heard of over in Switzerland, a Dr. Carl Jung. Those months would turn into eight years, leaving her "rich playboy" husband, as the papers called him, plenty of time to enjoy himself with a beautiful Polish opera singer.

In reality, Ganna Walska was known less for her singing skills than her knack of choosing rich husbands (she married six times, amassing an estimated $125 million along the way). However, she wanted to sing onstage, and upon hearing that Harold McCormick had, in his wife's absence, taken over her position as head of the Chicago Opera Company, she made her move. It didn't take Harold long to fall for her charms. He even proposed. But, while he was in Switzerland asking Edith to sign the divorce papers, his fiancée married someone else. Alexander Smith Cochran, "the world's richest bachelor," showered his new bride with gifts (famously, his wedding present to her was "to go with carte blanche to Cartier and choose anything" she desired), but it was a troubled marriage, and within a year, Ganna was back with Harold.

Ganna's marriage to Harold McCormick would last nine years, from 1922 to 1931, during which time she would become one of Cartier's best clients. She shopped in all three branches (there were even pieces that were the result of a collaboration between branches), but most of her important Cartier pieces were made in Paris, where the quality of the craftsmanship was still considered superior to elsewhere. An enormous admirer of Louis' take on the oriental Art Deco style, she bought the Shinto mystery clock in 1923 and a chimera bangle in 1928. Over time, she also came to know the Cartiers personally, and was as likely to be a dinner guest of Pierre and Elma's in New York (in 1937, she would also be one of their guests as they celebrated the British coronation in London) as to be meeting Jacques and Nelly on the mountains in St. Moritz.

In Conversation with Jean-Jacques Cartier

Paris was definitely the jewel in the Cartier crown. You see, France had a long history of jewelry making, it was home to the best ateliers in the world. You couldn't just replicate that over one generation. New York was fine for the smaller items, but Uncle Pierre would often order the very high-end jewelry from Cartier Paris.

By the late 1920s, Pierre's U.S. multimillionaire client list was the envy of luxury houses all over the world; he'd seen off Dreicer, his biggest competitor; and through ingenious marketing techniques, he had turned Cartier from an unpronounceable French word into a household name across America. Not that everything was straight-forward. At the time, Cartier Inc. was fighting an expensive, ongoing legal battle in the Court of Appeals against U.S. Customs over the correct duty to be applied to unfinished platinum jewelry. Still, it was with excitement and a fair degree of understandable pride that Pierre invited his elder brother, Louis, over to New York in the winter of 1927. Though Jacques and Nelly had spent a good deal of time in America with him and Elma, it would be Louis' first trip to the States, and Pierre was eager to show him all he had achieved.

A FIELD OF GOLD

Louis and Jacqui boarded the RMS *Aquitania* ocean liner at the French port of Cherbourg on a frosty January morning in 1927. They had left two-year-old Claude at home in Budapest with the nanny, and the six-day journey in front of them promised to be a relaxing one. Longer and wider than many other liners, the *Aquitania* offered its first-class passengers luxurious lounges, smoking rooms, and private suites. It also had the distinct advantage, as part of the British-owned Cunard shipping line, of being allowed to serve alcohol (unlike the American-owned liners burdened by Prohibition laws). Every evening, Louis and Jacqui would descend the grand staircase in their dinner jackets, long dresses, and diamonds for cocktails. Dinner was served in the immaculate Mewes and Davis–designed dining room (the same firm that had designed the Ritz in Paris and London), and dancing would follow. The *Aquitania* was known for its Charleston-playing band, and Jacqui, still in her early thirties and a fan of the dance floor, was in her element. Louis, though, was impatient to arrive. Fifty-one years old and officially "retired" (at least on his U.S. immigration form), he was eager to experience firsthand the land his brothers had been describing to him for years.

Pierre and Elma were the perfect hosts. Louis and Jacqui stayed with them at 15 East Ninety-sixth Street and were the guests of honor at dinners and cocktail evenings. Louis was riveted by what he saw: the rise of the United States, the vast wealth it was creating, and the artistic possibilities that would flow from that. Always looking for inspiration, he traveled around the country visiting galleries and museums. In Paris, his vast library included books on the histories of Egypt, China, and Persia; now he was hungry to learn about the heritage of the American Indians and their native art.

All through his life, Louis had considered Paris to be the center of the artistic world, but now he saw that America was catching up. "America is destined to become the great international art center within the next 25 years," he announced to the press in March. "Almost all great art creations have flourished in a field of gold. That is what the United States is today." He noted how Spain in the sixteenth century, France in the seventeenth, and England in the eighteenth had witnessed the flourishing of art coinciding with their periods of national prosperity. "It is now America's great opportunity to produce through its painters, sculptors, poets, goldsmiths, or jeweler craftsmen." He talked too of America gaining prominence in the jewelry world, observing that the country "already holds a monopoly of the world's most precious stones and jewels" and predicting a rise in their value.

To escape the bitter New York winter, in March, Pierre and Elma whisked Louis and Jacqui down south to Palm Beach. They stayed at Everglades, played golf looking out to sea, wandered along Worth Avenue to review the new store fit-out, and took a cruise in the southern waters. If Louis had needed any further evidence of the growing prosperity in America, this was it. Palm Beach had originally been envisaged as an alternative Riviera, but it was fast leaving its European inspiration in the shade. When Pierre discussed expanding the New York business, Louis understood his rationale. Later that year, Pierre would buy the building next to the Fifth Avenue store, expanding Cartier's New York footprint by three thousand square feet.

When Louis and Jacqui returned to Europe, they sent Pierre and Elma a thank-you note on a headed card. Only it wasn't a traditional pen-on-paper note. It was a card of gold, with the script engraved in black enamel: "Thank you with all our hearts for your charming welcome, and our wonderful stay with you. With all our affection,

Louis and Jacqui." There was even a hinged gold envelope addressed to "Monsieur et Madame P. Cartier" in New York, complete with postmark and stamp. Though impressed, privately Pierre had hoped for more of a response from his brother after his first trip to America. With their father no longer around, he was eager for Louis' approval, and the gold thank-you note, though fabulously stylish, wasn't the acknowledgment he craved.

Wanting more feedback, Pierre asked his brother-in-law, Jacques Worth, if he'd caught up with Louis since he'd returned to Paris. Writing back, Worth had to admit he hadn't heard much, but he knew that "Louis had only the most complimentary words to say on you and your organization." Pierre's brother Jacques reassured him too, reminding him that Louis had never been much of a letter writer. Whereas the rest of the family corresponded regularly, Louis tended to limit himself to an occasional card, telegram, or short letter.

Most recently, it had been Nelly writing to Elma at length, concerned about Marion's health after hearing she had contracted scarlet fever. Thankfully, Elma was happy to report, Marion was fully recovered, although it had been worrying for a time, even leading to the closing of the smart Spence School for Girls. Now the topic du jour was her debutante party—she would be turning eighteen the following year. They had plans to host a large dinner-dance to present Marion and her best friend, Reine, the daughter of Paul Claudel, the writer and the new French ambassador to the United States.

As it turned out, the party, with its prestigious guest list, would be a defining moment for Pierre in America. "The success of Marion's debutante party adds a new testimony to the position that you have conquered in New York," Jacques would write after reading about it in the newspapers, "and to the friendships that Elma and Marion have attracted by their qualities of heart and mind." Pierre, as he told his younger brother, had been delighted that Marion had chosen to share her debutante party with Reine Claudel. Admiring her father, Pierre encouraged their friendship wholeheartedly. But even he didn't have any idea quite how closely the two families would be linked in the years to come.

7

PRECIOUS LONDON: LATE 1920s

A FLOURISH OF HOSPITALITY

The British capital was a hive of activity. "All of society seemed to be *en fête*," the Duke of Windsor would later recall of the postwar years, as "most of the great houses in London . . . opened their doors for a flourish of hospitality such as will never be seen again." There were extravagant formal dinners, "served on gold or silver plates by footmen in the family livery with knee breeches, white stockings, buckled shoes, and powdered hair," and dancing under the light of thousands of candles. It wasn't unusual to receive up to four invitations a night and quite acceptable to move from one to the next. And when the private parties had finished for the evening, there were the West End nightclubs, "an almost continuous ball from midnight until dawn," where American dances like the Charleston were embraced by a nation hungry for entertainment.

Against the backdrop of endless high-end socializing, within an era of extraordinary wealth creation, Jacques found himself in the right place at the right time. He had moved to England from America when the brothers had decided, several years after the First World War, that the New York Maison was established enough for Pierre to manage on his own and that the London Maison really needed a Car-

Milton Heath, Jacques and Nelly's home in the English countryside, near Dorking

tier in residence full-time. With Nelly and the children, he'd left Rye, Connecticut, for the English market town of Dorking and, since 1924, had been happily installed in Milton Heath, a large country house about forty minutes from London. Made for entertaining, the stately red brick mid-nineteenth-century home was inviting and elegant, with expansive reception rooms, extensive grounds, and wonderful views over the wooded Surrey hills.

Inside, where Jacques had taken over the decorating, everywhere there was evidence of his artistic eye and travels. Indian rugs covered the oak floors, Egyptian figures held up a marble fireplace, a Chinese commode housed trinkets, and Cartier frames held pictures of loved ones on the piano. And of course, a country estate required staff. There were eight servants' rooms and cottages for the chauffeur and the groom. Only when guests brought many servants (as the maharajas were prone to do) would Jacques and Nelly have to ask their neighbors, Mr. and Mrs. Rees, down the road if they wouldn't mind taking the overflow into their house.

Every morning, as his elder son took the horse and trap to school, Jacques would travel the thirty miles up to 175 New Bond Street in his chauffeur-driven Rolls-Royce. Cartier London was inundated with clients. Along with the loyal aristocrats and heiresses, such as the Guinness sisters, Lady Granard, or Lady Sackville (known to pop in to buy gifts for her daughter, the writer Vita Sackville-West, after their famously momentous rows), there was a new generation of "bright young things." Satirized in novels of the time, from Nancy Mitford's *Christmas Pudding* to Evelyn Waugh's *Vile Bodies,* this fast-living wealthy bohemian group would have expense accounts at Cartier and dance all night in diamonds. There were also a growing number of financiers, industrialists, and entrepreneurs riding a wave of growth. As their newfound riches bought them a seat at the elite table, they knew they must look the part, and Cartier was on hand to help. Captain Alfred Lowenstein, for instance, who made millions by investing in the electric power and artificial silk businesses when those industries were in their infancy, would keep Jacques "very busy" with nonstop commissions until his controversial death in 1928 (he was said to have opened the wrong door to the bathroom on his private plane and plunged into the Channel below).

As soon as a new client entered the showroom, with its "walls draped in rose-pink moiré" and "discreet touches of gilt," a salesman would leap to attention and beckon to a chair at his leather-topped table. Each client had a dedicated salesman, but when new clients walked through the door, it could become something of a scrum. Salesmen, after all, worked on commission. More clients generally meant more pay.

In Conversation with Jean-Jacques Cartier

My father had two head salesmen, and they couldn't have been more different. Foreman was very English, formal, quite stiff. Knew everything there was to know about court life and royal etiquette. And then there was Bellenger—well, he was a French charmer, a hit with the ladies. My father had met him before the First World War and had offered him a job even though Bellenger knew absolutely nothing about jewelry at the time. He was very loyal to my father after that. And they became more than colleagues, they were friends. But Foreman and Bellenger couldn't stand each other!

It was a salesman's job to make his client feel comfortable. Instead of describing the clarity, color, or cut of a diamond, he would talk about her world (or aspirational world), from the season at Deauville to Lady Cunard's latest charity event. *Tatler* was obligatory reading, for he must be up to date on all the latest social news. Sometimes, when the client was less known to Cartier, the presale banter was designed to allow the salesman's assistant time to slip off into a back room to make a phone call. In an era before tight bank privacy laws, his role was to check on the lady's financial standing at her bank (or her boyfriend's bank). As it was quite normal to pay in installments, Cartier had to be assured that their client not only had the funds for the initial outlay but would also be able to keep up with the payments.

It went without saying that the well-dressed lady talking to her salesman should never know of any such behind-the-scenes activity. She, like Cherry Poynter from *Harper's Bazaar,* came to Cartier to be immersed in a world of beauty and calm, and nothing should detract from her pleasure: "It is always a joy to me to wander about the lovely Cartier salons in which something of the hush of a cathedral reigns and to see the respectful yet familiar way in which thousands of pounds' worth of pearls, emeralds, and diamonds are passed from hand to hand. Mr. Cartier knows each jewel and his memory is prodigious." In a nod to peaceful places of worship, Jacques had even selected the same wood paneling for the ceiling of the gallery that he had spotted in a Spanish monastery. Upstairs, though, it was a different scene entirely.

SPECKS THROUGH A BEAM OF SUNLIGHT

The workshop was the true place of worship for Jacques. Until the early 1920s, Cartier London had relied on Paris for its stock. The setup had worked well enough for a time, but as demand increased, Jacques proposed opening a significant in-house workshop above the New Bond Street store, and his brothers had agreed. Félix Bertrand, a talented jeweler (and musician) who had proved his skills setting up the American Art Works workshop under Pierre, was sent over to do the same in London. Notwithstanding his penchant for French wine at lunchtime ("the water curdles my stomach!"), he was a huge asset to the English company. Under his leadership, and that of a fellow Frenchman, Georges Finsterwald, a team of skilled mounters, setters, and polishers were hired.

Of course, building a fine jewelry workshop didn't happen overnight. Especially when one wanted to be the best. Jacques sought to hire top master craftsmen, at considerable expense, and then relied on them to teach the young apprentices. The firm took on about five or six apprentices a year, mainly Englishmen (Jacques felt strongly it was his duty to offer opportunities to the English workforce), of which only one or two made it through the first year of a six-year traineeship. Those who didn't make the cut soon discovered it was easy to find another job after having learned their trade at Cartier. Their training at English Art Works, as the 175 New Bond Street workshop was called, was increasingly recognized as among the very best in the industry.

Up on the very top floor was the design studio. This was one of Jacques' favorite places. An artist himself, he enjoyed being involved in the creative process and got along particularly well with the team of designers, who respected him for his love of their trade. He was, one of them recalled, "excitable, kind, and he lived for design." It was a jovial place to work and there was a sense of camaraderie among those in their white painting overalls who had made it up to the skylights of Cartier looking down onto New Bond Street below. But it wasn't without its stressful moments. On one occasion Jacques rushed upstairs to let the team know a particularly important maharaja client was in town. The Indian ruler had requested a design for a necklace by the end of that afternoon. Usually there would be one designer per design, but it had to be all hands on deck that time. Four senior designers frantically worked together—sketching, measuring, painting—to finish the small, perfect work of art.

Another time, it was a young apprentice, James Gardner, who had a trying day. He'd been working on designs alongside several trays of assorted diamonds. This wasn't unusual; it often helped the designer to conceive of the finished jewel with the actual gems in front of him or her (Jacques was unusual among his brothers in hiring a female designer, the very chic and nonchalant Ms. Winter). It was the role of Georges Finsterwald, the workshop manager, to sign out and back in again all gems that left his safe bound for the design department each day. A tried and tested system, it generally worked well, but not, as he would soon discover, every time. It had been a hot day, and Gardner, still working away in the stuffy top room during his lunch hour, had wanted some air. Standing on his desk to open the skylight, he pushed and pushed . . . until the jammed window suddenly crashed down into the room. In the blink of an eye, there not only were fragments of windowpane everywhere, but the trays of diamonds that had been sitting orderly on the desk were also catapulted into the air: "hundreds of specks sparkling as they filtered through a beam of sunlight."

If the diamonds had been large ones, they could perhaps have been spotted in the surrounding mess of broken glass. Alas, the task in front of Gardner was far harder. The young designer had been working with small rectangular-cut diamond "batons" and even smaller "mêlée" diamonds (which are so small they need to be weighed in bulk), both of which exactly resembled shattered glass. He thought for a long moment and came up with a plan. With everyone else still out to lunch, he locked the door to the department and stripped: Off came the shoes, the jacket, the waistcoat, the trousers and suspenders, the bow tie and the crisp shirt with the starched collar. Even the socks. Everything had to be shaken out to remove all trace of stray "sparklers" (both diamond and glass) that had made their way onto and into his clothes. Still undressed, he turned his attention to the surfaces all around him, meticulously wiping down each one in turn. Only then did he get dressed again, open the door, and call in the team to help him separate the diamonds from the glass.

The moment of truth came when the manager weighed out the retrieved diamonds. As Gardner had feared, they were well under weight. Fortunately, English Art Works was akin to a family—they looked out for each other. Giving the terrified Gardner a conspiratorial wink, the workshop manager opened the safe and withdrew a secret jewel supply he had put aside for emergencies. The loss was made up without anyone else's being the wiser, and Finsterwald simply told Gardner never to make the same mistake again.

KING TUT

For the first time in his working life, Jacques didn't have to depend on his brothers to oversee work from Paris or New York, and he loved the freedom that the London workshop gave him. He could pluck an ancient Egyptian faïence from an Eastern bazaar or a London antiques shop knowing exactly how he wanted to mount it as an

Art Deco brooch, and be confident that he had a team skilled enough to complete the work just as he envisioned it.

Ever since Jacques' first visit to Egypt in 1911 he'd been intrigued by the country and its remarkable history. So when the Egyptologist Howard Carter announced to the world in 1922 that he'd unearthed an opening to Tutankhamen's tomb, and with it the truths and artistic treasures of a long-shuttered mysterious past, Jacques was captivated. After 3,500 years, discovered deep within Egypt's Valley of the Kings were clues to a distant era. As photographs and articles made their way to the West, Jacques carefully cut them out of newspapers and folded them into his small black leather diary. Not many things made it into that diary, or stayed there for the remaining decades of his life, but this momentous discovery had revealed works of art on "a plane of excellence probably higher than has been reached in any subsequent period of the world." It was a humbling reminder of one's place in time, something of which the youngest Cartier brother was acutely conscious.

Jacques wasn't the only one inspired. Egyptomania swept Paris, London, and New York. After the deprivations of war, escapism was more welcome than ever, and ancient Egypt was suddenly all anyone could talk about. Fashion designers found inspiration in motifs like lotus patterns, the vibrant colors of Egyptian paintings, and the long, draped, and sometimes beaded garments in ancient depictions. Women heaped on the black eyeliner and put their hair up to more closely resemble the glamorous beauties of the past. Bright cocktails with names like King Tut became the drinks du jour (albeit secretly in Prohibition America) and Egyptian-themed parties were all the rage.

Theater performances of *Cleopatra* swept the West. In London, Jacques saw one with Nelly at Daly's Theatre and was so impressed with the lead actress, Miss Evelyn Laye, that "it occurred to him that she was worthy of the jewelry actually worn by Cleopatra," so the papers reported, "and as he possessed some, he decided to lend it to her for one evening." The jewels, estimated at $150,000 ($2.2 million today), were later delivered to the theater by a detective for the special performance and taken away afterward by an armed security guard. And while Miss Laye may have been the envy of all the ladies in the audience in Cleopatra's jewels, she wasn't the only one afforded the opportunity to wear genuine ancient Egyptian pieces. Cartier was creating a very special collection.

JEWELRY SPOTLIGHT:
EGYPTIAN-THEMED JEWELS

*Miss Evelyn Laye as Cleopatra in the
1925 London theater performance
attended by Jacques and Nelly.*

"Women interested in Egyptology, who desire to be in the Tutankhamen fashion, can
now wear real ancient gems in modern settings as personal ornaments," announced
The Illustrated London News in January
1924, alongside a full-page spread of Car-
tier London's Egyptian creations. These one-of-a-kind pieces
incorporated genuine antique treasures, sourced by the
Cartier brothers from European antiques shops and Eastern
bazaars.

The challenge was keeping the purity of the ancient style
while updating it for a modern audience. This wasn't to be a
whimsical attempt to follow the fashions of the day, it was
deeply rooted in authenticity. For a deep blue bead from 900
B.C., Jacques chose to enhance its color with the smallest
amount of diamond and onyx on its top and base, and to make
it into a simple pendant. A 600 B.C. figure of Isis and child was
set as a hatpin, practical yet not detracting from the original.
A sacred ram in a bright blue crescent-shaped glazed faïence
was brought into focus with a subtle border of diamonds and
onyx, and three-thousand-year-old stone carvings were
framed in black onyx. The focus was on a simple dressing up—
nothing fanciful. It had to be true to the original style and stay
classic. These were ancient artifacts that had survived thousands of years—they should not be turned into elaborate
pieces that might soon go out of fashion.

Louis and Jacques poured their energies into further understanding ancient Egypt, and their diverse illustrated libraries included tomes like the huge color edition of *The Book of
the Dead*. The combination of antique objects, intense his-

torical study, and skilled craftsmanship would result in some of the most rarefied of Cartier's jewels from the period. (Today, it is not unusual to see a single Egyptian-revival brooch reach over $1 million at auction.) Unsurprisingly, they were a hit with the stylish customers of the 1920s. They tapped into the excitement, bordering on obsession, for the exotic, and each one (the brothers limited their output to around 150) was entirely unique.

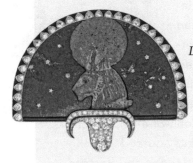

Designed as an Egyptian fan, this c. 1923 Cartier London brooch incorporates an ancient Egyptian green glazed faïence of the goddess Sekhmet, set against a lapis lazuli sky twinkling with diamond stars.

One client was so entranced she bought several pieces. At more than six feet tall, the beautiful, blond Iya Abdy was quite a presence as she flitted between Paris and London in the interwar period. A member of the Russian nobility, she and her family had been forced to flee their country during the revolution, and she later married an English baronet. Though the union lasted only five years, her husband, a wealthy shipowner and part-time art dealer known for his exquisite taste, brought impressive funds and contacts into his twenty-six-year-old bride's life. Iya became a model, tried her hand at acting, wore fantastically imaginative costumes, and counted Chanel and Cocteau among her close friends. An object of fascination, she was photographed by everyone from Man Ray to Cecil Beaton and in the December 1928 edition of *Vogue* appeared wearing one of her Egyptian brooches. "A Jewel Song from Paris," the caption read. "The Wearing of the Gem is an Ancient Art to which the Parisienne Brings Modern Interpretations." This idea of "ancient art" being shown in a modern light is what the Cartiers had set out to achieve.

Capable of coming up with unique ideas and able to follow them through without compromising on quality, Jacques was making a name for himself in London. His creations were the talk of the dinner party circuit up in town and in manor houses across the country. And it wouldn't be long before he became the jeweler of choice for one of the most important clients of the decade, a lady who loved gems so much that she changed her name to Emerald.

PAINTED KNEES

Lady Cunard was, according to *The Times*, "probably the most lavish hostess of her day." Born Maud Burke in San Francisco, she had hoped to marry the grandson of the last prince of Poland. After he jilted her, she settled for an English lord, Sir Bache Cunard, the grandson of the founder of the Cunard shipping line. Twenty years her senior and with a preference for a quiet life in the English countryside, Sir Bache wasn't perhaps the most obvious match for the outrageously outspoken American Maud. But he did have a handy fortune.

By 1911, Lady Cunard had moved to London with their neglected daughter Nancy in tow. It was here that she came into her own. Her gatherings were known for being crammed with everyone from the Prince of Wales and good friend Robert Abdy (along with his Egyptian-brooch-wearing wife) to lowly musicians and unknown writers: "indeed anybody so long as they were interesting." With an impressive knowledge and admiration of the arts, from French literature to German opera, Lady Cunard had a soft spot for creative types. There was even a rumor that the author George Moore was her daughter's father.

After separating from her husband, Lady Cunard fell for the conductor Thomas Beecham. Years later, Beecham would break her heart by marrying someone else in America, but while they were together in London, Lady Cunard was a huge supporter of his musical ventures. Not put off by the vocal disapproval of notable others (including the opera diva Nellie Melba), she tirelessly organized events to help Beecham out, regularly calling on friends and acquaintances to contribute to her worthy cause.

On one occasion, it was Jacques' turn to be prevailed upon. As Lady Cunard explained over lunch at Brown's Hotel in Mayfair, she was planning a December fashion show for Beecham's charity, the Imperial League of Opera. She already had the fashion houses Worth and Callot Sœurs on board, and the Parisian society hairdresser Émile. She just needed the jewels. Jacques didn't need long to make up his mind. One of the joys of being head of the London branch and having a workshop he knew he could rely on was not having to run every decision past his brothers. He accepted with pleasure. Not only was it for a good cause, but it would give him the chance to showcase his newest ideas in front of some of the best clients in London. "The idea," Jacques explained to Pierre, "was to show what women with short hair can wear, both now and when they start to grow their hair again."

Setting his team to work, Jacques proposed that his designers come up with ideas for bejeweled hair clips and modern headdresses. The prewar days of big hair up-dos (and tiaras that sat on top of the head) had been superseded by shorter haircuts that called for a change in accessories. Throughout the decade, Cartier London would produce a vast array of bandeaux designed to sit on the forehead, from simple diamond and platinum geometric bands to those with a splash of color: deepest red from Burmese rubies perhaps or a splash of sapphire blue.

Always stretching himself and his team, always thinking in terms of new design possibilities, Jacques came up with more unusual suggestions too, like the idea to combine bracelets to create a band for the hair. The Duke of York (later King George VI) would like this idea enough to buy one for his wife: five Art Deco bracelets, each one featuring a different gemstone (one with sapphires, one with emeralds, one with rubies, and two with diamonds), and a frame to convert any three of them to a bandeau. One particularly vibrant bandeau that could be broken into two separate bracelets was made from carved sapphires, rubies, and emeralds from India. An early example of Cartier's Tutti Frutti style, it was showstopping enough to be sold even before the fashion show. The buyer was the stylish and well-connected Lady Mountbatten, who would later, rather aptly given her choice of headdress, go on to become Vicereine of India.

When it came to novel ideas, Jacques didn't stop at the jewels. He also had an idea for how to make Lady Cunard's whole fashion show more memorable. He suggested that his designers might take their artistic talents to the models' knees, a part of the body that was considered risqué in 1920s polite society. Proposing that the models' stockings should be rolled down to just below the knee, his thought was then to decorate the knees with miniature paintings, which would be only half, tantalizingly, visible as the model swished down the catwalk in her slit skirt. One young Cartier designer, rather overexcited by the opportunity to be so close to a beautiful model, recalled offering his services to Jacques, only to find his brilliant idea wasn't without its challenges: "I took a deep breath, then, heady with the perfume vaporized by the warmth of her body, experimentally stroked her kneecap with a trembling thumb—to discover [that] the flesh on a goddess's knee joint puckers with a cobweb of tiny creases, then stretches taut, like any other." Taking his time, he got there in the end, and the resulting *Windsor Castle from the River* and *Arundel* miniature knee paintings were enough to propel Cartier's name into the dinner party gossip circuit that month.

Jacques didn't do things by half and the fashion show ended up being an enormous undertaking. He wrote to Pierre to update him on all the work that had gone into it: "In six weeks, the London workshop had executed, and executed well, a hundred items." The press, fortunately, was suitably impressed. *Tatler,* in a column about fashion, had to admit that "the jewels, introduced with the utmost discretion, seemed to cast a shadow over the triumphs of the dressmaker's art."

Like Louis, who had wanted his creations to be seen alongside haute couture in the recent 1925 Exposition, Jacques relished the opportunity to show his pieces as a living reality. Hoping that those watching the fashion show might be inspired to see the jewels in a new light, he played around with their placement on the mannequins. A leaf-shaped diamond brooch that one might have expected to dress up an evening gown appeared on a daytime black and yellow scarf; a square diamond watch "innocent of any bracelet" dressed up the sleeve of a Worth "black jumper frock"; and "in the chic little black beret gleamed a magnificent diamond brooch." For those without hats or bandeaux, "the hair ornaments, circles or crescents, were cleverly arranged on the tightly shingled heads." And there were wonderful creations making use of the many colored gemstones Jacques had sourced from the East. A "marvelous" ruby necklace was shown to best advantage against a gray satin dress by Callot and enhanced with "magnificent brooches in rubies and diamonds on the shoulder and on the hat." Emerald brooches were also a big theme, "and much interest was aroused in the fobs of emeralds with diamond surrounds; they appeared sometimes at the back and sometimes in front of the left shoulder."

In Conversation with Jean-Jacques Cartier

My father always insisted on using the highest-quality gemstones. He and his brothers operated on the belief that though the resulting piece might be expensive, if it was of good quality and lasted for generations, then the high price was soon forgotten. It was worth focusing on the best.

The press reports on the exhibition were better than Jacques could have hoped, with some critics even crediting him for starting new trends: "Diamond clip brooches on the shoulder were an effective new fashion," *The Sketch* announced in a column on "Woman's Ways," and "several evening dresses had these flashing diamond buckles on one side with a pendant to match suspended from a diamond chain." There was an unexpected bonus from all the publicity, too. "Mauboussin has opened opposite Boucheron on Burlington Gardens but I don't think it will do us much damage," Jacques reported to Pierre. "Luckily our exhibition at the Mayfair Hotel for the Opera Legion took place three days after his opening and totally eclipsed him." It was one of the few mentions of rivals that Jacques made in his letters. Though aware of the competition, the brothers did not tend to dwell on it. Their focus was on keeping ahead through innovation rather than looking over their shoulder at their peers, always following that same motto: "Never copy, only create."

From Lady Cunard's perspective, the fashion show was a great success, attracting publicity for her cause and raising £500 ($38,000 today) over two separate performances. Her loyalty to Jacques was assured. Through the 1920s and '30s, she would become one of Cartier London's best clients and a devoted patron. Jacques found he had a meeting with her almost every other week: In 1929 alone, there were more than forty orders to her account. Sometimes it was simply for repairs or to convert outdated pieces into something more à la mode, such as a vanity case into a stylish cigarette case. But she had a passion for gems, and she didn't hold back on buying showstopper pieces when the mood took her. As England-based clients during the 1920s went, she was hard to beat. But not impossible. There were several others over in India giving her a run for her money.

EASTERN ADVENTURES

In the autumn of 1926, Jacques boarded the large SS *Kashima Maru* bound for the East from the port of Marseilles. He took cases of heavily insured little red boxes to sell, and the details of clients and dealers dotted around both Ceylon and India. Knowing full well from his previous trip that life in the hot Indian subcontinent danced to a different tune, and that one meeting could very easily turn into several days of waiting around, Jacques had no detailed schedule in his diary. He would take each day as it came. Though there were a few specific tasks he wanted to accomplish (such as selling a particularly important necklace and tracking down high-quality Ceylon sapphires for a client in London), beyond that, he was open to whatever opportunities the three-month voyage might turn up.

In 1911, he'd made the same trip as a twenty-eight-year-old. Now, fifteen years and four children later, he was traveling with his wife, a great fan of overseas explorations. Jacques called Nelly's constant need to travel the "*va va*" (the go go). When he was working in London, she would often head off to far-flung lands with her great friend from school days, Madame Fournier. "*Raconte-moi ton aventures*" (tell me your adventures), Jacques used to say when she returned, as he settled down into his favorite armchair by the fireplace. This time, with Jacques heading east anyway and the children old enough to be left with the nanny, the couple could travel together.

Life on board was the first adventure. First-class travel was all very well, but there was no relief from the humid heat that turned cabins into saunas. Forced to sleep up on deck just to get some air, Jacques spent restless nights filled with vivid dreams: "Last night I dreamed I saw Father," he wrote in his diary on October 15, the first anniversary of his father's death. Above all though, it was the sameness of each day on board that was the hardest part of the three-week journey for a couple used to a varied and spontaneous life, with Jacques surprised at how all the passengers seemed to act as if life were under rule and regulation. "They bathe and dress for breakfast at 8 o'clock. They walk or play deck games until ten, then read or write in their deck chairs until near luncheon time, when they go to the bar for a drink or cocktail. The lunch is at 12:30. From one till three it is siesta time. . . . From three to six, exercise again, then bathe and dress. Dinner at 7, then some dance, most play cards."

The couple traveled with a small group of staff. After Jacques' first trip to India, he had promised himself that he would never again travel without his Rolls-Royce and Orr, his chauffeur. Nelly, with her eighteen suitcases, needed her personal maid, and because Jacques suffered from less than perfect health, they had also taken along the trusted Doctor Bonard. After eighteen long, repetitive days on board, the little entourage from the green verdant hills of Surrey finally spied their first destination in the distance. It was not the vast country of the maharajas but Ceylon, just south of India and home to some of the best sapphires in the world.

A HUNDRED BASKETS FOR ONE STONE

Jacques loved sapphires. Though it was hard to beat a perfect Burmese ruby or a vivid carved Mughal emerald, sapphires were his birthstone and he felt an affinity with them. The one jewel he wore constantly (apart from his wedding ring) was a simple platinum and cabochon sapphire ring on his little finger. So while Nelly settled into their sea-view suite at the Galle Face Hotel, he immediately set off into the wondrously busy, noisy, and vibrant capital city of Colombo, to look for them.

Though most of the best sapphires mined here would generally end up in India, where they would be cut, polished, and sold to international dealers, Jacques hoped to intercept some before they left their original home. Meeting with the local gemstone dealer Macan Mackar in his small, stuffy shop under the Grand Oriental Hotel opposite the main Colombo port, he was disappointed by the large markup: "Of precious stones I have found the prices high, and was confirmed in my opinion that the Indian jewelers can sell their goods dearer than we can obtain them for in Europe." Still, there were a few that seemed more reasonably priced than others. Wanting to remain on good terms with Mackar (who was also something of a local entrepreneur-tycoon), he bought a dozen or so that he envisioned making into buttons and a bracelet. In his diary, he sketched the pieces that interested him and wrote their prices in the Cartier code.

In Conversation with Jean-Jacques Cartier

I'll explain to you that code in my father's diary. We had a secret way of writing down prices, you see. It's not a secret anymore, I've even seen it in books. But back then it was top secret! The code word was CONFI-TURES. That always amused me, applying the French word for jam to jewels! Each letter was a number, you see. C was 1, O was 2, N was 3, and so on. And the letter K meant a repetition. So there in the diary, you see, the sapphire costs OI,SKS—well, that would have meant 25,000.

Most exciting of all in Mackar's little room was an enormous rectangular sapphire of around 350 carats. Not only was it one of the largest sapphires Jacques had ever seen, it was also of "very good color" and "pure" (free of the inclusions that detract from a gemstone's clarity). Mackar proposed a sale price of £25,000 ($1.8 million today). Jacques thought he could probably sell it on to a client in London for around £50,000, making a 100 percent profit. But it was a risk: £25,000 was a large outlay for a stone that might not sell quickly. He asked Mackar to hold on to it for him until the end of the season, by which time he would have had the chance to cable the London office and hopefully hear back from his client.

Eighty-eight years later, a large rectangular Ceylon sapphire of remarkably similar characteristics would resurface at a Christie's auction. Known as the Blue Belle of Asia and said to be the fourth-largest faceted blue sapphire in the world, it made headlines for being one of the most prestigious colored gems to come to market for many years. And then it made headlines again once the hammer came down—selling for $17.2 million in 2014, said to be a world record price for any sapphire sold at auction.

Back in the sticky heat of 1926 Colombo, Jacques asked the dealer another favor: He wanted to see the source of such a fantastic gemstone. Mackar agreed to take him the fifty-six miles southeast of Colombo to Ratnapura, the City of Gems, just as soon as the sapphire pits had dried out (recent rains had submerged them). A couple of days later, dressed smartly for their field trip in bow ties, blazers, and hats (a fez for Mackar, a pith helmet for Jacques), the men left the capital city early in the morning by car. Passing riverbeds on the way, Mackar pointed out the natives in turbans and loincloths knee-deep in the river shaking large round sieves and desperately looking for any glint of blue among the grainy brown pebbles. Intrigued, Jacques asked to stop and talk to the men to ask how much success they had finding sapphires that way. Not a lot, as it turned out. They showed him a few small gemstones but no good ones. It was the pits in Ratnapura that held the real treasure.

Pulling up at what looked like nothing more than a swampy paddy field, Mackar led Jacques over the mud on foot. They passed several mined pits before arriving at the newest one, essentially a ten-foot-deep hole, well timbered to prevent landslides. Two men at the bottom filled up alternate buckets with muddy, grainy earth, which were then hauled up on a pulley system, deposited in a large pile, and washed through sieves once a week. It was long, arduous work, and more often than not without reward. "They say that it takes a hundred baskets to get one stone," Jacques wrote back to his brothers in

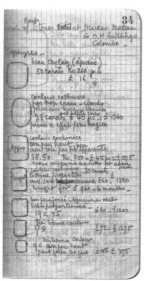

Jacques' visits to the East were filled with trips to gem dealers. This photograph
(left) was likely taken at Kanjimull Jewelers, Old Delhi, with the jeweler,
Mr. Kanjimull, seated second from right, front row. The image on the right
shows a typical page from Jacques' travel diary, filled with life-sized sketches
and descriptions of the gems he had bought or was considering purchasing
(in this case, sapphires in Ceylon).

surprise, "and of course there are lots of useless ones." Asking to see
some examples of what they had found, Jacques tried to buy a large
piece that he thought might be able to be cut as a star sapphire. As
was often the case, he was told it was not being sold on its own. It
formed part of a larger lot of sixty, mostly worthless, stones. He
bought them all, more for posterity than anything else.

Later, back in his smart Mayfair showroom, surrounded by clients eager for the next status-enhancing jewel, those imperfect little
sapphires would serve as a grounding reminder of the reality of gemstones. They may have ended up in a queen's tiara or on the décolleté
of some bright young thing, but they came from humble origins,
deep within the muddy earth. For now, though, they simply went
into Jacques' bag. He had a long trip ahead of him. After an evening
in the comfort of the Galle Face Hotel, Jacques and Nelly set off
again. They planned to drive north, past the cool air of Nuwara
Eliya and onward to the boat at Talaimannar that would take them
to India.

RAFTS, MONKEYS, AND PANTHER SHOOTS

The crossing to India was a rough one. The ferry, "simply like the Newhaven Dieppe boat, only smaller and topheavy," took them to Dhanushkodi, and from there they took the train to Madurai. "I got angry with the stationmaster who hadn't reserved as he was asked and we had to pile into a single compartment," an exasperated Nelly wrote to her children, "and what with 4 huge sleeping bags and 12 suitcases! And do you know who came to beg? Monkeys! quantities, swarms of them, all sizes and even some rascals would come right in by the windows."

Though Jacques and Nelly had the Rolls-Royce, trains were often the most efficient mode of transport. And on the occasions when they opted for the chauffeur-driven car, the experience was a far cry from any European road trip they'd ever taken. When the large silver Rolls encountered a stream unexpectedly blocking their road, rafts had to be made for the automobile. On another trip the salesman Clifford North took through mountainous terrain in Nepal, the locals would even go one further by literally disassembling the cars into their individual components and carrying the seats, wheels, doors, steering wheel, engine, and all separately over the mountains! The cars would then be reassembled once they reached the other side.

Places to spend the night were another unknown, especially as Jacques and Nelly usually didn't know where they were headed until a few days before. "You see we must move, not as the spirit guides us, but as JC's business plans develop," Nelly wrote to the nanny looking after her children back home. In the larger cities they booked themselves at the best hotels—Taj in Bombay (Mumbai), Maiden's in Delhi—but long distances between locations also meant stops in small rural areas: "We were again put up at the station house, which is the most primitive yet. Just whitewashed walls, 2 chairs, a dresser, and pegs to hang your clothes. As for beds?? Heavens preserve you! 4 steel feet and a frame that holds up a spring, which isn't a spring, only cords across a thin coco matting, so I simply couldn't lie on it, but got out our beds—and then only slept just 4 hours!"

By the time they arrived at the palace of Nawanagar, where Jacques hoped to sell a particularly magnificent necklace he had brought over from London, Nelly was beyond thrilled. "Dear Chicks all," she wrote to her children excitedly, "this is to show you we are honest to goodness in a palace of the Maharaja of Jamnagar, and His Highness certainly is a wonder as a host! . . . I hardly know how to begin to describe the luxury we live in. Indeed, what with one Rolls at our disposal and the suite in this palace built for the Prince of Wales's visit (which he never came to see and hurt most frightfully His Highness as you can imagine)." Invited to spend Christmas 1926 with the Maharaja, Jacques and Nelly would write home about the splendid celebrations, from a large banquet (although "no crackers or mince pies [to] make it a real Christmas atmosphere") to a "very very thrilling" panther shoot.

UNEQUALED EMERALDS

Of all his Indian clients, Jacques was closest to the Maharaja of Nawanagar. Sir Ranjitsinhji Vibhaji II, or Ranji, as he was known, had been educated at Eton and Cambridge and was famous in England for his world-class cricket skills. Within India, meanwhile, Ranji was respected as a progressive ruler and statesman. Having represented the Indian States at the League of Nations Assembly in 1920, he would go on to become a part of the first Round Table Conference (conceived in 1930 to consider constitutional reforms in India).

Over the time Ranji knew Jacques, he became not only one of his best clients but a good friend as well. Jacques described the link between himself and the Maharaja as "a business connection which became a friendship." The Maharaja had a house in England, but Jacques and Nelly would always offer to host him at Milton Heath. Occasionally he would take them up on the offer, turning up with an entourage of Indian staff in tow. He almost became part of the family. Jacques and Nelly taught their children to treat him with great respect, but to them he always seemed more an older-uncle-type figure (he was twelve years older than Jacques) than a prince. Blissful family summer holidays were spent at Ranji's Irish castle in Ballynahinch, where the Cartier children were allowed to roam free over the staggeringly beautiful seven-hundred-acre estate. A lover of fly-fishing,

the Maharaja had wanted a vacation home that allowed him to indulge his passion (he owned the entire Ballynahinch fishery).

In Conversation with Jean-Jacques Cartier

*Those holidays on Ranji's Irish estate were wonderful.
One time, my mother was rushing us all to the train at
the end of a holiday and Ranji told us there was no
need to rush—he would send word to the stationmaster to hold the train until we were all ready. I must have
been about eight years old at the time and had never
heard of a train waiting for anyone. Ranji certainly
went up in my estimation then!*

Jacques described Ranji as "a Prince really princely in his taste as
well as by the qualities of his mind and heart." At the root of the
men's close friendship was their shared love of gemstones. The stylish
Indian ruler would happily wait decades for the most perfectly deep-
red ruby or vivid green emerald. It didn't have to be huge and showstopping; he was far more interested in the quality and innate beauty
of the jewel than in making a statement. Like a true collector, he
would admire his gems even when alone, holding them in his hands
and studying them under different lights just for the pleasure of it.

Emeralds were a gemstone both men particularly admired. Within
India, they were in good company. In 1926, the Maharaja of Kapurthala, an ardent Francophile known for his excellent taste, commissioned Cartier Paris to make an emerald turban ornament for his
golden jubilee the following year. The resulting pagoda-style headdress, comprising fifteen large emeralds from his own collection (including a phenomenal 177.4-carat hexagonal emerald that formed
the centerpiece), elicited widespread admiration when he wore it in
front of hundreds of international guests at the opulent celebrations
in his Versailles-inspired palace in the Punjab. It was, the Maharaja
wrote in his diary, "a piece truly unique of its kind," and an image of
it was later used by Cartier in a 1931 advertisement.

Large emeralds of high quality are extremely rare. Incredibly fragile, the emerald crystal almost never survives the underground pressures of its creation to come up flawless and clear. Ranji dedicated many years of his life to collecting perfect specimens. He wasn't the wealthiest of the maharajas, but he was focused on his very specific task. And he succeeded, so Jacques would later assert, in assembling an emerald collection that was "unequaled in the world, if not in quantity, then certainly in quality."

Knowing of Ranji's love of emeralds, Jacques had the idea to create an exceptional necklace that he hoped the Indian leader might see fit to add to his collection. Contacting the world's best gem dealers, he tracked down some of the most fantastic emeralds on the market. Each one on its own was a collector's piece; together they were extraordinary. When he had more than a dozen, he asked that his designers work on ideas for a necklace incorporating as many as they saw fit, with the stipulation that the final creation should enhance each one without being overly showy or ostentatious. Ranji had excellent taste; if Jacques wanted the Maharaja to add this jewel to his collection, it must remain elegant.

It was a hugely important piece for Jacques and, unnervingly, not without its risks. The act of mounting large, fragile emeralds by fallible human hand was fraught with difficulties. The craftsman selected for the task had to apply exactly the right amount of pressure to each platinum claw that would hold the gemstones in place. Too much pressure and the emerald might well break; too little and any subsequent movement of the emerald might start a cleavage flaw. For such an intense task, Jacques would give the chosen craftsman two days off work before beginning the job to ensure he was totally relaxed. Fortunately, in the case of the Emerald Collection necklace, it had gone well.

Under Jacques' instruction, English Art Works had completed the necklace in time for his 1926 India trip. Throughout the journey east, Jacques had hoped he would find a buyer. In Bombay, he had put on an exhibition at the house of his good Parsi clients, the Dinshaw-Petits, but though the necklace had been much admired, it had failed to attract serious inquiries and Jacques had begun to wonder if his whole project had been in vain. But when he arrived in Nawanagar and slowly opened the red box containing the necklace, under the bright Indian sun, Ranji had been transfixed.

The price was £115,640 ($8.4 million today). Not able to afford the full amount immediately but desperately wanting the necklace, Ranji had offered to pay in two installments and to give Jacques a collection of pearls worth £45,000 ($3.3 million) as partial payment. The deal was done. Hugely relieved, Jacques telegraphed Fraser in the London office and his brothers to let them know that one of the most important missions of his trip had been accomplished. Pierre wanted more details. Not able to get hold of Jacques in India, he telegraphed Fraser: "I understand my brother has sold large emerald necklace in India STOP Please cable cost and sale price and terms of payment granted by my brother also name of purchaser."

Jacques may have managed Cartier London, but he owned just 5 percent of it. Pierre and Louis, meanwhile, owned 91 percent between them, making them particularly interested in how Jacques fared. When Pierre had heard about Jacques' idea to make such an expensive necklace, he had worried that his younger brother had been swayed more by his passion for gemstones and love of design than the realistic likelihood of finding a buyer. Once a buyer had been found, he feared his brother had not demanded a high enough profit. Fraser reported back that the sale had made a not insubstantial £40,000 ($2.9 million today).

The 54 percent markup on the cost price may not have been as much as Pierre himself would have charged, but Jacques understood his client, and he understood how to do business in India. Captivated with his friend's creation, Ranji would, in just a couple of years' time, go on to give Jacques the most important commission of his life.

In Conversation with Jean-Jacques Cartier

My father loved dealing with Ranji because he shared his love and knowledge of gemstones. But it wasn't always so easy in India. Some clients would ask my father to reset lesser-quality jewels that he knew would look better in their original settings. That put him in a difficult situation.

KILLER STONES

Sometimes, when Jacques was asked by clients he met in India to remount their family heirlooms in the Cartier style, he had to politely refuse. One Indian method of mounting involved placing the gemstones on a colored foil background to enhance their color. A ruby would be placed on a red foil, a sapphire on a blue, an emerald on a green, and so on. Though this had the beneficial effect of producing a gloriously vibrant end result, if the foils were to be removed, the gemstones would be revealed in their true colors. If they were then to be remounted using the Cartier method (not only without any foil but with maximum light behind the gemstones), Jacques knew their owners would be disappointed with how insipid the end result would appear. And yet when he tried to explain this to his clients, he was generally met with objections. They were the clients, he was reminded; *he* was a humble shopkeeper. He should do as they asked.

Refusing requests like this from Parsi clients in Bombay initially hurt Jacques' reputation. But after those same clients went to other jewelers (who did as they had requested, happy to pocket the large commission), they came back to him. He had been right, they admitted, and they were loyal to him after that, inviting him into their homes to see their family heirlooms.

For all the washed-out Indian gemstones brought to life with colored foil, there was, for those on the inside, a treasure trove of wonderful, bright, flawless gems lurking in the East. Never knowing where he might be shown gemstones for sale—it might be after dinner on a candlelit table, or in the shade of a market bazaar—Jacques would always travel with a pouch containing his trusty "killer stones." These were the most perfect examples of precious stones that he owned: a Burmese ruby, a Kashmir sapphire, a Colombian emerald, and a Golconda diamond. Color is a subjective matter; it changes depending on the time of day, different regions of the world, and whether it is viewed in natural or artificial light. Sometimes a dealer might reveal his gemstones under "the wonderful Indian sunlight" that Jacques so adored, but other times he might insist that they remain in a room with no windows for security reasons. Jacques' killer stones gave him the tools to look at gemstones in any situation, offering the perfect comparison to spot fakes and recognize quality.

With a few select trusted dealers, Jacques didn't need to worry about quality. By the 1920s, Imre Schwaiger, who had helped Jacques during the 1911 Durbar, had become Cartier's most important contact in India. He knew his clients' taste and was well connected enough to source pieces that Jacques, based in England for most of the year, would never have been able to find for himself. Toward the end of 1926, Jacques arranged to meet Schwaiger in Delhi, where he and Nelly had rented a large suite in the white neoclassical Maiden's Hotel, which was considered the best in the city. Tired of the long distances, Nelly was happy to stay put in comfort for a while. She even rented a piano and was amused to see it delivered through the busy cow-filled streets of the city on the backs of six strong men.

Schwaiger sold Jacques several gemstones that trip, but almost more important, he introduced his client to different dealers. One, the son of Schwaiger's Hindu collaborator Sunny Hal, was a young man called Manik whom Jacques had first met as a small boy on his first trip to India. It was these kinds of connections that would prove so crucial to Cartier's gemstone access going forward. India wasn't a country where a foreign jeweler from Paris or London could just turn up and buy high-quality gemstones at reasonable prices. To find the best pieces at the right price, one had to be on the inside. "Sahib Cartier is more full of work, business, and engagements than in London," Nelly would write back to her sister as Jacques traveled around meeting dealers and clients with whom Schwaiger had put him in touch.

After three months in the East, Jacques and Nelly packed their bags to return home. Jacques was already planning his next trip back. If he couldn't make it himself next year, he thought he might send someone else on behalf of Cartier. There were too many opportunities to leave them hanging. But for now, he was satisfied. He had sold many of the jewels he had taken out with him, and in their place his bags were full of gemstones he had bought and his head was buzzing with ideas for new creations. All the way through Ceylon and India, he had been sketching his surroundings: The scroll shapes on temple walls in Kandy ("the carving of the stone is quite remarkable for feeling expressed by the workers") would find their way onto tiaras; the interlocking ovals decorating an old ceremonial cannon would be-

come the basis for an Art Deco bracelet; and the red-and-green pais-
ley motif on a rug would be reborn as a brooch, vibrant in rubies,
emeralds, and diamonds.

Nelly, for her part, had soaked up the experience with abandon,
everything from the "extraordinarily good" mandarin fruit she found
while "roughing it in the south," to dinner and dancing at the Taj
Hotel and the indescribable luxury of the palaces. But it had been a
long few months away from their brood. They had missed seeing
their children's excited faces at Christmas and missed celebrating
their youngest's third birthday. It was time to go home.

A POLAR STAR IN THE MOUNTAINS

Jacques' voyages to India may well have provided Cartier with some
of the best gemstones and clients in the world, but he didn't always
need to brave boats, trains, and rafts to make an important sale.
Sometimes the perfect client was much closer to home. Henri Deterding was a Dutchman better known as "the Napoleon of Oil." It was
under his leadership that Royal Dutch Shell was created in the 1907
merger of Royal Dutch Oil and Shell. He was hugely admired in England and even knighted after the First World War for his work supplying the Allies with petroleum and his service to Anglo-Dutch
relations. By the time Jacques showed him one of the world's best-
known diamonds in 1928, he was sixty-two years old, a multimillionaire, and four years into his second marriage, this time to the
twenty-four-year-old Russian Lydia Kondayoroff.

Together with their young children, the Deterdings lived at Buckhurst Park, a magnificent English country estate near Ascot. By 1936
they would be divorced, and Sir Henri would go on to lose favor with
the British for his third marriage to a German Nazi Party member
and his subsequent support of Hitler's party (he was forced to resign
from Shell after allegedly offering the Nazis a year's oil reserves on
credit). Not to be outdone, Lydia would go on to have an affair with
Hitler. But back in 1928, when Jacques called on the happy couple at
Buckhurst Park, that was all yet to come.

The Polar Star, so named because of its eight-pointed star-like cut,
was a 41.28-carat diamond with an impressive heritage. It had be-

longed to Joseph Bonaparte, Napoleon's elder brother, and more recently to Prince Felix Yusupov. When Yusupov had met with Pierre in 1922 to discuss selling some of his jewels in New York, one of the most significant had been the Polar Star. Over the following months and years, Cartier had quietly shown it to a few select clients in New York, Paris, and London, but when no offers materialized, it had been deposited with pawnbrokers. The use of pawnbrokers was standard practice for clients waiting for their jewels to be sold. (Cartier might advance some of the money but would rarely take the risk of buying very expensive pieces outright in case no buyer could be found in the short term and they were left exposed to fluctuating markets and exchange rates.) In this case, the Polar Star was deposited, along with several other Yusupov jewels, with TM Sutton in London.

By 1928, with Cartier still unable to find a buyer, Jacques proposed remounting the Polar Star into a new necklace to make it more appealing to a modern audience. The Cartier London design featured it suspended from a necklace of thirty-three collet-set diamonds on a pendant that also held two of Jacques' favorite colored diamonds: the top one was a 26.26-carat cushion-shaped fancy blue diamond and underneath it, above the Polar Star, was a 22.97-carat cushion-shaped pink diamond. With the transformation completed, Jacques had three clients in mind who he thought would be interested. One of these was Henri Deterding.

Deterding had previously expressed an interest in the diamond, but it wasn't until his wife, Lydia, saw it in the new setting that he started asking more serious questions. Perhaps, given her heritage, she appreciated its Russian history, or maybe she was just spellbound by its size and shape. Either way, she wanted it. Sir Henri took Jacques off to one side for a quiet chat, man to man. He was tempted to buy the jewel, he explained, but was hesitating over the hefty £48,000 price tag ($3.5 million today). He often saw Jacques and his family skiing in the fashionable Swiss mountain resort of St. Moritz. He wondered if perhaps it could be arranged for Cartier to open an office there, so he might make the large payment offshore instead. Jacques promised to make some inquiries.

Jacques and his family had been visiting the Swiss Alpine resort of St. Moritz for the winter holidays ever since they moved to England. Villa Chantarella, the chalet they rented each year next to the large

Jacques, Nelly, and their children spent their winter holidays in St. Moritz throughout the 1920s and '30s. From left to right: Alice, Jean-Jacques, Jacqueline, Nelly, and Jacques. Jacques opened a seasonal Cartier showroom in St. Moritz in 1929.

hotel of the same name, became a home away from home. "Here we are again on top of the world in our Noah's ark full to the brim of growing ones," Jacques wrote to Pierre in January 1929. "The girls brought a friend, and we have a tutor for J.J., and Baroness Geress (our chum) [is] often over here with her 2 girls so it is pandemonium, but I am writing in my room looking out over the climb to the ski fields."

The children became avid skiers. Though Jacques' weak lungs prevented him from too much exertion, the doctors advised that the mountain air was beneficial. As the boys occupied themselves racing terrifyingly fast downhill, he and Nelly would meet friends for long, enjoyable lunches. Though generally these social engagements would be for pleasure, they often overlapped into work territory; St. Moritz, known as a glamorous winter retreat, was popular with many Cartier clients. Jacques and Nelly might be at a dinner with a motion picture star such as Gloria Swanson or Douglas Fairbanks one evening and at a party alongside the Deterdings or the famous Polish opera singer Ganna Walska the next.

As the 1920s progressed and Jacques' working life became busier than ever, he was taking more and more work with him on vacation.

"I'm doing some work for the Maharaja of Rewah at the moment," Jacques updated Pierre one Christmas holiday as he looked out at his happy children sledding. Later that afternoon, his son would walk into his father's room to find designs for the Maharaja's jewels spread all over the floor. Though pressed for time, Jacques included his son in the decision-making process, asking Jean-Jacques for his perspective and explaining what Jacques was trying to achieve. The boy would never forget that day, and his father's gentle manner and insights would shape how he ran the business in the decades to come.

But having designs all over the bedroom floor wasn't the most efficient way to be working, and suddenly Deterding's suggestion to open some kind of office in the snow was a reasonable one. Jacques had to admit it made sense on many levels: He was there for the season anyway; it was a fashionable winter resort, attracting a whole host of potential clients from the Nizam of Hyderabad to the Aga Khan; and it could satisfy the demands of non-domiciled clients of Cartier London who wanted the tax advantages of paying offshore.

The St. Moritz mayor was quick to approve Jacques' plan, even proposing that his son, Carl Nater, head up the new branch. Jacques, hiring Carl, formally created a Swiss company (named Jacnel, after Jacques and Nelly) that would allow him to open the seasonal branch. Enticingly located next to the famous Swiss confectioner Hauser, Cartier's new showroom in the mountains attracted a fair number of window shoppers over the few months it was open each year, even if, as Pierre had found with the Palm Beach branch, not that many people parted with serious amounts of money while they were on vacation.

COPENHAGEN TO CAIRO

Louis or his senior salesmen had traditionally met with Cartier clients on the continent, but by the late 1920s, Jacques was taking on more of these responsibilities himself. When big sales came off, it was worth the extra effort, but traveling all over Europe from London was time-consuming and often far from straightforward. Jacques would be summoned to Copenhagen only to be told the Grand Duchess Olga couldn't see him after all, or arrive in Paris to see the Yusupovs only to be told the Prince was traveling and his wife was "at a friend's house—says she's sick." More successful trips included one to Cairo in 1929, where Jacques presented a large collection of jewels for the French Exposition. King Fouad I of Egypt, a Francophile, famously kept his wife, Queen Nazli, under close guard in the royal harem but allowed her two consolations: visits to the opera and extravagant gifts of jewelry. "Everyone noticed," one British newspaper observed about Cartier's display at the exhibition, "that King Fouad I tarried long at this exhibit where His Majesty was received by Jacques Cartier." Just two weeks later, the Cartier brothers received news from Cairo's Abdeen Palace that their firm had been appointed as a royal warrant holder to the court of King Fouad I.

In Conversation with Jean-Jacques Cartier

I remember my father working for that Cairo exhibition. He took some of the designs with him to work on when we went to St. Moritz on holiday. Those events took a lot of preparation, you know. You didn't just turn up with the jewels—making enough high-end pieces to create an impression would tie up the workshop for many months.

The extensive travel started to wear Jacques down, especially as—even when back home—he rarely had a moment to recuperate. If he wasn't organizing events such as the Persian Gulf Pearl Exhibition in the summer of 1928 or the French Society's jewel and fashion parade with Lanvin and Worth in the spring of 1929, he was out hosting French visitors in his role as head of the Alliance Française, meeting clients at Browns in Mayfair, or discussing new ideas with the designers. Weekday evenings would be spent out at dinner, perhaps with Margot Asquith and friends in a Mayfair townhouse one night, with the salesman Bellenger and his fiancée in Putney the next, and with a visiting maharaja in the Savoy the one after that. And then there was the opera, the theater, and the charity events, while weekends were viewed as an opportunity to host friends and clients in Milton Heath. It was no more than Pierre was doing over in New York, but Jacques had suffered from weaker health since his tuberculosis and having been gassed in the war. He was in his mid-forties, but there were days when he felt decades older.

Pierre felt his younger brother deserved public recognition for all his work and proposed putting him forward for the French Légion d'Honneur. Jacques urged him to resist. "You are a very good brother to think of me for decoration, but I am not doing enough for the French in London now. I have helped organize events, and it has been appreciated, but not now." Instead, he said, he was focused elsewhere. The amount of work flooding in from Cartier's Indian clients was at an all-time high, and he had just returned from Paris, where he had "obtained a contract from the Maharaja of Baroda, a contract by which we are his official advisers, with Cartier S.A. and Ltd., for £TS,KSK." Eighteen years had passed since Jacques had been forced out of Baroda by the jealous court jewelers, but it was worth the long wait: £TS,KSK was Cartier code for £60,000 ($4.6 million today). And the Gaekwad of Baroda wasn't the only Indian ruler rewarding Cartier's patience with a significant commission.

JEWELRY SPOTLIGHT: THE PATIALA NECKLACE

In the summer of 1925, the head Cartier Paris salesman was summoned to the elegant Hôtel Claridge on the Champs-Élysées by a very distinguished client. One of the richest men in the world, Maharaja Bhupinder Singh of Patiala didn't do things by halves. With five wives and a world-renowned appetite for every conceivable type of luxury, from Rolls-Royces to aircraft to diamonds, he personified Eastern splendor. When Jacques had visited him in India fourteen years earlier, the Maharaja had been more interested in selling gems than buying them, but now he had decided to update his heirlooms into a collection that would put his fellow Indian rulers in the shade.

Knowing from experience that the Indian ruler didn't like to be kept waiting, M. Muffat had made his way briskly from 13 Rue de la Paix toward Claridge's. On arrival at the enormous royal suite, the salesman was shown through to the sitting room and asked to take a seat at a table by the window. As he waited for his esteemed client to appear, a large wooden box was carried over and placed in front of him. Several minutes later, the imposing thirty-four-year-old ruler entered the room and gave instructions for the box to be opened.

Maharaja Bhupinder Singh of Patiala, a ruler who personified excess and gave Cartier one of its largest commissions of all time, pictured here with six of his consorts. Seated on the left is Rani Saheba Gulerwale, who wears an important Cartier ruby, pearl, and diamond necklace.

Muffat peered inside. It was filled with what seemed to be hundreds of crumpled pages of newspaper. As he glanced up, confused, the Maharaja urged him to look closer. Muffat carefully opened one of the sheets of paper, and a large Burmese ruby fell onto the table. As the ruler nodded his approval, Muffat kept going. The next paper enclosed a diamond as large as his thumbnail. And then another. And another. There were white diamonds, yellow diamonds, brown diamonds, diamonds with a greenish tint, others with a hint of pink. There were deep red rubies and vivid green emeralds. There were bracelets, earrings, and necklaces. Muffat, a connoisseur of gemstones who had worked at Cartier for more than twenty years, tried hard to hide his awe and assume a professional expression.

The Maharaja of Patiala told Muffat that he was looking for his gems to be reset in a more modern style. He wanted, he explained, to have jewels worthy of a king. Muffat nodded respectfully and took out his notebook and silver pen. "What are you doing?" the Maharaja asked. Muffat replied that he was simply writing down each piece of jewelry and every individual gemstone in the box so there would be a record of all the jewels that the ruler was depositing with Cartier. "I don't need that!" the ruler responded quickly, never doubting for a second that Cartier was to be trusted. "Please just take them!"

It would take Cartier three years to turn the Maharaja's gems into a collection of jewels that would go down in jewelry history. There would be head ornaments, anklets, armlets, and traditional Indian jewels from a *hathpul* (worn on the back of the hand, linking bracelet and finger rings) to a diamond, ruby, emerald, and sapphire *nath* (nose ring). More than two hundred pearls were drilled to make a single bracelet. But the pièce de résistance was a necklace of such brilliance that it outshone everything else. Containing a staggering 2,930 diamonds and weighing over a thousand carats, it was mounted in platinum and enhanced by Burmese rubies. And at its center was the yellow 234.6-carat De Beers diamond, the size of a golf ball and the seventh-largest diamond in the world.

For all its splendor and importance, the Patiala commission didn't actually end up being financially that attractive for Cartier, primarily because the Maharaja supplied most of his own gemstones. But it did do wonders for Cartier's image in the West, where Indian rulers were the personification of untouchable magnificence. When Cartier displayed the Maharaja's gems in an exhibition on 13 Rue de la Paix, visitors flocked from all over the world to see them. J. P. Morgan, *The New York Times* reported, "was heard to say he had never seen anything like it." "We are transported into the world of the *One Thousand and One Nights*," the French magazine *L'Illustration* exclaimed. "This is a dream world, the incarnation of a fugitive Oriental dream! . . . The beauty and significance of this collection surpass the imagination." If there had been any doubt as to Cartier's prominence in the jewelry world, this made it crystal clear. "In America, where we are fond of naming Kings, Cartier would be the King of Precious Stones. If it has not formally received the title, still it exercises its sovereignty. On two sides of the ocean, in the old continent as well as the new, Cartier is the uncontested master of gems."

The Patiala necklace sparkled under the light of the Indian sun for two generations, a symbol of power, wealth, and exquisite European taste, but in 1948 it sparked controversy when it was reported missing from the Patiala royal treasury. Nothing was heard of it for a further thirty-four years, at which point the De Beers diamond mysteriously reappeared, without the necklace, at a 1982 Sotheby's auction (valued at $3 million). Sixteen years after that, part of the necklace appeared in a small antiques shop in London. Obviously, the De Beers stone was missing, but so were all the other big diamonds. It was bought by Cartier, who replaced the missing stones with replicas. It is said that if the necklace were in its original form today, complete with all the diamonds, it would be valued in the region of $30 million.

Maharaja Yadavindra Singh of Patiala, the son of Bhupinder Singh, in the Patiala necklace.

LOOKING FORWARD

Jacques was still thinking of opening a small branch in India. Traveling over occasionally or sending the odd salesman or gem expert when he couldn't make it was better than nothing, but he would get so much more work done over there if the traders, and clients, knew Cartier was always open for business, not just for a few months every other year. He had other ideas too. He wanted to buy a separate workshop in London to focus on non-jewelry items (like gold and silver cases, cigarette lighters, boxes, and watches) and also to invest in a small workshop in Paris. Though he and Pierre used Paris ateliers

when demand exceeded the in-house supply, they were often inefficient: "It takes months to complete what should be done in as many
weeks, and it holds up our gemstone stock for all that time, making
the work too expensive."

The Paris-based workshop that Jacques talked about setting up
would be run by the Vergelys, a trusted father-and-son team: "To test
it I ordered a diamond [and] coral head ornament that was not easy
to make, and they succeeded marvelously." Assuming Pierre was in
agreement with his plan, Jacques proposed to go halves with him,
"and you would have at your disposal a workshop in Paris which
will work under my direction." He hadn't, he explained in his letter,
warned Louis about the idea of the Paris workshop yet. Knowing his
elder brother could be mercurial, he wanted Pierre's answer first.

But for all Jacques' ideas and excitement for the future, there was
something gnawing at him: He might be master of his own Cartier
London kingdom in theory, but in practice his brothers were still the
main shareholders. When he'd first moved over to England, it hadn't
particularly bothered him. He'd been excited by the creative opportunity and driven more by his duty to the family firm and love of his
brothers than any financial reward. In his many letters, it is the personal bond that stands out: "My dear Pierre," he starts a typical one,
"Nelly and I rejoice that Elma has emerged victorious from this surgery and hope that she has fully recovered. You went through hard
times! The extraordinary courage and morale of your wife were, I am
sure, one of the elements of the success of the surgery." Only then
would he launch into four pages of work-related news before signing
off with affection. First and foremost, they were a family: "We will
think of you from our little roof covered with snow under a very blue
sky full of stars which shine down on your side too, saying it is
Jacques who sends you their good wishes with all his heart."

There were more and more moments, though, when even the almost Zen-like Jacques became frustrated. In 1928, wanting to expand the business, Jacques had proposed a capital increase in the
Cartier Ltd. company. Both his brothers blocked his request. Pierre
argued that it should be possible to fund the company from cash
flow. "The net profits of Limited [Cartier London] have always been
abnormally small in relation to the amount of sales . . . due to the
fact perhaps that your salesmen are allowed to grant a 10% discount

to the majority of customers." He counseled Jacques that "you should do away with this practice, which deprives the shareholder of fair dividends and the company of reserves for its natural growth and future development." Pierre even sent over his financial controller, a Mr. Dury, from New York to make a set of recommendations in London that, he insisted, must be "absolutely adhered to and strictly followed."

Understandably, at a certain point, this kind of control from his brothers—and their apparent lack of interest in investing for growth—became increasingly difficult and awkward for Jacques. Nelly felt it even more acutely. Seeing how hard her husband worked, she worried that his generosity of spirit was being taken advantage of by Louis and Pierre. Discussing it with him at length, she came up with a solution. She suggested lending him enough money so that he could buy a controlling share in Cartier London. She was by now an incredibly wealthy woman. After her father died in 1914, she and her siblings had become millionaires. With no need for her inheritance, she had watched as it had reassuringly accumulated in what was now Morgan & Co. Bank. Jacques initially dismissed her idea. He had promised her father he would never touch a cent of her money, and he intended to stay true to his word. Nelly disagreed. He wasn't spending her money, she pointed out, he was merely exchanging it for shares in his business—shares that she and their children would inherit.

Jacques eventually came around to his wife's perspective. Even if he didn't feel strongly that he needed to own the branch himself, he wanted his children to inherit Cartier London. He wrote to his brothers. Louis' initial response was noncommittal. Pierre indicated that he wasn't against the proposal; they just needed to firm up the details, and that was better done in person. They agreed to meet the following summer in Europe when Pierre was next over from America.

As the 1920s drew to a close, Jacques, in his late forties, was in a good place. He and Nelly, married for seventeen years, were still devoted to each other. Their four "chicks"—from sixteen-year-old Jacqueline to seven-year-old Harjes—were all healthy and at least mostly happy (Jean-Jacques wasn't convinced by his new Swiss boarding school), and Dorothy had given them a much-adored grandson.

Up in London, meanwhile, Cartier was buzzing. It may not have been run with as much focus on margins and dividends as Pierre would have liked, but Jacques was making an impression. And not just because of the quality of the rubies, emeralds, and sapphires on offer. Rather it was Jacques' understanding of exactly how to integrate the precious stones into modern yet timeless creations that elicited the admiration and loyalty of an ever-growing client base. The Polar Star diamond that he remounted to show the Deterdings, the multigem bandeaux and on-trend hair accessories he displayed at Lady Cunard's fashion show, the Egyptian revival brooches snapped up by Lady Abdy, and the Maharaja of Nawanagar's emerald necklace were among the most striking examples, but there were many more. And there were those too still waiting in the sidelines—Jacques' diaries were filled with sketches of ideas to transform into reality, like the amethyst brooch he planned for Nelly or the large diamond-plaited shoulder sash inspired by the pattern on an Egyptian vase. Confident after decades in the business, Jacques was fired up creatively and excited by what the future might bring. But his optimism would not last forever. It would not be long before he, and his brothers, were to be entirely caught off guard by the most devastating economic tsunami the twentieth century had ever known.

DIAMONDS AND DEPRESSION: THE 1930s

THE CRASH

The worst economic downturn in the history of the industrialized world began in October 1929. In just two days, the U.S. equity market lost a quarter of its value, devastating investors. But that was just the start. Over the next three years, as the Great Depression took hold, there would be wave after wave of banking panic with the effects rippling throughout society. At the top, some of the most well-known business leaders in the country, from General Motors founder William C. Durant to frozen foods entrepreneur Clarence Birdseye, saw their vast fortunes shrink to next to nothing. Later, when thousands of banks closed their doors and nine million savings accounts were wiped out, it was the middle-class professionals, all those who had dutifully saved for years, who were left ruined. But it didn't stop there. As the country's industrial production dropped by half, more than 85,000 businesses were forced to shut down. Unemployment, homelessness, soup kitchens, and bread lines swept through the cities. And while people starved, farmers, who could no longer afford harvesting, left their crops to rot in the fields.

"Eighty percent of our orders were canceled," Pierre would report

The Depression forced luxury firms to change their approach. Left: Clarence Mackay with his wife, Anna, in the large emerald necklace he bought on credit as a gift for their 1931 wedding.

to the press in 1930 about how Cartier New York had been affected. And for those clients that remained, "the Maison had to grant credits varying from six months to a year." Gone were the days of large cash purchases. Since the 1848 revolution, the Cartiers had survived multiple economic downturns, but this would prove the most trying period of all. The brothers had learned from their father to avoid taking on too much debt, but there was no escaping the calamitous impact of the Great Depression on their wider client base. In Pierre and Elma's case, many of their friends were suffering too.

Prior to 1929, Clarence Mackay had been an exceedingly wealthy American financier. Well-connected and generous, he was known for throwing incredible parties at his Long Island French-style château throughout the 1920s. Even the Duke of Windsor, not exactly used to frugality, had found one Mackay celebration "perhaps the most elaborate" event that he had attended that decade. Unfortunately for Mackay, it was not to last. In a spectacularly badly timed move, just a year prior to the crash, he sold his major source of income. Had the Postal Telegraph Company been sold for cash, it would have been fabulous timing, but Mackay had chosen to take stock in the acquiring company, ITT. A year later, his investment was worth just a fraction of its former value.

In 1930, aged fifty-six and about to be married for the second time, Mackay went to Pierre to ask about the possibility of buying a wedding gift for his new bride on credit. The two men had been friends for years. Regular dinner guests at the Cartier's 15 East Ninety-sixth Street townhouse, Mackay and his fiancée would reciprocate by inviting Pierre and Elma over to Long Island on the weekends. For most clients who came to Cartier during the Depression to ask for a sale on credit, Pierre would insist on an extensive background credit check. But Clarence Mackay was a loyal friend, and Pierre knew how important this gift was. The financier had fallen for the beautiful singer Anna Case fourteen years earlier, when she had performed at a private event at his house. Though he'd wooed her from the start with carloads of flowers and diamond bracelets, his Catholicism had prevented him from marrying her until his estranged first wife had passed away. Anna had patiently waited for more than a decade to be married, and Mackay refused to hold back on her wedding gift just because the economy was in chaos. With Pierre's help, he selected the perfect piece. Containing more than two thousand diamonds and thirty-five emeralds, the Mackay necklace was most extraordinary for its central stone: a jaw-dropping oval cabochon-cut Colombian emerald of 167.97 carats.

True to his word, though it took him two years, Mackay paid Pierre in full, selling some of his extensive collections of antiques and art to do so. Anna would proudly wear the necklace at important events with her adoring husband, but after all the years of waiting to be married, the couple would have only seven years as man and wife before Mackay died of cancer at the age of seventy-four. Anna would hold on to the necklace all her life, bequeathing it to the Smithsonian on her death in 1984.

POOR LITTLE RICH GIRL

Mackay had a good reason for wanting to shop at Cartier, but for most of Pierre's clients, the idea of spending money on expensive jewels had become either impossible or quite inappropriate. As unemployment rose to 30 percent of the workforce (almost 15 million Americans) and mothers struggled to feed their children, driving around in a Cadillac and wearing diamonds to dinner was severely frowned upon.

Not everyone, though, felt the need to exercise restraint. "Poor little rich girl" Barbara Hutton was turning eighteen in 1930. Heiress to the Woolworth retail dynasty, she had inherited $25 million ($375 million today) at the age of ten when her grandfather died. By 1930, thanks to the foresight of her father, who managed her trust and had liquidated much of it before the crash, she was richer than ever. While others were coming to terms with the loss of everything they owned, Barbara celebrated her debutante status with not one but three extravagant parties, including a ball costing $60,000 ($900,000 today). Four orchestras, two hundred waiters, two thousand bottles of champagne (despite Prohibition), one thousand seven-course midnight suppers, and one thousand breakfasts made up a party that guest Brooke Astor described as "to die from—the epitome of the big money deb affair." For two days and nights, workmen had transformed the entire lower floor of the Ritz into a jungle of flowers and trees. The party, taking place on December 21, had a Christmas theme, with mounds of artificial snow covering everything and the famous French actor and singer Maurice Chevalier greeting guests dressed as Santa Claus. His team of Santa's helpers were tasked with handing out party favors of small jewelry cases containing unmounted emeralds, diamonds, rubies, and sapphires. Barbara's aunt, Marjorie Merriweather Post (married at the time to Edward Hutton), was not the only one who was outspoken in her disapproval of the excess. But nothing was too good for Frank Hutton's only daughter.

It had been Barbara's father who had first ignited his daughter's love of jewelry. He had persuaded her to come with him to Europe in the summer of 1929 by promising her an item of her choice from Cartier. Just seventeen years old, she had known exactly what she wanted: a ruby ring. The salesman in 13 Rue de la Paix had pulled out trays of rubies for her to inspect and she had chosen the most expensive of the lot. At $50,000, it had been ten times the amount Frank Hutton had hoped to spend, but it did at least reassure him of his daughter's excellent taste in gems. From then on, Barbara was said to be entranced by jewels, and she would go on to have a far longer relationship with Cartier than with any of her many husbands.

Jules Glaenzer, Pierre's charming, larger-than-life leading salesman, made sure he was on hand to attend to Barbara's every need. Not one to disapprove of excess, he continued to hold parties in an attempt to cultivate relationships and boost sales. In 1931, he invited Barbara to a party he was throwing in honor of Edsel Ford and his wife (whom he had first befriended on a boat to Europe a decade earlier) The evening, as always with his parties, was designed to impress his top clients while never feeling like a sales pitch. Guests included the Astors, Cecil Beaton, the Condé Nasts, and the Huttons as well as Glaenzer's friends from the stage and screen like Fanny Brice, Richard Rodgers, and Douglas Fairbanks. High society came to be entertained, and the stars were more than happy to have their arms twisted into performing if they could mingle with the elite: "The roll of great names who have sung, played and clowned at Glaenzer's parties is a who's who of the theatre. Glaenzer cajoles them out on the floor by a mixture of bland praise, browbeating and reproving insistence. Nobody can resist him."

In 1933, after hearing from Barbara's uncle Edward Hutton that his niece was secretly engaged, Glaenzer made sure to invite the young girl and her father to Cartier to see some very special new jewels. That single wedding, the first of seven unhappy marriages for Barbara, would bring in enough business to boost profits for the year. After Cartier had conducted the necessary checks on their client's financial standing ("we consider F L Hutton a good moral risk but his health poor, although Insurance Company have accepted substantial increase in his life insurance policy after last year's physical examination"), Frank Hutton purchased with abandon. Later, Barbara Hutton would recall Glaenzer's effective selling technique: "his habit of carrying jewels round in his pockets—no security guards, no fancy jewellery cases. He would come round and turn his pockets inside out on a coffee table or bed. There was none of that razzle and dazzle with magic wands, kidskin gloves and stronghold boxes that charac-

Barbara Hutton, a lifelong client of
Cartier, wearing her 1933 jade
necklace that sold at auction
for $27 million in 2014.

terizes some of the other stores.
That's because Glaenzer had the
merchandise—you either bought
it or you didn't."

And the Huttons certainly did
buy. One necklace Frank Hutton
bought for his daughter, described
by the press as "one of the rarest
strands of pearls ever sold by Cartier," had previously belonged to
Marie Antoinette. Barbara's engagement ring was a black pearl
from Cartier, while the Cartier
tortoiseshell and diamond tiara
she wore as she said her vows was
inspired by the traditional wooden
headdresses she had seen on a re-
cent trip to Bali. For the wedding reception, she changed outfits but
stayed loyal to Cartier with a striking jadeite necklace consisting of
twenty-seven large bright green jade beads secured with a contrasting
ruby and diamond clasp.

A FIVE-DOLLAR DEPARTMENT

While Glaenzer was quite happy to support his clients' spending hab-
its, Pierre's public relations adviser, Edward Bernays, decided that
he could no longer work for a luxury business. It was wrong, he
felt, to be catering to the super-rich when so many others were facing devastation. It also seemed unhelpful for the firm's reputation
to focus on marketing at such a difficult time, as "the more people
talked about Cartier, the more ill-will might develop for the firm." To
Pierre's dismay, Bernays felt he had no option but to resign from the
Cartier account. Before he left, though, he offered a novel suggestion.
Recognizing that the luxury market was unlikely to bounce back, he
proposed "instituting a $5 and $10 department—a revolutionary innovation in a shop where $100,000 sales were routine."

Pierre swiftly implemented the idea. Just as the Fifth Avenue showroom had earlier introduced a stationery department to offer clients an entry at a lower price point, now it also offered economical non-jewelry objects like silver spoons, napkin rings, and gold toothpicks. If customers were to come into the store for one of these small items, they would receive the same luxury service, but their item would be gift-wrapped in a chic pale blue cardboard Cartier box instead of the standard red leather Cartier box. It was important, Pierre believed, not to devalue the higher-priced items.

Margins took a hit with the lower-priced pieces, but each time a client walked through the Cartier doors, even for the smallest purchase, Pierre saw it as a small victory. Recalling conversations he'd had as a young boy with his late grandfather about keeping the business alive through the tough revolutionary years, he knew the value of patience in a downturn. Purchases were kept to a minimum and stock was reorganized to keep pieces affordable.

Within the jewelry range, for instance, smaller brooches and rings were selected over larger necklaces. Across the industry it was particularly hard for skilled craftsmen: Their pay for "a specially designed bracelet that requires three weeks of work," one Cartier employee explained, had dropped to "$100, which is only about $30 per week." Previously, they had been paid over $2 an hour, "so that is a pitiful comparison especially since these offers of work at reduced rates are even so rather rare." Unfortunately, it wasn't showing signs of picking up anytime soon. "Tiffany cut salaries by 10–15% last month," was the 1931 report on the competition. And profits for Cartier New York were much worse in 1931 than they had been in 1930.

TIMID PROSPERITY

In July 1931, Pierre, Elma, and a twenty-year-old Marion took the boat from America across the Atlantic. Arriving in France, they found the country far more upbeat than the one they had left behind. A self-sufficient economy and extensive gold reserves had so far cushioned Paris from the worst effects of the Crash, and the French had been quick to point it out to their worse-off neighbors: "For our part let us rejoice in our timid yet prosperous economy as opposed to the presumptuousness and decadent economy of the Anglo-Saxon races."

As usual, Pierre and his family had been looking forward to spending their summer vacation in Europe, but this time there was the additional draw of a vast exhibition in the French capital. The 1931 Colonial Exposition aimed to display the diverse cultures and immense resources of France's forty-seven colonies to an enormous audience and Pierre had been heavily involved in promoting it in America. Along with fellow members of the French Chamber of Commerce, he had set up an American Committee, which placed a phenomenal 136,800 articles and 41,000 photographs in 2,400 newspapers across the United States and Canada. He hoped the publicity would translate into numerous visitors from across the Atlantic and, all going well, that he might be recognized for his efforts by the event president.

First up on Pierre's agenda, though, was a visit to 13 Rue de la Paix and his elder brother. Said to be "flying through Paris like a meteor," Louis was recently back from London, where he had displayed an important collection of Persian miniatures in a Mayfair exhibition. While there, he had seen Jacques, who had impressed him with the Cartier pieces he had recently lent to well-known socialites for the Jewels of the Empire Ball. Press reports had featured Lady Diana Cooper and Mrs. Henry Mond (notorious for commissioning a bronze relief that depicted herself and her husband naked) in "magnificent examples" of Cartier's "high craftsmanship."

The Hon. Mrs. Henry Mond (a client and a friend of the Cartiers) is pictured for *The London Illustrated News* in borrowed Cartier jewelry at the 1930 Jewels of the Empire Ball.

Pierre, proud of his younger brother, told Louis that he had put Jacques forward for a Légion d'Honneur. They hoped he would be successful; now that he had more control in the business, it was important he be recognized officially as they had been. The previous summer, when the three brothers had met in Munich to discuss the ownership structure of each branch, Pierre and Louis had conceded that Jacques should have the opportunity to buy a controlling interest in Cartier London. Grateful for their support, Jacques had promised that "the loyal co-operation" between the companies would continue and that he would "never hurt relations." In April, the agreement had been formalized. They all expected working life to continue largely as before with an ongoing sharing of ideas, clients, gems and staff but the new agreement would give each brother the autonomy to make his own decisions.

News of Pierre's arrival in Paris made the rounds of 13 Rue de la Paix. Before long, he was greeted by directors and employees, eager for updates from New York. René Revillon, who had spent so much time with the Cartiers when he had lived in New York, found it hard to believe Marion was already a debutante. It had been more than a decade ago that Pierre had introduced him to his wife, Anne-Marie, and he was now not only fully immersed in the Cartier family but also the firm. Louis, or *"le patron"* as he called him, had given him plenty of responsibility and he had developed from being a salesman to part of the committee that decided which designs should be executed. Money was tight, though. He hoped his salary might be increased before too long. Anne-Marie wasn't the most frugal of wives and they had two children to look after.

Pierre was pleased to see that the newer members of the firm were working out so well too. Louis Devaux had joined straight out of the prestigious École des Hautes Études Commerciales (HEC) business school a few years previously. Astute, organized, and ambitious, he had already become Louis Cartier's secretary and his composed, rational manner was proving to be a godsend when dealing with his sometimes irascible boss. Devaux had also been instrumental in Cartier's hire of Roger Chalopin, and the pair, who were good friends and shared a fierce intelligence, would each come to play an important role in the future of the Paris House. Paul Muffat, who had been placed in charge of the new Cartier Paris workshop at Rue Bachaumont, offered to show Pierre several pieces they had been working on. Preparations for the Colonial Exposition had absorbed most of their time recently, and there were innovative new items for stock that Muffat thought would go down well with Pierre's American client base.

Louis had long believed that "the jeweler gives free rein to his playspirit as well as to his serious creative side," and now he and Charles Jacqueau, previously trailblazers in Art Deco, were experimenting with an *art moderne* style. With the growing influence of machines on everyday life, Louis had been inspired to strip back the gem-heavy adornment and create pieces that were almost more machine-part than precious accessories. A ball-bearing bracelet with three rows of gold spheres and crenellated borders was shocking in its daring refusal to bow to conventional ideas of jewelry. Its focus on streamlined design over gems was a brave move for a firm known for its high jewelry. But as usual when it came to design, Louis had known what his clients would want before they knew it themselves.

There were a few interesting commissions going on for individual clients too. Most exciting for the firm as a whole was the contract Cartier had won to design its first academicians' swords.

JEWELRY SPOTLIGHT: THE ACADEMICIANS' SWORDS

It was, and remains, a great honor to be inducted into the Académie Française, the bastion of the French literary establishment. Since its founding under Cardinal Richelieu in the seventeenth century, its members (known as *les immortels*), have included some of the country's most eminent public figures, from novelists to philosophers to scientists. Given the infrequent induction of new *académiciens* (once elected, a member generally holds the position for life and there are no more than forty members at one time), the contract to design the new academicians' swords wasn't a guarantee of prolific work, but it was highly esteemed.

The brief to Cartier was that the decorative sword should reflect the recipient. Louis would assign only his most capable designers to the task. Part of their role was to come to know their client, not just in terms of his greatest professional achievements but also in a personal capacity. Only then could they create a sword that accurately reflected the academician himself. Georges Rémy, who was selected as the Cartier designer for several of the swords, explained his process: "I had many serious talks, real and imaginary, over a period of weeks with the future academician, immersing myself in his personality and his world, and we had many a chat, too, before I embarked on the job."

Cartier's first academician client was Duc Armand de Gramont, an aristocratic scientist and industrialist who had been a close friend of Marcel Proust. When he had married in 1904, Proust had notoriously given him the rather unusual wedding present of a revolver in a leather case inscribed with verses from the bride's childhood poems. Charles Jacqueau visited the Duc in his castle, the Château de Vallière, thirty-one miles north of Paris, for a weekend. Spending a couple of days with him in his home, seeing how he spent his free time, what he ate for breakfast, and his favorite topics to discuss over dinner, gave the designer an insight into the academician's motivations, passions, and family life as much as his notable public successes. Only then did he start designing several different options for a sword, in order that the Duc might choose his favorite.

The finished sword was inspired by the Duc's scientific career. Motifs of microscopes and range finders (which allowed the army to know the distances of their objectives) pointed to his specific accomplishments in the field of optics, while his services to astronomy were represented by constellations, the Milky Way, the North Star, and a comet. The sword was presented to the Duc de Gramont on his reception into the academy in June 1931.

Cartier would go on to create more than two dozen swords. One of the most significant was for a man who was not simply a client but also a friend of the Cartiers, and a source of inspiration. In 1955, the legendary sixty-six-year-old poet and artist Jean Cocteau was made a member of the Académie Française. He asked for his academician's sword to be made in accordance with drawings he had done himself, with materials supplied by his friends. The blade came from a swordsmith in Toledo, while the 2.84-carat emerald was donated by Coco Chanel. The other gems were a gift from the socialite Francine Weisweiller.

Cocteau's sword was to be a physical encapsulation of his work, bearing various symbols that related to his life. Like his writings, the sword was signed with a six-pointed star, but this one was made of diamonds and rubies. The handguard traced the profile of Orpheus, the mythological figure who was Jean Cocteau's muse. The scabbard had a pattern evoking the grille surrounding the gardens of the Palais-Royal, his place of residence, and at its tip, a hand clutched an ivory ball in reference to the snow-covered stone in *Les Enfants Terribles*, the 1950 film that Cocteau scripted from his 1929 novel. This sword, a symbolic work of art by, and for, a great artist, stands out as one of the firm's most prestigious commissions of all time.

Jean Cocteau at home, dressed in the uniform of the Académie Française and holding the Cartier sword he designed and was awarded in 1955 following his investiture as an académicien. Right: a close-up of the sword, with the handle in the shape of Orpheus's profile and fabric-like gold around the hilt suggesting the adornment of ancient theater.

TIGERS' TEETH AND EAGLES' TALONS

Set on more than five hundred acres in Paris's largest park, the 1931 six-month Colonial Exposition was the most extensive exposition in French history. Part of the government's propaganda effort to justify colonial enterprise, the event played host to twelve thousand exhibitors and vendors. Grand reproductions of huts and temples covered the park, and hundreds of natives from various Asian and African colonies performed for nine million visitors.

Within the jewelry category, Cartier displayed alongside many others, including Boucheron, Mauboussin, Van Cleef, and Mellerio. There were to be grand prizes decided by a judging panel that included Chaumet, and each fought for the prestige of winning. Everything had a colonial theme, from sumptuous Cambodian-style headdresses "executed with the best French taste" to necklaces in which diamonds were interspersed with ivory, "the most beautiful material that appears in the wild." There were ties that gave the impression of a serpent, circular Algerian-style brooches, and gold and enamel discs depicting African art. Most daring among the displays were the bracelets, necklaces, and belt clips that included real tigers' fangs, lions' molars, and eagles' talons, seductively combined with black enamel or onyx. They represented, the catalog of the exposition would note, an "invasion of the jungle into the modern woman's wardrobe."

For Louis and Jacques, with a shared history of using inspiration from different civilizations in their jewels, the exhibition offered them the chance to revive the public's taste for exoticism. A diamond Siamese-style tiara that Jacques had sent over from London and an Indian-themed emerald bead tiara were among the many jewels that elicited admiration for their originality and craftsmanship, and the Cartier display was awarded one of the most prominent prizes, the Grand Prix. Pierre, proud of his brothers' creativity, was equally thrilled to hear that he had been personally honored for a different reason.

On July 21, Pierre and Elma were the guests of honor at a luncheon given by the Colonial Exposition event president, Maréchal Lyautey. They had a busy summer in front of them, with a datebook full of dinners in Paris and a trip through Italy with their daughter in August, but this was the most important moment for Pierre. He had come bearing several huge volumes containing a third of all the clippings and articles published in the American and Canadian press about the exhibition. Presenting them to the Maréchal, he was applauded for his "excellent work." Elma looked on with pride as Lyautey awarded her husband the Black Star of Benin, the highest colonial decoration.

Less than five miles away, in the Hôpital Pasteur, Jacques' younger son, Harjes, awaited a diagnosis. Miss Edwards, his nanny, had rushed him to the capital after he had become ill on vacation in Houlgate and the local doctor hadn't taken it seriously. Jacques and Nelly, who had visited the Colonial Exposition when it first opened, were no longer in the country. They were in India again, on one of the many trips they would take there together during the 1930s as the support of the maharajas became even more important for Cartier during the Depression in the West. Nelly had been beside herself with guilt at being so far away when her little one needed her, but there was nothing she could do. Even if she did leave immediately, the voyage home would take three weeks. Jacques wrote to his brothers, who rushed to the side of their usually cheeky seven-year-old nephew. Speaking to the doctor, they discovered that Harjes had contracted polio. He wouldn't be that same sporty boy again, but he would live. Not everyone in the hospital was so lucky. The little African boy in the bed next to Harjes, also far from his parents, had fallen ill on the ship that had brought him over to France to perform in the Colonial Exposition. He would not survive the week.

A CONNOISSEUR'S DREAM

By the end of 1931, Jacques and Nelly were back in the comfort of Milton Heath, suitcases filled with Indian gifts for the children. It had been a volatile year, with Harjes being so ill and also from a business perspective, as Cartier London had struggled with the repercussions of the American financial crisis. In August, as Jacques learned he had been awarded the Légion d'Honneur, the British government had collapsed, sending the economy into a tailspin. By autumn, Britain had been forced to abandon the gold standard, with devastating effects on the currency. The price of imports had skyrocketed, and Jacques had feared for his firm's future. Thankfully, by year end, it wasn't looking quite as dire. There was no getting away from the ripple effects of the American Depression, but the recent election of the MacDonald national coalition in England promised short-term stability.

Against such a difficult backdrop, the trip to India had been a welcome respite. As Jacques had suspected, his Indian clients were largely unaffected by the economic crisis that was sweeping the West and saw no reason to rein in their spending. Already that year, Cartier had completed several important commissions from maharajas, including a fantastic ruby necklace for the Maharaja of Patiala and, most significant for Jacques, a colored diamond necklace for Ranji, the Maharaja of Nawanagar.

Ever since his 1927 trip to the palace of Nawanagar, when Jacques had sold Ranji the emerald necklace, the two men had been musing over the idea of creating a truly exceptional diamond necklace together. With Jacques' design expertise and Ranji's means to buy the best gemstones, it would be, they envisaged, like nothing else. They had made a start in 1929, but it had taken many months to track down some of the best quality white and fancy-colored diamonds in the world. Before purchasing each important gemstone, Jacques would check with Ranji that his client was in agreement. In the instance of the most important diamond of all, Ranji sought multiple opinions from experts before making up his mind.

One such expert was the diamond dealer Albert Monnickendam, who visited the Maharaja at his English house. After luncheon, Monnickendam was asked to accompany the Maharaja into a large room flooded with northern light, where a servant extracted from a safe a large gold jewelry box.

> His Highness asked me to sit near him and to my amazement opened the lid of the box and took out a magnificent diamond of about 130 carats set in a pendant. He placed it in my hands asking, "What do you think of this?" On examination I found the stone to be absolutely perfect, of the finest color and quality. Whilst I was examining the diamond, I felt the Maharaja's eyes continually watching me, and when I looked up there was an expression of pleasure and hope on his face. It was obvious he was greatly fascinated by the stone. When I was asked its value, I put it at approximately £250,000, though no true market price can be given for such a stone.

The Maharaja would end up buying the gemstone, the 136-carat, internally flawless Queen of Holland diamond, and it would form the centerpiece of Jacques' creation. But even with the major diamond decided upon, it would take a further year to finish the necklace. The problem, as Jacques explained to his young son, was that just as the design was approved, either he or his client would come across another fantastic diamond that simply must be added to the mix. And because the necklace had to be symmetrical, it then required finding another one of matching color and size for the other side.

There were a few particularly spectacular diamonds that didn't need a partner. These were suspended in a central pendant formation and included the Queen of Holland as well as the fancy blue and pink diamonds that Jacques had previously mounted into the Polar Star necklace (the Deterdings had ended up buying the Polar Star diamond without the entire necklace). There were also two more pink diamonds and an olive-green brilliant diamond of 12.86 carats—"A rare stone, indeed!" Jacques had exclaimed when he saw it. The overall effect was extraordinary, a unique cascade of colored diamonds. "Had not our age witnessed an unprecedented succession of world-shaking events," Jacques would later write, referring to the cumulative effect of the First World War, the Russian Revolution, and the Depression, "such gems could not have been bought at any price; at no other period in history could such a necklace have come into existence."

In Conversation with Jean-Jacques Cartier

I remember my father thinking for hours and hours about how to describe the diamond necklace he had made for Ranji. He had been asked to write the jewelry section for Ranji's biography, you see, and he so wanted to do it justice. I think the phrase he eventually came up with couldn't have been bettered: "The realization of a connoisseur's dream." Can you imagine that? A connoisseur, someone who knows so much about gems, well, this necklace was something that even such a person couldn't conceive of as reality.

When Jacques had traveled to India in 1931, he had been able to present his friend with the completed commission. It represented, at least in Jacques' own mind, the peak of his creative career. And yet, at the time, the necklace didn't receive the same acclaim as Patiala's jewels had sparked in Paris three years earlier. Displaying it in a grand exhibition wasn't Ranji's way. Jewels mean many things to many people. This necklace was born out of the love of gemstones, simply for their intrinsic wonder and beauty. Sadly, however, after all the work that had gone into it, Ranji did not have much time to enjoy the necklace, and Jacques did not see his friend wear it again. Just two years later, Ranji would die from heart failure.

UNDER THE RADAR

The 1930s were one of Cartier London's most creative periods as Jacques endeavored to offer his Depression-affected clients something they admired but could afford. Recognizing that many of the fashion-forward ladies who walked down New Bond Street wanted to make a statement without the huge price tag, he started experimenting with more economical gems. Semiprecious stones like aquamarines and topaz, for instance, were far less expensive than rubies and emeralds.

When it came to buying semiprecious stones, however, the Cartiers had to be careful. It was important—if they were to source good stones at reasonable prices—that neither the dealers nor their competitors caught on to their buying patterns. After deciding among themselves on a particular gemstone to create a collection around, the brothers bought under the radar over several months, or even years. Assuming it was topaz, they would gladly buy topazes when different gemstone dealers came to present their wares, but never too many at one time or from the same dealer. And they would never ask a dealer if he had any topazes for fear that would draw attention to themselves. If the market found out that the Cartiers were buying up topaz, it would start a trend for topaz, their competitors would jump in on the act, and prices would rise.

The idea was that over the course of a couple of years, they would have acquired enough of the chosen gemstone to make a collection.

And then, by showing topaz necklaces, earrings, bracelets, and bandeaux in their windows, they would make the topaz the gemstone du jour. By the time their competitors tried to copy them, not only would there be very few high quality topazes left on the market but also the dealers would have hiked their prices and it would become almost impossible for another jeweler to create a topaz collection on anywhere near the same scale.

In Conversation with Jean-Jacques Cartier

We couldn't stop other jewelers from copying Cartier designs, but we could make it harder for them. You see, by quietly buying one gemstone over the space of a couple of years, we could corner the market in that gemstone.

Not only were semiprecious gemstones considerably more economical, they were also more readily available in a variety of geometric cuts. This gave the designers the opportunity to come up with an almost architectural look in accordance with the fashions of the time. Through the 1930s, Cartier London became known for both its topaz and its aquamarine Art Deco jewelry. Topaz was generally combined with diamonds or gold: "The only requirement," *Vogue* would explain in its October 1938 issue, "is that topaz jewellery must look as important as if it were emeralds or rubies. That is the way Cartier has treated it." Often clients would request matching jewels: When the debutante Lady Elizabeth Paget was photographed for *Harper's Bazaar* in January 1935, she wore "Cartier's magnificent parure . . . of light and dark topaz," comprising necklace, bracelet, shoulder clip, and large pendant earrings.

But it was the combination of diamonds with aquamarines that Jacques particularly liked. It created, he felt, a look that was fresh and elegant and suited everyone from royalty to trendsetters. His clients agreed, as did many visiting Americans who ordered their jewels from his branch. Keeping up with demand was the problem: "We would mention that owing to the difficulty of obtaining quickly a supply of good color aquamarines," the London team updated their New York colleagues in the mid-1930s, "we are unable to fix a definite date for completion of the order, but we do hope to deliver in America in 2 months from receipt of order. As a matter of fact, we have for our own stock a number of partly completed necklaces, which we are unable to finish owing to lack of the necessary aquamarines."

As commissions for Cartier London's semiprecious jewelry poured in from home and abroad, Jacques' design team also found themselves busy with remounting requests. While many clients could not justify buying new jewels in a depression, they were open to recycling their old-fashioned necklaces and tiaras into more modern creations. In 1932, Lady Granard, daughter of the American financier Ogden Mills and wife of the Earl of Granard, commissioned an incredible necklace incorporating more than two thousand diamonds and an enormous rectangular emerald of 143.13 carats. All the gems were her own. Lady Granard, who had married into the English aristocracy at the age of twenty-six in 1909, had two passions: horse racing and jewels. When she made her debut in Parliament soon after her wedding, her jewels were said to have induced the jealousy of all the peeresses in the House of Lords. *The Washington Post* had even remarked that "after the Queen, who wore the crown jewels, no woman in the chamber wore so many splendid gems as the new American countess, and if the Queen had not worn the Cullinan diamonds for the first time, the American countess would have outshone Her Majesty." By the 1930s, she was already a very welcome client of Cartier London, known particularly for her commissions of *kokoshniki,* large Russian-style tiaras.

Despite the troubled economic backdrop since the crash, Jacques' problem was not so much a lack of demand as an inability to fund supply. The previous company structure (with the Cartier London majority owned by Louis and Pierre) had meant there were almost always funds available for large gemstone purchases. Since the financial control of Cartier London had passed to Jacques, there was far less capital available to him. To make matters even more difficult, the introduction of an import tax on gems between France and England had led to a dramatic reduction in the number of jewels that were exchanged between Cartier Paris and Cartier London.

Feeling less able to rely on his brothers for gemstones than he had in the past, Jacques looked for other ways to source capital and ended up joining forces with the bank Kleinwort & Sons. They agreed that the bank would fund Cartier London's purchases in return for a 50 percent share of the profit. It was a big slice of margin to give away, but Jacques was hopeful that the deal, at a time when his competitors were reining in spending, would give him the pick of the best gems. The 1920s had seen Jacques step out of his brothers' shadows, and now, with financial as well as artistic control of his company, he was proud to be taking it one step further. But the agreement among the brothers giving each of them independence would also have its drawbacks.

SIBLING HOSTILITY

In December 1930, Cartier London had sold a pearl necklace for £55,000 ($4.4 million today) to a client referred to as M.F. Cartier S.A. in Paris had supplied the pearls to Cartier Ltd. in London on the understanding that the profit would be split fifty-fifty between the two branches. Reflecting the terms with the client, most of the payment was to be deferred, with the balance payable in three years' time in pounds sterling (the British pound was the international reserve currency). To determine how much Paris was owed, a fixed rate of around 124 francs to the pound had been used, which had seemed reasonable at the time. The problem was that the British government's abandonment of the gold standard in September 1931 had since led to a massive decline in the value of sterling relative to other currencies.

Suddenly, the pearl deal was no longer a good one for Louis. The Paris firm would receive far less valuable pounds than expected. Louis blamed his younger brother for taking advantage of him. In reality, the exchange rate had been agreed upon at the time, and no one could have anticipated the currency collapse, but Louis had never been one to let the facts get in the way of his temper. The question was who should take the hit for the unforeseen currency losses. Jacques tried to reason with his older brother that Cartier London didn't have the funds to carry the burden, explaining that it could ruin him. "I would never ruin my own brother!" Louis replied, furious at the insinuation.

After taking advice from his financial controller (who confirmed that Cartier S.A. could bear the blow far better than Cartier Ltd.), Louis eventually accepted that his Paris branch should take the hit, but he did so with huge resentment. In a fit of anger he refused Jacques access to Cartier Paris and took him off the board of Cartier S.A. A senior Cartier employee, Georges Martin, tried to mediate but could not break through Louis' anger: "The worst aspect is the sanction taken by LC [Louis] with regard to JC [Jacques]—JC forbidden to enter S.A. locations at 4 or 13 Rue de la Paix. Cessation of all relations between the two companies, no S.A. stock to be sent, ordered, or repaired. Only current business to be conducted, no new business to be carried out."

Jacques didn't attempt to reason with Louis in his heated state, knowing from experience how pointless it would be. Pierre, too, chose to stay out of the argument as he waited for his elder brother's initial rage to subside. Deep down they realized that, although Louis might not have always seen eye to eye with his siblings, he would never betray them. And to the outside world, their bond should appear unbreakable. In the end he came round. A few months later, the fifty-six-year-old Louis had the first of several heart scares, and in the face of his own mortality, the dispute blew over.

In Conversation with Jean-Jacques Cartier

The trade knew how tight the Cartier brothers were. That was important. It was one of their strengths— when dealing with one, you were actually dealing with all three. They had a lot more bargaining power that way.

"THE MOST BRILLIANT WEDDING OF THE SPRING"

A year after the argument, relations between the brothers had been restored and Jacques was welcome again in the Paris Maison. Pierre was relieved; he'd hated mediating between his brothers, especially when he had so much on his plate. The economy in America was still far more challenging than in England or France, and he was working all hours trying to keep the business afloat. When Elma traveled to Miami to meet her siblings in 1931, she wished he could have gone with her, but he stayed in New York, living by the motto that, especially in the most difficult times, the Head of the House should be the first into the office and the last out.

He wouldn't take a vacation the following summer either. Instead, in 1932, they planned that Elma would travel with the now twenty-one-year-old Marion to London and Paris. When Elma returned, Marion would stay on in France until the fall with her good friend Reine, the daughter of the distinguished ambassador and writer Paul Claudel. Marion, an ardent horsewoman and budding artist, was looking forward to spending time at the Claudels' country house in Brangues, where she could paint to her heart's content. The entire trip was all worked out in advance down to the smallest detail. What Pierre and Elma couldn't have predicted, however, was how that one holiday would change their daughter's life.

Spending several weeks in the picturesque surroundings of the Château de Brangues, in the east of France near Grenoble, Marion fell in love. Unfortunately, Reine's cheerful, bespectacled older brother, Pierre Claudel, didn't seem to feel the same way. "A propos of Pierre—nothing new!" she confessed in a letter that summer. "He is always charming and treats me as a very beloved friend, but that is all." Refusing to dwell on it, she turned her focus elsewhere. Staying with the Catholic Claudels, she was, she explained, discovering God in a way that she had never before understood. "The world is blossoming like a flower petal by petal. The universe has a new and magnificent meaning."

Although the Cartier brothers were Roman Catholic, Marion had followed her mother into the Episcopal Church. During that long summer vacation, under the religious tutelage of Paul Claudel, her beliefs changed. "He explains so clearly and everything seems so simple," she wrote home, telling her father that she was preparing to convert to Catholicism in the local church that summer. And then, a few weeks later: "Dearest Papa . . . you cannot imagine how the fact of my conversion has changed everything!" Perhaps it was this

enormous enthusiasm that stirred
Pierre Claudel's affections, or simply the fact that she now shared
his religious faith. Either way,
something changed, and by the
end of Marion's holiday in September, the twenty-one-year-old
Pierre Claudel had proposed.

By October, the news had made
it into the papers on both sides of
the Atlantic. "I saw Marion in the
paper," Jacques wrote. "We're so
happy that she is engaged." Pierre,
thrilled to see his daughter so
happy, was himself delighted. An
ambassador's son was a worthy
match for his "Gem Princess," as
the papers dubbed her.

Marion Cartier and her fiancé,
Pierre Claudel, prior to their
marriage in New York in April 1933

The wedding was planned for the following spring. Pierre Claudel
was living in Paris where he was studying for the extremely demanding French diplomatic exams (he hoped to become an ambassador
like his father). He arrived in New York a couple of weeks before his
big day and was thrown into a whirlwind of celebrations. Pierre and
Elma held a formal afternoon reception with the French and Belgian
ambassadors, the Whitneys organized a large dinner at the Central
Park Casino, and Marion's aunt, Mrs. Bryson Delavan, hosted a dinner dance. There were opportunities for daytime photo shoots, too,
as Claudel visited his fiancée at her New York art class: "Claudel's
son picks a gem," the *Daily News* reported next to an image of Pierre
looking at Marion's work approvingly.

There were so many engagements and press appearances that by
the time the wedding approached, there were those who feared for
the bride's stamina: "How this busy young daughter of the Pierre
Cartiers manages to live through these hectic days preceding her marriage on Saturday to Pierre Claudel, son of the retiring French ambassador and Madame Claudel, is more than I can say." But manage it
she did. At 11:00 A.M. on Saturday, April 9, she appeared with her
father, to the excitement of the press and waiting crowds, outside the

Church of Saint Jean Baptiste at Lexington Avenue and Seventy-sixth Street. It was Lent, a period during which weddings were usually prohibited in the Catholic Church. On this occasion though, special dispensation had been given by the Pope because the father of the groom, Paul Claudel, was about to set sail to become the French ambassador to Belgium. Marion, recognizing that a Lenten wedding should show appropriate restraint, had dressed simply. Her V-necked ivory satin dress was accessorized with a discreet pearl necklace. She had presented each of her eight bridesmaids and her maid of honor with a simple diamond clip that they wore on their blue velvet turbans but had opted not to wear diamonds herself. Instead, real flowers took precedence, and her veil was secured by a half wreath of orange blossoms.

Five hundred guests waited to see the bride inside the church, but hundreds more cheered her on outside. Before Pierre walked his daughter down the long aisle, he instructed the police managing the hordes to let in enough onlookers to fill the empty pews at the back of the church. Just as he had wanted to make Cartier accessible to more than just the super-rich, now he applied the idea of democratization to his daughter's wedding. "A sailor from the USS *Pennsylvania,* an old woman peddling gum, a truck driver in torn pants, a sweatshirt, and a leather jacket, and a dozen aproned housewives with infants in their arms and small children clinging to their skirts, were among the throng that promptly acted upon the unexpected invitation. And since the doors of no Catholic church are ever closed, devout passers-by dropping into the church to say a few Lenten devotions remained for the most brilliant wedding of the spring."

Inside, society guests included the Rockefellers, the Whitneys, the Vanderbilts, and the Dukes. There were so many important figures from Washington that the press was quite overwhelmed by it all. *The New York Times,* the *Herald Tribune,* and the *New York American* were full of details of the many noted political figures at the "outstanding Lenten event." CLAUDEL WEDS A CARTIER AND WAS IT SWANK! declared *The Sunday Mirror,* reporting on a church filled with a joyously colorful congregation. There were "dowagers in pearl dog collars," French military attachés in "dark blue coats and gay scarlet trousers," diplomatic secretaries in "silk hats and long, picturesque capes," and American generals in "khaki, ribbons, and a bucket of decorations."

After the service, a beaming Marion and Pierre walked down the aisle, pausing as they left the church for the waiting photographers to catch their Sunday paper shot. Ushers directed the guests to the Waldorf Astoria, where a wedding breakfast on the roof terrace awaited them. Vintage champagne flowed, food was served, the large wedding cake was cut, and toasts were made. The newlyweds kicked off the dancing, swiftly followed by "everyone with tickling toes" unable to resist the Hungarian Gypsy band. Marion and Pierre eventually left the throng of friends and well-wishers to change. They had planned a honeymoon in South Africa before starting their new life together in Paris, and the ocean liner the *Conte de Savoia* was leaving that evening.

THE EX-KING AND THE JEWELRY KING

As Marion and her new husband started their married life together in Paris, not far away, another Cartier couple looked to be under pressure. Louis, already stressed at work as the effects of the Depression hit the French economy, was finding married life difficult too. In early 1934, it all came to a head when he accused Jacqui of having an affair. Her lover, he believed, was Alfonso XIII, the former king of Spain, who had abdicated a few years earlier. He was known for a lavish lifestyle, multiple mistresses, and at least six illegitimate children. When Louis discovered a telegram from the ex-king on his wife's boudoir table, he became suspicious and searched her belongings. On the discovery of "abundant correspondence with same foreigner," as he described it to Jacques, he flew into a jealous rage and demanded a divorce.

Jacqui insisted that while she and the ex-king knew each other well, they had only ever met "within the strict rules of social form." With Louis refusing to listen to her explanations, she left Paris for Budapest. "She is living in a sanatorium at Svabhegy," the Hungarian press reported in April, noting that she rarely showed herself in public. "Sometimes she asks her driver to take her, in her Delage car, into the city so she can visit a few friends. Otherwise she is living her life quietly in seclusion and waiting for her divorce to be finalized."

Suzanne, Louis' sister, urged him to give Jacqui another chance. She was suffering through an unhappy marriage herself. Her husband, Jacques Worth, was openly seeing another woman, but she had stayed with him for the sake of their four children and her Catholic faith. "God may not have blessed me with a perfect husband," she wrote to her siblings, "but he has blessed me with three wonderful brothers." Louis, though, was very different from his sister. Despite being no saint himself, the idea that his wife might be seeing a prominent society figure behind his back was the ultimate humiliation. He refused to back down. Louis "insists for divorce," Jacques telegraphed Pierre. "Asks me not to meddle as feels confident wife will accept conditions if not supported STOP Anne-Marie, PanPan [Toussaint], Dede have tried in view [sic] alter his mind."

Even the entreaties of Jeanne Toussaint, who had become fond of the Countess and recently found love herself with a French baron, could not dissuade him. The family tried to keep the news secret, but it wasn't long before the rumors started. By the summer of 1934, the press was having a field day. "Twelve years ago, the proud Countess Almásy married a king, a so-called king, the 'jewelry king.' In Budapest no one would be surprised if she would again marry a king. But this time a really blue-blooded one, an ex-king."

However, by the fall of 1934, Louis, to the surprise of his siblings, had changed his mind and decided to reunite with Jacqui. His nine-year-old son, Claude, had been terribly upset by his parents' separation, and it was partly his entreaties that had convinced his father to come home. "I only just learned of Louis' return to his wife," Suzanne wrote in October 1934. "In August, he had seemed so determined to me to go ahead with the divorce that I was not expecting this, but it has undoubtedly been brought about by Louis' son's intervention. What one doesn't do for one's children! I hope he will be rewarded for his generosity." Louis, true to the promise he had made to Claude, would make a go of his marriage with Jacqui. He had enough crises to deal with at work to warrant at least trying for stability in his home life. The situation in France was going from bad to worse. Rue de la Paix needed him.

"THE RUE DE LA PAIX IS LOSING LOTS OF ITS PRESTIGE"

France's relief at avoiding the worst of the Depression was short-lived. In 1932, European trade had fallen to one-third of its 1929 value, leaving many of Europe's most respected banking houses and currencies teetering on the brink of collapse. "Monthly figures for April-June disastrous," Louis' director Collin had reported in 1932. "The Rue de la Paix is losing lots of its prestige. If no improvement most of the jewelers and couturiers will close." Things hadn't been helped by lower-priced competition filling a gap in the market and attracting Cartier's traditional clients into the department stores: "Le Printemps and Galeries Lafayette have both opened jewelry departments which are doing well. They are selling diamond rings for 100 francs. Each maison losing 20 francs per ring, but it's a good advert."

Parliamentary instability in France became the norm, with five different governments elected between May 1932 and January 1934. In 1934 it all came to a head as a riot led to the fall of the government. As a populist leadership looked ever more likely, Louis feared for the future of his country. In 1935, he cleared out his Paris flat. Terrified of having his belongings seized, he moved them to Budapest, where Jacqui was living, and they chose to stay in a hotel when they were in the French capital.

To make matters worse for the business, there was a simultaneous jewelry market crisis. The steady rise in commercially available cultured pearls (from 1928 onward) had put the natural pearl market under increasing pressure. By 1930, prices of natural pearls had plummeted by 85 percent. Cartier, who still relied on natural pearls for the lion's share of its income, had joined with its old rival, Rosenthal, to fight for the fair classification of cultured pearls. They had asked that Mikimoto Kōkichi, the Japanese cultured pearl pioneer, should be forced to label his pearls as cultured, thus distinguishing (so they claimed) the real from the fake. Mikimoto insisted that his pearls, made by "seeding" the oyster with a small amount of mother-of-pearl, were no less real. Unfortunately for Cartier, many of their clients were willing to take his word for it.

Mikimoto would later decide to label his pearls as cultured, but by then, the damage to the natural pearl trade was already done. The

1930s jewelry market became awash with cultured pearls, and the majority of jewelry buyers, unable to tell them from natural pearls, were unconcerned with their origin. It wouldn't be until decades later that natural pearls were anywhere near as valuable again. The Cartier brothers refused to work with cultured pearls, despite their greater affordability in the midst of a depression. Yes, they could be large and perfectly shaped, but they were not, they felt, the result of nature. To them, the imperfections, color variations, and rarity of natural pearls were what made them so valuable.

In Conversation with Jean-Jacques Cartier

I had the impression from my father that the crash in natural pearl prices hurt us almost more than the effects of the Depression. You see, pearls made up such a large proportion of the jewels that Cartier's sold, and they were the most valuable gemstones by a million miles. To suddenly have that come crashing down, well, it made things very difficult.

In the absence of a stable economic backdrop, Cartier Paris was forced to be more creative in its offerings. Louis didn't feel Pierre's $5 bargain-offer technique would go down well in Rue de la Paix, but he did believe that "we must make it our business to build up an inventory that responds to the mood of the public by producing articles which have a useful function but which are also decorated in the Cartier style." Obviously, hugely expensive mystery clocks, which took months and months to make, were less appropriate in this market, but it was hard to take offense to functional watches or pocketknives.

Within the jewelry category, just two years before the Wall Street crash, Louis had predicted that "pearls, emeralds, very large rubies, sapphires, and diamonds" would dominate the fashion in jewelry. Now he had to change tack, and like Jacques, he started using more semiprecious stones. Among the devotees of Cartier Paris's semiprecious creations was the celebrity interior designer Elsie de Wolfe. In

1935, after selecting a geometric aquamarine and diamond tiara, she went for maximum shocking effect by dying her white hair (she was in her seventies at the time) a pale blue color to match.

Having previously started a trend for platinum, Louis was keen to explore new options for mounting metals. He instructed his technical department to come up with alloys that would be both lighter and better value than traditional mounts. With rose-tinted gold losing its noble appeal, his focus was on a more traditional yellow gold, or *"l'or Cartier"* as it became known. Experimenting by adding additional materials like cobalt, chromium, and beryllium, Cartier patented two new gold alloys in 1934. And ironically, just as so many of the maharajas had asked that their gold jewelry be reset in platinum in order to keep up with the fashions of the West, so Cartier's European clients switched their allegiance to gold.

But new innovations weren't limited to materials. The 1930s saw Cartier applying for more patents than in any other decade in its history. There were patents for objects like clip brooches (said to have been inspired by a clothes peg after Louis watched a washer woman hanging out clothes to dry) to those for techniques like the *serti mystérieux* that allowed the craftsman to set caliber-cut stones in a mosaic pattern by securing the underside of the stone with parallel metal rails. Louis would consider the new proposals from the design studio alongside a trusted committee comprising Edmond Forêt, Charles Jacqueau, Gérard Desouches, and, from 1935 onward, Jeanne Toussaint.

In 1933, Toussaint was promoted from Department S to a role focused on high jewelry. At the time, Louis had been away from the office more than usual, and worried that Cartier's creative output was suffering as a result. Although there were several senior personnel who shared his "sign-

A 1934 *Vogue* advertorial featured Cartier's innovative Diamants Mystérieux, worn as a head ornament.

off" authority when it came to choosing which designs to execute, Louis felt they lacked the imagination to push the design team in original directions. In 1933, after receiving several uninspiring designs by post from René Revillon, Louis replied to him with a suggestion: "As much as I am in favor of making rock crystal and diamonds, I would like to receive something tastier, or something new." The decision to use rock crystal alongside diamonds in the large bracelets favored by the Polish opera singer Ganna Walska and the Hollywood star Gloria Swanson had proved a great success over the past four years, but Louis was concerned that his firm was resting on its laurels. He didn't want to simply produce more of the same, however popular it was.

Wanting "something new" and yet unable to easily influence the creative process from afar, Louis explained to René he needed someone in Rue de la Paix to act on his behalf offering artistic direction. The first person who sprang to mind was Jeanne Toussaint, for her "great universally appreciated taste." Knowing her intimately for many years, he knew that she wasn't as tough as she pretended to be, and he admitted to harboring a fear that the extra responsibility might prove too much: "I am afraid of this new weight for her." Ultimately, though, he decided to take the risk and promote her: "I am ready to execute the stock drawings on her signature and under her responsibility." The team accepted Louis' word as law even if they didn't all agree with it (some felt Toussaint could be "very authoritarian"). Charles Jacqueau in particular was put out by the news, concerned Toussaint might use her new position to sideline his designs.

But Jacqueau did not need to worry quite yet. Louis was not ready to cede control entirely. When his niece saw him for dinner at the end of 1935, she reported back to her father, "he is in good spirits and told me again how much he loves his work." Toussaint may have been promoted, but he was still the boss, and when he was in Paris, he remained the driver behind the firm's artistic output. "I was pleasantly surprised to see how much the boss had worked on the models last month," René Revillon wrote in the spring of 1935. "We will be well fitted in advance of the season." And Louis wasn't just focused on new creations. Both his brothers had started seasonal branches, in Palm Beach and in St. Moritz, and he had long been tempted to do the same.

Believing there to be a slight uptick in the French economy, and hoping that it would bode well for future business, Louis traveled down to Cannes to explore the possibility of opening a showroom on the Riviera. It was here, on a sunny reconnaissance mission in early 1935, that he received a series of worrying telegrams from India. Jacques was gravely ill.

BARBARIC SPLENDOR

Jacques and Nelly had returned to India in March 1935. But this time, instead of settling into their usual sea-view suite, Jacques had been rushed to the hospital. "Jacques has hemorrhages on arrival Tajmahal Hotel Bombay," Nelly had telegraphed her husband's brothers on March 13 in fear. "Good doctor and nurses. Will keep you posted." A week later, it was looking less serious. Jacques had responded to treatment and "improvement continues." There was no way, however, that he was well enough to travel around India as planned. There would be no time in the gem bazaars, Schwaiger's shop, or the palace of Nawanagar. Both his doctors and Nelly insisted that he abandon the trip entirely and, as soon as he was well enough to travel again, return directly home.

Ten days after the couple's arrival in India, a hugely relieved Nelly wrote to the family to let them know that Jacques had been deemed well enough to return home and they would be setting sail by the end of the month. In early April, when the couple arrived at the port of Naples, Louis was there waiting to pick them up in his comfortable motor car to drive them to Paris. Later, as the brothers said goodbye in the city of their childhood, Louis made Jacques promise him he would take it easy. Work was far less important than his health, he insisted. Jacques, even more mindful of life's transience than usual, gave Louis his word. From Milton Heath his correspondence hinted at his philosophical mindset. In one letter to his then fifteen-year-old son, Jean-Jacques, he sent a small book of spiritual teachings: "The mind is a mill, the books we read are the grain brought to the mill, and our thoughts are the flour coming out of the mill. Therefore what you read you think and what you think you are. . . . This [book] will make you a better, stronger, and happier man than you would have been otherwise."

Despite his wife's urging him to stay at home and rest for a few weeks, it wasn't long before Jacques was back at work. He was, of course, relieved to be on the road to recovery but part of him was frustrated that the India trip had been curtailed before he had the chance to buy more gemstones. The Indian fashion was increasingly taking off in Europe, and the jewels he had been making since the 1920s from carved sapphires, rubies, and emeralds were more popular than ever.

JEWELRY SPOTLIGHT: TUTTI FRUTTI JEWELS AND THE COLLIER HINDOU

Cartier's brightly colored Indian-style jewels of the 1920s and '30s weren't given the "Tutti Frutti" name until the 1970s. At the time, Jacques called them his "Hindou jewels." Made up from carved gemstones he had brought back from the East, they combined the exotic with the modern and were an instant hit among the trendsetters of the day. They were also, perhaps surprisingly, more affordable than other similarly striking Cartier jewels, making them ideal for the Depression years.

A 1929 Tutti Frutti diamond bracelet with carved emerald and ruby leaves, buds, and flowers and black enamel vine motifs.

"Many of the Indian gems," Jacques revealed, "are not so flawless as those used here." But this was one instance when he was less interested in purity than in color. Focused on making an impact through the mix of colors, he was willing to sacrifice on each gemstone's clarity and translucency.

After returning from his Indian trips, Jacques' first port of call was Paris, where he would meet Louis and share the gemstones he had acquired. Both fascinated by Eastern cultures, the two brothers owned many of the same illustrated books on India (on subjects as diverse as rugs, traditional dress, and miniature paintings) in which they found inspiration for motifs that they would later use on their creations. But the books, often in black-and-white, didn't express the overwhelming explosion of color that Jacques had seen firsthand, and it was this that he wanted to capture in the Hindu jewels: "Out there everything is flooded with the wonderful Indian sunlight," Jacques explained. "One does not see as in the English light, he is only conscious that here is a blaze of red, and there of green or yellow. It is all like an impressionist painting. Nothing is clearly defined, and there is but one vivid impression of undreamed gorgeousness and wealth."

One rebellious lady particularly enamored with the Hindu style would prove pivotal in popularizing it. Daisy Fellowes, heiress to the Singer sewing machine fortune, was a celebrated society figure, admired and feared in equal measure. She was the embodiment of thirties chic, Jean Cocteau saying of her that she "launched more fashions than any other woman in the world," such as the avant-garde idea of wearing jewels with sweaters. But she could also be cruel, with a wicked wit and a penchant for "cocaine and other women's husbands." In 1933 she became Paris editor of *Harper's Bazaar* but left two years later because she found it boring. She preferred to be an icon of fashion herself, and in Cartier she saw a firm that made the trends rather than followed them.

In 1935, as Paris was "overrun with Maharajas, casually wearing fabulous jewels," Daisy held an Oriental Ball for which "all the precious jewels in Paris were taken out of the vaults." *Vogue* was quick on her heels, dedicating a double-page spread to "Eastern splendor" and the "barbaric" nature of Cartier's Indian-style jewels ("barbaric" because the gemstones were not cut in the smooth fashion that civilized American and European ladies were used to).

The following year, Daisy would go one step further, commissioning the Collier Hindou, perhaps the most spectacular example of Cartier's Tutti Frutti style. Reconstructed from Fellowes's own carved sapphires, emeralds, rubies, and diamonds, the necklace was unique both in terms of the sheer number of stones and for its ingeniously flexible design. And as with many jewels of the period, it was multipurpose: the central part of the necklace (formed from two large carved sapphire buds, diamond-studded emerald beads, carved ruby leaves, and navette diamonds) doubled as a removable clip brooch. In true allegiance to the Indian style, the Collier Hindou was designed to be secured around the neck with a black silk cord, but it did have one important difference from jewels made for Indian clients: Sapphires, rarely used in India because they were considered unlucky, appeared in abundance.

Daisy Fellowes in the Collier Hindou, photographed by Cecil Beaton in 1937.

After Daisy Fellowes's death, the necklace passed to her eldest daughter, the Comtesse de Castéja, who took it back to Cartier to be altered in 1963. The client's own gemstones were used to form a fixed collar, and the two large sapphires that had previously constituted the central part of the necklace comprised the new clasp.

In 1991, five years after the death of Castéja, the spectacular necklace, along with a pair of carved emerald and diamond earrings, came up for sale with an estimate of $650,000–$950,000. When the hammer came down at the Sotheby's Geneva auction, a new record was set for an Art Deco jewel. The final price was $2,655,172.

A ROYAL VISIT

The growing interest in Indian-style jewels helped boost Cartier's profile in all three branches, but in London, Jacques also had something his brothers lacked. The British royal family offered their country, in the midst of economic malaise, a spark of glamour and excitement. Financially, Cartier sometimes lost out in its transactions with the royals, but it always made up for it in terms of prestige.

The London branch's association with the British royal family had been bolstered back in 1933 when Queen Mary asked to exchange a gift she had been given from Cartier for a more valuable clip brooch. After Cartier made the exchange for free, the firm's reward was an offer from the Queen to tour the New Bond Street store. Her much-reported visit would help publicize the fact that although Cartier was a French firm, the London branch employed Englishmen. This was an important message to convey at a time when there was a backlash against firms in London employing foreign workers over British ones.

After looking through the showrooms and the various departments upstairs, "Her Majesty," Cartier's director Sinden recalled, "talked to quite a number of the workmen and the visit lasted an hour and a half." She had entered through the side entrance on Albemarle Street, but by the time she left, "the news had got round that Her Majesty was here and there were a number of people waiting to watch her leave." The Queen was particularly taken with a pair of antique earrings she had seen in the showroom and asked for them to be sent to the palace for a closer look. The following day, word came that Her Majesty would like to keep them but wanted to have them adjusted to wear on a necklace and brooch, so could Sinden pop down to the palace at midday? On his arrival, the Cartier director was greeted by the "extremely friendly" Queen, who "again expressed her enjoyment of the visit." He was also treated to a tour of her private suite, where she showed him all "the wonderful showcases containing various collections."

The royal visit in 1933 had been excellent for business. "Bond Street is busy," Jacques reported a couple of months later; "the workshop is blocked with orders." Not long after, much to Jacques' delight, the Queen's support would be mirrored by another member of her family. Prince George (who became the Duke of Kent) approached Cartier with a request. He was planning to propose to Princess Marina of Greece on holiday in Yugoslavia and needed a ring. After extensive discussions, the Queen's youngest son selected a square emerald-cut Kashmir sapphire of more than 10 carats set in platinum with a baton diamond on either side. "Prince George has displayed the most modern taste in his choice both of the ring and of the setting," Cartier announced when interviewed later by the press. "His selection will undoubtedly make sapphires the most popular ring for engagements this year."

The wedding took place in November (with the future Queen Elizabeth II as one of the bridesmaids). Princess Marina couldn't have been a better advertisement for Cartier. From the moment she set foot in England, she was adored. "Everyone is so delighted with her, the crowd especially, 'cos when she arrived at Victoria station, they expected a dowdy Princess such as unfortunately my family are—but when they saw this lovely chic creature—they could hardly believe it," Prince George told his future brother-in-law. "Even the men were interested and shouted 'Don't change—don't let them change you!' Of course, she won't be changed—not if I have anything to do with it."

Princess Marina would come to be considered one of the most beautiful and best-dressed women of her time, with "cool classical features in a perfect oval head held high on a straight column of neck, the topaz eyes, the slightly tilted smile, the apricot complexion, and the nut brown cap of flat silken curls." But she had a tough family to outshine, and before long she would have some serious competition from her future sister-in-law.

MRS. SIMPSON

Prince George's eldest brother, the Prince of Wales, had been entranced with Wallis Simpson ever since their first meeting over dinner at a friend's country house weekend in 1931. When he had asked her whether she missed the central heating of America, her cutting reply had somehow charmed him: "Every American woman who comes to England is asked the same question. I had hoped for something more original from the Prince of Wales." A year or so later, his frequent trips into Cartier (via the more discreet back Albemarle Street entrance and directly into the private client room away from prying eyes) were evidence of his growing affection. It was to Cartier's benefit that the Prince of Wales had favored Boucheron when buying gifts for his previous mistress, Freda Dudley Ward. When he started a relationship with Wallis, she wanted nothing reminiscent of Freda, and he was instructed to switch allegiance from one French jeweler to another.

It was no secret that the royal family did not approve of the future king's relationship with a married American woman. At the house of Lady Cunard, a fellow American in London who was friends with both the Prince and Wallis, the couple could, however, be assured of enthusiastic encouragement. Looking ahead to the day when her good friend would become Queen and all her support would be recognized, Emerald Cunard was said to be angling for the prestigious "Mistress of the Robes" title. At dinner parties throughout the rest of London, Mrs. Simpson was a source of endless fascination. When she appeared in the royal box at the opera with emeralds and diamonds glittering against her black dress, Marie Belloc Lowndes, a diarist of the day, declared that she must be wearing "dressmakers' jewels," since no one could possibly afford genuine stones so large. She was wrong. They were real.

Jacques often found himself being asked for his opinion of Mrs. Simpson. Always he was discreet, in keeping with the policy of the House, saying only that Mrs. Simpson had marvelous taste and a fantastic collection of jewels. The British media, for their part, also kept quiet about the affair, guided by the royal family, who hoped it would all go away. But after King George V died in January 1936 and as the Prince of Wales awaited his coronation to become King Edward VIII, gossip started to spread more vigorously, especially over in America, where word of the scandalous relationship escaped the self-censorship of the English press. When the couple took a Mediterranean cruise, Wallis was spotted wearing a rather special Cartier jewel, causing overexcited rumors. A diamond charm jewel with nine jeweled crosses, it didn't so much fuel speculation because of its value but rather because of its deeply personal nature: Each cross was engraved with various messages "handwritten" by the King.

With the coronation of the new king planned for the following year, Cartier London was inundated with new orders. Though keen to oversee the work, Jacques was not always well enough to make it into the office each day. "Sorry for delay, had to take to my bed for a few days on a slight relapse of my old trouble but all better now," he wrote in 1936. "Louis paid me a short visit and looked v well." Later, after a checkup, he wrote again, this time asking Pierre to find out about the best treatments in the United States for a blocked artery. In England, his doctor was recommending opening it with paraffin, he explained, but it was a very new technique and he wanted a second opinion. "Can you ask an American doctor their advice also? It seems to me that this paraffin could dissipate in the body and cause problems elsewhere." It had been less than two years since his last operation in India, and he was understandably concerned. Operations were not to be taken lightly, especially not one as serious as this.

A RISING TIDE

Reading his brother's letter, Pierre was worried. He knew how Jacques soldiered on and resisted resting as his doctors had advised. Pleased he would be able to see him the following summer for the coronation celebrations, he resolved to book rooms at the Carlton Hotel in London. From New York, he wrote back to Jacques with family news: Marion and her husband had moved to America.

Unfortunately, Claudel hadn't been successful in his diplomatic exams. Reflecting the terrible economy, the number of places on offer had been limited to three in 1935 and just two the year after. The political backdrop hadn't helped either. Pierre Cartier was well-connected to those in positions of authority within France, but with the unstable situation and endless changes of leadership in the country, this leverage had diminished. Claudel had studied diligently for three years, Marion had given endless teas and lunches to those ladies who might have some influence on those making decisions, and Pierre Cartier had supported them both as much as he could, but it hadn't been enough.

Instead, Pierre proposed that Claudel start work in the Fifth Avenue branch, and the younger man accepted, traveling to New York with his family in the summer of 1936. It was a good time to move away from France. "Business in UK and US and almost everywhere is on upward trend," Jacques wrote to his brother, "except France, where new laws will be noticeable to masses soon and expect strikes and workers' disturbances which may affect English and American services." Claudel was soon named vice president of Cartier New York and, like his father-in-law, became an officer of the French Chamber of Commerce.

Meanwhile the mood in New York was picking up. As the worst effects of the Depression subsided in America, an elite group of stylish individuals captured the imagination of the masses. Café society, as it was known, comprised the "beautiful people" who gathered in fashionable restaurants and cafés. The end of Prohibition in 1933 and the rise of photojournalism meant that this elegant set could not only entertain semipublicly but could also be photographed doing so. Simultaneously, the 1930s marked the start of the Golden Age of Hollywood as "talkies" replaced silent films. For all those struggling under the weight of the Depression, a trip to the movies offered affordable escapism and light relief, and suddenly those previously little-known actors and actresses on the big screen became international celebrities. Even blue-blooded Americans, from the Astors to the Vanderbilts, wanted to associate with the likes of Gloria Swanson and Marlene Dietrich, and café society epitomized this coming together of glamorous, and bejeweled, individuals.

The glamour of Hollywood soon inspired women to wear more jewelry. In black-and-white movies, colored gemstones didn't show up so well, but diamonds provided the necessary glitz. Before long costume jewelers were in on the act, creating cheap, sparkling alternatives out of rhinestone and nickel. Fortunately for Cartier, there were a few clients around who could afford the real thing.

Doris Duke had been in the American spotlight since her birth, when newspapers dubbed her "the richest little girl in the world." Thirteen years later, this prophecy had literally come true after the untimely death of her tobacco magnate father, when she inherited more than $100 million (over $1.4 billion today). A tall blond beauty, Duke didn't lack self-confidence or admirers, and she went after what she wanted. Though she owned several mansions, traveled the world, and shopped at all the best stores, she would also become a great philanthropist, a passionate gardener (she created one of the largest indoor botanical gardens in America), and one of the first female competitive surfers. In 1935, at the age of twenty-three, she married James Cromwell (who had divorced Delphine Dodge in 1928), and she would go on to finance his political career. Both Cromwell and

With the rise of Hollywood in the 1930s, a new group of actress celebrities became the perfect models for Cartier. Left: Marlene Dietrich, pictured for *Vogue* in Cartier silver earrings with yellow gold balls and a Cartier cuff bracelet. Right: Gloria Swanson, in her famous 1930 expanding rock crystal and diamond bracelets, pictured with William Holden promoting the film *Sunset Boulevard*.

Duke were New Deal advocates (much to the disapproval of her mother-in-law, Eva Stotesbury).

Fortunately for Cartier, along with Doris's many other interests, she also had a passion for jewels. Her mother, Nanaline, may have been more materialistic than nurturing, but she had taught her young daughter to appreciate beautiful gems. Doris was consequently known within Cartier for being very exacting in her jewelry requirements: "I spent last weekend at Doris's, and then lunched with her in New York and I got her to come into the office," Glaenzer reported in May 1937 after a summer weekend spent with his client in Rough Point, her Newport mansion. "She brought with her the briolette diamond earrings, saying the diamonds were too yellow." In this instance, Glaenzer managed to persuade her that her earrings were in fact very special. The diamonds, he explained, were an old Indian cut that was impossible to find in the U.S. and were intended to be "worn in the evening," as they looked lovely in candlelight. "In the end, Doris said O.K."

In anticipation of the 1937 coronation, to which she had been invited, Doris inquired about more jewels. Given the fashion for diamonds, she was particularly interested in a diamond fringe necklace, but before she committed to it, she wanted to wear it at a ball in Washington just to be sure. The week before the ball, however, she confided in Glaenzer that she couldn't possibly go anymore as her whole arm was covered with a rash and looked like a piece of "raw meat." Knowing that his role of salesman went well beyond simply supplying gems, Glaenzer promptly called his own doctor, tracked down the medicine that would take away the angry rash, "and, to make a long story short, she wore the necklace at the ball." The bill for $74,000 (close to $1.3 million today) was sent to her the following week.

And yet, though there were a few extremely wealthy clients, like Doris Duke, who were open to spending on jewels, America was still in the depths of the Depression. "The economic situation in the United States seems to be improving but don't forget that in the luxury business, we are still passing through a terrible crisis which has lasted almost seven years," Pierre would write to Jean-Charles Worth. Against this backdrop, the Cartier salesforce had to work harder than ever, both tracking down some of the country's richest ladies and enticing them to part with their (or their husband's) money.

From Palm Beach, Cartier's Paul Rosier was tasked with finding out any details that might help the New York branch approach his clients when they were back home after the holidays. Palm Beach had taken a hit during the Depression, with many forced to abandon their expensive holidays in the sun because funds were tight. By 1936, things were starting to pick up, and there were a few clients, such as the world's best-dressed woman Mona Williams (later von Bismarck), who were in the market for jewels. "She is looking for something ultra-modern and exotic that will startle society," Rosier explained to his boss in a message that was typical of the exchanges between branches. "I am under the impression . . . that she does not know herself exactly what she wants and perhaps this would be a good opportunity to create some business." Any hint that a new commission might be in the cards was worth pursuing, especially if (as in the case of Mona Williams) the client's husband was one of the richest men in America. The idea was that by the time Mona arrived in New York, Cartier would already have some unusual designs to show her, thereby achieving a jump start on the competition.

A GOOD JOLT OF BRANDY

Cartier salesmen were expected to be always on duty. From a boat to Europe, Glaenzer wrote that he had met the Dorrance family, owners of Campbell Soup, and that they would definitely be worth pursuing when back in America. He had also heard rumors that Barbara Hutton would soon be marrying again and they should be ready with some new jewels to show her. In the end she would buy the fantastic Romanov emeralds on the back of this tip-off in 1935.

The downside with Cartier salesmen's cultivating relationships with their clients outside the office was that they then owned these relationships. Being commercial by nature and highly aware of how much value these clients represented, the firm ran the risk that they might threaten to walk, especially when propositioned by jealous competitors offering more money. Despite his long history and bond with Pierre (he signed all letters to his boss *"ton ami, Jules"*—your friend, Jules), Glaenzer remained mercurial. In the summer of 1936, the director of Cartier's Palm Beach showroom wrote to Pierre to let him know that there was a very specific rumor "that a group of men from Cartier either had left or were going to leave and that the group was headed by Glaenzer and Lynch" (another Cartier New York salesman). It was said that the group planned to start their own business, backed by Edsel Ford, the only son of Henry Ford and a close friend of Glaenzer. "Naturally I made light of the whole matter but consider it my duty to bring it to your attention."

In the end, Glaenzer, who was already fifty-four and suffered from occasional bad health, opted to stick with the devil he knew. Like all senior salesmen at Cartier, he benefited from a decent commission on each sale he made, so as the market showed signs of recovery, he had more reason to stay put. He recognized too that Cartier had a reputation that couldn't be replicated overnight by a new firm. "When a man gets rich," he used to say, "sooner or later he comes to Cartier."

So instead of leaving, Glaenzer threw himself even further into sniffing out significant jewelry sales. On one occasion, he traveled six thousand miles to meet a client in Paris, only to be told she had gone to Freiburg, Germany. He then flew to Freiburg, only to be told she was in the hospital, and too ill to see him. He was forced to return to New York by ocean liner, empty-handed and frustrated. But the most memorable trip of all was in 1936, when Glaenzer traveled through America to try to sell a 22-carat diamond ring for $95,000 ($1.7 million in today's money) to a recently widowed client. He later wrote a letter explaining how "obstacles . . . hop up at the last moment in the path of an honest jeweler to hinder and retard his best efforts."

Glaenzer had taken the night boat to Fall River, Massachusetts. Not knowing exactly where the client lived, he went to her daughter's house, only to find that she was at the golf club. By the time he arrived at the golf club, he was informed that she had gone home. When he eventually found the mother's house, he was told she was in Boston, so, he later recounted, "I sat myself in a chair with a book in the cool ocean breeze and slept for two hours until lunchtime." Finally, the elderly lady came home to find—to her surprise—a Cartier salesman on the veranda. Turning on the charm, Glaenzer comfortably conversed with her on all manner of subjects, putting her at her ease. Only then did he bring up the ring, telling her how much he thought her late husband would have liked it.

Just as he was about to seal the deal, the phone rang. The widow listened to the voice on the other end for a couple of minutes before screaming "Oh my God!" Alarmed and baffled, Glaenzer took the phone. It was the superintendent at the cemetery. Apparently, the copper casket in which his client's deceased husband was buried in the mausoleum had just exploded in a freak accident. "You know, Pierre," Glaenzer wrote, "it is tough enough to try to sell a $95,000 ring without having the widower's body explode all over the place." Glaenzer told her that he had heard of a lot of similar cases, and that owing to the heat, a pocket of gas would have formed which had simply found a vent. "Got a good jolt of brandy in her and carried on!" he continued. This, he hoped, would give Pierre an idea of "the trials and tribulations of a jewelry salesman. . . . P.S. I sold her the diamond ring!"

Combined with the sale of the diamond necklace Cartier had made recently to Doris Duke, the ring purchase would put Cartier Inc.'s revenues well ahead of the previous year's. Glaenzer's commission was looking good too. Unfortunately, the news from Paris was not so upbeat. As Louis had feared, in May 1936, the Popular Front (made up of left-wing movements including the French Communist Party) had been voted in. The labor force greeted the news with a series of strikes to show their support, and many businesses, Cartier included, worried about the new government's policies.

To make matters worse, Louis had been ill. In February, after a terrifying episode of pleurisy, which affected his breathing, he was told to take bed rest for several weeks. The doctor repeatedly reiterated how important it was that his patient stay relaxed and quiet in order not to aggravate his heart troubles. Louis agreed to delegate more to others, like the increasingly capable Devaux, but a few months later, something would happen at Rue de la Paix that meant staying calm would be harder than ever.

WHAT'S MEANT TO BE IN THERE? PEARLS?

In August 1936, a valuable diamond necklace was stolen from Cartier Paris. The police were called but nothing was found. It appeared to have been an inside job. The necklace had been shown to a client, Madame Corrigan, in the showroom by a senior salesman. When Madame Corrigan had left, the necklace, still in its case, had been returned to the safe by the two *garçons* (errand boys). The following Tuesday, Jules Glaenzer, visiting from New York for a few weeks, had completed a stock check of all the items in the safe. On opening the red box that should have contained the diamond necklace, he found it empty.

In Conversation with Jean-Jacques Cartier

Robberies were very rare, especially inside jobs. I think people were generally proud to work at Cartier. I certainly never doubted the loyalty of those who worked for me.

After the *garçons* had been interviewed and deemed innocent, suspicion turned to Jules Glaenzer, who was asked to give a statement. Once he, too, had been found innocent, the police suspected the only other person in the room when Glaenzer had brought in the items from the safe: René Revillon. For years, Louis had given his son-in-law more responsibility than his age and experience warranted, mostly because he was family. Jacques had worried that it was a mistake, concerned that it had created feelings of jealousy and resentment among the other employees. But there had been no dissuading Louis. His own son, Claude, was still too young to join the firm and he wanted so much for Cartier to be a family-run business. Recently, though, the relationship between Louis and René had started to sour.

After hearing rumors that René was seeing other women, Louis became angry on behalf of his daughter. Anne-Marie was such a sensitive, fragile girl, and had been devastated. Her aunt had even advised her not to let on in public how upset she was, but Anne-Marie was known for her childlike behavior (ironically, it was this that René had found so attractive when they first met) and wasn't good at keeping her emotions in check. "Of course she is unbalanced," her relatives admitted to one another, but the only way to change her, they believed, was "by love and affection."

The matter of the robbery was kept quiet, with only the police and a handful of staff members informed. It turned out that not only had René been present with Glaenzer when the empty case had been opened, but he also had asked a surprising question: "What's meant to be in there? Pearls?" As a senior member of the team, he should have known that the box held a diamond necklace. There had also been a moment in the office when Glaenzer's back was turned, the implication being that René could have taken the necklace from its case and pocketed it. But there was no hard evidence.

Three weeks of discreet police investigation failed to turn up any more clues. Louis Cartier and Devaux decided to try to scare René into admission. Devaux mentioned to René, and only René, that the police had decided that if the necklace was not returned in two days, the matter would be taken to court. Miraculously enough, the necklace then turned up under a mat in the corridor. Now largely convinced it was the work of René, Devaux decided to set one more test. He mentioned to René that the necklace had been found and that, fortunately, the police had been able to collect fingerprints from it (this was untrue). René's response, Devaux later told Jacques, was not to be pleased, as an innocent man would have been, but to shake nervously.

And yet there was still no firm evidence either way. René continued to declare his innocence. Senior management, Louis included, were convinced of his guilt. Only Glaenzer, the other senior figure present when the robbery took place, remained supportive of him. René threatened to make the news public if he was fired, and as Jacques later wrote to Pierre, he had friends in high places, so they didn't want to risk that. And yet the few members of management who knew about the robbery and suspected him threatened to go on strike if he continued to come in to the office each day. Instead, Jacques suggested that René should take a long vacation and wait until the situation had calmed down.

For Louis, there was no hope of calming down. Furious, he went to see his daughter and demanded that she divorce René quickly and discreetly. "He was so fierce," Anne-Marie recalled later, "I could hardly be drawn to him. His brutality is so painful to me." Despite Louis' anger and her husband's past indiscretions, Anne-Marie stood by René, convinced of his innocence. In the end, Jacques stepped in to mediate, declaring that they must find proof before a conviction. "Even if he was capable of carrying out such an idiotic act, he shouldn't be made to lose both his job and his wife based on presumptions."

Jacques visited the Paris office and listened to all the evidence against René. There were suspicions about two previous robberies, including a sapphire stolen three years earlier. Digging deeper, Jacques discovered that those robberies had been investigated by one of the firm's directors, Collin, but not this one. He asked Louis for the right to interview Collin but Louis refused, saying the whole situation must be kept quiet. Here, unusually, Jacques went behind Louis' back. Convinced that his elder brother was being irrational, he wrote to Pierre suggesting that he speak to Collin about the previous thefts without mentioning the current one. Pierre responded immediately: "Approve your idea to interview Collin," he telegraphed back.

Pierre and Jacques had often despaired at Louis' temper, but they rarely went against his express wishes. This, though, they did for the good of the family and the firm. They didn't want the situation in the press ("we must consider the reputation of our House") and could see no other option but to take the investigations into their own hands, given the "infantile behavior" of their elder brother. The discussions with Collin failed to turn up new evidence but slowly more and more people within Cartier were learning about the scandal. It was hugely divisive. Those who suspected René were furious, while others were outraged at the baseless accusations. "There is no longer a family atmosphere in La Maison," Anne-Marie complained.

For his part, René continued to protest his innocence, writing about this "horrible nightmare" in which he found himself and blaming the accusation on the "jealousy, envy and wickedness of those in the office" who wanted to see a "diligent hard-working" young man disappear. Jacques considered trying to ease the situation by inviting René to London, but it was too close to Paris, the rumors would follow him there. Believing René to be either innocent or foolish, Jacques proposed that Pierre take him on in New York, at least on a trial basis.

Having known René for years, Pierre agreed, as did Louis (indicating that his son-in-law could stay as a director of S.A. until the next Board meeting in the spring). Just before Christmas 1936, René set sail from Le Havre on the SS *Normandie* bound for New York. Fifteen years earlier, he had taken the same journey with his new bride, hugely optimistic for the future. Back then, Louis had waved him and Anne-Marie off with the offer of a job in Paris whenever he wanted it. Now the only person waving him off was a tearful Anne-Marie. He was an exile, banished from Rue de la Paix.

A FAMILY TRAGEDY

René promised to send for Anne-Marie when he had found somewhere to live and had some money in his pocket. Pierre and Elma found him a hotel initially and Anne-Marie wrote to thank them: "I was brokenhearted when he left but he needs a change of life and atmosphere." Despite the fact that he had made her unhappy in Paris, she loved him deeply. She asked them to take special care of him, especially on the weekends when he had no work to keep him busy. "See that [he] is not lonely at night. . . . Tell him not to look too much at my photos, for his letters are sad."

Anne-Marie longed to visit him and waited impatiently for the confirmation that he was ready for her. He wrote often, sending small gifts—cigarettes for her, sweets for the children—but his letters were

pained. Anne-Marie, distressed by the enforced separation and concerned for her husband alone in the city, turned to her uncle in desperation. "I know that you have a wonderful influence over my
father," she wrote in January 1937, "so you might calm him down.
Jacqui does what she can but he is sometimes impossible." The situation in Cartier Paris was improving, she revealed, but it would take a
brave employee to go against the boss: "Everything depends on personal vindication by Louis."

Later she wrote again, thanking Pierre for dealing with her debts,
as her father had stopped giving her any money. Louis was under the
false impression, she wrote, that his ex-wife, Anne-Marie's mother,
Andrée-Caroline Worth, gave her plenty of money. The reality was
that "she gives me 5,000 francs on New Year's Day for myself and
the children." That's why she had debts, she explained, "but as in a
fairy tale, an uncle in America has arrived" to take an interest in her:
"Tu es un vraiment grand guy" (you are really a great guy), she wrote.
She didn't know how to thank him enough: "Money doesn't make
you happy . . . but it's a drag when you don't have it."

Meanwhile René, who missed his old job as Louis' right-hand
man, was receiving updates on business in 13 Rue de la Paix from
those on the inside. "The worst moment has passed, stay calm, be
patient, it won't be long until the situation all blows over," a junior
colleague reassured her old boss in January 1937, clearly believing in
his innocence. Louis, the colleague reported, was "very proud," but
he was already realizing his mistake and would soon be forced to
apologize.

Just as the incident began to blow over in Paris, in New York tragedy struck. It was a cold winter and as 1937 dawned, René became
ill. Worn down by the stresses of the previous few months, he developed a stomach ulcer that perforated, causing him severe pain. Pierre
and Elma looked after him, and their circle rallied around. May Birkhead, a journalist and one of Elma's best friends, was one of those on
hand as René was taken to the French Hospital on West Thirtieth
Street in Manhattan for surgery. It was serious, but everyone was
optimistic. Glaenzer, who had been with René when he had initially
been accused, telegraphed from Florida, "This ought to be an easy
fight for you after the one we went through last summer. . . . Your
devoted pal, Jules Glaenzer."

Anne-Marie, hearing of her husband's hospitalization, was desperate. Elma wrote that she was by René's bedside and praying for him. Tragically, the prayers would not save his life. The surgery on his ulcer led to further complications, and a blood clot passed to his lungs. He died three weeks later, in late February 1937. Overwhelmed with grief, Anne-Marie was prostrate for a fortnight at the shock of it all, and, as she later admitted to her aunt, wanted to die herself. Her children were the only reason she carried on (her eldest, René-Louis, who had just turned fifteen, already reminded her of his father).

Feeling helpless so far away, Elma asked her friend May Birkhead to check on her niece when she sailed back to France. On her arrival in Paris, Birkhead, who covered the Parisian social scene for *The New York Times* and "probably knew and was known by more cosmopolites and social personages of the two continents than any other reporter in Europe or America," went immediately to Rue de la Paix. Louis, returning from five months in Budapest, had only just heard the terrible news. "He has a calm exterior but is completely beside himself," she wrote.

Nervous about seeing his estranged daughter (with whom he had cut all contact since she had refused to divorce René the previous summer), Louis asked Birkhead to accompany him to Anne-Marie. He had, Birkhead discovered, "no hard feeling toward René anymore and said it was just one of those unfortunate things." In time, she believed, it would all have blown over. Anne-Marie, meanwhile, was broken: "Alone in bed and weeping her eyes out . . . She has a stack of René's letters by the bed." Louis sat there "white as a sheet." He was very sweet, Birkhead revealed, and brought Anne-Marie money, but "was more upset than he was prepared to admit to himself. . . . Poor Louis, I do think he regrets the whole thing."

Louis was joined by all his siblings at René's Parisian funeral. There, in the same church where René had said his marriage vows sixteen years earlier, a large congregation came to offer their support to his widow and three children. Anne-Marie was slowly reconciling with her father, but it would take some time. Soon after the funeral, Louis bade farewell to his daughter. Promising to do anything he could to help, he returned to Hungary, leaving Devaux in charge of matters at Rue de la Paix.

"TIARAS ARE ABSOLUTELY THE RAGE"

Jacques and Nelly were terribly shocked to hear of René's death. Thinking of Anne-Marie left behind with the children, they immediately wrote to invite her to Milton Heath whenever she felt ready to travel. Jacques worried about Louis too. His health had been weak for some time and this shock was not good for his already elevated stress levels. And yet, while he encouraged his elder brother to rest, Jacques had to admit that the Paris branch suffered without their boss around. And since the robbery, 13 Rue de la Paix lacked unity. Louis' long absences last year had been understandable, given his heart problems, but they had created something of a power vacuum in Paris and a "great amount of tension at the office."

In England, the British public had lived through an unprecedented few months in England. For most of 1936, the scandalous relationship between the King and Wallis Simpson was kept out of the British press. In October 1936, however, the King proposed to Wallis Simpson, and the following month he met with the prime minister, Stanley Baldwin, to announce his intention to marry her. Baldwin responded that the British public would never accept a divorced woman as their queen. "I think I know our people," he said. "They will tolerate a lot in private life, but they will not stand for this sort of thing in a public personage." In a series of meetings, he clearly spelled out Edward's options: The king must either renounce Mrs. Simpson or abdicate.

By December, the news that the future Edward VIII had chosen Wallis Simpson over the throne had hit the headlines around the world. In a poignant radio broadcast from Windsor Castle, he announced his abdication and left Great Britain. Lady Cunard, with her lofty plans to become a trusted confidante of Queen-to-be Simpson, was furious. "How could he do this to me!" she was heard to have wailed on hearing the news. As word of the abdication spread through British society, those in power decided that it would cause too many problems to cancel the forthcoming coronation entirely. It was only five months away; souvenirs were already on sale, the public had started making plans, and the guests had ordered their couture and jewels. To keep it all from going to waste, Edward's younger brother, George VI, would simply be crowned in May instead: "Same date, different king," he quipped. All those who had planned to travel to England for the celebrations, including Pierre and Elma, could stick to their original plans.

For the teams in Cartier London, the first few months of 1937 were manic. The head of the design studio, Georges Massabieaux, who had worked in 175 New Bond Street for more than two decades, divided new commissions among his team. George Charity and Frederick Mew were both artists who brought different perspectives to their work. Whereas Charity was more classically trained, Mew was responsible for many of the firm's more innovative geometric designs. In 1935, the London team had also been joined by the talented French artist and designer Pierre Lemarchand, whose move across the Channel was indicative of the shifting center of gravity away from Paris in the late 1930s.

In Conversation with Jean-Jacques Cartier

Lemarchand was very talented. Later he would become Toussaint's favorite designer—he did all the panthers for her—but before the war he worked in London and got along very well with my father. He did a lot of the Indian commissions. I remember visiting him in his artist's studio in Montparnasse—it was just as an artist's studio should be—paints and canvases all over the place.

For much of the 1930s, Jacques had been focused on how to create modern pieces without breaking the bank, but the coronation offered a departure from the financial restraint of recent years. Clients wanted expensive-looking jewels again. Somewhat surprisingly, after the trend for lighter bandeau headdresses in the 1920s, there had been a revival in larger tiaras since the Silver Jubilee of King George V in 1935. "Have you noticed lately that tiaras are absolutely the rage?" *Vogue* had observed. "Every woman wears one on the slightest provocation and they always seem to look their best in them." The coronation supercharged this. Cartier London made twenty-seven tiaras and head ornaments in 1937 (compared with seven in 1936 and fifteen in 1938).

Buyers included the royal family themselves as well as loyal aristocratic clients like Lady Granard, who, the political and social diarist Chips Channon noted, looked as if she "could scarcely walk for jewels." In 1936, Cartier made a diamond and platinum tiara with a cascading scroll design that the future King George VI would buy for his wife, Queen Elizabeth. This piece, known as the Halo tiara, would subsequently be worn by four generations of the royal family, making a special appearance in 2011 when Catherine Middleton (the future Duchess of Cambridge) wore it for her wedding to Prince William.

Indian clients coming over for the coronation also kept Cartier busy. Jacques missed Ranji, the late Maharaja of Nawanagar, who had given him his favorite commissions in the past, but his nephew and successor was fast becoming a good client too. Having inherited a fantastic collection of jewels from his uncle (many of which Jacques had originally supplied), Maharaja Digvijaysinhji of Nawanagar approached Jacques in the 1930s about remounting several in a modern Art Deco style. The men became friends, and Jacques invited him to stay in Dorking when he came over for the coronation. He and Nelly had recently bought the house adjoining Milton Heath and were in the process of decorating it to a high standard so that the Maharaja could have his own space when he visited. Jacques was particularly looking forward to showing him the turban ornament that English Art Works had been working on for him. With the 61.5-carat cognac-colored Tiger Eye diamond that Jacques had originally sold to Ranji at its center, it was truly magnificent.

THE GREATEST DAY OF SPLENDOR ENGLAND EVER SAW

The days in the run-up to the coronation were particularly busy, not least because several clients requested last-minute adjustments to their jewels. Doris Duke, who had brought her diamond necklace with her to wear for the big event, now wanted it to be shortened (previously she had asked for it to be lengthened). Writing in 1937 from New York, Glaenzer admitted that while he probably could have made the changes before she left, he had proposed that she have the work done in London. "I thought in this way it would again give you contact with her and give you a chance to show her what we have in London . . . would advise you getting in touch with her on Monday at the Dorchester."

Jacques and Nelly went to personally meet the Maharaja of Nawanagar off the train at Victoria Station. He was one of thousands of visitors, including Pierre and Elma, pouring into the British capital from all over the world. Though the Cartiers would not be in Westminster Abbey for the actual coronation, they wanted to be part of the wider festivities. To make the most of all his important friends and clients in town, Pierre had even organized a dinner in the Carlton Hotel, where he and Elma were staying. "Americans in London stay up late at Coronation Fetes," the *Chicago Tribune* reported, listing the guests of the Cartiers as including the New York politician Mr. Grover Whalen; M. Irigoyen, mayor of Biarritz and a friend of the Duke of Windsor; and the architect William Welles Bosworth, who had designed the Fifth Avenue store back in 1916.

Wednesday, May 12, 1937, Coronation Day, dawned cloudy with the threat of rain. Outside Westminster Abbey, guests known to the Cartiers, from Barbara Hutton and Princess Marina to the Maharaja of Kapurthala (in his emerald Cartier turban ornament) and Doris Duke started to arrive. As they made their way to their designated pews, the public tuned in their radios. From their hotel suite at the Carlton, Pierre and Elma welcomed those they had invited to join them in watching the royal procession from their well-positioned balcony. Jacques and Nelly were there with their daughters (their sons were away at boarding school), as were a selection of high-society friends and clients including Ganna Walska, Madame Vesnitch, and Lady Mond.

Inside the Abbey, "at the stroke of half past twelve, the hands of the venerable Cosmo, Archbishop of Canterbury, placed great Saint Edward's crown upon the kingly brow." Outside, the crowds erupted into patriotic applause. But the day was about more than the crowning of a king. It was a public spectacle, a display of the British Empire, described by the American press as "the greatest day of splendor England ever saw." Special trains had been laid on to take Britons from all over the country to the capital, and thousands lined the

After Edward VIII abdicated for love, King George VI and Elizabeth
were crowned in Westminster Abbey in 1937. Guests in the
royal box wear their obligatory tiaras.

streets. Many had even slept out the previous night in London's parks
and streets to get a prime position along the six-mile route. As the
King and Queen left the Abbey, the throngs of well-wishers cheered.
Pierre and Elma's party raised a glass of champagne as the clouds
burst into torrential rain and the King and Queen made their way to
Buckingham Palace in the famous golden coach.

Across the Channel, a couple listened to the celebrations over the
radio in a French château. Less than a month later, they would be
married there, becoming the Duke and Duchess of Windsor. For now,
she was just an American woman named Wallis Simpson, except for
the emerald on her left hand that symbolized the sacrifice a king had
made for her.

AN EMERALD TOO BIG TO SELL

Earlier in the 1930s, Jacques had sent a trusted salesman to Baghdad
to negotiate the purchase of several important gemstones. On his arrival, the salesman had been informed that the sale had to be conducted secretly and that he was forbidden to telegraph any details

back to London. All he was allowed to say was that he needed a large amount of money to be sent over as soon as possible. Trusting his employee, Jacques approved the sum and had it wired over without delay. For such a large price, he supposed, Cartier would be acquiring an enormous number of precious gems. But when his salesman returned, he had with him only a small pouch. Out of this, he brought one single gemstone. It was an emerald the size of a bird's egg.

Jacques was enthralled. As a gemstone expert, he marveled at the chance to see and hold one of the great emeralds of the world, a gem so magnificent it had once belonged to the Great Mughal. But as a businessman, he was dismayed. Years ago, before the Russian Revolution, they would have had no problem finding buyers wealthy enough to afford such a gem. But the 1930s was a very different era. The only option for Cartier to make their money back was to cut the emerald in two and repolish each half into a gleaming new stone. Though it pained Jacques even to consider splitting such a fantastic gemstone, he had to think of the business.

Not long after, the almost inconceivably brilliant emerald was divided in two. One polished half was sold to an American millionaire. The other, at 19.77 carats, was chosen by King Edward VIII to become the centerpiece for a platinum engagement ring for Wallis Simpson. Traditionally, emeralds are not used for engagement rings. Compared to diamonds, the stone is soft and can scratch easily with everyday wear. But King Edward VIII wasn't interested in tradition.

As with many of the jewels he bought for Wallis, the King had asked that Cartier engrave it with a personal message. This one read "WE are ours now 27 X 36." He had proposed on October 27, 1936, the same day Wallis had been granted her divorce from Ernest Simpson.

"THESE AMERICANS CERTAINLY DO STICK TOGETHER!"

As the coronation fervor subsided and the bunting came down, thousands of international visitors flooded out of England bound for Paris. Many of them who had traveled from far and wide to celebrate the crowning of a new king planned to make the most of their time in Europe. Second port of call after London was the much-anticipated

Exposition of Modern Arts and Technology about to open later that month in the French capital. Pierre, who had been heavily involved in promoting the event in America, traveled across the Channel with Elma, looking forward to the inauguration dinner. As always, his work for France would be noted. The following year the Légion d'Honneur would elevate him to the rank of Commandeur, its third-highest honor (after the elusive Grand Officier and Grand-Croix).

Meeting with colleagues in 13 Rue de la Paix, Pierre found them eager to hear about the coronation. From all they had seen in the newspapers, it had been a unique event. They were jealous of the English enthusiasm. Life in France was not so lighthearted. Industrial production was stagnant, unemployment was high, and the Popular Front was beginning to disintegrate, resulting in political uncertainty. "It is unfortunate that there is such a difference between the spirit of the English people and the French," senior Cartier Paris administrator, Georges Méry, had remarked, noting his belief that "after this troubled period, France will recover its traditional qualities."

There was a new young employee in the showroom who was especially keen to meet Pierre. Jack Hasey was a twenty-year-old American who had turned up at Cartier a year earlier to ask for a job. Hugely confident, he had known nothing about jewelry, as he had admitted to the two bemused directors interviewing him, but he did know how to sell. The interviewers, Léon Farines and Edmond Forêt, had been dubious at first, thinking he was just after a temporary job to fund a summer of good food and beautiful French women. But Hasey, a born salesman, had managed to convince them he was serious. After his American references had been checked out by the New York office, he was hired.

Since joining, Hasey had moved quickly up the ranks of the salesforce. Usually it took years for a junior salesman to deal with the important clients, but for Jack, in 1930s Paris, his nationality was a huge advantage. It all started when the actor Douglas Fairbanks had walked into 13 Rue de la Paix looking for a gift for a friend. Recognizing a fellow American, he had walked straight over to Hasey. Much to the chagrin of the more senior French *vendeurs,* the two Americans had chatted away about baseball and politics back home as if they had been friends for life. After Fairbanks made his purchase, he asked Hasey to deliver it to his friend at her hotel. The

The American salesman Jack Hasey helping a client, and the seasonal Cartier branch in Cannes where he worked for the summers of the late 1930s

friend turned out to be an actress Cartier had been hoping to secure as a client for years: Marlene Dietrich.

As the allure of Hollywood reached new peaks, the Cartiers, not blind to the growing influence of motion picture celebrities, were keen to attract as many of them through their doors as possible. Seeing the opportunity to impress his seniors, Hasey took the liberty of asking Fairbanks if he might perhaps suggest to the glamorous Marlene Dietrich that she pop in to 13 Rue de la Paix herself. He was new, he explained, and if a client like Dietrich came in asking for him, it could change his fortunes. The next morning, when Marlene Dietrich visited Cartier asking for Jack Hasey, his fellow salesmen were stunned. "That was the clincher," he recalled. In the eyes of the other *vendeurs,* "every star in Hollywood knew me either personally or intimately."

From then on, the young Hasey was given free rein when it came to American clients, and it was working out well. Pierre was pleased he'd encouraged the French team to hire him. The type of American clients visiting France had changed over the past few decades. The highly educated fluent French-speaking elite from Belle Époque days had been joined by straight-talking businessmen and actors who appreciated dealing with salesmen who not only spoke their language but also understood their culture.

There was another important change with Americans visiting France too: They weren't always headed to Paris. Whereas once the capital had been *the* place to spend the season, increasingly they were abandoning their opera boxes for the beach.

PEARLS ON THE CÔTE D'AZUR

The South of France had been fashionable among Americans for some time already, thanks largely to the composer Cole Porter, who had introduced it to his wealthy friends, Gerald and Sara Murphy. While the Côte d'Azur was originally considered a winter destination, the Murphys changed minds when, in 1923, they persuaded the exclusive Hôtel du Cap to stay open for the summer so they could invite their friends. Once guests like Man Ray, Hemingway, and Fitzgerald had experienced long-drawn-out picnics on the beach by day and fabulous garden parties in seaside villas by night, there was no going back. The Côte d'Azur became a summer destination spot and sunbathing became a fashionable activity. Sara Murphy even wore her pearls to the beach because, she explained, "they wanted sunning."

Coco Chanel had been one of the first Parisian luxury retailers to jump on the Riviera bandwagon when she had opened a Cannes branch in 1923. It offered her the opportunity to sell nautical-themed tops and swimming costumes while remaining in the vicinity of her lover, the Duke of Westminster (whose yacht *Flying Cloud* was often moored in the Mediterranean). By 1929, she had fallen in love with the area and bought land looking out to sea, where she built her own villa, La Pausa. The Duke would visit her there and bring extravagant gifts, but it was a stormy relationship. Chanel and he had many heated arguments, often about his other women. On one occasion, the Duke tried to make it up to her by offering her a large emerald while on board *Flying Cloud*. She accepted it, then casually dropped it overboard without a word. Another time it was a pearl necklace that she threw into the ocean in a jealous rage.

Alive to the potential, Cartier opened two Riviera showrooms, a Monte Carlo branch in 1935 and one in Cannes in 1938. At the start of each season, jewels from Cartier London and Paris were taken down to the coast. Hasey recalled the train ride from the French capital when "the garçon, the secretary, and I had three million dollars' worth of jewels in our baggage in a first-class compartment, and we worried and fretted until it was finally placed in the vaults of a store, a stone's throw from the Casino."

Having proved himself a reliable jewel mule, Hasey was later tasked with a similar journey from London to Cannes "with $3 million worth of stones in my grip to stock the store, and a revolver in my pocket to protect it." Like Paris, London in the summer months was often empty, and business was slow. It made sense to follow the money and try to make a sale where Jacques knew some of his most important clients were vacationing: "If you could renew connection between Ltd. [Cartier London] and the Duke of Westminster, it would be a splendid result of your trip," he telegraphed to his salesman Donald Fraser in 1937. In 1930, the Duke of Westminster, who had in the past showered Chanel with jewels, gave an enormous commission to one of Cartier's rivals, Lacloche, and Jacques was keen not to lose out again.

Selling jewels at the coast was more about seeking out the client than waiting for him to walk into the store. Sometimes this meant going to see the Duke and Duchess of Windsor in their Château de la Croë, the Maharaja of Indore in his hotel suite, or Princess Charlotte of Monaco in her palace. But other times, it meant tracking down new clients. Cartier bought their salesmen access to all the best clubs and expected them to be out and about, mingling and meeting people. Sometimes a chat with a tourist at a hotel bar could result in thousands of dollars of sales. The trick was always looking the part. Tails were essential during evening hours as "such exquisite jewelry at such high prices is not sold by common tradesmen." It could take a whole season to sell one important gemstone ("an account must be cultivated and nurtured as carefully and painstakingly as an orchid"), but that single sale might bring in several months' worth of profit.

Some salesmen were more formal in their approach than others. The old guard of Cartier Paris like Farines and Muffat, for instance, had been trained in the art of deference. But when Jack Hasey heard about a party on the yacht of a millionaire steelmaker, he simply dived from a pier in his bathing suit, swam to the yacht, joined the party, and made some friends. Before he left, he invited them to visit him in the Cartier store. Though his daring technique elicited disapproval among his dignified French colleagues, they had to eat their words when his fellow revelers turned up at the store a couple of days later wanting to buy a few items and asking if they could deal with "Jack" (he refused to be called "Monsieur Jack").

In September, the Riviera stores closed until Christmas and the salesforce would return to Paris, bringing with them any unsold jewels. Back in the French capital, business in the late 1930s was not easy, but there were a decent number of clients buying smaller items. Diana Vreeland, then working for *Harper's Bazaar,* recalled wearing her Cartier blackamoor brooches "in rows and *rows* . . . they were the *chic* of Paris in the late thirties." She wasn't alone. Cartier's talisman jewels, as they became known, also included brooches in the form of ladybugs (called *bon dieu,* or "good lord," beetles in France since the Middle Ages because they were thought to bring good luck) and turtles, which symbolized long life. And as with Vreeland and her blackamoors (although she admitted to mixing the genuine Cartier versions with the less expensive Saks copies), the fashion was for wearing several at one time, grouped together on one's hat, chest, lapel, or shoulder.

But those with serious money to spend on significant jewels were few and far between. Even the Duke and Duchess of Windsor, exiled from England and living mostly in Paris and on the Côte d'Azur, didn't always have the funds. On one occasion, the Cartier Paris workshop had gone to considerable trouble to make up a diamond and sapphire necklace that they felt was in the Duchess's taste, along with several new designs for crests to interest the Duke. This wasn't a commission, but rather an attempt by Cartier to tempt the couple into a significant purchase. Confident of an easy sale, a Cartier Paris salesman took the necklace and crests to their nine-room apartment at the Hôtel Meurice. The Duke was busy reading (amusingly, the book was entitled *Why Edward Abdicated*), so it fell to the Duchess to look at the jewels. She studied the necklace, agreed it was stunning, and then simply said that she didn't have the money, a response that left the salesman "dumbfounded."

As the Duke and Duchess of Windsor made France their new home (much to the delight of the French, who found their story terribly romantic), the sixty-two-year-old Louis was hardly in the country anymore. Dividing his time among his various houses, he largely left the control of the business to others. Pierre meanwhile had become more involved in the running of Cartier Paris from afar. Seeing the potential of the Riviera, he had also put forward almost half of the capital for the Monaco branch.

After his health scares, Louis' doctor told him to rest and stay calm for the sake of his heart, but circumstances were conspiring to make it very difficult. In 1936, civil war had broken out in Spain, with San Sebastián being one of the first areas to fall to the nationalist rebels. Louis, fearing for the town by the sea that he knew so well, had no idea when he might be able to return to his villa there or even whether it was still intact. While anxiously waiting for news, he had distracted himself with the renovation of another palace in Budapest. This time, the local press reported, Jacqui had the idea to rent it out furnished as a family home to foreign visitors who were bored with the city's drab and uniform hotel rooms.

But renovating and decorating Hungarian palaces couldn't distract Louis indefinitely. Especially with the increasingly bad headlines from Paris. In October 1937, France faced its first war scare after Mussolini visited Hitler and formed a fascist alliance. Against a backdrop of political unease, the franc became volatile. Severe currency fluctuations hurt businesses, and Cartier wasn't alone in converting francs into pounds and dollars, a move which would only make things worse.

A couple of months later, Louis would have another shock when he heard his younger brother had been hospitalized again. It was a repeat of the health issue Jacques had suffered on his trip to India, and he had to slow down for a while. "I am feeling quite well," he would later reassure his family, "but work only mornings, rest and walk in the afternoons, and go to bed before dinner. So that is living at only less than half speed." Fortunately, he had a good team in New Bond Street to help him manage the London business while he recuperated. Most important of them all was his head salesman, managing director, and friend, Étienne Bellenger.

THEY'VE GOT MY RINGS!

Étienne Bellenger prided himself on discretion. Five days before Christmas in 1937, however, something happened that catapulted his name into all the newspapers. Monday, December 20, had dawned particularly cold. Though fog and ice had caused disruptions to the trains, the forty-nine-year-old Bellenger had managed to make it in to work on the district underground line from Putney in time to give the salesmen a pep talk before the doors opened. He expected it to be a busy day, with all the last-minute Christmas shoppers, so it was all hands on deck.

Around three o'clock that afternoon, the Cartier London office had received a call from a guest at the nearby Hyde Park Hotel. Captain Hambro wanted to see some engagement rings as soon as possible. He was about to propose to a wealthy young woman and requested that a selection of Cartier's finest diamond solitaires be brought to his suite immediately. Recognizing the name Hambro, and reassured by the opulent hotel address, Bellenger jumped at the opportunity to secure a large sale (and the commensurate commission). He immediately selected nine rings, jumped into a London taxi, and was at the hotel within twenty minutes of the phone call.

Asking for Captain Hambro at the reception desk, Bellenger was directed to the third floor. In the hallway, he met a tall, well-spoken young man in a dark lounge suit, who introduced himself as Hambro and led the salesman to his suite, room 305, where he introduced another gentleman as his secretary. Bellenger took out the diamond rings and presented them in the natural light by the window. Seven were emerald cut (octagonal), two were rectangular, and their combined value was £16,000 ($1.3 million today).

After studying the rings, the men asked a few questions, and then requested to see them under a desk light. As Bellenger turned toward the desk, the secretary gave a signal. A third man, disguised in sunglasses and a bandanna, suddenly appeared from behind a closed door. He launched himself on Bellenger with a truncheon, raining blow after blow on his head. The salesman fought back, lashing out at his attacker. Shouting out "Finish it quick," the purported secretary joined the fight, tackling Bellenger, and it was only then that the middle-aged French salesman, always so polite and immaculately turned out, crumpled, collapsing to the floor in a pool of blood.

The three men made off with the rings. Half walking, half running down the hotel corridors, they carried their stolen treasures into a waiting car and made a speedy getaway. Meanwhile, a housemaid had alerted a waiter about unusual sounds coming from room 305. Entering the suite they found Bellenger, unbelievably still conscious despite a cracked skull but exhibiting all the signs of a brain injury: His left arm was paralyzed, and one side of his face was quivering uncontrollably. A doctor was called immediately. Bellenger's only thoughts were for the stolen jewels: "They've got my rings, they've got my rings!" he repeated over and over again.

As Bellenger was rushed to the hospital, the police investigation commenced. The men had given fake names, so the police released a bulletin describing the three thieves and attackers, "effeminate in manner," whom they sought for questioning. It was an unusual robbery. The press had a field day. Who had ever heard of such well-spoken, smartly dressed gentlemen committing such a brutal crime! Surely they didn't need the money? Cartier's insurers, Lloyds, issued a statement, offering a reward of £1,500 ($122,000 today) for any information leading to the capture of the ring thieves.

A member of the public gave the police the breakthrough they needed. Cyril Smith was a night porter at the Clarendon Hotel in Oxford. He had been surprised when three well-dressed men arrived from London at 6:30 A.M. on December 21 in a Jaguar. The timing had seemed peculiar to him. They must have left London around four in the morning to arrive in Oxford by then. And something else was strange, too. They were apparently unfamiliar with their car, a gray sedan, and had asked the porter to open the trunk for them. Once Smith's shift ended at nine that morning, he read the report of the previous day's robbery in the papers and went straight to the police with his suspicions. They caught the criminals. The stolen rings were recovered, and the Mayfair playboys, as they became known, were established to be "four men who gate-crashed parties, night-clubs and restaurants. All of good family, all four public school boys, one the son of a general."

During the court trial two months later, a still weak Bellenger amused the crowd and the tabloids with his matter-of-fact responses. When asked if he had been concerned, once in the hotel, that his rings would be stolen, he drew a laugh from the crowd with his response: "No, all I was afraid of was a dud cheque." Later, when the barrister asked him how many blows he had received before the secretary had shouted "Finish it quick," Bellenger elicited more courtroom amusement with his curt reply: "I was not counting them." Once convicted, the men were sentenced to prison as well as floggings. Headlines along the lines of swapping Savile Row suits for prison grey accompanied mocking commentary about how cockroaches would be replacing cocktails as a pre-dinner apéritif. Bellenger remained discreet, declining to comment, but pleased that his attackers were behind bars. He took a vacation in the South of France with his wife after the trial, which he credited with speeding his recovery. By April he was back at work, albeit with the occasional headache.

The following summer, things were looking up. Bellenger had recovered, Jacques was feeling much less drained, and they both, like many others, were planning to travel to Paris for the forthcoming royal visit of the King and Queen of England. As tourists streamed into the French capital in July 1938, morale was high and businesses received a much-needed boost. The French were in a celebratory mood and determined to show the world that they knew how to put on a show. Miles upon miles of flags and bunting decorated the streets, while newspaper headlines proclaimed Anglo-French friendship and peace. For three days it was incredible. "Old-timers said the Armistice could not compare with it. The visit of Edward VII, they said, was great, but nothing like this." But the good times were not to last. When the banners were brought down, the same difficult economy and rumblings of a potential European war still lurked in the background. And Cartier's salesmen were back to selling more cuff links and studs than diamonds and sapphires.

GAS MASKS AMONG THE GEMS

After the summer euphoria of 1938, as Cartier's salesmen returned from the seasonal Riviera stores with $2 million worth of unsold jewels in their bags, they were struck by a change in mood. Following his annexation of Austria in March, Hitler had become increasingly aggressive. In May 1938, he had ordered German troops into position along the border of the Sudetenland to intimidate the Czech government, and there had been a tense standoff throughout the stifling summer. France, not alone in fearing that Hitler would invade the Sudetenland, was in a state of heightened tension.

Paris was full of men in uniform. Sandbags were being put in place on important public buildings, and dim blue streetlights had replaced the previous white ones. The American embassy warned Americans to leave France. In Cartier, gas masks were distributed in the store and employees were required to be on alert twenty-four hours a day, ready to pack jewels for hiding at a moment's notice. Clients brought their gems into the store, asking their salesmen to hide them somewhere safe. Orders were canceled. Business between the three branches was largely suspended.

The mood in London was equally fearful. But there would be a few months of respite. On September 29, in a desperate last-minute attempt to avoid war, the British prime minister, Neville Chamberlain, convened a four-power conference. Hitler, Chamberlain, French prime minister Édouard Daladier, and Italian dictator Benito Mussolini all met in Munich to hash out the Munich Peace Agreement. When the Sudetenland in western Czechoslovakia was ceded to Hitler, the German Führer announced it was his last territorial claim in Europe, and it appeared that the threat of war had been averted.

The following day, Chamberlain arrived back in England. As the door to his British Airways plane opened, the crowds of thousands awaiting his return in the afternoon rain cheered wildly. He brandished the piece of paper signed by him and Hitler and read to the nation the brief agreement that affirmed "the desire of our two peoples never to go to war with each other again." He spoke of "peace in our time" and added, reassuringly, "Now I recommend you to go home and sleep quietly in your beds."

The Cartiers listened to the news with an enormous sense of relief. Jacques, who had recently returned from a visit to King Zog in Albania, had thought he would be canceling his forthcoming trip to India, but now he could write to his maharaja clients confirming the trip as planned for the end of the year. A month before he left, Louis visited him in Milton Heath, and the pair celebrated the news of peace together. Louis even made a donation to the local Dorking hospital "in gratitude for the heroic attitude of Mr. Chamberlain, the peacemaker." Pierre shared in his brothers' satisfaction. "That fool," he said, referring to Hitler, "has wrecked business now for six weeks."

By Christmas 1938, the mood was one of optimism. "In France a huge effort toward a moral and economic recovery has been initiated," Devaux wrote from 13 Rue de la Paix at the end of the year. The Christmas exhibition organized by Toussaint had been "a great success" and brought strong results. And January was also good: "In Paris we have handled a lot of business." The Cannes and Monaco branches were both open for the holidays, and there was talk of opening two more seasonal branches later in the summer, in the chic seaside resorts of Deauville and Biarritz.

Pleased with the improving situation in Paris, Devaux even felt it might be worth starting a perfume line. Chanel and Worth had both tried it and it had seemed to be successful for them. Pierre was open to the idea in theory, as was Toussaint; however, Louis "formally opposed" it, and Devaux planned to quietly do some more research into the idea before bringing it up with his boss again.

From America, Pierre sent regular updates back to Europe on the economic situation in his country. He feared that the "socialist policies" of the Roosevelt administration could be very negative for business. When Louis failed to respond to one of his letters (in which he had enclosed articles from *Baxter's International Economic Research Bureau*), Pierre became frustrated. The world was going through a time of major turbulence and his brother was hiding away in his Hungarian palace. "I will make sure he reads them," Devaux reassured Pierre; "he evidently doesn't grasp the seriousness of the situation."

The next cable Devaux wrote was from Budapest. He had been summoned there by Madame Cartier as Louis had fallen seriously ill due to heart problems "provoked by abnormal low [blood pressure]." The best doctor in Budapest was by Louis' side, and Devaux had asked an eminent heart doctor, Professor Laubry, to come from Paris. "Doctor more optimistic," Devaux reported the next day. The professor's recommendation was that the patient should remain under strict bed rest for a couple of months. Physically he was much better, Devaux reported, but "anxious particularly during nights." As per Pierre's instructions, the news of Louis' heart attack was hushed up. It wouldn't help to have people worried about the future of the company, particularly in such an uncertain time. Only a select few knew the truth, with Devaux giving the impression that the boss "just has to recover from stress."

As 1939 dawned, the sixty-one-year-old Pierre was planning his future. Hoping to return to live in Europe at some point, he was considering basing himself in Monaco and becoming more heavily involved in the Paris branch. With Louis so unwell, this made Pierre's plans even more relevant. He spoke about the logistics and details of the possible move with Devaux. He wanted to understand all the variables at play from the price of real estate in Paris to the difference in personal tax rates versus America, before making any decisions.

As part of his planning, Pierre investigated which salesmen in France were the most effective, which employees were signed up to long contracts, and who was considering leaving. If he moved to Europe, he wanted someone excellent to run the New York branch in his absence. Devaux didn't want to leave France but had suggested Edmond Forêt, and they were hammering out a deal that would see Forêt commit to relocating to New York later that year. Despite all this going on in the background, Pierre had so far avoided raising the subject with Louis. His elder brother still considered himself head of the Paris house even if, as Devaux observed in February 1939, "in reality, Louis has hardly managed the business actively for about two and a half years."

In February, Jacques wrote that he was on his way back from India. His trip had been successful, he reported, although he would have liked to stay out there longer to finalize several commissions. It

Jacques and Nelly in India prior to the outbreak of
World War II, at the palace of Nawanagar with one
of the Maharaja's children.

had been Nelly who had insisted they return home because of his health. In his place, he had left the Cartier salesman Clifford North, who had proved himself very capable dealing with leaders including the King of Nepal and the Maharaja of Jaipur on previous trips east. At the request of the Jodhpur royal family, Jacques had also cabled for the designer Pierre Lemarchand to travel out to Bombay immediately by air. The Maharani of Jodhpur had wanted jewels matching the ones he had designed for her the previous year, and Lemarchand spent a busy two days coming up with suggestions from which she might choose her favorites.

As they reached the port of Marseilles, Jacques and Nelly sent word to their son Jean-Jacques, who was engaged in his military service in the 1st Regiment of *chasseurs* near Paris. They hoped he could arrange leave to come and see them at Aunt Milly's house in Grasse, where they would stay a few days before heading back to England. Just inland from Cannes on the Côte d'Azur, Grasse was the sun-drenched perfume center of France, where fields of fragrant May rose and jasmine punctuated the views down the Mediterranean beyond.

Jean-Jacques, who hadn't seen his parents since he started military service the previous year, was granted forty-eight hours' leave and took the train down from Paris to Cannes. They planned to meet at the beautiful large white Hôtel Carlton on the Croisette, near the Cartier store. For Jean-Jacques, the wonderful light of the Côte d'Azur made an uplifting change from the rain and mud he'd endured over the winter with his cavalry regiment. The Riviera was warming up for the annual springtime battle of flowers that always drew crowds, and the first annual Cannes Film Festival was planned for that September. For a time at least, the mood was more one of excitement than trepidation.

As Jean-Jacques approached his parents sitting on the hotel terrace, his mother burst into tears. Overcome with emotion at seeing her little boy in army uniform, she leaped up and hugged him for what felt like an eternity. Jacques, waiting for his turn, shared a smile of understanding with his embarrassed son. Later he would write to Harjes, still at school, about how good it had been to see Jean-Jacques again, even if he was "very thin and smelling of horses and cowsheds!"

The initial reunion over, they had caught up on family news over coffee on the hotel terrace. Jean-Jacques' elder sister, known as Jacko, had recently returned to England from Argentina and was now planning a trip to America. She had been seeing a nice young man, Sylvester Prime, of Shelter Island. Harjes was getting into trouble at school again and Alice was pregnant in England. They all feared the rumblings of war but hoped desperately that peace would prevail. When Jean-Jacques left Villa Harjes the following day, after the most wonderful night's sleep and the best-cooked breakfast he could remember, he told his parents he couldn't wait for his military service to end so he could visit Milton Heath at the end of that summer. His optimism wouldn't last for long.

In March 1939, Hitler went back on his word and annexed the rest of Czechoslovakia. Chamberlain was humiliated. France and England were left fearful that the brown boots of the German Wehrmacht they had so dreaded marching their way the previous autumn might still be coming. Pierre Claudel, who was plugged in to the French political scene via his diplomat father, voiced his worries that there could soon be a war. Louis, intensely fearful of international conflict, proposed to travel across the Atlantic with some of his most precious possessions. His plan was to deposit them for safekeeping in Canada just in case there was a war and he was forced to flee without being able to take anything with him. Toussaint was "strongly opposed" to his even attempting a voyage in his weak state of health, but Devaux was equally worried about his staying in Hungary until the summer: "Could be running a big risk given the international situation."

In New York, Pierre received the updates from Europe with a rising level of uneasiness. To the outside world, he needed to appear bullish, especially against the backdrop of the World's Fair that was just opening in New York. Pierre was on the fair's organizing committee, ensuring Cartier a prime spot at an event intended to be the highlight of a difficult decade. Hosting multiple countries and welcoming 44 million people, the fair's "Dawn of a New Day" theme looked toward an exciting future far removed from the fears of war. Eye-catching exhibits included a futuristic car by General Motors, early televisions, and one of the first diners. For Pierre, "one of the outstanding features" was the House of Jewels in the French Pavilion that he had orchestrated with other leading jewelers. Cartier decided to focus on "the two distinctive characters of the Maison: originality of design and high-quality gemstones," displaying novel pieces like a bejeweled shoulder decoration sent over from Cartier Paris.

By the end of the 1930s, Cartier was one of the most well-known jewelers in the world. "In each of the three capitals," *L'Illustration* reported in 1939, "where civilization and modern culture take on the highest forms, a thoroughfare stands out, the center of luxury and taste. This is the rue de la Paix for Paris, 5th Avenue for New York and Bond Street for London, and in each of these three ways a name shines: that of Cartier." Pierre, meanwhile, had become one of the most respected business leaders of his generation. "No businessman in America is thought of more highly than Pierre Cartier," the journalist May Birkhead claimed. When he was called on to make a speech at the fair's opening in April, he understood the responsibility of his role as a spokesperson against such an uncertain backdrop and chose to sound a hopeful note: "For businessmen, who by definition are peace lovers, the World's Fair is a most important manifestation [that] world peace is through world trade." But the murmurs of military action were growing louder. "Stress building because of German-Italian pact," Devaux wrote in May from Paris. "Security devices on the Maginot Line are in place—absolutely impassable."

For the three brothers, each knowing firsthand the devastations caused by war, the growing sense of dread was particularly acute. They feared not only for one another this time, but for the next generation as well. And for the dream they had realized together. The easy confidence of youth that had seen them through the last world war had faded, replaced with the anxiety of age and the shadows of illness. Each of them desperately hoped for peace. But within six months of Pierre's optimistic speech at the World's Fair, the most devastating conflict in human history had begun.

PART IV

DRIFTING APART

(1939-1974)

Division in families creates ruin and misery. I command my heirs to maintain harmony among themselves and with their cousins.

—LAST WILL AND TESTAMENT
OF LOUIS CARTIER

THE WORLD AT WAR

(1939-1944)

A PARTY TO END ALL PARTIES

Before sending out the seven hundred invitations to her second annual circus-themed summer ball in 1939, the seventy-nine-year-old Elsie de Wolfe had jokingly announced that if the political situation didn't improve, she might have to replace RSVP with INW (If No War). There was to be no declaration of war, at least not before the July 1 party date. The American celebrity interior designer hostess, who had once proclaimed "I'm going to make everything around me beautiful—that will be my life," greeted her many high-profile party guests dressed in a Mainbocher butterfly-bejeweled ivory silk gown and a diamond and aquamarine Cartier tiara.

The party marked the end of the social season in the French capital, a last explosion of entertainment before everyone embarked on their summer holidays. Elsie de Wolfe, "Prominent in Paris society," as she was described by *The New York Times* in 1935, was not alone in being a sophisticated American who chose to base herself across the Atlantic. As a melting pot of ideas, parties, and new fashions, Paris had long attracted well-known figures from all over the world. In 1926, Elsie had married Sir Charles Mendl, the British attaché to Paris, but her devotion to the French capital had started well before then. In 1903, she had bought the eighteenth-century Villa Trianon (originally built by Louis XV as a retreat from the main Versailles palace) and lovingly renovated it until it became both a splendid palatial home for her and her female companion, Elizabeth Marbury, and the perfect venue for hosting others.

For the 1939 circus ball, duchesses and ambassadors, Hollywood stars and fashion designers were among the seven hundred guests who gathered excitedly in Elsie's magnificent Villa Trianon gardens on an unseasonably chilly July evening. "She mixes people like a cocktail," the Duchess of Windsor said of her friend and hostess, "and the result is sheer genius." On this occasion the cocktail included the French foreign minister and the German ambassador to Paris, a combination that *The New York Times* found truly shocking, given the political backdrop. But if anything, the feeling of impending doom helped propel the festivities to a whole new level. Elsie had conceived her party as a magical world away from the somber headlines of the time, and guests came together to be dazzled. Tightrope walkers leaped terrifyingly overhead, enormous elephants wandered through the gardens, and ladies in chiffon ball gowns danced elegantly with their white-tie dates in "the last grand gesture of gaiety and frivolity before the storm."

As the final few remaining guests summoned their chauffeurs to take them home at dawn, twenty-year-old Jean-Jacques Cartier, son of Jacques Cartier, was already up and feeding his horse in a far muddier, less glamorous corner of France. Nearing the end of his military service, he had spent the last few weeks hoping and praying war would not be declared so he could finally return home. It wasn't to be. Just two months later, on September 1, 1939, Hitler invaded Poland from the west, pushing France and England to join forces in declaring war on Germany. All military leave was canceled indefinitely. Jean-Jacques had absolutely no idea when, or even whether, he would ever make it home.

LA DRÔLE DE GUERRE

News of the declaration of war swept through Europe like a black fog. In France, a general mobilization on September 1 called up all able-bodied Frenchmen between the ages of eighteen and thirty-five to fight for their country. Cartier was not alone among Parisian jewelers in seeing a flurry of orders for engagement rings as men seized the opportunity to propose to their girlfriends before they left for their barracks. "Precious stones and jewelers are needed by a world that believes in love," Louis had once said in an interview. In spite of everything, that belief in love would translate into sales. "It may cost more, but men, in spite of new theories, continue to think love precious."

Those left behind in Paris faced a more regimented existence. A blackout was enforced to protect the population from enemy bombs. A curfew was put in effect from nine in the evening until five in the morning. Air raid sirens, designed to familiarize Parisians with the need to seek shelter, plagued daily life. The city's architectural landmarks were protected by sandbags. Fearing damage from German bombs, workers took down the stained-glass windows of the Sainte-Chapelle and packed away the Louvre's major works of art. The masterpieces, from the three-ton *Winged Victory of Samothrace* statue to Leonardo da Vinci's *Mona Lisa,* were transported in slow convoys (with truck headlights turned off) for safekeeping in the châteaux of the Loire Valley.

And then, after this initial surge of activity, nothing. No bombings, no invasions, no German attack on the capital. In the absence of any large-scale military action, the first few months of the war would come to be called a *drôle de guerre* (Phony War). "It does not feel like a proper War," the intellectual Simone de Beauvoir wrote in her diary, from Paris. "We are waiting, but for what? The horror of the first battle? For the moment, it seems like a farce—people looking self-important as they carry around their gas masks, the cafés blacked out."

When war had first been declared, cinemas, restaurants, and bars had shut their doors to the public. Over the following few weeks and months, however, with the continued absence of an air attack, Parisians started to relax. Their capital returned to an approximation of prewar normality. "We've forgotten the air-raid alerts . . . we hardly ever go out with our gas mask in its case. It's gone out of fashion."

As 1939 drew to an end, there was still no sign of fighting. Stationed in northeastern France, the philosopher and novelist Jean-Paul

Sartre summed up the feelings of many others when he wrote in No-vember, "The war has never been more elusive than it had these last few days. I am acutely aware of its absence, because, if there is no war, what the hell am I doing here?"

Cartier Paris stayed open, albeit with less stock (some of it had been taken into hiding) and reduced staff. Of those exempt from ser-vice who remained, the most important in Paris were Louis Collin and Paul Muffat. Both had been with the firm for decades and both knew well the dangers of war, having fought valiantly in 1914–18. They were good men to leave in charge. "Our dear businesses," Devaux wrote in 1940, "are well equipped in human terms to get through this difficult period." Not all jewelers were so lucky. "At Van Cleef, almost all staff have been mobilized," was the observation of those left at Cartier Paris.

At the news of war, Louis Cartier made the decision to base him-self in San Sebastián. He liked being by the sea where, his sister be-lieved, "the air of the Basque coast suits him" and had ambitious plans to reconstruct his Spanish villa damaged by the civil war. No one really understood why he was going to such expense during war-time but Marion suggested perhaps he wasn't thinking straight. He had been "very anxious," she reported, and was complaining of in-somnia. On his way down to Spain, Louis had collected his daughter Anne-Marie from Switzerland, where she was in a sanatorium after a nervous breakdown following René's death. She had been diagnosed with "a severe and progressive psychotic disorder that shuts her off from the real world." Deemed to need constant supervision, she couldn't go to San Sebastián with her father, so Louis moved her to a nursing home in France. Jacqui and Claude had joined Louis in Spain upon the declaration of war, but after the fourteen-year-old Claude had started at the local Biarritz lycée, Jacqui returned to Budapest to see her family, promising to return soon.

Louis did not plan to take up the management reins of Cartier Paris again. At the age of sixty-five, with a weakened heart, he was retired. For some time, it had been his trusted former secretary and now director, Louis Devaux, who had been holding the threads to-gether in 13 Rue de la Paix. Now, with the call to arms, the thirty-two-year-old Devaux had to swap his role heading up a temple of luxury for an arduous military campaign in the "intense cold: minus

24 at night and minus 17 by day." He was, he wrote from the front, concerned not just about dying but more about what would happen to Cartier if he were killed in the war. He had noticed "some clumsiness and thoughtless action in the financial management of the company" and felt that the whole area needed to be "firmly and personally monitored."

Devaux had proposed that the fifty-three-year-old Cartier director, Louis Collin, take charge in his absence. Collin was experienced but lacked the younger man's strategic brilliance. Devaux had tried to leave him with precise instructions but admitted that "the management of Cartier S.A. is full of pitfalls." He warned they needed to think about how to protect the real assets of the company. Several months before war had broken out, Louis, anticipating the worst in Europe, had talked of opening a branch in South America. He'd even proposed visiting Argentina to explore the possibilities over there in the summer of 1939. In the end, his ill health had prevented this but now Devaux suggested that they pursue the South American idea. Once the war was over, he felt, "Europe will be sick, and the world's center of gravity has every chance of establishing itself strongly in the new continent." It was only right that the firm should "take our place over there."

With Devaux off at the front and Louis barely involved in his business anymore, Pierre felt a responsibility more than ever to stay up to speed with the French operations. Trusting that Collin would keep on top of the financials in Devaux's absence, he was relieved that his son-in-law had yet to be called up to the front. Claudel had been working in 13 Rue de la Paix since the previous summer, when he and Marion had returned to Paris after three years in New York. As vice president of Cartier Inc., Claudel had been successful in America, but the couple had missed the "leisure and joie de vivre" of France and felt it made more sense to be based in Paris, the "grand center" of fashion and jewelry.

A WARTIME CHRISTMAS

Christmas 1939 was lonely for Pierre and Elma in New York. Friends, including the president's mother, Sarah Roosevelt, had urged them to bring their daughter Marion and grandchildren back to America from Paris, but it wasn't that simple. Just like her mother during World War I, Marion would not leave her husband alone in France during wartime.

Letters arrived from Pierre's siblings over the holiday period. His sister, Suzanne, wrote from her Ciboure vacation home, Villa Zuretzat in the Basque region of France, where she had chosen to sit out the war "because of the neutrality of neighboring areas." Five years previously, Suzanne's husband, Jacques Worth, had asked for a divorce after twenty-seven years of marriage. Suzanne, vehemently opposed to divorce because of her Catholicism and for the sake of her children, had been furious. For years, she had put up with her husband's errant ways in order to remain married. "My disgust is almost stronger than my sadness," she had written to her brothers at the time, talking of the "living nightmare" she found herself in. "I didn't expect this from Jacques after everything I have suffered because of him." Despite promising to treat his ex-wife well, Jacques Worth had distanced himself. When his son Maurice married earlier that year, he offered to pay for his future daughter-in-law's wedding dress, but, given the troubles in the Worth business at the time, he "would not have it made at Maison Worth." Suzanne would complain to her youngest brother that her husband "wanted his name on the wedding invitation of his son" but then "didn't even turn up."

Jacques Worth's behavior had the positive effect of bringing Suzanne closer to her three brothers. Louis, Pierre, and Jacques felt hugely protective toward their selfless younger sister, and they rallied around to offer their emotional and financial support. Incredibly grateful, Suzanne was happy to help them and their loved ones in a time of uncertainty. Villa Zuretzat would become something of a hub for the Cartier family in the early war years.

Her first wartime guest was Louis. Given the proximity of Villa Zuretzat to San Sebastián, Louis stopped off at his sister's house on his way to Spain during October 1939, leaving his granddaughter, Marie-Andrée, and her governess there. With Marie-Andrée's mother, Anne-Marie, in a sanatorium, and her father, René, having passed away, Louis wanted to ensure the little girl was somewhere safe. A couple of months later, Louis came back to Villa Zuretzat for Christmas with his son Claude. Jacqui had wanted them to go on to Budapest, but, not wanting to be exhausted by traveling, Louis decided "to stay where he is." Overall, Suzanne reported, the feeling was optimistic: "Morale is good in France . . . because we are certain of victory," but there was also a sense of deep sadness at being separated from those she loved during such a testing time. "We regret this distance that separates us, even though it is only water, and over the ocean our hearts meet in the same support for France."

Although Jacques and Nelly would later accept Suzanne's invitation to join her at Villa Zuretzat, for the Christmas period they would be in Paris. After war broke out, the couple had decided to close up their Milton Heath home and travel to France. Jacques believed that a man should be in his own country during a time of war. Although he had dedicated much of his life to England, he was a Frenchman and his son was fighting for France. While Nelly directed the domestic staff to cover the furniture, not knowing how long they would be away, Jacques summoned a meeting with his directors in London. He was, he had explained, leaving them in charge of 175 New Bond Street in his absence.

Not knowing how easily they would be able to communicate during wartime, he gave them authority to run the business as they saw fit. They should do all that was in Cartier's power to help the war effort. Clients' jewels should be safeguarded and the two senior directors, Bellenger and Foreman, should look after the employees like a family. He left Milton Heath at the staff's disposal, should anyone need to escape there.

Jacques and Nelly had left England in September, aiming for Paris, but Jacques' health had deteriorated en route and they had diverted down to the French spa town of Bourboule in the Auvergne. By December, when he was well enough to travel again, they moved to the capital, hoping that they might see Jean-Jacques, who was with his cavalry regiment just outside Versailles. He had been promised twenty-four hours' leave, and his parents proposed that they meet at the Hôtel Westminster, just above Cartier, where they had taken a suite.

Jacques, who knew firsthand the dangers of fighting at the front, was haunted by the image of his son in battle facing the threat of machine gun fire, on a horse. So far, he thanked the Lord, there had been no sign of widespread combat. "Army very focused," the Claudels had updated the family. "Everyone certain of victory. But will be a struggle. Morale excellent." As the Phony War continued, even business was reasonable. "Despite the war, there is business going on in France and in Rue de la Paix," was the report six months after war was declared. "The big fashion houses are happy." Though many restrictions were in place, it was still possible to treat oneself to the new season's fashions for Christmas 1939. Designers such as Jeanne Lanvin made chic cylindrical bags in which to carry one's gas mask around town. The war shelter at the Ritz became famous for its well-dressed Parisiennes in furs and Hermès sleeping bags.

Clients keeping Cartier busy included the Duke of Windsor, who "has been particularly obliging for the company." Over the summer, the Duke had enjoyed the social scene on the Riviera, where he had presided over glamorous jewel-filled events like Le Bal des Petits Lits Blancs (a charity ball in aid of children with tuberculosis). With the declaration of war, the festivities ground to a halt and he fled to England with his wife, only to find no royal residence at his disposal. The exiled couple duly returned to a city where he could mingle with friends and still live some vague semblance of the high life. "Paris is beautifully war gay," Noël Coward remarked. "Nobody ever dresses, and everybody collects at Maxim's."

Assigned to the British military mission just outside Paris, the Duke of Windsor continued to shop at 13 Rue de la Paix. Jacques, who had counted him among his good clients before his enforced exile, was pleased to see him again. It was in these early months of war that the Duke commissioned a large brooch, which would become one of his wife's favorite jewels. As he often did, the Duke chose to provide existing items of jewelry (a necklace and four bracelets) in order to make the new piece. This wasn't unusual; not only could the gems be recycled, but in wartime, the mounts were also required. With wholesale trade forbidden by the Bank of France in 1940, if clients wanted to commission a piece, they had to supply the full weight of the metal themselves (in the case of platinum, it was 135 percent).

Pierre Lemarchand, who had returned to Paris after several years in the London shop, apparently worked on the brooch's design (Frederick Mew may also have been involved). The brooch was to be a multigem flamingo with pavé-set diamonds for the flamingo's body and gloriously bright small emeralds, sapphires, and rubies for its

The Duke and Duchess of Windsor in Madrid, June 1940.
The Duchess is wearing her new Cartier flamingo brooch.

tail. The genius was in articulating the flamingo's leg so that when the Duchess bent down, it would not dig into her. She would first wear it in public on the Duke's forty-sixth birthday, June 23, 1940, at the Ritz hotel in Madrid. Her forty-fourth birthday, when she had received the brooch as a gift, had been just four days earlier.

AN END TO THE CALM

For Pierre Cartier, the spring of 1940, as he sought to hold the whole family and business together from across the Atlantic, was a testing time. After a series of reassuring family updates, the news coming in started to concern him. In March, he received word that Jacques was finding it hard to breathe. His younger brother had moved from Paris to the French spa town of Bagnoles after Christmas in an attempt to help clear the congestion in his lungs, but it hadn't helped. "His health has worried me greatly for a long time," Pierre confided in his long-time employee Paul Muffat, while agreeing with him about Jacques' inner strength. "He is endowed with remarkable physical and moral courage. . . . He is a man of character who even in the most serious circumstances, has never failed."

Jacques and Nelly moved again, this time to Montana in Switzerland, where they hoped the higher altitude might help Jacques' breathing. There they were visited by their younger daughter, Alice, and her children. Alice, who had married Carl Nater (the St. Moritz mayor's son Jacques had hired to run his seasonal branch), was sitting out the first part of the war in Switzerland with her husband's family. "Daddy doesn't give me a very good impression," she wrote after visiting her father in the spring of 1940. "He looks so well when he is in bed, and the moment he tries to walk, he breathes so badly." After Alice left, Jacques would have another relapse. Seeing his weakened state, the local doctor advised that he leave Montana for a lower altitude in order to relieve some of the pressure on his lungs. By the end of April, he had moved to Clinique Cécile, farther down the mountain in Lausanne.

As Jacques rested under the eyes of concerned doctors, it was his elder brother's turn for another health scare. In April 1940, an increasingly anxious Louis suffered a stroke. His niece visited him in the American Hospital in Paris and updated the family on his deterioration. Though Uncle Louis took a walk in the corridor, her impression was that "he will need to be cared for as an invalid." His convalescence, the doctors advised, would be long, and even several weeks later, he wasn't looking good: "The stroke was bad and his capacity will be reduced."

In Conversation with Jean-Jacques Cartier

I know my father and Pierre worried about Louis. Louis could become very anxious and it wasn't good for his heart. And don't forget he'd seen both his mother and daughter go into a nursing home—that weighed on him, I think.

From New York, as Pierre agonized over the health of his brothers, two invalids far away from him in a time of war, the news flash he had been dreading burst out over the radio waves. On May 10, 1940, after eight months of comparative calm, Hitler's army began its attack on Western Europe.

BIARRITZ: ALL OF PARIS IS HERE

Hitler unleashed his blitzkrieg invasion of the Low Countries and France with a fury. Within just three weeks, the British forces and French defenders were pushed to the English Channel and forced to abandon the continent at Dunkirk. Hitler's forces swept powerfully south. They drove before them the retreating French army and an estimated ten million refugees "as though," a Cartier Paris employee would later recall, "the German army wielded a monstrous brush and swept all loose people into the south of France raising a choking dust of panic in the very air."

Many of the wealthier international set, including Elsie de Wolfe, host of the extravagant prewar circus ball, had fled to America at the outbreak of open hostilities in the Netherlands during May. The Duke of Windsor was appointed governor of the Bahamas (mostly to keep him and his defeatist comments out of the way), and he and his wife sailed to Nassau by commercial liner in August 1940. Cartier Paris, however, initially stayed open. "Remaining open in Paris in line with government instructions," those left in charge wrote to the New York and London Maisons, asking that they continue sending correspondence to Rue de la Paix. But they did take important precautions, sending the company books, customer deposits, and some stock to Biarritz, in southwest France, where Cartier had installed a temporary showroom the previous summer. The salesman Muffat, who had survived a bullet in the neck in the First World War, had moved many of the jewels. Pierre wrote to thank him "for the dedication with which you and all our collaborators look after the interests of a Maison on which everyone's future depends." He noted too how "the transfer to Biarritz of the services and the goods" was, under such difficult conditions, "a masterstroke."

By June 10, 1940, the French government had fled Paris and set up an interim government in Bordeaux. Four days later, the German army occupied the French capital. Many of those who hadn't already left did so then, terrified of being taken prisoner if they remained. "I took the German advance as a personal threat," Simone de Beauvoir wrote on June 9, 1940. "I had only one idea which was not to be cut off from Sartre, not to be taken like a rat in occupied Paris." Against the backdrop of collective panic and millions of fleeing refugees, Parisian businesses that hadn't already closed their shutters and locked their doors did so now, including Cartier.

On June 22, 1940, France and Germany signed an armistice to end hostilities, albeit one dictated by Germany. Under the agreement, an unoccupied region in the South of France, the Zone Libre (Free Zone), was left relatively free to be governed by a residual French administration based in Vichy and headed by Marshal Philippe Pétain. To the north of the demarcation line lay the Zone Occupée (Occupied Zone), which had been invaded by German troops and so was under Nazi control. The French Army was mostly disbanded, reduced to a hundred thousand troops to maintain domestic order. Special papers, to be approved by the Gestapo, were required in order to cross the demarcation line. France was divided in two.

"All of Paris is here," Marion wrote to her family from the Biarritz area in May 1940 after refugees from the capital had descended on the seaside town by the thousands. After the Armistice, this area of France fell into the Occupied Zone, but the Cartiers had been among the many fleeing south for their lives before this was known (afterward, it would be nearly impossible to move back into the Free Zone). Within the Biarritz Cartier store, there was an atmosphere of camaraderie. "There was not space in a room, a closet or cupboard in the whole city," one employee recalled on his arrival. "People were sleeping three in a bed in small rooms, on billiard tables and on floors, and this remnant of proud Cartier's had made a home of the store. . . . Food was scarce but they had some stored in the back of the store, and a garçon cooked in the cellar."

Twenty kilometers away from the crowds in Biarritz, Marion and her children were staying with her aunt Suzanne. Her husband had been called up to "the Front somewhere" in April and she was five months pregnant and understandably fearful. "We can't go to the village because of the paratroopers," she wrote in May. "I can't dine in the little bistro or walk in the fields. Last night we were told to go to bed fully dressed with shoes on and a gun in our hand. I slept with one eye open." When Pierre and Elma wrote back, desperate with worry for their daughter, she reassured them that it was not as bad as it seemed. Suzanne was looking after her well. "I can't describe how kind she has been, and her villa is superb! I like the Basque country."

Perched upon a cliff, Suzanne's Villa Zuretzat was an imposing manor house in Ciboure, with staggering views of the Bay of Biscay on one side and the majestic Pyrenees on the other. Inside it was beautiful, all white walls, dark furniture, and fantastic artwork. Fortunately there was room for many guests because since Louis and Claude's visit the previous Christmas, there had been an endless stream of friends and family seeking refuge with Tante Suzanne. By June, it was full to the rafters—"there are forty-one of us here now!"—and news came from Switzerland that Jacques and Nelly were planning to join them too. Louis had already arrived in the area but was staying this time with Jeanne Toussaint, who had also fled south. Her partner, Baron Hély d'Oissel, had a nearby house, Villa Albaïcin.

After the ordeal of the journey from Paris, Louis was in a more celebratory mood than one of wartime restraint, much to the disapproval of his niece. "Uncle Louis arrived at Mlle Toussaint's last week. . . . It's not right to lead the life he leads when our country is defending civilization. He rides around in a magnificent American car which uses petrol like crazy."

MELANCHOLY MAGNIFICENCE

For Louis, his visit to family in the Basque region was something of a final farewell. Since the Occupation began, he had been more fearful of remaining in France than ever. Recently, he had made up his mind to escape to America, where he would be able to access the medical support he needed far more easily than in wartime Europe. Pierre meanwhile worried that if his elder brother (and Cartier Paris's principal shareholder) left France, 13 Rue de la Paix might be seized by the Germans. Though it was a genuine cause for concern, Jacques felt that they should not interfere with Louis' decision. Their elder brother, prone to angry outbursts at the best of times, needed to stay calm on account of his heart troubles. He wrote to Pierre in warning, explaining that "a cable to Louis from you would have a catastrophic effect" and might even "finish him off."

Toward the end of June, Louis said his goodbyes. His plan was to set off for Lisbon, where he hoped to collect a visa for America and take a ship across the Atlantic with his wife and son (his daughter

Anne-Marie would remain in the French sanatorium). Of all the fare-
wells, the one to Jeanne Toussaint was among the hardest. They
hadn't been lovers for many years, but they had remained soulmates.
And though she tried to hide it, Jeanne later admitted to Louis'
brothers how scared she was of his making the long journey in such
a fragile state.

In Conversation with Jean-Jacques Cartier

*Mlle Toussaint started off romantically involved with
Louis, but even when that part of their relationship
died down, they remained very close. She would have
done anything for him.*

As it turned out, Louis' journey to America would be a harrowing
nightmare from start to finish. Even before he got to the boat, there
were a series of complications that threatened his plans. First, he became sick with a virus and was admitted to a Portuguese hospital.
Then, in all the chaos, Jacqui and Claude lost their passports. To
compound matters, the wait for a visa was far longer than expected.
By late July, a month after leaving Biarritz, they still hadn't received
the necessary documents. Out of the hospital now, Louis was staying
in Lisbon's Hotel Aviz. It was a famously luxurious hotel but he was
"badly out of sorts" and frustrated beyond measure with the endless
wait.

One Los Angeles journalist who managed to secure an interview
with him was summoned to his hotel room to find the mighty jeweler
"in his bathrobe, sulking . . . He sits in Room 66 in melancholy magnificence, a handsome old gentleman with a pale, sagging face and
absent-minded eyes." The journalist, seemingly more interested in the
hotel's deluxe bathroom fittings than in Louis' anxious state of mind,
bizarrely tried to rile him by suggesting that surely it should be easy
for him to obtain a visa given his "great store" in New York. Louis,
terrifyingly close to another attack, rose to the bait. "With this salt
rubbed in his wounds, the great jeweler is superb. His handsome face
is tinted with a sudden rush of blood. He looks as if he is about to

cast himself upon his own sword in agony. 'What does it require,' he says, 'to get into your United States?'"

Fortunately, Louis wouldn't have to wait much longer. Within days of the unpleasant interview, Louis had his visa and was able to book a passage on the SS *Quanza* bound for America. Chartered by a mixed group of more than three hundred passengers desperate to flee Europe, many of them Jewish refugees, the ship left from Lisbon on August 9. The captain, doubting the validity of some visas, required many of his passengers to buy return tickets in case the United States rejected them. Louis traveled alone. Given the scarcity of boats to America and his ill health, he was desperate to leave while he still could. His wife and son, yet to receive their passports or visas, promised to join him as soon as possible.

The ocean crossing was another ordeal in itself, as a hurricane threatened to capsize the ship. When the *Quanza* finally arrived in New York City on August 19, 1940, Louis was among 196 immensely relieved passengers who disembarked. Not all on board were so lucky. The remaining 121 passengers, mainly Jews, were denied entry to America. The boat made headlines when it traveled to Mexico to deposit the final passengers only to find that 86 of them were again denied entry. When First Lady Eleanor Roosevelt heard of the inhumane decision to send Jews back, potentially to their death, she begged her husband to intervene. In the end, all those remaining on the ship were granted political refugee status and allowed to stay in America. They were the lucky ones. Assistant Secretary of State Breckenridge Long was upset by the president's unilateral decision and insisted that it must not occur again. After mid-1941, almost no European war refugees would be allowed into the United States.

Louis' boat was met by Pierre and Elma, who were shocked at how he had aged in the last two years. They arranged for him to see the best doctors and took him home, where he would stay for several weeks. Two months later, his fourteen-year-old son arrived in the country on a Pan Am Atlantic Clipper plane from Lisbon. After discussing American schooling with Pierre, Louis had decided to enroll Claude at St. Paul's, a Catholic boarding school in New Hampshire, starting in January 1941. "I like my school very much and am trying my best to work hard," he would later write.

Louis, by then recovered from his ordeal, considered traveling abroad. With his wife still waiting for a visa in Europe (she first had to travel back to her native Budapest for her passport and would not arrive in America until May 1941), he asked Pierre to be Claude's guardian. When Pierre accepted, Claude wrote from his school in New England, in thanks: "I promise I will not be a burden . . . and it has given my father enormous pleasure." As it turned out, Louis decided to stay in America, but spent the winter in Florida, where he saw Elma, who was on her annual break in Miami. "He is only interested in cars, sailing and parties," she observed, disapprovingly.

FREE FRENCH CRUSADERS

Back in England, Cartier London had remained open since the outbreak of war, albeit without many of its men. The workshop was asked by the government to make munitions, and many of the Cartier designers, deemed too old to fight, were sent off to more useful jobs. The designer George Charity swapped days designing maharajas' jewels for ones designing fighter planes. The few salesmen left in the office were tasked with selling what they could in a difficult environment. The head salesman and director, Étienne Bellenger, however, had more important matters on his mind than diamonds. A patriotic Frenchman, he had followed the news about the occupation of Paris with dismay. In his mind, the new French government at Vichy was no better than a puppet of the German occupiers. Inspired by the June radio broadcast of the renegade French general and decorated World War I officer Charles de Gaulle, he believed that France must fight back.

As undersecretary of national defense and war, de Gaulle had refused to accept the Vichy government's armistice with Germany, brokered by the French prime minister, Philippe Pétain, and had fled to London. After de Gaulle's BBC Radio address in which he had laid out his plans for a Free French movement, he had been branded a traitor by Pétain. Furious, the Vichy government tried de Gaulle in absentia. He was sentenced to death for treason and desertion.

For years, France would be bitterly divided by the split between de Gaulle with his Free French movement on the one side and Pétain with the Vichy government on the other. For Bellenger, the choice was clear. Having fought in the First World War, he felt strongly that France must resist Germany at all costs. For that reason, he saw de Gaulle as the last legitimate member of the French government and in early July, he went in person to offer his services to the general.

De Gaulle's son would later recount Bellenger's meeting with his father:

> One morning a middle-aged man called on the General and said, "I am Étienne Bellenger, manager of the London branch of Cartier's. I would like to offer you my services, but I must make two conditions . . ." De Gaulle, always haughty, cut him short with "People who pose conditions do not interest me." "Allow me, Mon Général, to finish my sentence: I want neither money nor medals." At that de Gaulle softened visibly. "I am not physically fit to fight," Bellenger continued, "but because of my position I know many important people here and I believe I can be useful to you. What would you like me to do?"

Bellenger started by driving the General around London in his comfortable Buick and progressed to helping him build up the Free French army from London. He even offered the Cartier boardroom as a temporary Free French headquarters. Before long, he was joined in the fight by another determined Cartier employee. Though American, the Rue de la Paix salesman Jack Hasey felt such an affinity with France that he had tried to sign up to join the French war effort in Paris. When his entry was refused on account of his nationality, he had formed an ambulance unit and headed straight to Finland when the Russo-Finnish War broke out in November 1939. Trying to help at the front, he had been hit by an explosive a few months later, which had shattered his right forearm. Even then, his arm in a sling, he had refused to give up. In the summer of 1940, he traveled from Lisbon to England hoping to join the Free French Forces.

Arriving in London, Hasey called Bellenger, whom he knew from summers selling jewels together on the Riviera. He'd heard of Bellenger's links with de Gaulle and asked to meet the General to offer his services. The elder salesman proposed that Hasey, after all he had been through, should relax first and insisted that he check out of his hotel and come and stay with him and his wife in Putney. Hasey

Cartier London was open for business as usual during the war (left: a couple choose a ring in 1941), but the firm's director, Bellenger, was also very involved with the Free French resistance movement. Right: General de Gaulle was offered Cartier London's boardroom as an initial HQ before he moved to Carlton Gardens (pictured here in 1941).

gratefully accepted. A few days later, comfortably installed with the Bellengers, he came downstairs for dinner only to find, to his great surprise, the General and his wife and daughter in the living room.

Hasey would later recall in his memoirs that de Gaulle was a very tall man, exceptionally so, and that though he wore the khaki French Army uniform of a general, "his chest was bare of the medals and decorations that had been awarded him." After the introductions, the small party enjoyed a home-cooked French meal and talked of France, of how Hasey had found Biarritz when he was there, and of de Gaulle's hopes for the Free French movement. Hasey was hugely impressed by the General: "He was honest and straightforward, his confidence in the French soldier still unshaken. He did not try to proselytize, or 'sell' me the Free French movement. . . . He was a pleasant dinner companion, who could not unshoulder for a moment the heavy burden of a problem that weighed down upon him."

By the end of the evening, Hasey was convinced he wanted to fight for de Gaulle. Bellenger told him to think carefully about the consequences of his decision: If Hasey enlisted, he would likely lose his American citizenship. But a few days later, the doggedly resolute

Hasey became the Free French Army's first American soldier. By September, he would be heading to Dakar in West Africa with the General himself.

Unfortunately for de Gaulle, not everyone shared Bellenger's and Hasey's immediate enthusiasm for his cause. By the end of July 1940, only about seven thousand soldiers had joined the Free French Army. One French admiral, loyal to Pétain and the Vichy government, voiced the opinion of many when, in June 1940, he explained why he would not order his ships to join de Gaulle: "For us Frenchmen, the fact is that a government still exists in France, a government supported by a Parliament established in non-occupied territory. . . . The establishment elsewhere of another government, and all support for this other government, would clearly be rebellion." His opinion was shared by many, including President Roosevelt, who saw de Gaulle initially as "a mere adventurer who could not claim to represent France, having no legitimacy of his own." According to Elliott Roosevelt, his father also worried that de Gaulle was a neo-Bonapartist: "De Gaulle is out to achieve one-man government in France. I can't imagine a man I would distrust more."

As Bellenger became increasingly involved in the Free French movement, he, too, faced opposition. He knew he had Jacques' support, but he worried that in New York, Pierre might not approve. In an attempt to explain himself, he sent Pierre a letter in July 1940: "Since de Gaulle came to London, I thought it was the least I could do for him, and for England, to give him all the support I could." He was eager to know "if you approve of my efforts in this direction," but had felt it was essential to demonstrate that, among the French, there were still those who are anxious to support England." He added how "really marvelous" it was the way English people, in turn, showed their support for the French cause: "I have had letters from different people in all walks of life, from servants to important members of the aristocracy in England."

Pierre wanted as much as anyone to rid France of the German occupation, but, like many others, he wasn't yet convinced by de Gaulle. Nor did he consider Pétain to be just a puppet of the Germans, but rather a man of character who had made a sacrifice to preserve what he could of France. Many of the Cartiers' friends were still pro-Vichy, some even involved in the administration. Pierre was a pragmatic businessman who was, above all, "for France" and was still unsure which way the political and military winds were blowing.

THE WAIT IS PAINFUL

In New York, where the Cartiers were endeavoring to "keep the flag of our Maison flying high and firm," business was difficult. "Despite hard work, the business isn't bringing in much revenue," Pierre reported back to those in the Paris and London Maisons. "Customers are very worried about the situation in Europe." He trusted that America, under Roosevelt (whom he greatly admired), would help out, but he was unsure of the timing of military support. "We can count on the moral and material help of the United States, but not on their immediate intervention. Perhaps later? Let's hope it's not too late."

In the summer of 1940, around the same time Bellenger was updating him on de Gaulle, there was troubling news from Marion. She had traveled to the French country house of her in-laws in the Free Zone at Brangues, but had not heard from her husband for several weeks. It was feared he might have been captured. She hoped her father or uncles might be able to find out where he was through their many contacts in France. Jacques tried to help through his links with the Red Cross but it was not easy; communication was so slow.

By the end of August 1940, the Cartiers learned that Pierre Claudel was a prisoner at Camp Élise in the Marne (northeast France) and was soon to be transferred to a prisoner of war camp in Germany. The family did everything they could to help have him freed, speaking to lawyers, exploring the possibility of repatriation to the United States, and writing to those they knew in the U.S. embassy in Berlin. It would, however, be an agonizing wait for news. Jacques and Nelly, knowing how much Pierre and Elma worried for their daughter, had suggested she might be better off in America with them, but she bravely refused. "Without Pierre [Claudel], it's a no."

Pierre and Elma were not the only ones sick with anxiety for their children. Jacques and Nelly, recently arrived at Suzanne's house, feared for their elder son. Jean-Jacques had recently been promoted

to *maréchal* (sergeant) in his cavalry regiment and assigned to the
Vichy army in the Free Zone. For the most part, his time in the cavalry had been thankfully devoid of real danger so far. His letters were
censored, so he had to be careful what he wrote and would draw
horses as a kind of secret code. For now, the horses were at rest, to let
his parents know his regiment was not under any threat, but it
wouldn't always be so calm.

WE PRETENDED TO PLAY THE GAME

After several months, Cartier Paris reopened in early August 1940.
The Cartier team in Biarritz, including the acting head, Collin; the
salesmen Marchand and Muffat; Jeanne Toussaint; and the designer
Charles Jacqueau, traveled back to the capital carrying merchandise
"of average importance." Though the Germans still occupied the capital, many shops had decided to open their doors again and business
would continue as close to normal as possible. "There has been no
friction with the occupying authorities who, particularly in Paris,
have no direct connection with the French."

But the main reason Cartier Paris had reopened (though it couldn't
be written about for fear of the letters being intercepted) was the risk
of 13 Rue de la Paix being taken over by the Nazis if it was left
empty. This had become an even more real threat since Louis, the
main shareholder, had left the country (a fact that the staff were told
to keep to themselves).

Cartier's fears of a German takeover were not unfounded. In June
1940, the only time Hitler visited Paris during the Occupation, he
made sure to be photographed in the Louvre so as to signal his plans
to expropriate French culture. His ambitions extended to fashion and
jewelry. That same summer, Nazi soldiers had broken into the Chambre Syndicale (the French trade association of high fashion), requisitioning the entire archive. Their idea was to move individual French
dressmakers to Berlin, with the aim that, within a generation, haute
couture would become German.

Fortunately, they were prevented in their initial attempt by Lucien
Lelong, a prominent French couturier. Lelong, who would later train
Christian Dior, explained why the plan was completely unworkable.

French haute couture was dependent on thousands of small ateliers, each specializing in a very skilled area, from embroidery to lace making. The skills were not transferable, he argued, because it took decades to reach the necessary levels of craftsmanship. The Nazis eventually backed down and returned the archive. Lelong had won the first skirmish, but there would be many more over the war period. As the occupiers repeatedly tried to relocate experienced fashion and jewelry personnel to Germany, those in charge in 13 Rue de la Paix also had to be on their guard. (Over the course of the war, there would be more than a dozen attempts to move Cartier employees to Germany.)

On the outside, it had to look as though the Cartier showroom was up and running as usual. The reality, however, was that Cartier's salesmen (not wanting to be forced to sell their best pieces to their occupiers) had taken the precaution of hiding their most important jewels. The salesman Léon Farines, who had been with Cartier for decades, had been particularly helpful, storing many of the precious items in his family's remote country house in the Free Zone, outside Perpignan, away from suspicion. "Business looked as usual but actually there was very little left," an employee would later reveal. "We pretended to play the game and put on display a large number of small items such as cigarette cases, oddities, lighters, small jewels. The important jewelry, big stones, necklaces and the like were safe in the unoccupied zone, thanks to friends and confidence in our personnel." Devaux later recalled that Cartier was only repeating a tradition Louis-François Cartier had begun during the war of 1870 when the Commune ruled Paris. Then too, its stock had gone into hiding.

The Paris workshop opened again and employed around twenty men who worked on items for stock and commissions. Most pieces were relatively small and insubstantial. "They should look good without having much substance," the serious bespectacled senior salesman Paul Marchand explained to his team. The reality was that it was a difficult market and finding gemstones and mounting metals was hard. Prices for precious stones, particularly rubies, were extortionate and wholesale trade in gold was forbidden by the Banque de France. "Gold and platinum are blocked by the refiners," Marchand reported, "only the purchase of old settings will provide the company with new metal." In Paris they were able to buy a few bracelets, necklaces, and brooches from private sellers at reasonable prices, but not many.

Before long, those left in charge were able to announce that there were "at present, about 20 visits a day" in 13 Rue de la Paix and that "life in Paris is gradually getting back to normal again, in spite of the absence of private cars, taxis and buses." Cartier was authorized to use a van to make its collections and deliveries as it had before the war, but although some clients remained the same, a great many had changed. "Important Jewish people have fled France or are living in the unoccupied zone," Marchand wrote in 1940, about a year before the Nazis began their terrifying roundups of Jews in Paris. The Americans who had kept Jack Hasey so busy in the late 1930s had long since returned home. In their place were the German occupiers, whom Cartier's salesmen were forced to grudgingly serve, fearful of giving them any reason to take over their company. While the store remained open ostensibly to sell to Frenchmen and Germans alike, every effort was made to discourage the Nazis. Knowing many of the Germans feared disclosure of their identities as purchasers of valuables, the Cartier salesmen would ask them a myriad of detailed and unnecessary questions in an attempt to put them off.

A TERRIFYING VISIT

Despite the efforts made to dissuade them, the German occupiers were enthusiastic buyers of jewelry, and each purchase made in "Occupation marks" hurt Cartier from a currency perspective. Several of the Nazis had taken lovers in the city, others wanted gifts for their wives, and jewelry, as ever, was the perfect token of affection. Chanel, who had closed her Rue Cambon boutique as soon as war was declared (announcing that "this is no time for fashion"), was one of many Frenchwomen to face widespread criticism for her relationship with a Nazi officer, Baron von Dinklage.

Of all the German clients who would visit Cartier in wartime Paris, the most terrifying was Hitler's designated successor, Marshal Goering. Goering was fond of jewelry; Hitler had even presented him with a Nazi baton encrusted in diamonds in February 1938. Stationed in the capital, he was living in opulence at the Ritz, having taken over several rooms and salons. "Last Monday," a Rue de la Paix employee reported, "Goering came to the shop (the 'great maison Cartier' as he put it)." He had first demanded a large number of gifts from small jewels to clocks and other little items, but his next command had been for something much harder to locate in wartime: "He wants to buy a thin platinum watch and a beautiful ruby." Terrified of angering the infamous Marshal, the employees of Cartier Paris were left with little choice but to comply: "We think it would be wise to try to satisfy him."

The Marshal was at the peak of his power and influence. He was commander in chief of the Luftwaffe (the German air force), the most senior military officer in the Nazi Party, and the designated successor to Hitler. Not a man to be trifled with, he had founded the Gestapo, was instrumental in creating the first concentration camps for political dissidents, and was rumored to have started the fire that burned down the Reichstag in 1933. Had Goering so commanded, Cartier could have been shipped off to Berlin, lock, stock, and barrel, in a heartbeat, with anyone who resisted deported into camps. Those in 13 Rue de la Paix may have hated everything the Marshal stood for, but—like many others in Occupied Paris—they were put in an impossible position. When Goering "requested" something, it was an order that couldn't be refused.

Reflecting the complexities of wartime morality, the terrifyingly powerful Goering could, it seems, also perform the odd small act of reciprocity. One day, he marched into 13 Rue de la Paix, and in the course of the conversation with a salesman, inquired about his family. The salesman replied that his son had been captured at the start of the war. Goering didn't respond. A few months later, however, the salesman's son walked into 13 Rue de la Paix. Elated to be home from the brutal prisoner of war camp, he had absolutely no idea why he had been singled out to be freed. Other Cartier staff members were not so fortunate; in total, around a dozen of them had been imprisoned (including Claudel, Chalopin, Devaux, Desouches, and Rémy). Pierre tried tirelessly to have them released, but it would be years before they were all freed.

Meanwhile, Cartier had decided to reopen its Cannes branch. "In all respects, this solution is judged the safest and best for unoccupied France." While both Paris and Biarritz were in the Occupied Zone, the Cannes showroom offered a base away from German control. Working in the Occupied Zone was difficult, not least because the German authorities forbade the passage of goods (including jewels) out of their zone and controlled all cash transfers, bank safes, gold bars, and currencies. Cannes made it possible to do business without the same restrictions, although "it goes without saying that only limited activity is envisaged." They would stock the showroom with a few of the Cartier items that had been taken into hiding, because now it was impossible for anything to leave Paris and the Occupied Zone.

LITTLE HOPE LEFT

From Suzanne's villa in the Basque country, Jacques heard about the opening of the Cannes branch from his old friend and employee Georges Massabieaux, who was heading over there to run it. Prior to the war, Massabieaux had run the London design team at 175 New Bond Street. He had also been a regular weekend guest at Milton Heath with the family. Jacques would have liked to go to Cannes to offer his support but his health had taken a turn for the worse again. He and Nelly were away from the hustle and bustle of the crowded villa in a lovely large bedroom looking out to sea, but the constant draft wasn't good for him. Despite the large sausage-shaped cushions against windows and doors, the strong Atlantic winds ripped through the house.

It was from this bedroom that Jacques also heard about the horrifying air attacks in England. The Blitz (German for "lightning") had been ordered by Hitler and Goering on September 6, 1940. All through the summer of 1940, the Battle of Britain had seen German and British sides fighting for air superiority. Goering was determined that his Luftwaffe should draw the British Royal Air Force into a battle of annihilation. From September 7, London would be systematically bombed for fifty-six out of the following fifty-seven days and nights. After October, Goering would order his Luftwaffe to attack only at night in order to evade the RAF, but those early weeks of the campaign were all the more terrifying for their around-the-clock approach. More than forty thousand civilians in England would be killed.

Back in Cartier London, Jacques' Swiss son-in-law, Carl Nater, was among those who took shifts on the roof of 175 New Bond Street each night ready with hoses to douse the fires that were spreading from the bombings. Those too young to fight, including the apprentice Joe Allgood, joined him. Jacques felt terrible for them all. He remembered hiring Allgood so recently: Bellenger had turned the young chap away for arriving late to his interview and Jacques, taking pity on the lad, had interviewed him himself. He had wanted to give him an opportunity, and now the boy was risking his life for the firm. Jacques and Nelly's large family home, meanwhile, lay empty, and they again offered it as a refuge for anyone who needed it. Fortunately, no one took them up on the offer: Milton Heath would be one of the million English homes damaged by German bombs, while Cartier London would remain miraculously unscathed.

Hearing that their Dorking home had been bombed, Jacques and Nelly's main feeling was one of relief that no one had been hurt. Many of the domestic staff had left at the outbreak of war, but those who stayed there, like Orr the chauffeur, were in smaller cottages on the estate that were not hit. Jacques and Nelly's second daughter, Alice, who had joined Carl in England, left for America with the children as soon as the bombing started. She would spend the remainder of the war with her sister, Jacko, on Shelter Island, New York. So instead of Jacques' own daughters, it was his niece Marion who visited him every day in his room at Suzanne's house, updating him on events. They would talk together of the family but also of shared passions: art, drawing, and horses. Jacques, close to his niece, tried to keep her spirits up. She may have made every effort to talk of other things, but he could see that she feared terribly for her captured husband. Then one day, she came with good news.

After countless appeals to everyone they knew in positions of authority, it looked as if the Cartiers might have finally secured the release of Pierre Claudel. "It is impossible to express my joy and gratitude," Marion wrote in September 1940. Her enthusiasm was premature. A month later, after an interview at the camp, it looked as though Claudel's case had been denied. "We have a bad feeling and little hope left." But they refused to give up. Weeks and weeks of desperate attempts continued until finally, three months later, in January 1941, came good news, and the family rejoiced with telegrams to one another: "Thank you Providence for the liberation of Pierre Claudel."

By the spring of 1941, Marion was reunited with her husband. The couple decided to work at 13 Rue de la Paix, while they waited for news on their journey back to America. Claudel was not an American citizen so the documentation was taking time to organize, but they had good lawyers on the case. They lived at the Hôtel Le Bristol in the Faubourg Saint-Honoré, walked to work each day, and generally lunched with Jeanne Toussaint.

And yet, though they were reunited and free, there was an undeniable sense of trepidation submerging their city. Nazi flags took the place of French ones (the flag of France was banned from its own capital) and every day, the occupiers marched along the Champs-Élysées, making absolutely clear who was in charge. Even within the sanctuary of 13 Rue de la Paix, an apprehension governed professional exchanges. And Claudel, like other Cartier employees who had been held prisoner by the Germans, now found himself catering to their jewelry requests.

Weekends were often spent traveling down through the Occupied Zone to see Uncle Jacques and Nelly in the southwest of the country. Their younger son, eighteen-year-old Harjes, was with them (he wouldn't be called up to fight on account of his polio-related disability), and they had moved out of Suzanne's house into the Hôtel Le Splendid in the nearby spa town of Dax. At one point it looked as if the prospect of Marion and her husband and children returning to America might encourage her uncle to do the same. Jacques didn't want to leave his country in wartime but he needed better medical treatment than he could find in France. He had been talking about making the voyage and had even booked a passage on a boat later in March, but first he wanted to see his elder son. Jean-Jacques had recently been demobilized from the cavalry regiment.

UNDER THE COVER OF DARKNESS

Desperate to see his parents again, Jean-Jacques had set off to find them. He knew they were in the southwest of France, but he was in the Free Zone and didn't have the necessary paperwork to cross zones. He traveled to the Cannes branch, hoping that someone there might help him. As he walked into the familiar Côte d'Azur showroom, Massabieaux leaped up in delighted surprise. The young soldier was different from the schoolboy the senior director remembered, but there was no doubting it was Monsieur Jacques' elder boy. He greeted him like a long-lost son with an enormous, and quite unexpected, hug.

When Jean-Jacques explained that he needed to travel through the Zone Côtière (Coastal Zone) to reach his parents in the Occupied Zone, Massabieaux didn't hesitate. Within twenty-four hours he had arranged and paid for a *passeur* (smuggler) to take him. Jean-Jacques would have to travel at night, he explained, under the cover of darkness, and he had to be careful. There was no knowing what the Germans would do if one was caught crossing zones without the right papers.

It was a frightening journey, especially because the other traveler was an elderly Jewish gentleman, visibly petrified about being caught. But they made it without incident, crossing just before dawn. Once in the Occupied Zone, Jean-Jacques easily made it on to Dax and the Hôtel Le Splendid. Walking past the German officers stationed in the lobby, he rushed up to his parents' suite. Nelly opened the door. Again overwhelmed by the sight of her boy in his war uniform, she burst into tears, squeezing him tight. Then it was Jacques' turn. Jean-Jacques' first thought was how thin his father felt in his arms. He had aged far more than he had been expecting.

Overjoyed to be reunited with their son, Jacques and Nelly wanted to know how he'd been and what the mood had been like in his regiment. Jean-Jacques filled them in as best he could, and for two weeks they shared stories. Jean-Jacques relished that holiday in Dax. For the past two years he had rarely had a minute to himself; now he woke early and wandered down to the village blissfully alone, sketchbook under one arm. He drew everything he saw—the market scenes, the children playing, and his favorite: the majestic horses of the German soldiers stationed there.

Nelly wanted Jean-Jacques to stay longer, but Jacques felt strongly that, after a decent time together, their son should return to Paris to start his apprenticeship. There were enough good senior employees left in Rue de la Paix to learn from, and it would be good for him to get some experience under his belt. If all went well, Jean-Jacques could then return to 175 New Bond Street with his new skills. But, should the war end badly and Cartier be forced to close, his son's training might become even more important. "I would like him to be able to earn a living as a jewelry designer," Jacques wrote to the head designer and Louis' protégé, Charles Jacqueau, in February 1941. "I want him to be able to support himself, should he find himself alone in life."

The day before he left Dax for Paris, Jean-Jacques and his mother ate lunch together on the hotel terrace while Jacques rested. At another table in the corner, Jean-Jacques spotted a pretty young lady with dark, wavy shoulder-length hair having lunch with her mother. Nelly had seen them too. Before her son could stop her, she stood up and walked over to introduce herself and ask if they might like to join her and her son for luncheon. With Jean-Jacques squirming over his baguette, the waiter was called to set up a table for four. It was a good meal. By the time the coffees came, Jean-Jacques was smitten.

Lydia Baels was the second child of Henri-Louis Baels, a senior Belgian Catholic Party official and the governor of West Flanders. The Baels family lived in the beautiful historic city of Bruges, but like Jacques and Nelly, they had relocated to what they had hoped would be relative safety in southwestern France. At thirty-four, Lydia was twelve years older than Jean-Jacques, a fact that concerned her. Still, it wasn't as if she was inundated with suitors during wartime. When Jean-Jacques asked if he might write to her from Paris, she agreed.

A FINAL BREATH

By April 1941, a twenty-one-year-old Jean-Jacques had started his apprenticeship in 13 Rue de la Paix. Jacques, who had asked that his son be trained "not as a future boss, but as a designer," was disappointed not to oversee the apprenticeship himself, but reassured his son was in good hands. From Monday to Friday, Jean-Jacques spent his mornings alongside the design team, and afternoons in the purchasing department, sorting gemstones by color and size. One had to understand gemstones as much as design, his father had explained, in order to create harmonious jewels. Each evening Jean-Jacques would walk through the streets of Paris to art school at the École des Arts Décoratifs, where he would soak up lessons in everything from sculpture to classical drawing to modern painting. An artist at heart, he loved it. School had been a struggle because of his dyslexia, but here he had a chance to make his father proud.

Jean-Jacques enjoyed life in 13 Rue de la Paix, especially after the past few years in a regiment. And it was only now that he realized quite how loved the Cartier brothers were, and how those who worked for them considered the firm like a family. Though Jean-Jacques had not known the senior team in Paris, they all, from Muffat and Collin to Lemarchand and Toussaint, made the effort to tell him how much they respected Monsieur Jacques. And all were greatly concerned for his health. Whenever Jean-Jacques took the train down south to see his parents on weekends, his small bag was filled with notes and small gifts for his father from the team.

Marion was especially pleased that Jean-Jacques had been able to see his father. She and her husband were leaving the following month for America and still hoped that Jacques and Nelly might go with them. Jean-Jacques thought his father was unlikely to be traveling anywhere, least of all to New York. He couldn't even make it down to lunch in the hotel most days. Each time Jean-Jacques left him after a weekend in Dax, he feared it could be the last.

The summer of 1941 was particularly hard on Jacques' health. In the heavy heat, he found it almost impossible to breathe, and he lacked the medical support he desperately needed. His son wrote to him almost daily from Paris, updating him on his apprenticeship and asking his advice on designs or gemstones. Most of all, though, he asked how his father was feeling, what he was doing, if he was still working on the same painting of the church in the distance outside his hotel window or if he had started another one. "Thank you for asking about me," Jacques replied at the end of August. "Don't think I am a 'knock-out.' I can read in bed and also draw a bit. I have a book that Lemarchand lent me, 'La Science de la Peinture' by Vilbert.

It's a good book about the technique of using colors. There's good advice, but nothing on how to use them." Then in Nelly's writing: "Daddy says 'more soon' but he's going to sleep now."

That was the last letter Jean-Jacques would receive from his father. Eight days later, as the intense summer heat finally started to subside and the leaves showed their first tints of autumnal reds and yellows, a priest would be called to a suite in the Hôtel Le Splendid to read the last rites. As the Lord was called on to "protect" his deeply spiritual follower "and lead [him] to eternal life," Jacques Cartier, with his adoring wife at his side, would draw his final breath. On September 10, 1941, the youngest of the three brothers who had dedicated their lives to realizing a shared childhood dream was the first of them to die. He was fifty-seven years old.

NOT AN ENEMY IN THE WORLD

Nelly was overcome with grief. A strong woman, previously immune to life's knocks, she couldn't begin to imagine life without her beloved Jacques. To make it worse, she was far from her family, with communication so bad that she didn't even know how to get word to them. Jean-Jacques was the first of the children to hear. It was a tearful Jacqueau who, very gently, broke the news to him in 13 Rue de la Paix. Jean-Jacques took the first train down to Dax. He knew he must be strong for his mother, but he felt broken himself. The admiration and love he had for his father were beyond measure. To have it all curtailed before its time was the harshest kind of injustice. All his life he'd been looking forward to working alongside his father. Now he would never have the chance.

There was little time to mourn. Arrangements had to be made for Jacques' body to be taken up to the Cartier family crypt in the Versailles cemetery. It required traveling through Occupied France, with all the controlling checks and soulless explanations that entailed. Jean-Jacques, already crushed by despair, had to assume the role of head of family. It was a journey that he would never forget, looking after his mother, ensuring that they made it through war-torn France to give his father the burial he deserved.

> ## In Conversation with Jean-Jacques Cartier
>
> *That was the most terrible journey. My mother was dis-*
> *traught, and I needed to be strong for her, but I was*
> *devastated to have lost my father. You may say I'm bi-*
> *ased, but my father really was the most wonderful man.*
> *I was full of admiration for him. I'd always looked for-*
> *ward to working with him, but instead I was transport-*
> *ing his coffin.*

In England, the news rippled through all those Jacques had known, from the domestic servants to the wealthiest clients and everyone in between. On September 17, Bellenger cabled Nelly and Jean-Jacques to express how "overcome we all are" by the tragic news, and again two days later to convey "the profound pain" felt by everyone working in the London House. "It is not always praiseworthy to say of a man that he had no enemies," Margot Asquith, Lady Oxford, would say of her friend, "but I do not think that Jacques Cartier had an enemy in the world." On September 25, a requiem mass was said at Westminster Cathedral. The day after, the full obituary, by Lady Oxford, appeared in *The Times:* "Jewellers are not always great artists, but this was not the case with M. Jacques Cartier. He was rarer than a great artist, or designer in precious stones: he was a wonderful friend. Completely unself-seeking, courteous to strangers, gay, kind and the best of ambassadors between the France which he loved and the England which he admired."

Across the Atlantic, Pierre heard about Jacques' passing via a Vichy telegram. He wrote immediately to Nelly on September 17, a poignant letter full of "deepest sorrow." He had hoped until the very last minute that Jacques would make it over to America and receive the "specialist care he needed in a calm environment." So on hearing the tragic news, he had been uncomprehending at first, stunned by grief. Jacques had always been, he offered, "a unique being of goodness, devotion and loyalty," and he and Elma well understood the "immensity" of Nelly's loss. He wanted her to know that not only were they all thinking and praying for her and her children, but also, on a more practical level, he and Louis would "do everything in our power to help you in the mission you have to prepare for the future of your children."

He also explained how he had taken it upon himself to tell Jacques and Nelly's daughters the terrible news. He had gone with Marion to first see Jacques' elder daughter, Jacko, on Shelter Island, but finding her heavily pregnant, they hadn't been able to break it to her. So they went straight on to her younger sister, Alice, who, on seeing her uncle's face, guessed immediately what had happened. She promised to tell Jacko herself. Several days later, on September 17, at ten o'clock in the morning, Pierre organized a memorial service at St. Patrick's Cathedral on Fifth Avenue for Jacques' family and friends in America.

Louis, in New York at the time, heard the news from Pierre. "Louis took it very badly, I feel quite worried," his wife confided to Nelly. "He is heartbroken, and these distances with no details makes the imagination work and never rest." Jacqui wrote Nelly a letter of condolence from the whole family on paper headed 653 FIFTH AVENUE, the Cartier New York address: "From the bottom of Louis', Claude's, and my heart to you. I know what you both meant to each other over all these years. . . . there is nothing I can say to you when you ache all over, words cannot console you. You are beyond that. But it does help to know our fondest love and thoughts and prayers don't leave you." Jacqui and Nelly were not that close, but as a woman who had lost her beloved first husband, Jacqui's sympathy and love for her sister-in-law was moving. Nelly, grateful, would always keep her letter with its kind words: "Life is cruel and brutal and you had your share of hardships, but nobody can rob you of what you had with Jacques. Darling Nelly . . . take care of your dear self for those who all love you. Kisses, Jacqui."

Correspondence in wartime was slow. "Conditions are so uncertain," Pierre noted in one letter, "that one never knows if letters are received." On October 16, 1941, just a month after his brother's death, Pierre wrote again to Nelly, asking her if she received his condolence letter and explaining that his last few letters to Jacques had just been returned to him unread. "I cannot tell you how sad I feel, to think that Jacques had been without communication from me at a time I wanted him to know that our thoughts were with him and you all." Ever the pragmatist, he went on to speak about Jacques' will, asking if she had an up-to-date version and wanting to know who his brother's executors were. He also inquired whether she was aware of the 1930 agreement between the brothers whereby it was decided that if one brother should die, the others would have an option to buy his shares. This time both he and Louis signed the letter to their "dear sister" with "affectionate greetings" while also requesting that Nelly transfer Jacques' remaining shares in Cartier S.A. to them within three months. Nelly in her raw state of grief was not yet ready to talk of the business.

In Conversation with Jean-Jacques Cartier

When my mother didn't respond to Pierre's request for the shares, he asked Louis Collin in the Paris office to speak to her about the transfer. In fact, Collin, who had been close to my father, advised her to hold on to them as whoever held those shares—though not many—held the crucial balance of power in the Paris Maison.

A SECOND TRAGEDY

Three months after Jacques' death, America entered the war. In December 1941, after Japan attacked the American naval base at Pearl Harbor, Hawaii, the United States decided it could no longer remain neutral and declared war on Japan, Germany, and Italy. Relieved that his adopted country was finally helping his home country, Pierre desperately hoped America's involvement would change the course of the conflict in France's favor. He continued to give generously to funds he thought would aid France's victory and to attend charity events in aid of the war effort.

Apart from transforming the odds against Hitler, the American entry into the war also boded well for the U.S. economy. Roosevelt's New Deal had mitigated the Great Depression but had not ended the economic crisis. By the summer of 1940, more than five million Americans were still unemployed. When the United States joined the conflict, drastic changes began to take effect, boosting what became a "command economy." The United States would quickly convert its struggling civilian economy into the most productive manufacturer of war materials on the planet. Unemployment fell dramatically as businesses moved into the production of war supplies and military vehicles. And as almost 20 percent of the population left to join the armed forces, millions of jobs opened up for those who had previously been denied employment opportunities. For Cartier, the U.S. economic recovery and involvement in the war effort would provide a spark of much-needed optimism. But morale, unfortunately, would not remain elevated for long. Any uptick in positive feeling was soon to be submerged by another devastating blow.

In the early part of 1942, Pierre, Elma, Louis, and Jacqui spent a couple of weeks in Florida together. Pierre and Elma ended up curtailing their trip after receiving an invitation from their friend Evalyn McLean, the now fifty-three-year-old owner of the Hope Diamond. "I am giving my really first dinner at my new Friendship and I would so love to have you and Mr. Cartier here with me. . . . Do try to come."

While Pierre and Elma rushed back to the snow for the "black tie very informal" party in McLean's Washington home, Louis and Jacqui stayed on in Palm Beach for another couple of months with his nurse and valet. The couple regularly appeared in the Palm Beach press as they made it out to the Everglades club, cocktail evenings, and dinner parties, such as the one in honor of Sir Charles Mendl and his wife, Elsie de Wolfe. In April, as Palm Beach shut down for another season, Louis and Jacqui returned to New York, taking up residence in the smart Westbury Hotel at 15 East Sixty-ninth Street, just a block from Central Park and about thirty minutes' walk from Pierre and Elma. But as summer approached, Louis' health deteriorated. He was sixty-seven years old with a weak heart. Just as with Jacques, the heat made breathing hard for him. By mid-July, the great Louis Cartier was near his end.

Louis left the world at 2:20 A.M. on July 23, 1942, with his wife and sixteen-year-old son at his bedside. The autodidact, the "incomparable teacher," the creative genius was gone. He had been a man of contradictions: controlling, impatient, short-tempered, and self-absorbed at times. But he had also been a brilliant visionary, a man whose legacy would transcend generations, and a leader able to spot and shape the talent of others. He was a man who chose not to marry for love, and yet he was a man who inspired great love in others. A well-read, erudite intellectual, who hungrily studied the world's civilizations for ideas and built up a remarkable library and collection of art and antiques, but who was also a pleasure-seeker drawn to fast cars and beautiful women.

Throughout his life, Louis had been restless and, at times, insecure. His concern for "honor" had almost led him to a duel to the death, yet he had possessed gifts that allowed him to almost single-handedly revolutionize an entire industry. Once chastised for having his "head in the clouds," he was miraculously able to transpose what he found in some distant realm of ideas into spellbinding creations that would long outlive him. "Louis knew what was beautiful," his grandson would later write, "he also knew how to convey his feelings, his demands, and his passion."

Since Alfred had died, Louis had adopted the role of family patriarch, infuriating at times but fiercely loyal. From those exciting years when the business was taking off, through the atrocities of war and the Depression, his brothers had relied upon his talents and sought his approval and advice. Now Pierre was the only one left. For him, the news of Louis' death was shattering, his pain all the more acute because the grief for Jacques was still raw. Two brothers gone within a year. More than siblings, they'd been business partners, confidants, and mentors. Together they'd made their dream come true. Now Pierre was left holding the realization of that dream alone.

The New York Times published an obituary the day after Louis' death, reporting that he had been "widely known for the innovations he introduced," particularly "the use of platinum alone for mountings, a change thought revolutionary at the time." He had, the paper recalled, retired ten years earlier because of a heart ailment and had moved to America just a couple of years previously. But he would be "known to many Americans who went to Europe after the Armistice and before the depression, buying jewels from him while abroad." Writing from New York, presumably with little information avail-

able from abroad, the writer chose to highlight the main connection
Louis had with New York, namely the 1933 Persian miniature show
at the Metropolitan Museum of Art, noting that he "was an expert
on Iranian art." It was a relatively short obituary, just a single column
and a small photograph of Louis in profile. Far less than his creative
genius deserved, but America was not his home and he was not so
well-known there.

In France, meanwhile, his first home, there was nothing. Pierre
made clear that the news of Louis' death must be kept secret from
those in Paris, and it wouldn't be until two months later that the team
in Rue de la Paix would hear about the loss. Perhaps mindful of the
censors, Marchand wrote to Pierre in September, obliquely referring
to "a painful event" that had "saddened your collaborators," especially those at Rue de la Paix who had had the privilege of working
with "the great man who is no longer with us." After the war, Louis'
body would be sent overseas to the Cartier crypt in Versailles, and
Cartier Paris would hold a memorial service. Those who attended
would describe it more as a state occasion for a king than a funeral
for a jeweler, as the solemn procession of employees paused for two
minutes' silence outside 13 Rue de la Paix.

For now, within 13 Rue de la Paix, it had to appear as though
nothing had changed. And yet, those who knew would later describe
how the building felt as if it had lost its soul. For Jacqueau, whom
Louis had discovered all those years ago up a ladder, seeing his vast
potential before the star designer had even realized it himself, a light
went out. Toussaint, Louis' "greatest disciple," was left devastated
without her teacher and soulmate. They were for once united in grief
for the mighty man whom they had both loved in their own way. The
jewelry king had been a demanding boss, but his genius was without
question; he had made Cartier what it was. The emptiness echoed
through the showroom. Louis' office was left exactly as it had been,
as if he might turn up at any moment. Partly this was for the Germans, who had to believe the company's principal shareholder was
still in charge, but equally those who knew he was gone could hardly
bear to acknowledge it as fact. There was an understandable fear for
many that without the great visionary behind 13 Rue de la Paix, the
whole enterprise might lose its sense of purpose.

MON PRÉSIDENT

Two months after Louis' death, Devaux returned to 13 Rue de la Paix to the news that his "incomparable teacher," the man who had taught him "so much about the arts, aesthetics, what makes the beauty of shapes and colors," was gone. Devaux, the senior director who had started out as Louis' secretary, had been away for three long years. Awarded a Croix de Guerre for being the first Frenchman to shoot down an enemy plane in the early months of the war, by 1940 Devaux had been captured after his generals had directed him to position himself and his cannons on the top of a large hill. "The generals had apparently forgotten that a gun can't shoot below the horizontal. The Germans had only to climb from below to seize the cannons. Unable to fight back effectively, he was taken prisoner." Pierre had campaigned tirelessly to have Devaux released, but it had taken more than two years. After being freed in September 1942, he had made it to Switzerland, from where he had cabled Cartier seeking safe passage into Occupied Paris. In the end, it was Louis' widow, Jacqui, who helped him. She contacted a friend in Bern, Switzerland, and was promised "all that is necessary in your interest." A week later, Devaux was back at 13 Rue de la Paix.

Years of occupation had taken their toll on the "City of Light" since Devaux had last been home. The wide streets, once filled with honking cars and buses, were eerily quiet and desolate in comparison. Those few cars that were left ran on wood gas rather than gasoline, and velocabs, effectively a seat pulled along by a bike, had replaced taxis. Food was increasingly hard to come by with many people surviving on rutabagas, a type of turnip usually fed to cattle. Dogs had been rounded up by the Germans in 1940 to de-mine the country, and cats had ended up in stews. Some sought to stretch out their rations by becoming first-time farmers, keeping chickens and rabbits in corners of small apartments.

And it was getting worse. As it became clear that America's entry into the war wasn't an immediate magical solution, desperate Parisians sank deeper into despair. Since March 1942, three months after America had committed its troops, the Germans had started to round up Jews in Paris. Mothers and their children had been forced into stadiums with no food, water, or working toilets. From there, families had been heartbreakingly separated, herded onto cattle trains, and sent off to unimaginable horrors. For those left behind, a sense of dread blanketed everyday life.

Recognizing that Cartier Paris needed a strong leader more than ever, Pierre asked Devaux to take on the role of company chairman. He was experienced in the inner workings of the company, reliable when it came to sharing information, and highly regarded within the company and the country. After his regiment's success in shooting down German fighter planes, he'd become something of a war celebrity, and like Pierre, he would become a trusted board member of multiple organizations. He was nominated over François Mitterrand, no less, for the position of president of the National Federation of Prisoners of War (FNPG), an organization that managed the return of prisoners of war. For the rest of his life, Mitterrand, the future president of France, would refer to his friend Devaux as *"mon président!"*

On the outside, Devaux's role was keeping the business operating as normally as possible in difficult circumstances. Business was slow, both in the occupied capital and in the Free Zone, in Cannes. "Here on the Riviera very little merchandise has been bought," a senior salesman reported in September 1942. Clients were hard to come by, money was uncertain, and prices were high: "It is difficult to compare the prices in New York with those of France. We are working in a closed circuit. The price of pearls is increasing. One must wait for peace to see the practical prices."

But beyond the day-to-day business concerns, the far more ominous threat of a German takeover of the company continued. Devaux, actively involved in the Gaullist resistance network, was absolutely determined to ensure the occupiers were unsuccessful. "If we had not resisted," Devaux would later write, "the House would have been dismembered and it would have been difficult to reconstruct it later." Devaux estimated the total number of jewelry craftsmen in France at around three hundred, of which Cartier's specialists numbered perhaps one third. Given the large proportion represented by Cartier, it was essential to "doggedly resist" the German attempts to transfer the company not just for the future of 13 Rue de la Paix but for the future of the entire French jewelry industry.

In Conversation with Jean-Jacques Cartier

Soon after I started my apprenticeship, I found out I was on the list of people called up to work in Germany. They had lots of different factories they sent people to, you know, not just munitions. Someone suggested running away but if I didn't turn up they would have just called someone else from Cartier. It was better I go, rather than anyone with children. So I learned my map of Germany like I never had in school, and I hid a few very small diamonds in my shaving brush cap, just in case I needed to sell them to survive. Before you went there was a medical check. This French doctor I saw said to me, "Cartier, Cartier, I know that name, are you part of the jewelry family?" "Yes, Jacques Cartier was my father," I told him. Later I found out I had been rejected. I have no idea what that doctor wrote on my form but I can only guess that he implied I had TB or something. The Germans were terrified about letting TB into the country, you see. Anyway, whatever he wrote, it meant I could complete my apprenticeship in Paris, thankfully.

Through the months and years of war, more employees returned slowly to Paris from prisoner of war camps. The designer Georges Rémy was trapped in freezing conditions in a Polish prisoner of war camp until Christmas 1943. "He was half starved, freezing, and made to do hard labor," his family recalled. Rémy, an artist, would draw in his free time. He sketched anything from his fellow inmates playing cards to the guards keeping watch. He spoke German, thanks to his school days in Switzerland, and some of the guards, recognizing his skill with a pencil and paper, asked him to draw their portraits. But one day, Rémy's artistic future came terrifyingly close to being ended forever. As he was doing hard labor out in the freezing cold, one of the heavy wagons he and his fellow prisoners were forced to push uphill came loose. His hands would have been crushed if it weren't for one of the guards, who took pity on his talented artist prisoner and pushed him out of the way just in time. "That guard saved his hands," his family would later recall, and Rémy would go on to use those skillful hands to design jewels for clients from the Duchess of Windsor to Barbara Hutton.

Rémy was one of the many thousands of prisoners profoundly affected by his time in captivity. For a long time afterward, he would paint only in grays and browns, as if he'd had the light stolen from within him. When he was well enough, he returned to work, where he joined his friends and colleagues. One of them, Lemarchand, who had been released from active duty several years earlier, had been creating wartime pieces for some time already. Occasionally, the pieces he made carried political significance. In 1942, at the request of a French client, Françoise Leclercq, who was engaged in the Resistance, the Paris workshop made a small six-pointed star brooch. Though a Roman Catholic herself, Leclercq would wear it throughout the German occupation as a sign of solidarity with her Jewish friends.

Better known among Cartier's controversial wartime pieces was one of Lemarchand's designs of a bird in a cage. Renowned for his animal designs, Lemarchand used this one to symbolize a city trapped by an oppressor. The bird represented the innocent French men, women, and children imprisoned by the Germans in their own city. Cartier daringly displayed the brooch in their Rue de la Paix window in 1942. Some reports suggest that the brooch led to Toussaint, as the head of High Jewelry, being taken in for questioning and held for a short time before her friend Chanel managed to have her freed.

As 1942 drew to an end, France was falling deeper under German control. In response to the Allies invading North Africa, Hitler had ordered the occupation of the South of France and Corsica. There would no longer be a Free Zone. All of France would be under the control of the German army. Cartier had previously reopened its Cannes branch in order to have a presence outside Occupied France. Now, fearing that all of their stock could be seized at any point, they needed another solution. Under Devaux's guidance, the director of the Cannes boutique, Massabieaux, started incorporating a new company in Monaco. Initially the Cartier Monte Carlo branch had belonged to Cartier Paris. Now the idea was to make it an independent company, more remote from the German authorities. In 1943 the new Cartier Monaco company was set up with Massabieaux and Collin as directors.

A WARTIME WEDDING

After his father's death, Jean-Jacques had been joined at the Hôtel Westminster in Paris by his mother. Whereas previously he had taken an attic room, Nelly rented a large suite with several windows looking out onto Rue de la Paix. For over a year, every third weekend, Jean-Jacques took the overnight train down to the southwest of France to meet with Lydia at her family house. He would save up his meager salary, then spend it all on a third-class return ticket on the sleeper train. It was a long, uncomfortable journey, and not without its dangers. He learned to jump from the moving train into a ditch a couple of miles before it arrived at Biarritz in order to avoid the German officers checking paperwork at the station. And by the time he arrived at Lydia's house, exhausted, on Saturday morning, he had only twenty-four hours with her before he had to head back to Paris.

As time went on, he knew that he had found the girl he wanted to marry. One weekend, he asked to take a walk with her after the family luncheon, and it was then, in her family's garden, that he proposed. For him, it was simple, he loved her and he promised to always look after her. She loved him too, but unfortunately for her, it wasn't so straightforward.

Henri Baels, Lydia's father, was skeptical of the match. Just as Jacques had faced the disapproval of the Harjes family all those years ago, so the governor of Flanders doubted whether this young Frenchman was worthy of his eldest unmarried daughter. He was particularly sensitive after the difficult period they had gone through with their youngest daughter, Lilian. Two years earlier, Lilian had secretly married the widowed King Leopold of the Belgians during the Nazi occupation of his country. It had caused huge controversy in the Belgian press, with headlines like SIRE, WE THOUGHT YOU HAD YOUR FACE TURNED IN MOURNING. INSTEAD YOU HAD IT HIDDEN IN THE SHOULDER OF A WOMAN. After seeing their youngest daughter suffer the pain of being vilified in the press, Lydia's parents were on their guard.

Jean-Jacques wished more than ever that his father were still alive. Jacques would have been able to talk to Monsieur Baels on equal terms, and no one could have failed to be impressed by his thoughtful manner. Fortunately, there was in the Paris office a huge admirer of the late Monsieur Jacques who offered to go in his place. Devaux, hearing of Jean-Jacques' plight, made the dangerous journey across France to speak to Governor Baels in person and convince him of Jean-Jacques' prospects.

In Conversation with Jean-Jacques Cartier

Whatever Devaux said to Pa Baels, it worked. I was so grateful to him for that. He was a wonderful man, so kind to travel all that way. I regret not thanking him more at the time.

The wedding took place on October 1, 1943, in a Catholic convent in Chatou, on the outskirts of Paris. Nelly and Jean-Jacques' half sister, Dorothy, were the only guests on the groom's side. Lydia's parents hosted a simple wedding breakfast after the service for them and the few members of the Baels family able to make it in wartime. It was a very small and informal affair but that suited Jean-Jacques, who hated being the center of attention.

Returning to Paris a married couple, Jean-Jacques and Lydia lived together in the small attic room at the top of the Hôtel Westminster. "Too hot in summer, too cold in winter," they would remember. Every day, Jean-Jacques went downstairs to continue his apprenticeship, every day hoping the war would end, Paris would be revived, and he might be able to return home to England.

I MAKE MY OBEISANCE

By the end of 1943, the rumors were that de Gaulle's Free French movement was gaining in strength. An overthrow of the Germans was becoming more than a distant hope. In May that year, de Gaulle and one of his fellow Resistance leaders, Jean Moulin, had united the eight major groups of the French Resistance into the Conseil National de la Résistance (CNR). Three months later, the CNR had merged with l'Armée d'Afrique (the French army of Africa) and de Gaulle had taken over all the Vichy territories in Africa, India, and the Pacific. The Free French emblem, the cross of Lorraine (chosen by de Gaulle for its association with Joan of Arc), was fast spreading through the French colonies.

Many of those who had initially doubted de Gaulle were increasingly ready to back him. In America, this included President Roosevelt, who had for so long insisted on supporting the Vichy government. In England, Churchill, who had described de Gaulle as "vain and even malignant" in the spring of 1943, was by the autumn of that year acknowledging that the General had won the struggle for French leadership.

Throughout the war, Pierre had worked hard at maintaining a good relationship with President Roosevelt, agreeing with his approach to support Pétain over de Gaulle. In 1943, he sent Roosevelt a gift of a Cartier clock. "My countrymen are particularly grateful for what you are doing for them," he explained in a letter to the president, "and we realize that it will be thanks to your efforts and marvelous leadership that France will again live." Pierre had engraved the magnificent onyx, nephrite, and silver timepiece with the initials FDR. The green and black colors, reminiscent of camouflage, were considered appropriate for the ethos of the time. The clock had five dials, the main one showing the time in New York and Washington, D.C., and four subsidiary ones labeled to keep the corresponding time in London/Paris, Berlin/Rome, San Francisco, and Tokyo: "I have thought that a clock which . . . will mark the hour of victory— might be a useful addition to your desk."

As 1943 drew to an end, Pierre turned his attention to de Gaulle. Before the war was over, Devaux later reported, Cartier would provide the French Resistance with more than 43 million francs (more than $9 million today) of funding. In July 1944, Pierre's old public relations manager, Edward Bernays, bumped into him and Elma at a reception for General de Gaulle at the Waldorf Astoria in New York. Elma was even wearing a diamond-encrusted Lorraine cross, the symbol of the French Resistance. Given Pierre's earlier support for the Vichy government, Bernays was surprised to see him there. "He seemed a little proud and a little embarrassed as he turned to us and said four words: 'I make my obeisance.'" Pierre's changing of sides gave Bernays and his wife, Doris, hope for the future: "Doris and I thought that M. Cartier's switch was a sign that de Gaulle would win. And he did."

Meanwhile, other parts of the wider Cartier firm and family had been doing their part for the war effort. When his first American recruit, Cartier salesman Jack Hasey, was shot in his larynx and jaw while fighting for the Free French in Syria, de Gaulle made sure that the devoted soldier was immediately sent to safety in America with all his medical treatment paid for by the Free French. Hasey was even decorated as "the first American to shed blood for the liberation of France."

"Jacqui is living in New York, busy with different war organizations and her son has volunteered in the US army," Pierre updated Nelly in November 1944. After finishing school, Claude had started a degree at Yale in September 1943 but had decided a few months later to enlist. After volunteering at the Aviation Cadet training center in Alabama, he was accepted in March 1944 and by August had started an intensive nine-week pre-flight course at Maxwell Field, Alabama, along with four other Yale students. Just eighteen years old, he missed his father. "We held a requiem mass for Daddy," he wrote a year after Louis' death. "It was simple but very sad. His departure still seems so recent to us." Pierre and Elma would invite Jacqui and Claude for meals when they were in New York, even if, as he wrote to Nelly in exasperation, "return invitations were not more frequent than rain in August on Long Island!"

LIBERATED BY ITS PEOPLE!

By mid-1944, the Free French army numbered four hundred thousand and had joined in the Allied attack, participating in the Normandy landings and also the invasion of southern France. From there, de Gaulle's forces would lead the drive to the capital. The liberation of Paris was not high on the Allies' list of immediate priorities (both because it had limited strategic value and, more worrying, because Hitler had ordered his troops to destroy the capital if it was invaded), but de Gaulle was not prepared to wait. The liberation of Paris was of huge symbolic value for him.

Those in the capital were facing increasing hunger and fear. "The supply is more and more difficult," Muffat wrote to his wife, Maria, in July 1944, "and we subsist by the black market. For a month we have not got wine, very few vegetables and fruits, 0.90 grams of meat per week of poor quality." And he was one of the lucky ones. On the black market a meal for four cost 6,200 francs (at a time when a secretary earned 2,500 francs a month). Electricity and gas were scarce, water was often cut off.

With de Gaulle repeatedly pushing to advance on Paris, the American general Eisenhower finally agreed to commit his troops. In the days leading up to the Liberation, Cartier shut its doors, as Muffat wrote: "On 18 August the Cartier firm closed (Friday night) until further notice. Monday morning, I'll see if it's open, because during the days of 22, 23, 24 and 25 we could not cross the Seine. The Germans occupied the Place de la Concorde and the Tuileries and fired on all the passers-by who wanted to cross over. For eight days all shops were closed."

On the night of August 24, 1944, the French Resistance and the Allied forces made their way into Paris, arriving at the Hôtel de Ville shortly before midnight. For those in the city it was a tumultuous and terrifying time. "We are currently living in historic hours," Muffat reported. "There is a lot of damage everywhere and yesterday evening the Germans sent us their bombing planes. . . . There was light in the street at 11 o'clock in the evening, the sky was fiery pink . . . the area has become dangerous, the Germans have no reason to spare us."

By August 25, Dietrich von Choltitz, the military governor of Paris, surrendered, famously disobeying Hitler's orders to destroy the capital's monuments and bridges. Spontaneous displays of joy erupted throughout the city as Parisians rushed out to hold impromptu street parties. De Gaulle gave a famous speech to a swaying mass of rapturous citizens at City Hall: "Paris! Paris outraged! Paris broken! Paris martyred! But Paris liberated! Liberated by itself. Liberated by its people."

It would be almost a year before Germany surrendered to the Allies, but for Paris, a cloud had lifted from the moment of Liberation. Pierre echoed the sentiments of many when he wrote to Nelly in relief: "Happily, with the new conditions and the leadership of men who have the interest of their country at heart and who are great patriots, France should be restored as a first-class power." To commemorate the 13 Rue de la Paix reopening after the Liberation, the talented Lemarchand created another bird brooch. This one featured a bird in France's national colors: red (coral), white (diamonds), and blue (lapis lazuli), in proud acknowledgment of the symbolism the Germans had apparently suspected but been unable to prove. And this time, the bird was outside the cage, wings spread and singing in joy. It was free.

COUSINS IN AUSTERITY

(1945–1956)

BREADLINES IN PARIS

When twenty-year-old Claude Cartier arrived back in France after the war, it was clear that the end of the conflict hadn't ended the hardships of Parisians. Strict rationing continued, housing was in short supply, and the city's bombed-out factories remained in ruins. "A pall of cynicism and futility hung over the inhabitants" was the bleak impression of the *New Yorker* writer S. J. Perelman. "Everywhere you went, you sensed the apathy and bitterness of a people corroded by years of enemy occupation."

Claude had inherited the wealth of his father, the aristocratic blood of his mother, and the good looks of them both. Tall, blond, and blue-eyed, he was self-assured and used to a life of privilege. And after five years in the bright lights of America, the prospect of lining up for the prescribed 350-gram daily allowance of rationed bread and 100-gram weekly limit of meat was exceedingly unappealing. After having to wait three years since the death of his father, Louis, to visit the Parisian business he had inherited, it didn't take long for him to decide that he didn't want to be there. While his father had felt his French identity keenly, Claude had grown up moving between homes and schools in Hungary, Spain, Switzerland, France, and most recently the United States. Throughout his life, he would feel a pull between his different nationalities, but young, single, and looking for excitement, it was perhaps not surprising that he identified far more with the buzz of America than the postwar bleakness of France.

Waiting for Claude in 13 Rue de la Paix were the men and the woman his father had entrusted with his business. Toussaint, Devaux, Collin, and Chalopin greeted him warmly, offering their support to train him in the business and vowing to do everything within their power to keep the name of the great Louis Cartier alive. It soon became apparent, however, that Claude did not want to start an apprenticeship in 13 Rue de la Paix. He didn't want to stay in Paris at all.

In Conversation with Jean-Jacques Cartier

It was no wonder, really, that Claude saw his responsibility to the business differently. He had a very different upbringing. For a start, he'd been moved from school to school nonstop. Now, that's hard for a child. And when it came to work, well, I had seen my father working all his life. But Claude didn't have the same role model; he had mostly known his father as a retired man.

Devaux, who had taken charge of Cartier Paris three years earlier, was disappointed. He'd been close to Louis and had hoped, in time, to build a similar relationship with his son. He could also have used the support of a Cartier family member to help quell political tensions in the Paris Maison. Louis' death left a large hole, and discord had been growing. Toussaint and Jacqueau had never been close, each jealous of the other's close relationship with Louis. Without their old boss around, the situation had gone even more downhill until, one evening after work, it had reached its lowest point yet.

TOUSSAINT "AT WORK"

As he often did, Charles Jacqueau had left work one evening to go to a gallery opening. He loved art, and as a designer it was part of his job to stay up to speed with the styles of the time. Armed with his invitation, he'd strolled out of 13 Rue de la Paix in the direction of the exhibition, but by the time he'd walked a couple of blocks, it had started raining. Suspecting it might turn into an almighty downpour, he turned around and headed back to Cartier to fetch his umbrella.

Entering through the employees' entrance as usual, he walked swiftly through the empty offices. Everyone had gone home for the day. He was just about to enter his office and grab his umbrella from its stand by the door when he stopped short. There were voices coming from inside. Surprised, he opened the door tentatively. There, sitting at his desk, holding a pencil over one of his exquisite designs, was Mademoiselle Toussaint. Jacqueau froze. In a corner of the room, there was a photographer, camera poised to take a photo of the great artiste herself applying the finishing touches to what she seemed to be implying was one of her own creations. Furious, Jacqueau erupted with anger. Not only had Toussaint consistently rejected his designs in favor of others, but now it appeared that she was claiming his work as her own.

It wasn't that Jacqueau wanted public recognition for himself. He was a modest man, quite happy with Cartier's policy of not disclosing its designers' names. He just couldn't believe that Toussaint was prepared to do this. He had no doubt that it would never have happened had *le patron* Louis still been around. And yet he had no power to stop her. In 1945, photographs of Toussaint "at work" appeared in *Harper's Bazaar* in an advertorial on Cartier's New Jewels. From her perspective, it was simply good marketing for the firm. She was the head of High Jewelry, and she felt it was only right that she should be associated with the art of the House.

Devaux tried to defuse the situation, but it was difficult. Not only had Toussaint and Jacqueau both shared a special relationship with Louis, but they were also older and had more experience. He feared upsetting either one of them and had hoped that having a family member back on the scene would help resolve the tension. But it

Toussaint's hands, complete with trademark large rings on her little fingers, with pencil poised above Cartier designs. This image appeared with other photographs in *Harper's Bazaar* in 1945, exacerbating a rift with the designer Charles Jacqueau.

didn't seem as though Claude was going to fulfill that hope. At least not yet. Not long after arriving in France, he'd said his goodbyes and returned to America. Eager to leave behind the gloom of a city ravaged by war, he was planning to apply for an MBA at Harvard. After that, he could come back to look after his inheritance. For now, the management of Cartier Paris would need to remain in the hands of the two remaining Louis, Devaux and Collin.

A TANGLED WEB

Elma, as she confessed to her sister-in-law, was worried for her husband. Pierre had worked hard all his life, that was who he was. "He came early and stayed late six days a week," his employees would recall. But at sixty-seven, he was no longer a young man, and the stress was wearing him down. Instead of easing himself into retirement, he was fraught with worries. After the First World War, the West had enjoyed a period of booming demand for luxury, but after this war, the pomp and splendor didn't seem to be coming back. Partly this was a function of wealth destruction caused by the years of conflict, but more worryingly, it also seemed to reflect a change in lifestyle and values. There was a sense that spending large sums of money on luxuries was no longer appropriate. And if even those with vast sums were inclined to spend moderately, luxury businesses would have to rethink their future strategy.

Pierre was kept up at night by the fear that the next generation of the family didn't understand the scale of the challenges ahead or appreciate the responsibility into which they'd been born. The three Cartier brothers, who had grown up together above their father's store in Boulevard des Italiens, had shared a dream to build an international jewelry business. That they had succeeded had largely been a function of their bond, but the unhappy consequence of their global success was that the next generation lacked that same closeness. Each brother had managed a branch in a different country, seeing one another only occasionally, so the cousins had grown up barely acquainted. Pierre had no idea how willing they would be to work together and listen to his advice.

In Conversation with Jean-Jacques Cartier

I went to the same school as Claude for a while [Le Rosey in Switzerland]. But he was much younger, so I didn't know him that well. I remember he was quite keen on letting others in his year know I was his cousin because I was quite a good skier—we used to spend the winter terms on the mountains. And he would ask me to help wax his skis for him so he could go faster! But other than that, I didn't see him much after all, a seventeen-year-old doesn't have much in common with an eleven-year-old.

The most serious concern for Pierre was the question of ownership of Cartier New York. The three brothers had long held a financial stake in one another's businesses. It was an arrangement that had been, they believed, a key reason for their global success, because it had given them an incentive to ensure that each branch performed well, not simply the one they managed. While Pierre had been more than happy to share the New York branch with his talented elder brother, it wasn't the same thing to share his life's work with a young nephew who didn't appear motivated by the same goals.

Louis had written multiple wills and left a sprawling fortune dotted around the world. There were properties and bank accounts in several countries and currencies. There were jewels, items of furniture, and near-priceless paintings (including his collection of Persian miniatures) that Louis, with his exceptional eye, had slowly, carefully collected over the years. But it wasn't the matter of Louis' belongings that concerned Pierre. Louis had left most of his estate to his son, Claude, and his wife, Jacqui. Anne-Marie was Louis' other main heir, but because she was in psychiatric care, her share passed to her son, René Louis Revillon.

And Louis, correctly predicting that the strong characters in his family might not see eye to eye, had shown the foresight to include provisions stating that should any family member contest the inheritance, their legacy would be revoked. Pierre felt that this was exactly as it should be and would not have dreamed of contesting his brother's wishes. What Pierre did have an issue with, as his brother's lifelong business partner, was the idea that this should impact the New York Maison.

In his 1935 will, drawn up in Paris, Louis had bequeathed all his shares in Cartier Paris to Claude but had not mentioned his large shareholdings in the other branches. A later will, drawn up in Budapest in February 1939, shortly after his heart attack, also named Claude as the primary heir for the Paris business but again failed to specifically mention his financial interest in the New York or London businesses. For Louis, the future of the Paris Maison, which he had developed and managed over decades, had been the priority. Knowing that "division in families causes ruin and misery," he had instructed his heirs to "keep harmony among themselves and cousins." He had even left specific instructions in his will about what should happen if one of them wanted to give up his claim to the Paris branch. As it turned out, the issue was not that Claude had wanted to give up his right to Cartier Paris, but rather that he also laid claim to his late father's shares in Cartier New York.

For his part, Pierre believed that he was the lawful owner of Louis' shareholding in the New York branch. "During the fifty years of our partnership . . . not even a written agreement existed," he would later write, noting that the agreement had been that when one brother died, "the controlling interest should be sold to his surviving brother."

Convinced he was right, Pierre felt that his nephew was behaving like a "carpet dealer" for disputing his perspective. In his mind, Claude had inherited his late father's share in the Paris branch, so he should not be meddling in Cartier New York's business. Meanwhile, Louis' widow, Jacqui, insisted that her son should inherit all his father's shares in all the branches. For the family, it was an unsettling and divisive time, and the debate would drag on for years.

In the midst of the heated argument with Claude, Pierre turned his attention to his other nephew. Jean-Jacques was the elder son of Jacques. Pierre hardly knew him, at least not as an adult, but he had received updates from others. Devaux had told him that he had taken his studies seriously, Jacqueau had suggested he had potential for design, and his nephew's action in the war spoke for itself. There were, however, understandable concerns. In London, Bellenger felt that some of the older employees might not take too kindly to having to work for a man still in his twenties. Even though they had unanimously respected Jacques, why should they feel the same loyalty to his son? Partly in response to Bellenger's concerns, Pierre came up with a proposal to create an international management committee. Comprising senior management figures from each branch, "Degecar," as it was known, was to oversee the global business while also enabling Pierre to keep an eye on his nephews. They hadn't needed such a structure when each branch was run by close brothers, but now that it was run by different generations of an extended family, it became more pressing.

At the end of 1945, soon after Jean-Jacques had been demobilized for the last time, Pierre asked him to come to America. He wanted to meet his nephew properly, to talk about the future and check firsthand how driven he was. He also wanted to tell him about his ideas and impress on Jean-Jacques the importance of working together as an international business. Cartier London wasn't as important to Pierre as Cartier Paris, but he still wanted to ensure it was in good hands. Clients had always considered Cartier to be Cartier, whether in Europe or America. He couldn't risk Jean-Jacques' not making a success of the London Maison—it could reflect badly on the entire firm.

AN UNCLE'S BLESSING

It had felt strange for Jean-Jacques to come home in the autumn of 1945. The last time he'd set foot on English soil had been six years earlier, when he'd visited his parents just before war was declared. It seemed like a lifetime ago. Since then, he'd fought in battle, trained under some of the best jewelry experts, lost his adored father, married Lydia, and become a father himself. Now he returned to England, twenty-six years old, with a family of his own to support, only "to find my home at Milton Heath, Dorking . . . damaged by Enemy action." His mother, Nelly, had wanted to repair the bomb damage and move back into Milton Heath but her lawyer had been adamant that the punitive postwar English tax rates would decimate her inheritance. At sixty-seven years old, she was being advised to sell up and move to Switzerland.

Not having a home of their own to move into, Jean-Jacques and Lydia spent their first few months in England sharing a small staff cottage with the groom and his wife. Later they would move into Sondes Field, a house close to Milton Heath that had previously belonged to his sister Alice. But it would take time for Jean-Jacques to get back on his feet again. Unable to retrieve his belongings from Milton Heath, he was even forced to write to the authorities to request clothing coupons, explaining that he and his wife had crossed the Channel with "only the mere necessary clothing in which to return to this country."

That first Christmas they spent in Dorking after the war was a meager one. And soon after welcoming in the new year, on January 4, 1946, Jean-Jacques boarded the SS *Sacramento*, a large cargo and passenger boat, bound for New York to meet with his uncle.

In Conversation with Jean-Jacques Cartier

I was terribly seasick. Each morning the ship's steward came into my cabin with an apple; each time I dutifully ate the apple, then promptly threw it up. "Don't worry, sir," the steward would say, "the captain's awfully sick as well." I doubted that! But I still remember that small act of kindness.

Jean-Jacques hadn't been keen on leaving his wife in a country she barely knew to go and meet Pierre, but his mother, who was already in New York visiting her elder daughter, Jacko, felt that it was what his father would have wanted. Jean-Jacques stayed with her at the Plaza and she spoke to him about the need for self-belief. She was the controlling shareholder of Cartier London, as, after lending Jacques the money to buy Cartier Ltd., she had inherited his shares after his death. It was ultimately down to her who ran the business, and her late husband would have wished his elder son to be at the helm. Yet Jean-Jacques couldn't help but feel nervous. He wanted to earn Pierre's trust and for his uncle to approve of his taking on his father's mantle. At the same time, he was in such awe of his late father that he doubted he would ever be able to fill his shoes. He had completed an extensive apprenticeship in Paris, but he knew little of the London business and feared Pierre would put him in his place.

He needn't have worried. In the past, Jean-Jacques had sometimes found his uncle to be overly formal, but he had been a child then. Now they met more as equals, and Jean-Jacques grasped the strength of the connection that the brothers had shared. From how Pierre spoke of Jacques, it was clear how much he had loved and admired his younger brother, and in that immense grief they both shared, the two men were united and the barriers of age came down. Pierre was there, he assured his nephew, to help in any way he could.

Pierre invited Jean-Jacques into his office to meet the New York team. He wanted his nephew to see the scale of the Fifth Avenue operation and to appreciate Cartier as a global business. He talked about the importance of the ongoing links between the three branches and shared his plans with his nephew. The international management committee would offer, he suggested, the guiding hand of experience, while also giving the senior employees comfort that there was still a Cartier brother overseeing the entire organization. Pierre moved on to discuss the challenges ahead in London. Business, and the creation of jewels, had dried up during the war as men had been called up to fight. Now that peace reigned, it was important to consider how best to restart the workshops.

By the time Jean-Jacques boarded the ship back to England, he felt better equipped to face the future. Pierre hadn't missed the opportunity to remind him that he was the Cartier patriarch, but he had also reassured his nephew that the bond of family was paramount. It was a sentiment that would be echoed in his correspondence over the months ahead: "Your letter confirms . . . the opinion I have always had of you. You are a real Cartier. Your affectionate attitude is similar to what your father always had toward me, and was reciprocated by me." His uncle had offered his blessing.

THE AGE OF AUSTERITY

In the years preceding the outbreak of war, Cartier London had been at the top of its game. While America struggled through the after-effects of the Great Depression and France faced political instability, the late 1930s luxury trade in England had blossomed, thanks to King George VI's coronation and continued patronage by the maharaja clients. Now the country's fortunes had reversed. After spending vast sums on the war effort and borrowing heavily from America through low-interest loans and the Lend-Lease program, England was mired in debt. Jean-Jacques started his career in a country that owed more than £20 billion (around $1 trillion today) and in a city littered with bomb sites and ruined buildings. The United Kingdom might have emerged victorious, but those who had been expecting life to quickly return to normal would be disappointed.

In the July 1945 general election, the Labour Party under Clement Attlee had won its first ever parliamentary majority in a shocking landslide victory. Unfortunately for the luxury trade, the new government's strategy to balance the UK's dollar deficit and fund the creation of a welfare state was to drastically raise taxes. It also focused on increasing exports, with the unhappy side effect of tightening rationing as British goods were prioritized for export markets. For the nation, to "manage without" had been acceptable during the war when there had been a certain pride in holding back for the good of one's country. But the idea that rationing should continue long afterward would be met with a growing sense of outrage.

For the jewelry industry, the most debilitating of all the government's postwar actions was the raising of the "purchase tax." Introduced in 1940 as a luxury sales tax to reduce wastage of raw materials during the war, it would continue until 1973, with devastating effects. Jewelry was not only exceptionally expensive to produce, as precious metals were still in short supply, but it also became eye-wateringly expensive to buy. Between 1940 and 1947, for instance, purchase tax rose from 30 percent to 125 percent, meaning that for every $100 spent on a bracelet, the buyer was forced to pay an additional $125. "I am afraid that Uncle Pierre will find that business conditions here are very much more difficult than one can realize

A youthful Jean-Jacques Cartier around the time he took over the management of Cartier London.

from a distance," Jean-Jacques wrote to his mother, awaiting his uncle's visit to London in July 1946, "and how hard it is to fight against the current red tape."

Jean-Jacques started off in New Bond Street by calling a company-wide meeting. He hated the idea of public speaking, especially to a group of senior employees who clearly knew far more than he did, but he felt it was important. After years dominated by uncertainty and tragedy, it was up to him to carry the business forward, and to do that effectively, he had to

inspire loyalty in his team. "Gentlemen," he said to the sea of expect-
ant eyes, sensing their skepticism. Many of them knew nothing more
of him than that he had gone to an expensive Swiss boarding school
and was taking over their business, at the age of just twenty-seven.
He wanted to convey how seriously he took his responsibility. "Besides a small experience gained during five years in Paris," he started,
"I bring an enthusiastic love for our profession, the sense of prestige
of the name I bear, and, along with the will to work and to understand, a vivid memory of my father, which I feel confident will keep
me on the right path."

Holding his carefully prepared notes, he outlined his plans for the
future. First, they would rebuild the workshops. During the war, the
large group of skilled craftsmen working for the three London workshops (English Art Works, Wright & Davies, and Sutton & Straker)
had dispersed, called up either to fight or to work in war-related
roles. Not all of them had returned. Some had tragically been killed
in battle or bombing raids, others had been sucked into alternative
professions, and some had simply reached retirement age. Jean-
Jacques promised to build a new team. It would be time-consuming
and expensive, he warned. It would also require the support of everyone there, as the senior craftsmen would be called upon to train the
new arrivals. But he was in no doubt that it was essential if they were
to continue making jewelry to the high standard for which Cartier
London was known.

Second, he spoke of the international management committee that
Pierre had set up, explaining that it would ensure that London continued to work in harmony with Paris and New York now that two
of the three brothers had passed away. As his father had always told
him, so now he told his team, that Cartier's strength lay in its bond
among the three Maisons. They needed to work together now more
than ever. He knew he was young and lacked his late father's experience, but this committee would enable the firm to draw on the experience of all three branches. From London, both Bellenger and Foreman
would be on the board: "I am not presumptuous," Jean-Jacques continued, "and I intend to lean on [their] strong experience."

Finally, Jean-Jacques spoke of his desire to continue his father's
legacy. He would work ceaselessly to create original items of the
highest quality. Even in a difficult economic climate, Cartier London

would not accept second best when it came to craftsmanship. And to the sales team, he stressed the need to "resolutely aim for an active future" and seek out new opportunities. Now was not a time to sit back; they had to fight to maintain the position Jacques had built. "This plan, gentlemen," he concluded, "will go smoothly into execution only if you will give me that wholehearted collaboration you gave my father, Monsieur Jacques." It was a speech that, as he humbly reported back to Pierre, "seemed to go down well," and he was excited for the future. Many of those who had worked for his father came to offer their support. Some, such as Joe Allgood, who had been hired just before the war, were incredibly loyal to the memory of Jacques and vowed to help his son in any way they could. Unfortunately, not everyone felt the same way.

After his speech, there was one immediate resignation, an English Art Works employee who felt he couldn't work for such a young boss with plans for change. But most significantly, Bellenger was still unconvinced. Prior to the outbreak of war, Bellenger had shared an office with Jacques. When Jean-Jacques had returned from war, he had assumed his father's old desk, but it was hard for both of them to work so closely together. While Bellenger offered to help his late boss's son, his paternalistic attitude only served to accentuate Jean-Jacques' feelings of inferiority. From the older man's perspective, Jean-Jacques seemed young and naïve. For years, Bellenger had been running Cartier London while simultaneously working with General Charles de Gaulle in his attempt to help the French win the war. Now he was expected to work for a young man fresh out of an apprenticeship with no real business experience.

Bellenger's grumblings were not unique, either within Cartier London or within the wider Cartier business. New York and Paris would face the same issues. In the time of Louis-François and Alfred, Cartier had been a small family business, so a transition to the next generation had been straightforward to manage. By the time Cartier had grown to the scale the firm had reached in the 1940s, it was inevitable that promoting an inexperienced young heir ahead of those who had dedicated their working lives to Cartier would ruffle feathers. Jean-Jacques consulted his uncle Pierre over the problem of Bellenger, and the two of them, agreeing that they could not afford to lose the London firm's leading salesman, not only increased his salary but also gave him a profit share in Cartier Ltd.

It was just at this troubled time that Charles Jacqueau arrived. Like a guardian angel from Paris, the enormously experienced and highly revered designer had come to help the young Jean-Jacques in his new role. Part of the reason for his decision to exchange 13 Rue de la Paix for 175 New Bond Street was to escape working alongside Toussaint (perhaps regretting the earlier episode, Toussaint would admit in a subsequent interview that she couldn't draw, explaining that Louis had told her not to learn because that would prevent her from being able to assess the designs of others). But Jacqueau's move to England was about more than just that. Before Jacques had passed away, Jacqueau had promised his friend he would look out for his son, and he had come to fulfill his pledge. For three weeks at a time, over the course of several years, Charles Jacqueau would work in the London branch and live with Jean-Jacques and his family in Dorking. It was an important relationship. Not only did Jacqueau become something of a mentor for Jean-Jacques, but the designer's presence in support of him as the new boss in 175 New Bond Street was an important signal to the rest of the team.

SWEETS FOR GEMS

Jean-Jacques had hoped to start his career in London with a stock-room filled with the most wonderful necklaces, headpieces, and brooches made under his father in the 1930s. Instead he returned to find that almost everything had been sold during the war at rock-bottom prices. The problem, as he would discover, was that the men his father had left in charge—Foreman and Bellenger—were sales-men, and salesmen usually wanted to sell, come what may. One of the buyers had been a lady who made toffees in the north of England. Providing sugary treats at a time when the nation was desperate for any tiny way to brighten their day had made this lady a small fortune. At the end of each month, she would travel down to London with her profits and head into Cartier. There she would ask the sales-men how business had been recently, and when they responded gloomily, she would propose to buy several pieces but for a knocked-down price. Happy to clinch a sale in a near-dead market, they usually agreed.

In Conversation with Jean-Jacques Cartier

I was furious to find out how much stock had been sold in the war! But I never let on. I was just joining, you see, and Bellenger and Foreman were much older men who had kept the firm going. They were my elders and I had to show them respect. Of course, they should probably have sent all the jewels away for safekeeping—we could have made much more money by selling them after the war.

Jean-Jacques, with his love for design, took over the artistic direction of the London house. As Toussaint had been doing in Paris, he oversaw the creations coming out of 175 New Bond Street, and like Toussaint, his challenge was to create a collection that better reflected the restrained postwar environment without losing sight of the classic Cartier style. Small bird and flower brooches were very different from the large diamond and emerald necklaces made under Jacques, but they still had to be recognizably Cartier. By working closely with Jacqueau and the designers his father had hired and helped train, Frederick Mew, George Charity, and Rupert Emmerson, Jean-Jacques sought to ensure that the original Cartier design aesthetic lived on. And when he added new members to the team, such as a young man by the name of Dennis Gardner, he made it very clear that they had to learn the rules of the established order.

Before the war, Dennis Gardner had worked as a teenage apprentice in London's jewelry center, Hatton Garden. Often tasked with deliveries in town, he used to walk past Cartier thinking that one day he would love to work there. After serving in the navy during the war, he'd decided to try his luck. Jean-Jacques, as inexperienced in the interview process as Gardner himself, recognized in the modest twenty-two-year-old a genuine passion for art and design. Gardner was hired in 1946, one of the first of a new wave of younger employees that would carry Cartier forward in the postwar era.

The starting salary of £6 a week was even less than Gardner's modest navy salary, but it was a prestigious position and he was grateful. Full of ideas, the young apprentice was excited to get started, but that first day didn't go quite as he had hoped. After a busy few hours putting pencil to paper, Jean-Jacques came over to look at the designs of his newest recruit and explained that, though rather lovely, they just weren't quite Cartier. "Look at the other designers, Gardner, learn from them. Try again tomorrow."

The next day Gardner did look at the others' designs. He studied the colorful flower drawings of Frederick Mew, who worked in a small office on his own because he had weak lungs and couldn't handle the cigarette smoke in the design studio. He looked closely at the intricate sketches of the cigarette boxes that Rupert Emmerson was working on. And he watched Charles Jacqueau in awe as he effortlessly drew brooch after necklace after bracelet. Over the course of the following few days, Gardner tried to absorb it all. The end of the week came, and proud of his new designs, he showed them to Monsieur Cartier. But they received the same response. "Very good, Gardner. Just not quite Cartier." Gardner went home discouraged. His wife, Mimi, had given up her job to look after him, making sure he looked the part every day in his pressed shirts, starched collars, and polished shoes. He couldn't let her down, and yet how could he succeed if he couldn't even grasp the fundamentals of the Cartier style?

He tried again. And again. For months and months this would continue. "Yes, that's very good, Gardner. You're getting there. Still not quite Cartier, though." It would take not one year, or even two. It would take three years. The day he finally had his work approved as "truly Cartier," he walked through his front door a different man. "I've got it! I've finally got it!" he roared to his somewhat perplexed wife. And that was it. "You see, the people at Cartier were wonderful," Dennis Gardner would later recall. "But it was the Cartier style that made a piece stand out from the competition. You had to really understand it to be a designer there. The symmetry, the Art Deco aspect mixed in with understated French elegance. That's what made Cartier so special."

JEWELRY SPOTLIGHT: THE CARTIER STYLE

"I have watched salesmen remove a jewel from a showcase," recalled an employee working under Jean-Jacques, "and reverently hand it to a client with the remark 'Madam, may I show you this? Here is something truly Cartier.'" This idea of a piece being "truly Cartier" is as evident as it is hard to define. First emerging under Louis in Paris, the Cartier style became, one designer recalled, "an essential attainment that every newcomer to the firm is trained to acquire."

At its crux was the understanding that everything comes from what came before. The Cartier brothers refused to imitate other jewelry designers ("never copy, only create"), but they could, and would, draw inspiration from their surroundings and from past civilizations. "The ten centuries that preceded our era," Jacques wrote in his diary, "are one of the most wonderful periods in the history of the world." Garland tiaras were inspired by Parisian balconies, an iconic watch was born out of a weapon of war, and jabot pins were based on ancient swords. Mythical creatures in oriental books were transformed into chimera bracelets, colorful ballet costumes inspired the use of sapphires and emeralds side by side, ancient Egyptian faïences picked up in antiques shops became the centerpiece for unique brooches, and antique jade animals formed the base of mystery clocks. Even tiny details, such as the shape of a brooch's clasp, were inspired by studying past works of art. When Jacques taught a young apprentice about drawing a perfect curve, he pulled out a book on Chinese furniture from his vast library and illustrated his point with a tight enclosing curve on a black-lacquered table leg.

For all the creative inspiration drawn from history, the style that first emerged in the late nineteenth century was not old-fashioned. It was Cartier's role to adapt and update. Sometimes the innovation would come from the use of new materials: platinum before it became a precious metal, a vanity case made of steel, or glow-in-the-dark hands on a clock. More often than not, though, it was in the design: Ideas from the past were valuable only if they could be reinterpreted and made relevant for a modern audience. So an Egyptian lotus-flower motif was reworked into an Art Deco 1930s diamond and platinum tiara, Chinese symbols were adapted to become more geometric as part of Art Deco desk clocks, and a panther illustration from a children's story was reworked in diamonds and onyx for the strong postwar woman.

This mix of past and present, of inspiration and innovation, was a classic hallmark of the Cartier style, but there was more that the designers had to learn. Underlying everything was an appreciation of proportion and symmetry and a focus on the highest quality. This is why even Cartier creations from over a century ago still accord with our understanding of beauty and elegance today, since "these are the characteristics that the discerning taste must find to make it happy," as Rupert Emmerson, one of Cartier London's greatest designers, once explained. "It cannot be fooled by the meaningless application of unnecessary twiddly bits which do nothing to emphasize the strength and beauty of correctly proportioned and well-balanced form."

As auction results continually reveal, the creations made under the three brothers have withstood the test of time. Partly this reflects the quality of the gems and the workmanship. "We used only the best quality gems," Jean-Jacques recalled, "and each jewel or case or watch had to be perfectly made, that is to say, it had to look as good from the back as the front. Even if a client never noticed it, it was important to us." But a large part of the enduring appeal is also due to that recognizable design style that across decades has been reflected in thousands of different items, from watches to necklaces to clocks and from letter openers to handbags. "It is a hard thing to explain" is the response of jewelry experts when asked how they can instantly recognize an antique Cartier piece as Cartier even before seeing its signature. But once they start talking, they will invariably refer to the subtle mix of old and new, the peerless workmanship, the timeless elegance, the lightness, and the subtle hints of Parisian style. And almost all would agree with Emmerson's succinct definition:

"It is simplicity too, this Cartier 'style.' ... Simplicity, restraint and a quiet confident look of quality."

While several designers focused on new items for stock and the showroom was slowly refilled, others were tasked with personal commissions. In 1947, these included one from the Indian royal family of Baroda. The glamorous Sita Devi, known as the Indian Wallis Simpson, had become the Maharini of Baroda after marrying Maharaja Pratap Singh Rao (Sayajirao III's successor) in 1943. A lover of gems, she was a welcome client of many jewelers, and a single order in Cartier London was enough to keep the London workshops occupied for several months. Happily for Jean-Jacques, it was followed by another large purchase from an Indian client in July 1947, when the Nizam of Hyderabad offered the then Princess Elizabeth two Cartier jewels of her choosing as a wedding gift. She picked out a floral diamond tiara set with leafy tendrils and a diamond necklace that had been modeled by the stylish Rose Greville, Countess of Warwick, in *Harper's Bazaar* in 1935. The Hyderabad necklace, as it became known, remains popular with the younger royals today.

Just a month later, in August 1947, the Indian Independence Act would presage an end to the opulent era of the maharajas. Over the years to come, extortionate Indian taxes on luxury items would prevent the rulers from buying jewels in any significant way or even wearing them in public. Gems that had been in the same families for generations, even centuries, would be secretly sold off, seized by the government, or tied up in lengthy disputes. For Cartier London, which had traditionally relied on the maharajas' custom in times of trouble, its loss was a major setback.

The vast changes in India did, however, also create opportunity. As the Romanovs had done after the October Revolution, the maharajas now sought to sell their jewels back to the firms that had once supplied them. Jean-Jacques suggested that his brother-in-law, the Cartier director Carl Nater, travel East to see if any of their clients were considering selling. Unfortunately, the process wasn't straightforward. When the Cartier brothers had bought back fabulous jewels after the Russian Revolution, Louis, Pierre, and Jacques had personally known the clients from whom they were buying. As a result, the

Russian princes, grand dukes, and grand duchesses had trusted Cartier more than most other European jewelers. The problem now was that those doing the buying were not those who had built the initial client relationship. The maharajas who had dealt with Jacques Cartier had never met Carl. Perhaps if Jean-Jacques had traveled to India himself, it might have been different, but given his more artistic leaning, his focus was on the creative side of the business.

SAYING GOODBYE TO AMERICA

In the summer of 1947, Pierre and Elma left America for retirement in Switzerland. Pierre was sixty-nine years old, and was both looking forward to the next chapter and wary of leaving the business behind, especially in such uncertain circumstances. The debate about Louis' inheritance didn't seem to be getting any closer to a resolution and his relationship with Jacqui and Claude was growing increasingly strained. Believing strongly that Cartier New York should remain a family firm, and his branch of the family at that, he left his son-in-law in charge. Claudel had worked under Pierre for some time as vice president and knew the ropes. But just as when Jean-Jacques had taken charge in London, there were those who feared that he lacked the exceptional skills and experience of his predecessor, and that the business could suffer as a result.

In Conversation with Jean-Jacques Cartier

Pierre Claudel was a nice chap, bright and very honest. I think he liked the sales side of the business. I'm sure he was good at it, he was easy to get along with, clients would have liked him. He wasn't as all-round a businessman as Pierre, but then no one was, really, apart from perhaps Devaux.

Before he'd left for Europe, Pierre had asked the best manager he knew to come out to New York and help Claudel run the business.

Devaux, who had managed the Paris branch for several years, was initially unsure. Neither he nor his wife wanted to leave France. But Pierre had been insistent. Devaux was not only well connected (when he visited Pierre in New York toward the end of the war, the pair had met with President Roosevelt to discuss "some confidential information" relating to Devaux's wartime roles in the Resistance), he also knew the inner workings of the Cartier business. And crucially, having worked closely with Louis, he truly understood the Cartier ethos.

When Devaux wavered, Pierre had pointed out that since Claude might take over the Paris house, his position there would be uncertain, as he would be likely to "surround himself with those of a similar ilk." In New York, meanwhile, Pierre was stepping down, and Devaux could head up the business alongside Claudel, who would focus more on sales. It had been a good pitch, and the thirty-eight-year-old Devaux eventually accepted, moving across the Atlantic in June 1947.

Devaux was very respectful of the shoes into which he was stepping. At the start of his trip, he stayed in Pierre and Elma's country home, Long Meadow Farm. "Every piece of furniture, every work of art in the many rooms of Long Meadow Farm reminds us constantly of your presence," he wrote back to Elma. It was a feeling that became even more acute, he confided, in the Cartier Fifth Avenue build-

An aerial view of the Cartier New York showroom in 1947, the hundredth anniversary of the firm. Though senior management changed when Pierre retired, for clients and employees, such as this craftsman setting a choker in the upstairs workshop, it remained the same Cartier it had always been.

ing, "where each detail reflects Monsieur Pierre's personality." It did not make life easy for him, being at times a reminder of "my own inability to replace your husband, whose indefatigable work I fully realize only now."

Pierre and Elma had bought a large Swiss property near Geneva that had been a part of Empress Josephine's residence. Villa Elma, as they named it, had a prime position on the shores of Lac Léman but was in need of extensive renovations. As they waited for the work to be completed, they stayed in hotels, initially in Lausanne and then in Geneva. Pierre kept up to date on news of all the branches via daily letters. Though officially retired, he would send regular counsel and instructions to his nephew in London and his son-in-law in New York. There was, for instance, advice to keep relations between the senior directors "harmonious" because "their collaboration is indispensable." There were also suggestions on whom to invite out for lunch, how to improve sales figures by the end of the year, and details on when specific clients were traveling back and forth between America and Europe.

That year, 1947, marked the centenary of the founding of Cartier. One hundred years after Louis-François had started the firm, his only surviving grandson, Pierre, wanted to ensure that it was marked appropriately. In Paris, there was an exhibition: "Dazzling, imaginative and new is the display at Cartier's in celebration of the company's one hundredth year anniversary," *The New York Times* reported. "Gone are the heavy gold rings, bracelets and necklaces of the war period, when a large part of the value of the piece was in the metal. This year . . . little metal is to be seen for it disappears under a paving of diamonds." Light and airy jewels led the way, from a choker with a cascade of diamond leaves and flowers to a diamond palm tree clip and Egyptian- and Hindu-inspired bib necklaces, where gold latticework was brought to life with amethysts and turquoise. In New York, too, there was a new collection on display: a mix of classic and modern pieces, from clips in the shape of tropical birds, squirrels, ducks, and butterflies to "a fabulous necklace with the 107 carat Alexander II emerald mounted in a detachable clip." An illustrated book, *Cartier 1847–1947,* was commissioned outlining the history of the firm, to be distributed to key clients, and Pierre suggested that each branch hold its own celebrations. "The success of the cocktail party to celebrate the centenary does not surprise me," he wrote after one such event, "but it is news that gives me great joy."

Struggling to fill the large hole Pierre left behind, Claudel came to rely heavily on Devaux. "They work together like brothers" was the report from those on the inside, with Devaux "having taken on all internal management at Fifth Avenue," and Claudel free "to concentrate his efforts on sales." Before long, however, there was tension in the American Maison. Devaux had spoken to Louis' son, Claude, to explain that he was working to honor Louis' memory but that Claude should stop making claims to a branch that was not rightfully his. Furious, Claude had reacted harshly toward Devaux, and the Cartiers had been appalled at his lack of respect. "The impudence of a boy of 22 not even being polite to a man of 40—and without Devaux what would he have had—it all seems so foolish." The reality, of which Claude may have been unaware, was that without Devaux's dedication to the firm, Cartier Paris might not have even survived the war years.

For Devaux, who had wanted to help his mentor's son, Claude's behavior had been a slap in the face, and he admitted to being "terribly hurt." Pierre, terrified he might leave in anger, reproached Claude for his "crude conduct" toward his senior and asked him to "make peace." Business was difficult enough without having to deal with internal strife as well. "We are experiencing a crisis in the luxury trade," Devaux reported in December 1947, confirming Pierre's earlier fears that in their new postwar world, extravagance was being judged more critically. It was a shift in society that would pose major challenges to a jewelry house that had always aspired to be the best. Not to mention a House that was increasingly divided.

AN EXCHANGE OF MAISONS

In October 1947, Claude started his MBA studies at Harvard. Pierre was pleased that his nephew was acting more seriously. "Better late than never!" he rejoiced. But the disagreements within the family continued. Pierre still felt that Claude "has not respected his father's wishes or the pact among the three brothers," and by early 1948, the situation had come to a head. "Claude refused to recognize the validity of his father's will," Pierre later wrote, "and his lawyer warned me that he would start a lawsuit against me if I decided to enforce the provisions."

Not wanting to entertain a public court battle or a scandal in the newspapers, Pierre proposed an alternative solution, namely to sell "my interests in the New York Firm, except the building" while simultaneously buying "the half interest that his father owned with me in the French company." His idea, quite simply, was to exchange stores. He would assume the controlling interest in Cartier Paris and Claude would control Cartier New York.

Claude would later tell his cousin that it had been his idea to exchange stores and that Pierre, unwilling at first, had agreed on the basis that Claude should pay him the difference in value between the branches (said to be one million dollars). In any case, by March 1948, the deal had been agreed upon. Claude wanted to stay in America and be head of the prestigious American branch even if (as he would later confide to Jean-Jacques) he felt he was paying too much.

In Conversation with Jean-Jacques Cartier

I never understood why Claude wanted to exchange Paris for New York. Well, I knew he preferred life in New York at the time and he feared that the Russians would overrun Europe, but to give up the Paris Maison? Cartier Paris was the jewel in Cartier's crown, and it was handed to him on a silver platter! Toussaint would have done anything to help him, but Claude wasn't interested. He could be like that, when he had made up his mind, there was no point trying to change it.

Pierre felt an understandable sadness that "our branch of the family, the one that founded the American House, is leaving the management of Inc." but, on balance, he was pleased to have reached a resolution. This would settle, at last, "the question of ownership, knowledge of which by the staff is indispensable to proper leadership." For many years he had considered taking over the Paris branch, and though the exchange was not without its risks, he was excited for the future and relieved that, some "six years since poor Louis' death," the years of family conflict would finally be over. He asked that Devaux and Claudel continue managing the New York branch until the transaction was finalized. After the difficult negotiations, it was important to him that they be there to keep an eye on things.

Claude, meanwhile, agreed to come over to Paris to train under the team there so that when he took over the New York branch, he would have a better sense of the global business. Pierre, who had arranged to meet him in the Ritz, had a "very serious conversation with him in the presence of his mother." It seemed to have had an impact. Everyone was delighted that he seemed to be taking his future responsibilities seriously. "No complaints about CC in Paris" was the report, "he is at meetings every morning, then goes to examine pieces." Claude, working hard, was realizing that "management is more complicated than he had thought." Pierre breathed a sigh of relief. Louis would be a hard act for his son to follow, but Claude surprised the team with his aesthetic sense: "He appears to have his father's eye!" After years of anxiety, Pierre dared to believe that the future of the family firm might work as he hoped.

Once the final exchange of the New York and Paris branches was completed in late 1948, the plan was that Claude would return to New York, where he would first become vice president and work alongside Devaux and Claudel for a three-month transition period. After that time he would assume the role of president of Cartier Inc., and Devaux and Claudel would return to Paris. Pierre had promised Claudel the role of president of the Paris branch and Devaux that of chairman, and he had enthusiastically told them that, together, they would be "the new engines" of Cartier S.A.

But just months after Devaux returned to France, he asked to see Pierre for a meeting. It was then, in early August 1949, that he resigned from Cartier, announcing he would be taking a new job as a senior director within the Shell Oil Company. Pierre was crushed. Devaux understood the business inside out. He'd been personally trained by Louis, and there was little doubt in Pierre's mind that he was the man to carry the business forward. But Devaux defended his position, explaining that when in New York, he had not been given free rein, and he found Claude "impossible" to work with. Those years in America, Devaux admitted, "undermined my faith in a future with Cartier," and he felt that he couldn't "bring about any practical developments in unfavorable psychological circumstances."

Pierre's disappointment soon turned to anger. Devaux's decision to quit felt like a betrayal of his late brother's memory. Upset by Pierre's critique, Devaux pointed out how he had run Cartier Paris without a break from 1935 until 1946 (the only interruption being the period he had spent in active service and as a prisoner of war). He had never sworn to "become involved with Cartier for life." In the end, they would make peace. Devaux, still wanting to help, agreed to stay on the board of Cartier S.A. as a non-executive.

PARIS: A CITY OF TWO HALVES

In the spring of 1949, the Claudels returned to Paris, and Pierre Claudel started his new role as president of Cartier S.A. Marion, delighted to be back in France, wrote to her family that she had "taken flowers to Versailles" (to the Cartier family crypt) and had tea at the Trianon as she used to do with her grandfather Alfred. She would later help her husband in Rue de la Paix, but not until the family was settled. The renovations of their apartment near the Bois de Boulogne were taking longer than they had hoped.

Paris was a city of two halves. Living conditions for many were far from ideal, creating a mood of discontent that sometimes erupted into angry strikes. "The economic and political situation is becoming more and more precarious," those in Paris would report in 1951. "It is possible to feel the rock moving under the shifting sands that cover terra firma." And yet, there were those who could afford to live well, and, particularly after the difficult years they had endured, they enjoyed dressing up and going out.

Through the postwar years, Paris was determined to maintain its position as the design capital of the world. French fashion would become an important export industry and foreign currency earner. Not long after the war ended, in February 1947, Christian Dior put on a major fashion show at his recently opened 30 Avenue Montaigne haute couture Maison. It was here that he first presented his "New Look," a reprise of mid-nineteenth-century fashions with billowing skirts below cinched-in waists, which transformed the spirit of postwar France. Since then, fashion shows had become quite a highlight in the Paris social calendar, and they were not limited to an elite few. More modest and relaxed than they would later become (models smiled and interacted with the audience as they walked down a usually small runway, around a showroom, or even through a private living room), they offered the designers an opportunity to showcase and sell their collections to buyers, editors, and the general public. Toussaint, who recognized, like Louis, that the jeweler designs "for the dressed and not the undressed woman," was often in attendance. She also took it upon herself to offer Marion an education in the world of fashion. "Tomorrow evening," Marion wrote to her mother, "we are going with Jeanne Toussaint to the Jacques Fath premiere." Another night, it would be the Revillon collection or to see the up-and-coming couturier Hubert de Givenchy.

The new generation of Cartiers were mingling socially with the same clients (or their descendants) that their fathers had spent time cultivating in the 1920s and '30s, and the Claudels found themselves at the center of a busy social scene. "It rains invitations," they wrote, with a typical week consisting of multiple evening dress events such as a ball for Princess Margaret or a party at the Louvre. And then there were lunches to host and attend with friends and acquaintances, including ambassadors' sons and socialites such as Eleanor Hutton (Marjorie Merriweather Post's daughter). The endless dressing up and going out could be exhausting, but equally it was recognized as an important part of the job.

In Conversation with Jean-Jacques Cartier

Marion was artistic, she enjoyed working on stained-glass windows, which is quite a specialized skill. But when it came to the business, the artistic direction of the Paris house was Toussaint's domain. Marion did more on the client-facing side, certainly more than I did.

Toussaint's sense of style was undisputed, but her challenge, as with Jean-Jacques in London, was selecting designs that would be affordable for the postwar public. Louis had said of her that she had something that he, for all his talent, could never have: a woman's eye. She understood that 1950s fashion called for a new style of jewels. Big brooches were important for accentuating the fitted bodice, large bib-style necklaces filled the décolletage, and bracelets worked both over gloves and without them. Matching sets of jewels were fashionable, as were pearl necklaces, and a trend for colored gemstones overtook the previous predominantly diamond look. "People may not have had as much money as before the war," one former Cartier designer recalled of the fifties, "but women were so elegant then. They simply didn't go out without jewels. I don't mean big expensive gems necessarily, but just a simple brooch or hatpin would finish off an outfit with such style."

Occasionally there were orders for large statement pieces, such as the Duchess of Windsor's iconic bib-style amethyst, turquoise, and gold necklace that she had commissioned from Cartier in 1947. But for the most part, Toussaint was tasked with overseeing a collection that appealed to a more subdued aesthetic (and thinner wallets). Her postwar collections were, as Pierre described them, "very sober and refined." Many Parisians, abiding by the 1950s fashion rules for multiple accessories but unable to afford the genuine article, opted for costume jewelry. Cartier, which refused to cater to this market, had to come up with alternatives to entice clients through their doors. The rings of the designer Georges Rémy, for instance, perfectly tapped into the demand of the time for a small, stylish luxury that was both relatively affordable and fashionable. "Rings are voluminous, but they can be seen through," *The New York Times* described Cartier's postwar creations. "Twisted threads of gold form a gossamer balloon shape like an inverted basket, and on this gold network, stones are sprinkled in various sizes." Toussaint, who wore Rémy's large rings on her little fingers, bestowed on him the title *le roi des bagues* (king of rings).

"Cartier, Paris' aristocratic jewelry house," an *Associated Press* report noted in January 1951, "have adapted their goods to suit the times and have said goodbye to the carriage trade and the million-dollar sales." The invisible settings of tiny diamonds used in pieces

The three Cartier branches adapted to the difficult postwar period with a range of more functional pieces. In New York, the store's Gold Room (right) was popular for gifts, while in Paris, a 1953 advertisement (left) focuses on the cigarette and vanity cases in front of the top model Bettina.

before the war were being replaced with gold mountings and settings. Semiprecious gemstones, favored in the post-Depression years, continued to sell better than their more expensive precious counterparts. "Today's customers have less to spend," senior Cartier salesman Jean Turpin told the journalist, before detailing how before the war an average "good customer" spent $25,000 to $35,000 and now it was more like $600 to $900. He blamed the postwar movement toward equality of income for the change. "Many of our best foreign customers cannot take enough money out of their countries to buy an expensive piece of jewelry," he explained. "High taxes, too, hold down big splurging."

And yet, though there wasn't the same level of top-end demand, there was still a reasonable volume of visitors to 13 Rue de la Paix looking to justify the three hundred–strong Cartier workforce. "As long as there are women," Turpin sighed, happily, "there will always be jewellery." Typical lower-priced jewels in the store included a bird with ruby eyes, gold beak, and sapphire breast for $886, and a bullfrog with diamond warts on its back for $700. There was even a sterling keyring for $5.50, while jewelry with a six-figure price tag was shown by appointment only.

"There are lots of foreigners," was the report from the Paris branch in 1951, "and the restaurants, theaters, and hotels are full. We are seeing a lot of them, and they are paying in dollars." The "international jet set," as they were known, were those who could afford the expensive airfares on the new, spacious passenger jets (previously most air travel had been on propeller planes). Many came from North America, but there were also those from South America, which, though volatile politically, was an exciting source of emerging wealth for the luxury industry. "The Comtesse Revilla has taken up her lovely apartment at the Ritz and Paris is prepared for a sparkling season."

Heiress to a Cuban sugar plantation, the Comtesse Revilla de Camargo traveled regularly to the French capital from her mansion in Havana. An ardent Francophile, she was one of the few big spenders of the postwar period and would buy dresses from Dior and jewels from Cartier. She was a woman who knew what she wanted and was quite happy to pay for it. In 1947, she had informed Cartier that she would be sailing to France on the *Queen Elizabeth* and requested, for when she arrived, "a pendant including a pear diamond between 32 and 35 carats, topped with a square or oval stone attached to a choker, this set being easily worn in the evening."

Other jetsetters of the period who came to epitomize an international postwar café society included the Prince Aly Khan and his wife, Rita Hayworth; Prince Sadruddin Aga Khan and his wife, Nina Dyer; Elsie de Wolfe; Cole Porter; and Mexican actress Maria Félix. For fashion houses and jewelers of the period, these were the perfect celebrity ambassadors for their creations, often photographed in the press (Elsa Maxwell even created *Café Society* magazine in 1953, with Zsa Zsa Gabor on the front cover of the one and only issue). Others appeared on screen or stage. Greek opera singer Maria Callas (not unlike Nellie Melba half a century earlier) performed to packed audiences all over the world. When she made her début at the Metropolitan Opera House in New York in 1956, ticket sales broke all records, and *The New York Times* reported that "never had so many Americans paid so much to hear an opera."

Within Cartier Paris, Pierre remained, as his father, Alfred, had been, the axis around whom everyone else turned. Though Elma may have hoped he would settle down into retirement, her husband couldn't let go of the business that had become his life. When he visited Paris, as he did quite often, he would spend time with the senior directors. Interested in dealings with any significant clients, he was pleased to hear that his son-in-law, before he had left America, had sent the recently inaugurated U.S. president, Harry Truman, a letter that expressed Cartier's feeling "of loyalty and cooperation" and a gift. Just as Pierre had offered Roosevelt a clock to mark "the hour of victory" during the war, so Claudel had sent Truman a silver table clock. "Many, many thanks to you and your associates," the president had replied, "for your gracious act of friendship in sending me such a lovely souvenir . . . this clock will make a very useful and decorative addition to my desk."

As Pierre well knew, growing and maintaining a luxury business was as much about networking as anything else. Even in his seventies, he would visit those clients whom he and his brothers had known for decades. Years of shared experiences, not least two world wars and the losses of those they had both known, had made them close. "Dear Pierre," the writer and artist Jean Cocteau wrote in March 1950, responding to an invitation. "You are kind. I'm hiding myself in the country a bit after the filming of Enfants Terribles. But I'll be back in Paris on the 20th, if you will allow me to appear in artist's overalls, stains and all. Yours, Jean Cocteau."

Jeanne Toussaint, once rejected by Pierre for her unsuitable background, was by now almost a member of the Cartier family. She shared not only Pierre's love of the late Louis and devotion to the firm but also a deep religious faith. Pierre would invite her to join Elma and him on their trips to the Vatican, where he, by virtue of his position within the religious Knights of Malta order, would meet with the Pope. And within 13 Rue de la Paix, partly as a result of Pierre's support, Toussaint still exerted significant influence. She may have ruffled a few feathers among the male employees, Jacqueau especially, but as Louis had always known, she did possess an ability to understand some of the world's most formidable trendsetting women. The Duchess of Windsor, for instance, would become such a good Cartier client partly because of her close relationship with Toussaint. Both women were possessed of an inner strength and both

JEAN-JACQUES CARTIER

1919–2010

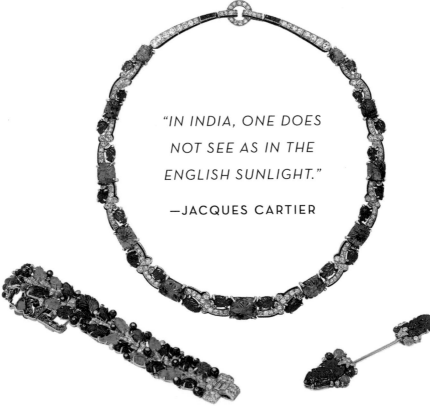

"IN INDIA, ONE DOES
NOT SEE AS IN THE
ENGLISH SUNLIGHT."
—JACQUES CARTIER

FOREIGN INFLUENCES

THE
1930s

"WE MUST MAKE . . . ARTICLES THAT
HAVE A USEFUL FUNCTION . . .
DECORATED IN THE CARTIER STYLE."

—LOUIS CARTIER

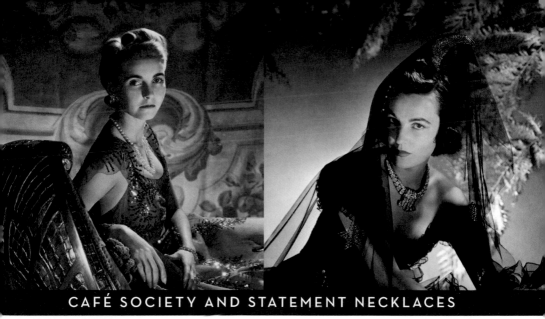

CAFÉ SOCIETY AND STATEMENT NECKLACES

A CHANGING WORLD

THE POSTWAR YEARS

"A JEWEL THAT IS CLASSIC IN DESIGN, THAT CONTAINS STONES OF GOOD QUALITY, ALWAYS REMAINS AN OBJECT OF BEAUTY. IT CAN BE WORN FOR YEARS AND BE ADMIRED AS MUCH TWENTY-FIVE YEARS AFTERWARD AS IT WAS WHEN IT WAS FIRST CREATED."

—PIERRE CARTIER

knew what it meant to overcome difficulties to occupy a prestigious position in society. Jeanne Toussaint would entertain the Duke and Duchess of Windsor at her chic Place d'Iéna apartment, where her attention to detail, on everything from the décor to the food to the wine, was known to be extraordinary. "This apartment," Cecil Beaton would recall, "is like a secret that few are privileged to share."

Jacqueau, meanwhile, was fading from the Cartier picture. His loyalty had, like that of so many, been to Louis, and after returning from London in 1949, he refused to work for Toussaint. He would design only client commissions for which he would be answerable to the client. In the new era, it was Pierre Lemarchand who became one of the most important designers in Paris. "He was Mademoiselle Toussaint's star," a fellow Cartier designer recalled: "She was always choosing his designs over the other designers'."

A talented artist first and foremost, Lemarchand focused on jewelry design a couple of days a week in order to pay the bills. Even then, he worked from his studio in Montparnasse (where he also gave Marion Cartier art lessons). He would come in to Rue de la Paix only once a week for the Tuesday design meetings chaired by Toussaint.

Toussaint and Lemarchand shared a "common love for animals and birds." Since the war, when he had created the iconic bird in (and out of) the cage, he had added larger animals to his repertoire. "He was a genius," one of his colleagues remembered. "He could sketch something on a scrap of paper in a second and it would be exquisite. He had such an ease with animals. They became real." In India, where he had traveled at the request of Jacques just prior to the outbreak of war, he had seen firsthand the majestic panthers and tigers. Now he turned them into jewels.

JEWELRY SPOTLIGHT: THE BIG CATS

It was Wallis Simpson who is said to have coined the mantra "You can never be too rich or too thin." After vying with Daisy Fellowes for the Best-Dressed Woman of the Year title throughout the 1930s and '40s, she posthumously won out when *Vanity Fair* proclaimed her best-dressed woman of all time. When she wore a Cartier diamond and onyx panther

*The Duchess of Windsor in
her 1956 Cartier tiger bracelet
(photographed in 1959), and
the 1952 articulated panther
bracelet that broke records
when it sold for $7 million
in 2010.*

brooch perched on top of an enormous
152-carat sapphire in 1949, the fashion glitterati
stood at attention, and Cartier panthers soon
became the accessory du jour among the world's
stylish elite.

The idea of a panther as a motif wasn't a new one
for Cartier. As early as 1914, Jacqueau had filled his
sketchbooks with images of panthers and created a
panther-motif watch strap from diamonds and onyx. And
from 1917, under the supervision of Louis, panthers had appeared on Cartier vanity cases and small jabot and tie pins.

A few years later, another of the Cartier brothers was also
being inspired by the big cats. Jacques had already marveled
at panthers in the wild in India, but it was as he read his small
son a bedtime story years later that the elegance of the beasts
impressed him again. Turning the pages of Rudyard Kipling's
The Jungle Book with his son, they paused at an illustration of
Bagheera the panther. Later that evening, Jacques took the
book down to his study with him. There he started making
notes in pencil in the margin, as he often did with the many
illustrated books in his library. Turning back to the chapter in
which Bagheera the panther was chased by a bear, he circled
the illustration in pencil, writing a little note to himself: *without the bear.*

Decades later, after the death of both Louis and Jacques, Jeanne Toussaint would build on the earlier idea of the panther and take it to a group of powerful women. Strong, driven, and at times terrifying, Toussaint perhaps felt an affinity with the big cat motif. Her "PanPan" nickname (likely to have been initially bestowed on her as early as 1913, when she visited Africa with her lover at the time, Pierre de Quinsonas) recalled the idea of a panther. Those who set foot in her exquisite apartment recalled magnificent panther skins decorating the floors, and others remembered that she had been an early adopter of the striking leopard-skin coat. Her own collection of Cartier pieces included a panther vanity case from 1917, when she had been in the early throes of her relationship with Louis.

In 1948, the Duke of Windsor, back in Paris after the war, commissioned Cartier to make a gold and onyx panther clip brooch for his wife. Not unusually for the Windsors, he supplied the main gemstone himself, in this case a 116.74-carat emerald upon which the big cat would sit. A year later, the Duchess bought a second panther brooch (this time it was one that had been made for stock): a panther in pavé-set diamonds with sapphire spots and yellow diamond eyes, sitting atop an enormous cabochon sapphire of 152.35 carats. She would wear it often, usually against a simple dress or coat. "I know women who put the most fabulous jewels on all over those beads," she would say. "To me, the jewels are finished."

From then on, there was no going back. The big cats kept coming. There were panther and tiger bracelets, clips, and even a lorgnette. "Wallis needed glasses to read a menu," Diana Vreeland recalled. Her 1954 tiger lorgnette with raised paw made it into *Vogue* in 1955 alongside the caption "The lorgnette has returned to fashion." In total, the Duchess of Windsor would acquire no fewer than twelve big-cat accessories from Cartier. And where Wallis led, others would follow.

Daisy Fellowes bought a diamond and sapphire spotted panther brooch, in which the articulated panther hangs from a central band of diamonds. Barbara Hutton bought a Cartier

tiger brooch to start with, before following it up with tiger earrings and a tiger bracelet. And after the beautiful Nina Dyer
married Prince Sadruddin Aga Khan in 1957, she was show-
ered with a parure of big cat jewels in diamonds, sapphires,
and emeralds. It is the Duchess of Windsor, however, who remains the Cartier client most associated with the big cats.
When her 1952 articulated panther bracelet was sold in 2010,
it reached £4.4 million ($7 million), breaking records and prov-
ing the world's ongoing fascination with the Cartier big cats
and the woman who wore them.

CLAUDE AS BOSS

Claude managed the New York Maison in his own way, with the select few who were in his circle of trust, including recent hires such as
"one of society's favorite unattached men," the aristrocrat Viscount
de Rosiere. Many of the employees who had worked under Pierre
had difficulty adjusting, however, and "PC wouldn't have done that"
was a common refrain whispered around the office. Pierre could be
haughty, but he had been universally admired. Claude mostly failed
to inspire the same loyalty. "Poor Claude has neither the courage nor
the imagination nor the competitive spirit for the recovery which is
necessary" was one of the less-than-glowing reports from the senior
management in New York.

To be fair to Claude, he had impossibly large shoes to fill. Comparisons with his uncle, who had dedicated his life to the business,
were unlikely ever to be in his favor. As a young man who had inherited a vast fortune, he had different priorities, and now that he
had tasted the good life, work wasn't always at the top of his list.
"It always seemed," one of his employees recalled, "that he couldn't
wait to leave those morning meetings he did make it in for, as though
he didn't want to be there." Newspaper gossip columns updated his
team on where "Claude Cartier of the jewelry millions" was holi-
daying: the Swiss mountains for a spot of skiing and bobsledding,
Rome with a former Miss America contestant, the Vigie Beach Club
in Monaco with fellow "international celebrities." In the summer of

1951, Claude traveled to the South of France for an extended three-month break. While he was there, his behavior caused serious alarm. Not unusually, he had borrowed money from the Paris branch for his vacation, but this time, there were "arguments relating to interest and devaluation." The outstanding amount was a sum of 1,500,000 francs (about $42,000 today). The Cartier firm had always been run on the basis of implicit trust underpinning financial matters among family members, but now there seemed a need "to abandon a family policy that has given such good results in the past."

Worst of all, a large scandal was threatening to break in the newspapers. In September 1951, when Claude had been on his way to catch the boat from Le Havre for America, there had been an accident. Having missed the train from Paris, and fearful he would miss the boat unless he moved quickly, he "took the wheel of his car and drove off with his chauffeur beside him." Driving too fast, Claude had swerved to avoid a car pulling out in front of him, and his own car had hit a tree.

Claude had emerged unscathed, but his chauffeur appeared to be injured and was rushed to a hospital, where he was diagnosed with bruising to the ribs. "As the chauffeur seemed fairly all right, Claude left for America," Jean-Jacques later recounted the story as he had heard it from his cousin. Concerned that he would miss his crossing to America, Claude booked a taxi plane to take him the one hundred miles to England so he could meet the boat when it docked there en route to America. Unfortunately, the situation was set to deteriorate. Several hours after Claude had flown to England, met his boat, and embarked for America, his chauffeur tragically died in the hospital of heart failure, thereby giving the world the (mistaken) impression that "Claude had left for another country after killing a man."

The Paris directors weren't sure how to deal with the situation. Everyone in the office had the same reaction—"Monsieur Pierre will be furious and upset, it's the kind of publicity he can't accept." An inquest would have to be opened, and the victim's representatives might allege hit-and-run. For Pierre, the situation was close to unforgivable. Even if Claude had left the country believing his chauffeur to be on the road to recovery, Pierre believed his nephew should still have appeared honorably in front of the authorities to explain his side of the story. "This mad mission you took to Le Havre, then from

Le Havre to Southampton, and finally the last dash to catch the boat," he wrote to Claude incredulously, "would almost be like something a film hero would do . . . but in your case it gave the impression of an escape from the authorities."

Pierre's long letter didn't stop there. It was as though he had finally found an excuse to speak his mind. It was ridiculous, he wrote, that Claude had claimed to need three months off in the summer to recover from the intense exhaustion of running Cartier Inc. and then spent that time in the busy party-filled resorts of Cannes and Biarritz. If he had worked in Cartier Paris, or at least in the Riviera branches, it would have gone some way to justifying his extended vacation, but instead he felt that Claude had now "added to your reputation as a playboy, . . . a disrespectful attitude." The fact that Claude had apparently left the Hôtel Carlton without paying, and had then asked Massabieaux, now head of the Monte Carlo branch, to pay on his behalf from company funds, was for Pierre the ultimate irreverence. "You must know [that] I would never ask Cartier Inc. to pay my expenses."

In the absence of Claude's having a father figure, Pierre took it upon himself to make clear "the consequences, serious for you and regrettable for us," of a bad reputation. The fun-loving Americans his nephew socialized with on the beaches and casinos of the Riviera would, he warned, report back to their banker friends in New York. And then, when Cartier Inc. needed to borrow money in the future, the credit would not be as forthcoming as in the past. He reprimanded Claude, too, for his excessive spending. Pierre ended his letter with several clear instructions for life. These ranged from practicing religion and living by the Golden Rule to "treat everyone as you would like to be treated," "forget the night life," and accept invitations only from serious people.

The commandments, as Pierre saw them, echoed his own values. And rules such as "Be the first person in to the office and last person out" and "Marry a soulmate" whose parents are "financially independent" were ones that he had followed. Finally, Pierre signed off with a reminder that, in his mind, Claude was "the owner of the best of our three Houses" and that he must be the "soul" of that House. The integrity of a House depended on the integrity of the boss. The three separate branches had to work together as one organization, but Claude was responsible for embodying the values of the New York branch.

If Pierre had hoped his nephew might take his letter to heart and change his ways, he was to be disappointed. For some time already, Claude had been feeling resentful that his uncle had made him pay such a large sum for the New York House, especially in such a difficult market. To receive a sermonizing letter, however justified it might have been, wouldn't go any way to improving relations.

In Conversation with Jean-Jacques Cartier

Claude and Uncle Pierre developed a difficult relationship. Pierre could be quite direct, and Claude wasn't good at being told what to do. I think Claude also felt he had been made to pay too much for the New York Maison. I never knew the details—but I imagine that Pierre wouldn't have done badly out of the deal, let's put it that way. He was a very astute businessman.

RUBIES IN BAGHDAD

With Britain suffering under the weight of postwar inflation, taxes, and ongoing rationing (which continued until 1954), Cartier London was forced to look overseas for clients. Right after the war, Jean-Jacques had explored opening a showroom in Canada, and Carl Nater had traveled over several times. They had been all ready to go ahead, and had even chosen the directors who would manage the new overseas branches, but ultimately the plan fell through when the UK government refused to allow the export of the capital required. It was disappointing, but it made the London salesforce even more eager to seek out large sales where they could.

Since the end of the war, 175 New Bond Street had seen an increasing number of Middle Eastern clients keen to convert their petroleum dollars into diamonds. When Carl Nater proposed attending a trade fair in Baghdad, Jean-Jacques agreed to give it a go, suggesting that Nater travel out there with the younger salesman Paul Vanson. One of the new recruits Jean-Jacques had hired after the war, Vanson had prior experience as a mounter and designer, and had experience of the Middle East (having spent the war as an officer at the British security mission in Beirut). In the autumn of 1954, the two Cartier salesmen took a flight to Baghdad. Between them they had two leather attaché cases containing a quarter of a million pounds' worth of jewels (more than $8.7 million today). Highlights included a 107-carat diamond mounted as a ring, and an emerald and diamond necklace that could separate into three bracelets and two brooches, but there were also many smaller items (from powder compacts to gold cigarette cases) designed to attract a wider client base.

When the plane refueled at Geneva and all passengers were asked to disembark, Nater and Vanson panicked. Taking their bags with them would attract attention to themselves, but it was a huge risk to leave them in the overhead compartments. Deciding quickly that it was, on balance, safer to leave them on board, they spent a very nervous hour in the airport and breathed a huge sigh of relief to find them still there when they returned.

Twenty-four hours later, those cases of jewels at stand number 187 of the British Trade Fair were attracting attention from all the right people in Baghdad. Four decades previously, it had been the Russian elite that Louis Cartier had striven to impress at Grand Duchess Vladimir's Christmas bazaar. Now it was the Middle Eastern rulers who were among the world's most important jewelry buyers, and this trade fair was the perfect place to reach them. After taking a particular liking to a diamond and ruby necklace, the nineteen-year-old King Faisal II of Iraq invited the Cartier salesmen to his palace that evening. It was a pleasant meeting but an uneventful one. The King didn't buy the necklace, and Vanson "took it back to my hotel in my coat pocket!"

A day later, after all the jewels had been packed up, cleared through customs, and sealed in their attaché cases, the King decided he did want the necklace after all. Carl Nater, not accustomed to the ways of the Middle East, told the younger salesman it was too late, and Vanson "had to convince him that here in Iraq, the King was the King and no customs official would stand in his way. Right enough, in thirty minutes, our necklace was out of customs with many 'salaams' from the Customs captain." It was a great boost to that year's sales, but the largest commission was yet to come. Sometime after the fair, the King traveled to London. Meeting his trusty salesman in 175 New Bond Street, he asked for a 10-carat rectangular diamond. He was engaged to marry an English lady, he explained, and the bridal registry would be at Cartier. Vanson was thrilled. But it was not to be. Just weeks later, in the summer of 1958, King Faisal II and his family were brutally murdered in a coup d'état. As with the Romanovs, the flip side to great wealth and power was inequality and, with it, social instability.

WITH THE SMOOTH PRECISION OF THE PARTS OF A GUN

While Claude inherited a fortune from his late father, Jean-Jacques had to work to make a living. Nelly was a very wealthy woman, but she believed, as had Jacques, that their children should not be spoiled with excessive wealth. Jean-Jacques didn't take his family on expensive vacations, and he had to save up when he wanted to buy an item of jewelry for his wife. His one extravagance was horses. He bought a hunter which he kept at the local stables, and each Saturday, in season, he would go on the local fox hunt.

But he wouldn't take a day off work. Each morning of the week there would be a different meeting to chair. One day it would be with the purchasing department, then the finance team, and another day sales. His favorite was the design meeting. He loved meeting with the senior designers, sharing sketches, discussing ideas, approving final designs, and proposing new pieces. If Easter was coming up, Jean-Jacques might suggest that they focus on bird brooches to form a seasonal window display. After looking at the gemstones they had in stock, he might ask that a citrine form the basis of an owl, an opal serve as the stomach of a kingfisher, or carved white chalcedony become a sparrow. He planned every display meticulously and liked to change them regularly.

In these small ways, through this obvious passion for his work, Jean-Jacques slowly gained the admiration of those employees who had once regarded him skeptically. And while he himself had been unsure in the beginning, over time he grew into his role as a leader.

He might never measure up to his father in his own mind, but he became very respected in his own way.

In Conversation with Jean-Jacques Cartier

Sometimes we planned exhibitions in-store to show a new collection. Well, I was insistent, of course, that everything had to be to the highest standard, but sometimes that meant we didn't always finish everything in time. I was furious with myself whenever that happened. I was the one responsible for the workshop, it was up to me to ensure everything was ready for the opening.

Since the end of the war, the London workshop had been slowly rebuilt to include some of the country's best mounters and setters. Each year, a handful of apprentices were hired to train under the master craftsmen. Just as in the time of Jacques, only one or occasionally two of the five or six would make it through the first year, and after that, there would generally be a further five years of intense training. "These craftsmen are men with nimble fingers, a keen eye and an infinite store of patience," a Cartier employee would later recall. "Add to these attributes a steady nerve, and you will describe the setter into whose charge may be entrusted a stone of value beyond price. An accident here, even a tiny chip, and the effect on this individual might be compared to the anguish of a surgeon whose slip or oversight makes him feel responsible for the loss of a life." As exacting as Jacques had been, Jean-Jacques put a strict process in place to ensure that only items of the highest quality made it into the showroom.

Once a jewel had been completed by the Cartier London workshop, the next step was to try it on. A female member of the staff would wear the necklace or brooch or earrings, while the backroom boys, as they were known, would be called in to observe. They were trained in what to look for. First, the big gemstones had to stand out. If they were too far from the center of the ornament, too concealed in the grouping of smaller stones, or not near enough to the highest point of relief, they would seem to disappear. Any prospective purchaser would expect to see where the jewels' value lay, and Jean-Jacques was adamant that the gemstones be shown to their best advantage. Even at the wax model stage, he would insist that they had to be attached at exactly the right angle.

The backroom boys would also be tasked with observing how the jewel changed when the wearer moved. As they walked around the model, or asked her to move, they would check that the necklace or brooch maintained a strong form and attractive appearance from all angles. Only then would it be passed to Jean-Jacques for his final approval. Everything, from the front of the jewel to the clasps at the back, merited the highest attention to detail. All of the tiny parts to which the client would barely give a second thought had to be simultaneously delicate and strong. They must move, as one designer recalled, "with the smooth precision of the parts of a gun."

By the time the jewel made it into the showroom, it would have passed under so many expert eyes that it was deemed worthy of the Cartier name. It was then up to Jean-Jacques to pass his own enthusiasm for the creation on to his salesforce. "If I can first 'sell' it to the

Left: Lilian, Princess of Réthy, in her Cartier jewels, including the diamond necklace designed by her brother-in-law. Right: Jean-Jacques with his wife, Lydia (Lilian's sister).

salesman," he told his senior designer, Rupert Emmerson, "I am half-way to selling it to the client!"

A PINK DIAMOND

Coronations had been big business for Cartier ever since Edward VII became king in 1902. Most recently, with the crowning of King George VI in 1937, Cartier's French and American branches had looked on in envy as Cartier London was inundated with orders for large tiaras and necklaces. But 1953, the year of the coronation of Elizabeth II, was not to be so prolific. Taxes on jewelry hovered between 50 percent and 75 percent for most of the 1950s, making large purchases prohibitive for most British residents. This time, coronation guests, for the most part, made do with wearing their existing jewels or, as in the case of Princess Margaret, borrowing from others (she wore her sister's, the Queen's, 1936 Halo tiara).

In fact, one of the firm's most important royal commissions completed in the coronation year was not intended to be worn at the coronation. In 1947, the then Princess Elizabeth had received a staggering 54.5-carat pink diamond as a wedding present from John Williamson, a Canadian geologist and fervent monarchist. The diamond, discovered underneath a baobab tree within Williamson's Tanzanian mining concession, was later cut into a brilliant-cut diamond of 23.60 carats. And five years after the Princess's wedding, just as she was preparing to become Queen, Cartier was tasked with incorporating it into a special brooch.

Frederick Mew, the head designer, was selected for the task. Good friends with Toussaint's favorite designer, Lemarchand, Mew shared the French designer's talent for naturalistic representations of flowers and animals. Jean-Jacques and he got along well, both quiet, modest men with a passion for art, and the pair discussed the royal brooch together. As with all commissions, multiple pencil sketch options were narrowed down to three or four final designs that would be painted in gouache, to scale, and presented to the client in order that she might select her favorite. On this occasion, the final approved design incorporated the large Williamson diamond as the

Her Majesty Queen Elizabeth II (then Princess Elizabeth) in 1951, wearing the Cartier necklace that was a wedding gift from the Nizam of Hyderabad (left); and wearing the Williamson brooch in a portrait with her children, Prince Charles and Princess Anne, in 1954 (right).

centerpiece of a flower with a stem of baguette-cut diamonds, petals of brilliant-cut diamonds, and leaves of marquise-cut diamonds. The Williamson brooch, as it became known, would appear many times on the Queen over the following decades, from the wedding of Prince Charles to Princess Diana in 1981 to a visit by the President and First Lady of the United States, Barack and Michelle Obama, in 2009.

In the same year as the coronation, with large commissions like the Williamson brooch harder and harder to come by, Jean-Jacques decided to open a boutique. Formal society was in decline and Cartier needed to attract a different type of client going forward. Debutante balls, for instance, once a highly esteemed invitation for daughters of the elite to be presented to the King or Queen at Buckingham Palace (and a source of great jewelry commissions for Cartier), had dwindled in prestige. By 1958, they had been abolished altogether (with Princess Margaret said to have remarked: "We had to put a stop to it—every tart in London was getting in").

In Jean-Jacques' mind, the boutique would appeal to a younger clientele who were looking for more affordable items. Similar to Louis' Department S and Pierre's lower-priced offerings in the Depression, Jean-Jacques' idea was that those who may have been daunted by the idea of walking into a showroom with million-dollar necklaces on display could feel reassured that nothing in the boutique cost more than £300 (about $10,000 today). To appeal to a younger, more modern demographic, the salesroom right at the back of the 175 New Bond Street store (previously used for stationery and handbags) was remodeled in light oak and glass. It could be accessed by its own entrance on Albemarle Street, and was headed up by Vanson and staffed by two saleswomen. Illustrated catalogs were printed detailing the items for sale, from £50 gold engine-turned cufflinks set with sapphires, to a £154 gold and ruby powder case "to take Max Factor Crème Puff pack." There were plenty of animal brooches for under £100 (from an agate and ruby butterfly to an agate owl with emerald eyes and a crystal and turquoise tortoise) and rings set with small gems. Gold charms were generally under £15 and gold ear clips were just £9. And yet, though the boutique selection was much more affordable than the jewels in the main showroom, Jean-Jacques would not risk tarnishing the reputation his father had worked so hard to achieve by selling anything that wasn't beautifully crafted.

Though the new Cartier boutique had its own Albemarle Street entrance, it was connected internally to the main high-end showroom, and one could walk through from 175 New Bond Street all the way out to Albemarle Street with almost nonexistent security. On one occasion, a young gentleman client had asked to see a top-quality diamond ring, studied it under the watchful eye of Vanson, then suddenly rushed out of the store, holding the valuable jewel in his hand. As he left, he shouted back that he was just off to show it to his friend, and Vanson, horrified, ran after him, trying to keep up. Once outside, he spied his client hurry across the road. "Held up a few seconds by traffic," Vanson would later recall, "I sprinted to the corner of the street opposite and at that moment my man rushed by me at top speed and sprinted back into the showroom. I did the same, and as I reached the showcase in the middle of the room, I saw him standing in front of my table looking for me. I slowed down to a casual pace as if I had never left the showroom and as he saw me, with delight, I simply said, 'Did your friend like the ring?' To which he replied, 'Yes, we will have it!' An unusual but honest Cartier customer—happily for my thumping heart."

"YOU'LL BE BACK, MONSIEUR CARTIER"

Jean-Jacques didn't usually meet with clients. "My father was more suited to the social side of the business than I was," he recalled. There were, however, a few exceptions, from the British royal family to important visiting clients, who appreciated meeting with "Monsieur Cartier" himself. There was also his sister-in-law, Lilian Baels, who, after marrying King Léopold III of the Belgians, had become Princess of Réthy.

In Conversation with Jean-Jacques Cartier

I wasn't a born salesman. I'd much rather have been with the designers or in the stone department than in the showroom. If I sold something, it was because my sincere appreciation for the quality of the object came through; it was the object that sold itself.

Lilian, known for her exquisite taste, loved jewelry. On one occasion, Léopold quietly mentioned to Jean-Jacques that he wanted to buy his wife a special diamond necklace and asked if his brother-in-law could visit them with a selection of diamonds and a proposal. Pleased with the commission in a difficult environment, Jean-Jacques didn't waste any time. Usually he would have sent one of Cartier's gem experts to source the stones, but this was family and he wanted to be involved at every step of the process. Traveling to Antwerp, the diamond capital, he met with leading dealers and bought around twenty large diamonds on consignment. Back in 175 New Bond Street, he worked on several designs for the necklace himself. He then wrote a detailed report that listed the characteristics of each diamond, noting every single tiny flaw he found. As usual, he was insistent that Cartier should be 100 percent transparent; nothing should be hidden. It was only when he had completed the list to his painstaking requirements that he set off for Belgium, loose gemstones and designs in his bag, hoping to have his proposal approved by Léopold and Lilian.

When he arrived in Belgium and declared the diamonds in customs (each one valued and documented by the four *c*'s: clarity, carats, cut, and color), the customs officer laughed at him. "You really think you'll sell those here in Belgium? You won't. You'll be back, Monsieur Cartier, mark my words." Smiling politely, Monsieur Cartier returned the diamonds to the bag and took a car to the Royal Palace of Laeken.

Warmly greeted by his brother and sister-in-law, Jean-Jacques updated them on family news before the conversation moved on to the necklace and Jean-Jacques took out the diamonds he had brought. They were impressed, and Lilian loved his designs, but as was to be expected with a purchase this significant, they asked for a second opinion. Jean-Jacques was directed into a room where the Belgian court gemstone expert and banker were seated at a table waiting for him. After looking through the diamonds, the expert announced that they were tinted (not as pure white as had been claimed). Jean-Jacques knew that while a couple of stones had a very slight tint, which he had noted on his report, for the most part they were of truly exceptional quality. But he wanted neither to get into an argument nor to influence the analysis; it was important to him that the Belgian expert make his report independently so there would be no arguments further down the line. Instead, he suggested that perhaps it would be worth asking for a room with a north-facing window (in the Northern Hemisphere, northern light is optimal for viewing gemstones, as it produces the least glare). They did. And sure enough, the stone expert admitted his mistake. There was no tint after all.

With the expert's positive report, Léopold and Lilian agreed to go ahead with the necklace (see photo, page 467). Jean-Jacques set off back to England, the loose diamonds safely back in his bag to be mounted into a necklace in English Art Works. Leaving Belgium, he was stopped by customs again. The same customs officer was on duty. On seeing Jean-Jacques' collection of diamonds, he chuckled. "You see," he said, "I told you you'd never sell those here!" Jean-Jacques smiled to himself, knowing he had just secured one of his most important commissions ever, at a time when the London business badly needed it.

CONVERSATIONS WITH PLEASURE SEEKERS

By the early 1950s, Claude, still just in his twenties, was questioning his earlier decision to buy the New York Maison. Though he liked the prestige of owning Cartier New York, the burden of running a large company especially in the face of difficult business conditions was considerable. In contrast, Paris, previously so weighed down by rationing and gloom, was now quite the place to be again. After his mother, Jacqui, passed away in 1952, Claude spent more and more time abroad. As one of the wealthiest and best-looking bachelors in New York, he enjoyed the international social circuit. In March 1954, it seemed he might settle down when news of his engagement to the Dior model with the "smallest waist in Paris," Miss Sylvie Hirsh, was announced in *The New York Times*. But by the following year, Claude was reported to be dating another model, and the engagement had been called off.

Fortunately, the team Pierre had built carefully over the years was strong enough to support the company even with a less experienced, less invested leader. And as in London, though new employees periodically joined the team, in general it was the older ones who continued to set the tone, passing down their experience and values to the new generation.

Sixteen-year-old Alfred Durante from Brooklyn had been at art school when he was called for an interview in 1953 with the head of the design department, Maurice Daudier. Cartier often recruited from art schools in London, Paris, and New York. Though schools such as the Chiswick School of Art in London or L'École Boulle in Paris or the Art and Design School in New York did not focus on jewelry design, they came to know the skills that Cartier was looking for in a young designer and could propose talented candidates. In the case of Durante, the young art student had never even considered jewelry design as a profession; he had always thought he would become an illustrator. But in the interview, when he was asked to sketch a flower

brooch, the fifty-one-year-old Daudier saw his potential and proposed that the boss, Claude, also interview him. Claude, clearly impressed, offered him a job. And Alfred Durante, with little idea what
it would involve or how it would shape the rest of his life, accepted.

After joining the firm, Durante was mentored by Daudier, who
took the time to train him not just in the art of jewelry design but also
in how to deal with clients. When Daudier was called to a meeting
with the Duchess of Windsor, he would bring Durante along with
him, not because he needed the young designer there, but because he
felt it would be good experience for him. Durante, who would remain with Cartier for many years, would remember those early years
as a special time, learning from the old-timers. Though he joined after
Pierre had left, the Cartier ethos that Pierre had instilled, that focus
on quality and respect for one's work, still dominated everyday life at
the firm.

The New York designers took their roles very seriously. While
Daudier focused on private commissions for important clients, Gerry
Muller was the designer one might go to with an old piece for remounting. His gift was the ability to listen intently to his clients so as
to redesign the jewel according to their taste. Durante, meanwhile,
started out designing family crests for the stationery department. It
was a far cry from the magnificent jewelry he would later create for
stars such as Elizabeth Taylor, but it was, he insisted, the perfect training, because he would have to understand the client and take the time
to research their family history.

Once the design had been approved, it was passed to the workshops. Cartier New York had two workshops in-house, set up years
earlier by Pierre. Marel Works made the gold objects, such as clasps
for handbags and tags with zodiac charms, while Vors & Pujol (which
had replaced American Art Works), just next door, made the top jewelry for sale in-store and clients' commissions. Experts such as the
quiet master craftsman Vors and the setter Larrieu ensured that Cartier New York still produced pieces that stood out from the American
competition. Vors would work through his lunch breaks making the
fashionable jewels that would later appear in Cartier's showroom,
such as the perfectly proportioned domed rings, large enough to
make a statement but not so protruding that they caught on one's
clothes. Larrieu was a master craftsman, trained in the French way.

He was incredibly skilled at constructing each tiny setting so that it was strong enough to hold the gemstone in place but delicate enough to allow the natural light to shine through. For a single diamond necklace, he would sit for hours with the diamonds laid out according to size on a piece of black felt in front of him while he made setting after setting—each one carefully designed and structured to fit the individual diamond for which it was made. His settings had a lightness that others struggled to replicate.

It was in-house craftsmen like these who ensured Cartier's reputation in a changing time. But the boom of the mid-1950s saw more jewelers coming to the market. As competition picked up, Claude and his senior management decided the branch must move with the times and start offering more cost-effective products. It was a similar thought to the one Jean-Jacques had in London, but the two cousins went about pursuing a wider client base in different ways. In New York, Henri Lebaigue, the debonair Head of Production, was instructed to look through jewelry brought in from external workshops and to buy pieces that he believed met the taste of the clientele. It was a way of adapting to the changing times, but as the New York Maison started to rely more heavily on external suppliers, there was an increased risk of quality discrepancy between the branches.

Claude's decision to appeal to the increasingly affluent middle class by offering more affordable items was, from a business perspective, understandable. America was a very competitive market and he had to adapt to changing times. Even Pierre admitted that his nephew's more modern approach might be what was required in a very different market from the one he had known: *"Autres temps, autres moeurs!"* (different times, different customs). Cartier already had worldwide allure, and Claude didn't face the same pressing need to build a reputation that previous generations had. The Cartier brothers, for instance, believed cultured pearls to be far inferior to natural pearls and had refused to sell them. Claude, however, instructed John Gorey in the purchasing department to start stocking them.

Some of Claude's ideas may well have been right for the times. In the case of pearls, even though to the older generation the idea of anything but natural pearls had been anathema, the world had moved on and the reality was that cultured pearls were extremely popular. The issue, for Pierre at least, was that his nephew's decisions were carried out without much consultation with the other branches, and without what he considered due diligence. "He seems to have decided everything with flair and authority," a Cartier director wrote of Claude's latest plan regarding a South American branch. "He doesn't read any newspapers or have any conversations with anyone except pleasure seekers."

The three brothers had inherited a deep-rooted sense of financial prudence from their father, and while they would open seasonal showrooms elsewhere (Palm Beach, St. Moritz, Cannes), this was never done without extensive discussions and preparation. Alfred, for instance, had vetoed the idea of both a Russian and an Indian branch, deeming them too risky. But in 1953, when Claude decided to open a branch of Cartier in Caracas, it was without consultation with the wider family. He'd visited Venezuela four years earlier with his treasurer René Pouech and been impressed. The country's per capita income was the highest in Latin America, the middle class was growing, and as Venezuelans migrated from the country to the city, a growing number of skyscrapers and modern apartment buildings dominated

Claude helps a Dior model with Cartier jewels for the
launch of the Cartier Caracas branch in 1953.

the landscape. It was a vibrant city with an exotic reputation, and he wanted to be a part of it.

The new Cartier Caracas store shared a building in the newly built Avenue Francisco de Miranda with Christian Dior. The sign above the entrance of the elegant stone building read both CHRIS-TIAN DIOR (above) and CARTIER (just below). On entering, clients would be directed to the right for Cartier's jewels and left for fashion. Rafael Cabrera, a Puerto Rican who had been hired at Cartier New York in 1948, was sent out to manage the showroom and would fly back and forth from New York with jewels to stock it. It would, however, prove a much more challenging and volatile period to be doing business in South America than Claude had imagined. The Cuban Revolution erupted in 1953, and several years later one of the firm's Caracas managers was killed in a plane crash. In part this was just bad luck, but Pierre's fears of his nephew's sometimes impulsive actions were being realized. In the minds of the clientele, Cartier had to be one firm. Claude didn't seem to grasp this, or that the decisions he made in America could have repercussions elsewhere.

SWISS EXASPERATION

In 1955, Pierre and Elma would welcome President Eisenhower to their Swiss home during the Cold War–era summit. The visit would make it into the papers (along with the news that the president had leased Pierre's 52-foot yacht) but the reality was that the president was only one of many well-known guests to Villa Elma through the 1950s. The Cartier couple's dinner books, listing seating plans and menus, reveal the myriad influential figures they continued to entertain in retirement. And family, of course, was always welcome too, especially their daughter and grandchildren but also nieces and nephews and their children. And Nelly, who had moved to a nearby house on the shores of La Léman, was a regular luncheon guest.

But while others may have visited Villa Elma for a relaxing retreat, Pierre couldn't switch off entirely. "Pierre is exasperated by the state of affairs in Paris," Jean-Jacques wrote to his mother. Feeling that Cartier Paris needed fresh management thinking to guide it through the very different postwar years, Pierre again approached the one man he thought could help. Repeatedly he had asked Devaux to leave his senior management position in Shell and come back to the firm, and time and again, Devaux had refused. But just before Christmas 1954, Pierre tried once more, this time with a better offer: He promised Devaux "extended powers" to take on the complete management of Cartier S.A.

Devaux promised to think about it, but ultimately, "in spite of all the benefits" on offer, he declined. In his mind, Cartier under the three cousins was a very different organization from the one under the close bond of the brothers. He felt he lacked the skills to pull it back together. When Pierre asked for advice on what he would propose, Devaux explained that the whole firm needed to "rethink its management structure, working methods, staff management, and commercial policy" but that the main problem was a "lack of authority and organization coming from Claude," and, he added, "perhaps from Pierre Claudel."

Later, Devaux went one step further with his advice. He proposed that Pierre realize his interest in the company by forming a syndicate of bankers to list the company on the Paris stock exchange. It was, he explained, "a propitious time now but it might not be in a few months," and it would avoid Pierre's having to invest additional capital while allowing him to retain an interest. The group of bankers could later possibly buy shares in the London and New York branches, "which would rebuild a united management which has been destroyed by the stupid blindness of Claude." Pierre would not act on Devaux's suggestion of listing the company on the stock exchange, primarily because he still hoped he could find a way to keep it in the family, but he did approach Claude with a proposal. As Claude later told Jean-Jacques, Pierre had asked him if he "might be a seller of Inc., if the conditions were worthwhile." Claude said no, as he "could not imagine anyone paying big money without obtaining the overall majority and control of the business." He wanted to stay in charge of Cartier New York, even if he didn't really enjoy working there.

While considering the idea of listing the firm on the stock exchange, Pierre was contacted by a "Mr. W.," interested in buying "either just Cartier S.A. or all three branches." Though neither of these possible outcomes would materialize, the ongoing uncertainty over the company's future was not good for morale. Management endeavored to keep it quiet from the staff, but there were a few employees who had heard rumors and were considering looking for employment elsewhere. "Calmette is obviously worried about his own future," Pierre was told about one of his senior administrators, "especially if the transaction you have in mind comes to pass."

CHANGING OF THE GUARD

Business in Paris rumbled on as normally as possible, albeit with a thinning out of the old guard. In 1954, Charles Jacqueau retired from the firm, aged seventy. The same year, in July, Jeanne Toussaint married her longtime partner, Baron Pierre Hély d'Oissel. The sixty-eight-year-old baron was a decorated hero of both world wars and the CEO of Saint-Gobain, a multinational construction company owned by his family. Toussaint, the same age as her new husband and by now a very wealthy baroness, wrote to Pierre proposing that she resign in 1955 from Cartier S.A. as she was too tired to continue and no longer felt useful to advise on production. She added, however, that if she could again render any service to Cartier S.A., which she had served for more than thirty years, she would do so with the greatest pleasure.

For Pierre, Toussaint was one of the last personal connections to his late brother. Wanting desperately to cling to some semblance of the glory days, he wrote warmly back to her: "I have the same admiration for your talent as a creator that I had for Louis'. What more can I say? Your departure would therefore be for me like a second separation from my brother." In the end, Toussaint would step down as a director of Cartier S.A., but Pierre's entreaties persuaded her to stay on as artistic director.

Within the sales team, too, there was change. Paul Muffat, who had joined fifty years earlier, retired in 1953 at the age of seventy. Prior to leaving, he trained the young André Denet, who would go on to become one of the firm's leading salesmen. Like his predecessor, Denet was known for being very demanding and clients came to trust him as much as they had Muffat. He was, as was the Cartier way, extremely respectful, but he was also easy to get along with, and it wasn't unusual for him to sell a parure of jewels one day and then be invited to a dinner where that same necklace, bracelet, and earrings would be glistening in a smart Bois de Boulogne dining room the next. In a sign of how far society had come from the very early days of Cartier, Denet and his beautiful wife were even invited to spend holidays with clients as significant as the King of Morocco.

Two of Denet's most important clients were known to be friends and rivals. Barbara Hutton and the Duchess of Windsor often requested their favorite salesman to visit them in their homes, but they would on occasion also come to 13 Rue de la Paix. Just before Christmas one year, Barbara Hutton wandered into Cartier with the intention of buying some gifts. Denet leaped to attention and assisted her as usual, but after some time, the Duchess of Windsor arrived for a prearranged appointment. Denet made his sincerest apologies and explained to Madame Hutton that he had already committed to meet another client at that time. When she saw who the "other client" was, she didn't take it well. So upset was she at being, as she saw it, jilted for the Duchess of Windsor that she stormed out of Cartier and across the road to Van Cleef & Arpels to do her Christmas shopping there.

It would take some time, but eventually Denet won back Madame Hutton's favor. He would visit her in her large, beautiful home filled with museum-worthy artifacts from jade to porcelain to the same screens that had decorated Versailles (along with the Rothschilds, she had helped fund the renovation of the palace). And when she was away, he would visit her old governess, Tiki, who lived with her and of whom Barbara Hutton was deeply fond. He hoped, Barbara's assistant would later recall, that if he told Barbara on her return that "he had spent a great deal of time seeing that Tiki was happy," she would forgive him. His dedication was repaid. Not only did Barbara come back to Cartier, but after her governess passed away, Barbara offered Denet's wife a spectacular pearl necklace that she had once given to Tiki. Madame Denet wore the pearls constantly, with one notable exception: When the Denets were invited to attend a dinner with the Duke and Duchess of Windsor, André suggested his wife remove them for the evening. The problem, he explained, was that they were superior to the Duchess's own pearls, and she would not be happy about that!

Denet was a man of integrity, a quality that endeared clients to him but could have repercussions for those who didn't play by the rules. On one occasion, he refused to receive an important aristocratic client because he discovered that she had been copying the jewels he had lent her in good faith. Cartier had long had a policy of lending pieces to clients for big events, deeming it a perfect way to market their high-end jewels. But on this occasion the client who had been borrowing the jewels had been taking them to a rival (presumably less expensive) jeweler to have them replicated. Outraged, Denet made it very clear that this type of behavior—however esteemed the client—would not be tolerated at 13 Rue de la Paix.

HOLLYWOOD GLAMOUR

When Marilyn Monroe sang "Diamonds Are a Girl's Best Friend" in the 1953 movie *Gentlemen Prefer Blondes,* she named Cartier as one of her New York jewelers of choice. When Daisy Fellowes masqueraded at the 1951 Venice costume ball, she gave her famous Collier Hindou necklace (commissioned in 1936) its most prominent public outing. And when the Duchess of Windsor attended the 1953 Versailles Gala in a Dior strapless dress and pale purple cape, she accessorized with her 1947 statement amethyst and turquoise Cartier necklace and matching earrings. The reputation of Cartier, which had taken three generations to build, was so far proving strong enough to withstand the challenges of this new era.

Elizabeth Taylor was one of the new generation of Hollywood stars who would become increasingly important to Cartier in the years ahead. In 1957 she recalled being given a Cartier ruby parure by her ~~second~~ third husband, Mike Todd, while they were vacationing in the South of France when she was just twenty-five years old:

I was in the pool . . . and Mike came outside to keep me company. I got out of the pool and put my arms around him and he said, "Wait a minute, don't joggle your tiara." Because I was wearing my tiara in the pool! He was holding a red leather box and inside was a ruby necklace, which glittered in the warm light. It was like the sun, lit up and made of red fire. First Mike put it around my neck and smiled. Then he bent down and put matching earrings on me.

Next came the bracelet. Since there was no mirror around, I had to look in the water. The jewelry was so glorious, rippling red on blue like a painting. I just shrieked with joy, put my arms around Mike's neck, and pulled him into the pool after me.

In a sign of the huge shifts in society from the early days of Cartier, in 1956, the world celebrated as a blue-blooded European prince announced his intention to marry an American actress. Grace Kelly had met Prince Rainier the previous year at the Cannes Film Festival, and their engagement was announced from her parents' Philadelphia home. She had not one but two engagement rings, both Cartier. The prince proposed with a ruby and diamond eternity band (the colors of Monaco), but shortly after, his fiancée was seen with a larger ring: a 10.47-carat rectangular emerald-cut diamond, flanked by two baguette-cut diamonds. The actress famously refused to take this one off, even onscreen. When she wore it in her final film, *High Society,* in which she played an engaged socialite just months before her real marriage, she made it one of the most famous rings in the world.

By the time Grace Kelly arrived in Monaco on the SS *Constitution* in the spring of 1956 to start her new life as a princess, the world was in a frenzy of excitement. Eighteen hundred photographers and reporters were waiting to capture the moment as the actress, complete with eighty bags and her dog, came to join her waiting prince. His wedding present to her was a Cartier three-strand necklace created from approximately 64 carats of emerald-cut and round-cut diamonds (more recently worn by her thirty-two-year-old granddaughter on the occasion of her marriage in 2019).

The civil wedding between Prince Rainier and his bride took place in Monaco's Royal Palace throne room on April 18, 1956, and lasted just fifteen minutes (although the subsequent reading of her new titles went on for closer to half an hour). It was the religious ceremony the following day, at Saint Nicholas Cathedral, that was the real show. Cary Grant, Ava Gardner, Aristotle Onassis, and even Claude Cartier were among the seven hundred guests who watched the fairy-tale bride walk down the aisle in an iconic dress by the costume designer Helen Rose. Having designed Elizabeth Taylor's first wedding dress six years earlier, Rose had been in no doubt as to how to create a robe worthy of an A-lister, and Kelly's high-necked, long-sleeved gown

Grace Kelly wearing her Cartier 10.47-carat diamond engagement ring in
her last film, *High Society;* Kelly with Prince Rainier of Monaco
in front of Cartier Paris, Rue de la Paix.

with a fitted bodice had been made by thirty seamstresses from 275
meters of antique Belgian lace, 23 meters of silk taffeta, and 90 meters of tulle. On her head, the bride wore a simple Juliet cap from
which a pearl-and-lace-adorned veil flowed, and in the place of a
traditional bouquet she carried a prayer book covered with lily of the
valley and pearls. There was also, unbeknownst to the hundreds
watching in the church and the estimated 30 million television view-
ers who tuned in from all over the world (televisions had only recently taken off), a single gold penny in her shoe for good luck.

Later that year, talk of a different wedding was giving the Cartiers
hope for the future. Claude had announced his engagement to Rita
Kane Salmona, an Italian American heiress. The wedding was set for
December 1956 in the basilica of Notre-Dame-des-Victoires in Paris.
With no parents, Claude turned to the only family he had and asked
Pierre, Elma, and Nelly to be there to support him, "as your presence
will make me feel my father is not so far away." They agreed with
pleasure. Despite the arguments, family came first, and Pierre particularly was happy that his nephew was finally settling down.

"It was an international high society event," the papers reported
on the wedding day. Guests including princesses, countesses, and earls
came to celebrate the union of "the son of the great Louis Cartier" to
"a delightful, well-cultured daughter of American high society." Un-

like fifty-eight years earlier, when Louis had married Andrée-Caroline Worth in a large Parisian society wedding, there was no need for an arranged marriage for the good of the family firm. Previous generations, aspiring to a better life, had done their part so that this generation, imbued with the "celebrity of the [Cartier] name," could reap the rewards.

Huge bunches of white and pink lilacs and the gentle flickering light of candles decorated the church. As the congregation filed in, Claude gave his arm to his elderly aunt and accompanied her to her pew at the front alongside the rest of his family and those who had been close to his father, including Jeanne Toussaint. Claude had asked Jean-Jacques to be his best man. With the organ starting to play Bach's *Fuga in Re Minore,* the cousins stood beside each other up by the altar. They shared a close bond that day. Both felt the absence of their fathers.

After the ceremony, Claude and his beautiful bride, wearing a Dior dress and carrying pure white roses, walked down the aisle with large smiles on their faces. The "sumptuous reception" took place at Paris's prestigious Hôtel de Crillon in Place de la Concorde, "the quintessence of elegance." It was, the papers reported, quite an affair: "It is rare to observe today in a reception so much splendor, pomp, and rigorous refinement!"

For all the extravagance, the wedding was also a day of great emotion. As Jean-Jacques stood up to give a toast, he asked the guests to raise a glass to those beloved members of the family who had passed away. Though he wasn't particularly close to his cousin, as much because of the geographical distance between them as anything else, Jean-Jacques sincerely wished the best for him that day. In the place of past disagreements, there was a sense of coming back together again, and a recognition of the strength of enduring family bonds. Before flying to New York with his bride, Claude bade his family goodbye. He would, he assured them, be back in Paris for Christmas and it seemed, for that moment at least, that the battles and mistrust of recent times could be put aside and a new cooperative spirit begun.

THE END OF AN ERA

(1957–1974)

THE BEST IS GOOD ENOUGH

Every morning, Jean-Jacques would take the 8:00 A.M. train from Dorking to London, dressed in his custom-tailored Savile Row Huntsman suit and bowler hat. Spotting the same commuters in the first-class carriage, there would be a suitably British "Morning, Cartier," "Morning, Smith" before they all settled down to read their papers in studied silence. From Victoria station, it was one stop on the underground to Green Park, then a short walk past the Ritz, over Piccadilly, past the back of the Royal Academy and Brown's Hotel to the same building that his father, Jacques, had transformed into the Cartier London showroom half a century earlier.

Those within 175 New Bond Street talked of it feeling like an extended family and in many ways it was. Jean-Jacques' brother-in-law, Carl Nater, once a salesman, was now in charge of the administrative side of the business, while Harjes, Jean-Jacques' younger brother, had joined the salesforce. Harjes was a much-loved character, a bundle of energy and laughter. He was popular both at work and out of it, known for tempting fellow salesmen to join him for cassoulet and good red French wine in London's best restaurants. But the Cartiers weren't the only ones who shared a bond of family within 175 New

Bond Street. There had always been father-and-son teams within the workshops and the showroom, right from the days when the first Cartier London employee, Arthur Fraser, had been joined by his son, Donald.

As the 1950s drew to an end, despite the occasional lavish commission, jewelry fashion in Britain was governed by elegant restraint. Partly this was due to the changing distribution of wealth since the Second World War. The wealth pyramid was lower in height than before and its base had widened (i.e., the rich were less rich than used to be the case but there were more of them). But also, simultaneously, aesthetic ideals were changing. Rather than beauty being linked only to luxury items, it was becoming more associated with the functional. Modern consumer durables (such as cars and household electrical items) became highly desirable, and design, in turn, would reflect a more industrial focus. Consumer preferences would move away from the purely decorative, like jewelry, to more useful items.

Despite the changing times, there was a sense of continuity and trust that management could be relied upon to look after its staff. When Jean-Jacques found out that one of the designers, Rupert Emmerson, was looking for somewhere to live, he offered him the vacant cottage on his estate in Dorking. Emmerson moved in with his family and would end up staying several years. "As to the relationship existing between management and staff throughout the organization," Emmerson would later observe, "I need point only to the length of service of the majority of the employees. I am entering my thirty-fourth year with the firm, working with colleagues—now approaching retirement—who are old enough in length of service still to refer to me as 'young Emmerson'—flattery indeed—were it only true!"

In the workshops, the older craftsmen trained the younger ones, continuing the legacy. The mounters and setters would sit at their cutout benches, the traditional jeweler's skin draped across their knees like an apron to prevent loss or damage from items falling on the floor. As they worked and chatted away, pipe smoke filling the room, these leather skins would become ingrained with minute particles of precious metals. When the skins became too worn to be of further use, they would be sent off to specialist firms equipped for the task of extracting that valuable dust.

Now in his forties, as Cartier London's managing director and its head of production, Jean-Jacques oversaw every aspect of the creative process, from the purchase of gemstones to the designing to the detailed craftsmanship in the workshops. That vertical integration is what gave the Cartier London jewelry of the period, one former employee remembered, the "sense of an organic whole." From the spark of an idea to the final polishing, the pieces had been made under one roof.

On one occasion, inspired by a bowl of nuts on the table at Christmastime, Jean-Jacques decided to create a small walnut-shaped pillbox. Usually the London workshops made everything by hand, but in this case Jean-Jacques suggested they cast a real walnut in gold. Nature had done such a perfect job that he wouldn't presume to better it. The workshop was all ready to go ahead when Jean-Jacques stopped them. They couldn't cast just any walnut, he explained, it had to be the ideal specimen. Sitting at his desk with a large bag of walnuts, he lifted each one out, studied it closely, then set it down. At the end of the bag, he still hadn't found what he was looking for, and he had to send out for another bag of walnuts. And another. To almost everyone else, a walnut was simply a walnut, but not to Jean-Jacques. In the end, it would take him three large bags to find the one impeccable walnut that was worthy of being preserved forever in gold.

At other times it was personal commissions from clients that stretched the workshops to their limits. Princess Lilian de Réthy didn't buy jewels exclusively from Cartier London, but she did keep Jean-Jacques' craftsmen busy. Appreciating her brother-in-law's aesthetic sense, she tended to go to him for the more creative pieces. When, for instance, she wanted a stag-shaped brooch, she invited Jean-Jacques to come hunting with her in Belgium to see for himself the majesty of stags close up in order to then convert that image into diamonds and gold. And when Lilian's stepson, King Baudouin, needed a birthday present for her, he asked to speak to Jean-Jacques personally.

The King of the Belgians knew he wanted to commission a vanity case with a hunting theme but wasn't sure exactly how it should look. Jean-Jacques, seated in the palace, took a piece of paper from his bag and instantly sketched how he saw the box: antlers with the royal crest and two intertwining L's for Lilian and Léopold. Inside there would be different compartments for makeup and cigarettes. He could try, he suggested, to do something original with this one. He had the idea to make the case out of steel, which would give the effect of gun-metal. The king approved the proposal on the spot, and Jean-Jacques set off back to London, excited by the creative challenge ahead.

He soon regretted how forthcoming he had been with a new idea. Unlike gold, silver, or platinum, steel was an incredibly difficult metal to work with when making a delicate object. It would end up taking multiple craftsmen many, many attempts before the desired effect was achieved. In terms of workshop hours, that piece ended up costing Cartier London more than it made them. But for Jean-Jacques, it was worth it. The result was both original and striking, with the blue-gray of the steel evocative of hunting, and the personalized design on the front in gold acknowledging Lilian's position and her love of the sport. She was thrilled with the gift. It was also one of the pieces of which Jean-Jacques was most proud because he'd pushed the boundaries of what was considered feasible.

In Conversation with Jean-Jacques Cartier

I was pleased with Lilian's vanity case that we made in steel. It ended up being an awful lot of work and I think the workshop would have killed me if I'd suggested they make another one! But the end result was quite something.

While his perfectionist streak was known to exasperate his team, for Jean-Jacques there was little point in creating something unless it was the very best it could be. It was a lesson that, over time, he passed down to others, with one of his salesmen, Poulton, known for his catchphrase: "The best is good enough." In 1958, Jean-Jacques even funded an award to acknowledge and reward exceptional jewelry skills. The Jacques Cartier Memorial Award, in memory of his father, was to be given by Goldsmiths (a guild from medieval times for the goldsmith trade in London), but only in a year when a craftsman had created a truly outstanding piece. At a time when the industry was suffering from the negative repercussions of high postwar taxation, it was an important signal of support for (speicalists) in the trade.

"We had some wonderful clients who gave us such fascinating work, really challenged us," a designer recalled of the period under Jean-Jacques. "No two days, or two pieces even, were the same." He recalled some of the clients' quirks: The comedian Peter Sellers had brought in forty photographs of his girlfriend's eye so that Cartier could create a ring with a stone of exactly the same gray-blue color (in the end, the only place they were able to find the perfect match was in an optician's drawer of glass eyes). The English actor Rex Harrison, who married six times, would come in repeatedly for engagement rings: "Here we go again!" he would say jovially as he discussed the latest commission. On another occasion, it was a trip to Downing Street that was particularly memorable.

Cartier had been asked to create a maple leaf brooch as a gift from the British prime minister, Anthony Eden, to the Canadian prime minister. Jean-Jacques had assigned Dennis Gardner the task of coming up with several design possibilities, which had been duly sent over to Downing Street for approval. The designs weren't, however, quite what the Prime Minister's wife had in mind and she had asked for Gardner to meet her at home in order to discuss her proposed changes in person. Dressed in his best suit, freshly pressed shirt, starched collar, and bowler hat, and armed with his briefcase of sketching paper and pencils, the designer took a taxi from New Bond Street with Bellenger. Though semiretired and in his seventies, Bellenger made a point of still making it in to the office to deal with the most prestigious clients.

Once they were all seated in the drawing room of 10 Downing Street, Mrs. Eden explained that she would prefer a less rigid maple leaf design, more "floating in the wind." Gardner, known to be particularly quick at his work, was able to immediately sketch it as she had envisaged and it was approved on the spot. As they said their respectful goodbyes, with Bellenger promising he would have the brooch ready in time for the Canadian visit, the Prime Minister's wife asked if she should call a member of the staff to show them out. Bellenger politely responded that there was no need: "This is not the first time we have been here, Madame." Nodding her approval, she let them find their own way out, whereupon, as Gardner later recalled, "we ended up in the kitchens!" In the taxi on the way back to the office, Gardner asked Bellenger when he had visited 10 Downing Street before, to which the senior salesman confided, "I have no more been there than to the moon!" Appearances, as ever at Cartier, were paramount.

COUSINS ON THE CRESTA

Whereas the three brothers had made a point of meeting up once a year, Jean-Jacques hardly ever saw his cousins. His Swiss brother-in-law Carl Nater and his younger brother, Harjes, would be far more likely to bump into Claude on the mountains in St. Moritz. Louis' son had a passion for the dangerous Cresta ice skeleton run. "Before the advent of the motor car and the aeroplane, Cresta riders were the fastest men on earth," a later writer would note. The idea of leaping onto a 75-pound toboggan and racing down a mountain ice channel at speeds of 80 miles per hour, with one's face five inches from the surface, is not for everybody, but Claude enjoyed it. On one occasion, an onlooker recalled, he went so fast that he flew through the air and ended up in a rock-strewn stream, astonishing everyone by emerging unscathed and upbeat.

Though those left behind at their desks in the office may have viewed tobogganing as a sport for rich playboys, it did require a level of skill: "Test pilots and students of aerodynamics are among those who have come nearest to mastering her sleek unyielding surface." Claude, who had joined the U.S. Air Force during the war, fitted the bill. In testament to his ability, he was selected to join the French world championship bobsled team and would also go on to coach the French Olympic bobsledding team. He became such an integral part of the St. Moritz Cresta scene that he started his own Claude Cartier Challenge Cup in 1955, which continues to this day. Harjes, meanwhile, loved the whole atmosphere on the mountains. He was known for boundless enthusiasm and also for generously driving a large van out to St. Moritz so he could collect the exhausted racers and take them to the top again.

In Conversation with Jean-Jacques Cartier

I didn't have much contact with Claude. He came to see us in Dorking only once, just before he got married, to introduce his new wife. And I didn't visit America apart from that trip out to meet Pierre after the war. Of course, there were dealings between the branches— New York often put in orders for our gold cigarette cases for instance, the London boxes seemed to be popular with American clients. But that would all be managed by the purchasing and orders departments.

Interaction between the three branches at this time mostly took place between employees. Jean-Jacques was saddened to hear that his cousin Marion had separated from her husband and that Claudel had stepped down from leading Cartier Paris. In May 1957, at Pierre's instruction, Paul Calmette, a longtime director of the firm, took over as the new Cartier S.A. president.

As a shareholder, Jean-Jacques had a presence on the Paris board of directors, and in 1957, Marion had asked to be more involved in Cartier Ltd. "I am very grateful to you for making me a director," she wrote to her cousin. "I really appreciate it and I will do all that I can to help you." It was, they both believed, important to maintain a consistency of approach between the London and Paris branches. Toussaint, meanwhile, wouldn't travel to London but she would send occasional updates on the latest creations from Paris, and likewise, each month, Jean-Jacques would send a selection of his team's latest designs to Rue de la Paix. If they appealed to Mlle Toussaint, she might pass them on to the Paris workshop and have them made for her clients.

Sometimes, Jean-Jacques would send his designers to Paris for a few days to interact with their French counterparts. On one occasion, Dennis Gardner recalled being escorted into Mlle Toussaint's office to make her acquaintance, only to be abruptly thrown out when she realized that he didn't speak French! Apart from the occasional board meeting, Jean-Jacques would rarely travel to Cartier Paris himself, feeling he was more useful in the London office. But he would visit his mother in Switzerland on a near-monthly basis. Already in her eighties, Nelly was as full of life as ever, but her health was not what it had been. She would famously greet guests, and there were many, with a smile and half a grapefruit on each knee ("for the arthritis," she would explain).

When staying with his mother, Jean-Jacques might drop in on his aunt and uncle on the other side of the lake. In the summer of 1958, Pierre and Elma celebrated their golden wedding anniversary. It had been fifty-one years since the young Miss Rumsey walked into 13 Rue de la Paix drenched from a summer's rain shower to steal the middle Cartier brother's heart. Now she was seventy-nine years old and frail. It would be her last big celebration. Just over a year later, she passed away. Pierre, who had looked after her tenderly to the end, was left alone. For almost two decades he had lived without his brothers; now he would have to continue without his beloved "pup." Nelly, too, was terribly upset. Elma had been like a sister to her, and they had shared so much being married to the Cartier brothers. Six months later there was more grief: Suzanne Worth, Pierre's last surviving sibling, died in May 1960. Now, of that incredibly close, dynamic generation of Cartiers, only Nelly and Pierre were left.

OUR LIFE'S WORK IS COLLAPSING

In New York, morale was low. When Pierre had founded the American branch, demand for chic gems from Paris had been enormous. Not only had there been no significant competition from other French houses in New York, but large displays of jewelry had been essential for marking one's position in society. Going into the 1960s, it was very different. There was far less wealth, and even those who did have important jewels struggled to find the opportunity to wear them. Coming back to manage the store after his wedding, Claude had faced a difficult economy and it seemed to be getting worse. "Customers are almost invisible," was one report in 1957, with "no appetite for the beautiful stones we are receiving every day." The following year, things had deteriorated even further, with business "quieter than ever"; and in May 1958, "Everything is so expensive, money hard to get. It doesn't make sense, the depression should make prices fall."

By 1960, the slowdown was reaching a nadir: "Money is becoming totally invisible." The stock market, which Jacques had called "the barometer of the jeweler," confusingly appeared to "have no effect on business," as it rose "despite depression and discontent." Even more worryingly, there was an undercurrent of fear that, with high unemployment in America, a difficult economy, and the Cold War threat from Russia (exacerbated by the success of the Cuban Revolution the previous year) it wouldn't take much to bring on "a total catastrophe." Against this backdrop, even Pierre would have felt the pressure. The thirty-five-year-old Claude, with limited business experience and a proud character (preventing him from asking his uncle for advice), was understandably out of his depth.

To Pierre's disappointment, marriage and children hadn't made his nephew any significantly more work-focused. Though Claude had bursts of being engaged with the business, he was often away traveling and pursuing his semi-professional sporting interests. By now, his staff were used to getting on with their roles with sporadic supervision. Jules Glaenzer, still working in his late seventies, maintained an impressive client roster that included Marilyn Monroe and Elizabeth Taylor. But where once he had been full of charm, those who worked with him in the 1960s recalled him becoming more pompous and self-serving. "Glaenzer liked being one of the most senior figures there and would lord it over others," one former colleague recalled. "He wasn't nice to the younger employees." Even Pierre, who had once seen Jules Glaenzer as his right-hand man, was no longer as close to him. He had been annoyed by a self-aggrandizing press article Glaenzer had masterminded some years earlier. Instead of adhering to the House's policy of discretion, he had name-dropped current clients in what Pierre considered to be very poor form.

Within the Fifth Avenue showroom, the type of jewelry on display wasn't dissimilar to that in Cartier London and Paris. For the past few years, some of the most popular items had been the smaller brooches, which tended to be either floral or animal-themed in design or governed by the same adherence to Art Deco principles for which Cartier had been known in the interwar years. While there were higher-priced items in the 1959 end-of-year catalog (from flower ear clips of marquise- and round-cut diamonds to a $5,000 wide gold and diamond bracelet), many pieces fell under the $1,000 or even $500 mark. An "envelope" watch in woven gold (where part of the bracelet could be opened to reveal the dial underneath) was $450; a flower clip with moveable mesh-gold petals and small rubies and diamonds was $475; and a ruby-and-turquoise-striped gold lizard brooch was $190. But many of those who came into the store did not come to buy jewelry at all. There was a selection of sterling silver objects (from $30 milk and juice cups "for the baby" to "enameled sugar tongs") and gifts for men such as tie clips and cigar piercers. There was also the Cartier stationery, and Alfred Durante, who had been set to work in this department, found himself busier than ever.

"Clients such as Barbara Hutton would come in with a picture of their house. I would sketch it and it would be stamped onto their writing paper," he recalled. Other clients would ask for their family crests to be used. It didn't matter if they didn't have one, Cartier would design one for them, and Durante would spend hours researching in the New York Public Library before coming up with a final design. It was not unlike the early days of the twentieth century, when rich American families would send their daughters off to marry a duke in England. Before, they were marking their position within society with tiaras and titles by marriage. Now the trend was for family crests.

For the most part, Claude was happy to leave his employees to work on their own. But he was also a man of contradictions who wanted to make his authority known, even if it was sometimes via strange decisions. "On one occasion he decided—for reasons that no one understood back then or now—that there should be no female employees on the shop floor at all," a female New York employee remembered. "It made things terribly difficult, of course, for employees like the pearl stringer and the women in the handbag department. That rule lasted only one week." Then there were times when he suddenly decided that a large number of previously approved designs should be immediately altered. Nobody understood why. It was this type of inconsistent leadership that his employees would later recall made day-to-day working life under him so challenging. Especially when compared to the clear, structured approach of his predecessor.

Some of the changes didn't go according to plan, as much due to bad luck as poor planning. His impulsive decision to open a branch in Caracas ("where he has influential friends," as one employee reported back) was reversed several years later. The branch was quietly wound down against a backdrop of huge political instability in South America (including revolution in Cuba and a 1958 coup d'état in Venezuela) and a management vacuum. Closer to home, the decision to fill Cartier's windows with valuable jewels overnight (a form of marketing to those strolling past after work) also backfired. An older employee, with the firm for forty years, had suggested that perhaps this wasn't such a prudent idea, especially after the robbery at Tiffany a couple of years earlier. But his counsel had been ignored and early one morning in June 1960, thieves, enticed by the glittering rings on display, "cut two padlocks" and broke "holes in the glass half an inch thick." After snatching the jewels, *The New York Times* dramatically reported, the "burglar dived through the open window of a car and it raced away." The goods, valued at $30,000, were subsequently recovered by the FBI, but the debacle was an unwelcome distraction for Cartier New York.

Fighting against a combination of increasing competition from rivals and the ongoing trend away from large items of jewelry, Cartier had to work harder than ever to maintain its profile in the eyes of the public. One tried-and-tested marketing strategy was lending pieces to high-profile clients. One day, it was Marilyn Monroe coming into the store to select earrings for a film premiere. Another day, a selection of bracelets would be sent to Jackie Kennedy from which she might choose her favorite for an evening gala. Then there were fashion shows at the Plaza for which Cartier supplied the diamonds to go with the ball gowns. But these efforts were starting to be eclipsed through the development of mass-market advertising techniques.

For decades, the Cartiers had predominantly relied on word of mouth, or discreet indirect press coverage, for marketing. Through the 1940s and '50s, they had experimented more with magazine advertising, but it was still on a relatively small scale. While Cartier was taking out full-page advertisements in *Vogue* and even collaborating with Cadillac (in one ad from 1956, two couples stand outside Cartier New York next to a pink and blue Cadillac), firms like De Beers were spending millions of dollars on far-reaching global advertising. Their "A Diamond Is Forever" campaign would later be named the slogan of the century by *Advertising Age* magazine.

Of all the New York jewelers, Tiffany was perhaps most resurgent in this period after the Swedish-born American businessman Walter Hoving had taken control from the family in the mid-1950s. In a July 1961 *Herald Tribune* article in which he discussed the "onslaught of mass production and mass distribution," he declared that "the rules of taste have nothing to do with price. A low-priced article can have just as much taste as a high-priced one if it is well-designed." One Cartier New York employee recalled that Tiffany became known for its more affordable pearl jewels: "Cultured pearls were coming up in the market in a big way. Tiffany was ahead in taking advantage of them in design and also in strung necklaces." Under Hoving's leadership, Tiffany also adapted its marketing approach by singling out the designer responsible for a collection. This went against Cartier's principles, but it did seem to appeal to the American clientele. Jean Schlumberger, one of Tiffany's most well-known designers, became enormously popular with those interested in fine colored stone pieces. On more than one occasion, a client even came into Cartier asking for a copy of one of Schlumberger's rings.

With the release of the classic movie *Breakfast at Tiffany's*, starring Audrey Hepburn, in October 1961, the competition became even more intense. SHARP PROFIT RISE SEEN FOR TIFFANY was the headline in *The New York Times* on December 22, 1961. Compared to its heyday under Pierre, Cartier New York seemed to be losing its edge—at least that was the view of those on the inside. "It wasn't always a nice place to work in the early 1960s," one employee recalled. "Everyone was worried for the future, scared they might lose their jobs. There was a lot of uncertainty." The American Maison needed strong leadership more than ever.

THE KENNEDY SLIDE

December 1961 saw the start of the "Kennedy Slide." Over the following six months, the S&P would plummet 22.5 percent, and the Dow Jones Industrial Average experienced its second-largest point decline on record. CONSUMERS CURTAILING SPENDING BECAUSE OF STOCK MARKET DIP, *The New York Times* reported in June 1962, noting that as a result of the "precipitous stock market declines," signs of belt tightening, including canceled orders, were being seen across "everything from auto, fur, and jewelry sales to the suburban real estate market." Possibly the largest order cancellation as a result of the "staggering stock market," the article noted, was to be seen at Cartier. In May, Mrs. Edward M. Gilbert, the ex-wife of a wealthy businessman, had placed a very significant order at Cartier New York. It comprised a necklace, a ring, and two clips, and the bill had come to $732,000 ($6.1 million today). She had taken the jewels home with her to try them out, but after several days they had neither been paid for nor returned.

As Cartier filed a lawsuit in an attempt to recover the jewels, Mrs. Gilbert explained that she had planned to fund them out of her divorce settlement, but her estranged husband, a lumber executive, was refusing to pay up. It transpired that Mr. Gilbert, who had been trying to pull off a company merger, had suffered such massive losses in the stock market collapse that he had been forced to flee the country. When a newspaper reporter caught up with him in Brazil, he admitted to being stunned by how quickly his fortunes had changed: "It happened so fast I couldn't believe it was happening to me." When questioned about his wife's large order, he replied that he was "not interested in discussing the purchase of any jewelry." Eventually, Cartier recovered the jewels, but the episode revealed the challenging environment within which the American jewelry business was operating.

There were "many finished pieces remaining in the shop for months," one employee reported. Most of the work was confined to insurance and estimates, with hardly any requests for new stock. "Fewer and fewer large pieces are being made. How times have changed." Claude, meanwhile, was stressed. "He would enter from the side entrance and walk through to the front of the store," his staff remembered. "We'd stand at attention and a whisper would pass through the building, 'CC is here, did you see what mood he was in?'" Among those who worked for him, there was a sense that although he didn't necessarily lack the skills to take the company forward, he did lack the drive. "Personally," one of them recalled, "I felt that if Claude was not immersed in his own life-style, he could have made a difference to the store."

When Pierre faced a terrible economic situation in the 1930s, he canceled his vacation to focus on the business. For Claude, whose life was about more than 653 Fifth Avenue, the difficult environment was a burden from which he wanted to escape. And as he raced down the Cresta run in St. Moritz or enjoyed cocktail parties in Paris, there was a sense among the staff left behind that perhaps their boss had had enough of managing the business. For years, there had been those who suspected he might one day sell his uncle's legacy, and now, as market conditions made business harder and harder, those rumors became louder.

THE ROTHSCHILDS OF JEWELRY

In December 1962, fifty-three years after Cartier New York had been founded, the Cartiers would learn that it had been sold. For 115 years, Cartier had been a family firm. Louis-François and Alfred and then the three brothers had survived almost everything life could throw at them to give the next generation a legacy to carry on. But Claude, disconnected from the sacrifices made by his ancestors and frustrated by the years spent arguing over his father's will, lacked that sense of familial duty. The news of the sale hadn't come as a total shock to Pierre. The previous month, after hearing rumors that a sale might be imminent, he had spoken to Louis' forty-year-old grandson. René-Louis Revillon (Anne-Marie's son) had agreed to fly out to America to meet Claude in person. Pierre, suspecting that Claude would be more open to an approach from René-Louis than himself, had wanted to find out whether his nephew would change his mind about the sale, or at least sell the business to a member of the family. They would, he maintained, be stronger together.

Six days after René-Louis left Paris for New York, on November 30, 1962, he telegraphed Pierre confirming that Claude's shares in Cartier Inc. were up for sale. They could perhaps make an offer, he proposed, but they were up against time and another bidder. For a short period, it looked as if there might be hope. But Claude's sale discussions with the other buyer were already well advanced, and he wasn't inclined to slow them down. Most disappointing of all, it seemed that Claude had no interest in selling to a family member. There may have been a moment of coming together at his wedding six years earlier, but since then, the old divisions had resurfaced.

Discussions with the other buyer were highly secret, and almost everyone, from Claude's staff to his family, was in the dark, both before the sale and immediately after it. "I tried to get some information at the shop discreetly on Wednesday," one employee wrote, "but no one seems to know. We are swimming in uncertainty." In the end, Jean-Jacques and Pierre would learn the details of the sale only when they appeared in the press, just like everyone else.

In Conversation with Jean-Jacques Cartier

I didn't know about the New York sale until after it had happened. The three brothers had a covenant that if one of them ever wanted to sell his branch, he must first offer it to the others. That was ingrained in the business. Claude should have offered it to a family member first.

CARTIER'S JEWELRY STORE SOLD TO BLACK, STARR AND FROST GROUP was the headline in *The New York Times* on Tuesday, December 4, 1962. The article, subheaded "Acquisition of Corporation by Syndicate," included the basic facts of the sale but no details on the financial terms. It noted that for some time "Claude Cartier has been interested in selling the Fifth Avenue store and returning to Paris" and that the sale "does not involve the Cartier stores in Paris and London, which remain in the ownership of the Cartier family."

Cartier was in new territory. When Pierre had talked to his nephews after the war, he had tried to impress upon them the importance of acting in unity with the other branches by explaining that they were more powerful together than apart. Now, with only two of the three branches unified, the family business had lost a pillar of support.

The syndicate that had bought the New York branch was made

up of three parties. Only one of them, Edward G. Goldstein, was in the jewelry business, "a Boston jewelry dealer with wide interests." The other two were reported to be financial investors: Benjamin Swig was a real estate developer who owned the Fairmont Hotel in San Francisco, and Ramco Enterprises Inc. was a diversified holding company that owned a shopping center and textile mills. The same syndicate had bought Black Starr & Frost Ltd., another Fifth Avenue jeweler, a year earlier, but they took pains to make clear in the new announcement that Cartier would remain "an independent and unaffiliated enterprise." They also confirmed that Claude would continue as president.

"What the Rothschilds are to banking, the Cartiers have been to jewelry," *Time* magazine reflected ten days later, in an article that made it across the Atlantic to Jean-Jacques in London:

> *In its handsome Fifth Avenue mansion, salesmen never push the merchandise; they discreetly "suggest." Last week Cartier's of Manhattan announced its biggest sale yet. At a price estimated to run between $4,000,000 and $5,000,000, a specially formed investment syndicate purchased from the Cartier family a major share of the store's stock. With the traditional reserve of the society jeweler, Cartier's would not discuss terms of the deal, [but] would only say that Claude Cartier, 37, a nephew of the founder of Cartier's of Manhattan, will stay on as president of the company. It did not take a jeweler's eyepiece, however, to see that Cartier's might be in for a change of character.*

As the news broke, letters came pouring in to the family. "I had a little emotional depression of my own," one friend wrote to Pierre. "I think [the firm] missed your presence and guidance very badly." Pierre responded with melancholy resignation, indicating that the news of the sale had not surprised him even though "of course I felt very sad that a company which had met with great success [had] left the family ownership."

Among the staff, there was anger and almost grief. "I am bitter, sad even," one Fifth Avenue employee wrote. "I had thought this magnificent organization would survive beyond me." And as with any sale, there was an understandable sense of anxiety for the future: "I feel sure they will sweep out the dead wood." But in the end, it was Claude himself who was the first to leave. On February 4, 1963, just three months after the sale and fourteen years after he had become president of Cartier New York, he resigned. Before he left, he went to see Alfred Durante to tell him that he had a job for life. Claude had written into the sale contract that no one could ever fire the young designer—one last goodwill gesture from this man of contradictions. "Why did he do it?" Durante would later wonder. "I have no idea, I was just twenty-three at the time, still learning from the other designers. But I owe him my career." On February 21, Claude walked around the showroom and workshops one final time, saying his goodbyes and promising to come back and see them all again soon. Not many believed him.

STUNNED DISBELIEF

Within 13 Rue de la Paix, news of the sale of Cartier New York was greeted with disbelief by the older employees. Those who knew what had gone into building the firm, and how close the brothers had been, were stunned that a Cartier would sell outside the family. But there was nothing to be done. Cartier Paris carried on as before with Pierre still delegating the management of the business to those he considered capable. Calmette, the president of Cartier S.A., was not particularly popular with the staff. Perhaps sensing dissension, he wrote to Pierre explaining "how much your presence and support are necessary." If Pierre also had doubts about the man he had left in charge, Calmette tried to alleviate them. He repeatedly thanked him for his trust, reiterating that he was "proud and happy to dedicate all my time and efforts to continuing your work."

By the early 1960s, after many difficult years, the economy in France was on an upward trajectory. Charles de Gaulle, who had been voted in as president in 1959, founded a Fifth Republic with a focus on reforming and developing the French economy and promoting an independent foreign policy. His two terms in power saw record growth rates unrivaled since the nineteenth century and the start of what was later nostalgically referred to as *"les trentes glorieuses"* (the thirty glorious years). In 1964, for the first time in two hundred years, France's GDP would overtake that of the United Kingdom, a position it would hold until the 1990s.

Cartier Paris still attracted the glamorous set. De Gaulle himself, loyal to Cartier after Bellenger's help in the war, bought a bracelet for President Truman's daughter that she described as "one of the dearest presents I ever received." The Duchess of Windsor, a client now for close to three decades, asked for her Cartier emerald engagement ring to be remounted in 1958, this time with the emerald enhanced by a stylized gold leaf border set with brilliant-cut diamonds. Daisy Fellowes passed away in 1963, but her daughter would ask for her late mother's jewels to be updated in a modern style. And María Félix, worked closely with the Cartier designer Gabriel Raton to create striking reptile jewels. In 1954, the Mexican actress, who lived part of the year in Paris, played the famous jewel-loving courtesan in the French film *La Bella Otero*. Like her turn-of-the-century character, María Félix was a strong, vibrant personality who knew exactly what she liked and always looked, one salesman recalled, "effortlessly stylish." On one occasion around 1950, she recalled walking into 13 Rue de la Paix unannounced with all her diamond jewels wrapped up in a handkerchief asking for them to be transformed into a serpent necklace (the snake represented eternity in Mexican mythology). On more low-key days, she might simply wear trousers, a sweater, and a pair of fantastic earrings. But when she dressed up, she went all out and became known for wearing multiple jewels all together for maximum effect.

Alongside the beautiful women modeling Cartier creations through the 1960s were a group of highly esteemed men. Georges Rémy worked on five new academicians' swords during the decade. These included those for the French neurologist and writer Jean Delay and the economist Jacques Rueff. His favorite, however, was the one he designed in 1964 for the Argentinian French journalist and novelist Joseph Kessel, a writer whom he admired enormously. Among the many symbols on the sword were a wing, symbolizing inspiration and adventure (Kessel had been a pilot in two world wars); a lion's head, representing one of the author's most famous works, *The Lion,* and the Lorraine Cross, which stood for his resistance during the war.

Toussaint, still the artistic director of the House, continued to mingle in artistic and fashion-oriented circles. Hubert de Givenchy praised her "lively, avant-garde and extremely elegant" creations and she retained loyal clients until the end of the decade.

Among the more notable high-jewelry pieces created under Toussaint's direction was a clock in a crystal bottle, created in 1960 and later described by one of her colleagues, Robert Thil:

> She particularly cared about a crystal flask which had been part of a travel case belonging to Louis Cartier. After much reflection, Jeanne said "slap a clock in it." To the objection of her colleagues, she replied, "Nothing is impossible, sailing boats are put into bottles." The clock in a flask was created and the gold stopper set with a cabochon sapphire served as the winder. "This is artisanal work at its best" was her reaction.

Now in her seventies, Touissant's health was not what it once was and she came in to the office less, often arriving in late morning just in time for a client lunch. Those who worked for her in this period recalled her exceptional taste but also that "she liked to be the one," by which they meant it was important to her to be acknowledged as driving the creative process. She would often entertain in the evening, hosting clients, designers, and colleagues. A younger saleswoman, one of the first women to work in a sales role in Cartier Paris, remembered the excitement of being invited by Mlle Toussaint to one of her elegant cocktail parties at which everything in her fabulous Place d'Iéna apartment, from the flowers to the champagne flutes to the canapés, was perfection. Toussaint's husband, Baron Hély d'Oissel, had passed away in 1959, just four years after they had finally married. She would not remarry.

From Geneva, Pierre might hear about Denet's latest sale to Barbara Hutton or the success of Rémy's most recent sword. He traveled to Paris less and less frequently. "I must live a very quiet life and see but very few people," he wrote at the age of eighty-five. Nelly was one of the few visitors. They had become closer than ever after the

Jeanne Toussaint, pictured here in her office in 1967, remained head of artistic
direction through the 1960s. "She was small," her family recalled, "but she had
the most enormous presence." Her team of designers included Georges Rémy,
pictured here discussing his designs with Gagniand, the head of the Paris workshop.

loss of loved ones and decades of shared history. "Dearest Brother
Pierre," she wrote to him in February 1963, "I've meant to drop in
and see you to thank you for a delightful lunch. . . . But alas, with all
this ice, I am afraid to be in the car. . . . See you soon I hope, with
much love from your old sister Nelly." It didn't suit Pierre, this "quiet
life," but he bowed to doctor's orders, noting that "at my age one
must become obedient to the [medical] faculty."

But from his Swiss lakeside home, Pierre remained passionately
engaged in the world outside. "Even when over 80, he followed international affairs, and in particular current affairs in France and at
the Holy See, with the zest of a young man," *The Times* of London
would later report. "Yet his memories took him back to Edward VII,
Pierpont Morgan, and the bejewelled Easter eggs of Russian grand
dukes."

And though the firm he had founded in America had changed
hands, Pierre was kept up to date on its development through devoted employees. It was an exchange of information for which he
was grateful, but it wouldn't last forever. In March 1964, one of his
loyal informants announced that he was among those who had been
let go from Cartier Inc. and he could therefore no longer keep "Monsieur Pierre" up to date with the New York branch. "I regret that I

have to give up my information service, the only thing that could give you a little satisfaction." Resigned that the world was changing in ways that he couldn't control, Pierre was increasingly shut out from what had been his life's work.

HE WAS HUMANITY ITSELF

On a cold autumnal morning in 1964, Pierre Camille Cartier passed away. He was eighty-five, a year older than his father had been when he died almost forty years earlier. For more than two decades, since the death of both his brothers, Pierre had carried the mantle of the Cartier name for the wider family. He had borne the responsibility heavily, feeling a duty to be as strong a patriarch as his father had been, but he didn't have endless strength, and the sale of the New York Maison less than two years earlier had devastated him. "Although he died of natural causes," the American employee Jack Hasey would later observe in a television interview, "those who knew him, including myself, know he died of a broken heart."

"He will be missed not only for the warmth of his personal kindness," *The Times* of London reported, "but for his shrewd judgment of men and events of today against the background of an active life spanning two wars and three generations." Over the following days, newspapers on both sides of the Atlantic were filled with his incredible achievements.

Pierre Cartier had, *The New York Times* reported, "built a jewelry firm of international distinction" with clients that spanned "Rockefellers, Fords and Astors and Mrs. John F. Kennedy, the Duchess of Windsor and Princess Grace," and jewels including "the Hope Diamond, earrings given by Napoleon to Josephine and a marriage crown worn by the last three Russian czarinas." He had been, the paper reflected, a "soft-spoken man of medium build who talked with his employees in a quiet, paternal tone." One of those loyal employees was quoted in the obituary: "Mr. Cartier started from practically nothing and built the store into one of the biggest in New York. He was a real merchant; he knew jewelry from A to Z and he had a wonderful personality. That combination made Cartier's what it is today."

The accolades didn't stop at Pierre's business success. Some talked of his charitable acts, such as donating his 15 East Ninety-sixth Street house in New York to a Roman Catholic order when he moved to Europe, and others focused on his "active role in efforts to spur better relations between France and the United States." As well as serving with the Alliance Française, the French Chamber of Commerce in the United States, and the Museum of French Art, *The New York Times* reported that he had also funded a number of scholarships to the Sorbonne. "I have used my best efforts," he once said, "to promote and develop, through Franco-American organizations, the closest economic and cultural relations between the United States and France. To me France and America are sister countries and will always remain so." A letter in *The Times* talked of his skill at connecting all types of different people, even in his retirement: "He was a generous host, whose table a British visitor was likely to share with the Vatican, the Red Cross, the French Army, the Swiss press, and the granddaughters home from skiing."

Expressions of sympathy poured in. Those who had worked for him revealed that he had been more than a boss. One spoke of how he "was like a second father to me." "I will leave it to the newspapers to summarize his many achievements," said another, "for me, he was simply better than good, he was humanity itself."

Jean-Jacques wrote to his cousin Marion in sympathy. Though the two cousins, who had always lived in different countries, didn't know each other particularly well, they had both had fathers who had impressed upon them the importance of family. For his part, Jean-Jacques was very sad to lose his uncle. Not only had Pierre been such a strong link back to his own father, but he had also been a patriarchal figure in the wider family, on whom Jean-Jacques had known he could rely for advice or support. He'd also known that with Pierre around, Cartier Paris would remain in the family. Now, the future was less certain.

In Paris, there was a large funeral attended by many of the people Pierre had touched during his very full life. Some, such as dignitaries, aristocratic figures, and artists, were well known, but others had simply benefited from his generosity over the years. Afterwards, Pierre's coffin was taken to Versailles and he was buried in the large family crypt, next to his adored Elma and alongside his grandfather, father, and brothers.

Over in New York, the city Pierre had called home for so many years, a memorial service took place in St. Patrick's Cathedral, organized by the executives of Cartier New York. A notice was placed in the paper by Jules Glaenzer, who had been promoted to chairman of the board, and John Gorey, its new president: "His associates and friends record with deep sorrow the death of Pierre C. Cartier, founder and past president of Cartier Inc. New York." A week after Pierre's death, on October 30, 1964, the Fifth Avenue branch closed for a day of mourning. It was a sign of respect that was echoed in the sentiments of many. "Never in all my life have I had a man stand out in my memory like Pierre Cartier," one friend recalled. "His charm and understanding and kindness were perfection.... If we had a few more like him around, the world would be a better place to live."

A TIME OF CHANGE

Outside the chic showroom on Rue de la Paix, Paris was in a state of flux. Suddenly high fashion, once such a staple of the Parisian scene, was coming under criticism. The French youth culture looked toward London, where trailblazers like Mary Quant (credited with popularizing the miniskirt) encouraged people to dress for themselves rather than according to convention. As ripple effects were felt around the world (in 1965, Vogue declared that a "youthquake" had hit the United States), the norms surrounding haute couture became less relevant. Yves Saint Laurent was the first couturier to open a "pret-à-porter" (ready-to-wear) boutique under his name in 1966. "I had had enough of making dresses for jaded billionaires," he is said to have declared. Whereas previously, member houses of the Chambre Syndicale were forbidden to use even sewing machines, now French fashion was expanding into mass manufacturing and marketing.

Cartier had a history of adapting to changing trends, often even being one step ahead, but the late 1960s were particularly difficult. The idea of a formal high jewelry salon was discordant with the trend toward more casual attire. Within 13 Rue de la Paix, the most popular jewels included animals: "turtles, dogs and mainly birds, their plumes and eyes shimmering with rubies, sapphires, and diamonds," but there were simply not enough clients coming through the doors. "The evolution of the business raises fears that, if the Company does not change its sales policy," a 1966 Cartier Paris financial report stated, "sales will stagnate and then drop."

The strategic challenge was twofold. First, "rich clients are becoming scarce in number and purchasing power." And second, "the counterpart of the prestige that Cartier still enjoys is the fear we inspire to an average clientele, who do not dare to enter our salons." The proposed solution was to expand the firm's product offerings to include lower-priced items to attract a wider range of clients. "This requires new manufacturing techniques, increased monitoring of cost prices," and "a considerable increase in the number of average-priced objects." There was also a plan, along the lines of the London boutique, to open "a new department of gifts at moderate or average prices, with a separate entrance from the main entrance."

In an early 1966 shareholder meeting, it was explained that, in order to carry out these strategy changes, a substantial capital contribution would be needed from the shareholders. They were being asked to commit millions of francs in further funding. This was at a time when Marion, now in her mid-fifties, was trying to wind down her father's affairs after his death. There were a multitude of different assets to sort out and, in some cases, sell, from properties to financial investments to artwork. There were auctions to organize, and plans for charitable donations and trusts. There was also her work as an artist. Marion had channeled her talents into designing stained-glass windows, and requests were coming in from various chapels and churches. She would even design the stained-glass windows for the Cartier crypt in Versailles.

Given her other commitments, Marion was understandably less interested than her father had been in owning a large business. And when she met two American businessmen brothers, she was open to talking about a possible deal. Harry and Edward Danziger were successful entrepreneurs. American born, they had made their name in England producing British films and TV shows throughout the 1950s and '60s. At one time, almost every British filmgoer and television watcher would have recognized the familiar "Produced by the Danzigers" credit up on the screen.

By 1956, the Danziger brothers had founded their own film

studios, the New Elstree Studios, by converting a former wartime airplane-engine testing factory in Hertfordshire. But they were more interested in seeking out investment opportunities than in remaining involved in any one industry, and by the mid-1960s, they had sold their film studios and changed focus. After buying Cordon Hotels Group, they became the owners of prestigious hotels such as the Mayfair and Grosvenor in London and the Metropole in Monte Carlo. Jewelry was a new avenue for them, but that didn't matter. They could sense when a struggling firm had potential, and they had an eye for turning businesses around. Cartier Paris seemed a good fit.

A few years later, *The Sunday Times* would report that after Marion had met Harry Danziger and his wife, Angela, on the ski slopes near her Swiss house, she had "entrusted her family's heritage" to them. Before doing so, however, she had turned to the Cartier Paris president, Calmette, for his advice. He had proposed that she not only accept the Danziger offer but also keep it secret, even from her cousin in Cartier London (the only remaining Cartier branch in the family). Previously, each Cartier brother had held significant shares in the others' branches as well as their own, so there was no way they could have sold without approval from one another. Now the structure had changed. The New York branch was separate, and Jean-Jacques was simply a minority shareholder in Paris.

In Conversation with Jean-Jacques Cartier

Marion didn't tell me she was considering selling the business. Later she told me that Calmette had told her to keep everything secret. Maybe he thought I would try to stop it and he didn't want that.

At the time, and for some time afterward, both the French and the international press were in the dark. The Danzigers had no desire to tell the world they had bought Cartier. They would own it and invest the necessary capital, but to the outside world, they felt it best if Cartier appeared to be the same family firm it had always been. Many of the more junior staff did not even know who their new owners were. Management was kept as before, with Calmette still in charge and Toussaint still head of the artistic direction until her retirement a few years later. The board of directors also remained the same. Everything was, to the outside world, just as it had always been. But now the only Cartier branch still owned and managed by one of the founder's great-grandchildren was Cartier London.

BOXES TO RIVAL FABERGÉ

At forty-seven years old, Jean-Jacques was as driven as ever to continue his father's legacy. Though deeply disappointed that both his cousins had now sold their branches, and that both had lacked the trust in him to tell him themselves, he was equally resigned to the fact that he couldn't change the past and must simply steer the London ship onward as best he could. His mother, Nelly, who still owned the controlling interest in Cartier London, had no intention of selling outside the family, and the reality, for those in 175 New Bond Street, was that not much changed after the sale of the Paris branch. Operations between London and Paris didn't suddenly cease. Jean-Jacques continued to share designs with Mlle Toussaint regularly and vice

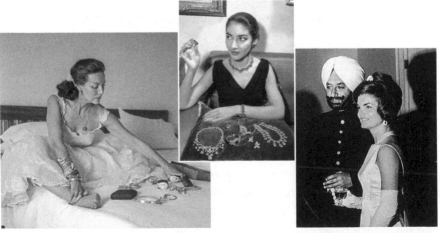

Glamorous clients in the 1960s included the film star María Félix (left), the opera diva Maria Callas (center), and Jackie Kennedy, pictured at right with the Maharaja of Patiala.

versa. Cartier London remained popular with foreign buyers who were exempt from the prohibitive purchase tax, and clients from Princess Grace of Monaco and Maria Callas to King Olaf of Norway and the Aga Khan continued to frequent both stores with little awareness that anything had changed.

Meanwhile, the other branches were moving forward with their strategies for growth. Cartier New York was expanding to include multiple points of sale across America. Under the Danzigers, Cartier Paris would open new stores in Geneva and Munich and as far afield as Hong Kong. From London, Jean-Jacques was left flying the family flag alone, knowing he had to adapt to survive but adamant that he wanted to hold on to the old values of quality and exclusivity.

175 New Bond Street remained a haven from the pressures of the outside world, just as it had been in Jacques' time. There was beautiful jewelry on display, flowers by Constance Spry, and salesmen dressed immaculately at their tables ready to greet those who entered. The daughter of one London salesman recalled visiting her father in the "very French, very discreet" showroom. "The only times my mother and I went into Cartier to see him were on the few Saturday mornings that they opened before Christmas, which were always very quiet because people went to their country estates on the weekend. Even so, you would always have your hair done, nails manicured, and be dressed in your best clothes because it was such a very smart place."

Jean-Jacques would rarely be in the showroom himself. And each lunchtime, instead of taking influential clients for a three-course meal at Brown's Hotel as his father had done, he took himself off to absorb the creative output of others. After a quick sandwich at the Italian deli down the street, he would wander over to Sotheby's or one of the other London auction houses to savor the latest works of art on display. Like his uncle Louis, he particularly loved Persian miniatures, but he was interested in everything from Chinese furniture to Indian rugs to British oil paintings (especially Alfred Munnings's horses). Though he rarely bought anything, sometimes the seed of an idea would be planted that would later make its way into his creations. He was an introvert who found being around people all day draining. Those quiet times wandering among beautiful masterpieces were rejuvenating for him.

> ## In Conversation with Jean-Jacques Cartier
>
> *You can't know where inspiration will come from. You don't go out looking for it. But look at that vase there, well, that's a beautiful curve, don't you think? That curve could work somewhere else. On a pair of earrings, perhaps.*

It was during a 1963 conversation with the James Bond writer Ian Fleming that the collector Peter Wilding came up with the idea of starting a new collection. The two friends were walking down Bond Street when they stopped to admire some Fabergé boxes. "I bet you couldn't get boxes made like that again," Fleming said to Wilding. And the collector, determined to win the bet, had paid a visit to Cartier.

Wilding's vision was to create a unique collection of decorative gem-set and enameled gold boxes, where each one would push the limits of its art. And his aim was not simply to win a bet, though that may well have been the catalyst, but to keep the goldsmithing trade alive at a particularly challenging time. "When Peter Wilding first came in," Cartier London director Joe Allgood recalled, "he talked about having special boxes made to prove that the art of the goldsmith and the art of the enameler were still alive, and that Cartier could produce cases as good as they could be produced, shall we say, fifty or sixty years before . . . even at that period, which was so difficult."

Wilding's plan, right from the beginning, was to leave the boxes to the British Museum. He didn't put a limit on the number of boxes and in fact tried to push Cartier to work faster because he wanted them to make more. Then in his fifties, he suffered from bad health and perhaps knew he didn't have long to live. Wilding asked for five boxes a year. Jean-Jacques, as an artist, loved the idea of the project but he also knew that, from the perspective of the business, he couldn't afford to tie up his best craftsmen on such a time-consuming project or everything else would suffer. He suggested that the workshop could not make more than one a year. In the end, they compromised on three boxes every two years.

Most Cartier clients explained their requirements to a salesman and waited for the accomplished designer to come up with some options from which they selected their favorite. Peter Wilding was one of the few who were allowed behind the scenes. Unusually, Jean-Jacques allowed him direct access to the head designer, Rupert Emmerson, and even to the craftsmen. "Mr. Wilding's downstairs" was a common refrain up in the workshops when the collector was in town, and Emmerson would despair of getting any other work done that day. But the two men enjoyed working together on such pinnacles of the art form. Sharing an appreciation for the earlier Cartier boxes of the 1920s and 1930s, they decided to use these as their basis for Wilding's collection.

Everything about the boxes was London-made. After a design was approved, it would be initially passed to Cartier's Wright & Davies workshop in Farringdon (which focused on the non-jewelry items, including the watch cases). "Given a good design," Emmerson explained, "these craftsmen will produce an article of such mechanical perfection that the hinge and opening cannot be felt, let alone seen. When the lid closes, the click of the catch engaging is almost inaudible, whilst a tiny puff of air escapes as the two surfaces brush gently together." Jean-Jacques was famous for testing the click made by a box when it closed. "I want the click to be better," he would say to his exasperated team if it wasn't absolutely perfect in tone and volume.

Many of the Wilding designs included complex geometrical patterns to be created using engine turning (effectively mechanical engraving). Jules Kneuss, Cartier's expert engine turner, would be called back from semiretirement to set up the templates based on Emmerson's intricate designs and then skillfully work the enormous engine-turning machine. He would create a rippling wave pattern on one box, or a moiré effect (with diagonal lines to achieve the watered-silk look) or a basket weave motif on another. The idea of engine turning in itself was not uncommon in the decoration of boxes, but the complexity of the patterns on the Wilding boxes and the use of the technique alongside enameling and gems were unusual. Kneuss, hugely respected within the industry, was known within Wright & Davies for his standard response when Emmerson turned up with his latest (often highly problematic) design: "It's impossible. Give me until lunchtime tomorrow." The enameling work was completed by experts such as Peter McCabe in the Kempson & Mauger workshop (although not officially part of Cartier, it worked almost exclusively for Cartier), while the gem-setting work was undertaken by the craftsmen in English Art Works (Wilding provided many of the gems himself).

In Conversation with Jean-Jacques Cartier

We had some of the best specialists in the country, in many different fields. Now, there's a reason not all jewelers had workshops like that. They took years and years to build up, and they were a considerable investment too. Especially in difficult times. But it did mean that one single piece could be worked on by multiple A-1 craftsmen, all at the top of their field. You simply couldn't find that under one roof elsewhere.

Cartier's boxes attracted discerning clients all over the world, many of whom also collected them, such as the Aga Khan (who bought back many of the boxes from the Art Deco era) and the owner of one of London's leading art galleries. But most clients would have little to do with the behind-the-scenes process of the box's creation. Wilding was an unusual collector in that he had the vision to start a collection of something that hadn't yet been created and the desire to shape that collection himself. "Collectors who claim some measure of participation in a rare object are themselves rare," reflected *Connoisseur* magazine in an article about Wilding's collection in August 1969.

The Wilding boxes were very expensive to make and Cartier did not make big margins on them. "Given the enormous work involved, he got a good deal," Jean-Jacques would recall. "They tied up some of my best craftsmen for months at a time." Wilding was pleased. By 1964, he wrote to a friend that he was "seriously in debt to my little jeweler [Cartier] but I cannot complain as our last production would make Fabergé sit up and take notice." Jean-Jacques, modest by nature, would claim that he couldn't begin to rival the work of his ancestors. But in this case, he could be justifiably proud. Wilding would live to see twelve boxes before he passed away, and five more boxes would be made after his death. Today, the seventeen Wilding boxes remain on permanent display in the British Museum, an example of bespoke British craftsmanship at its finest, just as Wilding had intended.

MECHANICAL MIRACLES

Through the 1960s, "Swinging London," as the capital was dubbed by American journalists, was at the front of a revolution in fashion, music, and consumer goods. The Mod subculture, with its roots in a group of rebellious young London-based "modernists," challenged the current trends. They danced all night, insisted on clothes suited to their lifestyle, and rode around town on motor scooters. By the mid-1960s, postwar austerity had well and truly made way for youth-focused fashion, psychedelic music, and vibrant pop art.

The fashion for opulent diamond tiaras was long gone, but even diamond necklaces were more rarely sold. The older salesmen would nostalgically tell the younger ones about the days when "money was no object" and Cartier jewels were the ultimate status symbol, but in the 1960s it was harder to entice people through the door, let alone make big sales. The pace was set by the young, who wanted the unexpected, bold, and new. In an interview, Joseph Allgood recalled a rather surprising visit to the 175 New Bond Street showroom by a group of long-haired gentlemen in jeans. He was later informed they were called the Beatles.

With couture deemed no longer relevant, trendsetting women demanded large jewels without the large price tag and even Dior started creating costume jewelry. While Jean-Jacques had no interest in costume jewelry, his lower-priced boutique offerings were proving more popular than the high jewelry in the main showroom (the boutique even ended up expanding over this period and taking over the Spanish gallery premises next door).

Often clients were after gold necklaces and bracelets or chunky brooches and rings with semiprecious gemstones such as topaz. Non-jewelry items were also popular, such as "the first handbags with detachable gold chains," which, one Cartier London salesman recalled,

Cartier London director Donald Fraser standing outside the entrance to the Albemarle Street boutique (left); the interior where one could find "gifts expressly designed to meet the economy of the day" (right).

"sold very well to the richest women in the world for £600 export" ($15,400 today). The idea was to offer three black bags—one in leather, one in ribbed silk, and another in plain black silk—with a gold chain strap that could be detached from one and reattached to another depending on the occasion. Fans included Elizabeth Taylor and Princess Margaret.

For Jean-Jacques, watches were a key focus. In the years since he had taken over Cartier London, he had dramatically expanded its watch offerings. In his father's time, a watch sold in London would have been identical to one sold in Paris. Jacques, fortunate enough to be busy with large commissions for maharajas' necklaces and coronation tiaras, hadn't prioritized the smaller timepieces. But Jean-Jacques faced a very different market, and, like his late uncle, he appreciated design and function being combined in one stylish object. Just as Louis had worked closely with Edmund Jaeger, so Jean-Jacques worked with his successor firm, Jaeger-LeCoultre (the Swiss supplier of Cartier's watch movements, considered top in their field). He loved thin watches that looked as if you were hardly wearing them, and he aspired to come up with the thinnest possible. "Often the artist sets the technician difficult problems," Devaux had written about Cartier's watchmaking division, "compelling him to some kind of mechanical miracles that he has achieved thanks to determination, care, and admirable science." The JJC model (standing for Jean-

Jacques Cartier) was one of the most popular styles in London. A re-working of the original Tank, it had more rounded edges, and in one of its many variations was one of the thinnest watches in the world.

From the bold maxi watches (the Maxi Oval retailed for £375 and now sells for closer to £70,000 at auction), to the double strap (inspired in part by the straps on a horse's bridle), to the his and her "pebble" models with their diamond-shaped dials, to Tanks in myriad different sizes and curved variations, multiple new models were introduced in this period. The Cartier London designers were known for their creativity, and for those clients seeking a more nonconformist aesthetic, they came up with off-center and elongated models, some with colored enamel dials and others with bold graphic designs. One of Jean-Jacques' favorites was the oblique model, or "driving watch," on which the case was set on the diagonal with the 12 and 6 in the top right and bottom left corners respectively, the idea being that with one's hands on the steering wheel of a car, the 12 would be pointing up (rather than to the left as in a traditional watch).

The process for making a Cartier London watch involved many craftsmen and departments. Once the design had been approved by Jean-Jacques in the weekly meeting, discussions would be opened with Jaeger-LeCoultre to find the perfect movement for the watch in question. Next the design would be passed to the Wright & Davies workshop on Rosebery Avenue (a location Jean-Jacques tried to keep secret to avoid the risk of robberies), where eight expert craftsmen sat at their benches by the window, converting precious metals into timepieces.

The first watch of any one design was always the hardest to make. Albert Mayo, known as Sam, was the head of the workshop, and it was up to him to make the prototype. He'd also make the watch templates (effectively the "secret recipe" for each watch model), which were stored in old tobacco tins piled up on shelves in the corner of the workshop. Everyone smoked—Jean-Jacques himself was never without his pipe—so there was no shortage of empty tins. Every tin was labeled with a different model of watch (one might read CLASSIC TANK, another JJC, another SMALL OVAL). Within each one were instructions on how much gold would be required (to be weighed out by Sam Mayo), a steel block template demonstrating the shape of the watch case, and other smaller templates (for everything from the dial to the movement to the curves, if required) in order that the crafts-man could make each watch to exactly the right dimensions.

Each watch case might take a senior craftsman thirty-five to forty hours to make. More complicated ones could take longer. And of course, given Jean-Jacques' high standards, if they weren't perfect, they would be sent back and remade. As well as the watch cases, the craftsmen would also be tasked with making the folding gold deployment buckles, first patented by Jaeger for exclusive use by Cartier in 1909. This fastening system, with the buckle invisible from the outside, was designed to look stylish on the wrist while remaining secure.

In a smaller room off the main Wright & Davies workshop sat Albert Penny, the leather craftsman. He would make watch straps to fit the client's wrist. Each week, the cases, deployment buckles, and straps that were finished were put into a briefcase and given to the apprentice to take to 175 New Bond Street. The young chap would jump on the 38 bus to Piccadilly Circus, then walk the ten minutes or so to Cartier. Entering through the staff entrance, the apprentice and his case would head upstairs to the small watchmaking division. Here, goldwork and straps from Wright & Davies would be combined with dials, movements, and winders and transformed into working timepieces.

"Cartier was the only firm to produce handmade, individual eighteen-karat watches with their special buckle fastener," one Lon-

Left: craftsmen at the East London Wright & Davies workshop.
Right: Prince Philip during a tour of English Art Works above
the London showroom (Jean-Jacques in background).

don employee of the period recalled, "even the cabochon sapphire winders were made by hand." Given the time-consuming nature of the work, the production of watches was limited. Clients from all over the world might have to wait, often for months, for their order to be ready. For the more original designs, Jean-Jacques might insist on reducing the output to twenty, or even fewer. Part of the luxury aspect, he felt, lay in the exclusivity of the pieces. In time, some of these watches would gain almost iconic status. The Crash, for instance, perfectly epitomized the rebellious creativity of the era while remaining an example of the high craftsmanship for which Cartier London had always been known.

JEWELRY SPOTLIGHT: THE CRASH WATCH

Stories abound about the provenance of the Crash watch. Created in 1967 under Jean-Jacques in London, its asymmetric shape was a departure from Cartier's more classic style. Some have claimed the idea came when a Cartier Maxi Oval watch (known as a Baignoire Allongée) half-melted in a car crash. Others have suggested that the inspiration must be Salvador Dalí's pocket watches in his surrealist 1931 painting *The Persistence of Memory.*

The reality was that the 1960s were a time of nonconformism in London. Several loyal clients, including the actor Stewart Granger, had been demanding a watch "unlike any other." Jean-Jacques, who worked closely with the designer Rupert Emmerson on watches and cases, discussed with him how they might try adjusting the popular Maxi Oval design to look as though it had been in a crash "by pinching the ends at a point and putting a kink in the middle." Emmerson then presented several variants of the proposed idea to his boss at their next design meeting, even one with a cracked-looking dial in order to make the crash theme more realistic. That was going slightly too far

The Crash watch, first launched by Cartier London, was conceived by Jean-Jacques Cartier and Rupert Emmerson as a reaction to changing times.

for Jean-Jacques, who, for all his openness to new ideas, still felt that the finished article should be an object of beauty. So Emmerson was asked to "tone it down" somewhat, the idea of a cracked dial was scrapped, and a final design was approved.

Creating the first Crash watch was far from straightforward. After Jaeger-LeCoultre had been consulted over the most appropriate movement to use, the design was passed to the highly skilled craftsmen in the Wright & Davies workshop. Here a template was created and the watch case was made from sheets of gold. A standard watch case may take thirty-five hours to make, but this one, with its irregular curves, was a major departure from the rectangular, square, and oval models and would take far longer. Once the case was completed, it was sent to Eric Denton, Cartier London's watchmaker, who would combine it with the movement, dial, and winder. It was here that the real complications started.

As Denton soon discovered, it was almost impossible to ensure that the numbers on the squashed dial remained at the right places to tell the time correctly. "That first Crash watch caused a lot of headaches. You see it's all very well coming up with a good-looking design, but it had to tell the time too! And because the dial was irregular, the numbers weren't at the standard places," Jean-Jacques recalled. The watch had to be deconstructed and the dial extracted and repainted by Emmerson (no easy feat, given that the numbers were painstakingly painted on by hand in a surrealist style). Once the watch was then put together with the new dial, it still didn't tell the time correctly, and the whole deconstruction, dial repainting, and reconstructing had to be undertaken again. And then again. In the end it took multiple attempts and far longer than anticipated.

An early Crash watch was sold to Stewart Granger, the actor who had previously requested something new and different. He took it home to try it but brought it back a week later, having decided that it was too unusual after all and that he wanted something more classic instead. Under Jean-

Jacques, Cartier London created only about a dozen Crash watches.

For all the enormous work involved, the Crash watches did not make the firm huge profits. The first one was sold for around $1,000 (approximately $7,500 today). "We should have charged more," Jean-Jacques later admitted. "Especially given how long each one took, tying up the workshop for an extended period. But you simply couldn't charge too much then. There wasn't that much wealth around. When I see what they go for today, oh my!" When a Cartier London 1968 Crash watch was sold in 2014, it went for more than ten times the estimate, reaching $130,000.

THE CARTIER DIAMOND

As the 1960s drew to an end, the situation of the Cartier business as a whole was, as Franco Cologni summarized, "a somewhat disconcerting one, with three perfectly legitimate companies marketing under the Cartier name, each manufacturing and distributing different products."

In some cases, the decisions made by one branch were unhelpful for the others. In 1971, Cartier New York would seek to reach a wider range of clients by creating a gold-plated Tank watch with a price tag of $150 (about $930 today). It was a move that proved popular in America but one that, at least in the eyes of some, including Jean-Jacques, risked "devaluing the Cartier name." On the other hand, when one branch attracted good publicity, it reflected well on the others too. In the eyes of the public, Cartier was still Cartier, and as in the days of the brothers, an important enough headline in one region generally made it overseas.

In 1968, the American branch made it into *The New York Times* again after it was sold for a second time. Claude had by now not been involved in the business for five years. He'd gone on to become a private investor and enjoyed his semi-professional interests of bobsledding and clay pigeon shooting. He was also a stamp collector but to the dismay of his cousin and several of those who had known Louis well, he had sold much of his father's collection of art and furniture. "All this has vanished in two sessions in the auction room," Devaux would exclaim in sadness at the thought of his late boss's "unique collection" disappearing into the hands of "indifferent people." "In fact," he would write to Jeanne Toussaint ruefully, the scattering of such a remarkable collection was "very unfair to the great Louis Cartier."

Meanwhile, the new buyer of Cartier New York was the Kenton Corporation, "a new holding company, which also owns the Family Bargain Centers, a discount-store chain." In an interview, Robert Kenmore, the company's chairman, dismissed suggestions that there might be any discounting of diamonds, explaining that Kenton was simply a holding vehicle for "companies with big names that haven't been fully exploited."

"You come away from the interview with Robert Kenmore," one journalist would remark in 1970, "with the distinct knowledge that you've just encountered one of the sharpest business brains in the world." Cartier New York, which had fallen within Kenmore's investment remit of firms that "needed new life and new blood," would be run independently from the discount chain. Standards, Kenmore implied, would not change, even if there were plans to expand the store footprint and target younger customers: "We want to get more young people into that store and then upgrade them as customers." The new Cartier Inc. president, Joseph Liebman, suggested that a change in approach, if not in strategy, was in the cards: "Cartier has been too damn formidable. We are going to make it more personal, more comfortable."

A year after the purchase, the new owners decided to bid for the twelfth-largest diamond in the world. Previously the record price for a diamond jewel at auction was $385,000 in 1957. Back then, it had been for a diamond necklace that formed part of the estate of Maisie Plant (or Mae Hayward Rovensky, as she was later known), with whom Cartier had exchanged the pearl necklace for the Fifth Avenue mansion. This time, the 69.42-carat diamond up for sale at a Parke-Bernet auction was expected to set a new record. It had already attracted interest from the Sultan of Brunei, Hassanal Bolkiah; the jeweler Harry Winston; and Aristotle Onassis (who was said to be interested in buying a diamond of more than 40 carats for the forti-eth birthday of his wife, Jacqueline Kennedy Onassis). It had also been flown to Gstaad in Switzerland so that the actress Elizabeth Taylor could see it close-up. When she fell in love with it, her hus-band, Richard Burton, had instructed those bidding for him to go as high as a million dollars.

The auction began at $200,000 with almost everyone in the room shouting "Yes!" but by $500,000 only nine people were still bidding. After $500,000, the sale proceeded in increments of $10,000. By $850,000 there were just two bidders left, Robert Kenmore for Car-tier and agents for Richard Burton. Kenmore had told the auctioneer at the start that he would remain in the bidding as long as his arms remained crossed. He simply leaned against a wall at the back of the room, looking entirely relaxed, and kept his arms crossed through-out. At $1 million, those bidding for Burton dropped out as instructed and the hammer came down at $1,050,000 to Kenmore for Cartier, a new record for a public auction of a jewel. "Men and women leaped out of their chairs as the bids climbed, turned to watch Mr. Kenmore in a back row, and cheered and applauded at the point of sale," re-ported *The New York Times*.

Burton's reaction was not so jubilant. "I turned into a raving ma-niac," he wrote in his diary, "Elizabeth was as sweet as only she could be and protested that it didn't matter, that she didn't mind if she didn't have it, that there was much more in life than baubles, that she would manage with what she had. The inference was that she would make do. But not me! . . . I screamed at Aaron [Burton's lawyer] that bugger Cartiers, I was going to get that diamond if it cost me my life or 2 million dollars whichever was the greater."

In the face of Burton's demands, Kenmore agreed to sell the dia-mond on one condition: It would first be displayed in Cartier New York as the "Cartier Diamond." After that it could be shipped to Burton and Taylor and they would be able to rename it. Burton agreed, and in a brilliant publicity coup for the firm, a large advertise-ment was published in *The New York Times* to announce the public viewing of the "Cartier Diamond" that had been bought by the world-famous movie star couple. An estimated six thousand people stood in line to see the diamond every day. Soon after, the diamond was shipped to the new buyers, and Elizabeth Taylor gave the enor-

Crowds queuing outside Cartier New York to see the "Cartier Diamond" in October 1969 just before it was sent to Elizabeth Taylor and renamed the "Taylor-Burton Diamond"; Taylor wearing the diamond as a necklace while presenting an Oscar at the forty-second annual Academy Awards ceremony in April 1970; a close-up of the diamond as a ring.

mous gemstone its first outing as the newly named "Taylor-Burton Diamond" at Princess Grace of Monaco's Scorpio-themed fortieth birthday party. The following year, in 1970, she wore it in front of a worldwide audience against a plunging blue dress at the forty-second Academy Awards ceremony. Though Cartier London at this time had little to do with the New York branch, that scale of publicity couldn't help but have a positive impact across the Atlantic as well. If Elizabeth Taylor herself didn't distinguish among the Cartier branches, regularly buying from London, Paris, and New York, then why should anyone else?

THE MOST DIFFICULT TIMES

Unfortunately, even the magic touch of Elizabeth Taylor couldn't transform the fortunes of what remained a troubled luxury industry in Britain. If anything, it was becoming even more difficult (the top tier of income tax reached 75 percent in 1971). "Cartier's showroom windows in Bond Street and in Albemarle Street are a focal point of interest to many people who are jewelry-minded," the designer Emmerson remarked around this time. "It is unfortunate that so many who are obviously in love with what they see are not sufficiently privileged financially to come inside and purchase."

In 1968, student rebellions swept the West. Protests, with their origins on university campuses, became widespread as the youth questioned their parents' traditional values. Spearheading the anti-establishment movement and expressing the need for freedom, the younger generation destabilized the pillars of bourgeois society. As an anarchic social scene combined hippiedom with futuristic space age dress, the wider luxury industry needed to adapt to a new outlook.

People were still interested in jewelry, they just wanted it to be more affordable—even if that meant mechanization as opposed to handcrafted pieces. As more machine-made items were produced, Albert Pujol, the head of Cartier's New York workshop, talked about the effect on the jewelry trade: "By the next generation, or thereabouts," *The New York Times* reported, Pujol feared that there might be "no new handmade jewelry."

The watch world was also about to be disrupted. In 1969, quartz watches, with their automated movements, started coming onto the market. Pioneered by the Japanese, they quickly became popular in the West. As Cartier's competitors, such as Bulgari, took advantage of the new technology, more affordable watches saturated the market. Suddenly, those handmade watches with manual movements, for which Cartier had always been known, were at risk of becoming obsolete.

In New York around this time, an Italian designer hired under Kenmore, Aldo Cipullo, was credited with inventing the love bracelet. This idea of singling out a designer marked a change from the previous Cartier policy of designer anonymity, but Kenmore believed it would resonate with an American audience (Tiffany had been doing it for some time already with success). Composed of two gold semicircles attached with two small screws (using the tiny screwdriver provided), the love bracelet was intended to be almost impossible to put on or remove by oneself. "Love," Cipullo said at the time, "has become too commercial, yet life without love is nothing—a fat zero. What modern people want are love symbols that look semi-permanent—

or, at least, require a trick to remove. After all, love symbols should suggest an everlasting quality." The love bracelet was big news from the start, as Cartier New York marked the 1970 launch by giving twenty-five pairs away to celebrity couples, including Elizabeth Taylor and Richard Burton, and soon everyone from Frank Sinatra to Sophia Loren to Cary Grant was in on the act. Not popular with airline security personnel (it caused delays at the X-ray machines when passengers left their screwdriver at home) or feminists (who saw it as akin to a chastity belt), the love bracelet was a great form of publicity for Cartier under Kenmore.

For his part, Jean-Jacques continued to pour his energies into handcrafted pieces. Cartier London was known as a firm of bespoke excellence, and he would steadfastly maintain that reputation. Despite his competitors' gaining ground on him with the sale of cultured pearls, for instance, he was known among his salesforce for never allowing a cultured pearl on the premises. And in the face of a dying trade, he insisted on continuing to offer apprenticeships within the Cartier workshops and went on funding the Jacques Cartier Memorial Award to encourage all craftsmen in the industry. He tried to boost sales by building brand awareness in England and farther afield. Plans included exhibiting in more fashion shows, a regular series of cocktail parties and exhibitions throughout the country (not simply in the London branch), and advertising in foreign glossy magazines so visitors to the United Kingdom would be reminded to stop by.

The sober reality was that however beautifully made the end product was, and however well it was marketed, it was very hard to make enough money from time-consuming unique creations at this time. Depressed high-end demand limited Cartier's pricing power, so, although margins were too low, Jean-Jacques couldn't increase prices without losing clients. Gone, sadly, were the days of the Indian maharajas shopping without regard for the cost or American heiresses bringing their fortunes to English dukes. The fundamentals of the luxury world were changing, and Cartier London was being left behind. The salesman Paul Vanson highlighted one aspect to this evolution: "My Cartier salesman's outfit was always a double-breasted black or dark suit tailored in Savile Row at Hawkes, the royal tailor; white shirt with stiff white collar collected and delivered every week

Jean-Jacques showing Princess Margaret and Lord Snowden a panther brooch.
Princess Margaret wears a diamond and ruby flower brooch and carries
a snakeskin Cartier bag (not pictured).

in special cardboard boxes at the staff entrance; a silk tie normally bought in Italy on my trips to Milan; slim handmade blade shoes from Church. . . . You can understand how it made me shudder to see . . . a young man in jeans walking into the boutique; someone told me he was the son of a duke, as if that made it all right!"

It was around this time, soon after creating a new collection of jewels intended to be elegant without being overly formal, that Jean-Jacques hired an external marketing agency to give feedback. The agency showed a mixed group of British consumers a booklet composed of unlabeled photographs of jewels from a variety of jewelers. When the consumers were asked to choose their favorite items, the results were disappointing. Not enough selected the Cartier items. It seemed that in an era of jeans and digital watches, understated elegance was no longer fashionable. "I blame the clientele," one old-school Cartier salesman was said to have remarked—"no taste anymore!" Jean-Jacques was disheartened. He was doing what he loved and had always done, but it was no longer working.

THE END OF THE FAMILY BUSINESS

At the start of 1972, Jean-Jacques heard that Cartier Paris had been sold again. This time the sale was more visible. Robert Hocq was a French entrepreneur who had been innovating in the field of gas cigarette lighters. His company, Silver Match, had become one of the leading lighter brands worldwide. Hocq had a vision for a luxury cigarette lighter and, having designed one, sought a prestigious name to endorse it. He had understood that "yesterday's luxury, ostentatiousness and the preserve of a privileged few, could no longer work. . . . It was necessary to combine luxury with functionality, up until now scorned by the coterie of great luxury houses."

After discussions with Van Cleef & Arpels apparently did not work out, Hocq approached Calmette at Cartier Paris and went on to market his lighter with the Cartier name (the firm was called Cartier Briquet S.A.). His Cartier-branded lighter saw rapid success, and, recognizing the larger potential, Hocq approached the Danziger brothers with an offer to buy Cartier Paris from them. He and his team saw that "although the prestige of the name remained unchanged," the House of Cartier was suffering "a crisis of succession and a crisis of adaptation, for decorative jewelry, objects beautiful for their own sake, had ceded to functional jewelry."

The Danzigers were open to the idea of a sale. Hocq, together with his business partner, Joseph Kanoui, put together a consortium (including an Italian hotel group, Sviluppo, and the French bank Paribas) to buy the business. By early 1972, the news of a buyout had made the papers. Reports in *Le Monde* and *L'Express* suggested that the Cartier Briquet company, with "its two hundred luxury outlets in France and its nine hundred points of sale in the world," would be responsible for managing the further diversification of Cartier into watches, pens, and lighters. They also noted that Cartier London was now the only Maison under family control.

Shortly after, during the summer of 1972, Nelly passed away. At the age of ninety, full of life and strong opinions right up until the end, she was the last of the older generation to go. Jean-Jacques, who had been particularly close to his mother, would miss her terribly. He may not have been able to work alongside his father, but for the twenty-seven years since he had taken over Jacques' mantle, his

mother had been there encouraging him in the background. In between his visits to see her in Switzerland, they had written to each
other regularly with updates on the family, daily life, and the business. She had seen Cartier London in its glory years, when Jacques
had found success by focusing on the same values that his son considered so important. She was one of the few who had understood why
Jean-Jacques had refused to compromise on quality, even if at the
expense of profitability.

The family traveled to France for Nelly's funeral and her burial in
Versailles. She was laid to rest in the same graveyard as her much-
adored Jacques, although not beside him. All her life, she had maintained her strong Protestant faith, and she was buried in the Protestant
Harjes vault, just around the corner from the Catholic Cartier one.
Here her name would be added to those of her parents, siblings, and
beloved daughter Dorothy, who had died some years earlier from
cancer.

After Nelly's death, events moved quickly. Hocq and Kanoui approached Jean-Jacques about buying Cartier London. Previously,
though Jean-Jacques had managed the London branch, Nelly held
the controlling interest. Now her estate was being divided among
numerous heirs. Jacques and Nelly's children, at retirement age themselves, had the opportunity for their capital to be released rather than
tied up. Jean-Jacques resisted for a while, but his siblings understandably wanted their share of the inheritance, and it was not easy to
continue building on his father's legacy without the support of his
mother.

To make matters worse, an oil crisis began in October 1973. Over
the course of six months, the price of a barrel of oil quadrupled as a
result of an embargo by the OPEC cartel, and the British economy
came under enormous stress. Within 175 New Bond Street, more clients seemed to be coming in to sell their jewels back than to buy new
ones. With profits for the firm uncertain, a difficult economic outlook, and pressure from his family, Jean-Jacques finally agreed to discuss the terms of a possible sale. It wasn't easy for him. But torn
between wanting to continue his ancestors' legacy and the fear that
in this market the company might not even survive, he felt lost. He
had tried to adapt, to appeal to a wider clientele, to open a boutique,
to travel overseas in search of pockets of wealth, to come up with in-

novative designs that would appeal to a more youthful client base. But the world had relentlessly moved on. New ideas were needed, and he worried that he wasn't the man for the job.

In the end, multiple factors convinced Jean-Jacques that he should sign the papers to end family ownership of Cartier. Among them was the possibility that all three branches might be reunited. Hocq and his investors already owned Cartier Paris, and he was talking of buying New York, too (which would happen a few years later). Even if it wasn't owned by the family, Jean-Jacques reasoned, Cartier would once again be one company. It was this point that the press focused on when the sale was announced in early 1974: "Cartier, the jewellers, are on the way to a reconciliation of the family interests," *The Times* reported, before quoting Jean-Jacques saying that negotiations had been completed for the restoration of "full cooperation" between the firms "in defence of Cartier's renown."

With a sale agreed, Jean-Jacques approached his employees. Almost three decades earlier, as a young, nervous, inexperienced manager, he had called them together to ask them all to give him their support in the business he was taking over. Now, at fifty-five, he had to explain why he was selling it. "We have always been a very happy community working together as a family business," he began, "but as events in the world around us have shown recently, it is now proving difficult, if not impossible, for family businesses to survive in this day and age, and I feel sure it will be greatly to your advantage to be working for a larger organization with considerable resources behind them." That speech was one of the hardest things he ever had to do. The craftsmen, stone experts, salesmen, and designers who worked for him were family. He felt a huge responsibility to them as much as to his father's memory, and he could see the disappointment on their faces.

Over the course of the following weeks messages of support and gifts poured in from those within the showroom and workshops. Jean-Jacques planned to retire. He knew the firm would need to change to survive, but it was too painful for him to watch that happen. Before he left, he made one more short speech. The staff had been, Jean-Jacques revealed, "a second family" to him. Incredibly moved by their kind words, he tried to express "the depth of my gratitude for all that you have been and all that you have made possible in the past."

It was the heartrending end to Cartier as a family firm. Jean-Jacques had held on as long as he felt he could. It had been more than a decade since Claude, now divorced and about to remarry, had sold the New York branch. It was almost eight years since Marion, now in her sixties, had decided to sell the Paris branch. Since then, Jean-Jacques had been flying the family flag alone. Perhaps, as a unified family, the Cartiers might have adapted to the changes sweeping through the luxury world, but apart and alone, they could not.

A LOST TRUNK

Two years after the sale of Cartier London, Jean-Jacques and Lydia moved to the South of France to begin their retirement. As he packed up the contents of their Dorking home into endless cases and boxes, Jean-Jacques felt terribly sad to be leaving the country he had called home for most of his life. Since selling the business, he had stayed in touch with many employees, some of whom would visit him and Lydia in France. He was, he promised them, "profoundly interested and concerned" in their future, and he missed the life they had shared in 175 New Bond Street.

But there was also a part of Jean-Jacques that was ready for a new chapter. It had been an incredibly trying period. Though he'd known that clinging to the ways of the past wasn't working, he couldn't help but feel disappointed by the way things had ended. It would be good to have a fresh focus. In his new French home, there was an enormous wasteland of a garden just waiting for his artistic eye to transform it into a magical paradise. For decades, he had been making flowers from gems; now he would turn his talents to the real thing. Over the following years, his sister Alice would visit him with suitcases full of seeds from England, and together they would plant a living work of art.

Over the following years, his grandchildren would visit him for long summer holidays and play happily in his colorful garden, mostly unaware of the full life he had led before becoming their grandfather.

Later, as they became older, he would sometimes talk to them of the past, dropping in entertaining family anecdotes over lunches on the sunny terrace. And as the jewels he and his ancestors had created were sold in record-breaking auctions, they would come to realize the importance of the legacy their modest grandfather and his ancestors had left behind. Though the business was no longer in the family, there was continuity through their creations. And the pieces they had brought to life would live on to tell their own unique story as they passed through new generations of owners.

Back in Dorking in 1974, among the many cases and boxes that were piled into the moving truck bound for France, there was one rather worn black trunk with brown leather straps. On its side were travel stickers from another era that hinted at an exciting life. But inside, hidden from view, was the real treasure. There, ordered into neat piles of letters, was a whole world of experiences and emotions, just lying in wait.

On arrival at his new home in France, when the furniture was arranged into the rooms, clothes unpacked into wardrobes, and paintings hung on the walls, this trunk would end up in a corner of the wine cellar, covered with more boxes. Later, once he was settled in his new home, Jean-Jacques would look for it, and, being unable to find it, would assume sadly that it had been one of the many items lost during the move from England. There, in a dusty corner of the wine cellar, the trunk would wait for more than three decades. Until one day, exactly ninety years after the birth of Jean-Jacques in Saint-Jean-de-Luz, his granddaughter would be searching for a bottle of champagne with which to celebrate his birthday. Spying a battered box in the shadows of the cellar, she would be overcome with curiosity. And a whole new journey would begin.

AFTERWORD

We shall not cease from exploration
And the end of all our exploring
Will be to arrive where we started
And know the place for the first time.
Through the unknown, remembered gate

—T. S. ELIOT,
"Little Gidding"

In most languages, there's a saying about the struggles of family firms through generational change. Whether it's "Shirtsleeves to shirtsleeves in three generations" in America or the musical-sounding *"Dalle stelle, alle stalle"* (from the stars to the stables) in Italy, the idea is the same. Success tends to contain the seeds of its own destruction. A Harvard study found that 70 percent of family-owned businesses either fail or are sold before the second generation takes over. Only one in ten remains an active privately held company for a third generation to lead. Cartier was unusual in enduring to the fourth generation as a family firm. But whereas three close brothers with complementary talents could survive the storms life threw at them, from a huge global conflict to a great depression, the cousins, lacking the same bond and shared upbringing, found the challenges of the postwar world overwhelming.

My grandfather was deeply upset after the sale. There was a sense of having let the family down. Of course, Cartier continued as a business after the Cartiers, and the firm would go on under new ownership to achieve more global success. For Jean-Jacques, however, perhaps not unlike the owners of stately houses who are forced to sell what has been their home for generations, there was a feeling of regret. For many years, he wouldn't talk about his past. It was too raw. I was born just a few years after Cartier London was sold, and growing up, the fact that the jewelry firm had been in our family was something we barely discussed and certainly always kept to ourselves. I knew that my grandfather was Jean-Jacques Cartier and that he had played a role in the firm's history, but to us he was just Grandpa, happiest around family and in his garden.

Finding the trunk of letters and recording my grandfather's memoirs opened up a long-closed window into the past. It was difficult for him at first, for he had been submerged in a kind of private grief after leaving the business. But once he started remembering farther back in time, those old wounds seemed to heal. As he talked about his father's trips to India or his uncle's creative vision or his grandfather's talent for buying gemstones, he rediscovered a sense of pride in what his family had achieved. Later he would thank me for pushing him to look back, grateful that his memories would be preserved so that these people he had so admired would not be forgotten.

I started this journey just wanting to record and capture some of the anecdotes my grandfather shared over the lunch table. An unexpected consequence was that I became closer to him than ever. But also, as I dug deeper and the history grew larger, I realized that the story of a family is about much more than just one family. For more than a decade, I have tried to meet or speak to the descendants of those my ancestors knew, because every story has multiple sides, and human memory is subjective. The variety of insights I have gathered have, I hope, made *The Cartiers* a more complete account of the past. But more than that, realizing how the family firm was, for so many, an extended family has been unexpectedly moving. An enduring bond remains, strong enough to transcend generations. As far afield as Sri Lanka, India, Paris, and New York, there are those who have, without question, invited me into their homes, treating me as one of their own. As photographs have been brought out, little red boxes opened, precious letters unfolded, and sketchbooks pored over, a feeling of a shared past has developed, a sense that our ancestors worked together to achieve something wonderful and that we have to play our small part by keeping that memory alive.

My journey back in time is one that encompasses many places and people, and I am grateful to all those who have added their own precious pieces to the enormous jigsaw puzzle of the past. With each new conversation, the history grows more colorful, and I suspect, and hope, that I will be adding to it for the rest of my life. For I have found that what I thought might be the end is actually another beginning. And never more so than in one place, not far from where it all started, where I was struck with an overwhelming sense of coming full circle.

About twenty kilometers from where Louis-François founded his first workshop, to the west of Paris on a road leading out of Versailles, next to a funeral parlor and just around the corner from the train station, is the Cimetière des Gonards. It's easy to walk past the entrance without seeing it. There are no obvious signs, just a little cross above a rectangular stone arch. Inside, however, the vast graveyard sprawls around corners farther than the eye can see, stretching over thirty-two acres and holding more than twelve thousand graves of multiple faiths. The upper part is laid out with walkways and planted with trees, but it is in the more crowded lower section, right in the northeast corner, where one large crypt stands proudly alone. Neoclassical in pale gray stone, it is more of a chapel, really, imposing and beautiful with stained-glass windows only vaguely visible from the outside behind dark iron grilles. Up high in the center, surrounded by stone swags and wreaths, is an inscription in block capitals that reads simply FAMILLE CARTIER.

To the left there is a rusty gate, behind which wildflowers compete with long grass in a small garden. And through here, on the side of the crypt that looks out to the fields beyond, is the tall, elegant wrought-iron entrance. Far away from the glamour and the celebrities and the window-shoppers, this is a very different door into the past. This is the resting place of my ancestors.

Inside, the vibrant stained-glass windows, designed by Marion Cartier, depict Saint Louis, Saint Pierre, and Saint Jacques. Facing the door, a large stone basin holds holy water under a cross. And leaning on the basin are the three small stone plaques that were dedicated to Alfred on his death from the three Maisons, in Paris, London, and New York. Each one is decorated with the same motif of a fern, the symbol of sincerity that, when it was made in diamonds and platinum at the turn of the twentieth century, helped to mark the emergence of the Cartier style. Louis, along with the distinguished architect Walter-André Destailleur, designed the chapel in 1927, two years after the death of his father, and his heightened aesthetic sense is visible in every detail. In this place of reflection, everything, from the eighteenth-century-style garlands and swags on the front of the building to the calming symmetry of the interior and the large, elegant marble plaques that bear the names of those inside, has been conceived to stay true to the Cartiers' relentless drive for beauty, timelessness, and high craftsmanship.

On each side of the chapel are stairs leading down to the crypt below. Here, in the central area, are eighteen stone plaques. Not all are inscribed, but those that are bear the name and dates of the Cartier who lies in the coffin behind. A decade of research had taught me untold facts about my family, things they probably didn't even know about one another, but it wasn't until I arrived here that I felt a true jolt of connection with them. There were times when my exploration into the past had seemed like a race, with mad dashes across oceans to meet those connected with the times of old before it was too late. But down in that cool, dark room, surrounded by a deep peace, time stood still for a while.

I left the crypt different from before. The story I was telling felt more like mine to tell. Yes, I was collating the stories of others, but on that day, two hundred years after the birth of my great-great-great-grandfather, I felt closer to understanding the family's legacy. To the outside world, the Cartiers helped to redefine the shape of luxury. They took a local business onto an international stage in an era before globalization, and today the iconic pieces they created are coveted the world over.

But as I stood in their final resting place in that green corner of Versailles, I was struck by another aspect of the Cartiers' legacy. Not just the exceptional jewels they created, or the luxurious showrooms they opened, but the values they passed down and the strong bonds that they instilled. For though the world today is very different from the one they inhabited, their philosophy remains profoundly relevant. Underpinning their life's work was a focus on taking care, in both senses of the phrase. "Be very kind," Louis-François had written to his son, and over generations, this respect for others would play its part in building not just a loyal client base but also a devoted team of employees. Young apprentices would go on to dedicate the rest of their working lives to the firm. They were looked after, and in turn they cared themselves. And this is the other part of the taking-care mindset: a resolute belief that "the best is good enough," that there is no point cutting corners for it is worth taking years to learn a skill, and months to fashion a single piece, in order to create something truly exceptional. A conviction that every item, from the smallest tie pin to the most extravagant mystery clock, deserves the attention and care of expert craftsmen trained in their discipline and aspiring to perfection. And, finally, an unshakable faith in originality, an understanding of the subtle balance between taking inspiration from the old and relentlessly innovating for the future: "Never copy, only create."

ACKNOWLEDGMENTS

Researching this book has brought numerous people into my life, and I am indebted to many of them. This list is not conclusive, not least because there are those who wish to remain anonymous, but I am hugely grateful to the following:

Those I have been fortunate enough to meet who worked at Cartier when it was still under family ownership: especially the late Joe Allgood, along with his daughter Suzanne, Glenn Chapman, Alfred Durante, the late Dennis Gardner and his lovely wife Mimi, David McCarty, Albert Middlemiss, and Elizabeth Trillos for so generously sharing their own stories in order that I may gain a more complete— and very human—picture of the past.

The descendants of multiple former Cartier employees, including: Felix and Charles Bertrand, Roger Chalopin, George Charity, Paul Cheyrouze, Maurice Daudier, Andre Denet, Louis Devaux, Rupert Emmerson, Leon Farines, Arthur and Donald Fraser, Alexandre Genaille, Jules Glaenzer, Joseph Hartnett, Jack Hasey, Charles Jacqueau, Henri Larrieu, Paul Marchand, Jean Mayeur, Gerald Mayo, Frederick Mew, Paul Muffat, Clifford North, Douglas Poulton, Georges Remy, Maurice Richard, Jeanne Toussaint, and Paul Vanson for offering their recollections, passed-down stories, and precious correspondence. With special thanks to Catherine, Colin, Dany, Fanny,

Gillian, Kate, Laurent, Mark, Martin, Michel, Ruth, Veronique, Wendy, Yves, and Yvette.

The descendants of the gem dealers with whom my ancestors worked, including Talal Mattar, Fawzi Ahmed Kanoo, Reza Macar, Siddharth Kasliwal, and Ralph Esmerian for their perspectives. Also the families of my great-grandfather's Indian clients, including: from Baroda, H.H. Maharaja Samarjitsinghrao Gaekwad, H.H. Maharani Radhika Raje Gaekwad, and H.H. Rajmata Sahiba Shubhangini Raje Gaekwad; from Patiala, Raja Randhir and Rani Sahiba Vinita Singh, and Yuvraj Sahib Raninder Singh; and from Kapurthala, Brigadier H.H. Sukhjit Singh, for graciously welcoming me into their homes and opening my eyes to the wonders of a country that Jacques held so dear.

I am conscious that in writing this book, I tread on territory common to other members in my extended family, and I have tried to be mindful of this while remaining true to my grandfather's memories. I am especially grateful to Princess Esmeralda of Belgium, Alain Cartier, Nelly Cartier, Jean Dousset, Gabriel de Kasa-Hunyady, Henri Krainik, Jean-Philippe Lemoine, Lee Rumsey, Matt Tee, Jean-Philippe Worth, and Olivia Worth for helping me see new sides to the family story.

Having started this project without a jewelry history background, I sought out the expert opinions of others, and I owe a debt of gratitude to those who offered their time, knowledge, introductions and material in order that I might better place my family story in context. Chief among them is Diana Scarisbrick, whose encyclopedic grasp of history and extraordinary gift for summoning at will the most enlightening fact, anecdote, or quote has been a constant source of inspiration. I have loved our sessions delving into lives past and half-forgotten times, and I thank her for her wisdom, encouragement, and unwavering support, even when she was so busy herself. Special mention must also be made to Usha Balakrishnan, Stephen Bartley, David Beasley, Viren Bhagat, Michèle Bimbenet-Privat, Rene Brus, Humphrey Butler, Martin Chapman, Stephen Clarke, James Danziger, Richard Edgecumbe, Angel Elechiguerra, Harry Fane, Marion Fasel, Adhil Fouz, Cynthia Meera Frederick, Jean Ghika, James de Givenchy, Geoffrey Good, Caroline de Guitaut, Joanna Hardy, Jan Havlik, Amin Jaffer, Sophia Kai, Clive Kandall, Claire Martin, Kieran McCarthy, Dennis Meyers, Geoffrey Munn, Estelle Nikles, Jonathan, Francis, and Nicolas Norton, Stefano Papi, Matthew Pizzulli, Alex Popov, Jeffrey Post, Gaelle Rio,

Justin Roberts, Judy Rudoe, Richa Goyal Sikri, Richard Spicer, Kristian Spofforth, Sue Stronge, Karen Stone Talwar, Simon Teakle, Graeme Thompson, Christophe Vachaudez, Minal Vazirani, David Warren, Margaret Young-Sanchez, Adam Zebrak, Wilfried Zeisler, and John Zubrzycki, who have all contributed in their own way: by adding pieces to the puzzle of the past, pointing out new avenues to pursue, shedding light on the wider context, or bringing the detail to life.

To Her Majesty the Queen for the use of images from her private collection. Also to His Highness Sheikh Hamad bin Abdullah Al Thani, to the auction houses Bonhams, Christie's, and Sotheby's, and to the many professionals and private collectors who have generously shared images and information about their jewels. I also owe thanks to the knowledgeable individuals in the following organizations who helped me mine their archives and libraries for illuminating details. In England: the British Library, the Goldsmiths Company, the National Art Library, and the Royal Collection; in France, the Archives de Paris, Bibliotheque Forney, Bibliotheque Nationale de France, Ecole Stanislas, the Louvre, Le Petit Palais; in Monaco, the Audiovisual Institute for images from the Prince's Palace of Monaco. In America: the Benson Ford Research Center, the Colony Club, the Everglades Club, the Franklin D. Roosevelt Presidential Library, the Harry S. Truman Presidential Library, the Library of Congress, the New York City Municipal Archives, the New York Public Library, the New York State Archives, and the libraries of Harvard, Yale, and Stanford universities; and further afield: the Russian State Archives, the Budapest Metropolitan Archives, and the Cotroceni National Museum in Romania. I am especially grateful to Father Biondi, Bridget Fletcher, and John Waide at St. Louis University for their invaluable help navigating the fascinating Marion Cartier archives and for making me and my family so welcome during our stay there. More thanks must go to those who have helped out with research, especially Joan, Jasmine, Kirill, Laurence, Liz, Pam, and Sylvain, and to Sophie for her read-throughs.

The scope of this book is limited to the period of the firm under family ownership but the fact that Cartier remains a name revered today is due to many, many employees, both past and present. Of those who have played a part in keeping the history alive, I thank Michel Aliaga and Bernhard Berger for their time. It would also be remiss of me not to acknowledge the late Hans Nadelhoffer, whose definitive Cartier book, written in the 1980s, is an extraordinary work of scholarship, the scope of which continually amazes me.

I had no idea when I started out what a vast amount of work happens behind the scenes to bring a book into existence. This one would not have been possible without the fantastic team at Penguin Random House. In particular, I am grateful to my editor, Pamela Cannon, at Ballantine for believing in this project as I saw it: a human story across four generations with its inevitable highs and lows. I thank her for never pushing me to prioritize the glamour ahead of the story and its characters, for admirably coping with my many manuscript changes, for always being available, and for her incisive edits and suggestions. Special thanks also to Lexi Batsides, Nancy Delia, Jo Anne Metsch, and Robbin Schiff. Also to Carol Poticny for her brilliant help with sourcing images. And, of course, to my agent, Grainne Fox, for guiding me through what was a very unfamiliar process with clarity, humor, and a colossal amount of patience. She miraculously knew exactly when to step in and when to leave me to it. I couldn't imagine anyone I would rather have championing my cause.

Finally, it goes without saying that this labor of love would not have been possible without the recollections and blessing of my late grandfather, Jean-Jacques Cartier, but it was the kindness and encouragement of my close family and friends that sustained me through the last year of all-consuming writing. I am especially grateful to my other grandfather, Gordon Stevens, a brilliant historian and businessman who always made the time to talk, even when he was nearing the end, and whose thoughtful perspective on the past has made this a more informed book. I am also enormously thankful to my mother, father, and siblings for whole-heartedly supporting this project from the outset and for coming to the rescue on numerous occasions; to my in-laws, Claire and Andrew, for putting their lives on hold to host the perfect New Zealand writing retreat, and to my children for their pushed-to-the-limit patience. But most of all, I am indebted to my husband, for his enthusiasm and understanding. Not only has he been on hand when combining motherhood with publishing deadlines all got to be too much, but he has also been the best sounding board I could have wished for. This book would not have been finished on time without him, and it certainly wouldn't have been half as much fun. For that, and a million other things, I thank him.

TIMELINE

This is a timeline of events that are important to the Cartier family or that feature in this book.

- 1819—Birth of Louis-François Cartier

- 1847—Foundation of Cartier; Louis-François Cartier buys Rue Montorgueil workshop; first maker's mark registered

- 1848—Year of European revolutions

- 1853—Cartier moves to 5 Rue Neuve-des-Petits-Champs

- 1859—Cartier buys Gillion and moves to 9 Boulevard des Italiens

- 1867—"Eureka" diamond discovered in South Africa, leading to the rapid growth of the diamond industry

- 1870–71—Siege of Paris; Louis-François flees to the Basque region; Alfred travels to London to sell jewels

- 1873—Alfred Cartier takes over the business from his father

- 1875–84—Birth of the three Cartier brothers: Louis (1875), Pierre (1878), and Jacques (1884)

- 1898—Alfred goes into partnership with Louis as Cartier et Fils (Cartier and Son); Louis marries Andrée-Caroline Worth

- 1899—Cartier moves from Boulevard des Italiens to 13 Rue de la Paix; early emergence of the "Cartier style"

- 1902—Cartier showroom opens in London at 4 New Burlington Street; coronation of King Edward VII

- 1903—Pierre visits America for the first time

- 1904—King Edward VII grants Cartier a royal warrant; Pierre visits Russia for the first time; death of Louis-François Cartier

- 1906—Cartier Frères established; Jacques joins the firm and takes over London showroom from Pierre

- 1908—Pierre marries Elma Rumsey

- 1909—Cartier branch opens in New York (712 Fifth Avenue); Cartier London moves to 175–176 New Bond Street; the designer Charles Jacqueau joins Cartier Paris; Louis divorces Andrée-Caroline

- 1910—Ballets Russes performance of *Scheherazade;* Louis travels to Russia and displays Cartier's wares at Grand Duchess Vladimir's Christmas bazaar

- 1911—Exhibition of nineteen tiaras at Cartier London in advance of the coronation of George V; Jacques' first visit to India; Cartier's first wristwatch for men, the Santos, available to the public

- 1912—Jacques investigates the pearl trade in the Persian Gulf; Cartier Paris expands to include number 11 Rue de la Paix; Jacques marries Nelly Harjes

- 1913—Launch of the first mystery clock; Jacques admitted to Cartier Frères

- 1914—Outbreak of World War I; all three brothers return to France

- 1915—Pierre and Elma return to America

- 1916—Pierre exchanges a pearl necklace for 653 Fifth Avenue; Cartier moves in the following year

- 1917—Russian Revolution

- 1919—Cartier Ltd. set up as a separate company in London; Cartier Inc. set up in New York; launch of the Tank watch; postwar fashions inspire more modern Art Deco jewels, vanity cases, and cigarette cases. Cartier exhibition in San Sebastián, Spain

- 1920—Louis serves as expert in Princess Lobanov Rostovsky's auction and purchases Tsar Nicholas I pearl necklace

- 1921—Incorporation of Cartier S.A. (Paris)

- 1922—First of the figurine mystery clocks created in Paris; discovery of Tutankhamen's tomb inspires Cartier's Egyptian jewels

- 1923—Department S (Silver) launched in Cartier Paris; seasonal store first opened in Palm Beach

- 1924—Louis marries Jacqueline Almásy; Cartier Paris creates trinity ring and bracelet; Jacques and family move to England from America; Cartier New York acquires Thiers pearls

- 1925—Cartier exhibits 150 pieces in the landmark Art Deco show in Paris; death of Alfred Cartier

- 1926—Jacques visits Ceylon (now Sri Lanka) for the first time

- 1928—Cartier Paris displays the remounted Maharaja of Patiala jewels

- 1929—Cartier seasonal showroom opened in St. Moritz; Jacques travels to Cairo for French Exposition; Wall Street Crash

- 1931—Cartier exhibits at the Colonial Exposition; creates first *académicien's* sword

- 1933—Marion Cartier marries Pierre Claudel

- 1935—Cartier seasonal showroom opened in Monte Carlo

- 1936—Collier Hindou commissioned by Daisy Fellowes marks pinnacle of Cartier's Tutti Frutti jewels; Romanov emeralds sold to Barbara Hutton; Edward, Prince of Wales, buys emerald engagement ring for Wallis Simpson

- 1937—Coronation of King George VI after abdication of Edward VIII

- 1938—Cartier seasonal showroom opened in Cannes

- 1939—Cartier exhibits at the World's Fair in New York; outbreak of World War II

- 1940—Louis Cartier moves to America

- 1941—Death of Jacques Cartier in Dax, France

- 1942—Death of Louis Cartier in New York

- 1943—Jean-Jacques Cartier marries Lydia Baels

- 1945—Jean-Jacques returns to England after the war and takes over Cartier London

- 1948—The Duke of Windsor commissions the first three-dimensional panther jewel for his wife

- 1948–49—Claude and Pierre exchange stores (New York for Paris); Claude becomes president of Cartier New York, Pierre Claudel becomes president of Cartier Paris

- 1953—Coronation of Queen Elizabeth II; Cartier London opens Albemarle Street boutique; Claude Cartier opens a store in Venezuela

- 1955—Creation of Jean Cocteau's *académicien* sword for his election to the Académie Française

- 1956—Claude Cartier marries Rita Salmona

- 1962—Sale of Cartier New York by Claude Cartier to a consortium led by Edward Goldstein

- 1963—The first of seventeen Wilding boxes is produced by Cartier London

- 1964—Death of Pierre Cartier in Switzerland

- 1966—Sale of Cartier Paris by Marion Cartier to the Danziger brothers

- 1967—Launch of the Crash watch by Cartier London

- 1969–71—Cartier Paris opens stores in Munich, Hong Kong, and Geneva; Robert Kenmore buys the Cartier Diamond and sells it to Richard Burton and Elizabeth Taylor

- 1972—Cartier Paris sold to a consortium led by Robert Hocq and Joseph Kanoui

- 1974—Sale of Cartier London by Jean-Jacques Cartier to Robert Hocq / Cartier Paris consortium

- 1979—Cartier Monde unites Cartier Paris, London, and New York

For a more detailed jewelry-focused timeline, see Nadelhoffer, page 343.

AUTHOR'S NOTE

Writing this book has taken far longer than I expected. Wanting to tell a complete story, I dove into a sea of sources only to discover that the more I learned, the more there was to find out. In some cases, the findings I had taken for granted early on were contradicted by later research, which then required burrowing down new rabbit holes in an effort to work out where the pockets of truth were hidden. As a result, the story as I know it now is not the same one that I thought I knew ten, five, or even two years ago. Sharing my family's perfectionist streak, this realization was frustrating at first—I had set out to unearth the real story but with each new finding, the ground of history kept shifting.

In the end, it was the people who have shown such interest—family, friends, experts, those who came to my lectures, those who contacted me via my website or on social media and kindly asked when the book would be out—who made me see the choice before me: to keep working for a likely impossible level of certainty, or to share the history as I understood it as of now. The reality is that my research is not over, but I have come to see the story's continuous evolution as something to be embraced, and in fact, one of my hopes is that this book will reach those who can add their own insights to the history.

And so I started writing, accepting the error and shortcoming that Theodore Roosevelt warned was inevitable when moving from the sidelines into the arena. Of course, it was my ancestors who were truly the ones in the arena, who, graced with great talents but not immune to human flaws, strove to reach the "triumph of high achievement." I just hope that this account will keep their memories alive, or better still, convey a fraction of the wonder I felt as I listened to my late grandfather bring to life the highs and lows of a very different time.

NOTES

These notes focus on published works. Unless otherwise stated, the letters or diaries I have referenced are from my archives, the archives of other Cartier family members, or the archives of former Cartier employees, kindly shared with me by their families.

Although most of the people who played key roles in the history of the Cartiers have passed away, some are still living. The fact that I've not mentioned them is not to ignore their contribution, but out of respect for their privacy. Similarly, reflecting my grandfather's wishes, I have not discussed any living clients, with the respectful exception of the royal family.

For expanded versions of some notes, please refer to my website: the -cartiers.com.

Introduction

xix   **his work at Cartier:** In English, many names have been used to refer to the Cartier family business, including Cartier's, Cartier Brothers, Messrs Cartier, Messrs Cartier's, Messrs A. Cartier, A. Cartier & Son, and simply Cartier. Of all of them, the most common firm name when it was under family ownership was probably Cartier's or Cartier. For simplicity, this book generally uses the name Cartier throughout.

Chapter 1: Father and Son: Louis-François and Alfred

3   **Maharajas & Mughal Magnificence:** This auction took place on June 19, 2019, at Christie's New York, Rockefeller Center (see in particular lots 224, 225, 227, 228, 271, 272, 274, 277, 383, and 388).

5   **as the eldest son:** Louis-François Cartier was born May 31, 1819, on Rue des Juifs in the Marais. He was the second of five children, and the eldest boy.

5   **Monsieur Bernard Picard:** Although it has been written that Louis-François was Adolphe Picard's apprentice, Picard's was a father-son business, led by Bernard Picard (b. 1800). His son, Adolphe (b. 1825, six years younger than Louis-François), formally joined his father in partnership in 1853 and later broke off on his own.

5   **31 Rue Montorgueil:** By 1831, Picard had moved to Rue Montorgueil from Rue de la Tabletterie (where he had been living since at least 1822). Only from 1834 was he listed as a *fabricant* (a maker of jewels) in the Didot-Bottin Paris Trade Almanac (*Annuaire-almanach du commerce*).

5   **"no pupil has ever learnt without one":** Franz Birbaum was the Swiss-born chief designer of Fabergé. In his memoirs (discovered in 1990), he told the story of an elderly craftsman delivering a set of jeweler's tools to a Grand Duke customer. When asked why it contained a leather strap, the old man explained, "Your Highness, it is the first and most important instrument. No pupil has ever learnt without one." See Geza von Habsburg and M. Lopato, *Fabergé: Imperial Jeweller* (London: Thames & Hudson, 1994), pp. 444–460 (Birbaum Memoirs: introduction and notes by Marina Lopato).

5   **when he'd been captured by Wellington's army:** Hans Nadelhoffer, *Cartier: Jewellers Extraordinary* (London: Thames & Hudson, 2007), p. 13. The story of Pierre Cartier's capture while fighting in the Siege of Zaragoza in Spain is also told in the Cartier centenary book *Cartier 1847–1947*. A review of British military records suggest that Pierre may have been captured later during the siege of Ciudad Rodrigo in early 1812 and held on the *San Damaso* prison hulk in Portsmouth Harbor. The elder Cartier was later awarded the Médaille de Sainte-Hélène during the Second Empire to recognize his participation in the campaigns led by Emperor Napoleon I.

6   **found work as a metalworker:** Pierre referred to himself on his marriage certificate, and on the birth certificates of his children, as a metalworker (*tourneur en métaux*). Multiple books, including the 1947 Cartier centenary book *Cartier 1847–1947* (Paris: Société d'Étude, 1947), suggest that Pierre was a powder horn manufacturer, but no source is given.

6   **their master's *poinçon*:** Bernard Picard registered his maker's mark in 1825.

7   **fashionable Palais-Royal part of town:** At 29 Rue de Richelieu, Picard set up as a *bijoutier en résidence* (a jeweler retailing from home) before later opening a showroom.

7   **Louis-François designed a simple lozenge shape:** Arminjon, Beaupuis, and Billimoff, *Dictionnaire des poinçons de fabricants d'ouvrages d'or et d'argent de Paris et de la Seine 1838–1875* (Paris: Imprimerie Nationale, 1991, record 02834).

7   **"successor to M. Picard":** Cartier is listed at 31 and 29 Rue Montorgueil in the 1847–1853 entries for Didot-Bottin. Number 31 later became number 29: see Jeanne Pronteau, *Les numérotages des maisons de Paris du XVᵉ siècle à nos jours* (Paris: Ville de Paris, 1966), p. 36.

8   **(including the royal jeweler, Fossin):** In 1847 alone, Fossin's records show no fewer than nineteen items bought from Cartier. But as well as buying from Cartier, Fossin also supplied Cartier (Louis-François bought a Byzantine bracelet from him in 1853); see Nadelhoffer, *Cartier,* p. 17. For a history of Fossin in the period (at 62 and 78 Rue de Richelieu, not far from Picard), see Henri Vever, *La bijouterie française au XIXᵉ siècle 1800–1900* (Paris: H. Floury, Libraire-Éditeur, 1906), vol. II, pp. 182–184.

8   **the disturbances continued:** In 1849, Louis-François' younger brother, then an assistant to a Parisian notary, narrowly avoided being shot, while his boss was shot in his hat.

10   **From his new second-floor showroom:** In this book, American conventions are used consistently for references to floor level, "first floor" being synonymous with "ground floor," "second floor" being the first level above the ground floor, and so on.

10   **Silver tea sets:** Franco Cologni and Ettore Mocchetti, *Made by Cartier: 150 Years of Tradition and Innovation* (New York: Abbeville Press, 1993), p. 21. See also Nadelhoffer, *Cartier,* pp. 13–19; both works give examples of the early output of Cartier.

10 **"Through the chapel, Sire"**: Jane Stoddart, *The Life of the Empress Eugénie* (New York: E. P. Dutton, 1906), p. 40.

11 **"mingled their pure loveliness"**: Ibid., p. 63, and *Every Woman's Encyclopaedia* (London: s.n., 1912).

11 **a select few jewelers**: Mellerio, Lemmonier, and Ouizille-Lemoine; see Germain Bapst, *Histoire des joyaux de la couronne de France* (Paris: Librairie Hachette, 1899), p. 654.

12 **new role as a retailer**: Jean-Jacques Cartier believed that his great-grandfather (Louis-François) was primarily a retailer. However, see also Judy Rudoe, "Cartier in the Nineteenth Century," *Jewellery Studies* 9 (2001), pp. 29–50, which indicates that the firm bought gold and silver from Lyon Alemand in the 1850s, so it may be that Louis-François was still manufacturing some items and/or undertaking repair work.

12 **Over the next three years**: Nadelhoffer, *Cartier,* p. 13, gives details of the Comtesse de Nieuwerkerke's purchases.

12 **"inspired by an old jewel"**: This account appears in the 1947 Cartier centenary book *Cartier 1847–1947,* but the apparent triangular relationship between Princesse Mathilde, the Countess, and her husband perhaps strains credulity.

12 **"Had it not been for the great Napoleon"**: Jean-Philippe Worth, *A Century of Fashion,* p. 98.

12 **After a short-lived and stormy marriage**: The Demidoffs owned extensive platinum mines in the Ural mountains of Russia. (This is where Jean-Jacques recalled his father saying that Cartier sourced much of its platinum.) For background, see "The Demidoffs and the Mining Industry of the Ural," author not stated, *Practical Magazine,* vol. 1, no. 6, pp. 406–9 (1873).

13 **"the home and centre of Parisian"**: Princess Caroline Murat, *My Memoirs* (New York: G. P. Putnam's Sons, 1910), pp. 70–71.

13 **"le plus beau décolleté d'Europe"**: Robert Burnand, *La vie quotidienne en France de 1870 à 1900* (Paris: Librairie Hachette, 1947), p. 30.

13 **There would also be**: Nadelhoffer, *Cartier,* p. 14, and François Chaille, *Cartier Creative Writing* (Paris: Flammarion, 2000), p. 36.

13 **those bought by the Count**: Such as an imperial eagle in 1857, per Nadelhoffer, *Cartier,* p. 14.

14 **Fellow students included other jewelers**: Vever, *La bijouterie française,* p. 252. They included Robin, Nattan, and Pourée (later a supplier to Cartier).

15 **8,500 francs a year**: Currency translations have been done using the Measuring Worth.com website for U.S. dollar translations over time, and using the Historical Statistics.org website for foreign currency translations into U.S. dollars (e.g., French francs).

15 **amounted to 40,000 francs**: "Cartier in the Nineteenth Century," p. 32, citing account books. Cartier family records suggest that the entire cost of the Gillion transaction was higher (65,000 francs). This may have included deferred consideration and/or prepaid rent.

15 **"There are also these sumptuous dishes"**: "La Mode," *Bulletin des modes,* 1846.

16 **"a talent of undeniable supremacy"**: Dargaud et Palouzié, eds., *Le Cocher, Journal des Annonces* (September 1846).

17 **"on a scale worthy"**: Jacques Cartier, "Modern Jewellery," *Encyclopaedia Britannica* (14th edition, London, 1929), vol. 13, pp. 34–35.

17 **"The Empress had a beautiful ballroom"**: Princess Pauline Metternich, *My Years in Paris* (London: Eveleigh Nash & Grayson, 1922), p. 136.

18 **Chambre Syndicale**: The Union was set up in 1864; two years later, Louis-François was the group's secretary. By the late 1860s, Louis-François' place in the Parisian jewelry world was established enough that he was called on as an expert in important auctions.

19 **"Mr. Cartier Gillion"**: *Le Siècle,* September 20, 1864.

19 **"It is a double fortune"**: *L'Artiste: Journal de la littérature* (1864, vol. 2), p. 136.

20 **Was successful in his own right**: Prosper worked in, and jointly owned with Louis-Victor Robert, a shop on Rue Lafayette selling *nouveautés* (novelties) and women's clothing.

21 **Notable Commerçant:** Didot Bottin, 1870 entry, Annuaire de Commerce (Commercial Register of Paris). It is interesting to contrast the generally short and sparse Didot-Bottin directory listings for Cartier during the late nineteenth century with the more extensive entries of Boucheron, or even Bourdier, who appears more prestigious, even as late as 1902.

23 **"Business for France is everywhere":** *Times* of London, 1870, edition 12, cited in the *Journal of the Society of Arts*, April 5, 1872 (Royal Society of Arts).

23 **"Anyone would think":** Ludovic Pissarro, *Camille Pissarro: Son art—son œuvre* (San Francisco: Alan Wofsy, 1989), p. 24, citing 1871 letter from Duret to Pissarro.

23 **"to watch the Prussians parading":** Nadelhoffer, *Cartier*, p. 50, citing Louis-François Cartier.

24 **"with the grave and imposing bearing":** Katie Hickman, *Courtesans* (London: Harper Perennial, 2003), p. 2, citing Comte de Maugny.

24 **"*Je souis [sic] le Vénus de Milo*":** Frédéric Loliée, *La fête impériale: Les femmes du Second Empire* (Paris: Félix Juven, 1907), p. 240.

25 **"What, did you not tell me":** Loliée, *La fête impériale*, p. 259.

25 **Relieved, the future king:** John Van der Kiste, *Alfred: Queen Victoria's Second Son* (Stroud, Gloucestershire, UK: Fonthill Media, 2014), chapter 6.

26 **Lord and Lady Dudley:** Lord Dudley, who lived in Dudley House on Park Lane, was already a client by 1869, when Louis-François was making him a ring. See Lord Dudley obituary, *Times* (London), May 1885, and Lady Dudley obituary, *Times* (London), February 1929.

27 **"And I, ladies, am sleeping":** Loliée, *La fête impériale*, p. 240. See also Nadelhoffer, *Cartier*, pp. 15, 120, and 330.

27 **"Prosper is drawing in the sales ledger":** Nadelhoffer, *Cartier*, p. 330, citing Louis-François Cartier writing to his son, Alfred, dated August 25, 1873, referring to his son-in-law, Prosper.

28 **And not forgetting his lucky escape:** Sale transfer deed between Louis-François Cartier and Alfred Cartier. Family records show that, in descending order of value, the stock Alfred bought consisted of rings, earrings, brooches, miscellaneous stones, bracelets, goldwork and silverware, necklaces, lockets, miscellaneous jewels, chains, and pins.

29 **In 1872, it had been valued:** This was according to the Bourdier-Griffeuille marriage contract. It's not clear whether this amount included stock. If not, it was more than six times the value. Excluding stock, Cartier was valued at 45,000 francs in 1873 (even if it was for an intrafamily transfer, for which the valuation may have been lower).

30 **"footman, powdered concierge, imposing staircase":** Émile Zola, "Quartier Haussmann et rue de Prony," in *Carnet d'enquêtes. Une ethnographie inédite de la France* (Paris: Librairie Plon, 1986), p. 311.

31 **"inspiration and taste":** Jacques Cartier, "Modern Jewellery," p. 34.

31 **Cartier saw profits of just 39,200 francs:** Nadelhoffer, *Cartier*, p. 15. Liquid capital in 1875 was only 186,630 francs (it would grow to 500,000 by 1890).

31 **favored couture over jewels:** Nadelhoffer, *Cartier*, p. 50, citing a letter from Louis-François Cartier. Louis-François had written that "dress is becoming more magnificent by the day; on the beach at Étretat at eight o'clock this morning, women from the demimonde spread out more silk, satin, and lace than a queen herself would need for her entire trousseau."

32 **"Worth was launched":** Metternich, *My Years in Paris*, p. 59.

33 **a series of early impressionist oil paintings:** Two of these paintings can be seen in the Metropolitan Museum of Art: *The Parc Monceau 1876* and *1878* (59.206 and 59.142).

34 **Alfred's brother-in-law, Prosper Lecomte:** *Le Figaro*, May 22, 1887.

35 **Cartier's income fell by 30 percent:** Nadelhoffer, *Cartier*, p. 15.

36 **Bourdier was awarded a gold medal:** Aucoc, president of the Jewelry Union, was also awarded a gold medal. Boucheron was awarded the Grand Prix, along with Vever.

37 **Andrée-Caroline was a love child:** Chantal Trubert-Tollu, *The House of Worth, 1858–1954: The Birth of Haute Couture* (London: Thames & Hudson, 2017), p. 182. Her mother's name was Alice Paulet. This book gives an in-depth account of the Worth family history.

39 **more important gems:** Though it would be years before the introduction of the first men's wristwatch, pocket watches, chatelaines, and small watch bracelets for women were popular.

39 **acclaim for presenting an enamel egg:** *Le Monde Illustré,* July 4, 1891. See also the *Moniteur Universel* of July 6, 1891.

40 **struggling finances of aristocratic landowners:** The wealth of Britain's landowners declined after the Corn Laws repeal in 1846, which made it cheaper to import grain.

40 **"invariably produced a violent headache":** Consuelo Vanderbilt Balsan, *The Glitter and the Gold* (London: Hodder & Stoughton, 2012), p. 58.

41 **enormously confident:** Louis' governess nicknamed him Louis XIV. Alain Cartier and Olivier Bachet, *Cartier: Exceptional Objects,* vol. 1 (Hong Kong: Palais-Royal, 2019), p. 18.

Chapter 2: Louis

47 **"deliciously pretty":** "Mariages," *Le Gaulois,* May 1, 1898.

47 **that the groom of Andrée-Caroline:** *Le Figaro,* May 2–3, 1898.

49 **"bought clothes in Paris":** Michael Teague, *Mrs. L.: Conversations with Alice Roosevelt Longworth* (New York: Doubleday, 1981), p. 114.

49 **stylish ladies and wealthy admirers:** In her memoirs, Consuelo Vanderbilt Balsan describes these wealthy foreign shoppers: "How gay were those years at the turn of the century when in Paris there gathered cosmopolitan society come from Rome, Berlin, Saint Petersburg, Vienna and London, with the sole object of spending money and finding amusement!" Balsan, *Glitter and the Gold,* p. 116.

50 **He wanted "inventors":** Laurent Salomé and Laure Dalon, eds., *Cartier: Style and History* (Paris: Réunion des Musées Nationaux–Grand Palais, 2014), p. 203, citing a letter from Louis Cartier to Jeanne Toussaint, 1934.

52 **eighteenth-century France as a source of inspiration:** This wasn't groundbreaking in itself. Since Empress Eugénie had had her jewels reset in the 1850s by Bapst and Lemonnier in the style of Marie Antoinette, there had been a fascination with the Louis XVI era.

52 **would fill notebooks:** Ibid. Alain Cartier writes that between 1905 and 1925, Louis filled four notebooks with ideas, sketches, and sources of inspiration.

52 **"France's past brilliance and influence":** See Cartier and Bachet, *Cartier: Exceptional Objects,* vol. 1, p. 31.

53 **"It was not until we studied the mechanics":** "America to Become Great International Art Center, Says French Jeweler," *Jewelers' Circular* (New York: Jewelers' Circular Pub. Co.), February 23, 1927, p. 39.

54 **"The use of platinum":** Ibid., p. 39. Louis-François had sold small pieces, like studs and buttons, that incorporated platinum as far back as 1853. But it had been difficult to take it further than occasional experimental usage. As Jacques would note in his article for the *Encyclopaedia Britannica,* p. 34, "Platinum had been used experimentally since the 18th century, but it was only in 1900 that it started to be used exclusively in the setting of diamonds and found favour on account of its brightness and its superior hardness, which permitted of considerably lighter settings." According to Nadelhoffer, *Cartier,* p. 48, the Cartier platinum was an alloy of which the Picq workshop was particularly proud.

54 *devant de corsage:* Unlike tiaras, which had to obey the strict conventions of court, *devants de corsage* could be freer in their use of motifs.

56 **Jean-Philippe had promised:** According to their marriage contract, the total dowry amounted to some 720,000 francs (about $4 million in today's money).

56 **It was a rather efficient way:** Hugo, *Vingt ans maître d'hôtel chez Maxim's,* edited by Roland Toutain (Paris: Amiot Dumont, 1951), pp. 32–33.

57   **Cocteau is said to have recalled:** Jean Cocteau describing dining with Otéro and
      Lina Cavalieri, around 1913. With thanks to the Maxim's Museum. See also Mauduit,
      Maxim's: L'Histoire d'un rêve.

58   **a "technically astonishing" diamond and platinum *collier résille*:** Judy Rudoe, *Car-
      tier: 1900–1939* (London: British Museum Press, 1997), p. 68.

58   **She supplied many of the gemstones:** Ibid. *Collier résille* translates literally as "hair-
      net necklace." The design, with its knotted ribbons and tassels, was a nod to the
      notorious necklace that had ended up contributing to Marie Antoinette's downfall.

58   **"The prize was given one night":** Hugo, *Vingt ans,* p. 33.

60   **the other's innovative streak:** King Léopold of Belgium awarded the aviator a Cartier
      pocket watch in 1901, according to Cologni, *Made by Cartier,* p. 73.

60   **Here one was as likely to be seated:** Paul Hoffman, *Wings of Madness: Alberto
      Santos-Dumont and the Invention of Flight* (London: Fourth Estate, 2003), p. 1.

62   **The aviator was a global celebrity:** Ibid., p. 7.

62   **It wouldn't be until 1911:** Cologni, *The Cartier Tank Watch* (2017), p. 23. Louis
      released the Santos watch, known as the Santos II, in Cartier's Rue de la Paix store
      in 1911.

62   **Since 1903, the forty-five-year-old watchmaker:** Ibid., pp. 16–17; see the discussion
      of the March 1907 supply agreement between Pierre, Louis, and Edmond Jaeger.
      According to Nadelhoffer, *Cartier,* p. 292, Louis Cartier and Edmond Jaeger were
      introduced by Joseph Vergely, a watchmaker from Auvergne renowned for his gold-
      coin watches and who headed up the Paris office of the European Watch and Clock
      Company.

62   **solidifying this agreement four years later:** Under this fourteen-year 1907 agreement
      with Jaeger, the Cartier brothers undertook to guarantee minimum orders for a sum
      of 250,000 francs. In return, Jaeger undertook to deliver exclusively to Cartier his
      production of flat anchor watches. It was also agreed that any new creations, includ-
      ing watch mechanisms and shapes, would remain the property of Cartier.

62   **"produce a series of exceptional watches":** Cologni, *Cartier: The Tank Watch,* p. 19.
      Other than the Santos and the Tank, other innovative watch models pre–World
      War II included the barrel-shaped Tonneau (1906), the more compact tortoise-
      inspired Tortue (1912), the slim Tank Cintrée and the Asian-inspired Tank Chinoise
      (both 1921), the round-angled Tank L.C. and the church bell–shaped Cartier Cloche
      (both 1922), the Tank Savonette and Petite Tank Rectangle (both 1926), the "jump-
      ing hour" Tank à Guichets (1928), and the square-faced, bullet-lugged Tank Obus
      (1929). The 1930s saw the arrival of the ladies' Baguette Form Tank, the Tank 8
      Jours, and the waterproof Tank Étanche (all 1931), the reversible Tank Basculante
      (1932), and the Tank Parallelogram (1936), later known as the Tank Asymètrique.

64   **timepieces:** "At the turn of the century he [Louis] read an article about radium and
      radioactivity which led to the production, several years later, of desk clocks and
      wristwatches with hands and numerals coated in radium so they could be seen in the
      dark." Cartier and Bachet, *Cartier: Exceptional Objects,* vol. 1, p. 19.

64   **In 1911, he engaged Maurice Couët:** Maurice Auguste Couët (1885–1962) was an
      exceptional talent, born in Rouen to a family of clockmakers. After working for the
      Prévost workshop, he started supplying table clocks exclusively to Cartier starting in
      1911. Couët set up a new workshop at 53 Rue Lafayette with thirty specialists in 1919
      producing marvels like the 1920s mystery clocks. His team included his brother
      Rene Couët, the designer Alfred Loquet (1884–1967), Alexander Diringer (1893–
      1981), and Gaston Cusin (1897–1986) who patented the Ruc Reaumur. See Nadel-
      hoffer, pp. 266–276.

65   **"terrified of him in the workshops":** For an extensive discussion on the workshops
      used by Cartier Paris during Louis' reign (including Louis Mathey, Edmond Char-
      pentier, Verger Frères, Robert Frontin, and Robert Linzeler), see Cartier and Bachet,
      Cartier: Exceptional Objects, vol.2, p. 31. In this period, Henri Lavabre was perhaps
      Cartier's largest supplier, manufacturing all types of objects, from tiaras to clocks, in
      Rue Tiquetonne. Another key supplier was Henri Picq, who supplied high jewelry
      pieces, including (in part) the 1906 Fabergé-style egg (now in the Metropolitan Mu-
      seum of Art).

65 **Recently, one of these models:** See lot 393 of the Doyle New York 13JL02 sale (available online, April 15, 2013): a "Model A" mystery clock from the estate of Consuelo Vanderbilt Earl (1903–2011) was sold for $515,000.

65 **first royal warrant:** This was followed by King Alfonso of Spain (1904), King Carlos of Portugal (1905), King Rama V of Siam (1907), Tsar Nicholas II of Russia (1907), King George I of Greece (1909), King Peter of Serbia (1913), the Duke of Orleans (1914), King Albert of Belgium (1919), King Victor Emmanuel III of Italy (1920), Prince Albert of Monaco (1920), Edward, Prince of Wales (1921), Queen Marie of Romania (1928), King Fuad I of Egypt (1929), and King Zog of Albania (1939).

66 **The grand dukes:** Wilfried Zeisler, "From Moscow to Paris," in *Moscow: Splendours of the Romanovs*, edited by Brigitte de Montclos (Paris: Skira, 2009), p. 193, quoting Mme Ekaterina Khmelnitskaia.

66 **Countess von Hohenfelsen:** In 2009, Sotheby's Geneva sold a collection of jewels from the collection of Olga, Princess Paley (Countess Hohenfelsen), which included a 1912 Cartier aquamarine and diamond aigrette tiara (lot 283), which sold for CHF566,500 (about $522,000), more than triple the estimate.

66 **not unusual to visit Cartier:** Wilfried Zeisler, *Vivre la Belle Époque à Paris: Olga Paley et Paule de Russie* (Paris: Mare & Martin, 2018), p. 167; see the diary entries for April 11, 1912, and May 21, 1904.

66 **welcomed the Dowager Empress:** The Dowager Empress Maria Fedorovna may have known Cartier for many years already. Ian Vorres recounts how, as a child, "Grand Duchess Xenia, a great favourite with her mother [the Empress Maria Feodorovna], happened to be in the Empress's rooms when two ladies-in-waiting were unpacking cases of jewelry and bibelots sent by Cartier from Paris. Xenia, aged thirteen, had not yet decided what she would give her mother. But suddenly she saw a filigree scent bottle, its stopper studded with sapphires. She snatched at it and begged Countess Stroganov not to give her secret away. That scent bottle must have cost a small fortune and Xenia duly presented it to her mother on Christmas Day. A little later, the Empress made it known that boxes arriving from Cartier and other jewellers could be admired by the children and no more." *The Last Grand Duchess: Her Imperial Highness Grand Duchess Olga Alexandrovna* (Toronto: Key Porter Books, 2001), p. 28. The accuracy of this recollection is questionable, as by 1888 Cartier was not yet revered enough in Russia to be regularly sending jewels to St. Petersburg.

67 **"Bring me any woman in Europe":** Julia Gelardi, *From Splendor to Revolution: The Romanov Women, 1847–1928* (New York: St. Martin's Press, 2011), p. 129, quoting John Logan, *In Joyful Russia* (New York: D. Appleton and Co., 1897), p. 27.

67 **depressed demand "for the most diverse objects":** Léonard Rosenthal, *Faisons fortune* (Paris: Payot, 1924), p. 98.

68 **"Outside his own country, the Russian is indecisive":** Nadelhoffer, *Cartier*, p. 111, citing Sarda report.

69 **"I'm in with the government":** Letter from Paul Cheyrouze to Cartier, December 1908, cited in Geza von Habsburg, *Fabergé-Cartier: Rivalen am Zarenhof* (Munich: Hirmer Verlag, 2003), p. 439.

69 **"Today I am attached":** Letter from Cheyrouze, 1908, Russian State Archives. Interestingly, Cheyrouze also asked the Empress to try to persuade Louis to open a store.

70 **"so as to give the impression that he has come":** Nadelhoffer, *Cartier*, p. 105. When Nadelhoffer refers to this marketing technique, it is unclear whether he is referring to the 1907 or 1908 Christmas sales.

70 **Sarda (on the ground):** Ibid., p. 107. Louis and Pierre would also visit, although Pierre's visits tailed off after he opened the New York branch.

71 **"elegant dancing evening":** *Le Figaro*, January 1907.

72 **It was a traumatic time:** *Le Petit Troyen*, September 23, 1908 (this is one of several newspaper reports of the accident).

72 **quizzed by the press for details:** See "Les Bijoux d'Abdul Hamid," interview with Alfred Cartier, in *Le Petit Courrier*, November 12, 1909. While stressing confidentiality, Alfred confided, "I can tell you, however, that there are very pretty things in the lot that I had to examine in the cellars of the Ottoman Bank, old objects of art, some

of which are of French origin," and highlighted a few items: "the narghiles are very beautiful, diamonds of a considerable size, the emeralds are quite remarkable. I can also mention a number of fancy diamonds and ancient golcondas; there is an admirable collection of pearls in Muslim rosaries in three groups of thirty-three."

73   **greatest designer up a ladder:** With thanks to Charles Jacqueau's family for this story.

75   **offered the younger man a job:** To start off with, Jacqueau worked predominantly on precious objects, moving to jewelry design only later. Chazal and Chazal, *Bijoux parisiens,* p. 150, citing Jacqueau's *Livre de raison.* Given his chance to shine, Jacqueau wrote that he daringly chose to design creations that were "the exact opposite of the house [style], white with a few splashes of color," presenting instead "the most whimsical pieces: color with a few splashes of white. . . . Mr. Louis was thrilled, and so were the sellers. All my designs were made up."

76   **"extraordinary scenery, the even more extraordinary dresses":** A review in *Tatler,* 1914 (after the controversial *Rite of Spring*).

76   **"uncanny instinct for predicting":** Cecil Beaton, *The Glass of Fashion: A Personal History of Fifty Years of Changing Tastes and the People Who Have Inspired Them* (New York: Rizzoli ex libris, 2014), p. 131.

76   **"Recruited for the creation of precious objects":** Gilles Chazal and Martine Chazal, *Bijoux Parisiens: French Jewelry from the Petit Palais, Paris* (Memphis: Dixon Gallery & Gardens, 2013), p. 150, citing Jacqueau's *Livre de raison.*

77   **emerald and sapphire ring:** Of course, not all the credit for these color combinations within Cartier's jewelry lies within the Eastern-inspired Ballets Russes and Jacqueau. Louis had long been interested in the exoticism of the East (his collection of Persian miniatures later became one of the most important in the world).

77   **A brooch of little ruby and emerald fruits:** Rudoe, *Cartier,* p. 222, referring to the brooch made in 1913 by Picq and designed by Jacqueau. For the next item (again, designed by Jacqueau), see Rudoe, *Cartier,* p. 96.

77   **In a promotional masterstroke:** Nadelhoffer, *Cartier,* p. 82. Discussing the Persian balls of 1911 and 1912, he notes that "the heyday of the Cartier aigrette coincided with those years preceding the First World War when Oriental influences were most clearly felt."

77   **"nearly everyone prominent in Paris society":** "Ball in Paris like Arabian Night Tale," *New York Times,* May 31, 1912.

78   **"Many a man would be willing":** Gelardi, *From Splendor to Revolution,* p. 48, quoting Knox, "A Gala Night in Russia," in *Harper's Bazaar New Monthly Magazine,* January 1875, vol. 50, p. 266.

79   **"parures of diamonds, emeralds, rubies":** Balsan, *Glitter and the Gold,* p. 136.

80   **"one only met the prettiest and smartest women":** Meriel Buchanan, *Victorian Gallery* (London: Cassell, 1956), p. 57.

80   **wasn't entirely without blame:** Tatiana F. Fabergé, Eric-Alain Kohler, and Valentin V. Skurlov, *Fabergé* (Geneva: Slatkine, 2012), pp. 101–102, citing several of Louis' letters as evidence that "Louis Cartier tried to avoid taxes and control." In contrast, Nadelhoffer, *Cartier,* p. 110, gives him credit, noting that "the insignificantly small quantity" of gold that Louis brought with him could have been "inadvertently not declared." Another contemporaneous, if indirect, account of the incident appears in Birbaum's memoirs where he refers to Grand Duchess Vladimir affording all-powerful protection to foreign jewelers (cited in Géza von Habsburg, *Fabergé: Imperial Jeweler,* p. 455).

81   **"I learned this evening":** Fabergé et al., *Fabergé,* pp. 101–102, citing letter from Louis Cartier to Captain Sawurski, December 1910 (Russian State Archives).

82   **The whole experience:** Tony Faber, *Fabergé's Eggs* (London: Pan Books, 2009), p. 192. The Goldsmiths' Company brought a court case in 1910, which Fabergé lost.

82   **Fabergé's London business:** For more on this topic, see Kieran McCarthy, *Fabergé in London: The British Branch of the Imperial Russian Goldsmith* (Woodbridge, UK: ACC Art Books, 2017). As McCarthy points out, the outbreak of World War I was also an important factor in the closing of Fabergé London.

82 **"One hundred years after Napoleon":** Fabergé et al., *Fabergé*, p. 103.

83 **"cathedral-like setting":** Nadelhoffer, *Cartier*, p. 110, citing Louis Cartier.

83 **"welcom[ing] everybody who approached":** Buchanan, p. 58.

83 **"The crowd of onlookers surged everywhere":** Nadelhoffer, *Cartier*, p. 110–111.

85 **Cartier's Russian-inspired creations:** Some of Cartier's pieces were remarkably similar to Fabergé's over the same period, close enough for accusations that Cartier "shamelessly" copied its rival. The reality is more nuanced. These objects were in demand, so jewelers found a way to create them, often sharing the same suppliers. Generally Fabergé was more revered for its objets d'art and Cartier for its jewels. In her memoirs (p. 139), Consuelo Vanderbilt Balsan explained how she saw the difference. Speaking about the houses of the St. Petersburg nobility, she said, "to me these palatial interiors, in which the ikon with its flame and the steaming samovar were the only distinctly Russian features, lacked the perfect taste one finds in France. One could not imagine oneself in a French house any more than one could mistake a Fabergé jewel for one set by Cartier."

85 **Grand Duchess Vladimir spent:** Cartier invoice from Russian State Archives; this order, from March 1910, was offset against 75,000 francs' worth of gemstones the Grand Duchess was providing to Cartier (one lot of diamonds, pearls, sapphires, and emeralds).

85 **This was a moment of particular satisfaction:** Théodule Bourdier had passed away in 1898 at the age of sixty-one, and 8 Rue de la Michodière was in the hands of his son, Georges.

86 **"as is fitting, we are now the leading firm":** Nadelhoffer, *Cartier*, p. 106.

87 **Known as "PanPan" Toussaint:** Toussaint was one of the demimondaines mentioned in the autobiography of Philippe de Rothschild as he recalled a debauched New Year's Eve when he was sixteen. See Joan Littlewood, ed., *Baron Philippe: The Very Candid Autobiography of Baron Philippe de Rothschild* (New York: Crown, 1984), p. 67.

87 **ladies of the night:** Hickman, *Courtesans*, p. 2. The concept of a demimondaine is a hard one to translate accurately for a modern audience. Essentially, they were very grand and expensive "ladies of the night," albeit in a socially acceptable way: "These were highly cultured women; rich, famous and, most remarkably, independent females."

87 **"My dear PanPan, I'm sorry":** Letter from Pierre de Quinsonas to Jeanne Toussaint, sold in Haynault Ventes Publiques auction in June 2018, original letter date unknown.

91 **She was joined by Jean Cocteau:** Sue Rose, *In Montparnasse: The Emergence of Surrealism in Paris from Duchamp to Dali* (London: Fig Tree, 2018), chapter 3.

92 **There's a pencil sketch Louis drew:** Haynault Ventes Publiques auction, June 2018.

95 **one of their key salesmen, Léon Farines:** Léon Farines (1883–1948) was a *grand vendeur* who played a key role in the early years of Cartier. Spanish-born, from Tarragona, he spoke Spanish, German, English, and Russian. He was heavily involved in sales to the leading royal families of Europe, especially the Spanish royal family and the Romanovs. He accompanied Louis Cartier to Kiev and Moscow in 1911; he also signed—from St. Petersburg—a March 1910 sapphire and diamond *devant de corsage* invoice for 150,000 francs (about $670,000 today) to Grand Duchess Vladimir. Farines also ran the Monte Carlo branch, and his house in Baixas also served as a "safe house" for the Cartiers during World War II. He died suddenly in October 1948, when he was about to depart on a work trip.

96 **"How many of them risked":** Léonard Rosenthal, *Au jardin des gemmes: L'Émeraude, le rubis, le saphir* (Paris: Payot, 1922), p. 274.

96 **They would become friends:** Jacques was friends with Eugène Fabergé, for example.

97 **"in the twinkling of an eye":** Account of Armistice Night by Australian soldier Herbert Goddard (7th Reinforcements to the 33rd Battalion), available online at thecourier.au/story/5749007.

97 **"It was the night, however":** Ibid.

97 **"work of art destined to become a historical object":** "Échos," *Le Figaro*, August 25,

1918. This was recognition for Foch's key role in halting a renewed German advance on Paris.

97   **These historical souvenirs:** "Les joyaux de la victoire," *Écho de Paris,* October 29, 1919, p. 2 of 4. In the autumn of 1917, Cartier had also offered a square pendant (set with a ruby, pearls, and diamonds and supported by a string of pearls) as part of a charity auction organized by the Press Association for war veterans.

97   **First, her mother, who had been living:** Marie Toussaint died of pneumonia in Lambeth, London, April 1915, age sixty-three. Her death certificate suggests that she, or her late husband, was a laundry proprietor.

97   **her former lover, Comte Pierre de Quinsonas:** Reported in *Le Petit Parisien,* July 21, 1917. Pierre was killed in an accident at Villacoublay Air Base, south of Paris, when a friend in a plane decided to swoop down low over him as a prank and miscalculated. Pierre sustained grave spinal injuries and died in a Versailles military hospital. See also Paul Morand, *Journal d'un attaché d'ambassade 1916–1917* (Paris: Gallimard, 1948), pp. 290, 293.

98   **her adored older sister, Clémentine:** Although it has been written that Toussaint's sister was named Charlotte and married into the English aristocracy, discussions with her family and a review of genealogical records suggest that those details are fictitious. Jeanne Toussaint was the youngest of five children; her siblings were Arthur (b.1880), Édouard (1878), Clémentine (1875), and Rosalie (1873). Clémentine (1871–1919) married a Parisian motor mechanic Émile Henri Dumarcay (1875–1931), in 1911.

99   **In mid-November 1919, the first Tank:** Cologni, *The Cartier Tank Watch* (2017), p. 38.

Chapter 3: Pierre

100   **at the 1915 Arts Décoratifs exhibition:** After lobbying by the Society of Decorative Artists, in 1911/1912, the French Chamber of Deputies had in 1912 agreed to host an international exhibition of decorative arts in 1915. With the outbreak of World War I, the plans were put aside, then later revived. The Expo was first rescheduled for 1922, then postponed because of a lack of building materials to 1924 and then 1925.

102   **Nothing too old-fashioned:** Diana Scarisbrick, *Ancestral Jewels* (London: André Deutsch, 1989), p. 179, quoting the novelist Elinor Glyn, who writes about Americans who "crossed the Atlantic twice a year to have their dresses fitted, and whose jewels were perfect, not a bit like the English sticking to their hideous Victorian settings."

102   **Forget aspiring to outshine her countess friends:** Martin Chapman, *Cartier and America* (Munich: Prestel, 2010), p. 16: Taken as a whole, "the overall effect of these glittering white diamonds placed at the bosom, neck and head would have been similar to that of the jewels worn by royalty of the day, such as Queen Alexandra of England."

103   **society ladies even had their tiaras:** Geoffrey Munn, *Tiaras: A History of Splendour* (Suffolk: Ace Art Books, 2001), p. 332. "Possibly because they lacked a royal family of their own, the enthusiasm of American ladies for European monarchy was intense." See also the 1911 Cartier exhibition invitation on p. 13.

103   **"The third morning," so the American press:** *Detroit Free Press,* September 1906.

105   **the cinema star had not yet eclipsed:** Balsan, *Glitter and the Gold,* p. 112.

105   **Together with top salesman M. Buisson:** Nadelhoffer called him Alfred, but contemporaneous records suggest that his name was Claude Alfonse Buisson (b. 1876) and that he was a close friend of Henri Lavabre (b. 1875) and Louis Lecomte (b. 1877).

105   **Cartier's business into Germany:** Cartier's early internationalization efforts didn't always go smoothly. In the winter of 1903, a number of newspapers reported that Mr. Cartier had gone to Berlin and sold many thousand dollars' worth of jewels, including to Prince Albert of Prussia and Prince Hohenlohe, when suddenly, one afternoon, three police officers called at his hotel and informed him that on no account would he be allowed to sell his goods. His jewel cases were sealed and they and their

owner were sent back across the frontier, without further explanation. A review of German archive records suggests that although the newspapers referred to Mr. Cartier, it was likely to have been the salesman Buisson who was deported, owing to the lack of a trading permit.

105 **used the smart Hotel Cecil:** On the site now occupied by 80 Strand, the Hotel Cecil was a thousand-room grand hotel, at one time the biggest in Europe, between the Thames Embankment and the Strand. Its builder, a notorious Victorian fraudster named Jabez Balfour, had fled to South America.

106 **the Worths and the Cartiers would be able to afford the lease:** The launch in early 1902 of Worth, "the King of Dressmakers," at 4 New Burlington Street was noted in the English press, with Worth reported as having paid this tribute to English beauty: "The English people are among the most beautiful in the world and to design dresses for them is a real pleasure. The great thing in all my costumes is the quality of the material, the workmanship, and above all, the simplicity of the taste" (*Brighton Gazette,* February 27, 1902). In 1911, Worth would move to 11 Hanover Square; see *The Sketch,* September 27, 1911.

107 **"he [Cartier] says no Queen or Empress has anything finer":** "Cartier and the Diva," in Margaret Young-Sanchez, *Cartier: The Exhibition* (Canberra: NGA, 2018), exhibition catalog, pp. 49–57.

108 **the Duchess of Portland would have stood out:** See Laurits Regner Tuxen's oil painting *The Anointing of Queen Alexandra at the Coronation of King Edward VII,* signed and dated 1902–3, Royal Collection Trust. Devastatingly, the Portland tiara, which had remained in the same family for generations, was stolen in 2018 from the family house (Welbeck Abbey) in Nottinghamshire, England.

108 **"After the monotony which had blanketed London":** Beaton, *Glass of Fashion,* p. 27.

108 **Dickens in a Cartier setting:** Edward, Duke of Windsor, *A King's Story,* p. 58.

108 **one side by Worth and Cartier:** Nadelhoffer, *Cartier,* p. 26.

109 **"society completely by storm":** William Cavendish-Bentinck, *Men, Women and Things: Memories of the Duke of Portland* (London: Faber and Faber, 1937), p. 68.

109 **"dressed as carefully":** Evalyn Walsh McLean and Boyden Sparkes, *Father Struck It Rich* (Lake City, CO: Western Reflections, 1999), p. 130.

109 **"He never said":** Edward Bernays, *Biography of an Idea: Memoirs of Public Relations Counsel* (New York: Simon & Schuster, 1965), p. 327.

110 **Cartier et Fils (Cartier and Son) became Cartier Frères:** At the firm's founding in 1906, this meant Louis and Pierre. Their much younger brother, Jacques, was not included until 1913.

111 **The days were filled with:** In 1904, the banker J. P. Morgan bought one of the first Cartier sun tiaras; he would add a winged tiara to his collection in 1909.

112 **It would take many months:** Robert F. Bruner, *The Panic of 1907: Lessons Learned from the Market's Perfect Storm* (Hoboken, NJ: John Wiley & Sons, 2009), pp. 127–133.

113 **Moses Rumsey, Jr.:** Originally from New York, Moses was the president of the L. M. Rumsey Manufacturing Company, having founded the business with his older brother.

113 **"uncommonly likeable girls":** *St. Louis Post-Dispatch,* June 25, 1905.

114 **thirty-three-year-old spinster aunt:** In 1906, her older sister, Marion (who lived by then in New York), had her only child, a daughter she named Elma after her sister.

114 **"Their taste in jewelry and method of wearing it":** Pierre Cartier interview, November 8, 1907.

114 **"Well, I hardly know how to describe him":** "Miss Rumsey to Wed as Soon as Fiancé Has Time," *St. Louis Post-Dispatch,* December 22, 1907.

114 **"HEIRESS TO WED FOREIGNER":** *New York Times,* December 22, 1907.

116 **"the only private residence I ever cared to own":** "New York: Day by Day," *Nebraska State Journal,* May 23, 1931.

117 **"The onlooker must be blind indeed":** *New York Times,* April 24, 1910.

117 **"the Rue de la Paix is being moved to Fifth Avenue":** *New York Times,* April 4, 1909.

118 "Since the House of Cartier is destined to lead the world": Salomé and Dalon, eds., *Cartier: Style and History*, p. 20, citing Cartier board meeting minutes 1910–12.

118 When one saleswoman: Rosenthal, *Faisons fortune*, p. 177, tells this story about a young Frenchwoman who was sent to New York to sell dresses. She told her boss in Place Vendôme that within three months she would speak English without an accent. "Don't do that," he replied. "We have hired you as a French saleswoman, and it is advisable that you keep ... your faults of language. They affirm your Parisian origin which is your first quality."

118 who exchanged Rue de la Paix for: Muffat originally went to New York on a two-year-contract, negotiated directly with Alfred Cartier and signed in September 1909 (it was later extended by ten years, to 1921). His wages were $50 per week plus a 0.5 percent commission on turnover plus a 2 percent commission on his sales. He was given a return voyage to France every two years. Interestingly, the contract also guarantees return fare for his family and a salesman role in Paris in case of the failure of Cartier New York, showing the uncertain prospects in those early years.

118 multilingual gemstone expert Muffat: Paul Muffat was a key figure working for Cartier for five decades. In 1903, he joined from Worth, initially working in both Paris and London (New Burlington Street) before moving to Cartier New York in 1910 where he became a sales director. He returned to work in Cartier Paris in 1921 before retiring in 1953 (his retirement album somehow turned up at auction in 1996, and his descendents would like to locate it in case anyone knows of its whereabouts).

119 The fun-loving Glaenzer: Although Jules was born in America, his father was a French Alsatian who immigrated to the United States in 1870. Glaenzer met Pierre Cartier in 1899 and started at Cartier in 1907. He would retire from Cartier in 1966.

119 King of Siam: Glaenzer visited Siam for the King's fortieth jubilee in 1909. Maurice Zolotow, *It Takes All Kinds: Piquant Pen Portraits of Some Picturesque People* (London: W. H. Allen, 1953), p. 153, recalls the King of Siam's visit to 13 Rue de la Paix in 1907 when he had wanted to see some bracelets. Glaenzer brought out tray after tray, but the King shook his head. Finally Glaenzer brought out a tray of the rarest and costliest bracelets. The King gave a sign, and the interpreter said: "His Majesty has chosen this one." "Which one?" asked Glaenzer. "The whole tray," came the reply. The value was $450,000 (a few years later, the Hope Diamond was sold for $180,000).

119 Alexandre and Georges Genaille: The seasoned Cartier Paris designer Alexandre Genaille came over to New York in 1909, followed by Maurice Duvallet in 1911, Émile Fauré in 1912, and his brother, Georges Genaille, in 1914.

120 "all dressed in the most expensive, magnificent frocks": Elinor Glyn, *Elizabeth Visits America* (New York: Duffield, 1909), ebook.

121 "The man who 'kept a shop'": Edith Wharton, *A Backward Glance* (New York: D. Appleton and Co., 1934), p. 11.

122 "We must never lose": Salomé and Dalon, eds., *Cartier: Style and History*, p. 20, citing Cartier board meeting minutes 1910–12.

123 "There are those who say": "Remarkable Jewel a Hoodoo: Hope Diamond has brought trouble to all who have owned it," *Washington Post*, January 19, 1908.

123 "It is no use to anyone": McLean and Sparkes, *Father Struck It Rich*, p. 222. Evalyn was the daughter of Thomas Walsh, an Irish immigrant miner who made his fortune when he discovered the Camp Bird gold mine near Ouray, Colorado.

123 "thing I craved at sight": Ibid., p. 117.

124 "His manner was exquisitely mysterious": Ibid., p. 130.

124 He shipped the gemstone to America: *New York Times*, March 9, 1911; the Hope arrived in Washington toward the end of 1910.

124 changed the setting: The stone setter for the Hope Diamond was Louis Maîtrejean (Nadelhoffer gives his name as Paul), who had come over to New York from Cartier Paris.

125 "For hours, that jewel stared": McLean and Sparkes, *Father Struck It Rich*, p. 134.

125 The price was $180,000: While the markup looks significant, this may be distorted

by historical exchange comparisons; furthermore, the costs involved with the Hope transaction were substantial. In the end, the Cartiers would even admit to having taken a small loss.

125 **"extreme precautions"**: *New York Times,* March 9, 1911. The newspaper tried repeatedly to reach him, but even they were forced to admit defeat.

125 **a previous wearer of the diamond:** May Yohe, ex-wife of Lord Francis Hope, warned against the curse in a March 1911 article in the *New York Evening World* newspaper.

126 **"Upon examining our legal expenses":** Gilberte Gautier, *Cartier: The Legend* (London: Arlington Books, 1983), p. 132, citing Cartier board minutes of November 23, 1912. Note: Gautier is cited only where she quotes key sources directly, as her book is not reliably accurate on the Cartier family.

127 **"through the station so fast":** McLean and Sparkes, *Father Struck It Rich,* p. 226.

127 **high security of the Smithsonian:** Harry Winston donated it to the national museum in 1958. Amusingly, he sent the gemstone in a brown paper package through the mail.

127 **the Hope Diamond proving more charmed:** The unfortunate subject of this story was Mr. Berdoulay, the head of the Order Department for decades.

128 **Legal battles aside:** *Washington Post,* December 5, 1914. Simultaneously, Cartier was fighting a case against Howard Gould, the son of Jay Gould, a notorious American railroad speculator, in the U.S. Supreme Court for nonpayment for jewelry bought by his ex-wife. Despite the suit's starting in 1908, the Cartiers were still fighting it by the time World War I broke out, facing by that time a counterclaim for $200,000.

129 **of Mrs. Bryson Delavan:** Elma's sister, Marion, was married to a surgeon, David Bryson Delavan, known as the dean of American laryngologists, and lived in New York City.

129 **"wealthy Frenchman":** *New York Times,* April 15, 1911.

129 **They even extended their "Our Home" property:** Just before the war, they enlarged their already expansive home by buying an adjacent property from the founder of Automobiles Delaunay-Belleville (at the beginning of the twentieth century, these were among the most prestigious luxury cars in the world).

130 **"We brothers are very close":** Bernays, *Biography of an Idea,* p. 323.

130 **nearby American hospital in Neuilly-sur-Seine:** This hospital had been founded by the American community in Paris in 1908, including John Harjes (the chairman), who was linked to the Cartier family through his daughter, Nelly Harjes, who married Jacques Cartier.

130 **Pierre was appointed as a chauffeur:** Pierre also spent time working for other offices and with the 14th Automobiliste Division in Cherbourg, but he ultimately turned down a position as a driver for an army administrator to stay with Ponsard, whom he admired.

132 **Even in war:** *Boston Daily Globe,* February 14, 1915, mentions the Gould lawsuit.

132 **everything from lawsuits to staff changes:** "Loban is very fond of you," he told his younger brother; "do you think he has the right qualities to be part of our firm? . . . One person who I am considering now is my old colonel of the 23rd, Ponsard. I think he would in part replace our father on the technical side, buying stones etc."

136 **Jules Glaenzer and Victor Dautremont:** Jules Glaenzer was an American, while Victor Dautremont had been excused from fighting for the French in the war because of weak lungs.

137 **"Give me your townhouse":** This is the story as told by the society columnist Nancy Rudolph in 1954. According to the family of Paul Muffat, it could have been Muffat who proposed the deal (although the timeline is confusing given his extensive war role). Even if the details remain uncertain, this confirms that the swap took place, as does the 1917 Deed of Sale.

137 **"A pearl necklace was exchanged for a set of keys:** Initially the building was leased, but by mid-1917 when the building work was nearing completion, the final exchange took place. See *Jewelers' Circular,* vol. 74 (1917), p. 73.

138 **renovating the new building:** According to the Deed of Sale (a copy of which is held

in the New York Municipal Archive), when the work was nearing completion, the final exchange took place in mid-July 1917.

138 **He asked both Louis and his sister-in-law:** Nelly's father, John Harjes, founded Morgan Harjes Bank in Paris and had recently begun a move to 14 Place Vendôme.

140 **"Men who I could only assume were salesmen":** Bernays, *Biography of an Idea,* pp. 321–322.

142 **His very capable president was Joseph Hartnett:** Joseph P. Hartnett had been the secretary of the L. M. Rumsey Manufacturing Company (Elma's family's firm) until 1917. See his obituary in *The New York Times,* May 30, 1937.

143 **became the company secretary:** According to the notice, Pierre's vice presidents at the time were Paul Muffat, Jules Glaenzer, and Louis Lecomte, Pierre's cousin.

143 **"for the purposes of becoming an American institution":** *Commercial and Financial Chronicle,* vol. 110 (1920), p. 80. The *Jeweler's Circular* also notes that the net liquid assets of the American business were $4.4 million and that profits for the years 1917–19 were more than three times the sum required to pay the annual dividend.

Chapter 4: Jacques

145 **Jacques became closer to his brothers:** Louis' and Pierre's early letters are addressed simply to *"Mon cher frère Jacques"* (my dear brother Jacques), but by the time their younger brother reached his late twenties, they started referring to him as *"vieux Jacques"* (old/wise Jacques), a term of affection that stuck for the rest of his life.

146 **"an almost palpable sense of satisfaction":** Adrian Fort, *Nancy: The Story of Lady Astor* (London: St. Martin's Griffin, 2014), p. 106.

146 **Bobby, as he affectionately called his sister:** Cassel's sister was named Wilhelmina. Widowed for more than twenty years, Cassel had depended on Wilhelmina's help in bringing up his motherless child, alongside her own two fatherless children.

147 **175–176 New Bond Street was leased as an art gallery:** Arthur Tooth & Son were a once renowned firm of art dealers. Before that, it was part of the Clarendon Hotel. Number 175 New Bond Street, still the Cartier London store today, is a Grade II listed building (List Entry Number 1224555, https://historicengland.org.uk/). The historical background of this listed building, including old photos and a 1909 site plan, is detailed in various planning consent documents filed over the years in the Westminster Council Planning archive (ref no 15/01647/LBC).

148 **a pearl necklace restrung (recommended twice a year):** In her book about Nancy Astor, the lady's maid Rose explains keeping watch while the pearls were restrung and polished. See Rosina Harrison, *Rose: My Life in Service to Lady Astor* (New York: Viking Press, 1975), p. 103.

149 **The design sketchbooks:** Salomé and Dalon, eds., *Cartier: Style and History,* p. 26 and p. 386 (note 24). It is unclear whether all the notebooks are in the handwriting of Louis Cartier; perhaps authorship was shared with key collaborators such as Charles Jacqueau.

149 **Instead of the then fashionable diamond and pearl dog collar:** Rudoe, *Cartier,* pp. 53–55, citing the "Cahier des Idées, 1906–7."

150 **To his consternation:** Toby Faber, p. 192. Fabergé's move from 48 Dover Street (which Fabergé had moved to in 1906), in collaboration with Henry C. Bainbridge, took place in 1911.

150 **"ever brought together":** *New York Times,* April 9, 1911. See also *London Daily News,* March 27, 1911. The later estimate of £2 million ($200 million today) seems unlikely.

152 **was married to Charles Messenger Moore:** Moore was an American who had started his career working for Tiffany in New York. In the 1880s, he moved to France to manage the Paris branch of the firm and married Nelly's older sister, Louise Harjes, in 1886. Moore made a name for himself in 1887 by securing some of the French crown jewels at auction in a brilliant marketing coup for Tiffany.

153 **"very attractive young woman":** *New York Times,* August 7, 1901.

154 **After being rescued by her father:** *New York Times,* November 29, 1908. The grounds given were that Lion had misconducted himself with a woman by the name

of Ida Loomis (whom he later married) at the Glenmore Hotel at Fifty-fifth Street and Broadway.

156 **weddings for their pets:** Javier Moro, *Passion India: The Story of the Spanish Princess of Kapurthala* (New Delhi: Full Circle, 2008), p. 164.

156 **"They scattered pearls as confetti":** Ann Morrow, *Highness: Maharajas of India* (London: Grafton, 1986), p. 37.

157 **the Taj Mahal Palace:** Built in 1903 for £250,000 (around £34 million today), the Taj was the best hotel in Bombay. Now it is next to the Gateway of India, but only the foundation stone had been laid by 1911.

159 **"First was the Nizam":** Charles Allen and Sharada Dwivedi, *Lives of the Indian Princes* (London: Century Publishing, 1984), p. 210.

159 **Imrie Schwaiger, whom he had met:** Béla Kelényi, "Two Trunks from London: Hungarian Aspects of the 'Discovery' of Nepalese Art," *Ars Decorativa* 24 (2006), pp. 123–145, describes how Schwaiger came to India and became one of the first dealers in Nepalese art.

160 **they didn't want discreet little bracelets:** There were a couple of exceptions to the lack of female clients, including the wife of the Crown Prince of Kapurthala, who bought a blue and gold enameled watch.

164 **"He was weighted—head, neck, chest":** W. H. Russell, *The Prince of Wales' Tour: A Diary in India, 1877* (New York: Lovell, Adam and Wesson, 1877), p. 137.

167 **Léonard Rosenthal's fortune:** Born in the Caucasus region of Russia, Rosenthal had immigrated to Paris at the age of fourteen. He had been forced to scrape together an income as a small-time trader in the Paris auctions. Before long, he had made enough in pearls to start a company with his brothers: Rosenthal Frères.

168 **On the day the ship arrived:** Léonard Rosenthal, *The Pearl Hunter: An Autobiography* (New York: Henry Schuman, 1952), p. 68. Rosenthal also describes in his biography how, given that the locals were unacquainted with any European money other than pounds sterling in gold, "the defile [*sic*] of donkeys aroused their imagination and respect. We became in their imagination, the richest men in the world, and from then on, the finer lots of pearls were offered to us without the least hesitation. We had won the battle." By 1910, the Rosenthals were bringing back 4 million rupees' ($20 million) worth of pearls a year and were considered to be a "weather-cock of the market." See Matthew S. Hopper, *Slaves of One Master: Globalization and Slavery in Arabia in the Age of Empire* (New Haven, CT: Yale University Press, 2013), pp. 93–95.

171 **a temporary branch in Delhi:** The Cartiers never set up a branch in India, but it did sell items out of Schwaiger's shop, outside Maiden's Hotel, with a sign advertising that Cartier jewels were sold there.

172 **"Among the collections which I saw":** "Interview with Jacques Cartier," *Sheffield Evening Telegraph*, May 29, 1912.

174 **just days after returning to work:** Jacques and Nelly lived a couple of blocks west of the Harjes house at 62 Avenue Henri Martin.

175 **remembering lunches at the Colony Club:** Nelly was a member, and had been on the committee, of the Colony Club, a women-only private New York social club that still exists.

175 **He started off by organizing:** On November 11, 1913, he put on an exhibition in New York displaying a "Collection of Jewels Created by Messieurs Cartier from the Hindoo, Persian, Arab, Russian and Chinese." Of the fifty pieces on display at the 1913 New York exhibition, twenty were in the Indian style.

180 **"an Ali Baba hoard" of jewels:** James Fox, *Five Sisters: The Langhornes of Virginia* (New York: Simon & Schuster, 2001), p. 100, quoting Nancy Astor's son.

180 **"When she was dressed up to the nines":** Rosina Harrison, *Rose: My Life in Service to Lady Astor* (New York: Viking Press, 1975).

181 **Though they showed commendable courage:** "Jacques Cartier Dies, Jewelers' London Partner," *Herald Tribune*, September 1941.

181 **Passing through Rheims and seeing the large cathedral:** Cartier and Bachet, *Cartier: Exceptional Objects,* vol. 1, p. 21, citing this August 1917 letter from Jacques to Louis Cartier.

181 **The pieces of glass could be set into jewelry:** Alain Cartier and Olivier Bachet, *Cartier: Exceptional Objects*, 2 vols. (Hong Kong: Palais-Royal, 2019), p. 21, citing an August 1917 letter from Jacques to Louis Cartier.

184 **Cartier Ltd. was created:** Cartier Ltd. articles of incorporation, Companies House, July 1919.

Chapter 5: STONES Paris: Early 1920s

188 **"the *nouveaux pauvres"*:** Nadelhoffer, *Cartier*, p. 243.

188 **impressive head start:** Chaumet opened a New York branch in 1920. Van Cleef & Arpels tried to enter the American market in the 1920s but it was mostly in the 1930s that the firm "began applying itself seriously to the New World" (per the https://www.vancleefarpels.com website). Van Cleef opened a boutique in Palm Beach in 1940 and then in New York—at 744 Fifth Avenue—in 1942.

189 **Andrée-Caroline had enabled:** In 1909, soon after divorcing Louis, Andrée-Caroline Worth married a doctor named Roussel. She divorced him in 1916, then married Pierre Jomini, a businessman, in 1919.

189 **they had been formally registered:** The growing complexity of international tax planning—with separate luxury taxes introduced in France, the United States, and the United Kingdom at the end of the war—had made it important to have country-specific structures.

189 **replaced with Cartier S.A.:** When Cartier S.A. was set up in 1921, it was capitalized at 25 million francs ($21 million today). See *Côte de la Bourse*, July 27, 1921. "Deposit of the statutes and Declaration of subscription and payment of the Cartier S.A. company," June 17, 1921 (Paris Archives). See section 5 for the term. The new company was dedicated to "all operations involved in jewels, watches, leather, gold & silver objects, trade of precious stones, pearls, art and valuable objects."

191 **Founded in 1723:** Marcel Sexé, *Two Centuries of Fur-Trading 1723–1923: Romance of the Revillon Family* (Paris: Draeger Frères, 1923). The Rue de Rivoli fur maison became Revillon Frères when Louis-Victor Revillon merged his business with Givelet in 1839.

195 **"It's not so much what France gives you":** Quoted in Joseph Amber Barry, *The People of Paris* (Garden City, NY; Doubleday, 1966), p. 122.

195 **"a luxury in Montparnasse":** Letter from Jean Cocteau to Georges Ribemont-Desaignes, April 22, 1956 (sold at Drouot Paris auction, April 7, 2011).

196 **"Do we not design for the dressed":** *Jewelers' Circular*, February 23, 1927.

198 **"I'll certainly be going to Cartier's":** René Gimpel, *Diary of an Art Dealer* (London: Hamish Hamilton, 1986), p. 122, citing December 1919 letter.

199 **"The day before yesterday":** Gimpel, p. 296, quoting a letter from Proust to Gimpel.

199 **Louis had been forced to hold off buying precious gemstones:** A letter to Jacques Cartier said, "Mr. Louis will buy the grey pearls for 32 or 33,000 francs, but for white pearls, he can't give a response right now."

200 **"the only hiding place that could not":** Rosenthal, *Au jardin des gemmes*, p. 275.

200 **in a James Bond–style heist:** Gelardi (2011), p. 337. See Bertie Stopford, *The Russian Diary of an Englishman: Petrograd, 1915–1917* (London: William Heinemann, 1919).

200 **Gladstone bags bursting with jewels:** See Bertie Stopford, *The Russian Diary of an Englishman, Petrograd, 1915–1917* (London: William Heinemann, 1919). They weren't the only precious items Stopford helped smuggle out of Russia. In 1918, he ensured the safe passage of two of the Duchess's pillowcases stuffed full of objets d'art and jewels to the Swedish legation in Petrograd. From Petrograd, they were hidden among government archives in Sweden, eventually discovered only in 2008. Auctioned by the Grand Duchess's descendants at Sotheby's, the sale items went for a staggering $11.8 million. (At nearly $10,000 apiece, the Grand Duchess' pillowcases almost certainly set records for the most expensive ones ever sold.) For more about Bertie Stopford, see his anonymous autobiography, *The Russian Diary of an Englishman, Petrograd, 1915–17* (London: William Heinemann, 1919).

200 **the beach's rocky crevices:** Ian Vorres, *The Last Grand Duchess: Her Imperial High-*

ness Grand Duchess Olga Alexandrovna (Toronto: Key Porter Books, 2001), p. 153. Olga marked the spot where she had hidden the jewels with a white dog skull and would regularly go down to the beach to check on them. One day, she found that the skull had been moved. Watching her husband searching every possible crevice, she felt "cold drops of perspiration. . . . What a relief when he finally pulled a cocoa tin rattling with jewels out of one hole!"

201 **"I had no doubt"**: Rosenthal, *Au jardin des gemmes*, p. 282. The English, he claimed, didn't share his French integrity. Whatever the murky backstory, "the English closed their eyes, believing that sooner or later, these gemstones on the market would be sold well."

202 **A lover of jewelry**: Nadelhoffer, *Cartier*, p. 105. The Princess's first Cartier purchase in 1900 was "a delightful pansy brooch in amethyst and diamonds, followed by three boa pins."

202 **"They are wise investments"**: M. Henri Baudoin and Georges Berg, eds., *Catalogue des joyaux, colliers de perles, joailleries, perles et brillants* (Lausanne: Lausanne Palace, 1920), p. 14. Berg cites in the introduction: *"Ce sont des placements avantageux; je ne gaspille rien; au contraire, j'édifie une seconde fortune."*

202 **the Princess died in Switzerland**: This date for her death is taken from a contemporaneous newspaper account (*Le Gaulois*, May 17, 1919) of her funeral arrangements, despite more modern references suggesting that she died in 1914.

202 **Dealers, experts, and important members of society**: Christie's, *Magnificent Jewels* (Geneva: Christie's, November 15, 2016), lot 53.

202 **"reached nearly double the figure that we had hoped for"**: Cartier and Bachet, *Cartier: Exceptional Objects,* vol. 1, p. 66, citing a letter from Louis Cartier to Alfred Cartier.

202 **"Pearls, emeralds, very large rubies"**: *Jewelers' Circular*, February 23, 1927.

205 **"Young, slender, with skin as milky white"**: *Lincoln Star*, July 15, 1934, giving a fairy-tale account of their meeting some years after the fact.

205 **Growing up, Jacqueline and her cousins**: See Catherine Karolyi, *A Life Together: The Memoirs of Catherine Karolyi* (London: George Allen & Unwin, 1966), p. 50; see also Countess Karolyi's books in Hungarian titled *Together in Revolution* and *Together in Exile*.

206 **One cousin married the man**: This was Countess Catherine Károlyi, née Andrassy (1892–1985), the wife of Count Mihály Károlyi, who served as prime minister, then president, of the First Hungarian Republic after the First World War. She was known as the Red Countess. The other cousin, who inspired *The English Patient*, was the Hungarian count and desert explorer László Almásy (1895–1951)

206 **she had become a war widow**: Almásy was married in October 1917 to Count Charles Bissingen-Nippenburg (1891–1918), killed during World War I by an Italian aircraft bombing.

207 **his accusers wrong**: Louis tried without success to have his first marriage annulled.

207 **Louis Cartier officially became**: This amendment was made "by decision of the Court of Justice of Senlis" on Louis' birth certificate on August 14, 1923—and on that of Alfred.

207 **The marriage, the article reported, had been kept**: *Le Gaulois*, July 9, 1924.

207 **those early years of married life were happy ones**: A relative of Jacqui's recalled being told that Louis had been considered a particularly good catch by the Almásy family.

208 **"The Cartiers' life in Paris was a most glamorous one"**: *Lincoln Star*, July 15, 1934.

209 **he didn't enjoy being tied down with administrative functions**: The decision to step down from the board may have been linked to not wanting to be a resident of France. The timing coincided with Louis' buying a house in San Sebastián (a move that was tax-driven).

209 **"the hiring and laying off of workers"**: Minutes of February 15, 1924, Cartier S.A. board meeting (Cartier Paris archives). M. Revillon was first appointed for one year by this decision, then reconfirmed in subsequent meetings, including that of December 17, 1925.

209 **sold to museums and important collectors**: Géraldine Lenain, *Monsieur Loo: Le*

roman d'un marchand d'art asiatique (Paris: Philippe Picquier, 2013), gives a detailed account of the life of Ching-Tsai Loo (1880–1957), an influential dealer in Chinese artifacts.

209 CHINESE FASHIONS CAPTURE EUROPE: *Brooklyn Daily Eagle,* November 18, 1923.

210 **"other Asian dealers":** Louis also frequented Michon in Boulevard Haussmann, La Compagnie de Chine et des Indes on Rue de Londres and Yamanka, the Japanese dealer in New York.

210 **a woman caught smoking:** The exception being in Russia, where the practice was more accepted. Grand Duchess Maria Pavlovna was an avid smoker.

210 **"a mirror that may be carried":** *Jewelers' Circular,* February 23, 1927.

211 **Jacqueau worked on many of the designs for the cases:** When he later taught my grandfather the trade, he explained why he enjoyed making cases so much: They offered a little canvas on which a designer could create his own bejeweled picture.

213 **"to whom every great line of poetry":** Arthur King Peters, *Jean Cocteau and His World: An Illustrated Biography* (New York: Vendôme Press, 1986), p. 9, quoting Edith Wharton in 1934.

213 **By 1924, Louis was able to present his friend:** "Les Bijoux Mythiques . . . La Bague Trinity de Cartier," *Le Parisien,* February 19, 2010, citing Cartier design records.

213 **"captures fragments of the moon on a thread of sun":** Cocteau, p. 47; "*Cartier qui fait tenir, magicien subtil, / De la lune en morceaux sur du soleil en fil.*"

213 **his lover, the poet Raymond Radiguet:** Radiguet wrote at seventeen a masterpiece, *Le Diable au corps,* but tragically died three years later at age twenty in Paris of tuberculosis.

213 **Natalia Pavlovna Paley:** Natalia aka Natalie Paley (1905–1981) was the daughter of Grand Duke Paul Alexandrovich of Russia and Louis' excellent turn-of-the-century client Countess Hohenfelsen. She was given the title of Princess Paley in 1915.

213 **The first triple bracelet:** *Le Parisien,* February 19, 2010.

214 **"cut from one piece of onyx":** "The New Jewellery: The Very New Trinity Bracelet and Ring," *Vogue* (American edition), vol. 65, no. 1, pp. 50–51.

214 **"I hardly feel as though I am lowering myself":** François Chaille, *Cartier: Creative Writing* (Paris: Flammarion, 2000), p. 88.

215 **mechanical pencils:** Noël Coward bought one of these in 1934. A button on the tip turned on the light inside.

216 **Villa San Martin:** This became his official residence in 1924, per an official Consulat de France document dated October 20, 1924, and when Louis traveled to New York in 1929, he gave San Sebastián as his primary address.

216 **the stylish resort town of San Sebastián:** Louis' villa was situated next to the funicular railway, which took visitors up Monte Igueldo to a fashionable restaurant, casino, and gardens.

216 **"the Best View in the World":** "La Vista Más Bella del Mundo" in *La Voz de Guipúzcoa,* August 25, 1912.

217 **"satisfy the anxiety of the restless spirit of Louis Cartier":** "*La Intelligencia y el Arte*" (Spanish magazine article/interview, 1928).

217 **enraging his cook:** This story is related in Cartier and Bachet, *Cartier: Exceptional Objects,* vol. 1, p. 23.

217 **thriving cosmopolitan town:** The city's Belle Époque was not to last. From 1924, San Sebastián suffered under the Miguel Primo de Rivera dictatorship, which banned gambling.

217 **filled with a fashionable crowd:** Balenciaga opened his first boutique in 1917.

217 **Originally from Ceylon:** In 1913, Cartier added this 478-carat sapphire to seven other sapphires to form a magnificent necklace. Later that year, the smaller sapphires were moved to focus on the large sapphire drop attached to a pendant ring of calibré-cut sapphires. In 1919, the sapphire drop was transferred to a diamond sautoir, which was bought by Queen Marie of Romania.

217 **"Only the nouveaux riches can afford such luxuries":** Nadelhoffer, *Cartier,* p. 243.

217 **Louis still enjoyed mingling with the aristocrats:** As one example, Louis Cartier had been a guest at the 1922 wedding of Count Henri de Rochechouart-Mortemart to Isabelle de Chabrillan (the daughter of Countess Aynard de Chabrillan)

218 **"an obviously superior servant"**: Marcel Haedrich, *Coco Chanel: Her Life, Her Secrets* (London: Robert Hale, 1972), p. 191.

218 **"one of the gaudiest ornaments"**: "The Refugee Rothschilds," *Arizona Republic,* June 1941. His aunt had been Baroness Adolphe.

218 **a vast Parisian townhouse**: Hôtel de Pontalba on Rue du Faubourg Saint-Honoré was an *hôtel particulier* (a very large townhouse), now the official residence of the U.S. ambassador.

219 **"What are you doing here?"**: *Indianapolis Sunday Star,* October 2, 1927.

219 **Chanel herself claimed that the invitation was**: Haedrich, *Coco Chanel,* p. 190.

220 **"The affair still hangs in suspense"**: *Duncannon Record,* October 6, 1927.

221 **The mystery clocks**: See Nadelhoffer, *Cartier,* p. 281. Comparing them to Fabergé's eggs, he notes that "although they lacked the symbolism of dynastic commissions, these figurative mystery clocks . . . are today considered the most valuable of all collectors' items with the Cartier signature."

221 **freestanding oriental gateways**: Between 1923 and 1925, six "Portico" shrine gate clocks were created (in which the movement is housed above the dial instead of in the base). They feature a twelve-sided rock crystal dial, diamond hands, rock crystal columns, and a black onyx lintel/base, usually with a rock crystal figure on top (though this is not the case for clocks number 2 and 3). Clock number 1 (1923) was sold to Ganna Walska and acquired by Robert Hocq at a Christie's auction in 1973. Number 3 was sold at auction by Sotheby's in 1988. Cartier Portico clock number 4 was sold by Antiquorum in Geneva in 1996 for CHF1.8 million (then about $1.5 million). For more details, see Nadelhoffer, *Cartier,* p. 281, and Sotheby's, "Portico Mystery Clock Number 3, Cartier Paris 1924" (auction catalog)

221 **a jade goddess**: See *The Cartier Museum at the Goldsmiths' Hall Foster Lane* (London: Goldsmiths' Company, 1988), p. 31. Originally, twelve figurine or animal mystery clocks were supposed to have been made from 1922 to 1931: a jade "Mandarin Duck" clock (1922); the first agate chimera clock (1924); a Chinese jade twin carp clock, a jade vase clock with bird and flowers, and a crystal turtle clock (all three 1925); a second agate chimera clock (1926); a clock with the Chinese goddess Kuan Yin holding a branch of flowering ling-shi (1926); a crystal chimera clock (1927); a jade elephant clock sold to the Maharaja of Nawanagar (1928); a Buddhist lion clock (1929); a coral chimera clock (1930); and a Kuan Yin goddess in jade with jade chimera, coral trees, and a jade vase (1931). However, a thirteenth example from 1928, Le Ciel, turned up at auction with Bonhams in 2006 (it was sold again at Christie's and Sotheby's). Since then there have been reports of a fourteenth.

222 **"seemingly woven from moonbeams"**: *Gazette du Bon Ton,* no. 10 (1925).

222 **"an exquisite little thing"**: Loelia Lindsey, *Grace and Favour: The Memoirs of Loelia, Duchess of Westminster* (New York: Reynal, 1961), p. 232.

223 **Louis, who had been working on the Exposition**: Alongside his rival Louis Boucheron, Louis Cartier was appointed as one of three vice presidents for the Parure (Jewelry) category.

223 **"exhibit gem jewelry, fine timepieces, etc."**: Salomé and Dalon, eds., *Cartier: Style and History,* p. 162, citing an official exhibition admission form submitted by Louis in 1923.

223 **His firm's creations were designed to be worn with haute couture**: Cartier also retained a subsidiary stand in the Grand Palais alongside the other jewelers, but the main display was in the Pavillon d'Élégance.

224 **"Modern decorative art in all its forms"**: Nadelhoffer, *Cartier,* p. 188, citing exposition documentation, *"L'exposition des arts décoratifs et industriels modernes"* (1923).

224 **Jacqueau had been experimenting**: Chazal and Chazal, *Bijoux parisiens,* p. 150, citing Jacqueau's *Livre de raison.*

225 **"Among the outstanding pieces"**: Rudoe, *Cartier,* p. 289, citing Fouquet, *La bijouterie, la joaillerie: La bijouterie de fantaisie au 20e siècle* (Paris: Évreux, 1934), pp. 189–190 (see also the subsequent quote).

225 **"fastened at intervals to the corsage"**: *Vogue* (American edition), September 15, 1925.

225 "Cartier sponsors this new jeweled ornament": Ibid.
225 "necklace shoulder ornament": Rudoe, *Cartier*, p. 316, quoting how it is described in Cartier archives. The Berenice name was given only later when it appeared in an illustration in a special 1925 edition of the *Gazette du Bon Ton* on the Pavillon d'Élégance.
225 an illustration of a short-haired blond model: "Le Pavillon d'Élégance," *Gazette du Bon Ton*, no. 7, 1924–25.
226 In mid-September 1925: *Comoedia*, September 15, 1925.
227 Baron de Meyer: *Harper's Bazaar*, New York, March 1926.
227 "without doubt among the *bijoutiers-joailliers*": Rudoe, *Cartier*, p. 289, citing Fouquet, *La bijouterie, la joaillerie*, pp. 189–190.

Chapter 6: MOICARTIER New York: Mid-1920s

228 "Up to a few months ago": *New York Herald Tribune*, October 16, 1925.
229 "personalities from the world": *Le Gaulois*, October 18, 1925.
231 "This nation has definitely become": United Press, April 4, 1927 (*Dunkirk Evening Observer*).
231 the savvy redheaded Dodge brothers: Howard and his brother were 10 percent minority shareholders in the Ford Motor Company and sued Ford for accumulated dividends. After losing the lawsuit, Ford bought out the remaining stockholders in July 1919, including $25 million for the Dodge brothers (they had also earned more than $5 million in dividends).
231 "the richest man at J. P. Morgan": Stephen Birmingham, *The Grandes Dames: The Wonderful Uninhibited Ladies Who Used Their Wealth and Position to Create American Culture in Their Own Images—from the Gilded Age to Modern Times* (Guilford, CT: Lyons Press, 2016), p. 22.
231 "the most beautiful [tiara] ever seen": Ibid., p. 27, quoting *The Bulletin*.
232 "Father was the show-off": Birmingham, *Grandes Dames*, pp. 42–43.
232 "Not long before the wedding": Ibid., p. 40–41. The price paid was exaggerated in this anecdote; it was actually $825,000.
233 It was said to have been owned at one time: The necklace, apparently part of Catherine's personal jewelry collection, had been passed down to successive Romanov rulers and was eventually smuggled out of Russia by a related aristocratic family.
234 courtesy of two reputed Egyptian art dealer brothers: See the *New York Times* obituary of Vitali Benguiat (trader of oriental carpets in Paris, London, and New York), March 18, 1937.
234 Claiming that the necklace had in fact been sold: *Boston Globe*, January 13, 1922, and response in *New York Times*, January 14, 1922.
234 In the end, the matter was resolved: *Daily News*, January 1922. Howard Bloomer, chairman of Dodge's board of directors, made public a letter he had written to Cartier Inc. Howard bought the necklace in May 1920 for $825,000 (more than $8 million today).
234 Ten years later, in 2018: Bonhams, *Fine Jewellery*, New York, December 16, 2008; New York Christie's, *Magnificent Jewels* (Geneva, November 13, 2018), lot 305. This appears to be the same set of 305 pearls, even if it was split into two necklaces in the latter auction.
235 Pierre hired the marketing consultant Edward Bernays: His retainer was $6,000 a year.
235 "If we understand the mechanism and motives of the group mind": Edward L. Bernays, *Propaganda* (London: Routledge, 1928). He would later call this scientific technique of opinion molding "the engineering of consent."
235 "the illusion that Monsieur Cartier's decisions": Bernays, *Biography of an Idea*, p. 324.
235 flanked by his secretary and chief of staff: Pierre's chief of staff was Armand Eugène Sieper (1882–1934), a Frenchman who came to the United States in 1909. He was general secretary of the French Chamber of Commerce in the United States. Miss Stella Engler (b.1875) was Pierre's devoted secretary, an American from Indiana,

who lived in Paris before the First World War. She also maintained his database of clients. Later, his secretary was Eugenia Munson.

237 **Dreicer's storefront had been designed:** Anna W. Rasche, *Dreicer & Company: Forgotten Jewelers of the Gilded Age* (New York: Cooper Hewitt, Smithsonian Design Museum, 2018), p. 60.

237 **a number that would later grow:** Rudoe, *Cartier,* p. 44. Maîtrejean's son Philippe also later worked for Cartier.

237 **Alexandre Genaille, who by now was senior enough:** Alexandre Charles Genaille (1884–1947) attended the École Nationale des Arts Décoratifs before joining Cartier Paris as a designer in 1906. A talented artist, he worked for Cartier New York from 1909 to 1930, becoming head of the design department in 1919. As a Cartier designer, Genaille created a variety of objects, including desk accessories, clocks, and jewelry. His archive has been preserved at the Bibliothèque Forney. See also the *Bénézit Dictionary of Artists* (available online at oxfordartonline/benezit).

238 **Pierre expanded his in-house supply capabilities:** Further details of Marel Works are given in New York State Department of State, Corporation / Business Entity database, DOS ID21732 (see also DOS ID18420 for the Bombay Trading Corporation).

239 **It would feature:** *New York Times,* April 20, 1924.

240 **"working now with might":** "Jusserand Opens French Exposition," *New York Times,* April 23, 1924.

240 **There were, *The New York Times* continued:** Ibid.; also March 31 and April 20, 1924.

240 **"anticipated by years corporate image building":** Bernays, *Biography of an Idea,* p. 329.

242 **Designed by the fashionable architect:** Ogden Codman, Jr., had co-authored in 1887 (with Edith Wharton) *The Decoration of Houses,* an influential text in American architecture, as well as decorating mansions for New York's elite, including Cornelius Vanderbilt II.

242 **She had lived in her Ninety-sixth Street mansion:** *New York Times,* February 1915.

242 **when the opportunity arose six years later, bought it:** "Dahlgren House Sold," *New York Times,* August 11, 1927; see also *Brooklyn Daily Eagle,* September 11, 1921.

242 **There were carved fireplaces:** Edward T. Mohylowski, *Lucy D. Dahlgren House Designation Report* (New York: NYC Landmarks Preservation Commission, June 19, 1984).

243 **"brought his love of Mediterranean architecture":** *New York Times,* August 1, 2008, citing Paulette Koch.

244 **In 1923, he took a long-term lease:** *Palm Beach Post,* March 20, 1925.

245 **Cartier's had established a seasonal store:** Letters suggest that 249 Worth Avenue was the original Cartier location (after Lake Trail). It was replaced years later by another site at 340 Worth Avenue (and after that, 214 Worth Avenue).

245 **There was no in-house workshop:** One Cartier Inc. designer recalled his work trips to the Palm Beach sunshine—there he would listen to the client's requirements, sketch up a couple of examples for her to consider, and, once she had selected one, return to New York with the design sketch. The piece would be priced and, if approved, made up. For the most part, though, Cartier Palm Beach was frequented more for repairs and remounting.

245 **"You can't conceive of the amount of jewels":** Marjorie Merriweather Post interview by Nettie Leitch Major, 1965.

245 **Not only was she knowledgeable:** Later, she favored the art of Russia (particularly after spending time there once her third husband, Joseph E. Davies, became ambassador to Russia).

245 **Born to a pioneer in the hugely profitable cereal industry:** "Obituary," *New York Times,* September 13, 1973.

245 **He met Marjorie at a Palm Beach houseboat party:** Nancy Rubin, *American Empress: The Life and Times of Marjorie Merriweather Post* (New York: Villard Books, 1985).

246 **Marjorie enjoyed entertaining:** In the 1950s, Marjorie Merriweather Post bought Hillwood in Washington, D.C., which remains a museum filled with her collection today.

246 "Its 110,000 square feet glinted with gold leaf": Rubin, *American Empress*, p. 161.
248 "Perhaps the most outstanding new":"The Chic of Jewels," *Vogue America*, June 1, 1926, p. 50.
248 It is likely Marjorie's dresses: The brooch is featured in a 1929 portrait of Post and her daughter by Giulio de Blaas (see photo insert).
248 hoping others might gain the same enjoyment: Along with dressing up and entertaining, Marjorie did a huge amount for charity. "There are others better off than I am. The only difference is I do more with mine. I put it to work," she once told an interviewer.
248 "one of the last of a rapidly disappearing": Maurice Zolotow, *It Takes All Kinds: Piquant Pen Portraits of Some Picturesque People* (London: W. H. Allen, 1953), p. 129 onward.
248 "His studio in New York": "Jules Glaenzer Obituary," *New York Times*, August 1977.
249 "considered so important socially": Zolotow, *It Takes All Kinds*, p. 132.
250 "very swank" farewell party: *Daily News*, January 18, 1925.
250 their engagement was announced: "King of Diamonds Takes a Queen in Florida Romance," *Daily News*, March 31, 1925.
251 Emergency affidavits of his good character: These were arranged, at least in part, by Pierre's nephew-in-law, René. The president in question was Thierry Mallet.
251 United States Attorney William Hayward: *New York Times*, April 10, 1925.
251 watching as his beautiful bride in ivory satin: *New York Times*, April 24, 1925.
252 "telegrams from Jules prepared Louis Cartier": Nadelhoffer, *Cartier*, p. 29.
252 "On Tuesday, he [Glaenzer] telephoned me": Bernays, *Biography of an Idea*, p. 328.
252 "Nothing can be added to fine pearls": Another saying was that a fine pearl necklace is the one piece of jewelry a woman could wear twenty-four hours a day and remain in good taste.
253 "Nothing could save them": "Uncanny Recovery of the Lovesick Pearls," *Butte* [Montana] *Miner*, Sunday, August 10, 1924.
254 All were bid on: The longest strand, containing 55 pearls, reached 5 million francs from the Parisian jeweler Oscar Kahn. The middle, 49-pearl strand reached 3.2 million francs from an M. Henry, and the shortest, 41-pearl strand reached 2.7 million francs from Baron López de Tarragoya, a reputed Spanish pearl merchant based in Paris.
254 a Mr. Esmerian: This was presumably the father of Raphael Esmerian (1903–1976). Paul Esmerian had worked as a lapidary in Constantinople before relocating to Paris in 1890. His son Raphael entered the business in 1919 and became a leading European gem dealer, and a major supplier of stones for Cartier, also later in the United States. His collaboration with the Cartiers helped create some of the most important pieces of the Art Deco period.
255 the press was able to report: Nadelhoffer, *Cartier*, p. 118; see also *New York Times*, April 10, 1924; June 25, 1924; June 19, 1924; July 6, 1924; and January 12, 1925.
255 "An inner salon": *Kane* [Pennsylvania] *Republican*, July 21, 1924.
255 "No, they are too poor": "Thiers Pearls Too Costly for Poor Queens," *Buffalo Times*, July 17, 1924.
255 "passed the customs": *Hartford Courant*, January 13, 1925.
255 the Big Sisters organizations: *Coshocton* [Ohio] *Tribune*, Monday, July 21, 1924.
256 "New York society, the wealth of America": *Morning Call*, March 16, 1925.
256 "Dazzlingly fair, with lovely features": Balsan, *Glitter and the Gold*, p. 123.
257 "see the country, meet the people": Terence Elsberry, *Marie of Romania* (New York: St. Martin's Press, 1972), p. 136.
257 "whistle of steamers, roar of guns": Constance Lily Morris, *On Tour with Queen Marie* (New York: Robert M. McBride & Company, 1927), p. 13.
258 "horse shows and balls and luncheons": Julia Gelardi, *Born to Rule: Granddaughters of Victoria, Queens of Europe* (London: Headline, 2005), p. 324.
258 "very eager that I should visit": Marie, Consort of Ferdinand I, *America Seen by a Queen: Queen Marie's Diary of Her 1926 Voyage to the United States of America* (Bucharest: Romanian Cultural Foundation, 1999), p. 66. See also Marie, Consort of Ferdinand I, *The Story of My Life* (New York: Charles Scribner's Sons, 1934), and

Diana Mandache, ed., *Later Chapters of My Life: The Lost Memoir of Queen Marie of Romania* (Stroud, Gloucestershire, UK: History Press, 2004).

258 **"On this chair sat her Majesty":** Bernays, *Biography of an Idea*, p. 326.

259 **"At the time, I was in":** Henri Delgove, *Le monde et les cours: Mémoires de S.A.R. le Prince Christophe de Grèce* (Paris: Plon, 1939), p. 59.

260 **Yusupov described sailing to America:** Nadelhoffer, *Cartier,* p. 124, gives a different date, 1922. Yusupov's account appears in the second volume of his memoir, *En Exil,* published in 1954, in which he wrote, "*par un beau jour de novembre 1923, chargés de tous nos bijoux et collections de bibelots, nous montions à bord du paquebot Berengaria, à destination de New York. . . . Comme rien ne se vendait, je finis par confier le tout à la maison Cartier. Je connaissais personnellement Pierre Cartier. C'était un homme serviable et loyal et sur qui je savais compter pour agir au mieux de nos intérêts.*

260 **"a helpful and loyal man":** Felix Yusupoff, *Prince Felix Yusupoff: En Exil,* vol. 2 (Paris: Plon, 1954), p. 72.

260 **the richest man in Russia:** The vast Yusupov fortune had been acquired through extensive land grants in Siberia as well as mines and fur trading posts.

260 **"as I had always seen them":** Yusupoff, *En Exil,* p. 71.

260 **"I ended up entrusting everything to the Cartier House":** Ibid.

261 **Mathilde Townsend:** "Mrs. Gerry Buys Youssoupoff Necklace of 42 Black Pearls for $400,000," *New York Times,* January 25, 1924.

261 **the $75,000 advance:** Nadelhoffer, *Cartier,* p. 124, suggests that for this advance, Yusupov had also deposited a second necklace of thirty-one pearls.

263 **"the finest collection of emeralds available":** *St. Louis Star and Times,* January 15, 1936.

264 **"The legendary joining of two great American fortunes":** Birmingham, *Grandes Dames,* p. 136.

265 **"My dear, don't you realize":** Ibid., p. 129.

265 **"appearing more annoyed by the interruption":** Birmingham, *Grandes Dames,* p. 130.

266 **Walska was known less for her singing skills:** The United Press Association, 1936, reported that she was "estimated to have married fortunes totaling $125,000,000 in her marital ventures. . . . She likewise was believed to have spent one-twelfth of this sum in attempting to further her great ambition to become an opera star."

266 **"the world's richest bachelor":** Birmingham, *Grandes Dames,* p. 139.

266 **"to go with carte blanche to Cartier":** Ganna Walska, *Always Room at the Top* (California: Lotusland, 2015), p. 175.

266 **most of her important Cartier pieces:** Her remarkable collection came to light in April 1971 when, in her eighties, she consigned the collection to auction with Parke-Bernet to raise funds for her historic Lotusland estate near Santa Barbara. See *New York Times,* April 2, 1971 (report on the auction), and the description of her collection in Sotheby's, *Magnificent Jewels* (Geneva: Sotheby's, November 13, 2013).

266 **she bought the Shinto mystery clock:** This clock was the first in a series of six in the oriental-style "portico" (gateway) form, made by Cartier between 1923 and 1925, containing the movement in the lintel. Number 3 in the series (1924) was sold by Sotheby's New York in October 1998. For the other clocks, see *The Magical Art of Cartier* (Paris: Antiquorum, 1996), pp. 302–315.

267 **Cartier Inc. was fighting an expensive, ongoing legal battle:** *United States v. Cartier Inc.,* U.S. Customs Court of Appeal, December 5, 1927.

267 **it would be Louis' first trip to the States:** In press reports, Louis indicated that it was his first trip to America, but, confusingly, his immigration form stated that he had visited in 1911.

268 **"It is now America's great opportunity":** *Palm Beach Post,* March 7, 1927.

268 **expanding Cartier's New York footprint:** In 1927, Pierre bought 4 East Fifty-second Street from the grocery magnate Harry James Luce. The following year, Pierre would buy another neighboring building, 647 Fifth Avenue, the former home of Robert Goelet, occupied by the Gimpel & Wildenstein galleries. See *New York Times,* May 30, 1928.

269 **They had plans to host:** *New York Times,* December 1, 1929.
269 **a defining moment for Pierre in America:** "Debutante Party for Marion Cartier," *New York Times,* December 1, 1929.
269 **Admiring her father:** Pierre Cartier had held a dinner for the incoming French ambassador, Paul Claudel, in April 1927 ("Mr. and Mrs. Cartier Hosts," *New York Times,* April 22, 1927). Paul Claudel served as the French ambassador in Tokyo (1922–1928), then Washington, D.C. (1928–1933), then Brussels (1933–1936).

Chapter 7: PRECIOUS London: Late 1920s.

270 **"All of society seemed to be *en fête*":** Edward VIII, Duke of Windsor, *A King's Story: The Memoirs of HRH the Duke of Windsor* (London: Pan Books, 1957), pp. 161 and 188.
271 **Only when guests brought many servants:** Jacques would later thank Mrs. Rees for her trouble by offering her small uncut gemstones acquired on his travels.
272 **Captain Alfred Lowenstein:** In the summer of 1928, the fifty-one-year-old Lowenstein took his private Fokker plane from Croydon, England, back to Belgium. Getting up to use the lavatory, he walked to the back of the plane but never returned. When his private secretary, Baxter, went to check that all was well, he found the lavatory empty and the door opposite it (to the outside) flapping in the slipstream. Two weeks later, Jacques read in *The Times* that what was believed to be his client's decomposed body had been discovered in the English Channel, identifiable only by an engraved gold wristwatch. The standard story was that Lowenstein, increasingly suffering from absent-mindedness, had opened the wrong door and plunged to his death. But knowing his client, Jacques doubted that that was possible. Conspiracy theories abounded, with suggestions that Lowenstein had been murdered (possibly even by his own wife), faked his own death, or committed suicide (there were rumors his companies were on the brink of collapse)
272 **"walls draped in rose-pink moiré":** Gardner, *Elephants in the Attic,* p. 11.
273 **"It is always a joy to me":** Cherry Poynter in *Harper's Bazaar,* 1937.
273 **Félix Bertrand, a talented jeweler:** Félix Bertrand (1880–1952) was a French jeweler who moved to New York in 1910 before moving back to Cartier London in 1921 and eventually running English Art Works. His son, Charles, also worked as a setter for Cartier London from the 1920s.
274 **"excitable, kind, and he lived for design":** James Gardner, *Elephants in the Attic: The Autobiography of James Gardner* (London: Orbis, 1983), p. 13. Apprenticed from 1923, Gardner worked at Cartier's until 1929 and then spent the 1930s traveling abroad.
275 **"hundreds of specks sparkling":** Ibid., p 15. Gardner became a renowned designer and graphic artist. He would also undertake ship design work, including the *Queen Elizabeth II,* an ocean liner, in the late 1960s.
276 **"a plane of excellence probably higher":** *New York Times,* December 22, 1922.
276 **Jacques wasn't the only one inspired:** In Paris, Jacqueau had been experimenting with the Egyptian style since about 1910, using motifs like the lotus in his Art Deco designs.
276 **"it occurred to him":** "Real Cleopatra Stuff," *Leader-Post,* Regina, Sask., Canada, October 3, 1925.
277 **European antiques shops:** Nadelhoffer, *Cartier,* p. 146; Rudoe, *Cartier,* p. 137. In 1914 a Paris antiques dealer named Kalebdjian sold Louis Cartier a series of antiquities, mostly faïence figures.
277 **their diverse illustrated library included tomes:** The *Book of the Dead* is one of many books in Jacques' library containing bookmarks revealing the path of his creative journey.
277 **The combination of antique objects:** Vivienne Becker, *Highlights from "Magnificent Jewels": Five Rare Egyptian-Revival Jewels,* Sotheby's.com; "These cerebrally beautiful and strikingly original compositions, possessing a powerful and imposing presence, are amongst the most rarefied of Cartier jewels from this period."

279 **"the most lavish hostess":** "Lady Cunard Obituary," *Times* (London), July 12, 1948, p. 7.

279 **"indeed anybody so long as they were interesting":** Alan Jefferson, *Sir Thomas Beecham: A Centenary Tribute* (London: MacDonald and Jane's, 1979), p. 39.

280 **it would give him the chance to showcase:** *Tatler*, December 12, 1928.

281 **"I took a deep breath":** Gardner, *Elephants in the Attic*, p. 17.

281 **"executed well, a hundred items":** Those he didn't sell immediately he would take to the Cairo French Exposition in March, where he attracted the attention of King Fouad I.

281 **"the jewels, introduced with the utmost discretion":** *Tatler*, December 12, 1928.

282 **"and much interest was aroused":** *Tatler*, December 12, 1928.

282 **"*The Sketch* announced in a column:** *The Sketch*, December 19, 1928.

286 **a world record price:** Sotheby's, *Magnificent Jewels* (Geneva: Sotheby's, November 11, 2014), lot 348; US$17,295,796. The Blue Belle was 392.52 carats; Jacques said the one he saw was close to 350 carats, but it's possible that the weighing equipment was inaccurate. Certainly, judging by the description of its color, purity, and shape, it appears to be the same stone. If so, it was then sold in 1937 to the British motor magnate Lord Nuffield (1877–1963), founder of the British car company Morris Motors and of Nuffield College, Oxford.

288 **When the large silver Rolls:** This is described in Clifford North's extensive 1932 travel diary of his trip for Cartier to Nepal (with thanks to his family). Clifford North joined Cartier London at the start of the 1930s and traveled extensively to India throughout that decade, including with Jacques Cartier in 1939. After the war, he continued to work as a salesman out of Bond Street until his retirement in 1960 (on his sixty-fifth birthday).

289 **Jacques was closest to the Maharaja:** The Maharaja Jam Sahib of Nawanagar, Shri Kumar Ranjithsinhji Vibhaji Jadega (1872–1933), leader since 1907.

289 **"a business connection which became a friendship":** Jacques Cartier, in the afterword to Rowan Wild's *Ranji: The Biography of Colonel His Highness Shri Sir Ranjitsinhji* (London: Rich & Cowan, 1934), p. 326.

290 **shared love of gemstones:** They agreed on almost everything, except the perfect color for a ruby. Whereas Jacques thought it should be deep red, Ranji preferred a slight purple hue, although by the end of his life, Ranji would come around to Jacques' way of thinking.

290 **Versailles-inspired palace in the Punjab:** According to *The Times*, October 11, 1927, visitors were housed in a huge camp in front of the Maharaja's residence, with tents "fitted in palatial style, with luxurious reception and sitting rooms, baths and all the comforts of home." There were garden parties, excursions, sports, fireworks, and banquets. See also Francis de Croiset, *Nous avons fait un beau voyage* (Paris: Grasset, 1930), p. 79.

290 **"a piece truly unique":** Nadelhoffer, *Cartier*, p. 169, citing the Maharaja of Kapurthala's diary entry of September 27, 1926.

290 **1931 advertisement:** An advertisement titled "For the Brow of a Great Prince" in *Spur* magazine, described the Maharaja as "one of the most enlightened of Hindu princes." See Nadelhoffer, *Cartier*, p. 162.

294 **"Sahib Cartier":** Jocularly, Nelly used the Hindi honorific to refer to Jacques while in India.

295 **"Napoleon of Oil":** Paul Hendrix, *Sir Henri Deterding and Royal Dutch–Shell: Changing Control of World Oil, 1900–1940* (Bristol, UK: Bristol Academic Press, 2002), p. 121, citing Lord Fisher.

295 **Lydia would go on to have:** Massimo Gargia and Allan Starkie, *Jet Set: Mémoires d'un International Playboy* (Paris: Michel Lafon, 2000), pp. 152–155.

296 **with TM Sutton in London:** in 1927, Yusupov offered Cartier London various pearl jewels, including the La Pelegrina pearl (later bought by Elizabeth Taylor), that had been mortgaged at TM Sutton between 1927 and 1929, with Cartier and TM Sutton jointly advancing the £37,807. See Nadelhoffer, Cartier, p. 124.

296 **Deterding had previously expressed an interest:** Christie's, *A Casket of Magnificent*

Jewels: The Collection of the Late Lady Lydia Deterding (Geneva: Christie's, 1980). In 1980, the Polar Star was sold by Christie's for $4.6 million, at that time a record price for a single gem. It was bought by an anonymous Indian collector from Mumbai and has not been seen since.

297   **"Ganna Walska the next"**: Ganna Walska, *Always Room at the Top*, p. 292. While in St. Moritz, Walska asked Jacques Cartier whether Lady Louis Mountbatten's pearl earrings were real (he replied that they were not)

298   **created a Swiss company**: From 1929, the St. Moritz branch was open in the winter season and also in the summer months. It closed down after World War II. See *Schweizerisches Handelsamtsblatt*, December 30, 1929, no. 305, p. 2566, referencing the setup of JacNel Aktiengesellschaft (JacNel Limited) a week earlier

299   **King Fouad I of Egypt**: Fouad I (1868–1936) had become Sultan of Egypt in 1917 (later King in 1922). Queen Nazli was born to Egyptian parents with French ancestry. She accepted the king's advances after he fell in love with her at the Cairo Opera in 1919. In 1927, they had made a state visit to France. See *L'Écho d'Alger,* March 7, 1927.

299   **Cartier's display at the exhibition**: M. Georges Philippar, ed., *Exposition française au Caire: Égypte–France* (Paris: Délégué du Gouvernement Français, 1929). For the most part, the French Exposition in Cairo was dedicated to industrial companies like Schneider and de Wendel, but there were a few fashion-focused stands. Egyptian-style designs were only a part of the exhibit, as Jacques sought to demonstrate the full range of Cartier's craftsmanship. In an interview at the time, he stated: "You could say that a jewellery business like ours is equally equipped to furnish a woman's shoulder with a gorgeous necklace as to fill her handbag with a powder compact, a mirror, a small comb, and even visiting cards, and each and every item carries the same stamp of originality and art."

301   **white diamonds, yellow diamonds, brown**: Rosita Forbes, *India of the Princes* (New York: Book Club, 1939), p. 127. Patiala's legendary collection is also described in A. Kenneth Snowman, ed., *The Master Jewelers* (New York: Thames & Hudson, 2002), p. 89.

302   **"What are you doing?"**: My thanks to the Muffat family for sharing this story with me, as told to his grandchildren.

302   **yellow 234.6-carat De Beers diamond**: The Maharaja had inherited the De Beers diamond from his father, Maharaja Sir Rajinder Singh. Rajinder had purchased the pale-yellow diamond after seeing it exhibited at the Paris Exposition of 1889.

302   **financially that attractive for Cartier**: Katherine Prior and John Adamson, *Maharajas' Jewels* (Paris: Assouline, 2000), p. 172. According to this book, not only did the Maharaja supply his own gemstones, but he tended to be a slow payer (in 1929, his debts totaled £1.5 million, much of it owed to European luxury suppliers)

302   **he had never seen anything like it:** For a detailed account of the Patiala exhibit by May Birkhead, a friend of Pierre and Elma, see "Paris Is Amazed by Oriental Gems," *New York Times,* October 21, 1928. She reports that "Cartier is now showing at an invitation affair, set diamonds which probably surpass any single collection ever assembled in the Occident. They are the property of an Indian sovereign who is delighted by the setting contrived for these amazing baubles." She indicated that the jewels, carefully guarded, were worth around $10 million (close to $150 million today)

303   **to buy a separate workshop**: By 1930, he had acquired Wright & Davies, a longtime supplier.

305   **now Morgan & Co. Bank**: It had been renamed after the tragic early death of her brother, Hermann—then lead partner—a few years earlier.

306   **the amethyst brooch**: See Estelle Nikles Van Osselt, *Asia Imagined in the Baur and Cartier Collections* (Geneva: Fondation Baur, 2015), exhibition catalog, p. 65.

Chapter 8: Diamonds and Depression: The 1930s

307   **"Eighty percent of our orders were canceled"**: Georges Dovime, "La Bataille Electorale aux États-Unis," *Action française* (1930), Marion Cartier archive, Saint Louis University.

308 **avoid taking on too much debt:** The French designer Paul Poiret was forced to close in 1929. See Jaclyn Pyper, "Style Sportive: Fashion, Sport and Modernity in France, 1923–1930," *Apparences* (July 2017).

309 **"perhaps the most elaborate":** Edward VIII, Duke of Windsor, *King's Story*, p. 195: "The art treasures alone would have sufficed the needs of an ordinary museum, and I particularly remember a vast hall lined with figures in armor that had been obtained from various old European collections."

309 **A year later, his investment:** After receiving nearly $300 million (over $4.4 billion today) in shares, ITT's share price plummeted, from $149 in 1928 to $17.5 a year later and just $3.45 by 1937 (see *New York Times,* November 1938).

310 **"Poor little rich girl":** *Sioux City Journal,* January 1926: "What in the world will that poor girl do with all that money, so much more than she has any possible need of?"

310 **"to die from—the epitomy of":** Heymann, *Poor Little Rich Girl,* p. 49.

311 **"The roll of great names":** Zolotow, *It Takes All Kinds,* p. 160. The American composer Richard Rodgers recalled Glaenzer's gratitude: "As an appreciator of your efforts, Jules is second to none. . . . Jules doesn't only tell you—he looks it, he feels it with his whole body. His sincerity and gratification are tremendous. Often, he'll have tears in his eyes."

311 **"his habit of carrying jewels round":** C. David Heymann, *Poor Little Rich Girl: The Life and Legend of Barbara Hutton* (Secaucus, N.J.: Lyle Stewart, 1984), p. 130.

312 **"one of the rarest strands":** Nadelhoffer, *Cartier,* p. 125. The Barbara Hutton / Marie Antoinette pearl necklace sold for $580,000 at a Christie's auction in Geneva in May 1992. Seven years later, it reached $1.47 million at a November 1999 Christie's auction in Geneva.

312 **a striking jadeite necklace:** Sotheby's, *Magnificent Jewels and Jadeite* (Hong Kong: Sotheby's, April 7, 2014), lot 1847. In 2014, this necklace was sold for more than $27 million.

312 **"instituting a $5 and $10 department":** Bernays, *Biography of an Idea,* p. 332.

313 **"a specially designed bracelet":** Sylvia Neely and David E. Cassens, *The Legacy of Elma Rumsey Cartier* (St. Louis: Saint Louis University, 1995), p. 10, citing a letter from Ed Kehren to Pierre Cartier, September 6, 1931.

313 **profits for Cartier New York were much worse:** Ibid.

313 **"For our part let us rejoice":** *Le Figaro,* October 7, 1931.

314 **set up an American Committee:** May Birkhead, a journalist from St. Louis who wrote for a Parisian newspaper, said that the strong interest in the United States for the exhibition was attributable to "an American committee, in which the most active spirits are leaders of the French Chamber of Commerce in New York." For the figures cited, see Neely and Cassends, p. 10.

314 **a Mayfair exhibition:** This was an exhibition in Burlington House. After decades of collecting, Louis had one of the most highly regarded collections of Persian miniatures in the world. Ironically, one of the only other collectors who could have competed was Maurice de Rothschild, the man who still hadn't responded to Louis' request for a duel.

314 **"magnificent examples" of Cartier's "high craftsmanship":** *Illustrated London News,* November 1930.

315 **Roger Chalopin:** Chalopin had graduated from the prestigious École Polytechnique before joining Cartier and becoming an administrator (later a director). His family recalled that he used to finish his work in half the time expected and would happily then stretch himself by translating engineering manuals into Latin or ancient Greek for pleasure.

315 **new Cartier Paris workshop at Rue Bachaumont:** Cartier Paris opened a workshop at 17 Rue Bachaumont in 1929, then bought the Robert Linzeler silver workshop at 9 Rue d'Argenson in 1932. Both workshops were united into Cardel (which combined the names of Cartier and Claudel) on Rue d'Argenson in 1949. Only in 1954 did this workshop move into Rue de la Paix. Cartier and Bachet, *Cartier: Exceptional Objects,* vol. 2, p. 42; and François Chaille et al., *The Cartier Collection: Jewelry* (Paris: Flammarion, 2019), vol. 1, p. 125.

317 **"I had many serious talks":** Nadelhoffer, *Cartier*, p. 309.

317 **Duc Armand de Gramont:** The 12th Duc de Gramont (1879–1962) was a noted French industrialist making precision optical instruments to help France compete with the German military.

317 **more than two dozen swords:** The 1988 *Cartier Museum at the Goldsmiths' Hall* catalog lists twenty-six Cartier swords between 1931 and 1986, including those of François Mauriac (1933), Georges Duhamel (1936), Jacques de Lacretelle and James Hyde (1938), André Maurois (1939), Pasteur Valéry Radot (1945), Henri Mondor and Maurice Genevoix (1947), Julien Cain (1953), and Duc de Lévis-Mirepoix (1954). Jacques Rueff is listed as 1947 but this appears to have been 1965 (per the Académie Française website). See *The Cartier Museum at the Goldsmiths' Hall,* p. 89.

319 **"invasion of the jungle":** See the 1929 Exposition catalog: Philippar, *Exposition française au Caire.*

319 **the Cartier display was awarded:** Nadelhoffer, *Cartier*, p. 175; Rudoe, *Cartier*, p. 23; Munn, *Tiaras*, p. 382. In the jewelry class, they won the Classe 95 Grand Prix.

321 **"His Highness asked me to sit":** Albert Monnickendam, *The Magic of Diamonds* (London: Hammond, Hammond & Co., 1995), pp. 103–105.

322 **flawless Queen of Holland diamond:** The Queen of Holland diamond's origin is a mystery. Jacques thought it was from South Africa. However, some experts speculate that it was from Golconda, the famous Indian mine.

322 **it would form the centerpiece:** Prior and Adamson, *Maharajas' Jewels*, p. 163.

322 **the Deterdings had ended up:** Nadelhoffer, *Cartier*, p. 319. See also John Herbert, ed., *Christie's Review of the Season 1981* (London: Weidenfeld & Nicolson), p. 270.

322 **"such gems could not have been bought":** Rowan Wild, *Ranji: The Biography of Colonel His Highness Shri Sir Ranjitsinhji* (London: Rich & Cowan, 1934), pp. 323–326, citing Jacques Cartier, "The Nawanagar Jewels," p. 323: "The Jam Saheb himself loved jewellery, and would fondle precious stones with the touch of an artist. He began to pit his knowledge against the opinions of the experts. He already envisaged the possession by the State of the finest collection in India. It took twenty-three years to fulfil that ambition."

322 **"The realization of a connoisseur's dream":** Wild, *Ranji*, p. 324, from the chapter "Nawanagar Jewels," written by Jacques Cartier.

323 **This necklace was born out of the love of gemstones:** A necklace based heavily on the 1931 Nawanagar diamond necklace was the subject of a 2018 Hollywood film in which it was referred to as "the Jeanne Toussaint necklace." My grandfather, however, recalled that it had been designed by his father. Furthermore, at the time it was made, Jeanne was running Department S in Paris, not London.

324 **an almost architectural look:** See Rudoe, *Cartier*, p. 284.

324 **"The only requirement":** Rudoe, *Cartier*, p. 261–63; cites *Vogue*, October 1938 (p. 52).

324 **"Cartier's magnificent parure":** Rudoe, *Cartier 1900–1939*, p. 261, citing *Harper's Bazaar*, January 1935, p. 59.

324 **as did many visiting Americans:** Ibid., p. 263: "Much of Cartier's aquamarine jewellery seems to have been made by the London branch, where it appears in the records from 1932. Aquamarines were popular not only with the London clientele but also with the American clients of both the London and Paris branches." De Wolfe bought this tiara at Cartier Paris in 1935, aged seventy.

324 **"We would mention that":** Rudoe, *Cartier*, p. 263.

325 **"As a matter of fact":** Christie's, *Magnificent Jewels* (Geneva: Christie's, May 16, 2007), lot 125, citing letter from Cartier London to Cartier New York, December 1936.

325 **"after the Queen, who wore the crown jewels":** "Almost Outshone Queen," *Washington Post*, February 21, 1909.

326 **bank would fund Cartier London's purchases:** Letters from Cartier Ltd. to Kleinwort Sons & Co., 1930–32 (London Metropolitan Archives). The agreement was that while the property in the jewels was transferred to Kleinwort's, they remained insured by Cartier and would be sold by Cartier. The profit was then to be divided

between Kleinwort's and Cartier. Cartier could sell at any time without reference to Kleinwort's, provided a specified net minimum profit was shown.

326 **a client referred to as M.F.:** This may have been Marshall Field III, heir to the Chicago Marshall Field department store fortune.

326 **A massive decline in the value of sterling:** It fell 30 percent against the U.S. dollar.

328 **"A propos of Pierre—nothing new!":** Neely and Cassens, *The Legacy of Elma Rumsey Cartier,* p. 13, quoting letter from Marion Cartier to Pierre Cartier, August 28, 1932.

328 **"The world is blossoming":** Ibid.

329 **Pierre Claudel had proposed:** Their engagement took place on September 25, 1932.

329 **"How this busy young daughter":** *New York American,* Tuesday, April 4, 1933; there had been an "adieu" call to her fellow students at the Art Students League, fittings of gowns, sittings for photographs, "and a series of luncheons, receptions, dinners and dances that would wear out the hardiest debutante."

330 **"outstanding Lenten event":** *New York American* and *New York Times,* both Sunday, April 9, 1933: "many diplomats . . . wore the uniforms of their respective countries."

331 **Her lover, he believed, was Alfonso:** Alfonso XIII (1886–1941) was king of Spain from birth until the proclamation of the Second Republic in 1931.

331 **a lavish lifestyle, multiple mistresses:** His marriage to the English princess Victoria Eugénie of Battenberg (later Queen Victoria Eugenia of Spain) had broken down after their first son was born with hemophilia.

331 **"She is living in a sanatorium":** *Magyarorszag,* April 25, 1934.

332 **"Twelve years ago, the proud Countess":** "King Alfonso Starts Tongues Wagging," *Oakland Tribune,* July 15, 1934.

334 **"we must make it our business":** Nadelhoffer, *Cartier,* p. 201, cites Louis Cartier. Louis' directive to combine form with function always played a role in the firm's creative strategy from the early twentieth century, but it became even more relevant in the Depression years.

335 **Cartier patented two new gold alloys:** In 1937, Cartier patented a different alloy, platinex, said to be as pliable as platinum but more affordable.

335 **Gérard Desouches, and, from 1935:** Gérard Desouches (1909–2000) was an important figure in Cartier Paris in the mid-twentieth century. In addition to a role on the design committee, he is listed on a number of patent applications (e.g., 1931 and 1948). In 1939, he opened the pop-up store in Deauville with Jacques Guyot and Jack Hasey (who remembered him as "blond and very nice-looking") and postwar, he was involved with the Cardel workshop. Gérard's uncle Robert Desouches also painted a famous watercolor of Rue de la Paix in 1924.

335 **Louis had been away:** 1933 alone saw Louis travel to Budapest, Spain, London, and New York, where he displayed his Persian miniatures at the Metropolitan Museum of Art.

337 **that it would bode well for future business:** Around this time, Louis Cartier gave an interview to the *Comoedia* newpaper (May 21, 1935), along with Louis Boucheron, "two great jewellers," about the state of the Parisian luxury trade. Interestingly, Louis Cartier focuses in the interview not on design and fashion trends, or on the need for skilled craftsmen, but firmly on taxation, arguing that the industry's problems were not specific to the luxury trade but rather the result of the national tax burden. Since 1925, taxes had become excessive and the state raised more than half of the national income in this way. The consequence was an increase of unemployment and social disorder. The solution, he argued, was to restore purchasing power through tax relief and the adjustment of French prices against world prices.

339 **heiress to the Singer sewing machine fortune:** Christened Marguerite Séverine Philippine and born in Paris in 1890 of American and French extraction, Daisy Fellowes's mother was Isabelle Blanche Singer and her father was the fourth Duc Decazes et de Glücksberg, descended from Louis XVIII's chief minister. James Pope-Hennessy, *American Vogue,* 1964, observed that "she could rely on four major assets: very great beauty, a subtle, exquisite and barbed sense of humor, an inborn taste for dress, and a considerable fortune."

339 **a penchant for "cocaine and other women's husbands":** The *Daily Mail*, March 29, 2014, reported that Fellowes "lived on grouse, cocaine and other women's husbands." See also Mary S. Lovell, *The Riviera Set, 1920–1960: The Golden Years of Glamour and Excess* (London: Little, Brown / Abacus, 2016), p. 117, which details her use of narcotics and reports that "her lovers numbered in the hundreds and she appeared to regard the serial purloining of other women's husbands as normal behaviour.

339 **"overrun with Maharajas, casually wearing fabulous jewels":** *London Vogue*, August 7, 1935.

339 *Vogue* **was quick on her heels:** Judy Rudoe, "The Taste for 'Barbaric Splendour': Daisy Fellowes and Her 'Hindu' Necklace," *Jewellery Studies*, vol. 9 (2001), p. 90, citing *London Vogue*, August 1935.

339 **example of Cartier's Tutti Frutti style:** The Tutti Frutti style really came into its own in the late 1920s and the 1930s, but there were a few early Indian-inspired examples, like the 1912 exotic aigrette with an Indian *sarpech* motif. Also, as far back as 1901, Cartier created an Indian-style necklace for Queen Alexandra to wear with the Indian-style embroidered silk dresses given to her by Lady Curzon, wife of the viceroy of India.

339 **Reconstructed from Fellowes's own:** She asked Cartier to dismantle two bracelets and a necklace to make it. The necklace had been made in 1928 by Cartier, one of the bracelets was made in 1929 by Cartier, and the third bracelet is unidentified. The design for the 1928 bracelet was signed off by René Revillon.

339 **the necklace was unique:** Sotheby's, *Magnificent Jewels* (Geneva: Sotheby's, May 15, 1991), lot 390; in 1991, the necklace surfaced at auction.

340 **the Collier Hindou was designed:** Later, when it passed to Daisy's daughter the Countess de Castéja, the Collier Hindou's design was changed slightly to give it less of a classic Indian bib shape and a sapphire clasp in place of the cord. "I preferred her original necklace," Jean-Jacques Cartier admitted many years later. "That silk cord and bib shape were so classically Indian."

340 **one important difference:** Rudoe, "Taste for 'Barbaric Splendour,'" p. 87, points out that the necklace was most likely based on the Maharaja of Patna's 1935 Cartier necklace but with the addition of sapphires (Maharajas did not tend to favor sapphires, which were traditionally considered unlucky in India).

342 **"His selection will undoubtedly make sapphires":** *Guardian* and *Dundee Courier*, September 13, 1934.

342 **"cool classical features in a perfect":** Roy Strong and Cecil Beaton, *Cecil Beaton: The Royal Portraits* (London: Simon & Schuster, 1988), p. 71.

342 **"Every American woman":** Edward VIII, Duke of Windsor, *King's Story*, p. 248.

343 **he was instructed to switch allegiance:** Anne Sebba, *Les Parisiennes: How the Women of Paris Lived, Loved and Died in the 1940s* (London: Weidenfeld & Nicolson, 2016), p. 350; she indicates that both Cartier and Van Cleef were patronized in place of Boucheron.

343 **Wallis was spotted wearing a rather special Cartier jewel:** Diana Cooper, *The Light of Common Day* (London: Hart-Davis, 1959), p. 175. A number of photographs—which appeared in the international press—caused intense speculation as to the true nature of the couple's relationship.

344 **"Claudel hadn't been successful":** A February 1935 report in *Aux Écoles du Monde* suggesting nepotism ("Everyone knows that two places are already reserved to the sons of two ambassadors: one for the son of Georges Roux and one for the son of Paul Claudel") may have worked against Claudel.

344 **traveling to New York with his family:** Neely and Cassens, *Legacy of Elma Rumsey Cartier*, p. 16.

345 **"the richest little girl in the world":** Stephanie Mansfield, *The Richest Girl in the World: The Extravagant Life and Fast Times of Doris Duke* (New York: Pinnacle Books / Kensington Books, 1999).

346 **Fortunately for Cartier, along with Doris's many other interests:** At a Christie's auction in June 2004, Doris Duke's jewelry collection—including the pieces she had in-

herited from her parents and grandmother—fetched more than $12 million. A 1908 Belle Époque necklace that her father had bought, providing Cartier with some of the larger stones himself, sold for more than double the estimate, reaching $2.4 million. An Art Deco bracelet that had been bought by her mother in 1927 went for $1.2 million.

347 **Mona Williams (later von Bismarck):** Mona Williams von Bismarck (1899–1983) was an American socialite and fashion icon. In 1933, Mona was named "Best Dressed Woman in the World" by Chanel, Molyneux, Vionnet, Lelong, and Lanvin, the first American to be honored in this way. She was an important Cartier customer; her famous 98-carat sapphire necklace, designed by Cartier, is on display at the National Museum of Natural History of the Smithsonian Institution (also the home of the Hope Diamond) in Washington, D.C. Her personal papers are preserved by the Filson Historical Society in Louisville. See also the 1925 Cartier jadeite, onyx, ruby, and diamond pendant/brooch featured in the "Magnificent Jewels and Noble Jewels" sale in Geneva in May 2017 (lot 362)

347 **the client's husband was one of the richest men in America:** Her third husband, the entrepreneur Harrison Williams, was well known for funding trips to the Galápagos and Greenland, for having a volcano named after him, and for accumulating a fortune of $680 million in 1929 (about $10 billion today). Williams later faced investigation into his securities dealings, but in the mid-1930s, he was still riding high.

351 **he wanted so much for Cartier to be a family-run business:** As early as 1924, his son-in-law René Revillon had been made a director of Cartier S.A. at the relatively young age of thirty-four.

355 **He died three weeks later:** According to his death certificate, René died of a pulmonary embolism following an operation for the repair of a perforated duodenal ulcer.

355 **"probably knew and was known by":** "May Birkhead, 55, Paris Writer, Dies," *New York Times,* October 29, 1941.

356 **"I think I know our people":** *Newsweek,* vol. 44 (1952), p. 52, citing Stanley Baldwin.

356 **"How could he do this":** Richard Kenin, *Return to Albion: Americans in England, 1760–1940* (New York: Holt, Rinehart and Winston, 1979), p. 218.

357 **"Have you noticed lately that tiaras":** Diana Scarisbrick, *Tiara* (San Francisco: Chronicle Books, 2000), p. 35, citing *Vogue* (1935).

358 **Cartier London made twenty-seven tiaras:** Rudoe, *Cartier,* p. 258; of these, fifteen were produced in April and early May, nine for stock and six for special orders.

358 **"could scarcely walk for jewels":** James Robert Rhodes, *Chips: The Diaries of Sir Henry Channon* (London: Weidenfeld & Nicolson, 1967), p. 116.

358 **Maharaja of Nawanagar:** Digvijaysinhji Ranjitsinhji Jadeja (1895–1966) was the Maharaja Jam Sahib of Nawanagar from 1933 to 1948, succeeding his uncle.

359 **"at the stroke of half past twelve":** *Boston Globe,* May 12, 1937, and *Santa Cruz Evening News,* May 12, 1937.

359 **"the greatest day of splendor":** Frank H. King, writing for the Associated Press, published in the *Boston Globe,* May 12, 1937, inter alia.

362 **Exposition of Modern Arts and Technology:** This event was known in French as the Exposition Internationale des Arts et Techniques dans la Vie Moderne and was held from May 25 to November 25, 1937.

363 **"That was the clincher," he recalled:** John F. Hasey and Joseph F. Dinneen, *Yankee Fighter: The Story of an American in the Free French Foreign Legion* (New York: Garden City Publishing, 1944), p. 47.

364 **"they wanted sunning":** Justine Picardie, *Coco Chanel: The Legend and Life* (New York: HarperCollins, 2011), p. 168.

364 **Chanel and he had many heated arguments:** Ibid., p. 176.

364 **one in Cannes in 1938:** Records indicate that the Cartier Cannes store had been set up at 59 Boulevard de la Croisette by early July 1938.

364 **"the garçon, the secretary, and I":** Hasey and Dinneen, *Yankee Fighter,* p. 37.

365 **"with $3 million worth of stones":** Ibid., p. 64.

365 **It made sense to follow the money:** In 1936, Cartier London displayed in the Monte

Carlo store a significant diamond that had previously belonged to the Duke of Westminster. The 80.6-carat triangular Nassak jewel (said to have been taken from the eye of a temple god) had in 1933 been proposed by Jacques as the central stone in a turban ornament for the Gaekwad of Baroda. When that project didn't materialize, the diamond had been incorporated by the designer Frederick Mew into a five-string pearl and diamond necklace, and it was this piece that was displayed in Monte Carlo. When it didn't sell during the season, it was returned to London, and the diamond was recut as a more fashionably shaped rectangular stone of 47.41 carats. Rudoe, *Cartier,* p. 35; Baroda abandoned the project in 1935 (after eight years' work) when he was seventy-two years old.

365 **"an account must be cultivated":** Hasey and Dinneen, *Yankee Fighter,* p. 39.

366 **"in rows and *rows"*:** Diana Vreeland, *D. V.* (Boston: Da Capo Press, 1997), p. 53.

367 **another palace in Budapest:** Jacqui in her early forties was very social and would regularly invite friends to stay. In the autumn of 1937, one of these was Lois Sturt, Lady Tredegar, who had been one of the Bright Young Things of the 1920s. Just a week after Lady Tredegar arrived at the Cartier palace, she started to feel unwell. Jacqui called for a doctor, but before he arrived, her thirty-seven-year-old friend had collapsed. An autopsy would later confirm that Lois had died from a heart attack brought on by a severely restricted diet. See *Western Mail,* September 22, 1937.

368 **their combined value was £16,000:** Angus McLaren, *Playboys and Mayfair Men: Crime, Class, Masculinity, and Fascism in 1930s London* (Baltimore: Johns Hopkins University Press, 2017), p. 17, citing Metropolitan Police telegram, December 20, 1937.

368 **After studying the rings:** Ibid., citing statement of E. Bellenger, December 20, 1937.

368 **The three men made off:** Ibid., citing statement of Enrico Larenti (the waiter who found Bellenger), December 20, 1937.

369 **the police investigation commenced:** Ibid., citing *Police Gazette,* December 21, 1937.

369 **The press had a field day:** *Times,* January 28, 1938; *Daily Telegraph,* February 16, 1938.

369 **"four men who gate-crashed parties":** *Daily Mail,* February 19, 1938.

369 **Bellenger amused the crowd:** *Daily Mail,* July 3, 1939.

370 **with the occasional headache:** The story attracted the attention of Britons of all classes. Even King George VI mentioned that he was saddened that the case had led to a decline in public trust and cited as an example a recent meeting at the palace. It was customary for the royal family to buy their jewelry presents from Cartier. Not long after the Hyde Park Hotel robbery, the palace called Cartier as usual and asked for a salesman to be sent with a selection of jewels. "And what do you think?" the King cried. "They sent up two men. Two men! I could see that they were not going to trust me!" See *Yorkshire Evening Post,* February 6, 1937.

370 **The French were in a celebratory mood:** *Paris Soir,* July 1938; Jacques and Nelly, who had planned to come over for the event, almost didn't make it when their suitcases, containing over £5,000 worth of jewels ($300,000 today), were stolen from the automobile outside their London flat.

370 **"Old-timers said the Armistice could not compare":** Hasey and Dinneen, *Yankee Fighter,* p. 64.

371 **"in gratitude for the heroic attitude":** *West Sussex Gazette,* October 13, 1938.

371 **"That fool," he said, referring to Hitler:** Hasey and Dinneen, *Yankee Fighter,* p. 70.

374 **Aunt Milly's house in Grasse:** The generous Milly cared for her parents in their old age rather than marrying, and her father passed his vast Grasse residence down to her in thanks.

Chapter 9: The World at War (1939–1944)

379 **seventy-nine-year-old Elsie de Wolfe:** Elsie de Wolfe, known as America's first interior decorator, authored the influential 1914 book *The House in Good Taste* and was a prominent figure in New York, Paris, and London society. Openly lesbian, she shocked everyone at the age of sixty-seven when she married her platonic friend, Sir Charles Mendl.

379 she might have to replace RSVP with INW: Jane Smith, *Elsie de Wolfe: A Life in the High Style* (New York: Atheneum, 1982), p. 279.

379 "I'm going to make everything": Ibid., p. 280.

380 "She mixes people like a cocktail": Elsie de Wolfe, *The House in Good Taste: Design Advice from America's First Interior Decorator* (New York: Charles Scribner's Sons, 1914), p. 37.

380 "the last grand gesture of gaiety": Charlie Scheips, *Elsie de Wolfe's Paris: Frivolity Before the Storm* (New York: Abrams, 2014), p. 103.

381 "It does not feel like a proper War": Simone de Beauvoir, *Wartime Diary, September 1939 to January 1941* (Urbana: University of Illinois Press, 2009), p. 677.

381 "We've forgotten the air-raid alerts": David Drake, *Paris at War: 1939–1944* (Cambridge, MA: Belknap Press of Harvard University Press, 2015) quoting Charles Braibant, a wartime diarist (see also the Archives Nationales, 366AP).

382 "The war has never been more elusive": Ibid., p. 31, citing Jean-Paul Sartre's diary, November 20, 1939.

382 some of it had been taken: In August 1939, as war had seemed ever more likely, the salesman Hasey had been ordered to hide some of the most important jewels.

382 "a severe and progressive psychotic disorder": Declaration by Roger Worth about his cousin Anne-Marie, Court of the First Instance, August 1945.

386 The war shelter at the Ritz: Sebba, *Les Parisiennes*, p. 13.

386 Le Bal des Petits Lits Blancs: Mary S. Lovell, *The Riviera Set, 1920–1960: The Golden Years of Glamour and Excess* (London: Abacus, 2016), p. 192.

386 "Paris is beautifully war gay": Noël Coward, *The Letters of Noël Coward* (London: Knopf, 2007), p. 78. Coward wrote to Gladys Calthrop in the tense days before France fell.

386 the Duke of Windsor continued: Sebba, *Les Parisiennes,* p. 40. The Duchess of Windsor had volunteered for a short time, delivering bandages and cigarettes to hospitals.

386 the Duke commissioned a large brooch: This jewel was commissioned in March 1940 and given to the Duchess as a birthday present in May 1940.

386 wholesale trade forbidden: Nadelhoffer, *Cartier*, p. 312.

386 worked on the brooch's design: Lemarchand was officially demobilized from the artillery service in Saint-Cloud in August 1940, but he may have returned to work earlier.

389 "the German army wielded a monstrous brush": Hasey and Dinneen, *Yankee Fighter,* p. 147.

389 "I took the German advance": Sebba, *Les Parisiennes,* p. 46, quoting Simone de Beauvoir.

390 "There was not space": Hasey and Dinneen, *Yankee Fighter,* p. 149.

391 Pierre meanwhile worried: According to an order of the occupying authorities, if it had been known that the shareholders of the company were in the United States, a German commissioner would have been appointed for Cartier Paris. This would have been a disaster, potentially allowing seizure of stock and even repatriation of the workforce to Germany.

392 "badly out of sorts": "What Comes After War," *Los Angeles Times,* July 30, 1940.

392 "in his bathrobe, sulking": Ibid.

393 When First Lady Eleanor Roosevelt heard: Blanche Wiesen Cook, *Eleanor Roosevelt*, vol. 3: *The War Years and After, 1939–1962* (London: Viking, 2016), p. 313.

395 "One morning a middle-aged man": Pierre Galante, *The General* (London: Leslie Frewin, 1969), p. 110.

395 Bellenger started by driving the General: Before long, Bellenger was helping de Gaulle in multiple ways. When two hundred young men arrived from France to offer their support, he was disappointed to discover they were still too young to join the Free French army. Rather than having them wait out the time before they turned eighteen in London, "where they were mixed with a very rough crowd," he arranged for them to be moved to a boy scout camp in Wales where they could continue their studies. Several Cartier London clients like Lady Arthur Peel and Mrs. Crawshay had helped.

396 "his chest was bare": Hasey and Dinneen, *Yankee Fighter,* p. 179.

396 "He was honest and straightforward": Ibid., pp. 183–184.

397 "would clearly be rebellion": Max Hastings, *All Hell Let Loose: The World at War 1939–1945* (London: Knopf, 2011), p. 125, citing Admiral René-Émile Godfroy.

397 "a mere adventurer": Claude Fohlen, *De Gaulle and Franklin D. Roosevelt* (London: Palgrave Macmillan, 1992), p. 34.

397 "De Gaulle is out to achieve one-man government": Elliott Roosevelt, *As He Saw It* (New York: Duell, Sloan and Pearce, 1946), p. 83.

398 "the flag of our Maison": Around this time at Cartier Inc., aside from Jules Glaenzer and Edmond Forêt, other longtime employees included the sales director and VP Jean E. Grelet (who later joined Lentheric, the perfume house), the salesman William F. Lynch, Victor Pujos, Henry G. Richard, Paul Rosier (who was running the Palm Beach store), René Pouech, Renée Besson, Lee M. Rumsey, and John J. Gory, not to mention Edmond Kehren (who, corresponding frequently with Pierre, was his "eyes and ears" in New York for many years). Other employees were Henry Duru (a salesman who joined in 1921, son of the New York workshop manager, Paul Duru) and John E. Davis (credit manager, who joined around 1929).

400 The skills were not transferable: Valerie Steele, *Paris Fashion: A Cultural History*, p. 230.

400 Over the course of the war: Louis Devaux war notes, unpublished. See also Jean Védrine, *Les prisonniers de guerre, Vichy et la Résistance, 1940–1945* (Paris: Fayard, 2013).

400 Devaux later recalled: "Cartier's in Paris Hid Gems from Foes," *New York Times*, June 3, 1945.

400 senior salesman Paul Marchand: The Frenchman Paul Marchand (1887–1956) worked for Mellerio in Madrid before joining Cartier as a salesman (specializing in diamonds) in Paris after World War I. He worked at Cartier Paris for the rest of his life.

401 the German occupiers were enthusiastic buyers: "Occupation marks" (worth 20 francs) were inflated in value and circulated only in the Occupied Zone. They could be exchanged for francs at the Banque de France, but each time the French did so, they took a loss.

401 "this is no time for fashion": Picardie, *Coco Chanel*, p. 230.

402 "wise to try to satisfy him": In a *Sunday Times* article in October 1970 (p. 48), Marcelle Decharbogne—who had worked at Cartier for forty-five years—recalled that Hermann Goering had ordered and paid for a Cartier tiara. She also recalled being surprised that Goering was much smaller than she had imagined.

404 Carl Nater, was among those: The new Cartier Ltd. recruits such as Joe Allgood and Paul Vanson, still too young to join the war effort, also recalled standing guard with hoses.

410 "Jewellers are not always great artists": "Obituaries," *Times*, September 26, and September 18, 1941.

413 more than five million Americans were still unemployed: This was far fewer than the 11.5 million in 1932 but still a vast number of suffering citizens.

413 Louis left the world at 2:20 A.M.: "Louis Cartier Obituary," *New York Times*, July 1942. See also his death certificate.

414 presumably with little information available: The date of the London store opening, for example, is incorrect.

415 Toussaint, Louis' "greatest disciple": As Devaux would later call her, in a note to Madame Toussaint (Toussaint family archive, undated but 1960s by context).

416 "generals had apparently forgotten": In conversation with the family of Louis Devaux.

417 "*mon président!*": Philip Short, *Mitterrand: A Study in Ambiguity* (London: Bodley Head, 2013), p. 119; also in conversation with the family of Roger Chalopin.

417 Gaullist resistance network: Devaux also headed up the Aid Centres National Committee and covertly worked for the Gaullist resistance intelligence network called Vélite-Thermopyles that had been founded in 1941 by Pierre Piganiol and Raymond Croland.

417 **"If we had not resisted":** War files compiled by Louis Devaux (unpublished).

419 **Leclercq would wear it throughout:** Salomé and Dalon, eds., *Cartier: Style and History,* p. 328. For Françoise Leclercq's story of resistance, see Union des Femmes Françaises, *Les Femmes dans la Résistance* (Monaco: Éditions du Rocher, 1977), pp. 168–170.

419 **Some reports suggest that the brooch:** This story is noted by several sources but is not referenced. Perhaps unsurprisingly, given the censorship, it is not mentioned in family letters. A brief review of the Paris police archive of foreigners (Toussaint was Belgian) arrested during the war (*répertoires de notifications de procès-verbaux et arrestations d'étrangers, côtes 289W7 et 289W8, 1940–1943*) did not reveal any mention of Toussaint, unlike Devaux or Collin, who were actively known to Paris police as Cartier's representatives at the time (Chanel also had a file). It may be that if Toussaint was taken into custody and then released soon after, her name wouldn't have been recorded.

420 **Two years earlier, Lilian had secretly married:** Lilian married King Léopold on December 6, 1941, after a secret religious ceremony on September 11, 1941.

420 SIRE, WE THOUGHT YOU HAD YOUR FACE TURNED IN MOURNING: HRH Princess Lilian of Belgium, *Daily Telegraph* Obituary, June 10, 2002 (name of original Belgian paper not given in this article).

422 **"I have thought that a clock":** 2007 Sotheby's press release, citing Pierre Cartier.

422 **Cartier would provide the French Resistance:** Philip Short, *Mitterrand: A Study in Ambiguity,* note 169.

423 **"Doris and I thought that M. Cartier's switch":** Bernays, *Biography of an Idea,* p. 334. This is likely to have been the reception given for de Gaulle on July 10, 1944.

423 **"the first American to shed blood":** Hasey and Dinneen, *Yankee Fighter,* p. 292–293.

424 **"Paris! Paris outraged! Paris broken!":** Charles de Gaulle speech to the crowd from the Hôtel de Ville, August 25, 1944.

Chapter 10: Cousins in Austerity (1945–1956)

426 **"Everywhere you went, you sensed":** Harvey Levenstein, *We'll Always Have Paris: American Tourists in France Since 1930* (Chicago: University of Chicago Press, 2004), p. 98, citing S. J. Perelman in *The New Yorker.*

426 **the prospect of lining up:** Antony Beevor and Artemis Cooper, *Paris After the Liberation: 1944–1949* (London: Penguin, 2007), p. 153. By the summer of 1945, the rationing allowance was still just 350 grams of bread a day, 100 grams of meat a week, and 500 grams of fat a month. In April 1945, the city's population was said to average only 1,337 calories a day.

426 **Claude had grown up moving:** Although Hungarian-born, Claude had been awarded American nationality after serving in the U.S. Air Force during World War II.

428 **Not only had Toussaint consistently rejected his designs:** My thanks to the family of Charles Jacqueau for sharing this story.

428 **photographs of Toussaint "at work":** The article in question was "Paris: Cartier's New Jewels," *Harper's Bazaar,* October 1945. Photos by Henri Cartier-Bresson, but some photos were taken earlier by the French Slovakian photographer François Kollar.

429 **"He came early and stayed late six days a week":** Bernays, *Biography of an Idea,* p. 323.

430 **spending large sums of money:** Cologni and Mocchetti, *Made by Cartier,* p. 170.

431 **Louis had written multiple wills:** Jersey Heritage Reference: D/Y/A/120/72, November 17, 1948; contains a copy of the first and second wills of Louis-Joseph Cartier.

431 **his collection of Persian miniatures:** This collection was later sold by Claude Cartier and bought by John Goelet, who donated them to Harvard in 1958 (accessible online).

431 **carefully collected over the years:** Before the war, Louis had hidden some of his precious silverware and porcelain in an English country house in Yorkshire. Valued at £40,000 ($2.2 million), it made the newspapers in December 1945 after it was re-

ported stolen, and then again seven months later when it mysteriously reappeared dumped on the side of the road. *"Dix-neuf millions d'objets précieux sur le bord d'une route en Angleterre," L'Aube,* July 9, 1946.

431 **Louis had left most:** Jacqui was given a quarter of her late husband's belongings and named sole heir to the Budapest palace. However, by the time she came to inherit the palace, it had already been sold in the war and virtually destroyed by Russian forces.

431 **left specific instructions in his will:** The will specified that they must first offer the rights to the other heirs, and then to Louis' two brothers or their direct descendants. If neither option was feasible, the rights should be offered to his most trusted Cartier S.A. employees, namely Louis Devaux, Jeanne Toussaint, Gérard Desouches, and Roger Chalopin; he envisaged them taking 80 percent of the shares, with the balance split equally among the four other employees: Jean-Baptiste Turpin, Paul Marchand, Louis Bezault, and Marcel Marson (5 percent each). See the associated court documents included in Jersey Heritage Reference: D/Y/A/120/72.

435 **the Lend-Lease program:** Under the Lend-Lease program, the United States donated equipment for the war effort but required that anything left over at the end be paid for.

435 **England was mired in debt:** Niall Ferguson, *Civilization: The West and the Rest* (London: Penguin, 2011), p. 309. By the end of World War II, Britain had amassed an immense debt of £21 billion, more than 270 percent of GDP, most of it owed to the United States.

439 **Toussaint would admit . . . that she couldn't:** *Le Jardin des Modes,* October 1948.

441 **the cigarette boxes that Rupert Emmerson was working on:** Rupert Emmerson (1909–1996) trained at Chiswick School of Art and was one of Cartier London's most talented postwar designers.

444 **tied up in lengthy disputes:** Five years later, in 1952, Indira Gandhi stripped India's maharajas of their titles, their privy purses, their first-class train tickets, and their 13-gun salutes.

447 **part of Empress Josephine's residence:** The property used to be the boathouse of the Château de Penthes before being rebuilt and renamed Villa Elma.

447 **"Dazzling, imaginative and new":** "Parisian Cartier's Mark 100th Year," *New York Times,* December 22, 1947, and "100th Year Is Hailed by Cartier's Store," *New York Times,* November 11, 1947.

449 **said to be one million dollars:** Cartier and Bachet, *Cartier: Exceptional Objects,* vol. 1, p. 466.

453 **iconic bib-style amethyst, turquoise, and gold necklace:** The Duchess of Windsor's décolletage-spanning bib necklace, a special order from Cartier Paris in 1947, contains twenty-eight step-cut amethysts, one oval faceted amethyst, and a large heart-shaped amethyst, all suspended from a rope-like gold chain. The Duke commissioned the piece, supplying his own diamonds and amethysts, but Toussaint is said to have convinced him that the necklace would benefit from dozens of turquoise cabochons (see the *Telegraph,* June 10, 2016). This necklace went up for auction in April 1987 at Sotheby's Geneva. See the *New York Times* report, April 3, 1987, "Windsor Jewels Bring an Auction Record." There was a matching Cartier bracelet, purchased in 1954. See Nadelhoffer, *Cartier,* p. 241.

453 **"Rings are voluminous":** *New York Times,* December 22, 1947.

454 **"Today's customers have less to spend":** *The Orlando Sentinel,* "Famous Jewelers Install Bargain Counter," January 21, 1951, cites Associated Press article.

456 **"of loyalty and cooperation":** Correspondence between President Truman and Pierre Claudel, January 1949, Truman Presidential Library, PPF 4604: Cartier, Inc.

457 **"This apartment . . . is like a secret":** Beaton, *Glass of Fashion,* p. 328.

457 **"common love for animals and birds":** Nadelhoffer, *Cartier,* p. 233, citing Jeanne Toussaint's tribute to Lemarchand in 1949.

458 **filled his sketchbooks with images of panthers:** Perhaps best known in Paris for a love of big cats in the late 1920s and 1930s was Joséphine Baker (1906–1975), the American-born French entertainer who was a star of exotic cabarets like the Folies Bergère. Baker was joined in her act by a cheetah named Chiquita, in a diamond

choker. Diana Vreeland tells an anecdote that one hot July, she had gone to a Montmartre cinema. When the lights came on at the end, she had been shocked to find she was sitting next to Chiquita. Josephine had brought the animal for an outing to see the cheetahs in the film.

459 a 116.74-carat emerald: Nadelhoffer, *Cartier,* p. 229, gives this weight for the emerald, but the Sotheby's auction catalog (1987) estimates the emerald at 90 carats (lot 55).

459 "I know women who put": Menkes, *Windsor Style,* p. 179.

459 "The lorgnette has returned to fashion": Portrait by René Bouché of the Duchess of Windsor with her Cartier tiger lorgnette in *Vogue,* May 1955.

460 "one of society's favorite unattached men": *Daily News,* October 6, 1955.

460 "Claude Cartier of the jewelry millions": *Cincinnati Enquirer,* September 4, 1953.

460 Rome with a former Miss America contestant: *Lima News,* April 13, 1955.

460 with fellow "international celebrities": *The Sketch,* September 26, 1956.

461 docked there en route to America: This incident was reported in *The New York Times,* September 27, 1951; see also *Le Monde,* September 27, 1951 (according to the article, the driver was still alive at that point).

469 "every tart in London was getting in": Although the famous remark "We had to put a stop to it, every tart in London was getting in" is possibly apocryphal, it has often been attributed to the late Princess Margaret, including by the Queen's cousin, Margaret Rhodes, in her autobiography, *The Final Curtsey: A Royal Memoir by The Queen's Cousin* (London: Birlinn, 2014).

470 Though the new Cartier boutique: Inside the Albemarle Street boutique, one could find a variety of gifts from a £7 lipstick holder to an £18 cigarette case or a £45 gold and ruby ring.

473 "smallest waist in Paris": *New York Times,* March 9, 1954.

474 replaced American Art Works: American Art Works is said to have been dissolved in May 1941. See Decisions and Orders of New York State Labor Relations Board, vol. 5, 1942, pp. 14–19. The list of parties in that case gives an insight into the management structure of Cartier New York at the time: As well as Cartier Inc. and American Art Works, Inc., the complaint was filed against European Watch & Clock Co., Bombay Trading Corp., Pierre C. Cartier, Leo [sic] M. Rumsey, Pierre L. Claudel, Rene J. Pouech, John E. Davis, E. Foret, and Hilden & Sons, Inc.

475 purchasing department to start stocking them: Occasionally larger, more impressive ones made the cut, but these would pass through a separate jewelry trading entity known as the Bombay Trading Company (kept separate but in-store).

477 Cartier Caracas store shared a building: The Caracas store is said to have been in the old Galipan building on Avenida Francisco de Miranda, between Chacao and Campo Alegre.

477 leased Pierre's 52-foot yacht: *New York Times,* November 13, 1959, on the death of Elma, looking back at their retired life in Switzerland.

477 Nelly, who had moved to a nearby house: She was accompanied by her maid, Libbie Evans.

478 "Mr. W.": Based on previous correspondence, this may have been Harry Winston, but it's not clear in the text.

479 "I have the same admiration": Salomé and Dalon, eds., *Cartier: Style and History,* p. 23, citing a letter from Pierre Cartier to Jeanne Toussaint, January 1955.

479 artistic director: Greffe du Tribunal du Commerce de la Seine, Cartier S.A. Régistre du Commerce 1955, "Déclaration de Modification de Société"; see also Salomé and Dalon, eds., *Cartier: Style and History,* p. 372.

480 stormed out of Cartier: Mona Eldridge, *In Search of a Prince: My Life with Barbara Hutton* (London: Sidgwick & Jackson, 1988), p. 10.

480 helped fund the renovation of the palace: *New York Times,* "Gerald Van der Kemp, 89, Versailles' Restorer," January 15, 2002.

480 "he had spent a great deal": Eldridge, *In Search of a Prince,* p. 10.

481 "I was in the pool": Elizabeth Taylor, *My Love Affair with Jewelry* (New York: Simon & Schuster, 2002), p. 29.

482 **ruby and diamond eternity band:** For more on Grace Kelly as a Cartier client, see Salomé and Dalon, eds., *Cartier: Style and History*, p. 354; also Chapman, *Cartier and America*, p. 174.

483 **televisions had only recently taken off:** In 1948, only 300,000 television sets had been sold, and *Fortune* estimated that "90 per cent of the citizenry has not yet seen a television program." In the 1950s, television went mainstream. In 1950, more than 7.3 million TV sets were sold in the United States.

Chapter 11: The End of an Era (1957–1974)

486 **always been father-and-son teams:** There were also father-son teams in English Art Works, such as the skilled setter David Bisford and his son Andrew. When Imre Schwaiger's son, Ernest, wanted to work in England in the jewelry trade, Jacques proposed he join Cartier London. Though not as skilled as his father when it came to gemstones, Ernest became a top salesman, if sometimes pushy—on one occasion, a client had to tell him "It's okay, Schwaiger, you can stop selling now, I said I would take it." His wife, Adele Dixon, was a well-known actress, and her wearing of Cartier jewels in celebrity circles was, as always, good for business.

486 **more useful items:** See Franco Cologni (1998), pp. 120–127, for a discussion on this point.

487 **made under one roof:** Although Cartier Ltd. was a fully integrated operation, not all the Cartier workshops were actually under the same physical roof—for example, the Wright & Davis workshop was in East London.

488 **his perfectionist streak was known to exasperate his team:** Jean-Jacques' team in Cartier London included, on the sales side, Donald Fraser (later a director), Ernest Schwaiger, Clifford North, Douglas Poulton, and Kenneth Forbes (whose brother Norman worked in the ordering department). London designers included Frederick Mew, Rupert Emmerson, Ernest Frowde, and Dennis Gardner, while Charles Ambrose worked as a modeler. The directors of the workshops were Carl Nater, Jean-Jacques, Arthur Bergner, and, in the case of Sutton & Straker, George Henry Straker.

488 **"The best is good enough":** With thanks to the family of Douglas Poulton, known as DWP. Joining in 1930, DWP worked as a Cartier salesman for more than three decades. Clients included the Queen Mother, the Maharaja of Jaipur, Noël Coward, Salvador Dalí, the Duchess of Bedford, and Maria Callas. He also delivered Wallis Simpson's engagement ring to Buckingham Palace.

488 **The Jacques Cartier Memorial Award:** In the fifty-nine years since it was introduced, the award has been given thirty-eight times. The award was first made in 1958 to C. E. Geere for a beautiful silver box. Geere later worked for Cartier.

490 **"Before the advent of the motor car":** Michael Seth-Smith, *The Cresta Run* (London: Foulsham, 1976), p. 6.

490 **Harjes, meanwhile, loved:** He also created an award, the Harjes Cartier Silver Chip (also known as the Poor Man's Curzon), to be awarded to the winner of the runner-up competition. His nickname was Chips, and the award, a small silver chip (first given in 1963), remains much coveted today.

491 **new Cartier S.A. president:** Greffe du Tribunal du Commerce de la Seine, Régistre du Commerce, May 7, 1957.

491 **she would send occasional updates:** Nadelhoffer, *Cartier*, p. 253.

493 **traveling and pursuing semiprofessional interests in sports:** During the late fifties and early sixties, Claude raced for the French world championship bobsled team; later he served as chief coach of the French team in St. Moritz and became a juror of the National Federation of Bobsledding.

495 **management vacuum:** In June 1956, the Caracas branch manager, John Pilar, was killed in a plane crash on his way to Venezuela. In 1964, the head of the Caracas venture, Rafael Cabrera, joined Cartier's rival, Van Cleef & Arpels.

495 **"burglar dived through the open window":** *New York Times*, June 26, 1960; *Daily News*, June 26, 1960; *Indianapolis Star*, September 1, 1960.

495 **the debacle was an unwelcome distraction:** This robbery contrasted with the absence

of publicized robberies in the Paris branch. "Cartier has never been robbed," the *Spokesman Review* reported in January 21, 1951, of Cartier Paris. "A heavy iron curtain seals off the entire store during non-business hours." In reality, although the Rue de la Paix store had never been broken into, there were unexplained losses of jewels, such as the 1930s incident involving René Revillon. There was also a theft in the late 1920s when Cartier Paris sent a $250,000 necklace to London through the post and it never arrived (it was later found to have been stolen by a postal clerk). See the *Brooklyn Times Union,* April 16, 1928.

495 **favorite for an evening gala:** In conversation with the former Cartier New York designer Alfred Durante.

495 **firms like De Beers were spending millions:** Though De Beers itself could not trade directly in the United States because of antitrust laws, it had an enormous budget to promote the sale of diamonds by retailers.

496 **"A Diamond Is Forever":** Between 1939 and 1979, De Beers's wholesale diamond sales in the United States increased from $23 million to $2.1 billion. Over those four decades, the company's ad budget soared from $200,000 to $10 million a year.

496 **slogan of the century:** See the Edward Jay Epstein article in the February 1982 issue, which analyzed the groundbreaking De Beers campaigns.

496 **perhaps most resurgent:** "Sharp Profit Rise Seen for Tiffany," *New York Times,* December 22, 1961.

496 **had taken control from the family:** "Hoving Takes Control of Tiffany; Held 118 Years by the Same Family," *New York Times,* August 19, 1955.

496 **"have nothing to do with price":** Walter Hoving, "Mass Production is no excuse for poor design," *Herald Tribune,* reported in *Janesville Daily Gazette,* July 12, 1961.

497 CONSUMERS CURTAILING SPENDING: "Consumers Curtailing Spending Because of Stock Market Drop," *New York Times,* June 23, 1962.

497 **It comprised a necklace:** This comprised 2 pear-shaped emeralds, 2 black pearls, 16 round diamonds, 19 square emeralds, 20 pear-shaped diamonds, and 32 triangular diamonds.

497 **neither been paid for nor returned:** "Jewels Approved but Unreturned," *Dayton Daily News,* May 10, 1962.

497 **"It happened so fast":** *Cincinnati Enquirer,* June 2, 1962 (interview with Edward Gilbert). He had been trying to raise funds to prevent forced sales of Celotex Corporation.

498 **wanted to escape:** From 1960 to 1962, immigration forms show Claude traveling back and forth to Europe multiple times, as well as his trips to Bermuda, Venezuela, and the Bahamas. This was no mean feat in the early days of air travel.

499 CARTIER'S JEWELRY STORE SOLD TO BLACK, STARR: *New York Times,* December 4, 1962; *Bridgeport Post,* December 4, 1962.

500 **"a Boston jewelry dealer with wide interests":** See *Boston Globe,* December 6, 1962; *Tampa Tribune,* December 6, 1962. Goldstein was reported as heading up Jewelsmiths Inc. of Boston, as well as having interests in "Tecla Pearls Inc.," also of Fifth Avenue, and Marcus & Co., which operates the jewelry departments in various Gimbels Brothers department stores."

500 **"an independent and unaffiliated enterprise":** *New York Times,* December 5, 1962.

500 **"What the Rothschilds are to banking":** *Time,* December 14, 1962.

502 **"one of the dearest presents":** Cartier and Bachet, *Cartier: Exceptional Objects,* vol. 1, p. 467, quoting President Truman's daughter describing the gift: "[My father] had brought me the most beautiful present, which General de Gaulle had given him to give me as a token of friendship from the people of France. It was a Cartier piece and started a whole new trend in Cartier jewelry. I still wear it with joy—a heavy gold bracelet, studded with rubies, emeralds, sapphires, and diamonds, with a tiny watch in the center, surrounded by diamonds."

502 **striking reptile jewels:** Félix's largest commissions included a 1968 diamond serpent articulated necklace (with black, green, and coral plaques on the snake's underbelly symbolizing Mexico's colors) and a 1975 crocodile emerald and yellow diamond necklace.

502 **Jacques Rueff in 1965:** The full list was Jean Delay (1960), Joseph Kessel (1964), Jacques Rueff (1965), Maurice Druon (1967), and Pierre-Henri Simon (1967). See *Épées de Joaillier, Cartier* (Paris: Cartier, 1972).

503 **a clock in a crystal bottle:** Cartier and Bachet, *Cartier: Exceptional Objects,* pp. 344–345.

504 **"Even when over 80":** Sir Michael Wright, writing in *The Times,* October 1964.

505 **"those who knew him, including myself":** *The House of Cartier,* A&E Network's Lap of Luxury series documentary, 1999, citing Jack Hasey.

505 **"built a jewelry firm of international distinction":** *New York Times,* Obituary, October 29, 1964.

506 **"He was a generous host":** Sir Michael Wright, writing in *The Times,* October 1964.

506 **"was like a second father":** Condolence letters, Marion Cartier archive, Saint Louis University.

507 **"turtles, dogs and mainly birds":** See "Suzy 'shops' Cartier's—Jeweler to Royalty," *Journal Herald,* December 7, 1963, reporting on a meeting with Marcelle Decharbogne, said in the article to be Cartier Paris's public relations lady, though her actual role was far broader. For examples of Cartier's birds in the postwar period see Nadine Coleno, *Amazing Cartier: Jewelry Design Since 1937* (Paris: Flammarion, 2009), p. 28–44.

508 **"evolution of the business":** Greffe du Tribunal du Commerce de la Seine, Dépot du 12154, June 28, 1966, citing "Cartier SA Assemblée Générale, 1 février 1966." Despite the negative outlook, not all parts of the business were suffering. Cologni (1988) notes on p. 230 how Parisian watch production increased significantly in this period; 1,519 watches were sold by Cartier Paris in 1966 (of which 596 were Tanks), compared with around 250 a year in the 1950s (of which 30–40 were Tanks). The pre–World War II peak was 1920 for wristwatches overall (720 units) and 1926 for Tanks alone (135 units).

509 **no desire to tell the world:** My thanks to the Danziger family for helping me understand this period. See also "58 Shopping Days to Christmas," *Sunday Times,* October 18, 1970.

512 **"I bet you couldn't get boxes":** Judy Rudoe, "Cartier Gold Boxes: A Visionary Patron and a Bet with Ian Fleming," *Journal of the Decorative Arts Society* 37 (2013), p. 121, citing the late Mrs. Anne Hay, Peter Wilding's sister.

512 **at a particularly challenging time:** Because Wilding was not a UK resident (he had moved to the West Indies for health reasons), his boxes were exempt from the high purchase tax.

512 **"When Peter Wilding first came in":** Rudoe, "Cartier Gold Boxes," p. 121.

513 **including the watch cases:** According to Arthur Withers, most of the boxes were made by Dick Richards, Jack Perry, and Charlie Geere (the winner of the 1958 Cartier prize). The engine turning was done by Jules Kneuss and his pupil, Gerald Mayo.

514 **"Collectors who claim some measure":** "Twelve Gold Boxes," *Connoisseur* (August 1969), p. 227.

514 **"seriously in debt":** Rudoe, "Cartier Gold Boxes," p. 121.

515 **group of long-haired gentlemen . . . called the Beatles:** Interview in *The House of Cartier,* Lap of Luxury series documentary, 1999.

515 **more popular than the high jewelry:** Stefano Papi and Alexandra Rhodes, *20th Century Jewellery and Icons of Style* (New York: Thames & Hudson, 2013), p. 210.

517 **"as in a traditional watch":** Cartier London led the way in watch innovation through the 1950s and '60s, with the JJC models, the Half Tank (1962), the Tank Oblique (1963, based on the Tank Asymètrique), the Off-Centre case (1963), the Elongated Curved Tank (1966/69), the Crash (1967), the "Maxi Oval" (1968/69), the rare Cartier Pebble watch, and the experimental Double-strap (early 1970s). Postwar models from Paris included the gold-dial Tank Rectangle (1952) and a curved oval-shaped watch (1956), later named the Baignoire after the French for bathtub, while the 1960s saw the arrival of discreet "mini" models for the female audience, like the Mini Tank Allongée and Mini Tank Louis Cartier. For more information, see Cologni (1998), especially pp. 226–232.

517 CLASSIC TANK: See Cologni, *Cartier: The Tank Watch,* pp. 226–227, for a list of some key Cartier London models in the 1950s and 1960s.

518 This fastening system: See Ibid., p. 36, for early drawings of the folding buckle and the patent (number 409891) from December 1909.

518 small watchmaking division: Called Sutton and Straker, this was originally a gold-smiths' workshop in Clarendon House, Bond Street.

519 might have to wait: With eight craftsmen making about four a month (fewer if there was other work going on), only thirty or so watch cases would be made each month.

521 "a somewhat disconcerting one": Cologni, *Cartier Tank Watch,* p. 148.

521 creating a gold-plated Tank watch: Ibid., p. 148.

521 it was sold for a second time: "Cartier, Inc. Acquired by Holding Company," *New York Times,* November 9, 1968.

521 a stamp collector: On Claude's death, his rare collection of British North America and West Indies stamps would be sold by Stanley Gibbons Auctions for £443,310 ($3.8 million today). See *Classics from the Claude Cartier Collection,* April 21, 1977, sale number 5438.

522 "You come away from the interview": *Morning News,* October 27, 1970.

522 "Cartier has been too damn formidable": "Cartier's Won't Discount Diamonds," *Akron Beacon Journal,* November 24, 1968.

523 "I turned into a raving maniac": Richard Burton and Chris Williams, *The Richard Burton Diaries* (New Haven, CT: Yale University Press, 2013), p. 279.

523 Kenmore agreed to sell the diamond: Reports vary as to the exact price Burton paid for the diamond. The press reports $1.1 million, but some of those who worked at Cartier at the time recalled it being sold for less than Cartier's cost in exchange for the publicity.

523 brilliant publicity coup for the firm: Not everyone was so positive about the diamond. One *New York Times* editorial remarked that "in this age of Vulgarity marked by such minor matters as war and poverty it gets harder every day to see the heights of true vulgarity. But given some loose millions it can be done—and worse, admired!" Quoted in Kitty Kelley, *Elizabeth Taylor, the Last Star* (New York: Simon & Schuster, 1981).

525 mechanization as opposed to handcrafted: See Ashok Som, *The Road to Luxury: The Evolution, Markets, and Strategies of Luxury Brand Management* (Hoboken, NJ: John Wiley & Sons, 2015), especially pp. 163 and 244, for a discussion of how up until the early 1970s, the luxury industry was facing the challenges of globalization, i.e., "maintaining a balance between the values that luxury stands for (tradition, know-how, precious materials, scarcity, craftsmanship, and others) with economic requirements ('industrial scale' production, focus on costs, economies of scale)."

525 "By the next generation, or thereabouts": "Hand Craftsman Vanishing Breed," *New York Times,* July 6, 1969.

528 "yesterday's luxury, ostentatiousness and the preserve": This period is discussed in more detail in Anne-Marie Clais and Stéphanie Busuttil-César, *Les Must de Cartier* (Paris: Assouline, 2002), pp. 8–14. See also the "Indestructible Cartier" interview in *Journal de la Fondation de la Haute Horlogerie,* July 5, 2018, which discusses the subsequent developments for Cartier in the 1970s (which lie outside the scope of this book as a family- and family-firm-focused work).

528 "although the prestige of the name": Clais and Busutil-César, pp. 11–12.

528 "its two hundred luxury outlets": See for example "Cartier à l'Italienne," *L'Express* no. 1076, 21–27 February 1972, p. 78.

529 With profits for the firm uncertain: Cartier Ltd. annual accounts filed at Companies House (company no: 00157267) in the late 1960s and early 1970s illustrate the difficult trading environment. The year 1966, for example, was particularly difficult: Cartier Ltd. accounts for the year show a net loss, and both the preferred and ordinary dividends were waived.

530 buying New York, too: "Cartier Agrees to Sell Business to Foreigners," *New York Times,* December 19, 1975 (see also *New York Times,* November 27, 1975). For

other interviews in the 1970s about Cartier under the Hocq family and their investors, see the *Lincoln Star,* October 10, 1976; *The New York Times,* December 2, 1979; and *The New York Times,* December 10, 1979 (the latter article reports on Robert Hocq's death in a car accident).

530 **"Cartier, the jewellers":** "Family Interests of Cartier May Soon Reunite," *Times,* March 1, 1974.

Afterword

533 **a third generation to lead:** "Avoid the Traps That Can Destroy Family Businesses," *Harvard Business Review,* January–February 2012.

BIBLIOGRAPHY

Aga Khan, Princess Catherine, and Pierre Rainero. *Jeweled Splendours of the Art Deco Era: The Prince and Princess Sadruddin Aga Khan Collection.* London: Thames & Hudson, 2017.

Alison, Archibald. *Travels in France, During the Years 1814–15.* Ann Arbor: University of Michigan Press, 1817.

Allen, Charles, and Sharada Dwivedi. *Lives of the Indian Princes.* London: Century Publishing, 1984.

Antiquorum Auctioneers. *The Magical Art of Cartier.* Paris: Étude Tajan, 1996.

Arminjon, Catherine, and James Beaupuis. *Dictionnaire des poinçons de fabricants d'ouvrages d'or et d'argent de Paris et de la Seine 1838–1875.* Paris: Imprimerie Nationale, 1991.

Arnaud, Claude. *Jean Cocteau: A Life.* New Haven, CT: Yale University Press, 2016.

Arnold, Philippe, et al. *Saumur, l'école de cavalerie: Histoire architecturale d'une cité du cheval militaire.* Paris: Éditions du Patrimoine, 2005.

Arwas, Victor. *Art Deco.* New York: Harry N. Abrams, 1992.

Bainbridge, H. C. *Twice Seven: The Autobiography of H. C. Bainbridge.* London: George Routledge & Sons, 1933.

Balsan, Consuelo Vanderbilt. *The Glitter and the Gold: The American Duchess—in Her Own Words.* London: Hodder & Stoughton, 2012.

Bapst, Germain. *Histoire des joyaux de la couronne de France.* Paris: Librairie Hachette, 1889.

Barry, Joseph Amber. *The People of Paris.* New York: Doubleday, 1966.

Baudoin, M. Henri, and Georges Berg, eds. *Catalogue des joyaux, colliers de perles, joailleries, perles et brillants.* Lausanne: Lausanne Palace, 1920.

Beaton, Cecil. *The Glass of Fashion: A Personal History of Fifty Years of Changing Tastes and the People Who Have Inspired Them.* New York: Rizzoli ex libris, 2014.

Becker, Vivienne. *Art Nouveau Jewelry.* London: Thames & Hudson, 1985.

Beevor, Antony, and Artemis Cooper. *Paris After the Liberation: 1944–1949.* London: Penguin, 2007.

Belgique, Esmeralda de, and Patrick Weber. *Lilian: Une princesse entre ombre et lumière.* Brussels: Racine, 2012.

Benaïm, Laurence. *Dior: The New Look Revolution.* Paris: Rizzoli, 2015.

Bénézit, Emmanuel. *Bénézit Dictionary of Artists*. Oxford: Oxford University Press, 2011. oxfordartonline/benezit.

Bérard, Emilie. *Mellorio: Le Joaillier du Second Empire*. RMN, 2016.

Bernays, Edward L. *Biography of an Idea: Memoirs of Public Relations Counsel Edward L. Bernays*. New York: Simon & Schuster, 1965.

——. *Propaganda*. London: Routledge, 1928.

Birmingham, Stephen. *The Grandes Dames: The Wonderful Uninhibited Ladies Who Used Their Wealth and Position to Create American Culture in Their Own Images—from the Gilded Age to Modern Times*. Guilford, CT: Lyons Press, 2016.

Bonhams. *Fine Jewellery*. New York: Bonhams, December 16, 2008. Auction catalog.

Bruner, Robert F., and Sean D. Carr. *The Panic of 1907: Lessons Learned from the Market's Perfect Storm*. Hoboken, NJ: John Wiley & Sons, 2009.

Brus, René. *Crown Jewellery and Regalia of the World*. Amsterdam: Pepin Press, 2011.

Buchanan, Meriel. *Victorian Gallery*. London: Cassell, 1956.

Bugeaud, Pierre. *Militant prisonnier de guerre*. Paris: L'Harmattan, 1990.

Burnand, Robert. *La vie quotidienne en France de 1870 à 1900*. Paris: Librairie Hachette, 1947.

Burollet, Thérèse, ed. *The Art of Cartier: Musée du Petit Palais, October 20, 1989–January 28, 1990*. Paris: Paris-Musées, 1989. Exhibition catalog.

Burton, Richard, and Chris Williams. *The Richard Burton Diaries*. New Haven, CT: Yale University Press, 2013.

Cartier 1847–1947. Paris: Société d'Étude, 1947.

Cartier, Alain, and Olivier Bachet. *Cartier: Exceptional Objects*. 2 vols. Hong Kong: Palais-Royal, 2019.

Cartier, Jacques. "Modern Jewellery." Vol. 13. *Encyclopaedia Britannica*, 14th ed. (1929).

Cartier: London. Paris: Assouline, 2002.

Cartier: New York. Introduction by Marion Maneker. New York: Assouline, 2001.

Cartier: 13 Rue de la Paix. See Trétiak, Philippe.

Cartier Treasures: King of Jewellers, Jewellers to Kings. Beijing: Palace Museum, 2009. Exhibition catalog.

Cartier: Vintage Aircraft Exhibition. New York: Seventh Regiment Armory, March 15–20, 1979. Exhibition catalog.

Cavendish-Bentinck, William, 7th Duke of Portland. *Men, Women and Things: Memories of the Duke of Portland*. London: Faber & Faber, 1937.

Centre Pompidou. *Jean Cocteau sur le fil du siècle: The Exhibition*. Paris: Centre Pompidou, 2004.

Chaille, François. *Cartier: Creative Writing*. Paris: Flammarion, 2000.

——. *High Jewelry and Precious Objects by Cartier: The Odyssey of a Style*. Paris: Flammarion, 2013.

——, et al. *The Cartier Collection: Jewelry*. Paris: Flammarion, 2019.

Chambers, Anne. *Ranji: Maharajah of Connemara*. Dublin: Wolfhound Press, 2002.

Chapman, Martin. *Cartier and America*. Munich: Prestel, 2010.

Chazal, Gilles, and Martine Chazal. *Bijoux Parisiens: French Jewelry from the Petit Palais, Paris*. Memphis, TN: Dixon Gallery and Gardens, 2013.

Chazal, Martine, ed. *Art Deco Jewellery: Charles Jacqueau, Genius Jewellery Designer and the Brilliant Age of Boucheron, Lalique etc.* (in Japanese). Kyoto: Art Consultant International, 2006. Exhibition catalog.

Christie's. *Casket of Magnificent Jewels: The Collection of the Late Lady Lydia Deterding*. Geneva: Christie's, 1980. Auction catalog.

——. *The Collection of Elizabeth Taylor*. Vols. 1 and 2. Christie's, December 2011. Auction catalog.

——. *Jewellery and Objects by Cartier*. Geneva: Christie's, May 27, 1993. Auction catalog.

——. *Jewellery by Cartier*. Geneva: Christie's, May 21, 1992. Auction catalog.

——. *Magnificent Jewels*. Geneva: Christie's, May 16, 2007. Auction catalog.

——. *Magnificent Jewels*. Geneva: Christie's, May 14, 2014. Auction catalog.

——. *Magnificent Jewels*. Geneva: Christie's, November 15, 2016. Auction catalog.

——. *Magnificent Jewels*. Geneva: Christie's, November 13, 2018. Auction catalog.

———. *Three Magnificent Art Deco Cartier Clocks*. New York: Christie's, April 25, 1990. Auction catalog.

Clais, Anne-Marie, and Stéphanie Busuttil-César. *Les Must de Cartier*. Paris: Assouline, 2002.

Claudel, Paul. *La Perle Noire: Textes recueillis et présentés par André Blanchet*. Paris: Gallimard, 1947.

Claudel, Pierre. *Out of the Blue: Dessins de Marion Cartier-Claudel*. Paris: Camille Bloch, 1934.

Claudel, Violaine Bonzon. *L'accueil amical: Aquarelles de Marion Cartier Claudel et partitions de Darius Milhaud*. Paris: Bleulefit, 2017.

Clifford, Colin. *The Asquiths*. London: John Murray, 2003.

Cocteau, Jean. *Oeuvres Complètes*. Vol. 2. Paris: Marguerat, 1946.

Coleno, Nadine. *Amazing Cartier: Cartier Jewelry Design Since 1937*. Paris: Flammarion, 2009.

Collins, Larry, and Dominique Lapierre. *Is Paris Burning?* New York: Simon & Schuster, 1965.

Cologni, Franco. *The Cartier Tank Watch*. Paris: Flammarion, 2017.

———. *Jaeger-LeCoultre*. Paris: Flammarion, 2006.

———, and François Chaille. *The Cartier Collection: Timepieces*. Paris: Flammarion, 2006.

———, and Dominique Fléchon. *Cartier: The Tank Watch*. Paris: Flammarion, 1998.

———, and Ettore Mocchetti. *Made by Cartier: 150 Years of Tradition and Innovation*. New York: Abbeville Press, 1993.

———, and Eric Nussbaum. *Platinum by Cartier: Triumphs of the Jewelers' Art*. New York: Harry N. Abrams, 1996.

———. *Splendeurs de la joaillerie*. Paris: Bibliothèque des Arts, 1996. Exhibition catalog.

Cook, Blanche Wiesen. *Eleanor Roosevelt*. Vol 3: *The War Years and After, 1939–1962*. London: Viking, 2016.

Cooper, Diana. *The Light of Common Day*. London: Hart-Davis, 1959.

Coward, Noël. *The Letters of Noël Coward*. New Haven, CT: Yale University Press, 2007.

Croiset, Francis de. *Nous avons fait un beau voyage*. Paris: Grasset, 1930.

———. *Voyages aux fêtes de Kapurthala*. Paris: Éditions Kra, 1929.

de Gaulle, Philippe. *Mémoires accessoires, 1921–1946*. Paris: Plon, 1997.

Delgove, Henri, trans. *Le monde et les cours: Mémoires de S.A.R. le Prince Christophe de Grèce,* Paris: Plon, 1939.

"The Demidoffs and the Mining Industry of the Ural." *Practical Magazine,* 1873.

Dentu, E., ed. *Exposition Universelle de 1867 à Paris: Catalogue Général*. Paris: Palais-Royal, 1867. Exhibition catalog.

Devi, Gayatri, and Santha Rama Rau. *A Princess Remembers: The Memoirs of the Maharani of Jaipur*. New Delhi: Vikas, 1976.

de Wolfe, Elsie. *The House in Good Taste: Design Advice from America's First Interior Decorator*. New York: Charles Scribner's Sons, 1914.

Drake, David. *Paris at War: 1939–1944*. Cambridge, MA: Belknap Press of Harvard University Press, 2015.

Duras, Marguerite. "Le Bruit et le Silence." Preface to *Yves Saint Laurent et la photographie de mode*. Paris: Albin Michel, 1988.

Eden, Clarissa. *A Memoir from Churchill to Eden*. London: Weidenfeld & Nicolson, 2007.

Edward VIII, Duke of Windsor. *A King's Story: The Memoirs of H.R.H. the Duke of Windsor*. London: Pan Books, 1957.

Eldridge, Mona. *In Search of a Prince: My Life with Barbara Hutton*. London: Sidgwick & Jackson, 1988.

Elsberry, Terence. *Marie of Romania*. New York: St. Martin's Press, 1972.

Épées de Joaillier, Cartier. Paris: Cartier, 1972.

Every Woman's Encyclopaedia. London [s.n.], 1912.

Faber, David. *Munich: The 1938 Appeasement Crisis*. London: Simon & Schuster, 2009.

Faber, Toby. *Fabergé Eggs: One Man's Masterpieces and the End of an Empire*. London: Pan Books, 2009.

Fabergé, Tatiana F., Eric-Alain Kohler, and Valentin V. Skurlov. *Fabergé*. Geneva: Slatkine, 2012.

Fane, Harry, Hans Nadelhoffer, and Eric Nussbaum. *Reflections of Elegance: Cartier Jewels from the Lindemann Collection*. New Orleans: New Orleans Museum of Art, 1988.

Ferguson, Niall. *Civilization: The West and the Rest*. New York: Penguin Press, 2011.

"58 Days Until Christmas." *Sunday Times Magazine,* October 18, 1970.

Fitzgerald, F. Scott. *Tender Is the Night*. London: Penguin Group, 1998. First published 1934.

Fohlen, Claude. *De Gaulle and Franklin D. Roosevelt*. London: Palgrave Macmillan, 1992.

Forbes, Rosita. *India of the Princes*. New York: Book Club, 1939.

Fornas, Bernard, and Chor Lin Lee. *The Art of Cartier*. Singapore: Cartier, 2006.

Forster, Jack. *Cartier Time Art: Mechanics of Passion*. Milan: Skira, 2011.

Fort, Adrian. *Nancy: The Story of Lady Astor*. New York: St. Martin's Press, 2013.

Foster, Norman. *Cartier in Motion*. London: Ivory Press, 2017.

Fouquet, Alphonse. *Histoire de ma vie industrielle*. Paris: Michels et Fils, 1899.

Fouquet, Georges. *La bijouterie, la joaillerie: La bijouterie de fantaisie au 20e siècle*. Paris: Évreux, 1934.

Fox, James. *Five Sisters: The Langhornes of Virginia*. New York: Simon & Schuster, 2001.

Galante, Pierre. *The General: A New and Revealing Portrait of the Man Who Is France*. London: Leslie Frewin, 1969.

Gardiner, Juliet. *The Thirties: An Intimate History*. London: Harper Press, 2010.

Gardner, James. *Elephants in the Attic: The Autobiography of James Gardner*. London: Orbis, 1983.

Gargia, Massimo, and Allan Starkie. *Jet Set: Mémoires d'un International Playboy*. Paris: Michel Lafon, 2000.

Gautier, Gilberte. *Cartier: The Legend*. London: Arlington Books, 1983.

Gelardi, Julia P. *Born to Rule: Granddaughters of Victoria, Queens of Europe*. London: Headline, 1999.

———. *From Splendor to Revolution: The Romanov Women, 1847–1928*. New York: St. Martin's Press, 2011.

Gibbons, Stanley. *Classics from the Claude Cartier Collection*. London: Stanley Gibbons Auctions, April 21, 1977. Auction catalog.

Gimpel, René. *Diary of an Art Dealer*. London: Hamish Hamilton, 1986.

Glyn, Elinor. *Elizabeth Visits America*. New York: Duffield, 1909.

Goldsmiths' Company. *The Cartier Museum at the Goldsmiths' Hall, Foster Lane, London*. London: Goldsmiths' Company, 1988.

Gregorietti, Guido. *Jewellery Through the Ages*. London: Hamlyn, 1970.

Gregory, Alexis. *Paris Deluxe: Place Vendôme*. Paris: Rizzoli, 1997.

Haedrich, Marcel. *Coco Chanel: Her Life, Her Secrets*. London: Robert Hale, 1972.

Harrison, Rosina. *Rose: My Life in Service to Lady Astor*. New York: Viking Press, 1975.

Hasey, John F., and Joseph F. Dinneen. *Yankee Fighter: The Story of an American in the Free French Foreign Legion*. New York: Garden City Publishing, 1944.

Hastings, Max. *All Hell Let Loose: The World at War, 1939–1945*. New Haven, CT: Yale University Press, 2011.

Hendrix, Paul. *Sir Henri Deterding and Royal Dutch–Shell: Changing Control of World Oil, 1900–1940*. Bristol, UK: Bristol Academic Press, 2002.

Herbert, John, ed. *Christie's: Review of the Season*. London: Weidenfeld & Nicolson, 1981.

Heymann, C. David. *Poor Little Rich Girl: The Life and Legend of Barbara Hutton*. Secaucus, NJ: Lyle Stewart, 1984.

Hickman, Katie. *Courtesans*. London: Harper Perennial, 2003.

Hoffman, Paul. *Wings of Madness: Alberto Santos-Dumont and the Invention of Flight*. London: Fourth Estate, 2003.

Hopper, Matthew S. *Slaves of One Master: Globalization and Slavery in Arabia in the Age of Empire*. New Haven, CT: Yale University Press, 2013.

Horts, Stéphanie des. *La Panthère*. Paris: JC Lattès, 2010.

The House of Cartier. A&E Biography. With Jack Perkins. A&E Networks. March 3, 1999.

Hugo. *Vingt ans Maître d'Hôtel chez Maxim's.* Edited by Roland Toutain. Paris: Amiot Dumont, 1951.

Jackson, Anna, and Amin Jaffer, eds. *Maharaja: The Splendour of India's Royal Courts.* London: V&A Publishing, 2009.

Jackson, Julian. *De Gaulle.* Cambridge, MA: Belknap Press of Harvard University Press, 2018.

Jaffer, Amin, ed. *Beyond Extravagance: A Royal Collection of Gems and Jewels.* New York: Assouline, 2013.

———. *Des Grands Moghols aux Maharajahs: Joyaux de la Collection Al Thani.* Paris: Réunion des Musées Nationaux, 2017.

James, Robert Rhodes, ed. *Chips: The Diaries of Sir Henry Channon.* London: Weidenfeld & Nicolson, 1967.

Jefferson, Alan. *Sir Thomas Beecham: A Centenary Tribute.* London: MacDonald and Jane's, 1979.

The Jewels of the Duchess of Windsor. Geneva: Sotheby's, April 2–3, 1987. Auction catalog.

Josephy, Helen, and Mary Margaret McBride. *New York Is Everybody's Town.* New York: G. P. Putnam's Sons, 1931.

Kanoo, Khalid M. *The House of Kanoo: A Century of an Arabian Family Business.* London: London Centre of Arab Studies, 1997.

Károlyi, Catherine. *A Life Together: The Memoirs of Catherine Károlyi.* London: George Allen & Unwin, 1966.

———. *On m'appelait la Comtesse Rouge.* Paris: Les Éditeurs Français Réunis, 1977.

Kelényi, Béla. "Two Trunks from London: Hungarian Aspects of the 'Discovery' of Nepalese Art." *Ars Decorativa* 24 (2006): 123–145.

Kenin, Richard. *Return to Albion: Americans in England, 1760–1940.* New York: Holt, Rinehart and Winston, 1979.

Kurin, Richard. *Hope Diamond: The Legendary History of a Cursed Gem.* New York: Smithsonian Books, 2007.

Laurillard-Falot, Salomon-Louis. *Souvenirs d'un médecin hollandais sous les aigles françaises, 1807–1833.* Paris: La Vouivre, 1997.

Lenain, Géraldine. *Monsieur Loo: Le roman d'un marchand d'art asiatique.* Paris: Philippe Picquier, 2013.

Leslie, Anita. *Edwardians in Love.* London: Hutchinson, 1972.

Levenstein, Harvey. *We'll Always Have Paris: American Tourists in France Since 1930.* Chicago: University of Chicago Press, 2004.

Lindsey, Loelia. *Grace and Favour: The Memoirs of Loelia, Duchess of Westminster.* New York: Reynal, 1961.

Littlewood, Joan. *Baron Philippe: The Very Candid Autobiography of Baron Philippe de Rothschild.* New York: Crown, 1984.

Livres Précieux: Provenant de la bibliothèque Louis Cartier. Paris: Hôtel Drouot, 1962. Auction catalog.

Logan, John. *In Joyful Russia.* New York: D. Appleton and Co., 1897.

Loliée, Frédéric. *La fête impériale: Les femmes du Second Empire.* Paris: Félix Juven, 1907.

Lovell, Mary S. *The Riviera Set, 1920–1960: The Golden Years of Glamour and Excess.* London: Little, Brown Abacus, 2016.

Lowndes, Marie Belloc. *Diaries and Letters of Marie Belloc Lowndes, 1911–1947.* Edited by Susan Lowndes. London: Chatto & Windus, 1971.

Mandache, Diana, ed. *Later Chapters of My Life: The Lost Memoir of Queen Marie of Romania.* Stroud, Gloucestershire, UK: History Press, 2004.

Mansfield, Stephanie. *The Richest Girl in the World: The Extravagant Life and Fast Times of Doris Duke.* New York: Pinnacle Books / Kensington Books, 1999.

Marie, Consort of Ferdinand I. *The Story of My Life.* New York: Charles Scribner's Sons, 1934.

———. *America Seen by a Queen: Queen Marie's Diary of Her 1926 Voyage to the United States of America.* Bucharest: Romanian Cultural Foundation, 1999.

Marin, Sophie. *High Jewelry and Precious Objects by Cartier: Biennale des Antiquaires, Grand Palais Paris 2012*. Paris: Flammarion, 2012.

Marly, Diana de. *Worth: Father of Haute Couture*. New York: Holmes & Meier, 1990.

Mattar Jewelers. *The Story of Pearls: A Bahraini Family Relationship with Natural Pearls*. Bahrain: Mattar Jewelers, 2014.

Mauduit, Jean. *Maxim's: L'Histoire d'un rêve*. Paris: Éditions du Rocher, 2011.

McCarthy, Kieran. *Fabergé in London: The British Branch of the Imperial Russian Goldsmith*. Woodbridge, Suffolk, UK: ACC Art Books, 2017.

McLaren, Angus. *Playboys and Mayfair Men: Crime, Class, Masculinity, and Fascism in 1930s London*. Baltimore: Johns Hopkins University Press, 2017.

McLean, Evalyn Walsh, and Boyden Sparkes. *Father Struck It Rich*. Lake City, CO: Western Reflections, 1999.

Menkes, Suzy. *The Royal Jewels*. London: Grafton Books, 1985.

———. *The Windsor Style*. London: Grafton Books, 1987.

Metternich, Princess Pauline. *My Years in Paris*. London: Eveleigh Nash & Grayson, 1922.

Meylan, Vincent. *Archives secrètes Boucheron*. Paris: Éditions SW Télémaque, 2009.

———. *Christie's: The Jewellery Archives Revealed*. Woodbridge, Suffolk, UK: ACC Art Books, 2016.

———. *Van Cleef & Arpels: Treasures and Legends*. Woodbridge, Suffolk, UK: ACC Art Books, 2014.

Mitford, Nancy. *Christmas Pudding*. London: Thornton Butterworth Ltd., 1932.

Mohylowski, Edward T. *Lucy D. Dahlgren House Designation Report*. New York: New York City Landmarks Preservation Commission, June 19, 1984.

Monnickendam, A. *The Magic of Diamonds*. London: Hammond, Hammond & Co., 1955.

———. *Secrets of the Diamond*. London: Frederick Muller, 1941.

Moore, Lucy. *Maharanis: The Lives and Times of Three Generations of Indian Princesses*. London: Penguin Books, 2005.

Morand, Paul. *Journal d'un attaché d'ambassade, 1916–1917*. Paris: Gallimard, 1948.

Moro, Javier. *Passion India: The Story of the Spanish Princess of Kapurthala*. New Delhi: Full Circle, 2008.

Morris, Constance Lily. *On Tour with Queen Marie*. New York: Robert M. McBride & Company, 1927.

Morrow, Ann. *Highness: The Maharajahs of India*. London: Grafton, 1986.

Munn, Geoffrey C. *Tiaras: A History of Splendour*. Woodbridge, Suffolk, UK: Antique Collectors' Club, 2001.

Murat, Princess Caroline. *My Memoirs*. New York: G. P. Putnam's Sons, 1910.

Nadelhoffer, Hans. *Cartier*. London: Thames & Hudson, 2007. First published 1984.

Neely, Sylvia, and David Cassens. *The Legacy of Elma Rumsey Cartier*. St. Louis, MO: Saint Louis University, 1995.

Newton, Charles Manfred. *A Barrel of Diamonds*. Privately published, New York, 1980.

Norris, William. *The Man Who Fell from the Sky*. New York: Viking, 1987.

Papi, Stefano. *The Jewels of the Romanovs: Family and Court*. London: Thames & Hudson, 2013.

———, and Alexandra Rhodes. *20th Century Jewellery and the Icons of Style*. New York: Thames & Hudson, 2013.

Paredes, Liana. *Spectacular: Gems and Jewelry from the Merriweather Post Collection*. Washington, DC: Hillwood Estate, 2017.

Pereira, João Castel-Branco. *Cartier 1899–1949: The Journey of a Style*. Milan: Skira, 2007.

Peters, Arthur King. *Jean Cocteau and His World: An Illustrated Biography*. New York: Vendôme Press, 1987.

Philippar, M. Georges. *Exposition française au Caire: Égypte–France*. Paris: Délégué du Gouvernement Français, 1929.

Picardie, Justine. *Coco Chanel: The Legend and Life*. New York: HarperCollins, 2011.

Pissaro, Ludovic, and Lionello Venturi. *Camille Pissarro: Son art—son oeuvre*. San Francisco: Alan Wofsy, 1989.

Potter, Caroline. *French Music Since Berlioz*. London: Routledge, 2006.

Prague Castle Administration. *Cartier at Prague Castle: The Power of Style*. Paris: Flammarion, 2010.

Prior, Katherine, and John Adamson. *Maharajas' Jewels*. Paris: Assouline, 2000.

Pronteau, Jeanne. *Les numérotages des maisons de Paris du XVᵉ siècle à nos jours*. Paris: Ville de Paris, 1966.

Proust, Marcel. *À la recherche du temps perdu*. Paris: Gallimard, 1992. First published 1913–27.

———. *Articles et Lettres*. Paris: Arvensa, 2009.

Pyper, Jaclyn. "Style Sportive: Fashion, Sport and Modernity in France, 1923–1930." *Apparences*, July 2017.

Rasche, Anna W. *Dreicer & Company: Forgotten Jewelers of the Gilded Age*. New York: Cooper Hewitt, Smithsonian Design Museum, 2018.

Rhodes, Margaret. *The Final Curtsey: A Royal Memoir by the Queen's Cousin*. London: Birlinn, 2014.

Richardson, Joanna. *The Courtesans: The Demi-Monde in 19th-Century France*. London: Weidenfeld & Nicolson, 2000.

Riott, Pat. *The Greatest Story Never Told: Winston Churchill and the Crash of 1929*. Montgomery, IL: Nanoman Press, 1994.

Roberts, Glyn. *The Most Powerful Man in the World: The Life of Sir Henri Deterding*. New York: Covici-Friede, 1938.

Roe, Sue. *In Montparnasse: The Emergence of Surrealism in Paris from Duchamp to Dali*. London: Fig Tree, 2018.

Roosevelt, Elliott. *As He Saw It*. New York: Duell, Sloan and Pearce, 1946.

Rosenthal, Léonard. *Au jardin des gemmes: L'émeraude, le rubis, le saphir*. Paris: Payot, 1922.

———. *Faisons fortune*. Paris: Payot, 1924.

———. *The Kingdom of the Pearl*. London: Nisbet & Co., 1920.

———. *The Pearl Hunter: An Autobiography*. New York: Henry Schuman, 1952.

Rothschild, Guy de. *The Whims of Fortune: The Memoirs of Guy de Rothschild*. New York: Random House, 1985.

Rottenberg, Dan. *The Man Who Made Wall Street: Anthony J. Drexel and the Rise of Modern France*. Philadelphia: University of Pennsylvania Press, 2006.

Rubin, Nancy. *American Empress: The Life and Times of Marjorie Merriweather Post*. Lincoln, NE: iUniverse, 2004.

Rudoe, Judy. *Cartier: 1900–1939*. London: British Museum Press, 1997.

———. "Cartier Gold Boxes: A Visionary Patron and a Bet with Ian Fleming." *Journal of the Decorative Arts Society* 37 (2013): 114–135.

———. "Cartier in the Nineteenth Century." *Jewellery Studies*, vol. 9 (2001): 29–50.

———. "The Taste for 'Barbaric Splendour': Daisy Fellowes and Her 'Hindu' Necklace." *Jewellery Studies*, vol. 9 (2001): 78–94.

Russell, W. H. *The Prince of Wales' Tour: A Diary in India, 1877*. New York: Lovell, Adam and Wesson, 1877.

Salomé, Laurent, and Laure Dalon, eds. *Cartier: Style and History*. Paris: Réunion des Musées Nationaux–Grand Palais, 2014.

Santos-Dumont, Alberto. *My Airships: The Story of My Life*. London: Grant Richards, 1904.

Scarisbrick, Diana. *Ancestral Jewels*. London: André Deutsch, 1989.

———. "The Pursuit of Perfection." In *Christie's: Jewelry and Objects by Cartier*. Geneva: Christie's, 1993, pp. 19–23.

———. *Rings: Jewelry of Power, Love and Loyalty*. London: Thames & Hudson, 2013.

———. *Tiara*. San Francisco: Chronicle Books, 2000.

Scheips, Charlie. *Elsie de Wolfe's Paris: Frivolity Before the Storm*. New York: Abrams, 2014.

Sebba, Anne. *Les Parisiennes: How the Women of Paris Lived, Loved and Died in the 1940s*. London: Weidenfeld & Nicolson, 2017.

Seth-Smith, Michael. *The Cresta Run: History of the St Moritz Tobogganing Club*. London: Foulsham, 1976.

Sexé, Marcel. *Two Centuries of Fur-Trading 1723–1923: Romance of the Revillon Family*. Paris: Draeger Frères, 1923.

Short, Philip. *Mitterrand: A Study in Ambiguity*. London: Bodley Head, 2013.

Smith, Jane. *Elsie de Wolfe: A Life in the High Style*. New York: Atheneum, 1982.

Snowman, A. Kenneth, ed. *The Master Jewelers*. New York: Thames & Hudson, 2002.

Som, Ashok, and Christian Blanckaert. *The Road to Luxury: The Evolution, Markets, and Strategies of Luxury Brand Management*. Hoboken, NJ: John Wiley & Sons, 2015.

Sotheby's. *Magnificent Jewels*. Geneva: Sotheby's, May 15, 1991. Auction catalog.

———. *Magnificent Jewels*. Geneva: Sotheby's, May 11, 2010. Auction catalog.

———. *Magnificent Jewels*. Geneva: Sotheby's, November 13, 2013. Auction catalog.

———. *Magnificent Jewels*. Geneva: Sotheby's, November 11, 2014. Auction catalog.

Sotheby's New York: Portico Mystery Clock Number 3; Cartier Paris 1924. Text by A. Alfred Taubman et al. October 18, 1988. Auction catalog.

Sottsass, Ettore, and Franco Cologni. *Cartier Design Viewed by Ettore Sottsass*. Milan: Skira, 2002.

Spotts, Frederic. *The Shameful Peace: How French Artists and Intellectuals Survived the Nazi Occupation*. New Haven, CT: Yale University Press, 2008.

Steele, Valerie. *Paris Fashion: A Cultural History*. Oxford: Berg, 1998.

Stoddart, Jane T. *The Life of the Empress Eugénie*. New York: E. P. Dutton, 1906.

[Stopford, Bertie]. *The Russian Diary of an Englishman: Petrograd, 1915–1917*. London: William Heinemann, 1919.

Stronge, Susan. *Bejewelled Treasures: The Al Thani Collection*. London: V&A Publishing, 2015.

Succession de Monsieur Claude Cartier provenant de la collection de ses parents Monsieur et Madame Louis Cartier. 3 vols. Monaco: Sotheby Parke Bernet, November 25–27, 1979. Auction catalog.

Taylor, Elizabeth. *My Love Affair with Jewelry*. New York: Simon & Schuster, 2002.

Teague, Michael. *Mrs. L.: Conversations with Alice Roosevelt Longworth*. New York: Doubleday, 1981.

Thomas, Dana. *How Luxury Lost Its Lustre*. London: Penguin, 2008.

Trétiack, Philippe. *Cartier*. New York: Thames & Hudson, 1997.

———. *Cartier: 13 Rue de la Paix*. Paris: Assouline, 2005.

Trubert-Tollu, Chantal. *The House of Worth, 1858–1954: The Birth of Haute Couture*. London: Thames & Hudson, 2017.

Union des Femmes Françaises. *Les femmes de la Résistance*. Monaco: Éditions du Rocher, 1977.

Van der Kiste, John. *Alfred: Queen Victoria's Second Son*. Stroud, Gloucestershire, UK: Fonthill Media, 2014.

Van Osselt, Estelle Nikles. *Asia Imagined in the Baur and Cartier Collections*. Geneva: Fondation Baur, 2015. Exhibition catalog.

Various. *L'Artiste: Journal de la littérature et des beaux-arts*. Paris: Imprimerie de Béthune et Plon, 1864.

Vaughan, Hal. *Sleeping with the Enemy: Coco Chanel's Secret War*. New York: Vintage Books, 2011.

Védrine, Jean. *Les Prisonniers de guerre Vichy et la Résistance 1940–45*. Paris: Fayard, 2013.

Vever, Henri. *La bijouterie française au XIXe siècle 1800–1900*. Paris: H. Floury, Libraire-Éditeur, vol. 1 (1906), vols. 2, 3 (1908).

von Habsburg, Géza, ed. *Fabergé-Cartier: Rivalen am Zarenhof*. Munich: Hirmer Verlag, 2003.

———, and Marina Lopato. *Fabergé: Imperial Jeweller*. London: Thames & Hudson, 1994.

Vorres, Ian. *The Last Grand Duchess: Her Imperial Highness Grand Duchess Olga Alexandrovna*. Toronto: Key Porter Books, 2001.

Vreeland, Diana. *D.V.* Ecco/HarperCollins, 2003.

Walska, Ganna. *Always Room at the Top*. Santa Barbara, CA: Lotusland, 2015.

Weigold, E. *Peconic Bay: Four Centuries of History on Long Island's North and South Forks.* Syracuse, NY: Syracuse University Press, 2015.

Weill, Alain. *Parisian Fashion: La Gazette du Bon Ton 1912–1925.* Paris: Bibliothèque de l'Image, 2000.

Wharton, Edith. *A Backward Glance.* New York: D. Appleton and Co., 1934.

Wild, Rowan. *Ranji: The Biography of Colonel His Highness Shri Sir Ranjitsinhji.* London: Rich & Cowan, 1934.

Worth, Jean Charles. *A Century of Fashion.* Boston: Little, Brown and Company, 1928.

Young-Sanchez, Margaret. *Cartier: The Exhibition.* Canberra: NGA, 2018. Exhibition catalog.

Yusupov, Felix. *Prince Felix Yusupov: En Exil.* Paris: Plon, 1954.

Zeisler, Wilfried. "From Moscow to Paris: Russian Clients and Commands in France." In Brigitte de Montclos, ed., *Moscow: Splendours of the Romanovs.* Paris: Skira / Monaco: Grimaldi Forum Monaco, 2009. Exhibition catalog.

———. *L'objet d'art et de luxe français en Russie (1881–1971): Fournisseurs, clients, collections et influences.* Paris: Mare & Martin, 2014.

———. *Vivre la Belle Époque à Paris: Olga Paley et Paul de Russie.* Paris: Mare & Martin, 2018.

Zola, Émile. "Quartier Haussmann et rue de Prony." In *Carnet d'enquêtes: Une ethnographie inédite de la France.* Paris: Plon, 1986.

Zolotow, Maurice. *It Takes All Kinds: Piquant Pen Portraits of Some Picturesque People.* London: W. H. Allen, 1953.

PHOTO CREDITS

All images in this book are from family archives, unless otherwise stated below.

14 Left, Nina Slavcheva/Alain Cartier; right, RMN Grand Palais (Château de Versailles)/ Franck Raux
16 Left, Alamy/Library of Congress; right, Wartski Ltd. (with thanks to Kieran McCarthy)
33 Gallica/Bibliothèque nationale de France
38 Left, Ministère de la Culture—Médiathèque de l'architecture et du patrimoine, Dist. RMN-Grand Palais/Paul Nadar
46 Left and right, Dist. RMN-Grand Palais/Atelier de Nadar
53 With thanks to Princesse Esmeralda de Belgique
60 Everett Collection Historical/Alamy
75 Left and right, Petit Palais—Musée des Beaux-Arts de la ville de Paris
79 Graf Hilarion Woronzow-Daschkow collection, "Album of the Masquerade Ball at the Winter Palace in February 1903," Hoover Institution Archives
94 Clockwise from top left, Timothy A. Clary/AFP/Getty; Dist. RMN-Grand Palais Paul Nadar; United Artists/Collection Suns/Sunset Boulevard/Corbis; David Cairns/ Express/Getty;
126 Left, Topical Press Agency (Getty); right, Associated Press
137 Left, portrait by Alphonse Jongers (1872–1945), with thanks to the Preservation Society of Newport County; right, Museum of the City of New York
165 Top left and bottom; Maharaja Samarjitsinh Gaekwad: Royal Gaekwad Collection, Baroda
168 Bottom left, © Look and Learn
194 Left, Keystone-France, Gamma-Keystone/Getty; right, Georges Goursat, dit Sem, 1863–1934/White Bottoms de 1927, plate 35, with thanks to L'Association Sem
210 LA Collection Privée
212 Mr. Pure Zheng, Courtesy of Zebrak
221 Courtesy of Barbra Streisand
222 Courtesy of Bonhams
243 Left, The Granger Collection; right, Milstein Division, The New York Public Library

247 Top left, Hillwood Estate Museum and Gardens; top right, Alpha Historica/Alamy; bottom right, Gado Images/Alamy

250 Left, Library of Congress Prints and Photographs Division, New York World—Telegram and the Sun Newspaper Photograph Collection, LC-USZ62-126710; right, Edward Steichen/Condé Nast/Getty

257 Courtesy of the Cotroceni National Museum of Romania

261 Left, Archive PL (Alamy); right, John Vachon, Library of Congress Prints and Photographs Division, Look Magazine Photograph Collection, LOOK—Job 52-101

263 Cecil Beaton Studio Archive (Sotheby's Picture Library)

277 Hulton-Deutsch Collection/Corbis/Getty

278 Sotheby's

301, 303 With thanks to His Highness the Maharaja of Patiala

308 Top right, Bettmann (Getty); left, courtesy of Gregory Gillette

312 Paul Popper/Popperfoto/Getty

314 Mary Evans/The Image Works

318 Left and right, Frank Scherschel/The LIFE Picture Collection/Getty

329 Bettmann/Getty

338 Courtesy of Bonhams

335 Horst Horst/Condé Nast

340 Cecil Beaton Studio Archive (Sotheby's Picture Library)

346 Left, Horst Horst/Conde Nast/Getty; right, Silver Screen Collection/Getty

360 © Alpha Press

363 Left, Alfred Eisenstaedt/The LIFE Picture Collection/Getty

387 Hulton Royals Collection/Getty

396 Left, Hans Wild/The LIFE Picture Collection/Getty; right, Cecil Beaton Studio Archive (Sotheby's Picture Library)

429 Dist. RMN-Grand Palais/François Kollar

446 Left and right, Alfred Eisenstaedt/The LIFE Picture Collection/Getty

454 Left, Jean-Philippe CHARBONNIER/Gamma-Rapho/Getty; right, Alfred Eisenstaedt/The LIFE Picture Collection/Getty

458 Top left, Age FotoStock Spain SL; right, Sotheby's

467 Left, Bridgeman Images

469 Left, Royal Collection Trust/Her Majesty Queen Elizabeth II 2019; right, Royal Collection Trust/All Rights Reserved

476 Studio Willy Rizzo

483 Left, Clarence Sinclair Bull/Mgm/Kobal/Shutterstock; right, Jack Nisberg/Roger Viollet/The Image Works

504 Left, Henry Clarke/Condé Nast (Getty)

510 Left, Emilio Ronchini/Mondadori (Getty); middle, dpa Picture-Alliance GmbH; right, with thanks to His Highness the Maharaja of Patiala

518 Right, © Alpha Press

519 © 2006 Christie's Images Limited

524 Top left, Paul Slade/Paris Match/Getty; top right, Bettmann/Getty; below, TopFoto/The Image Works

527 TopFoto/The Image Works

PHOTO INSERT CAPTIONS AND CREDITS

All images are from the author's private collection unless otherwise stated below.

FIRST INSERT

Page 1

THE CARTIER STYLE

Clockwise from top: Cartier New York 1936 arrow-shaped clasp with tassels of diamonds, designed to be worn with the low-backed evening gowns of the thirties (partly visible are four strands of Marjorie Merriweather Post's pearl necklace, remounted with Caro Yamaoka pearls in 1963); Cartier Paris c. 1925 Art Deco diamond and gem-set dragon brooch; Cartier Paris c.1921 single-axle Mystery Clock in gold, rock crystal, onyx, ebonite, cabochon turquoise, platinum, and rose-cut diamonds; Cartier London c.1930 "Tutti Frutti" gem-set bracelet; Cartier Paris c.1925 *laque burgauté* and gem-set compact; Cartier London c.1923 Egyptian Revival faience brooch. **Center:** Cartier London c.1925 Art Deco diamond and enamel lapel watch.

Image credits: © Hillwood Estate Museum and Gardens, photographed by Edward Owen; Private Collection (photo © 2012 Christie's Images Limited); Nina Slavcheva; Private Collection (photo © 2012 Christie's Images Limited); Courtesy of Bonhams; © LA Collection Privée.

Page 2

Sources of inspiration included (**top left**) eighteenth-century pattern ledgers whose fabric weave suggested geometric engravings, such as on this c.1920 gold, emerald, and enamel compact; (**top right**) a letter from Louis during the world war that inspired the Tank watch; (**bottom row, left to right**) an Egyptian vase where the central motifs inspired Jacques to sketch how a similar plait shape could be converted into diamonds, worn here as a diadem by opera singer and actress Lina Cavalieri, declared by *Tattler* in 1909 to be the "loveliest prima donna in the world."

Image credits: **Top left:** © LA Collection Privée; **top right:** Timothy A. Clary/AFP/Getty Images.

Page 3

Top left: Performances by the Ballets Russes (pictured here: Léon Bakst's set for *Scheherazade*) inspired the use of bold colors through the 1920s and beyond, as in (**below**) this 1922 emerald, sapphire, and diamond belt brooch meant to complement the low-waisted dresses of the 1920s. **Top right:** Wrought iron designs inspired Art Deco onyx and diamond jabot pins. **Bottom left:** the *Book of the Dead* was consulted when designing the Egyptian Revival jewels, such as this 1920s "Sekhmet" brooch (purchased by Lady Abdy). **Bottom right:** Jean-Jacques' favorite childhood story, *The Jungle Book,* inspired his panther bookplate, similar in form to the Duchess of Windsor's 1952 panther bracelet.

Image credits: **Top left:** World History Archive/Alamy; **below:** © The Al Thani Collection 2013 (all rights reserved, photographs by Prudence Cuming). **Top right** jabot pins: Courtesy of Bonhams. **Bottom left and right** jewels: © Sotheby's.

Page 4

LA BELLE ÉPOQUE: 1898–1919

Clockwise from top left: c.1915 diamond and natural pearl bracelet; early-twentieth-century pocket watch/pendant watch in enamelled gold case; 1912 platinum and diamond garland-style *devant de corsage* commissioned by Solomon Joel. a c.1910 gold onyx, diamond, and pearl vanity case. Early-twentieth-century diamond and platinum wristwatch **Bottom, left to right:** Louis Cartier sailing on Lake Geneva with his Jack Russell terrier c.1910; Alfred Cartier valuing the deposed Sultan's jewels in Istanbul in 1909 (the Sultan's infamous treasures were said to have once included the Hope Diamond—see opposite page.)

Image credits: **Clockwise from top left:** Courtesy of Bonhams; Private Collection. © The Al Thani Collection 2015 (all rights reserved, photographs taken by Prudence Cuming). LA Collection Privée. Private Collection. Granger. TopFoto/The Image Works.

Page 5

Top left: Queen Alexandra wearing her 1904 Cartier diamond and platinum *résille* necklace; **top right:** Grand Duchess Vladimir wearing her 1909 Cartier sapphire *kokoshnik* tiara (with a 137-carat cabochon sapphire at its center). **Center left to right:** the 45-carat, notoriously cursed blue Hope Diamond sold by Cartier to Evelyn McLean in 1912; enamel, blue hardstone and silver carriage clock given to King George V for his coronation in 1911 by his mother Queen Alexandra and inscribed: "May God lead you and protect you"; c.1900 rose quartz rabbits in the Royal Collection (though these are thought to have been acquired by Queen Alexandra, it is possible they were a gift from her sister, the Dowager Empress Maria Feodorovna, who bought two hardstone rabbits on her first visit to 13 Rue de la Paix in April 1907). **Bottom:** 1909 garland-style tiara with detachable pear-shaped diamonds within wreaths of laurel suspended from lover's knots.

Image credits: **Top left:** Royal Collection Trust/© Her Majesty Queen Elizabeth II 2019; **top right:** Historic Images/Alamy. **Center left:** Smithsonian Institution (Chip Clark); **center and right:** Royal Collection Trust/© Her Majesty Queen Elizabeth II 2019. **Bottom:** © Wartski.

Page 6

THE JAZZ AGE: 1920S

Top left: Mme Jean Larivière in five-row pearl necklace with rectangular diamond and ruby motif, 1928; **top right:** back-of-head shot for *Vogue,* 1924, featuring jewels that worked with the fashionable short haircut: diamond bandeau, pear-shaped emerald earrings, and diamond-clasped pearl necklace. **Center:** Art Deco diamond bandeau. **Third row, left to right:** nephrite, onyx, and diamond pendant; natural pearl and diamond necklace; Art Deco diamond ear pendants.

Image credits: **Top left:** © Edward Steichen/Condé Nast/Getty Images; **top right:** © George Hoyningen-Huene/Condé Nast/Getty Images. **Center:** © LA Collection Privée. **Third row, left to right:** Courtesy of Bonhams; © 2015 Christie's Images Limited; © LA Collection Privée.

Page 7

Top row, left to right: lady's diamond wristwatch on black cord strap; enamel, diamond, pearl, and onyx pendant watch; onyx and diamond ear pendants. **Center:** coral, onyx, and diamond fan brooch suspending a rock crystal ring. **Bottom row, left to right:** diamond, onyx, and coral fob watch; blue and white enamel desk clock with Art Deco agate pedestal base; diamond, coral, platinum, and emerald brooch.

Image credits: **Top row, left to right:** Courtesy of Bonhams; © LA Collection Privée; Private Collection (photo © 2012 Christie's Images Limited). **Center:** Courtesy of Bonhams. **Bottom row, left to right:** Private Collection (photo © 2012 Christie's Images Limited); © 2018 Christie's Images Limited; © LA Collection Privée.

Page 8

Top left: the Duchess of Manchester in 1912 wearing her late mother-in-law's 1903 eighteenth-century-inspired tiara; **top center:** the actress Alden Gay in 1924 wearing Cartier emerald, pearl, diamond, and sapphire jewelry; **top right:** the model Helen Bennett in 1939 wearing Cartier pearl and diamond jewelry. **Bottom left:** the Duchess of Windsor wearing her 1947 Cartier amethyst and turquoise bib-style necklace at a 1953 gala in Versailles; **bottom right:** Jackie Onassis in the 1970s wearing her Tank watch with jeans in New York.

Image credits: **Top left:** Library of Congress Prints and Photographic Division [Lc-DIC-ggbain-06373]; **top center and right:** © Edward Steichen/Condé Nast/Getty Images. **Bottom left:** photo © AGIP/Bridgeman Images; **bottom right:** photo by Art Zelin/Getty Images.

SECOND INSERT

Page 1

JEAN-JACQUES CARTIER: 1919–2010

Top, left to right: Jean-Jacques as a child with his father and grandfather; as a twenty-year-old soldier on leave with his mother; and with his trademark pipe in his English country garden. **Below, encircled:** during retirement in his South of France garden. **Bottom:** various sketches and designs from his personal collection, including **(left)** a c.1965 chalcedony and sapphire owl brooch, **(center)** the 1953 Williamson flower brooch commissioned by Her Majesty Queen Elizabeth II, and **(right)** a c.1970 coral, diamond, and enamel ladybird brooch.

Image credits: Jewels on top of family sketches, **bottom, left to right:** Private Collection; © Royal Collection Trust/all rights reserved; Courtesy of Bonhams.

Page 2

FOREIGN INFLUENCES

Top, left to right: the Maharaja of Kapurthala wearing his 1926 Cartier emerald turban ornament; 1923 carved emerald pendant brooch in its 1928 remodeled form; Marjorie Merriweather Post wearing the brooch in a portrait with her daughter (she would also wear it as a pendant attached to her 1928 Indian-inspired emerald necklace). **Center:** c.1925 necklace where the articulated band is designed as a pavé-set diamond undulating branch with black enamel trim, enhanced by carved ruby and emerald leaves and berries. **Third row, left:** c.1930 diamond, sapphire, ruby and emerald "Tutti Frutti" bracelet; **third row, right:** c.1930 sapphire, emerald, ruby, and diamond "Tutti Frutti" jabot pin. **Bottom:** restrung ruby, pearl, and diamond choker, formerly part of a larger 1931 necklace made for the Maharaja of Patiala.

Image credits: **Top left:** photograph by Karam Puri, courtesy Cynthia Meera Frederick; **top center and right:** © Hillwood Estate Museum and Gardens. **Center:** Private Collection (photo © 2012 Christie's Images Limited). **Third row, left:** © Sotheby's; **third row, right:** Courtesy of Bonhams. **Bottom:** © The Al Thani Collection 2013 (all rights reserved, photographs by Prudence Cuming).

Page 3

Top left: ivory, mother-of-pearl, enamel, turquoise, and ruby dragon compact; **top right:** c.1925 *laque burgauté* cigarette case. **Center, left to right:** 1937 multigem and diamond maharaja clip brooch once owned by Daisy Fellowes; c.1925 Oriental motif red enamel, diamond, and onyx brooch; c.1923 Egyptian glazed faience brooch designed as temple entrance and framed with diamonds and colored gemstones. **Bottom, left to right:** Jacques Cartier in India, 1911; c.1930 diamond and platinum temple brooch; Daisy Fellowes wearing the 1936 Collier Hindou at a 1950 dinner at the Hotel Lambert.

Image credits: **Top left:** © LA Collection Privée; **top right:** Albion Art. **Center, left to right:** © LA Collection Privée; © 2016 Christie's Images Limited; © Sotheby's. **Bottom center:** Private Collection (photo: © 2012 Christie's Images Limited). **Bottom right:** Robert Doisneau/Gamma-Rapho via Getty Images.

Page 4

THE 1930S

Top: the Duchess of Windsor's 1930s Cartier charm bracelet featuring nine gem-set inscribed crosses. **Bottom, clockwise from top right:** a 1930s gold Tank Cintrée with buckle *déployant* (this slim curved-case style of Tank was introduced in 1921); gold compass and clock cufflinks; emerald-inset enameled silver-mounted agate letter opener watch; a gold and enamel lighter; a black silk brocade and gold evening bag with rose quartz clasp; a ball-bearing bracelet in gold and silver (an example of Cartier's Art Moderne style), favored by Marlene Dietrich and the Duchess of Windsor; a gold, enamel, sapphire, and diamond desk clock.

Image credits: **Top:** © Sotheby's. **Bottom, clockwise from top right:** Courtesy of Bonhams (watch); Courtesy of Bonhams (cufflinks); Courtesy of Bonhams (letter opener); Courtesy of Bonhams (lighter); © Sotheby's (handbag); Courtesy of Bonhams (bracelet); © LA Collection Privée (clock).

Page 5

CAFÉ SOCIETY AND STATEMENT NECKLACES

Top: Barbara Hutton (left) in 1939 and Mrs. Alfred Gwynne Vanderbilt (right) in 1940, wearing Cartier jewels. **Center, left to right:** diamond and platinum necklace with detachable double-drop diamond pendant (created c.1935 and known as the Hyderabad necklace after it was presented by the Nizam to the then Princess Elizabeth for her wedding in 1947); the Greville chandelier earrings, incorporating the modern diamond cuts commissioned in 1929 and bequeathed to Queen Elizabeth the Queen Mother (then Queen Consort) in 1942; a Cartier London c.1935 diamond and aquamarine necklace that doubled as a tiara; **Bottom left:** the Cartier New York emerald and diamond necklace that Clarence Mackay gave to his new bride in 1931. **bottom right:** Cartier New York sapphire, diamond, and platinum fringe necklace commissioned by Marjorie Merriweather post (then Mrs. J. E. Davies) in 1937.

Image credits: **Top, left and right:** © Horst P. Horst/Condé Nast / Getty Images. **Center, left and center:** © Royal Collection Trust/all rights reserved; **center right:** © 2018 Christie's Images Limited; **Bottom left:** © Smithsonian Institution (Chip Clark). **bottom right:** Hillwood Estate Museum and Gardens.

Page 6

A CHANGING WORLD: THE POSTWAR YEARS

Top, left to right: Audrey Hepburn's c.1950 swizzle stick (one side of heart charm signed AUDREY, the other GIGI); freed bird brooch to symbolize the Liberation of Paris, 1944; c.1945 ivory, diamond, and quartz flower brooch. **Second row, left to right:** c.1965 lapis lazuli and diamond turtle brooch; 1963 gold walnut clock. **Center:** Marlene Dietrich's c.1940 tricolor gold and lapis lazuli bracelet. **Bottom left:** the actress Romy Schneider wearing her Baignoire watch; **bottom right:** 1968 Cartier London Maxi Oval watch with visible buckle deployment.

Image credits: **Top, left to right:** © 2017 Christie's Images Limited; © 2006 Christie's Images Limited; © Sotheby's. **Second row, left and right:** Courtesy of Bonhams; **center:** © Sotheby's. **Bottom left:** © Jean-Pierre Bonnotte/Gamma-Rapho/Getty Images; **bottom right:** Courtesy of Bonhams.

Page 7

Top left: 1958 *The Sketch* cover featuring Cartier jewels; **top right:** 1950 *Vogue* cover featuring a Cartier compact. **Center, left to right:** c.1950 bangle typical of the fashion for gold and diamond jewelry in the postwar period; c.1960 gold, emerald, and diamond bombe ring of rope-twist design; c.1952 gold, platinum, and diamond vanity case. **Bottom left:** Marjorie Merriweather Post's 1950 Cartier New York amethyst, turquoise, diamond, gold, and platinum necklace; **bottom right:** 1947 Cartier London emerald, gold, and diamond necklace.

Image credits: **Top left:** © Mary Evans/Image Works; **top right:** © Vogue Paris. **Center, left to right:** © Sotheby's; Courtesy of Bonhams; © LA Collection Privée. **Bottom left:** © Hillwood Estate Museum and Gardens; **bottom right:** © Sotheby's.

Page 8

Top, left to right: Elizabeth Taylor receiving her ruby and diamond parure from Mike Todd on the Côte d'Azur in 1957; Princess Grace of Monaco wearing her ruby cabochon and diamond tiara (which doubles as a necklace) and three-row diamond necklace; Princess Grace of Monaco's 10.47-carat diamond engagement ring. **Center:** the 1936 Halo tiara. **Bottom, left to right:** Four royal generations wearing the Halo tiara: Queen Elizabeth the Queen Mother, then Queen Consort, in 1937; Princess Margaret in 1958; Princess Anne in 1970; and the Duchess of Cambridge on her wedding day in 2011.

Image credits: **Top, left to right:** © Eve Johnson/Archive Films Analog Collection/Getty Images; © Georges Lukomski (1959)—Archives du Palais de Monaco; © Geoffrey Moufflet (2018)—Archives du Palais de Monaco. **Center:** © Royal Collection Trust/all rights reserved. **Bottom, left to right:** © Mary Evans/The Image Works; TopFoto/The Image Works; © William Lovelace/Daily Express/Getty Images; Alamy.

INDEX

Page numbers of illustrations and their captions appear in italics.

Key to use of first names:
Alfred = Alfred Cartier
Claude = Claude Cartier
Jacques = Jacques Théodule Cartier
Jean-Jacques = Jean-Jacques Cartier
Louis = Louis Joseph Cartier
Marion = Marion Cartier
Pierre = Pierre Camille Cartier

ABOUT THE AUTHOR

A graduate in English literature from Oxford University, FRANCESCA CARTIER BRICKELL is a direct descendant of the Cartier family. Her great-great-great-grandfather founded Cartier in 1847. Her late grandfather Jean-Jacques Cartier was the last of the family to manage and own a branch of the world-famous family firm. She is a sought-after international lecturer on Cartier's illustrious history and has given talks for major auction houses, museums, and societies. This book is the result of a decade of the author's independent research into her family and the business they founded. She lives with her husband and children in London and the South of France.

the-cartiers.com
Twitter: @cescacartier
Instagram: @creatingcartier

ABOUT THE TYPE

This book was set in Sabon, a typeface designed by the well-known German typographer Jan Tschichold (1902–74). Sabon's design is based upon the original letterforms of sixteenth-century French type designer Claude Garamond and was created specifically to be used for three sources: foundry type for hand composition, Linotype, and Monotype. Tschichold named his typeface for the famous Frankfurt typefounder Jacques Sabon (c. 1520–80).